DAVIS POLK & WARDWELL

2007 Alumni Reception

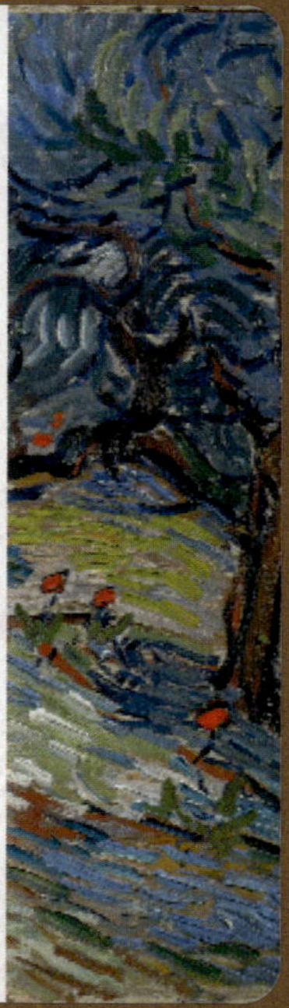

With Our Compliments

Vincent van Gogh
~
Painted with Words

The Letters to Émile Bernard

Leo Jansen
Hans Luijten
Nienke Bakker

Rizzoli
NEW YORK

IN ASSOCIATION WITH
THE MORGAN LIBRARY & MUSEUM, NEW YORK
VAN GOGH MUSEUM, AMSTERDAM

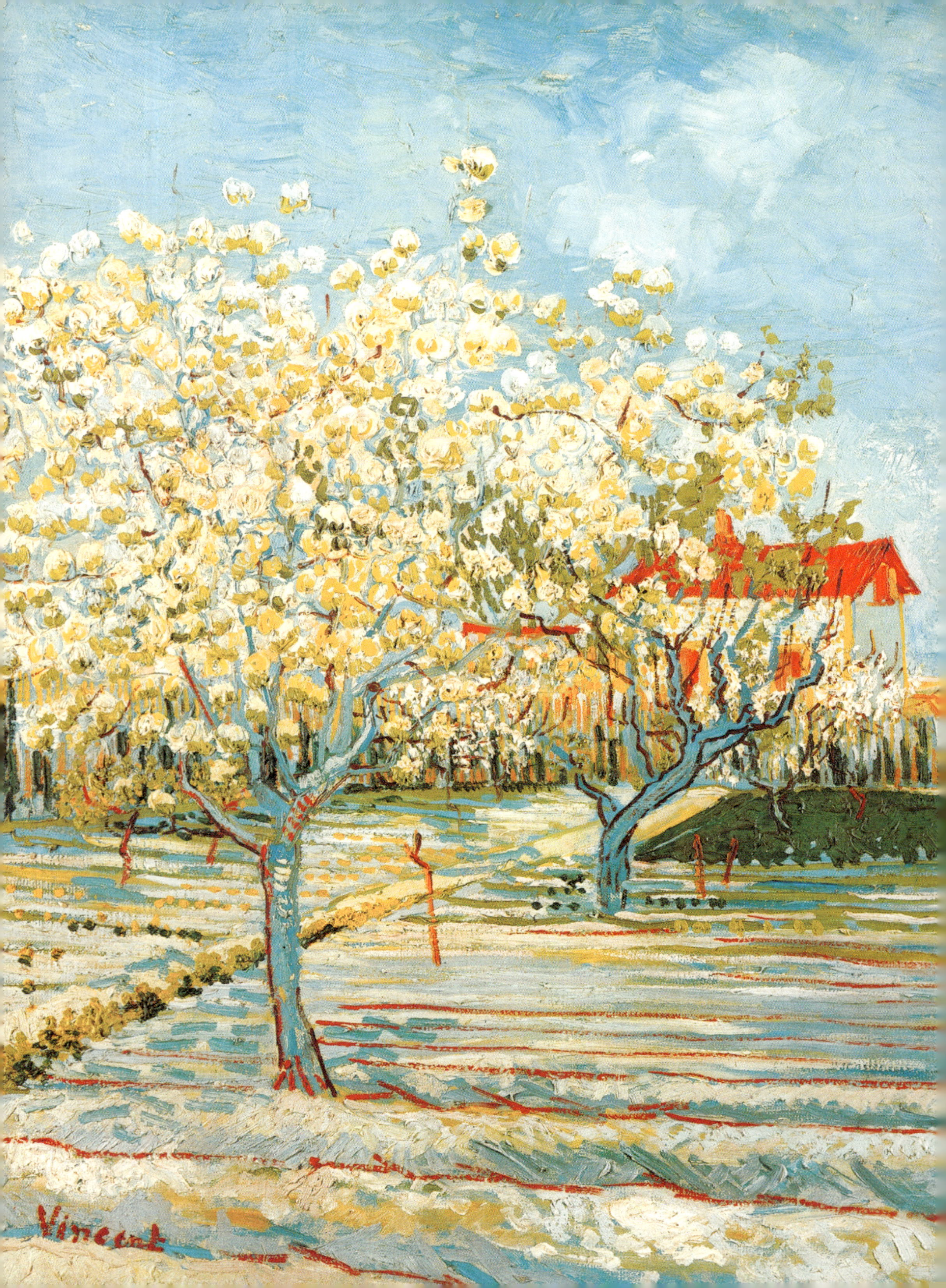
Vincent

Contents

5 Directors' Foreword

7 Introduction

25 Notes to the Reader

34 The Facsimiles

126 The Letters

357 Epilogue

357 Appendix 1: Letter from Vincent van Gogh to Paul Gauguin

360 Appendix 2: Article by Émile Bernard, with a Letter to Albert Aurier

366 List of Works Exchanged by van Gogh and Bernard

368 Descriptions of the Manuscripts

370 Notes

374 Concordance of Published Letters from van Gogh to Bernard

375 Works Cited in Abbreviated Form

378 Index

382 Credits

383 Authors' Acknowledgments

aussi intéressant & aussi difficil
bien dire une chôse que de peindre
chôse Il y a l'art des lignes & co
mais l'art des paroles y est et y re
pas moins.

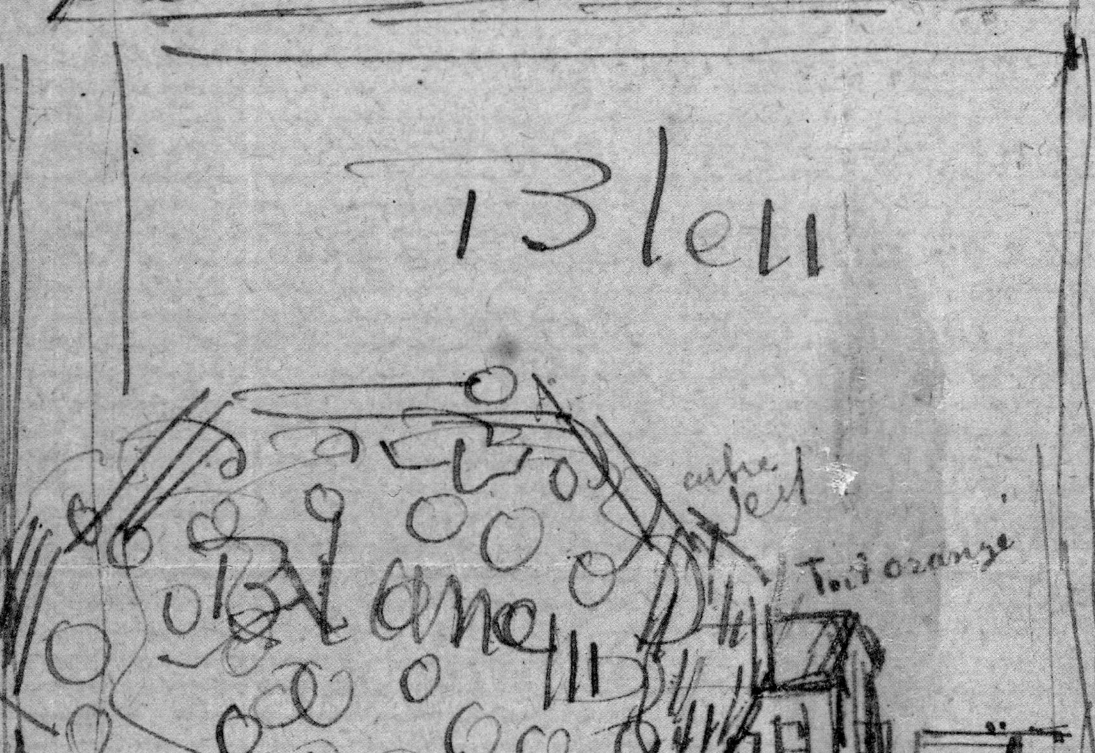

Voici un
verger as
comme co
un arbre bla
petit arbre
un coin d
carré -
lilas un
un grand
ai neuf
en trai
un blanc
rose un r
rouge un
un rose gr
vert et ro

J'en ai éreinté une hier d'un cér
contre ciel bleu les jeunes pous
des feuilles étaient de l'orangé et
les touffes de fleurs blanches Cela co

Directors' Foreword

Vincent van Gogh possessed twin talents that have both contributed to his worldwide renown. As an artist he left behind a magnificent oeuvre of paintings and drawings that made him one of the founding fathers of modern art. In addition, he was blessed with considerable talent as a writer that found its expression in his correspondence. The hundreds of letters by his hand not only tell the story of an eventful and moving life in which art and literature stood central, but they also convey the rich world of ideas that informed van Gogh's art.

Within this correspondence the twenty-two letters that van Gogh wrote to the French artist Émile Bernard occupy a special place. They contain the essence of his views during the period 1888 to 1889, when he worked in Arles in the south of France and had reached the peak of his creativity. Some of the masterpieces of those years include *Sunflowers*, *The Bedroom*, and *Starry Night*. The letters attest to his love of the light and colors of Provence, his admiration for Rembrandt and Millet, his preference for spontaneous brushwork, and his hope for collaboration among artists.

When, in 2002, nineteen of the letters to Bernard arrived at The Morgan Library & Museum as a promised gift of Eugene and Clare Thaw, they had existed in complete obscurity for more than half a century. Egbert Haverkamp-Begemann, who was then acting head of the department of Drawings and Prints, immediately contacted the editors of the Van Gogh Letters Project, who since 1994 had been working at the Van Gogh Museum in Amsterdam on a new scholarly edition of the complete correspondence. It was to become a fruitful transatlantic collaboration between our two institutions. Not only were the researchers given the opportunity to be the first to study the manuscripts extensively and to transcribe them, but early on, during the researchers' first visit to the Morgan, the plan also emerged to publish the letters jointly and to mark the event of the publication with an exhibition at the Morgan in 2007.

The present book is the result of this plan. It provides the reader with an ideal guide to penetrate the world of van Gogh: accurate transcriptions of the letters, facsimiles, a new English translation, and extensive annotations and illustrations of as many as possible of the works by van Gogh, Bernard, and others that are mentioned in the letters. Never before has the publication of an artist's correspondence been approached in such an exhaustive manner. *Painted with Words* gives a taste—and, it is hoped, whets the appetite—for the complete edition of van Gogh's letters that will appear in 2009 on the Web as well as in print.

As ever, a project of this kind relies on the support of many people. We owe a debt of gratitude to Egbert Haverkamp-Begemann, who established the contact between our two institutions and who lent the project his continuing support. At the Morgan the researchers benefited greatly from the extensive expertise of Margaret Holben Ellis, director of the Thaw Conservation Center. We also wish to thank Jennifer Tonkovich, associate curator, department of Drawings and Prints, who is the curator of the related exhibition that will be held at the Morgan from 28 September 2007 to 6 January 2008. Thanks are also due to Karen Banks, publications manager, who has shepherded this publication through its various stages, and Patricia Emerson for her thoroughness and expertise at editing the manuscript. At the Van Gogh Museum, we are extremely grateful to the editors of the Van Gogh Letters Project—Leo Jansen, Hans Luijten, and Nienke Bakker—who enthusiastically embraced the project and applied their considerable expert knowledge and experience to produce the publication you are holding in your hands.

Charles E. Pierce, Jr.
Director
The Morgan Library & Museum

Axel Rüger
Director
Van Gogh Museum

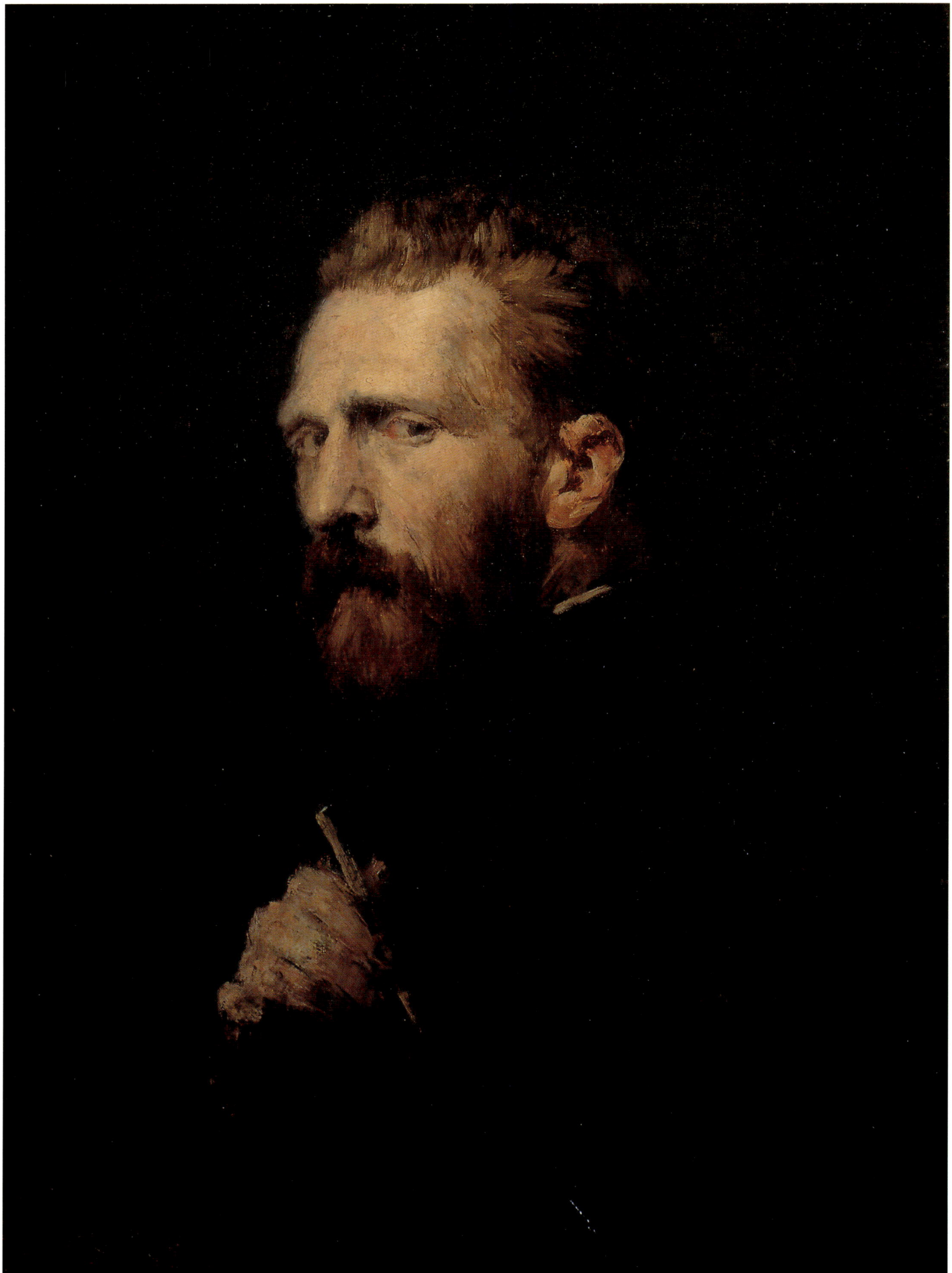

Introduction

An Artists' Friendship

There's the art of lines and colors,
but there's the art of words that will last just the same.

Vincent van Gogh's letters provide a fascinating account of an artist's eventful and inspirational life. Their fame spread rapidly around the world after his death in 1890, and during the twentieth century the complete correspondence was published in many editions and languages. The letters to Émile Bernard have a status of their own because they are typical artists' letters, in the sense that as part of the exchange of ideas between two colleagues they deal at great length with numerous artistic questions, some of which have proven fundamental to modern art.

Twenty-two of the approximately eight hundred surviving letters by van Gogh were addressed to Bernard, and they are quite simply the most spontaneous of them all. As surely and diversely as van Gogh wielded his brush and draftsman's pen, he found the words to express the problems and ideals that concerned him as a human being and artist. The style is very direct, perhaps because French was not his native language, even if the tone and mood do range from the exuberant and boisterous to the reflective and melancholy. Contrary to the myth of van Gogh as the unworldly genius, he was essentially a seeker with a rational approach to the questions he posed as a painter and draftsman as well as a human being. His quest yielded the wealth of insights and doubts to which these letters bear witness. Bernard himself characterized them with the words, "There, pulsating with life, one would find the whole of him."[1]

The Morgan Library & Museum is the curator of nineteen of these letters to Bernard—an admittedly small but nonetheless very special part of the collection. They are now being published with the three others that became separated from the main group over the years. The letters were written between December 1887 and November 1889. For art historians, this correspondence contains priceless information about an extremely creative period in the life of one of the most important painters of the modern era. At the same time, though, the letters were written with a passion for art and life which no reader—whether a specialist or not—could find anything but infectious. According to W. H. Auden, "there is scarcely one letter by van Gogh which I, who am certainly no expert, do not find fascinating."[2] Many consider van Gogh's written legacy to be a part of world literature. There could hardly be a greater compliment from a writer than that bestowed by Charles Bukowski: "Van Gogh, of course, was never insane. He simply realized the world was elsewhere. And his style, the purest of styles."[3]

Acquaintance

The friends Vincent van Gogh (1853–1890) and Émile Bernard (1868–1941) last saw each other on the evening of 18 February 1888, when they hung Japanese prints on the walls of the Paris apartment of Vincent's brother Theo.[4] Van Gogh left for Arles the next day. Their last epistolary contact

1. John Peter Russell, *Portrait of Vincent van Gogh,* 1886. Amsterdam, Van Gogh Museum (Vincent van Gogh Foundation).

dates from ca. 26 November 1889, when van Gogh took Bernard severely to task over the results of the latter's search for a new kind of religious painting, which van Gogh regarded as a "setback" (Letter 22).

Paradoxically enough, we know of two fairly exact dates marking the end of their friendship, but the moment when they first met is not so precisely documented.[5] Van Gogh arrived in Paris in early March 1886 and immediately got in touch with Theo, who was then living at 25, rue Laval. At the beginning of June, the brothers moved to a larger apartment at 54, rue Lepic, also in Montmartre (Figs. 1 and 2). A little over three months before his arrival he had rounded off his self-taught apprenticeship in Holland by enrolling for a course at the art academy in Antwerp. There, though, he discovered that he had somewhat overestimated his ability to adapt to academic discipline. He had two goals in Paris. Having worked in isolation for years, he now wanted to live where he could meet other artists and experience the "friction of ideas," as he put it, and discover what was going on in the art capital of Europe, where there was apparently something called "impressionism." He planned to work for a year, if necessary, in the studio run by Fernand Cormon. He had also been aware for some time that his application of the color theory of Eugène Delacroix, whom he admired greatly, was not leading to the lighter palette he was seeking. He hoped that he would get on the right track by studying the colorist's work in such museums as the Louvre and the Luxembourg.[6]

Bernard, fifteen years his junior, had already been studying with Cormon for eighteen months when van Gogh arrived in Paris but had been sent packing for "insubordinate behaviour" (Fig. 3).[7] This was typical of Bernard. He was energetic, fiery, nonconformist, and looking for his place in modern painting. He also wrote poems with a modern feeling for life and a Baudelairean "spleen."

Bernard's later writings are the main source of information surrounding the circumstances under which he met van Gogh, but he gave differing accounts. He related in the periodical *Les Hommes d'Aujourd'hui* (1890) that he met van Gogh "for the first time in Cormon's studio," and went on: "Then at Tanguy's shop, that fervent little chapel whose old priest has the kindly smile of misunderstood honesty. When he [van Gogh] emerged from the back shop, with his high, broad forehead, he was so striking I was almost frightened; but we soon made friends and folders from Holland and portfolios of studies were opened. [. . .] On the table, among some Japanese prints, balls of wool, whose interlaced threads played unforeseen symphonies" (Fig. 4).[8]

Bernard told a similar story in 1893 in his introduction to the publication of fragments from the letters in the leading monthly periodical on art and literature, *Mercure de France*. It can be deduced from these and other remarks about this episode that they really did first meet in Cormon's studio in March 1886, albeit briefly. Bernard must have returned there after van Gogh had started taking lessons. The meeting in the color shop of "Père" Tanguy in the rue Clauzel marked the actual beginning of the friendship. This must have been after Bernard's return from Brittany in the autumn of 1886. Julien Tanguy was a dealer in art supplies who also exhibited and sold the work of young artists. For them it was a popular meeting place, and van Gogh was almost one of the family.

The contact between van Gogh and Bernard in Paris is poorly documented, for van Gogh's correspondence, otherwise such an important source of information, was reduced to a minimum during this period (because he was living with Theo and therefore didn't have to write to him). All the same, we do know something about how they spent their time together and made themselves known on the art scene. For instance, van Gogh visited the home of the Bernard family in Asnières,

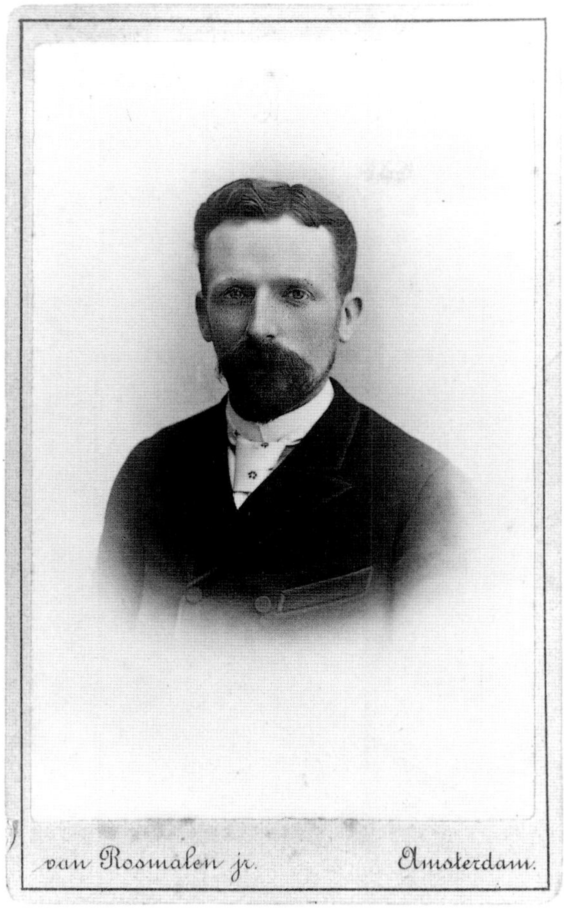

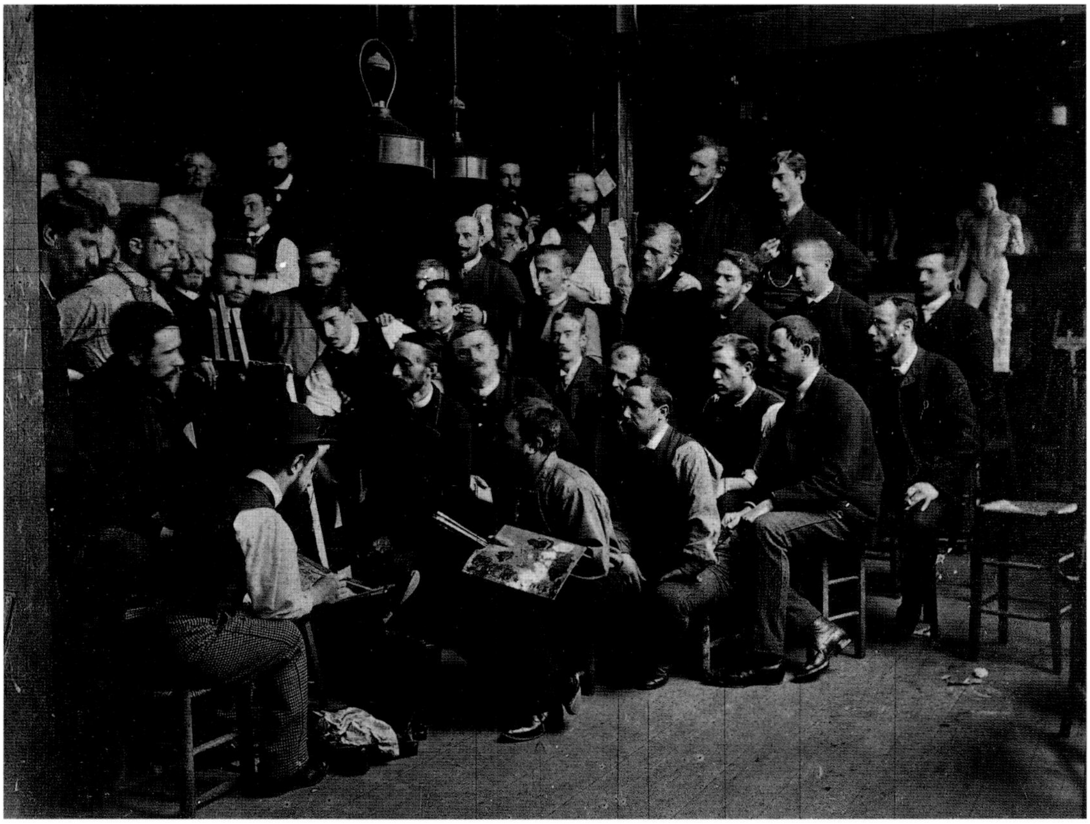

2. *Portrait of Theo van Gogh,* 1889. Amsterdam, Van Gogh Museum (Vincent van Gogh Foundation).

3. *Atelier Cormon Around 1883–85.* Amsterdam, Van Gogh Museum (Documentation).

then still a rural suburb north of Paris, near Montmartre (Fig. 5). Bernard wrote that in 1887 he often met van Gogh in the wooden studio that had been built for him in the family garden, where they worked together on portraits of Père Tanguy. He also related that van Gogh put his version under his arm, still wet, after a dispute with Bernard's father over Émile's future.[9]

Their time at Cormon's was important for both artists. At first van Gogh mainly sought the company of other foreigners who, like him, were a little older than the rest, such as Frank Myers Boggs and John Peter Russell, with whom he exchanged works.[10] Bernard became friendly with Henri de Toulouse-Lautrec and Louis Anquetin, and in 1886 they were exploring neo-impressionism. It was only after Bernard had introduced van Gogh to this avant-garde at the end of 1886 that the Dutchman became actively involved with the new group.[11] Van Gogh called them the painters of the "petit boulevard," to distinguish them from the impressionists, who were becoming established artists in the 1880s and whose works were sold in the art galleries on the "grands boulevards."

There was no question of any unity among the avant-garde. Van Gogh argued for collaboration and tolerance, but that clearly did not interest Bernard, with his youthful anarchism. In 1887 he and Anquetin demonstratively distanced themselves from the "divisionism" of Seurat and Signac (Fig. 6). According to them, this attempt to dissect observed color into little dots and dabs reduced its intensity and resulted in static, wooden figures. They had experimented with the method but found it unsatisfactory and decided to change course. Line and contour governed their work, and they sought the solution to color in large, simplified areas instead of small dots. This synthesizing style, which became known as cloisonism, was heavily influenced by Japanese printmaking.[12]

Van Gogh's affiliation with innovations of this kind from the end of 1886 emerges, among other things, from two exhibitions that he organized. In the spring of 1887, he was allowed to use Agostina Segatori's Le Tambourin café and restaurant for a show of Japanese prints, of which he and Theo had built up a sizable collection.[13] He had initiated Anquetin and Bernard into this art form by taking them to the gallery run by Siegfried Bing, who had huge stocks of Japanese prints.[14] In November that year he organized an exhibition in the Grand Bouillon-Restaurant du Chalet on the avenue de Clichy with work by himself, Toulouse-Lautrec, Bernard, Anquetin, and the Dutchman Arnold Koning. Although it attracted little attention, it did have an impact, in the first place because it was visited by Gauguin, Seurat, Guillaumin, and Camille Pissarro. And because, as van Gogh later wrote to his brother, not without pride, "Bernard having sold his first painting there, Anquetin having sold a study there, I having made the exchange with Gauguin, we all got something" (*CL* 510). Theo, who was manager of the Boussod, Valadon et Cie gallery in the boulevard Montmartre, was also keen to bring the new art to the public's attention, although in his own gallery he had to confine himself to less controversial artists like Gauguin and Toulouse-Lautrec.[15]

Relationship

Van Gogh and Bernard undoubtedly got on well together, and one can safely assume that they, sometimes accompanied by Toulouse-Lautrec, enjoyed the bohemian pleasures to be had in Montmartre. Cafés-chantants and cabarets like Aristide Bruant's Le Mirliton, and the anti-bourgeois Le Chat Noir, were famous and notorious; the district was full of bars, restaurants, artists, prostitutes, musicians, and actors.[16] These surroundings gave rise to the frank language of van Gogh's letters to Bernard. The friends were on familiar territory when speaking about brothels, pimps, and whores, the relationship between the artistic life and sex, and so on. As far as style is concerned, there is a very marked contrast between the letters to Bernard and those to Theo. In the few cases that such

subjects were raised in his correspondence with his brother, it was done in far more guarded terms.

Van Gogh's letters to Bernard provide clear evidence of the way he regarded his younger counterpart. He himself came from a Dutch vicar's family, and by nature tended to reason and moralize. The difference in their ages also prompted him to play the part of the older and wiser brother, the more experienced adviser and guide. He encouraged Bernard, praised or criticized his paintings, drawings, and poems, talked him out of ideas that he considered wrongheaded and suggested others—whether concerning how he should have behaved toward opponents such as Signac, the military service that he would have to do in Africa, the value of the old masters, the importance of good health, or the significance of Christ.

Van Gogh's appreciation of his friend's work is clear from the letters. When, in Arles, he considered the possibility of organizing an exhibition in Marseille, he wanted it to include work by Bernard. He is unreserved in his admiration for some of his portraits and still lifes, and when Bernard sent drawings to Arles he was often delighted with them, just as he assumed that Theo would display drawings by Bernard that he had sent him (*CL* 502). And when Gauguin arrived in Arles and showed him Bernard's *Breton Women in the Meadow* (see Fig. 103), van Gogh was full of praise. He called it superb and wrote to his brother: "Have you seen the studies that Bernard brought back from Brittany? Gauguin has told me many things about them. He himself has one which is simply masterly. I think that buying one from him, from Bernard, would be doing him a service and that he really deserves it" (*CL* 558a).[17] The fact that he made a watercolor copy of it speaks volumes (Fig. 7). On top of that, the artists exchanged works on several occasions. When Bernard sent his self-portrait for an exchange in 1888, van Gogh roundly declared: "As for your portrait—you know—I like it very much—I actually like everything that you do, as you know—and perhaps nobody *before* me has liked what you do *as much* as I do" (Letter 19).[18]

It is a thousand pities that we do not have Bernard's letters, for van Gogh's are partly a reaction to them, and many of the remarks and topics must have been prompted by what Bernard had written. Bernard's later written reminiscences are almost the only source of information about how he regarded the friendship and correspondence.[19] Van Gogh valued Bernard's letters, as he told Theo: "I'm keeping all Bernard's letters, they're sometimes really interesting, you'll read them some day or other; they already make quite a bundle" (*CL* 538).[20] The intensity and liveliness of their written discussions is also clear from Bernard's description: "I replied to him no less lengthily, also filling my letters with sketches of my canvases in progress. We had formed this plan of drawing as one writes, and with the same fluency as would a Hokusai or an Utamaro."[21]

In addition to these reminiscences, there are one or two contemporary witnesses who supply details about the relationship between the two artists. One of them is Gauguin, who was a friend of theirs. Both Bernard and van Gogh accorded him a leading place in their joint quest for innovation and admired his work. Back in Paris, in November 1887, van Gogh had exchanged two of his still lifes, both titled *Two Cut Sunflowers* (New York, The Metropolitan Museum of Art; F 375 / JH 1329; Bern, Kunstmuseum; F 376 / JH 1331) for Gauguin's *On the Shore of the Lake, Martinique* (see Fig. 17). A month later, Theo van Gogh bought his *Among the Mangoes* (see Fig. 18) for the brothers' collection.[22] Those two works were Bernard's first encounter with Gauguin's exotic scenes, and in his opinion they were very good indeed.[23] Bernard and Gauguin first met in the summer of 1886, but only got to know each other in the summer of 1888, when they worked together in Pont-Aven. Bernard had enormous respect for Gauguin. It was during that period that Gauguin wrote to van Gogh, rather paternalistically: "I am studying young Bernard, whom I do not know as well as you do; I believe you'll do him good, and he needs it. He has suffered, of course,

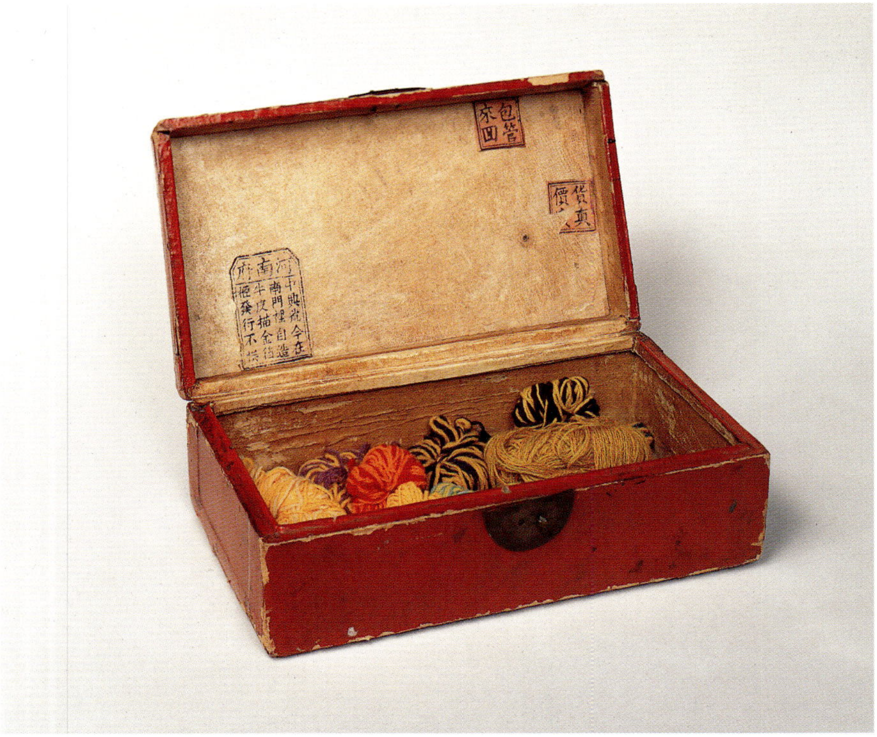

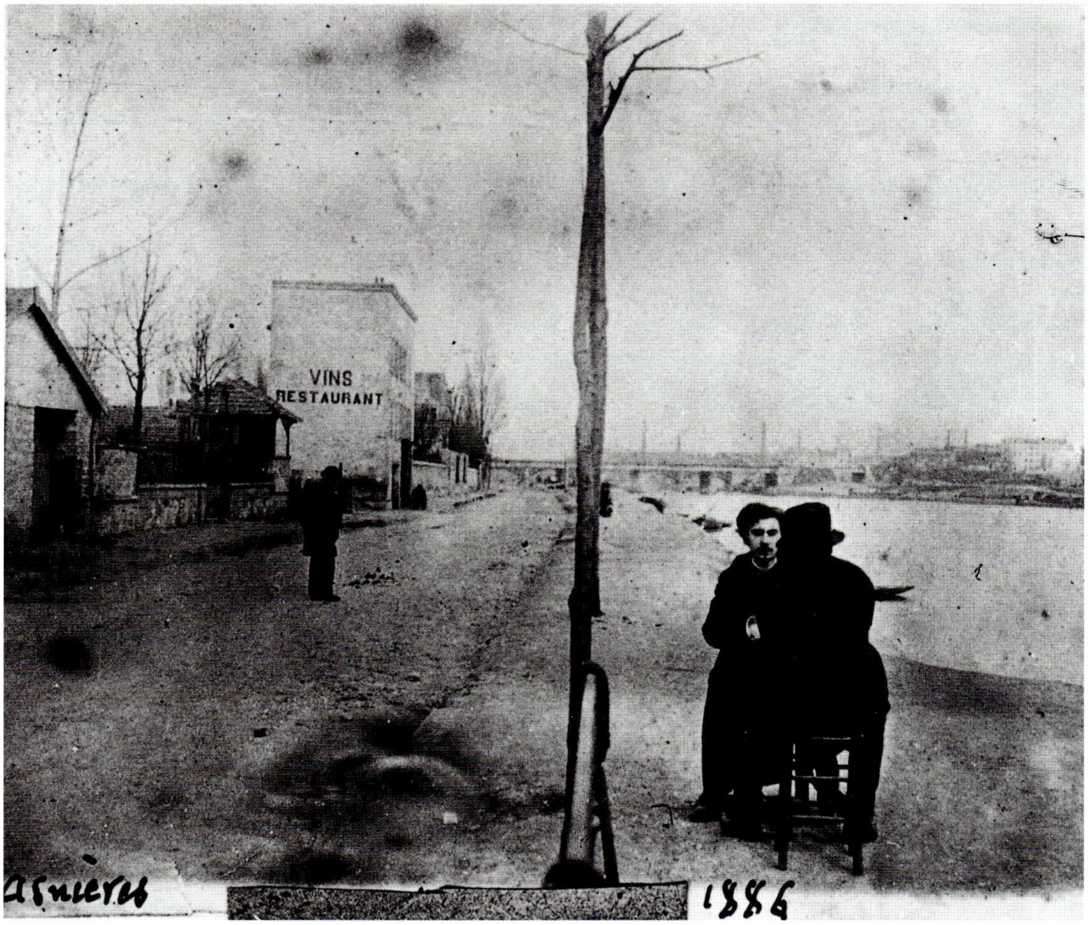

4. Red lacquered box containing sixteen small knots of wool. Amsterdam, Van Gogh Museum (Vincent van Gogh Foundation).
5. *Émile Bernard and Vincent van Gogh in Asnières*, dated by Émile Bernard 1886, probably 1887. Amsterdam, Van Gogh Museum (Documentation).

and he's starting out in life full of bile, ready to see man's bad side. I hope that with his intelligence and his love of art he'll see one day that goodness is a force against others and a consolation for our own ills. He likes you and respects you, so you can have a good influence on him. We need to be very united in heart and in intellect if we wish the future to put us in our true place" (GAC 31).[24] So the older Gauguin, the self-appointed leader of the group of Pont-Aven, really did see some promise in "young Bernard"; his words also indicate that the latter had spoken approvingly of van Gogh. That enthusiasm also emerged from the fact that Bernard put some drawings he had received from van Gogh in an album that he showed to Gauguin (*CL* 526).

Another contemporary source consists of Bernard's other correspondence. Van Gogh's letter of 19 April 1888 (Letter 4), which he found when he arrived in Saint-Briac in Brittany, prompted him to write to his parents:

On arriving I found a very interesting letter from Vincent which I read and re-read to divert myself, because with the wind that's blowing, the rain and the cold, the countryside, although very wild, is still really dreary. Vincent congratulates me on my decision about Algeria, and tells me that he will perhaps also go to see me there himself. He advises me to build myself up before going for my service, which I also believe very necessary, although my constitution is not as strong as it looks. In short, he's a very good friend, very sincere, and all his southern exuberance expresses itself (in a northerner) in a deep sincerity. But (there's always a but), he blows up too quickly over unimportant things. He has spoken to me a lot about the lines of verse I sent him, and says, "it's not as good as your painting, but you must definitely continue with sonnets. There are many pals who think it's bad to write. Well! I say that it's just as interesting to paint with words as with a brush. So continue."[25]

On 11 June 1888 he again wrote to his parents about his friend. "He's a lad with a great artistic temperament, but too independent, with a deeply developed scientific side; in spite of that, I don't despair of seeing him come back with some really good things. He has a quick understanding, and in short has a highly developed artistic side (that's so rare!)."[26] This shows that Bernard did not blindly admire the declamatory Dutchman but had a mind of his own.

One remarkable counterpart to these private testimonies was Bernard's attempt to champion van Gogh in public as well. As early as the summer of 1889 he sent a short article about his friend to the symbolist writer and critic Albert Aurier, whom he had met in Saint-Briac the previous year. Aurier was the editor of the modern art journal *Le Moderniste Illustré*. Bernard's article was never published, but the manuscript was preserved and is now in The Morgan Library & Museum, together with the cover letter (see Appendix 2).[27] In it, Bernard explained the reasons for his initiative, which he had taken while van Gogh was being cared for in the asylum of Saint-Rémy. "As much as possible, I am eager that my good friend should be talked about a little, in the sense that he is truly an artist who ought to be spoken of in our times, not that his work is something absolutely complete, but nevertheless because of the surprising insights that he sometimes has." It is striking how the simplicity of his motivation and wording is entirely in van Gogh's mold. Those sentences could have come from the older artist's pen, had he been intervening on behalf of one of the artists of the "petit boulevard."

In January 1890 van Gogh's name suddenly became much more widely known as a result of the publication of an article devoted entirely to him by Albert Aurier in his series "Les isolés" in the *Mercure de France*.[28] He placed van Gogh right in the middle of the avant-garde artists of the day, something that van Gogh found a little difficult to accept, judging by his letter of thanks

to Aurier, although that did not stop him giving the critic his painting *Cypresses* (F 620 / JH 1748; Otterlo, Kröller-Müller Museum).[29] Given the importance of that article, it is understandable that Bernard wrote to Aurier again in the summer of 1890 to draw attention to his friend but under sadder circumstances: van Gogh's death on 29 July 1890. In his letter, written two days later, Bernard gave a subdued but nonetheless very moving account of what he had heard about the circumstances surrounding the suicide and of the funeral that he had attended on 30 July in Auvers-sur-Oise.[30]

Bernard would later look back on his friendship with van Gogh on more than one occasion. In 1890 he wrote an article for *Les Hommes d'Aujourd'hui* in which he sketched a portrait of van Gogh from his own recollections as an energetic and impassioned artist. He recalled that shortly after they met, among other works, van Gogh showed him *The Potato Eaters* (see Fig. 7C), which he described as "remarkably ugly and disturbingly alive."[31] His drift is obvious: the Dutchman had come from afar both literally and figuratively. It was only after he had experimented with new techniques and ideas in Paris that van Gogh found an authoritative style and a very pictorial, individual technique in Arles. Bernard used him in passing to comment on a topical subject by saying that van Gogh was tormented by "a nascent symbolism." A work may look "unfinished" in itself, but van Gogh's oeuvre as a whole attests to his complexity. Bernard wrote a little apologetically: "his invariable turbulence of spirit gave him a unity that, in the long run, shows him very balanced, very logical, very aware. Some people saw insanity in the last canvases. But what is it when it reveals itself in its present form, if not genius?"[32]

In September 1891 Bernard published an evocative portrait of his friend in *La Plume*.

Red-haired (goatee beard, ragged moustache, cap of close-cropped hair), with a piercing gaze and an incisive mouth, so to speak; of medium height, stocky without being overweight, his gestures lively, his gait jerky, that was van Gogh with, always, his pipe, a canvas or an engraving, or a folder. Vehement in his discourse, given to interminable explanations and a great developer of ideas, not much given to controversy—all that is him, too; and dreams, ah! what dreams! Huge exhibitions, philanthropic phalansteries of artists, the foundation of colonies in the south and elsewhere, the gradual penetration of public domains in the interests of the celebrated reeducation of the masses, who, nevertheless, knew art in the past . . . [33]

In a later article, Bernard asserted that van Gogh "intrigued everyone with his fierce, absorbed manner."[34] His remarks laid the groundwork for the later reception of van Gogh's work and life as an artist.

One interesting piece of writing that presents Bernard's view of their friendship is the introduction he wrote for the first complete edition of van Gogh's letters to him, which appeared under the imprint of the Paris art dealer and publisher Ambroise Vollard in 1911. Bernard portrayed himself there as a comrade in the struggle, a devoted friend who, unlike most people, believed in van Gogh's talent from the very start. He held him up as a model to the French, who were more interested in luxury and fashion in 1911. Here was an independent figure who nevertheless regarded Mauve, Rembrandt, and Delacroix as his great models, briefly took lessons at the academy, experimented with different techniques and palettes (impressionistic, divisionistic), but who always broke free of them to strike out on a new path of his own. The tragedy of van Gogh's final years was that, as a spiritual northerner, he had ended up among the inhabitants of the south of France, with their Latin temperament. He was still, according to Bernard, preoccupied with social, religious, and mystical questions, which made him, a rational thinker, lonely in his southern surroundings.

"Oppositions frequently create unexpected conflicts of this kind and resolve them in an inner tragedy, hidden from everyone's eyes." Moreover, as a result of the onset of his mental breakdowns, the elation in the sun supposedly gave way to melancholy.[35] Here, once again, we have the portrait of the tormented genius that became integral to the van Gogh myth.

Bernard's essay shows that he tried to foster understanding for his friend, but here and there his wording also reveals his reservations, particularly regarding technique. Van Gogh occasionally lost himself in excessive impasto, his use of color was not always right, his style was sometimes weak, and he was unable to paint hands, but his painter's temperament and expressive frenzy made up for all of that.[36] Reservations are also evident when, after describing the crisis that led to van Gogh cutting off part of his ear, Bernard remarked: "I do not describe it all without sharing his horror and without understanding how far the incompleteness of his art, marked by an undeniable genius, demands indulgence and forgiveness." Yet after this, Bernard believed, came van Gogh's best work, because he had shaken off his naturalism and had come to identify with simple people and objects.

He is less preoccupied with technique, he paints better because he is no longer playing scales but following the development of his inner visions. His mysticism leads in the direction of a pity that makes him love his suffering brothers, the underclass and the poor, the lowest of the low, the sick, the lost; in nature itself he is touched by the sight of the old tree covered in ivy, the fountain in the park, from which the water is missing, and which the leaves fill with their faded mantle.[37]

The Role of the Letters

Bernard and van Gogh had ample opportunity to meet and speak in Paris, so there is only one letter from that period (Letter 1). Van Gogh's departure for the south of France put an end to their companionship. They kept in touch from March 1888 by letter—a medium that both used avidly in their contact with others.[38] In the spring of 1888 letters were actively and immediately exchanged.

Bernard himself described the role of the letters as:

the bond that joins us together; they enabled us to love each other, to know each other, during this separation. He liked writing me long letters. I was, I believe, after Gauguin, his only friend; I have seen the letters he addressed to him, they were shorter, because more respectful. Gauguin was his elder, and in his eyes occupied a position superior to his own: he had known the impressionists and come into conflict with them. So only to me did he entirely let himself go; I was fifteen years younger, and although he spoke of my works—those of an eighteen-year-old—with consideration, he could adopt a counseling, protective voice toward my youth; that is why, despite my total independence from any influence, one will find in these letters the tone allowed a man of ripe years toward a young man.[39]

Here he touched on a few key points. Van Gogh was indeed very isolated in Arles and had hardly any artistic contact other than by correspondence.[40] The written dialogue with his brother Theo prior to his arrival in Paris was revived in the south of France and was of course an important safety valve. It was, however, far less concerned with artistic matters than were the letters to Bernard published here. In fact, van Gogh did not write to anyone else so expressly on this level. What has survived of his correspondence with Gauguin shows that, as one would expect, they discussed similar subjects but they did not expound their ideas at such length; their exchange was more formal and less spontaneous. Gauguin was reserved by nature, and van Gogh had too much respect for him to express himself freely. Anthon van Rappard had been a valued correspondent in

the Dutch period, but van Gogh's ideas were still taking shape at that point. His self-appointed role as Bernard's mentor challenged him to put into words his increasingly crystallized artistic, social, and religious views. These letters thus constitute a catalogue of van Gogh's view of the world from 1887–89 and as such are unique in his surviving correspondence. They expound the grand ideas that have proved to be so characteristic of his idealistic vision of the future: the search for fraternization and collaboration among artists; the hope of a renaissance in painting to counterbalance the decadence he saw around him; the social exclusion of the artist, which was unavoidable if anything innovative was to be created; the physical and psychological sacrifices that the artist had to make for the sake of his art.

It would, however, be wrong to judge the letters solely on the basis of their function as an outlet for the writer and their importance for our knowledge of his world of ideas. They must also have been a very valuable support for the young Bernard at the time, because in the early years of his career they contained recognition of his aspirations and achievements. Van Gogh had involved his friend in exhibitions back in Paris, and from Arles he praised his drawings and paintings, his plans, his immersion in the Bible, his poetry. Both were well-informed about the history of art and literature, and both were prone to admire, even to gush. Van Gogh satisfied Bernard's hunger for knowledge, and one can see from his introduction to the publication of parts of the letters in the *Mercure de France* that he profited from what van Gogh had to offer him.

As much theology as sociability. As much criticism as painting. Just compare these letters one with another, and see how they form the similar links of a single chain, and that harmony that comes from similarity. The greatest geniuses are endlessly quoted in them. Names of gods, saints, apostles, scholars, painters, Jesus, Rembrandt, Giotto, Delacroix, etc. Each of these names evokes a world of ideas that respond to one another, add to one another, and, creating unison, lead you towards the sublime.[41]

Van Gogh did not mince his words and could be severely critical if he felt he had good cause. It seems that Bernard was usually able to take it. He was definitely an advocate of discussion and innovation. "In fact, someone who has suffered, loved, battled, has lived, has lived to the full. To struggle is to live. Eternal harmony is certainly admirable but it is inert; it engenders nothing. There must be ebb and flow in everything, that's the law, the rhythm, the beat."[42] The same names and thus the same differences in appreciation keep coming to the surface. While van Gogh cited Dickens, Balzac, Zola, Rembrandt, Delacroix, and Millet, Baudelaire, Cézanne, and the Italian primitives appealed to Bernard. The differences in their cultural backgrounds and traditions is abundantly clear. And the generation gap probably played a part, too. Bernard said that the difference in their ages lay at the root of the difference between his own absolutism and van Gogh's eclecticism.[43]

The exchange was fairly continuous from March 1888, but after van Gogh's letter of 1 or 2 November of that year, when Gauguin was staying in the Yellow House, a silence fell that lasted almost a year, for reasons that are not entirely clear. Bernard may have felt that van Gogh was not overly enthusiastic about having him come to Arles for the winter of 1888–89, and once it had been decided that Gauguin would come, he was the only guest whom van Gogh could or wanted to think about. Nevertheless, while this was under discussion—around summer of 1888—the correspondence continued as usual, as did the exchanges of drawings. Moreover, Bernard was certainly very much in the minds of van Gogh and Gauguin when they were planning the studio of the south. The last letter before the silence was in fact written by the two elder artists.

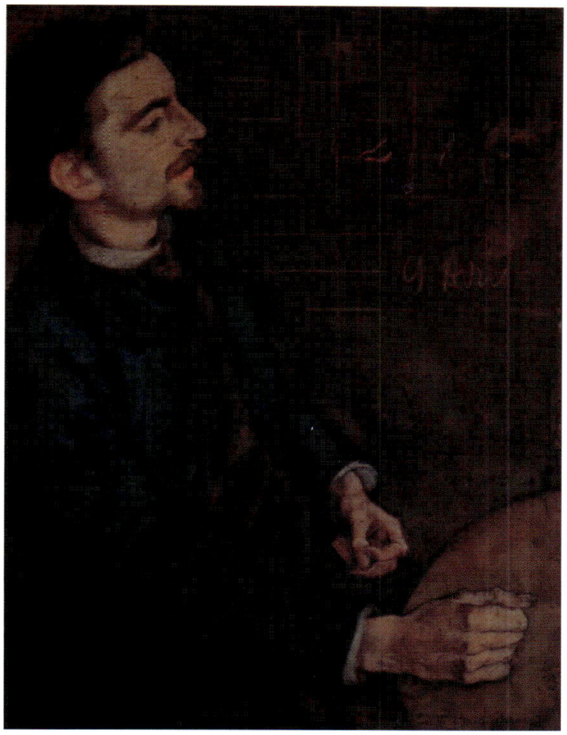

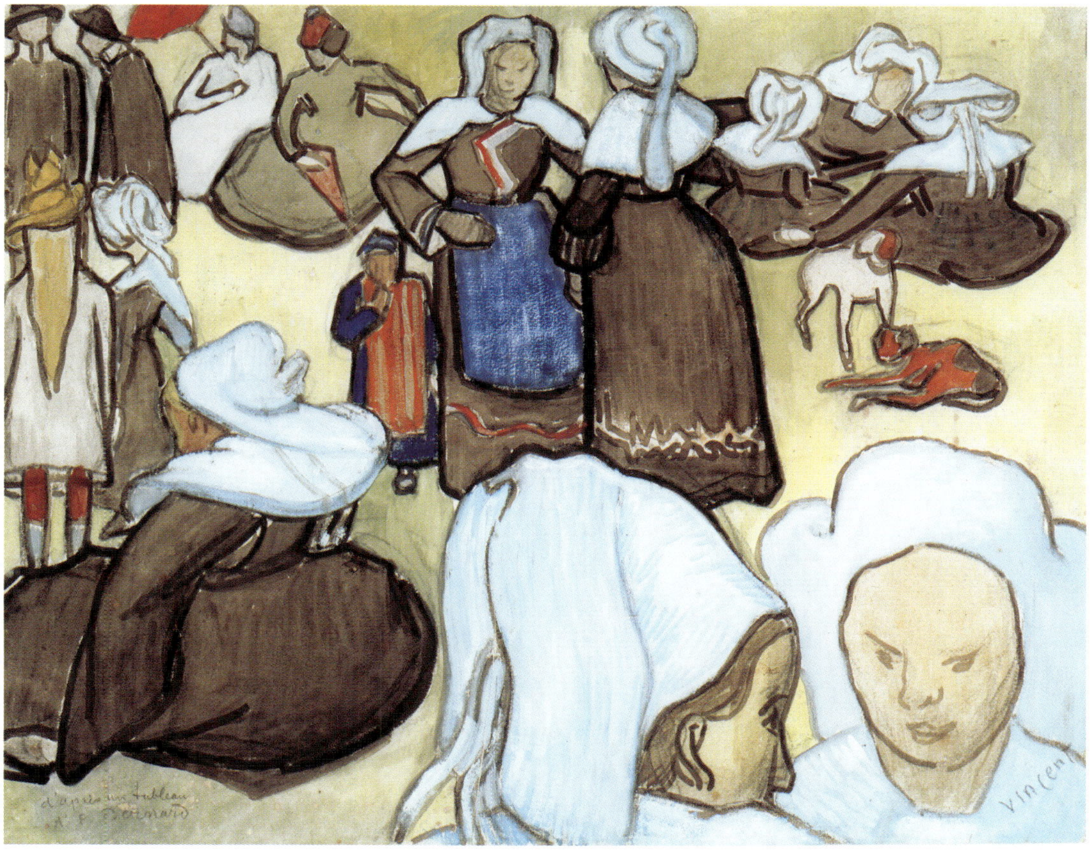

6. Louis Anquetin, *Portrait of Émile Bernard,* 1887. Amsterdam, Van Gogh Museum.

7. Vincent van Gogh, *Breton Women, After Bernard,* 1888 (F 1422 / JH 1654). Milan, Civica Galleria d'Arte Moderna.

Gauguin's stay ended abruptly at the end of December, when weeks of growing tension between them boiled over, with van Gogh slashing his ear. He then entered a long period of frequent hospitalizations in which his mental health seesawed. It seems only logical to consider this one of the causes of the broken contact.[44] Against that, though, is the fact that he did continue corresponding with Theo and his sister Willemien, albeit with a few interruptions. Bernard, for his part, longed to hear from van Gogh, as is clear from the letters to Theo.[45] In addition there was his above-mentioned proposal to Aurier in the summer of 1889 to have something published about van Gogh.

All in all, then, there is no reason to assume that their feelings of friendship had diminished. When the correspondence resumed in October 1889, after a break of almost a year, van Gogh's involvement was as intense as it had ever been. What is striking, though, is that in the two letters that follow he addressed his friend alternately with their customary *tu* form and the more formal *vous.* This seems to be a symptom of the uncertainty that had gradually taken hold of van Gogh. From an artistic point of view, the fiasco of the collaboration with Gauguin was a major setback, and the prospects for his mental and physical health were far from reassuring.

As far as the contents of the letters are concerned, there is no sign that the bond had weakened. Van Gogh is obviously pleased that Bernard had gone to look at recent work at Theo's, he inquires after Bernard's progress, and asks for information about the world's fair being held at the time. But in the last letter, of November 1889, he is so scathing about Bernard's religious paintings that for a while he must have killed off any desire on Bernard's part to continue with the correspondence. Underlying van Gogh's criticism was an issue that kept cropping up between him, Bernard, and Gauguin, which was whether an artist was better able to express an idea by taking reality as the basis for a work of art or to paint from the imagination. Bernard and Gauguin tended to use the imagination, memories. They deliberately dispensed with reality and employed polyinterpretability, mystery, and enigma to suggest the idea behind the work. Van Gogh had experimented with this, particularly while Gauguin was staying in Arles, but it provided a rude awakening. He simply could not do it, and he held fast to reality, nature in the broader sense, although he also depicted that as seen through his temperament, in accordance with the principle of Zola, whom he admired so much.[46] That is why Bernard's religious scenes provoked such a severe attack, as if van Gogh had been personally insulted by the unrealistic nature of the figures in *The Adoration of the Shepherds* and *Christ in the Garden of Olives* (see Figs. 100 and 106), of which Bernard had sent photographs.[47]

But although this contretemps put an end to their correspondence, van Gogh's criticism cannot be seen as his final judgment on Bernard, for in the same period he often wrote about him at length to his sister Willemien. It is true that he repeated his objections to the religious works, but he praised others highly (*CL* W16). Therefore, from his point of view, the friendship had not ended, and in January 1890 he wrote that he wanted to write to Bernard, and that he was expecting a letter from him (*CL* W19).

Another possible reason for the break in the correspondence is that things were not going well for Bernard either; he was depressed after an unhappy love affair and had money worries. In December 1889 he went to Lille, where his grandmother lived, to work for six months as a textile designer.[48] This explains why they could not meet during the few days in May 1890 that van Gogh spent in Paris on his way to Auvers-sur-Oise. When Bernard arrived there on 30 July 1890 to attend his friend's funeral, the lid of the coffin had already been closed.[49]

The History of the Letters

Publication History

Despite the reservations that Bernard later aired about van Gogh's views and technique, he was one of the main champions of his friend's work in the decade following his death. He assisted Theo, who began making plans for a retrospective exhibition immediately after his brother's suicide. Theo first sounded out the renowned art dealer Paul Durand-Ruel, who after some hesitation turned the offer down. It was then decided to hang as many works as possible in the apartment at 8, cité Pigalle, where Theo lived with his wife, Jo van Gogh-Bonger, and their infant son, and Bernard was asked to help with the hanging.[50] In April 1892 Bernard organized an exhibition in the Galerie Le Barc de Boutteville in the rue le Pelletier in Paris, where sixteen works were put on display for a month (Fig. 8).[51] He also urged Jo to leave the collection in France (it had remained in Paris for some time after Theo's death in January 1891), because he felt that that would be the best way of securing van Gogh's reputation.[52]

Bernard also recognized the remarkable power of the letters early on. They provided an insight into van Gogh's mental world, which is why he had used them to provide Albert Aurier with information for his "Les isolés" article in January 1890. Bernard even claimed to be the one who had kindled Aurier's enthusiasm for van Gogh's work. "I had won him over to Vincent at my first meeting with him, at Saint-Briac [in the summer of 1888]. [. . .] I showed him [. . .] the letters from van Gogh that I had recently received, the drawings in them charmed him and their text enthralled him."[53] The critic Gustave Geffroy had also made similar use of the letters to Bernard in 1888, but that did not result in an article.[54] So the letters were already gaining currency during van Gogh's lifetime—something that few people realize.

But naturally Bernard also saw their intrinsic value as *documents humains* and understood that they could be of interest to a wider public. He had already pointed out in his article in *Les Hommes d'Aujourd'hui* that an edition of his letters from van Gogh "would have novelty and appeal." In 1893 passages from them were published in several installments in the *Mercure de France*, Bernard's purpose being, as he later wrote, "to try to make Vincent appreciated by revealing his spirit, his struggle, his life. There was nothing more powerful than his letters. After reading them, you would doubt neither his sincerity, nor his character, nor his originality; you would find everything there."[55] The first four installments, which appeared in the months April to July, were taken from the letters to Bernard himself, who wrote in the introduction: "He was the noblest human character one could meet: frank, open, alert to the possible, with a certain trace of comical mischievousness; an excellent friend, an implacable judge, utterly without egoism or ambition, as his so simple letters show, in which he is as much himself as in his countless canvases."[56]

The humble editing work that he had to undertake for the *Mercure* publication cost him a great deal of time and worry. A passage in a letter to Theo's friend and Jo's brother Andries Bonger of 31 December 1892 is revealing. "I copied out part of the letters, it's very time-consuming and fiddly work. I am often forced to complete unfinished sentences and to follow ideas through impenetrable mazes. At other times it's as clear as water from a spring. What do you think of this idea, for example: Luther is the great light of the Middle Ages. Luther in the Middle Ages and an assertion of that kind, that could damage Vincent . . . Should such things be included? Tell me frankly what you think."[57] In other words, Bernard wanted to protect van Gogh from his presumed mistakes and exaggerations, which is why he replaced *moyen-age* with *la Renaissance* in the *Mercure* version.[58]

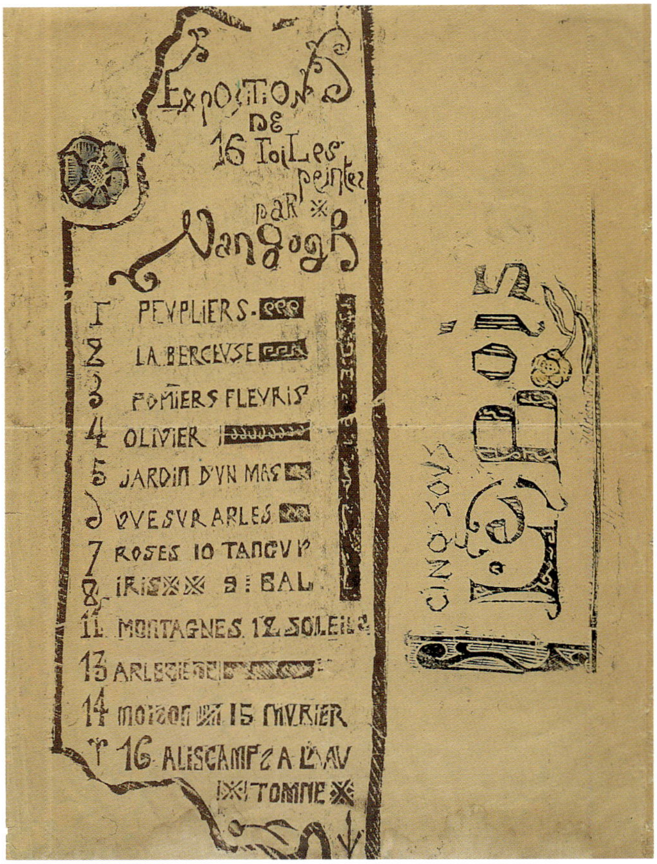

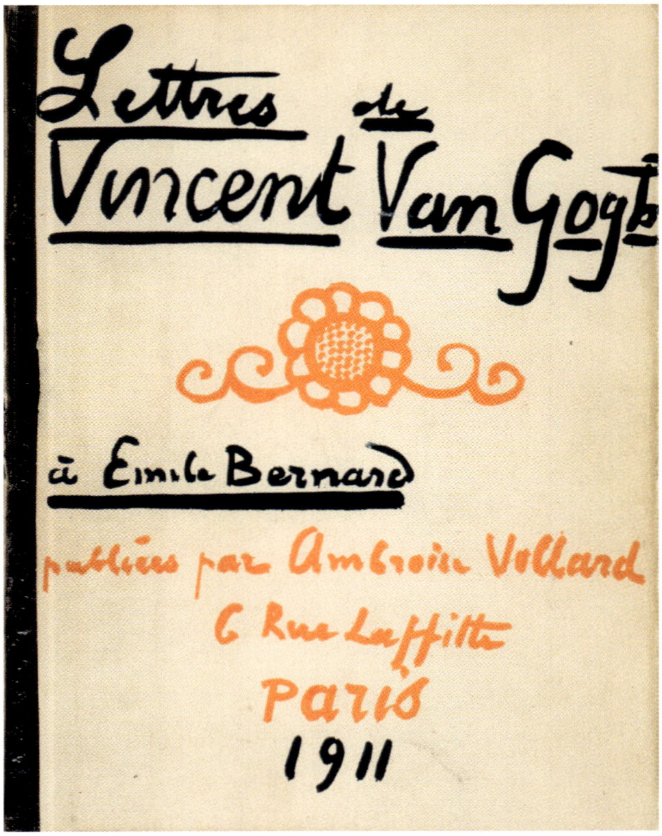

8. Émile Bernard, *Catalogue for the van Gogh Exhibition at Galerie Le Barc de Boutteville, Paris*, 1891–92. Amsterdam, Van Gogh Museum (Vincent van Gogh Foundation).

9. Front cover of *Lettres de Vincent van Gogh à Émile Bernard*. Émile Bernard, ed., Paris (Vollard), 1911. Amsterdam, Van Gogh Museum Library.

Regarding the selection of the passages, he said in the integral edition of the letters published in 1911 that he had avoided touching on personal matters concerning himself or others. "Rather than publishing all of them straightaway, it was necessary, so to speak, to extract only their essence, so that the desired goal might be attained through cautious contact between the public mind and van Gogh's mind. In publishing these fragments in the *Mercure de France*, I therefore took the position of reproducing nothing that could wound through coarseness of language, crudity of expression, of publishing nothing relating to myself, of giving only the initials of friends involved in our lives in those days."[59]

And indeed, the fairly arbitrary sequence of the passages reveals almost nothing about private affairs or intimacies; the scabrous tone of some of the letters was also absent. Bernard did dare include the following passage: "Painting and loving women are not compatible; and that's what's really damned annoying." The original text, though, is a good bit coarser: "Painting and fucking a lot are not compatible; it weakens the brain, and that's what's really damned annoying" (Letter 7). Bernard highlighted several of the main themes running through the correspondence: seventeenth-century Dutch painting, modern painting, descriptions of van Gogh's work and progress, van Gogh's reactions to Bernard's work, and observations about religion and society. Each installment was illustrated with works by van Gogh—mainly letter sketches and drawings.

The Bernard letters were followed by passages from some of those to Theo in nine installments spanning the period August 1893 to February 1895, with a delayed postscript in August 1897. This series was also edited by Bernard, who had been loaned the letters by Jo van Gogh-Bonger since her return to the Netherlands after Theo's death.[60]

The *Mercure de France* was not the only periodical to publish van Gogh's correspondence. In 1893 fragments also appeared in the August issue of the Flemish avant-garde journal *Van Nu en Straks*. This, however, was no more than a minor miscellany selected from the letters written in Dutch and one or two in French; in addition the journal had a far smaller circulation. The *Mercure* was read throughout Europe. It was the prime mover in the unstoppable advance of van Gogh's letters and the eventual legend of his life. At first it was just modern artists and writers who recognized a great artist and writer in his letters, but gradually they began to reach a wider audience. In the first decade of the twentieth century, the Berlin art dealer and publisher Paul Cassirer produced a book containing all the fragments that had appeared in the two journals in a translation by Margarethe Mauthner, a collector of van Gogh's work. The book went through many reprintings and had sales in the tens of thousands. One consequence of this, of course, was that the readers got only a very limited insight into van Gogh's Dutch period, with the emphasis being on the letters written in French, which make up only one third of the total and mainly cover the later years of the artist's life. One must remember, though, that it was mainly the innovative work of van Gogh's French period that attracted attention abroad, with his Dutch oeuvre being treated as a curious footnote.

That was still the case when Ambroise Vollard, the Paris art dealer and publisher of art books, decided to issue an integral edition of the Bernard letters, which can be described as the prototype of the present book. A contract was drawn up on 25 January 1910, under which Bernard, the owner of the manuscripts, sold the publication rights for six years for 2,000 francs. During those six years Vollard could print as many copies as he wished, provided he adhered to the approved design and sold the copies for no less than 10 francs. On 18 October 1911, Bernard wrote out a receipt for the agreed sum. Strangely enough, Vollard paid him an additional 840 francs on 23 January 1912: "for full payment regarding the edition of van Gogh's letters to him."[61] It appears that Bernard received a sum for each copy sold, although there is nothing about that in the contract.

It is also possible that the payment was for the introductory material that Bernard had supplied for the edition.

It is not known how many copies Vollard put on the market. His surviving sales ledgers are far from complete and offer little to go on. What they do show is that most copies cost around 70 francs, although there was a very sizable discount for a batch of 100 copies sold in November 1923 for 1,500 francs.

The layout was very generous, with wide margins, 100 reproductions of drawings, letter sketches, and paintings by van Gogh in black and white, as well as two color reproductions *hors texte.* Forty copies were printed on Japanese paper. The cover, designed by Bernard, had a simple ornament, the title, and the publisher's name in script, printed in orange and blue (Fig. 9). The text ratios are remarkable, with a little over eighty pages reserved for the letters, and seventy pages for the prefatory material. The latter consists of a 43-page preface that Bernard wrote specially for this edition, and four other articles on van Gogh: the two introductions for the series of letters to Bernard and to Theo published in the *Mercure de France* (both of 1893), a previously unpublished introduction written in 1895 for an unrealized edition, and the essay on van Gogh that had appeared in *Les Hommes d'Aujourd'hui.* It is not likely that Vollard's edition reached very many people, for the design was of a bibliophilic luxuriousness. Today it is a collector's item.

Bernard wrote in his introduction that the letters were being published in full, complete with all the peculiarities of van Gogh's French and the occasionally coarse language, which according to him was sometimes attributable to alcohol.[62] Whatever his protestations, though, he did censor here and there by replacing names with initials or an *X,* and by giving only the first letter of coarse or indecorous words followed by dots, which just made them more prominent. Perhaps he thought that he had to do so in order to protect the pure reputation of his friend. He must also have been the source for another explanation, however, which Douglas Cooper recounted in his 1938 English edition of the Bernard letters. "Bernard himself, it is true, wanted to publish the whole text, but at the last minute M. Vollard for personal reasons, partly on account of Degas, saw fit to omit several words, not to mention whole sentences and paragraphs."[63] But in other places, too, the Vollard text is not entirely accurate. Cooper added a five-page list of Emendations to the Published Text after studying the original manuscripts.

Cooper's *Letters to Émile Bernard* appeared in an English edition published by The Cresset Press in London and an American licensed edition under the auspices of the Museum of Modern Art in New York.[64] Cooper made an important contribution to the dissemination of van Gogh's ideas with this edition, for these letters were the last of those known at the time that had not yet been published in English. In addition, Cooper improved on the chronology of the letters in Vollard's 1911 edition. It was republished unaltered in later editions of van Gogh's complete correspondence, and the letters were given their distinctive B numbers. Cooper's edition was also the first, and so far only one, in which the letters were annotated.[65] Together with the editorial improvements mentioned above, his edition can be regarded as innovative in the field of van Gogh studies.[66]

The History of the Manuscripts

Almost all the letters that van Gogh wrote to his brother Theo remained in the possession of the latter's descendants, from whom they came to the Van Gogh Museum. Many letters to other people, however, went on unpredictable peregrinations, which are often difficult or impossible to trace, from the original recipient to their present location. For example, the originals of fifty-five very

important letters to Anthon van Rappard surfaced recently and fortunately the Van Gogh Museum was in a position to acquire them for its collection, while other letters became dispersed among the collections of private individuals, some of them anonymous, and among museums in Europe and the United States.

In the case of the Bernard letters, only one fact about the provenance is unclear—when and how Bernard disposed of them. Letter 20 is the exception, for he gave it to Aurier as background material for his article on van Gogh in the *Mercure de France*.[67] Since it had become separated from the rest it was not included in the 1911 edition, nor in Cooper's publication of 1938. Aurier died in 1892, and his estate, together with the letter, passed to a cousin, Eliane Williame-Mahé in Aix. On her death it was passed on by inheritance, and its present whereabouts are not known to us.[68]

Although it is conceivable that Bernard thought that the time had come to sell the letters after their integral publication in 1911, they were still in his possession in 1926, for in that year some of them were included in *Lettres de Vincent van Gogh, Paul Gauguin, Paul Cézanne, J.-K. Huysmans, Léon Bloy, Elémir Bourges, Milos Marten, Odilon Redon, Maurice Barrès à Émile Bernard*, which was published by Bernard himself under the imprint of his own publishing house, Editions de la Rénovation Esthétique in Tonnerre.[69] In addition to the fact that a facsimile was included in the book, it can be deduced from Bernard's foreword that he still had the originals.[70]

We are on firm ground again in 1929, but now the scene moves to Berlin, where the wealthy ex-diplomat, art lover, and bibliophile publisher Count Harry Kessler noted the following in his diary on 8 December.

Dined at Baby Goldschmidt-Rothschild's on the Pariser Platz. Eight to ten people, intimate dinner, extreme luxury, four priceless masterpieces by Manet, Cézanne, van Gogh and Monet on the walls. After the meal, thirty letters by van Gogh, in an excessively ornate, horrible binding, were handed round with the cigarettes and coffee. Poor van Gogh! In the end one thinks pogromishly: these people should be beaten to death. Not out of jealousy but disgust at the falsification and degradation of intellectual and artistic values to mere materialistic values, objects of "luxury."[71]

It is absolutely certain that it was the Bernard letters that Mrs. Goldschmidt-Rothschild—"Baby" to her friends but born Marianne von Friedländer-Fuld—was showing off, to Kessler's irritation, which verged on anti-Semitism. She is identical to "the Baroness de Goldschmidt-Rothschild" whom Douglas Cooper thanked in his English edition of the Bernard letters "for her kindness in allowing me to consult and photograph the manuscript originals in her possession."[72] It is doubtful whether the "thirty" should be taken literally, for since 1911 there have never been more known letters than those published in the Vollard edition (and in the present publication). Kessler's figure was probably an estimate.[73]

So Bernard sold the letters from van Gogh after his 1926 publication. The fact that they ended up in Berlin raises the question of whether the art dealer Paul Cassirer was involved in some way, possibly through Ambroise Vollard, with whom he regularly did business. That, though, is guesswork, and there is no trace of any such transaction.[74] What is certain is that the baroness kept the letters, although two did become separated over the course of time. The first was Letter 11, now in the Lugt Collection in the Fondation Custodia in Paris, which she donated to that institute in 1966. The second to leave the corpus was Letter 15, which opens with the famous cry from the heart: "I want to do figures, figures and more figures, it's stronger than me." It is not known who

bien cela m'a énormément amusé
faire cet intérieur sans rien
e simplicité à la Seurat

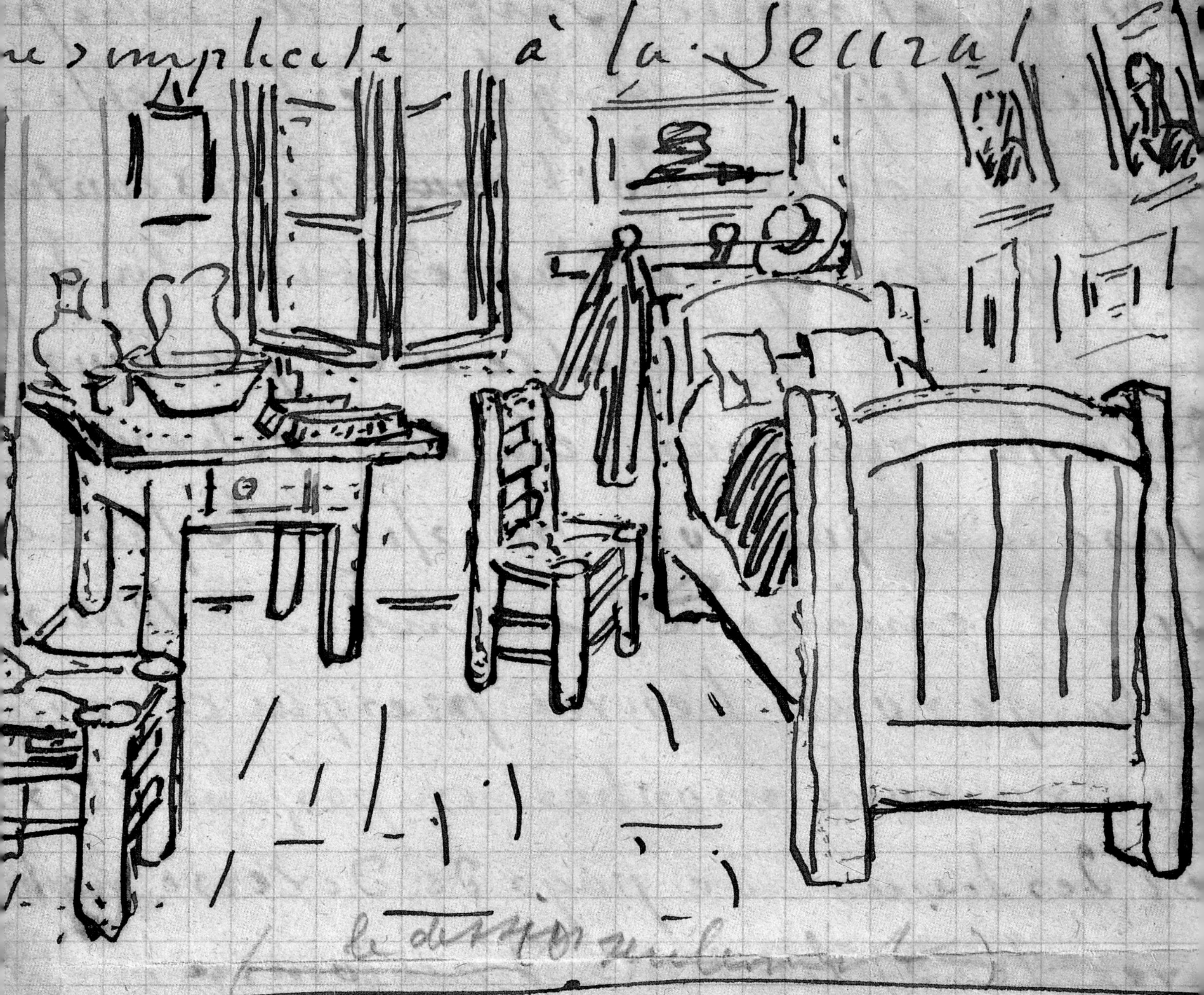

teintes plates mais grossièrement brossé
pleine pâte les murs lilas pâle
sol d'un rouge rompu et fané les
uses et le lit jaune de chrome les ore
drap citron vert très pâle la couvert
... la table à toilette orangé

acquired this letter, or when. All that is known is that it was auctioned by Drouot in Paris on 15 May 2001 and now belongs to Anne-Marie Springer.[75]

So depending on when Letter 15 started out life on its own, Mrs. Goldschmidt-Rothschild still had twenty or twenty-one letters, which passed to her heirs on her death. They first sold the manuscript of one letter separately, with the magnificent sketch of *The Bedroom*. Being a letter to Gauguin, it was in fact a *corpus alienum* in the collection of Bernard letters (see Appendix 1). The buyer was the American collector Eugene Thaw, who in late 2001 succeeded in acquiring the remaining pièce de résistance, and was so generous as to present the entire group to The Morgan Library & Museum as a promised gift. Without that gesture, much new information about these letters would have remained unknown, and this book would never have been published.

Notes to the Reader

The letters from Vincent van Gogh to Émile Bernard are numbered from 1 to 22. General references to them use these numbers only (for example, Letter 22). Letter numbers preceded by an abbreviation refer to the following publications:
CL: The Complete Letters of Vincent van Gogh. 3 vols. Boston, Toronto and London, 1958.
GAC: Douglas Cooper, *Paul Gauguin: 45 lettres à Vincent, Theo et Jo van Gogh*. The Hague, 1983.
The dates of the letters in this publication are those that have been assigned to them in the forthcoming new edition of the correspondence.

This book contains all the known letters that Vincent van Gogh wrote to Émile Bernard. The artists corresponded from 1887 to 1889, but only van Gogh's side of the exchange has survived. Even that is incomplete, for on 8 September 1888 he told his brother Theo that he had written to Bernard and Gauguin, but there is no trace of the letter or letters in question. Although there are no other indicators of this kind, it is possible that van Gogh wrote even more letters to Bernard.

Above all, this is a source edition, the purpose of which is to publish a faithful text and to clarify its content. The methods and their implementation have not been applied to this publication alone but are an integral part of the basic principles of the Van Gogh Letters Project, which was launched by the Van Gogh Museum in Amsterdam in 1994, in collaboration with the Huygens Institute (part of the Royal Netherlands Academy of Arts and Sciences). The project objective is to publish a scholarly, annotated edition of the complete correspondence of Vincent van Gogh. The principles and methodology applied in the project will be detailed at length in the integral edition. They are outlined here in brief.

Detail of Appendix 1.

The Texts of the Letters

The reader is presented with three versions of van Gogh's letters to Bernard: in facsimile, as edited transcription, and in English translation.

To the extent possible, the facsimiles are printed in full size, unless otherwise indicated. The present whereabouts of Letter 20 are not known, so the black-and-white photographs held in the Documentation Department of the Van Gogh Museum had to suffice.

The edited transcriptions reproduce the manuscripts as faithfully as possible, meaning that all the slips of the pen, inconsistencies and peculiar spellings are included as written. Diacritical marks were used in the transcriptions to indicate which letters or words were crossed out, which ones became illegible as a result, which passages were added later, and so on. Van Gogh also wrote some words atypically (larger, with extra space between the letters, thicker letters) in order to give them added emphasis. Significant features of this kind were documented in the transcriptions.

Such a transcription may preserve many graphic details, but it is not a pleasure to read. The edited transcription is therefore an adaptation. Here we were helped by the Romance language scholar Wouter van der Veen, who edited all the French transcriptions in accordance with the rules established for van Gogh's letters in Dutch, while making the necessary adaptations dictated by the difference in language.

First the diacritical marks were removed, but it was also desirable to make several other modifications, as detailed below. Graphic characteristics are inevitably lost when converting from manuscript to printed page. Textually, though, we have endeavored to remain as close to the original as possible. The letters were not written for publication but to tell the recipient something, be it of a practical, artistic, or intellectual nature. It was the content that counted, not copperplate handwriting or the rules of spelling. The liberties that van Gogh took in these areas were typical of him. Punctuation, accents, and apostrophes are often missing, along with capital letters at the beginning of a sentence or a name. When compiling the edited transcriptions, we tried to do justice to van Gogh's insouciance while remaining within the bounds of readability. To put it another way: we wanted to correct him as little as possible. In addition, we applied the following basic principles.

The edited text represents the final version of the letter. The final reading of the letter is printed, omitting passages that van Gogh wrote over or crossed out (with the exception of a few interventions and emendations, which will be treated below). Needless to say, deleted text or the fact that something was added later can sometimes be revealing, and where we believed that readers might be interested in such passages we have included them in the annotations.

The edited text must be comprehensible and must not lead to misunderstandings. Comprehensible does not mean faultless, and most of van Gogh's lapses do not, in fact, compromise understanding, which is why inconsistencies in spelling, the use of capitals, and missing punctuation marks are not *automatically* corrected. That said, though, the most faithful reproduction of the text of a letter must not leave it up to the reader to tease out the intended meaning from the context. We have made emendations in those cases where, in our opinion, errors and sloppiness could result in incomprehension or misunderstanding. This is explained in further detail in the following section.

The edited text should reflect the distinctive features of van Gogh's style of writing as closely as possible. In addition to grammatical errors and spelling mistakes, and the lack of care over a letter's appearance, there are words, expressions, and forms of spelling that have to be regarded as part of van Gogh's personal idiom, and it would be irresponsible to correct them. Not only is it impossible to lay down an objective norm, it would also detract from the spontaneous and intimate nature of

these private documents. We have therefore not emended incorrect spellings and expressions, such as *néamoins* (in Letter 22) and *en tant que quant à* (Letter 13 and others), because they are typical of the way this Dutchman in France wrote, and do not cause misunderstanding.[1]

The text must be quotable and translatable. This goes without saying and is an important reason for not using diacritical marks. Moreover, language, spelling, and structure must be such that students, scholars, and translators have no need of special graphic devices in order to reproduce passages for papers, articles, or books. In addition, such a passage must be able to stand on its own as a text and be comprehensible. The author or translator should not be forced to accompany a quotation or translation with an explanation of van Gogh's manner of writing.

The Emendations

Our textual interventions can be divided into two groups: the changes we have made without drawing attention to them and those that are mentioned in the textual notes. The former involve issues that occur so frequently that a specification of the changes we have made would lead to unacceptably long lists. The categories are as follows.

Capital letters. Van Gogh did not always use capital letters where they are customary. Nevertheless, taking the correspondence as a whole, he did generally follow the conventions. Moreover, because capitals provide important signals to the reader, we have replaced lowercase letters with capitals in the names of people and places. This has been done tacitly.

Accents. In roughly one-third of the cases, van Gogh made mistakes when writing acute, grave, and circumflex accents. As far as the three criteria of comprehensibility, readability, and quotability permit, we have preferred not to intervene. Some incorrect accents may be typical of a Dutchman writing in French, such as *rémédier* and *pretention.* Mistakes with accents can, however, create ambiguity and make it difficult to understand the text. For example, *a* and *à* have different meanings, as do *du* and *dû*, *sur* and *sûr*, *la* and *là*, *ou* and *où*, *après* and *âpres*. This category also includes words like *represente* and *dessine*, where the omission of acute accents leads to confusion. In order to avoid that, emendations are always made in such cases without drawing attention to them, because van Gogh certainly knew what was right and in most cases used accents correctly. We have not intervened when an alternative reading is very unlikely, as in the case of *meme*, which will usually be read as *même.*

Hyphens. Van Gogh was also inconsistent with his hyphens. In French, however, they often have a semantic function. For instance, the hyphen linking *même* to a pronoun, as in *lui-même*, governs the syntax of the sentence. This also applies when the hyphen connects *là* with a noun, for there is a difference in meaning between *cet artiste-là* and *cet artiste là*. Such omissions are confusing, so the hyphen has simply been inserted without comment.

Apostrophes. Van Gogh's use of apostrophes regularly deviates from the rules in two ways, either by being omitted altogether or being put in the wrong position. In many cases this was undoubtedly just carelessness, but sometimes it would have been ascribable to confusion with the Dutch use of the apostrophe. A typical example of this is found with elision, with the apostrophe being placed before instead of after the remaining letter: *je 't écris* instead of *je t'écris* and *'t ai* instead of *t'ai,* analogous to the perfectly correct Dutch usage in *'s morgens* (in the morning). In our opinion, the omission or incorrect positioning of an apostrophe often disturbs the flow, so any such errors have been corrected.

Punctuation. One of the most striking features of van Gogh's cavalier approach is his carelessness with punctuation marks, especially periods, commas, quotation marks, and dashes.

We have not gone so far as to fill in all the omissions. That is not always necessary from the point of view of comprehensibility, and it would obscure the authenticity of van Gogh's style. On the other hand, the absence of punctuation sometimes hampers readability and can foster obscurity or ambiguity. Partly with a view to the basic principles outlined above, we have therefore felt it necessary to make some improvements on this front.

All other emendations are listed under the heading Textual Notes. They usually relate to uncategorized alterations, corrections of confusing slips of the pen or the elimination of redundant words. The relevant places are marked in the text with notes in the form of superscript a, b, c, and so forth. The notation used is as follows. First we give the emended text, followed by a < mark, and behind that the manuscript version or the editors' comment, or both. Those comments are italicized to set them off from the letter extract. For example, the reader will find the following in the textual notes of Letter 9:

affaire < à faire

This means we changed *à faire* into *affaire*. The following is an example of an editorial comment in Letter 7:

Je connais *[. . .]* possible < *Van Gogh put a frame around this passage.*

In one or two cases, manuscript text is missing or has been lost. Wherever possible we replace it between square brackets thus:

e*[*n*]* < *Text lost due to paper damage.*

Translation

When new text research reveals all sorts of discrepancies with previously published letters, it is self-evident that a new translation is essential. That is certainly true in van Gogh's case, for his letters are regularly studied closely, for example, to resolve questions surrounding the identification and dating of named works.

The translation of the Bernard letters was made by Imogen Forster and edited by Wouter van der Veen and Michael Hoyle (the latter being the general translation editor of the Van Gogh Letters Project), in close consultation with the editors. The objective was to provide the closest possible rendering of the meaning of van Gogh's words. In other words, this is not a literary or interpretive translation.

It is inevitable that shades of meaning get lost in translation, but needless to say we have tried to keep that to a minimum. A more troublesome area concerns a few specific features of van Gogh's use of language. His French was better than that of many foreigners, but it was not his native tongue. Some unusual phrasings are due to his Dutch. This occasionally led to idiosyncrasies in spelling, sentence structure, and wording that could not possibly be reflected in the translation. Consequently, no attempt has been made to replicate inconsistencies, errors or un-French French, since the solutions would be arbitrary and result in unnatural English.

On the other hand, there are some instances that cannot be passed over, because they are associated with important concepts in van Gogh's language and thought. For instance, he uses the French word *nature* in several senses (precisely as he does the Dutch equivalent, for that matter), among them "natural surroundings," "landscape," and "reality." Translating it consistently with the English *nature* would cause confusion at some points, or obscure van Gogh's meaning. In those cases we have therefore opted for the suitable equivalent, such as *reality*.

The verb *navrer* and its derivative *navrant* undergo a slight shift in meaning with van Gogh, which can be explained by the fact that *navrant* is a loan word in Dutch. Depending on the

context, however, van Gogh gave these words several different meanings. We have translated them according to their intention within the context.

A third instance of van Goghian French is the use of *abstrait* and *abstraction*. Apart from the normal meaning in an expression like "art is an abstraction," van Gogh used them where *distrait* or *distraction* were intended. In other words, they have become ambiguous. Once again, we have translated in the intended sense.

Finally there is the word *midi,* which can refer both to the south of France and to the area around the Mediterranean in general. In the first case the *m* should be capitalized, in the second case it should not. Van Gogh always used a lowercase *m,* and generally used the word in its general sense, even including north Africa in the *midi.* For that reason we have translated the word with the general term, *the south.*

Proper and topographical names have been capitalized without comment in the translation and comply with general usage (*de Gas* in the edited text becomes *Degas* in the translation).

Numbering of the Pages

For the most part, the letters take two forms, single and double-page spreads. In either form, each page of the letter is identified: number side: number. The first number indicates the sheet, the side is indicated by r (recto) or v (verso), and the number following the colon refers to the page in the letter. Recto stands for the front of a page and verso for the back of a page.

For example, all the letters have a page numbered 1r:1. This means the page is on the recto of the first sheet, and is the first page in the letter. Another example, which appears in the single page letters, is 2v:4. This means this page is on the verso side of the second sheet, and is the fourth page in the letter.

Single-page letters: 2, 3, 6, 7, 8, 9, 12, 13, 21, Appendix 1. These letters follow the standard pattern of 1r:1, 1v:2, 2r:3, 2v:4. The front of the first sheet is page 1, the back is page 2, the front of the second sheet is page 3, and the back is page 4. Some letters do not have a second page, and therefore end at 1v:2. One exception to this single-page identification formula is Letter 4, which is identified 1r:1, 2r:2, 2v:3, 1v:4. This means that the front of the first sheet is page 1, the front of the second sheet is page 2, the back of the second sheet is page 3, and the back of the first sheet is page 4.

Double-page letters: 1, 5, 10, 16, 17, 18, 19, 22. These letters are patterned 1r:1, 1v:2, 1v:3, 1r:4. The whole letter is contained on a single sheet, with page 1 and page 4 on the front of the sheet (page 1 on the right and page 4 on the left), and page 2 and page 3 on the back of the sheet (page 2 on the left and page 3 on the right). The exception to this double-page identification formula is Letter 14, which has two sheets. The first sheet follows the same convention as above, but the second sheet is labeled 2r:5, 2v:6, meaning the front of the second page is the fifth page of the letter, and the back of the second sheet is the sixth page of the letter.

Other letters: 11, 15, 20. These three letters are not in the Thaw Collection, The Morgan Library & Museum. All three are single-space letters; the first is in Paris, the second is in a private collection, and the location of the third is unknown.

Typography and Layout

Although writing letters is usually bound by time-specific conventions, any correspondent is free to take liberties, and it will come as no surprise to learn that van Gogh did precisely that. The textual aspect has already been discussed, but anyone looking at some pages from the correspondence will see at a glance that he was not always consistent in his placement of the salutation and signature,

in the way in which additions were made and text struck out, and in his handwriting. He did as he pleased. The letters are reproduced in facsimile in this publication, so the reader can see how they look. Moreover, it is an illusion that printed matter can reproduce the layout of a manuscript. It is for this reason that we have partially diverted from the graphic image in the edited transcriptions. Stock elements like salutations, closing formulas and signatures, paragraph indentations, letter sketches, and so on, are reproduced in the same typographical way in all the letters.

One element requires further explanation. Van Gogh had various ways of emphasizing words. As almost everyone did in those days, when writing was done by hand, he underlined important words. They are printed in this book as roman in the transcriptions and as italics in the translations. Van Gogh, however, often underlined twice or even more times, wrote some words larger or much larger than other ones, or in a different script. One also finds combinations of these emphasizing techniques. In a printed text there is a limited number of ways of reproducing such gradations. We have used italics and roman, small capitals, and full capitals, respectively, to indicate three grades of increasing emphasis. There is inevitably an arbitrary element to this, but we have of course taken the context into account, as well as relying on our findings in the other letters by van Gogh.

Annotations

The planned new edition of van Gogh's complete correspondence will be the first to have extensive annotations. We have applied the same basic principle to the present book: the annotations serve to improve understanding and elucidate the original function of the letters within van Gogh's circle. We provide factual information formulated in a concise and neutral way. The annotations themselves relate to specific passages in a letter and consist of explanations of references: names, the titles of works of art and publications, dates, the background to events, quotations, literary allusions, quotations from or references to the Bible, and historical, topographical, and geographical data.

Many will regard this as self-evident, but it also implies that we have decided not to include references to all the secondary literature in which passages from the letters are discussed. As already noted, this is a source edition. A historiography of the research into van Gogh's letters not only would be an unwarranted amplification—the completeness of which could not be guaranteed—it would be obsolete the moment the book was published.

That does not mean that we do not refer to discussions about important or recurrent problematic topics. For example, the reader will find references to the most important literature on the problem of the timing of van Gogh's visit to Saintes-Maries in Letter 6. In cases, too, where the identification of works has a history of discussions, such as the composition of the batch of drawings sent with Letter 10, the relevant literature will be given.

The literature consulted is given in short-title form, the full titles being found in Works Cited in Abbreviated Form on p. 375. The full names and dates of individuals are in the Index on p. 378. Mentions of works by van Gogh are followed by their present location and their numbers in the oeuvre catalogues: Faille 1970 (F) and Hulsker 1996 (JH), for example: *Zouave, Half-Length* (Amsterdam, Van Gogh Museum; F 423 / JH 1486). Mentions of works by Paul Gauguin are followed by their numbers in the catalogues raisonnés Wildenstein 2001 and Wildenstein 1963.

This is also the place to mention the most important standard literature that we have used. Van Gogh research is like a *perpetuum mobile*, with scholars benefiting from the work of their predecessors and colleagues. We are no exception.

The founding father of research into the letters was Jan Hulsker, who did pioneering work with his *Van Gogh door Van Gogh* of 1973 by making a chronological arrangement of all the correspondence known at the time and by dating the letters. He and others later made corrections and additions to his initial ordering, but his study was of fundamental importance. Tsukasa Kōdera was the first to make a thorough study of the background to van Gogh's religious ideas in *Vincent van Gogh: Christianity Versus Nature* (1990). Roland Dorn discussed everything related to the series of paintings that van Gogh made for the Yellow House in Arles in *Décoration: Vincent van Goghs Werkreihe für das Gelbe Haus in Arles* (1990). The standard works on van Gogh's French period include the catalogues that Ronald Pickvance wrote for exhibitions in The Metropolitan Museum of Art in New York: *Van Gogh in Arles* (1984) and *Van Gogh in Saint Rémy and Auvers* (1986). An essential work for the Bernard letters is Mark Roskill's article, "Van Gogh's Exchanges of Work with Émile Bernard in 1888" (1971). Finally, needless to say, we were guided on several occasions by the exhibition catalogue *Émile Bernard 1868–1941: A Pioneer of Modern Art* (Mannheim and Amsterdam 1990) and by the very first annotated van Gogh publication: Douglas Cooper's English edition, *Letters to Émile Bernard* (1938).[2]

Mention must also be made of Fred Leeman, who while preparing his forthcoming monograph on Émile Bernard discussed ideas with us on many occasions and on all kinds of subjects, and who also commented on the manuscript of our book. We profited greatly from his knowledge and helpfulness.

The annotations accompanying each letter are preceded by more general information. In the first place, under *Date* we explain our reasons for the date we have assigned to the letter. This is the date on which it was written, not when it was sent or received. When we use *ca.* we mean that it could have been written a day earlier or later. The second category is *Sketches,* which lists the sketches drawn in the letter or sent with it. If a sketch contains text, such as color notations, they are transcribed literally and given in translation. Any other points of interest that do not belong in these categories will be found under the heading *Additional details.*

Normal annotations are indicated with a note number in the edited transcription. Lettered notes (a, b, etc.) are used when an annotation relates solely to the French text, for example to explain a grammatical problem or clarification of van Gogh's idiosyncrasies.

Introductory Texts

The letters published in this book are necessarily isolated from the rest of the correspondence. The full edition will contain useful information in intervening letters or their annotations, but that context is missing in this partial edition. As well as supplying supplementary information in the annotations themselves, we have written short linking texts that briefly describe the events and questions that arose between two letters relevant to an understanding of van Gogh's written exchange of ideas with Émile Bernard.

Back Matter

In addition to the surviving letters from van Gogh to Bernard, this book contains a number of documents, which will be found in the appendices. The first is a letter from van Gogh to Gauguin that has traditionally been published with these letters (Appendix 1). Bernard added it at the back of his *Lettres à Bernard* of 1911 because by chance he had the manuscript. That practice was followed in later publications, including *Letters to Bernard* of 1938, which is why the letter has always had a B number. It, too, is on deposit at The Morgan Library & Museum. Its inclusion in the

present book means that all the van Gogh letters in this collection have been brought together in the same publication.

The Morgan also has a fine piece of testimony to Bernard's attempts to gain recognition for van Gogh's work in the shape of an article that he sent to Albert Aurier for publication in *Le Moderniste Illustré* (on this see the Introduction, p. 13). That short piece, together with the cover letter to Aurier, constitutes Appendix 2.

The back matter also contains a list of the works that the two artists exchanged. It is divided into groups according to the degree of certainty of the identifications. The list is incomplete in that it is known that both artists had more works by the other, but they are unidentifiable.

Details about the manuscripts have been kept out of the annotations and will be found in the list of physical descriptions. By and large we have confined ourselves to the size of the paper, a rough indication of its type (including any watermarks), the writing materials, and in a few cases annotations in a hand other than van Gogh's. Experience has shown that a lengthier physical description, which is very time-consuming to compile, rarely yields important clues for, say, dating a letter or ordering the sheets.

There is also a concordance of letter numbers to make it easier to find the relevant letter in earlier publications. In this edition, the letters are numbered consecutively by date. In the complete edition of van Gogh's correspondence, they will be inserted chronologically and renumbered.

The book closes with a bibliography and an index, which contains the names of people and places. Works of art and publications by the individuals are listed under their names.

The Facsimiles

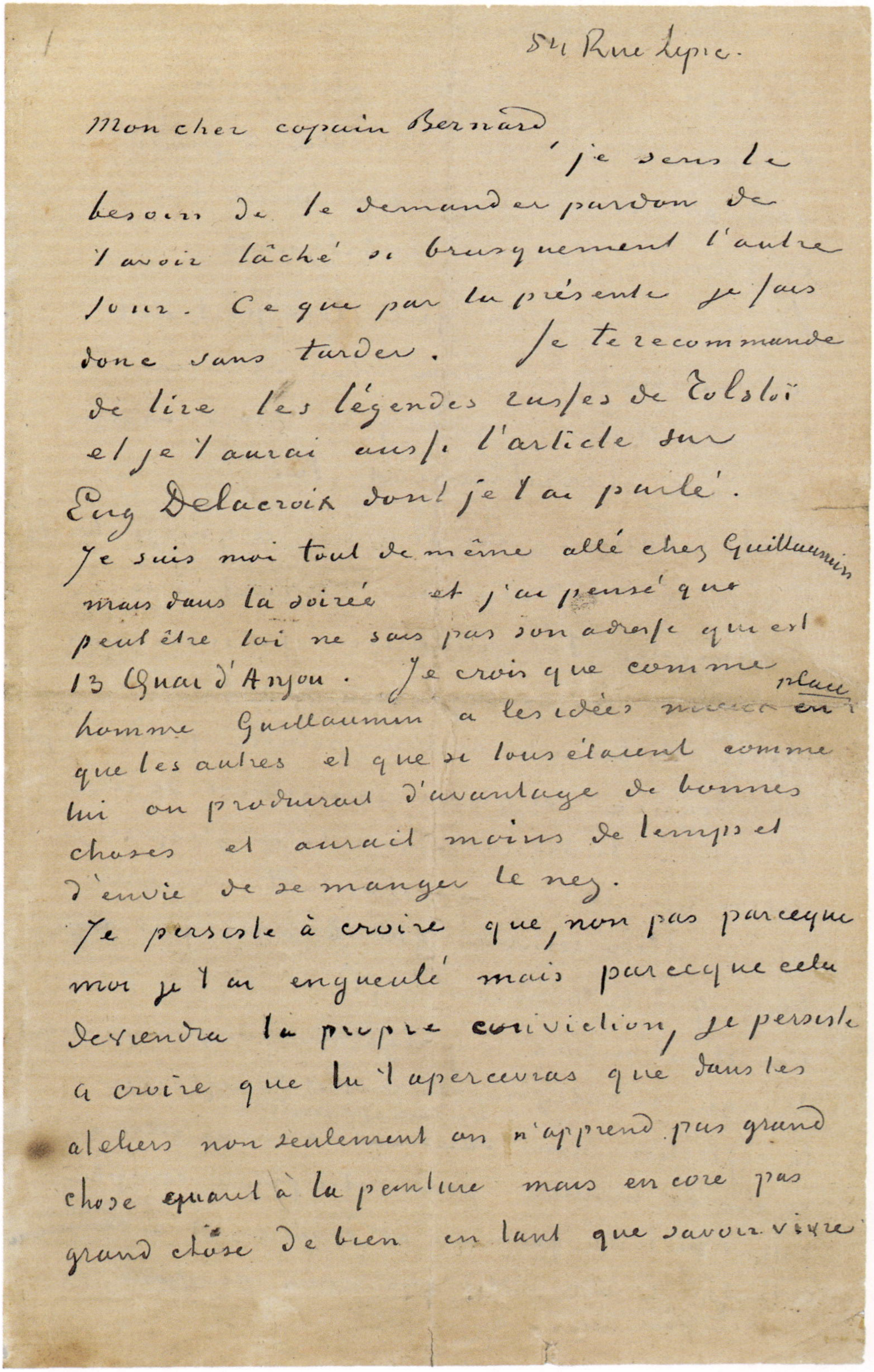

54 Rue Lepic.

Mon cher copain Bernard,
je sens le besoin de te demander pardon de t'avoir lâché si brusquement l'autre jour. Ce que par la présente je fais donc sans tarder. Je te recommande de lire les légendes russes de Tolstoï et je t'aurai aussi l'article sur Eug Delacroix dont je t'ai parlé.

Je suis moi tout de même allé chez Guillaumin mais dans la soirée et j'ai pensé que peut être toi ne sais pas son adresse qui est 13 Quai d'Anjou. Je crois que comme homme Guillaumin a les idées ~~mieux~~ plus en place que les autres et que si tous étaient comme lui on produirait d'avantage de bonnes choses et aurait moins de temps et d'envie de se manger le nez.

Je persiste à croire que, non pas parceque moi je t'ai engueulé mais parceque cela deviendra ta propre conviction, je persiste a croire que tu t'apercevras que dans les ateliers non seulement on n'apprend pas grand chose quant à la peinture mais encore pas grand chose de bien en tant que savoir vivre

1r:1

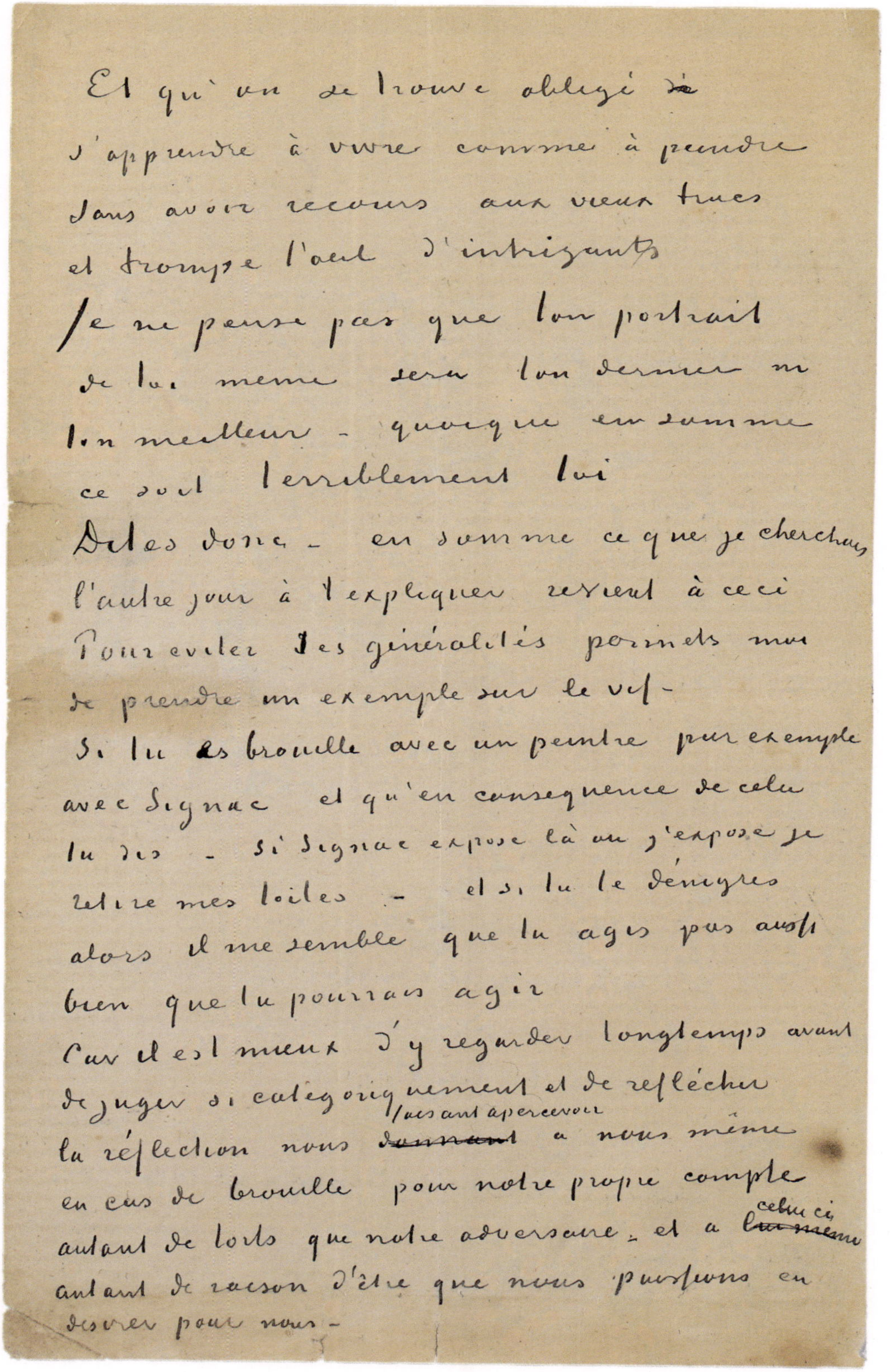
Et qu'on se trouve obligé ~~de~~
d'apprendre à vivre comme à peindre
sans avoir recours aux vieux trucs
et trompe l'oeil d'intrigants
Je ne pense pas que ton portrait
de toi même sera ton dernier ni
ton meilleur – quoique en somme
ce soit terriblement toi
Dites donc – en somme ce que je cherchais
l'autre jour à t'expliquer revient à ceci
Pour eviter des généralités permets moi
de prendre un exemple sur le vif –
Si tu es brouillé avec un peintre par exemple
avec Signac et qu'en consequence de cela
tu dis – si Signac expose là ou j'expose je
retire mes toiles – et si tu le dénigres
alors il me semble que tu agis pas aussi
bien que tu pourrais agir
Car il est mieux d'y regarder longtemps avant
de juger si catégoriquement et de refléchir
la réflection nous ~~donnant~~ laisant apercevoir à nous même
en cas de brouille pour notre propre compte
autant de torts que notre adversaire – et à ~~lui même~~ celui ci
autant de raison d'être que nous pussions en
desirer pour nous –

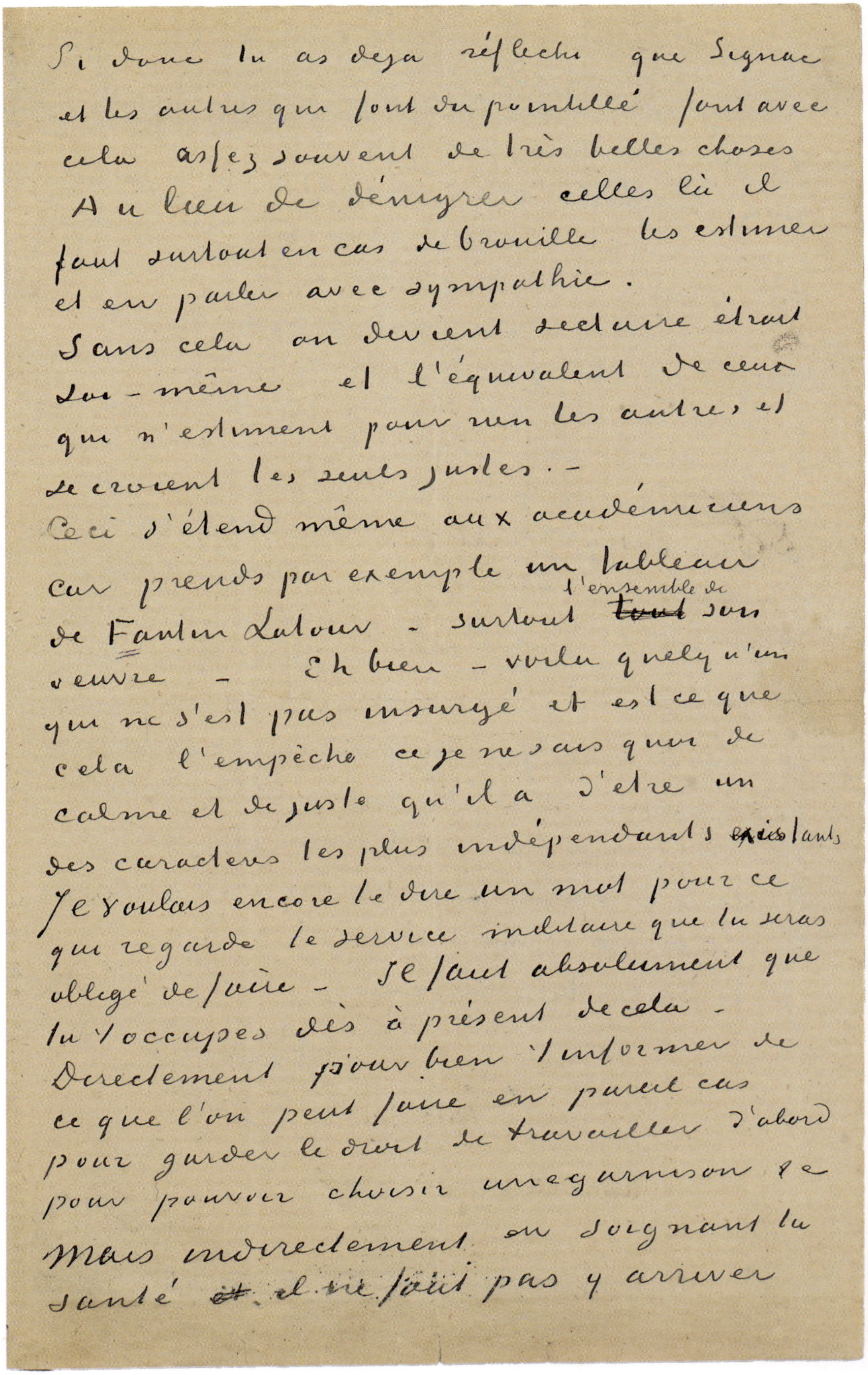
Si donc tu as deja réflechi que Signac
et les autres qui font du pointillé font avec
cela assez souvent de très belles choses
Au lieu de dénigrer celles là il
faut surtout en cas de brouille les estimer
et en parler avec sympathie.
Sans cela on devient sectaire étroit
soi-même et l'équivalent de ceux
qui n'estiment pour rien les autres et
se croient les seuls justes. –
Ceci s'étend même aux académiciens
car prends par exemple un tableau
de Fantin Latour – surtout ~~tout~~ l'ensemble de son
oeuvre – Eh bien – voila quelqu'un
qui ne s'est pas insurgé et est ce que
cela l'empêche ce je ne sais quoi de
calme et de juste qu'il a d'être un
des caractères les plus indépendants ~~exis~~ existants
Je voulais encore te dire un mot pour ce
qui regarde le service militaire que tu seras
obligé de faire – Il faut absolument que
tu t'occupes dès à présent de cela –
Directement pour bien t'informer de
ce que l'on peut faire en pareil cas
pour garder le droit de travailler d'abord
pour pouvoir choisir une garnison &c
Mais indirectement en soignant ta
santé ~~et~~ il ne faut pas y arriver

1v:3

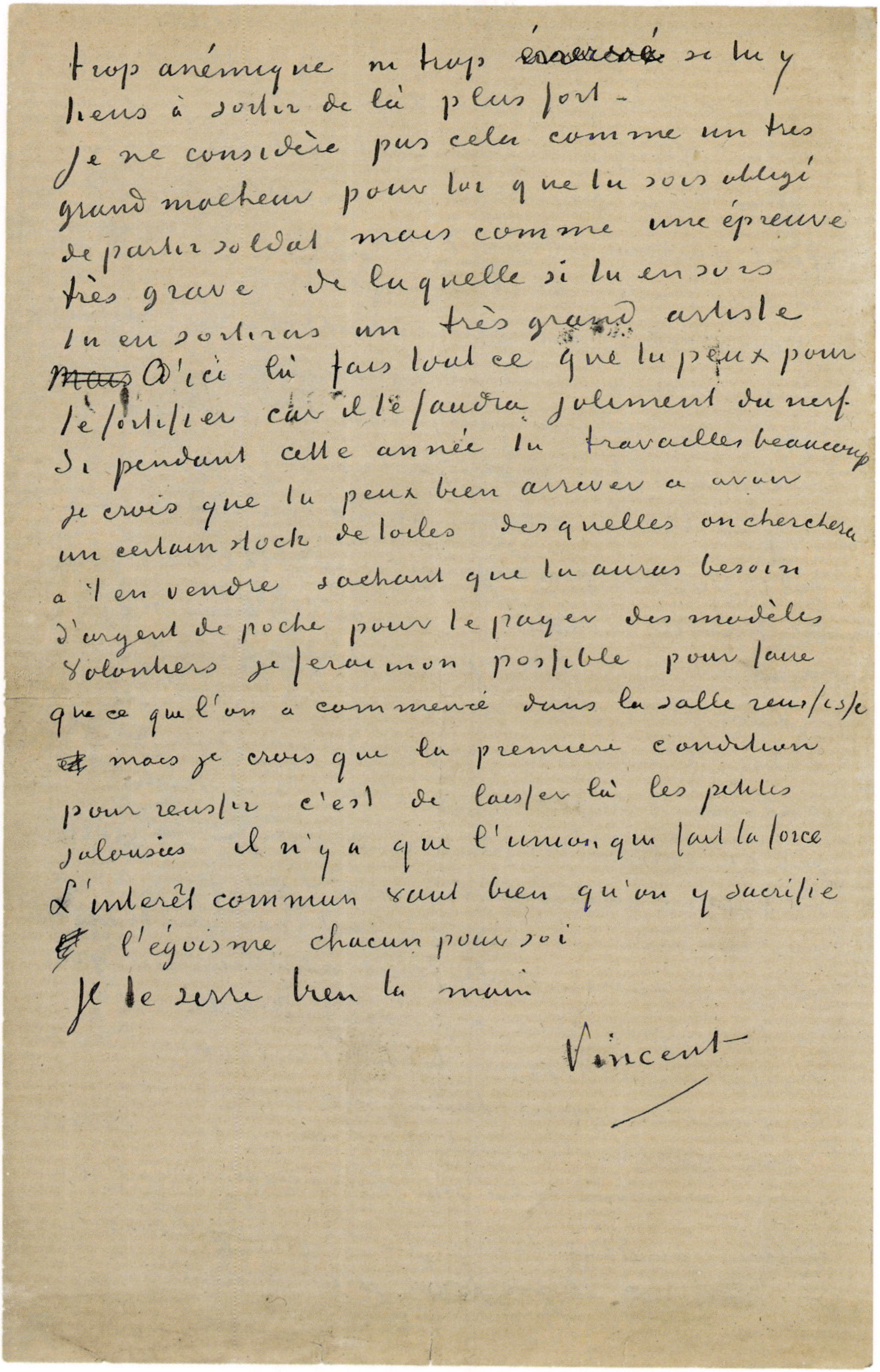
trop anémique ni trop ~~énervé~~ si tu y
tiens à sortir de là plus fort -
Je ne considère pas cela comme un très
grand malheur pour toi que tu sois obligé
de partir soldat mais comme une épreuve
très grave de laquelle si tu en sors
tu en sortiras un très grand artiste
~~mais~~ D'ici là fais tout ce que tu peux pour
te fortifier car il te faudra joliment du nerf
Si pendant cette année tu travailles beaucoup
je crois que tu peux bien arriver à avoir
un certain stock de toiles desquelles on cherchera
à t'en vendre sachant que tu auras besoin
d'argent de poche pour te payer des modèles
Volontiers je ferai mon possible pour faire
que ce qu'on a commencé dans la salle réussisse
~~et~~ mais je crois que la première condition
pour réussir c'est de laisser là les petites
jalousies il n'y a que l'union qui fait la force
L'intérêt commun vaut bien qu'on y sacrifie
~~l~~ l'égoïsme chacun pour soi
Je te serre bien la main

Vincent

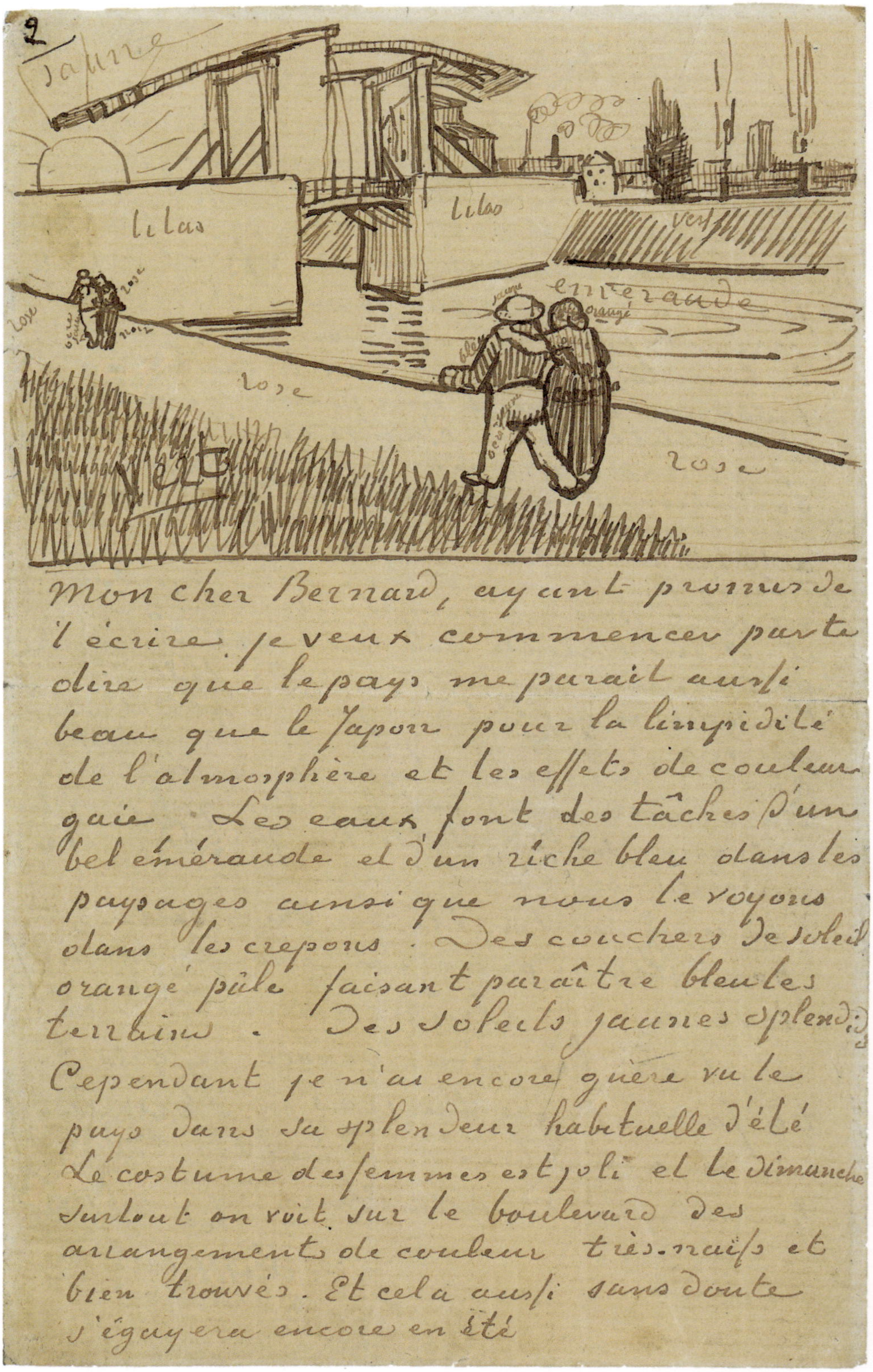

Mon cher Bernard, ayant promis de
t'écrire je veux commencer par te
dire que le pays me paraît aussi
beau que le Japon pour la limpidité
de l'atmosphère et les effets de couleur
gaie. Les eaux font des tâches d'un
bel émeraude et d'un riche bleu dans les
paysages ainsi que nous le voyons
dans les crepons. Des couchers de soleil
orangé pâle faisant paraître bleus les
terrains. Des soleils jaunes splendides.
Cependant je n'ai encore guère vu le
pays dans sa splendeur habituelle d'été.
Le costume des femmes est joli et le dimanche
surtout on voit sur le boulevard des
arrangements de couleur très naïfs et
bien trouvés. Et cela aussi sans doute
s'égayera encore en été

1r:1

je regrette que la vie ici n'est pas
à si bon marché que je l'avais espéré
et je n'ai pas trouvé moyen jusqu'à
présent de m'en tirer à aussi bon
compte qu'on pourrait le faire à Pont Aven
J'ai commencé par payer 5 fr et maintenant
je suis a 4 francs par jour. Il faudrait
savoir le patois d'ici et savoir manger de
la bouillabaisse et de l'aïoli alors on
trouverait surement une pension bourgeoise
peu coûteuse. Puis si on était à plusieurs
on obtiendrait, je suis porté à le croire, des
conditions plus avantageuses. Il y aurait
peutêtre un réel avantage pour bien des
artistes amoureux de soleil et de couleur
d'émigrer dans le midi. Si les Japonais
ne sont pas en progrès dans leur pays
il est indubitable que leur art se continue
en France. En tête de cette lettre je
t'envoie un petit croquis d'une étude
qui me préoccupe pour en faire quelque
chose - des matelots qui remontent avec
leurs amoureuses vers la ville qui profile
l'étrange silhouette de son pont levis sur
un énorme soleil jaune
J'ai une autre étude du même
pont levis avec un groupe de
laveuses. Serai content d'un
mot de toi pour savoir ce que
tu fais et où tu iras. Poignée
de main bien cordiale à
toi même et aux amis   bien à toi
Vincent

mon cher copain Bernard merci
de ta bonne lettre et des croquis
y inclus de ta décoration que je trouve
bien drôle – Je regrette parfois de
ne pas pouvoir me résoudre à travailler
davantage chez moi et de fantaisie
Certainement – l'imagination est
une capacité qu'il faut developper
et elle seule peut nous faire arriver
à créer une nature plus exaltante
& plus consolatrice que ce que
le clin d'oeil seul sur la réalité (que
nous apercevons changeante passant
vite comme l'éclair) nous fasse
apercevoir –

Un ciel étoilé par exemple tiens –
c'est une chose que je voudrais essayer
à faire de même que le jour
j'essayerai à peindre une verte
prairie étoilée de pissenlits
Comment pourtant y arriver à
moins de me résoudre à travailler
chez moi et d'imagination – Ceci
donc à ma critique et à la louange –

Actuellement je suis pris par les
arbres fruitiers en fleur pêchers
roses poiriers blancs-jaunes

1r:1

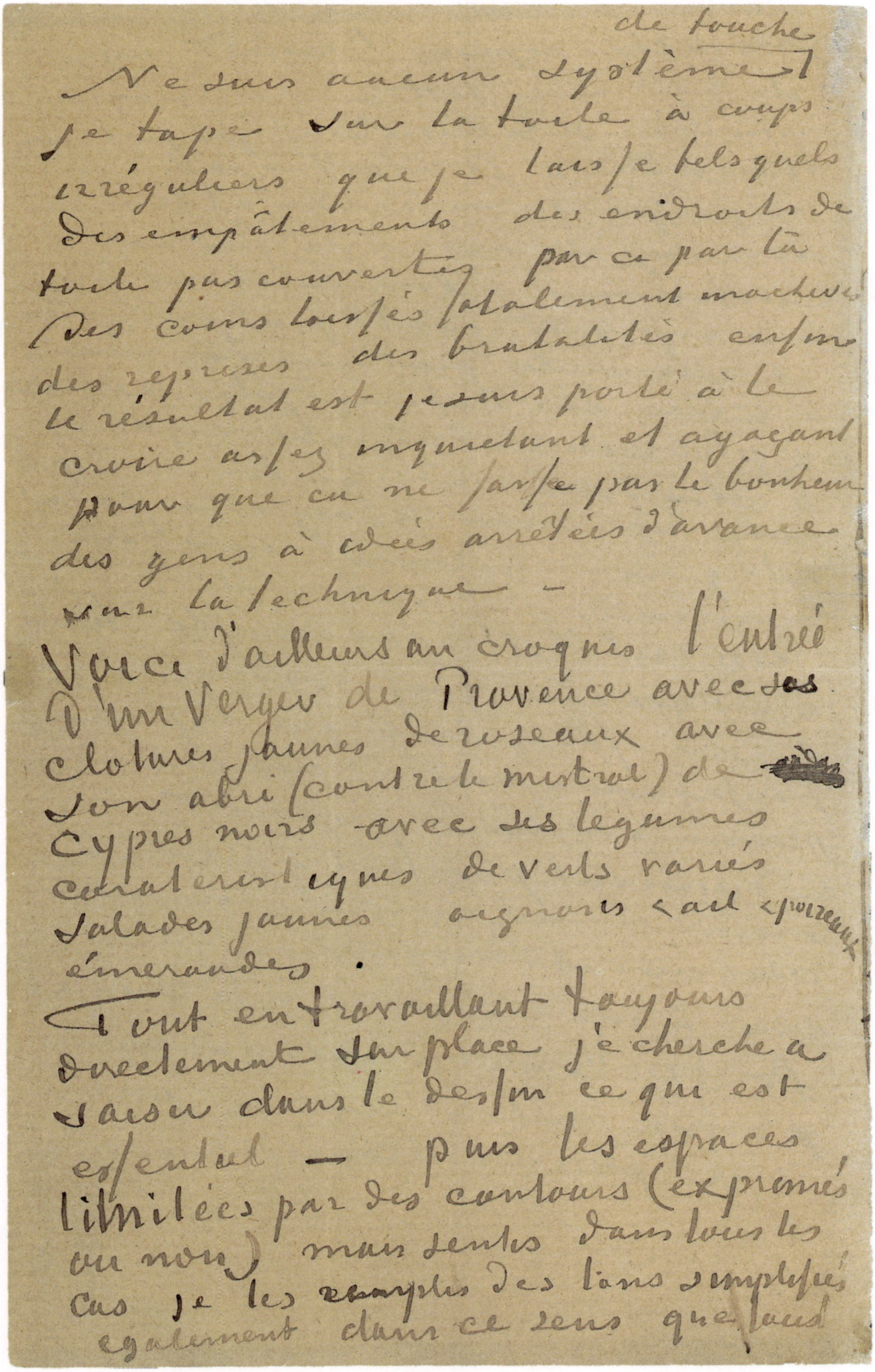
Ne suis aucun système de touche
je tape sur la toile à coups
irréguliers que je laisse tels quels
des empâtements des endroits de
toile pas couverte par ci par là
des coins laissés totalement inachevés
des reprises des brutalités enfin
le résultat est je suis porté à le
croire assez inquiétant et agaçant
pour que ça ne fasse pas le bonheur
des gens à idées arrêtées d'avance
sur la technique —
Voici d'ailleurs un croquis l'entrée
d'un verger de Provence avec ses
clotures jaunes de roseaux avec
son abri (contre le mistral) de
cypres noirs avec des legumes
caracteristiques de verts variés
salades jaunes oignons ail et poireaux
émeraudes.
Tout en travaillant toujours
directement sur place je cherche à
saisir dans le dessin ce qui est
essentiel — puis les espaces
limitées par des contours (exprimés
ou non) mais sentis dans tous les
cas je les remplis des tons simplifiés
également dans ce sens que tout

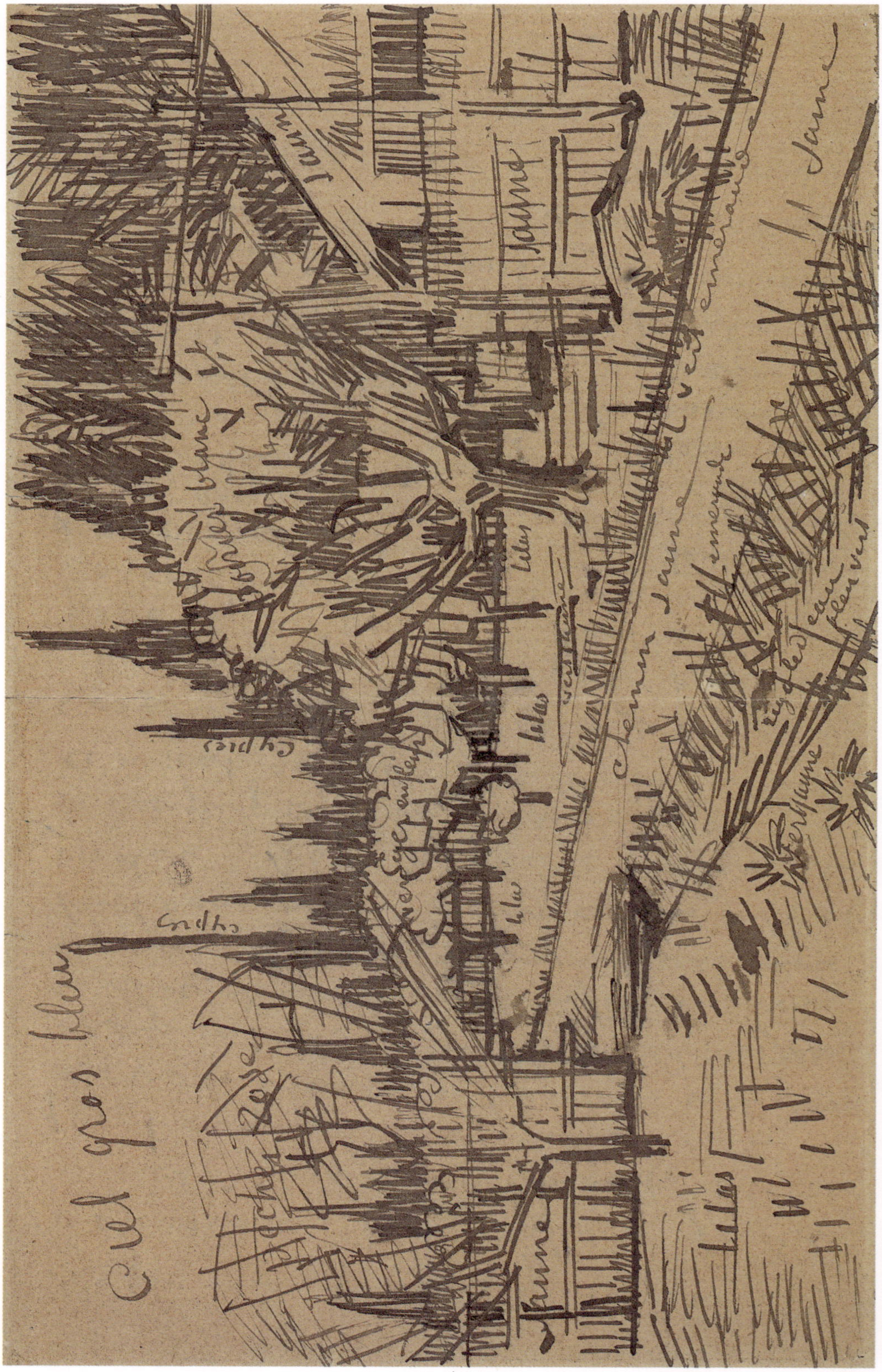

1v:3

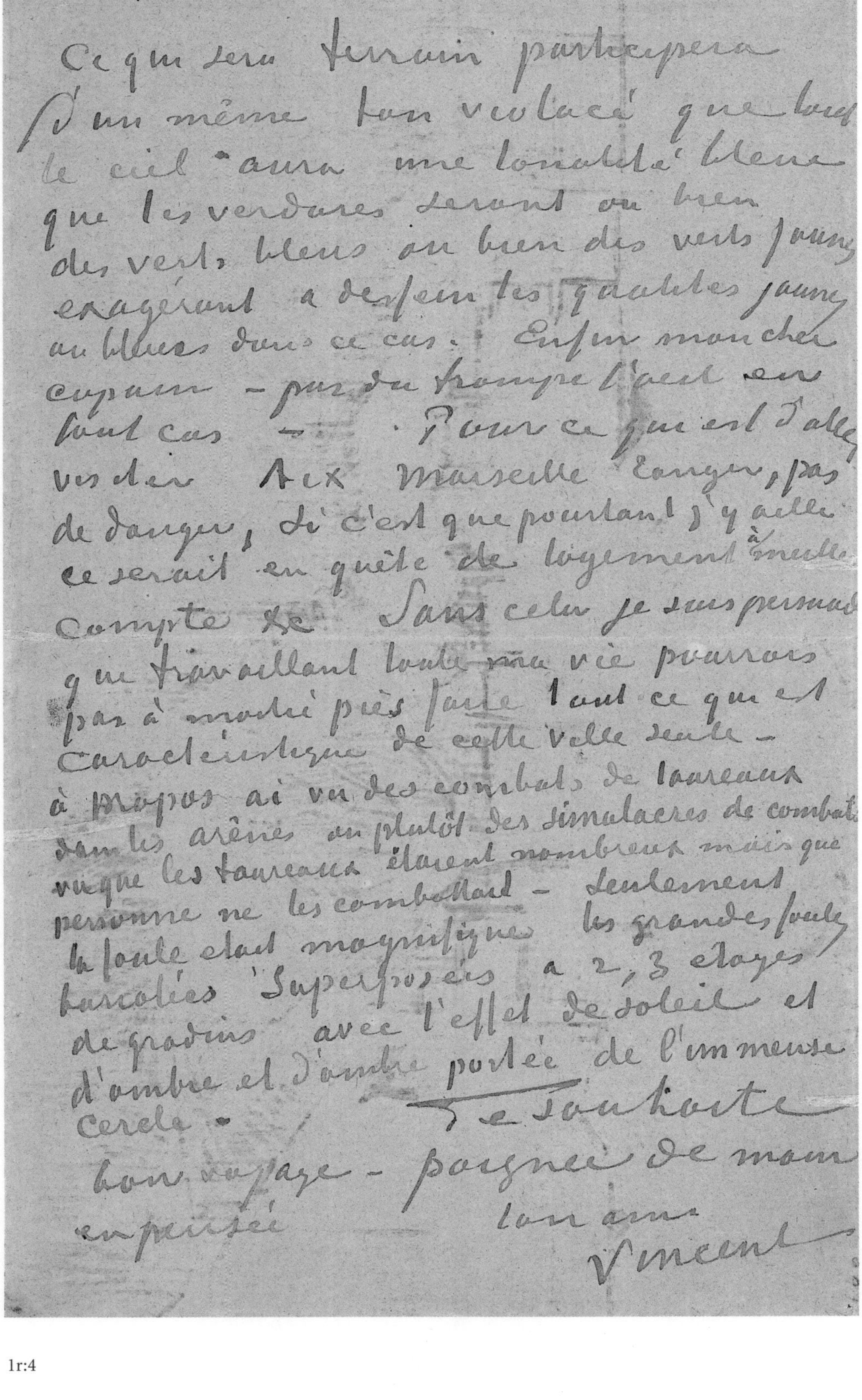

Ce qui sera terrain participera
d'un même ton violacé que tout
le ciel aura une tonalité bleue
que les verdures seront ou bien
des verts bleus ou bien des verts jaunes
exagérant à dessein les qualités jaunes
ou bleues dans ce cas. Enfin mon cher
copain – pas de trompe l'oeil en
tout cas –. Pour ce qui est d'aller
visiter Aix Marseille Tanger, pas
de danger, si c'est que pourtant j'y allais
ce serait en quête de logement à meilleur
compte — Sans cela je suis persuadé
que travaillant toute ma vie pourrais
pas à moitié près faire tout ce qui est
caractéristique de cette ville seule –
à propos ai vu des combats de taureaux
dans les arènes ou plutôt des simulacres de combats
vu que les taureaux étaient nombreux mais que
personne ne les combattait – seulement
la foule était magnifique les grandes foules
bariolées superposées à 2, 3 étages
de gradins avec l'effet de soleil et
d'ombre et d'ombre portée de l'immense
cercle.
Te souhaite
bon voyage – poignée de main
en pensée
ton ami
Vincent

1r:4

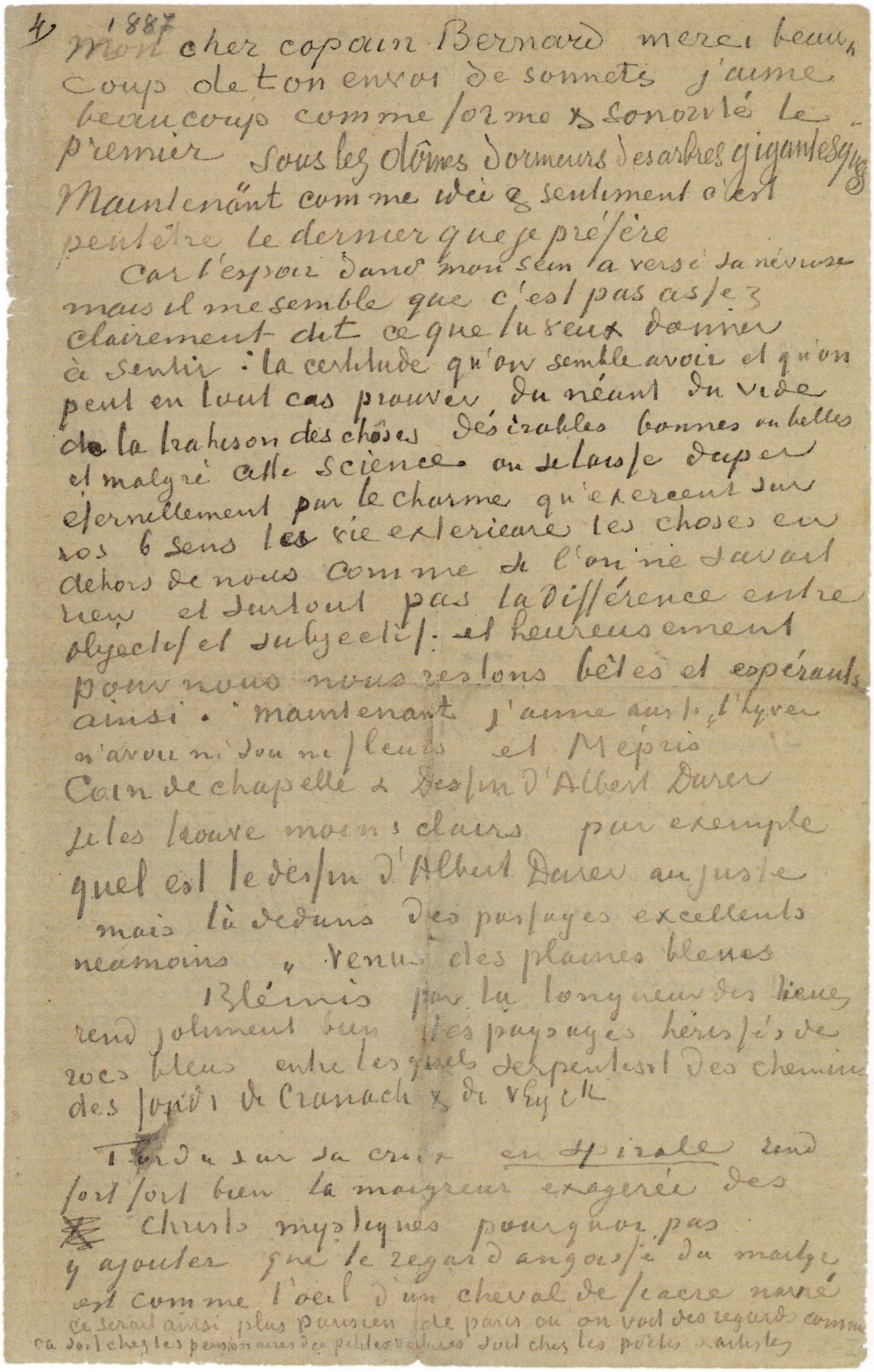

4) 1887 Mon cher copain Bernard merci beau-
coup de ton envoi de sonnets j'aime
beaucoup comme forme & sonorité le
premier sous les dômes d'ormeaux des arbres gigantesques
Maintenant comme idée & sentiment c'est
peutêtre le dernier que je préfère
Car l'espoir dans mon sein a versé sa névrose
mais il me semble que c'est pas assez
clairement dit ce que tu veux donner
à sentir : la certitude qu'on semble avoir et qu'on
peut en tout cas prouver, du néant du vide
de la trahison des choses désirables bonnes ou belles
et malgré cette science on se laisse duper
éternellement par le charme qu'exercent sur
nos 6 sens la vie exterieure les choses en
dehors de nous comme si l'on ne savait
rien et surtout pas la différence entre
objectif et subjectif. et heureusement
pour nous nous restons bêtes et espérants
ainsi. maintenant j'aime aussi l'hyver
n'avoir ni sou ni fleurs et Mépris
Coin de chapelle & Dessin d'Albert Durer
je les trouve moins clairs par exemple
quel est le dessin d'Albert Durer au juste
mais là dedans des passages excellents
néamoins , Venus des plaines blêmes
Blémis par la longueur des lieues
rend joliment bien ces paysages hérissés de
rocs bleus entre lesquels serpentent des chemins
des fonds de Cranach & de Van Eyck

Tordu sur sa croix en spirale rend
fort fort bien la maigreur exagérée des
Christs mystiques pourquoi pas
y ajouter que le regard angoissé du martyr
est comme l'oeil d'un cheval de fiacre navré
ce serait ainsi plus parisien de paris où on voit des regards comme
ça soit chez les pensionnaires de petites voitures soit chez les poètes artistes

1r:1

mais en somme c'est pas si bien que
ta peinture encore n'importe ça viendra
et faut surement continuer les sonnets
Il y a tant de gens surtout dans les copains
qui s'imaginent que les paroles ne sont
rien au contraire nest ce pas c'est
aussi intéressant & aussi difficile de
bien dire une chôse que de peindre une
chôse Il y a l'art des lignes & couleurs
mais l'art des paroles y est et y restera
pas moins.

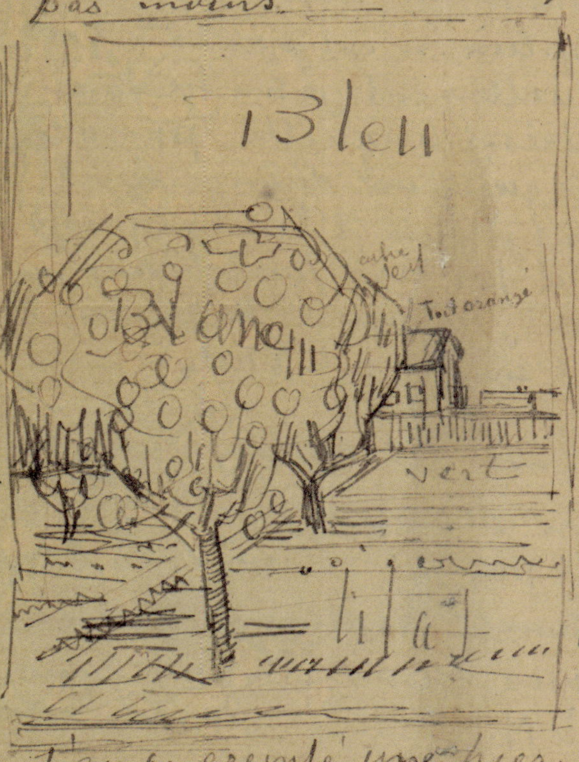

Voici un nouveau
verger assez simple
comme composition
un arbre blanc un
petit arbre vert
un coin de verdure
carré — un terrain
lilas un toit orangé
un grand ciel bleu
ai neuf vergers
en train
un blanc un
rose un rose presque
rouge un blanc & bleu
un rose & gris un
vert et rose

J'en ai éreinté une hier d'un cérisier
contre ciel bleu les jeunes pousses
des feuilles étaient de l'orangé et de l'or
les touffes de fleurs blanches cela contre
le bleu vert du ciel était rudement glorieux
malheureusement voilà la pluie aujourd'hui
qui m'empêche de revenir à la charge.

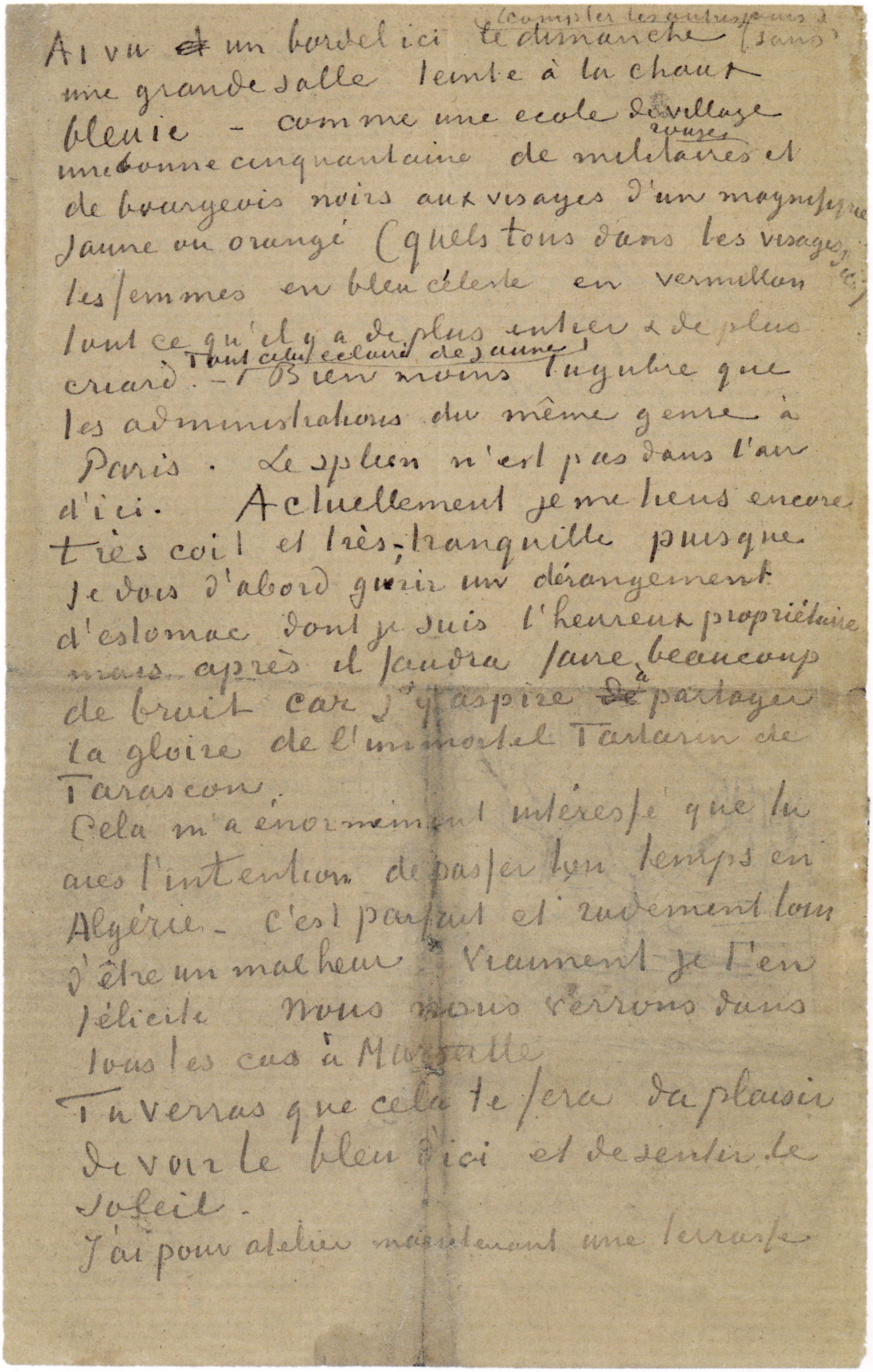
Ai vu un bordel ici le dimanche (sans compter les autres jours)
une grande salle teinte à la chaux
bleuie — comme une école de village
une bonne cinquantaine de militaires rouges et
de bourgeois noirs aux visages d'un magnifique
jaune ou orangé (quels tons dans les visages d'ici)
les femmes en bleu céleste en vermillon
tout ce qu'il y a de plus entier & de plus
criard. — Tout cela éclairé de jaune. Bien moins lugubre que
les administrations du même genre à
Paris. Le spleen n'est pas dans l'air
d'ici. Actuellement je me tiens encore
très coi et très tranquille puisque
je dois d'abord guérir un dérangement
d'estomac dont je suis l'heureux propriétaire
mais après il faudra faire beaucoup
de bruit car j'y aspire à ~~de~~ partager
la gloire de l'immortel Tartarin de
Tarascon.
Cela m'a énormément intéressé que tu
as l'intention de passer ton temps en
Algérie. C'est parfait et rudement loin
d'être un malheur. Vraiment je t'en
félicite. Nous nous verrons dans
tous les cas à Marseille
Tu verras que cela te fera du plaisir
de voir le bleu d'ici et de sentir le
soleil.
J'ai pour atelier maintenant une terrasse

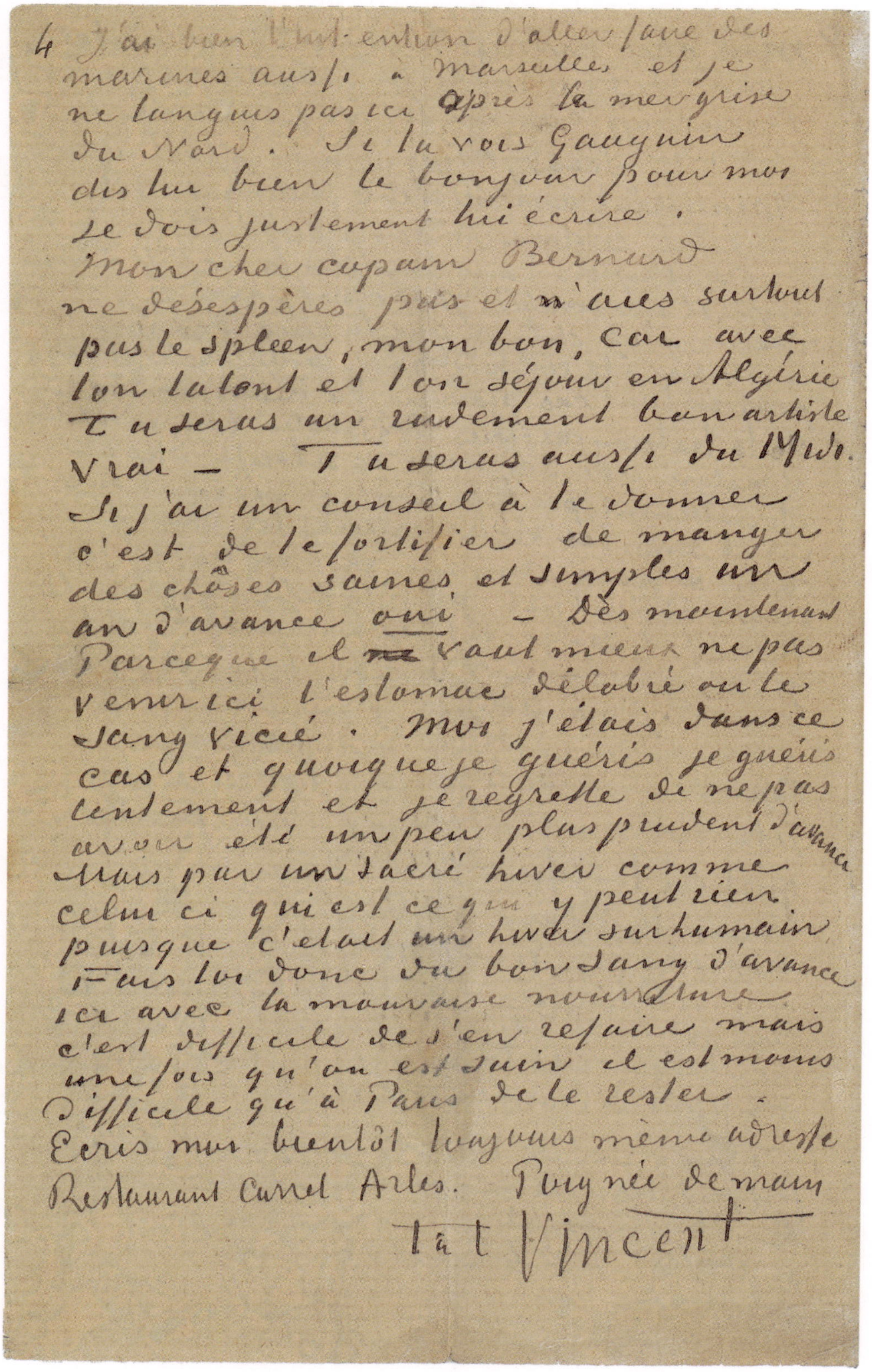

4 J'ai bien l'intention d'aller faire des
marines aussi à Marseille et je
ne languis pas ici après la mer grise
du Nord. Si tu vois Gauguin
dis lui bien le bonjour pour moi
je dois justement lui écrire.
Mon cher copain Bernard
ne désespères pas et n'aies surtout
pas le spleen, mon bon, car avec
ton talent et ton séjour en Algérie
tu seras un rudement bon artiste
vrai — Tu seras aussi du Midi.
Si j'ai un conseil à te donner
c'est de te fortifier de manger
des choses saines et simples un
an d'avance oui — Dès maintenant
Parceque il vaut mieux ne pas
venir ici l'estomac délabré ou le
sang vicié. Moi j'étais dans ce
cas et quoique je guéris je guéris
lentement et je regrette de ne pas
avoir été un peu plus prudent d'avance
Mais par un sacré hiver comme
celui ci qui est ce qui y peut rien
puisque c'était un hiver surhumain.
Fais toi donc du bon sang d'avance
ici avec la mauvaise nourriture
c'est difficile de s'en refaire mais
une fois qu'on est sain il est moins
difficile qu'à Paris de le rester.
Ecris moi bientôt toujours même adresse
Restaurant Carrel Arles. Poignée de main
t à t Vincent

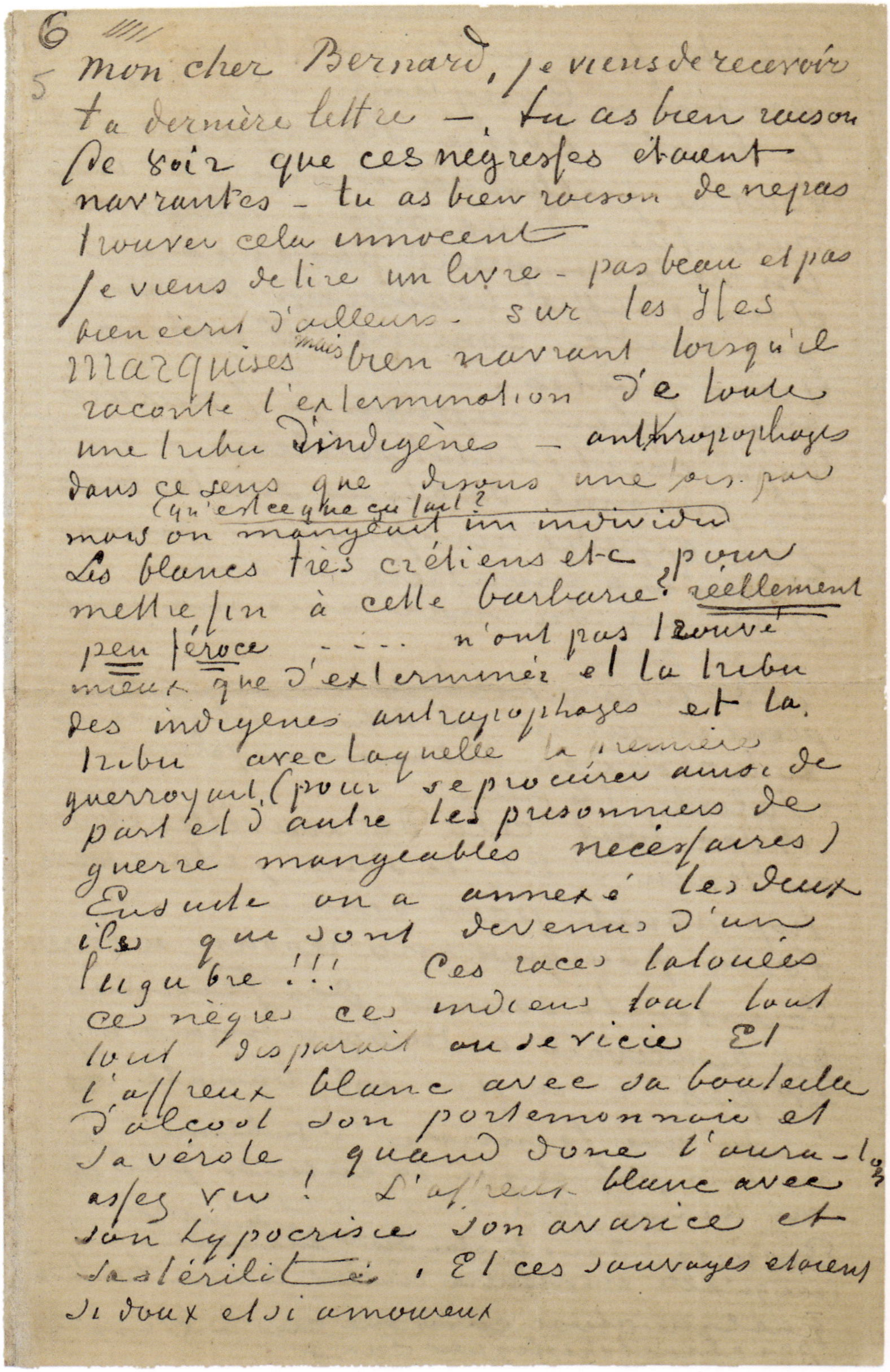

6 ////
5 mon cher Bernard, je viens de recevoir
ta dernière lettre – tu as bien raison
de voir que ces négresses étaient
navrantes – tu as bien raison de ne pas
trouver cela innocent
je viens de lire un livre – pas beau et pas
bien écrit d'ailleurs – sur les Iles
Marquises mais bien navrant lorsqu'il
raconte l'extermination de toute
une tribu d'indigènes – anthropophages
dans ce sens que disons une fois par
(qu'est ce que ça fait?)
mois on mangeait un individu
Les blancs très crétiens etc, pour
mettre fin à cette barbarie? réellement
peu féroce ... n'ont pas trouvé
mieux que d'exterminer et la tribu
des indigènes antropophages et la
tribu avec laquelle la première
guerroyait (pour se procurer ainsi de
part et d'autre les prisonniers de
guerre mangeables nécessaires)
Ensuite on a annexé les deux
iles qui sont devenues d'un
lugubre!!! Ces races tatouées
ces nègres ces indiens tout tout
tout disparait ou se vicie Et
l'affreux blanc avec sa bouteille
d'alcool son portemonnaie et
sa vérole, quand donc l'aura-t-on
assez vu! L'affreux blanc avec
son hypocrisie son avarice et
sa stérilité. Et ces sauvages étaient
si doux et si amoureux

1r:1

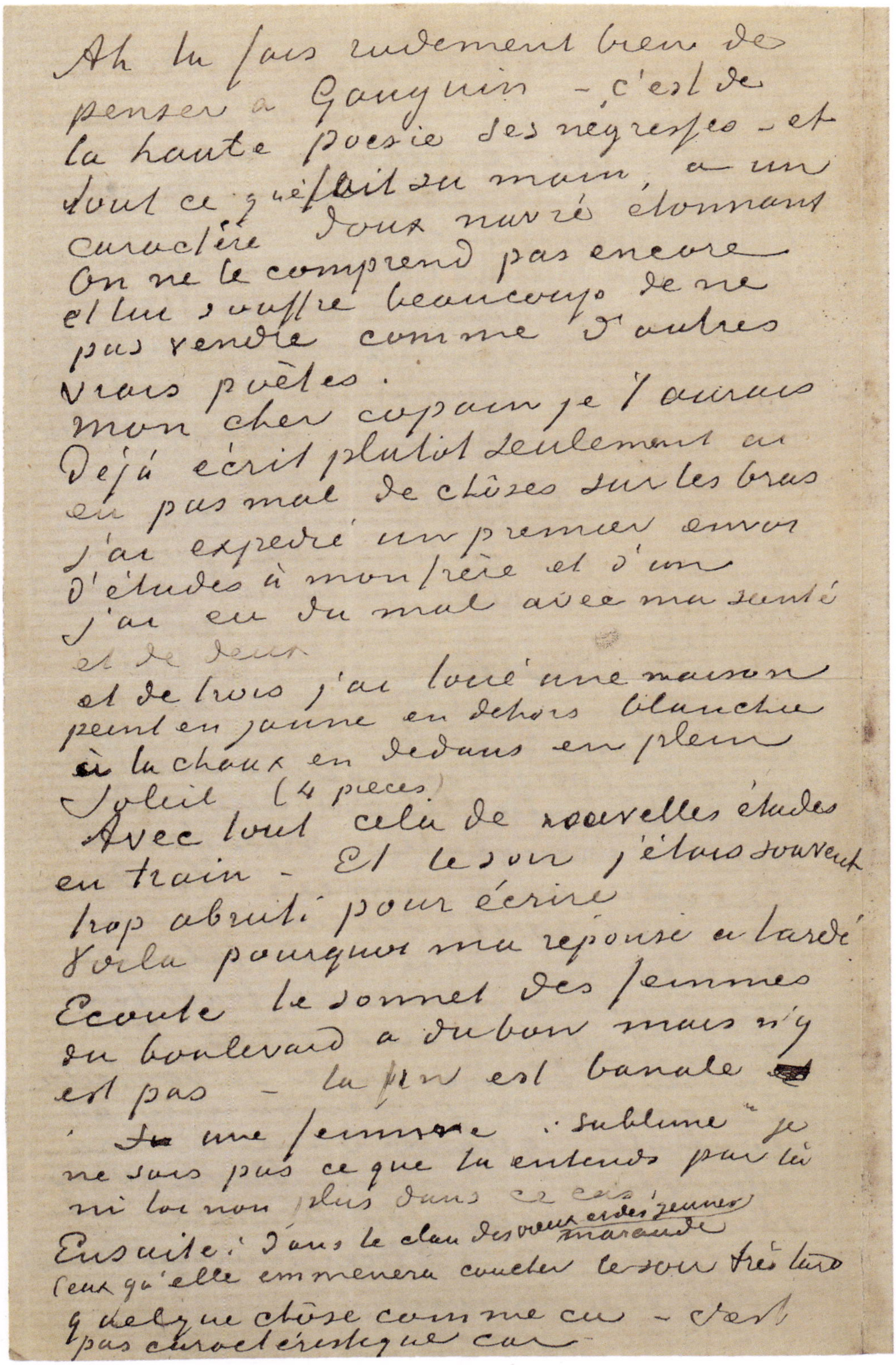
Ah tu fais rudement bien de
penser a Gauguin – c'est de
la haute poésie ses négresses – et
tout ce que fait sa main, a un
caractère doux navré étonnant
On ne le comprend pas encore
et lui souffre beaucoup de ne
pas vendre comme d'autres
vrais poètes.
Mon cher copain je t'aurais
Déjà écrit plutot seulement ai
eu pas mal de choses sur les bras
j'ai expedié un premier envoi
d'études à mon frère et d'un
j'ai eu du mal avec ma santé
et de deux
et de trois j'ai loué une maison
peint en jaune en dehors blanchie
à la chaux en dedans en plein
soleil (4 pieces)
Avec tout cela de nouvelles études
en train – Et le soir j'étais souvent
trop abruti pour écrire
Voila pourquoi ma réponse a tardé
Ecoute le sonnet des femmes
du boulevard a du bon mais n'y
est pas – la fin est banale
"une femme sublime" je
ne sais pas ce que tu entends par là
ni moi non plus dans ce cas
Ensuite: dans le clan des voueurs aidés jeunes maraude
ceux qu'elle emmenera coucher le soir très tard
quelque chose comme ça – c'est
pas caractéristique car

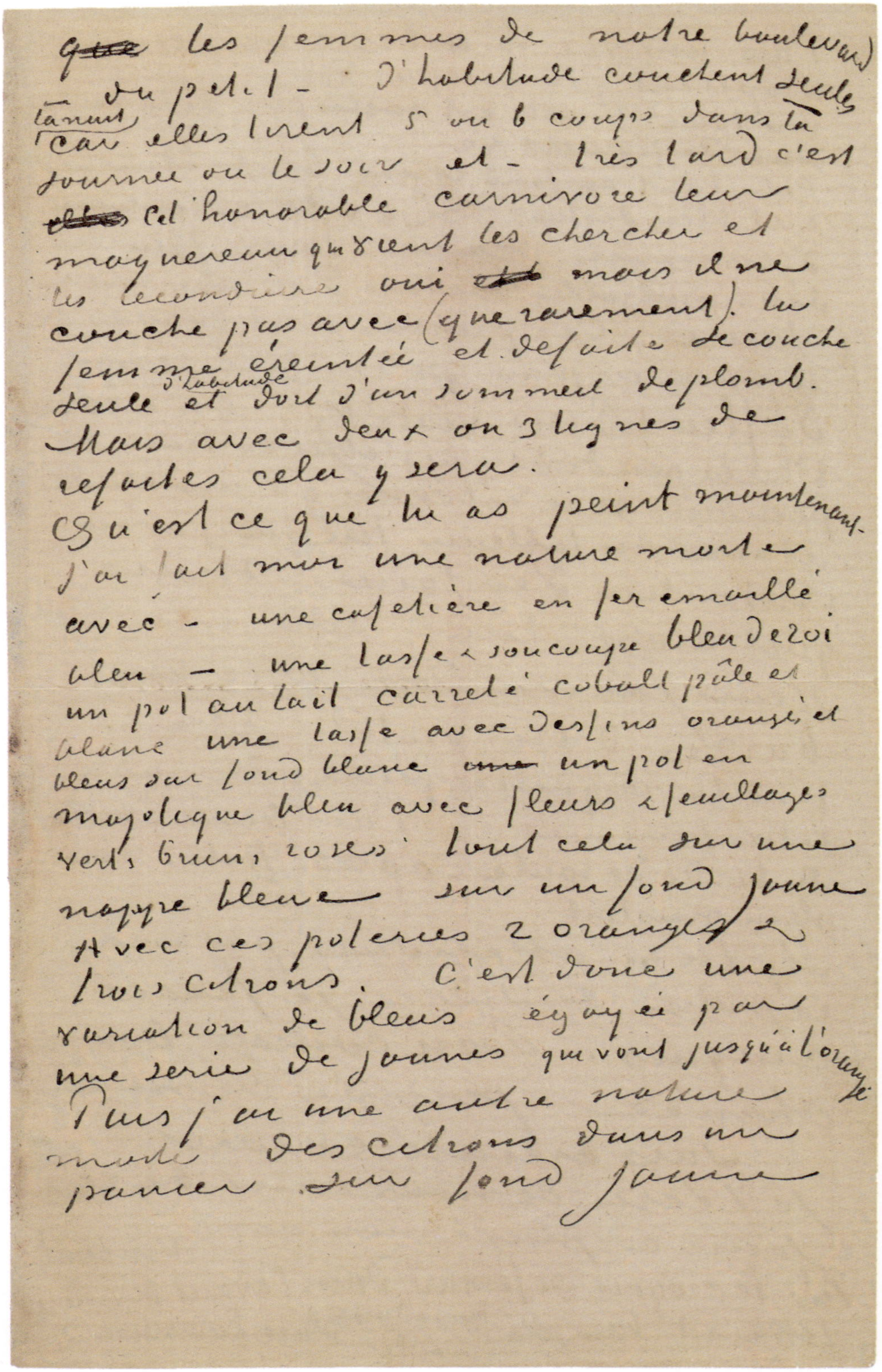

~~Que~~ les femmes de notre boulevard
du petit — d'habitude couchent seules
tandis ~~car~~ elles tirent 5 ou 6 coups dans la
journée ou le soir et — très tard c'est
~~elles~~ cet honorable carnivore leur
maquereau qui vient les chercher et
les reconduire oui ~~et~~ mais il ne
couche pas avec (que rarement). La
femme éreintée et défaite de couche
seule d'habitude et dort d'un sommeil de plomb.
Mais avec deux ou 3 lignes de
retouches cela y sera.
Qu'est ce que tu as peint maintenant.
J'ai fait moi une nature morte
avec — une cafetière en fer émaillé
bleu — une tasse & soucoupe bleu de roi
un pot au lait carrelé cobalt pâle et
blanc une tasse avec dessins orangés et
bleus sur fond blanc ~~une~~ un pot en
majolique bleu avec fleurs & feuillages
verts, bruns, roses. Tout cela sur une
nappe bleue sur un fond jaune
Avec ces poteries 2 oranges &
trois citrons. C'est donc une
variation de bleus égayée par
une serie de jaunes qui vont jusqu'à l'orangé
Puis j'ai une autre nature
morte des citrons dans un
panier sur fond jaune

1v:3

Puis une vue d'arles — de la ville on
n'apercoit que quelques toits rouges et
une tour le reste est caché par de la verdure
~~[illegible]~~ de figuiers &c.
Cela tout au fond et une bande étroite de
ciel bleu dessus. La ville est entourée
d'immenses prairies toutes fleuries
d'innombrables boutons d'or — une mer
jaune — Ces prairies sont coupés sur
le premier plan par un fossé rempli
de fleurs d'iris violettes. On a coupé
l'herbe pendant que j'étais en train de
peindre ce n'est donc qu'une étude
et non un tableau fait que j'avais
l'intention d'en faire. Mais
quel motif — hein — cette mer de
fleurs jaunes avec une
barre d'iris violets et au
fond la coquette petite ville aux
jolies femmes. Puis deux études
de bords de route — après — faites en
plein mistral.
Si tu n'attendrais pas ma
réponse de suite je ferais
croquis. Bon courage bonne
chance poignée de main
Je suis éreinté ce soir
je t'écris de nouveau de ces
jours ci plus à mon aise
Vincent
P.S. le croquis de femme dans l'avant dernière
lettre est bien joli | mon adresse Place Lamartine 2
Arles.

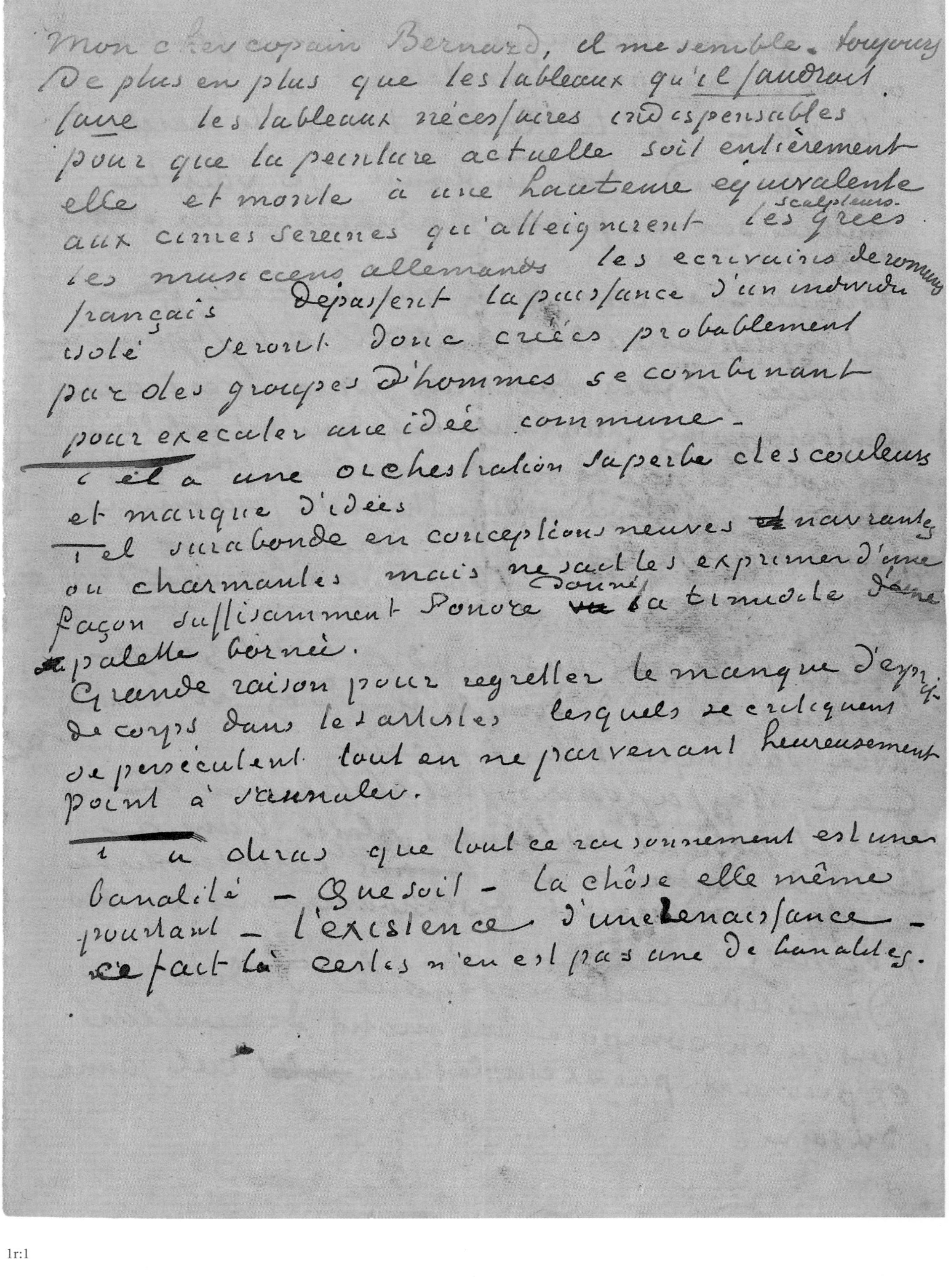

Mon cher copain Bernard, il me semble toujours
de plus en plus que les tableaux qu'il faudrait
faire les tableaux nécessaires indispensables
pour que la peinture actuelle soit entièrement
elle et monte à une hauteur équivalente
aux cimes sereines qu'atteignirent les sculpteurs grecs
les musiciens allemands les écrivains de romans
français dépassent la puissance d'un individu
isolé seront donc créés probablement
par des groupes d'hommes se combinant
pour exécuter une idée commune.

Tel a une orchestration superbe des couleurs
et manque d'idées
Tel surabonde en conceptions neuves navrantes
ou charmantes mais ne sait les exprimer d'une
façon suffisamment sonore donné la timidité d'une
palette bornée.
Grande raison pour regretter le manque d'esprit
de corps dans les artistes lesquels se critiquent
se persécutent tout en ne parvenant heureusement
point à s'annuler.

Tu diras que tout ce raisonnement est une
banalité — Que soit — la chose elle même
pourtant — l'existence d'une renaissance —
ce fait là certes n'en est pas une de banalités.

Une question technique - Dis moi un peu ton
opinion dans prochaine lettre.
le noir et le blanc tel que le marchand
nous les vend tout simplement je vais le
mettre sur ma palette hardiment et les employer
tels quels
lorsque - et remarques que je parle de
la simplification de la couleur a la japonaise -
lorsque je vois dans un parc vert aux
sentiers roses un monsieur qui est habillé de
~~en~~ noir et juge de paix de son métier (l'~~i~~ le juif arabe
dans Tartarin de Daudet appelle cet honorable fonctionnaire
zouge de paix) lequel lit l'intransigeant
Au dessus de lui ~~même~~ & du parc un ciel d'un
simple cobalt -
Alors pourquoi pas peindre le dit zouge
de paix avec du simple noir d'os et l'intransigeant
avec du simple blanc tout cru
Car le japonais fait abstraction du
reflet posant ses teintes plates l'une a
côté de l'autre - Des ~~lignes~~ traits caractéristiques
arrêtant naivement des mouvements ou des
formes.
Dans une autre catégorie d'idées
lorsqu'on compose un motif de couleur
exprimant par exemple un ~~soleil~~ ciel jaune
du soir

le blanc cru et dur d'un mur blanc contre le ciel à la rigueur s'exprime et d'une façon étrange par le blanc cru et ce même blanc rabattu par un ton neutre. Car le ciel même le colore d'un ton lilas fin.

Encore dans ce paysage si naïf lequel est censé nous représenter une cabane blanchie entièrement à la chaux (le terrain aussi), posée sur un terrain orangé – certes car le ciel du midi et la méditerranée provoquent un orangé d'autant plus intense que la gamme des bleus est plus montée de ton

Sketch 1

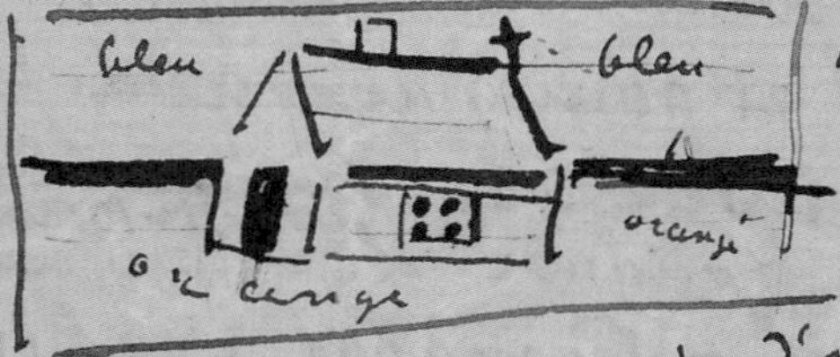

la note noire de la porte, des vitres, de la petite croix sur la faîte, font qu'il y ait un contraste simultané de blanc & noir agréable à l'oeil tout autant que celui du bleu avec l'orange.

Pour prendre un motif plus amusant supposons une femme habillée d'une robe carrelée noir & blanc dans le même paysage primitif d'un ciel bleu & d'une terre orangée. ce serait assez drôle à voir je m'imagine. Justement à Arles on porte souvent du carrelé blanc & noir.

Sketch 2

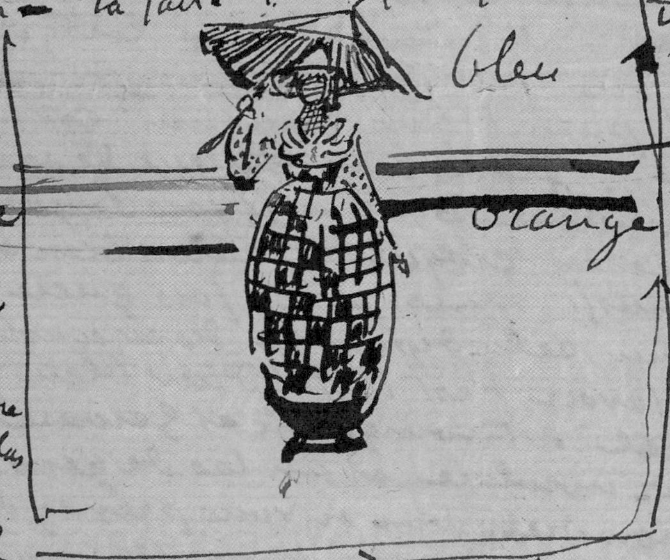

Suffit que le noir et le blanc sont des couleurs aussi plutôt dans bien des cas peuvent être considérés comme couleurs car leur contraste simultané est aussi piquant que celui du vert & du rouge par exemple.

la partie encadrée seulement

Les Japonais s'en servent d'ailleurs – ils expriment merveilleusement bien le teint mat & pâle d'une jeune fille et le contraste piquant de la chevelure noire avec du papier blanc et 4 traits de plume sans compter leurs buissons d'épines noires étoilés de mille fleurs blanches

J'ai enfin vu la Méditerranée laquelle c'est probable tu franchiras avant moi. ai passé une semaine à Saintes Maries et pour y arriver ai traversé en diligence la camargue avec des vignes des landes des terrains plats comme la Hollande Là il y avait des filles qui faisaient penser à Cimabue et à Giotto minces droites un peu tristes & mystiques. Sur la plage toute plate sablonneuse de petits bateaux verts rouges bleus tellement jolis comme forme & couleur qu'on pensait à des fleurs un seul homme les monte ces barques là ne vont guère sur la haute mer – ils fichent le camp lorsqu'il n'y a pas de vent et reviennent à terre s'il en fait un peu trop. Il paraît que Gauguin est toujours encore malade. Je suis bien curieux de savoir ce que tu as fait dernièrement moi je fais toujours encore du paysage ci inclus croquis. J'aurais bien envie de voir l'Afrique aussi mais je ne fais guère de plan fixe pour l'avenir cela dépendra des circonstances.

Ce que je voulais savoir c'est l'effet d'un bleu plus intense dans le ciel. Fromentin et Gerome voient le terrain du midi incolore et un tas de gens le voient tel. Mon dieu oui si vous prenez du sable sec dans votre main & si vous allez regarder cela de près. l'eau aussi l'air aussi considérés de cette façon est incolore. Pas de bleu sans jaune et sans orangé et si vous faites le bleu faites donc le jaune & l'orangé aussi n'est ce pas. Enfin tu vas me dire que je ne t'écris que des banalités Poignée de main en pensée t à t Vincent

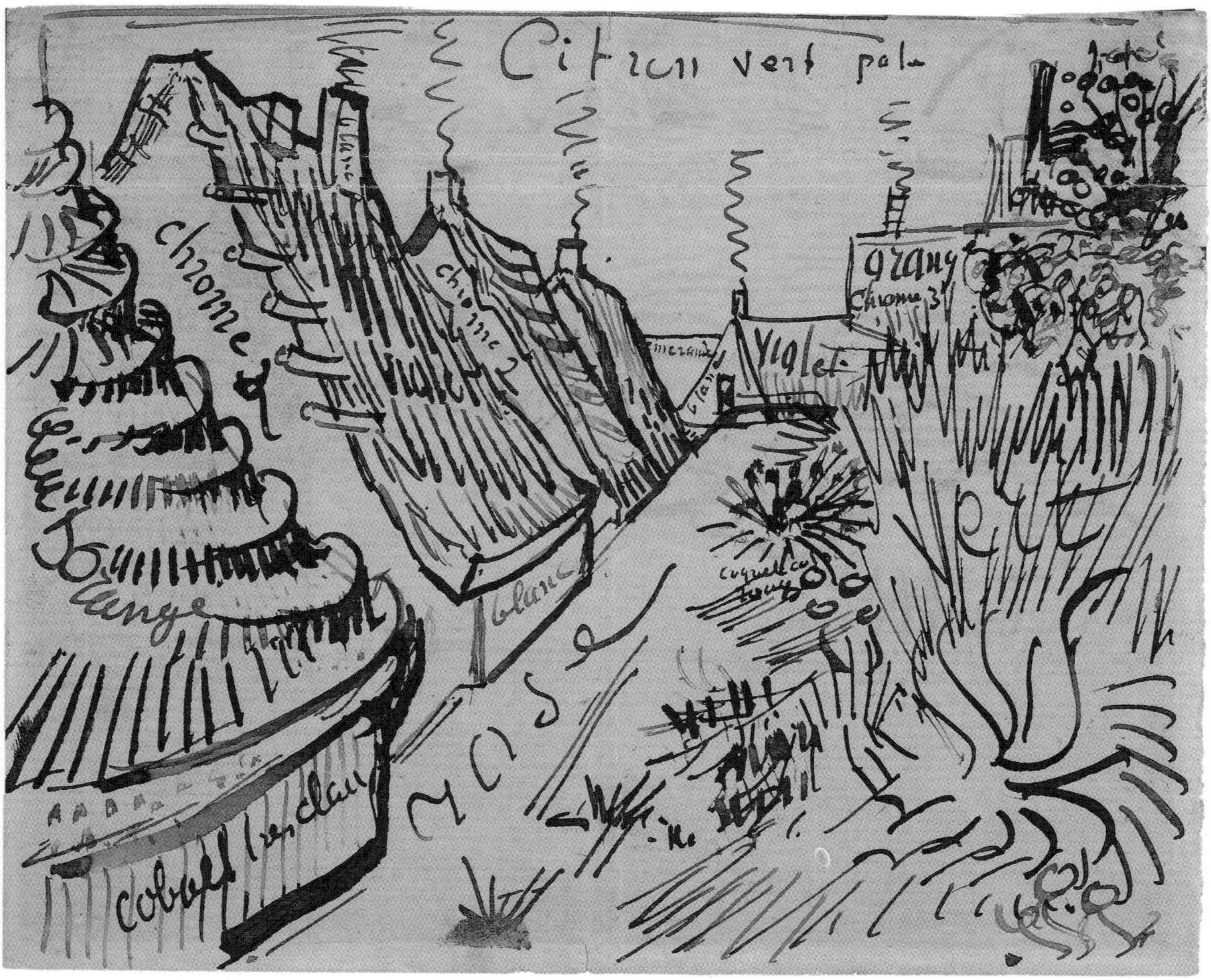

Sketch 3

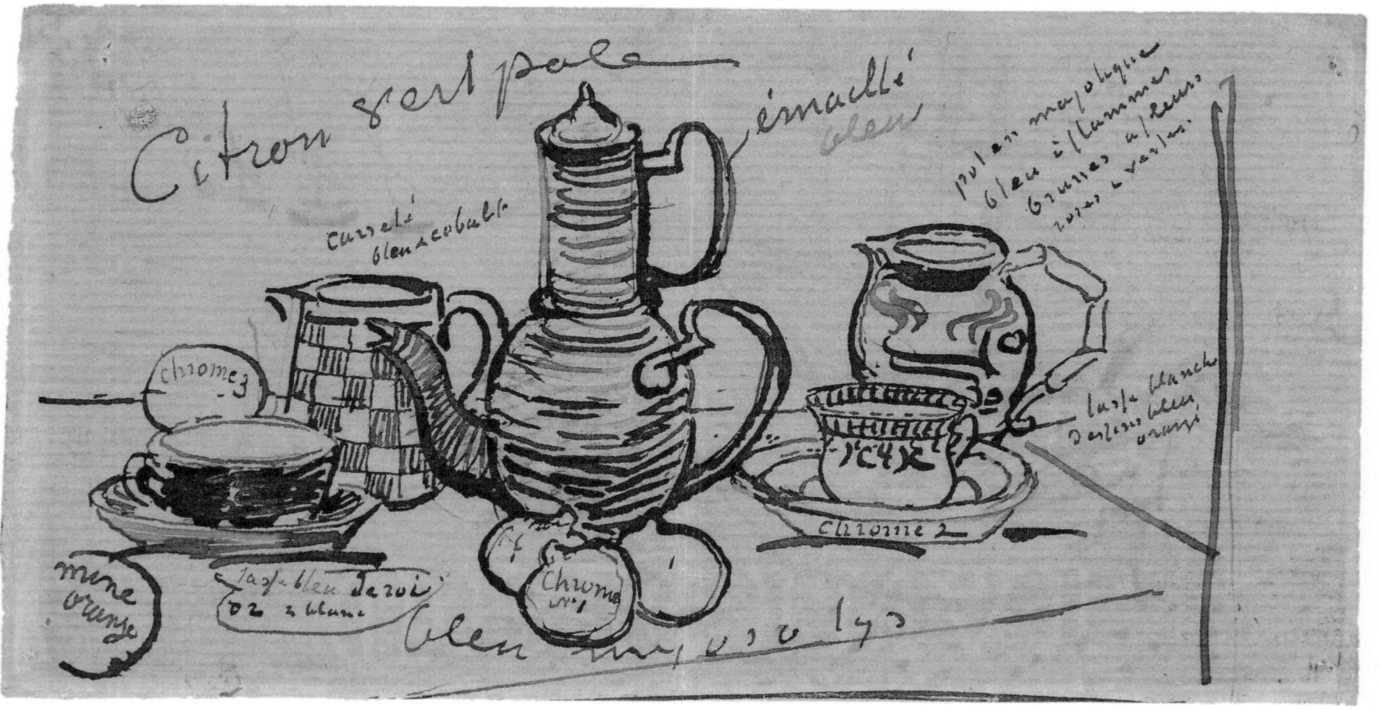

Sketch 8

Sketch 4

Sketch 5

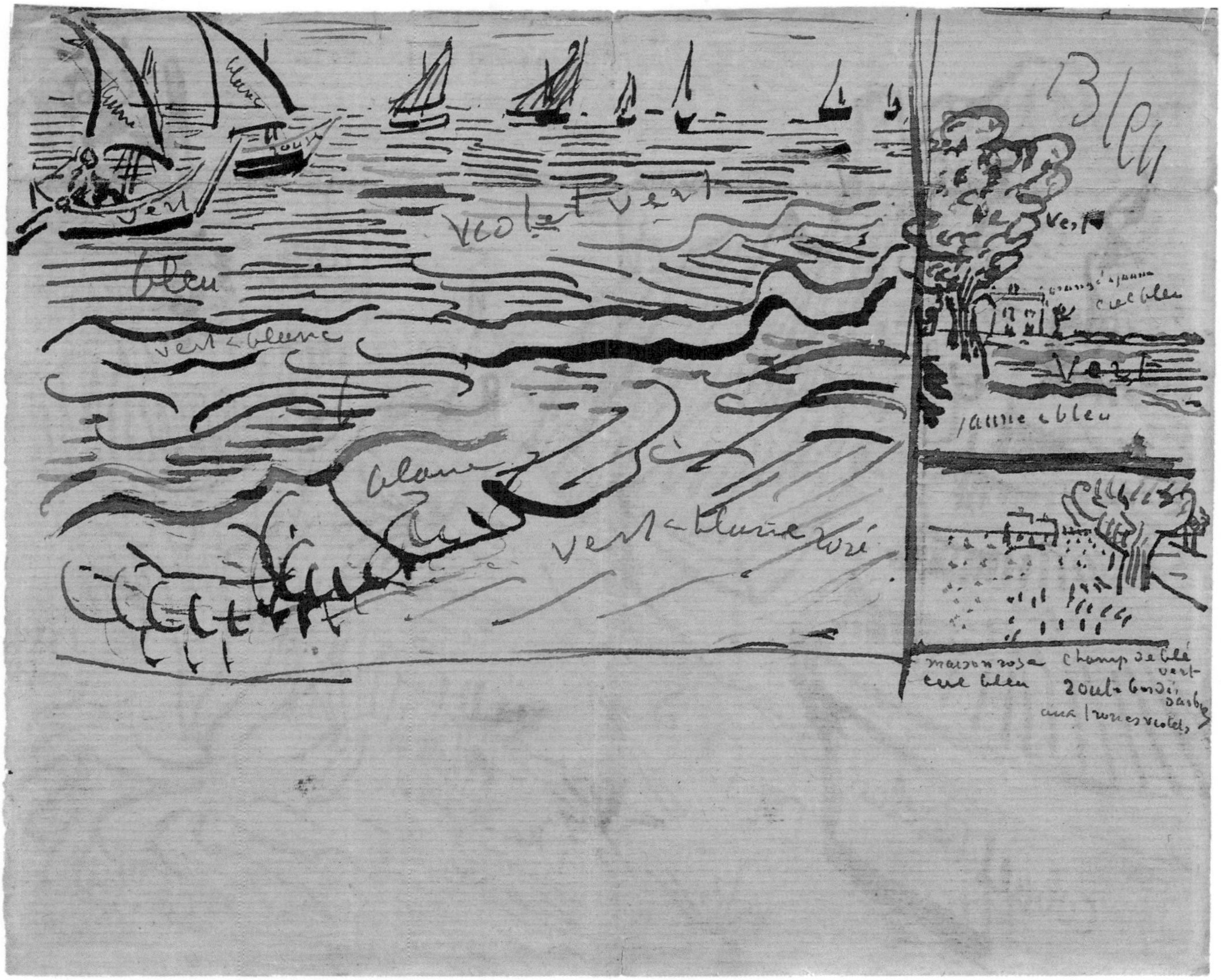

Sketch 6

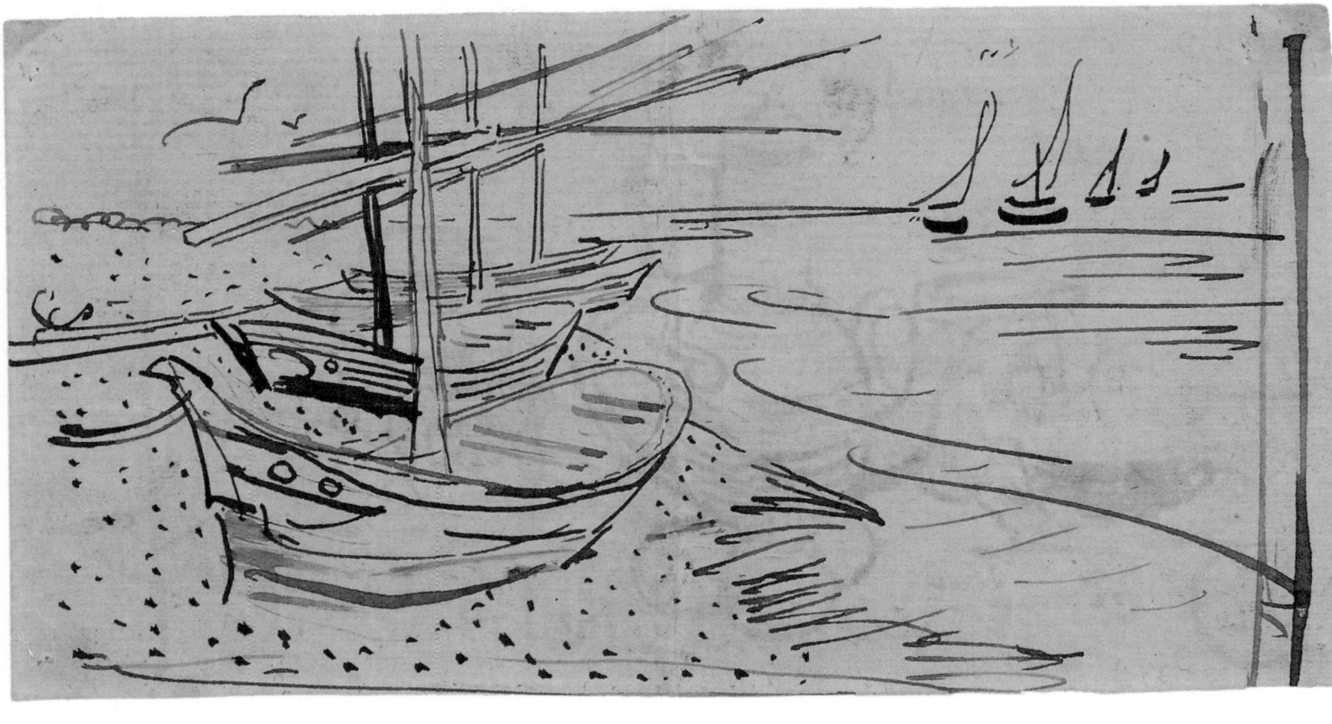

Sketch 7

7 mon cher Bernard Pardonne moi si j'écris bien à la hâte je crains
que ma lettre ne sera point lisible mais je veux te répondre tout de suite
Sais tu que nous avons été très bêtes Gauguin toi et moi de ne pas
aller dans un même endroit. Mais lorsque Gauguin est parti moi
j'étais pas encore sur de pouvoir partir Et lorsque toi tu es parti
il y avait cet affreux argent du voyage et les mauvaises nouvelles
que j'avais a donner des frais ici qui l'ont empeché. Si nous étions
parti tous ensemble vers ici ce n'aurait pas été si bête car à trois
nous eussions fait le ménage chez nous. Et maintenant que je suis
un peu mieux orienté je commence a entrevoir des avantages ici
Pour moi je me porte mieux ici que dans le nord - je travaille même en
plein midi en plein soleil sans ombre aucune dans les champs de blé et
voilà j'en jouis comme une cigale. mon dieu si à 25 ans
j'eusse connu ce pays au lieu d'y venir a 35 — à cette epoque
j'étais enthousiasmé pour le gris ou l'incolore plutôt ~~[illegible]~~
je revais toujours de millet et puis j'avais des connaissances en Hollande
dans la catégorie de peintres Mauve Israels &c.

Sketch 1

Voici croquis d'un
semeur.
Grand terrain de mottes
de terre labourées
franchement violet en
grande partie
Champs de blé mur d'un
ton d'ocre jaune avec un
peu de carmin
le ciel jaune de chrome 1
presque aussi clair que
le soleil lui même qui
est jaune de chrome 1 avec
un peu de blanc tandis que
le reste du ciel est jaune
de chrome 1 et 2 melangés
très jaune donc
la blouse du semeur est bleue
et son pantalon blanc
toile de 25 carrée

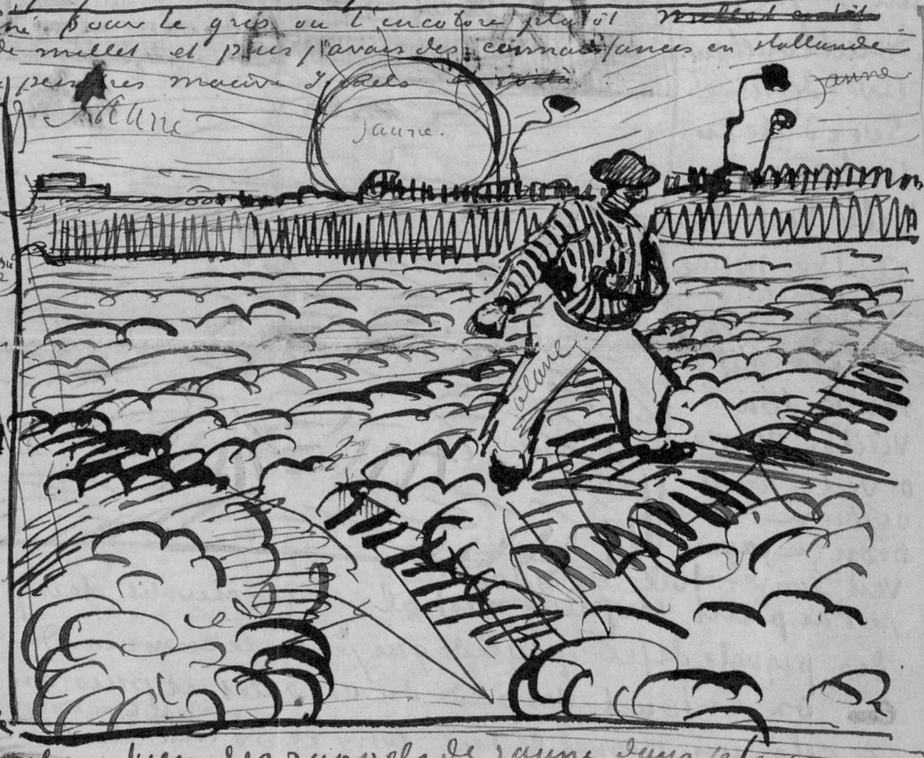

il y a bien des rappels de jaune dans le terrain
des tons neutres resultantes du mélange du violet avec le jaune mais
je me suis un peu foutu de la vérité de la couleur. faire des images naives
d'almanach plutôt_de vieil almanach de campagne ou la grêle
la neige la pluie le beau temps sont représentés d'une façon tout à fait
primitive. ainsi qu'Anquetin avait si bien trouvé sa moisson
Je ne te cache pas que je ne déteste pas la campagne — y ayant été
elevé des bouffées de souvenirs d'autrefois des aspirations vers cet infini
dont le Semeur la gerbe sont les Symboles m'enchantent encore comme
autrefois

1r:1 (reduced to 85 percent of actual size)

mais quand donc ferai je le ciel étoilé ce tableau
qui toujours me preoccupe. – helas helas c'est bien
comme dit l'excellent copain Cyprien dans « en ménage » de
J K Huysmans : les plus beaux tableaux sont ceux que l'on rêve
en fumant des pipes dans son lit mais qu'on ne fait pas. S'agit
pourtant de les attaquer quelqu'incompétent qu'on se sente ~~en~~ vis a vis
des ineffables perfections des splendeurs glorieuses de la nature.

mais comme je voudrais voir l'étude que tu as fait au bordel
je me fais des reproches à n'en pas finir de ne pas encore avoir fait
de figures ici

Voici encore
un paysage
Soleil couchant?
Lever de lune?
Soir d'été en
tout cas.
Ville violette
astre jaune
ciel bleu vert
les blés ont
tous les tons
vieil or cuivre
or vert or rouge
or jaune
bronze jaune
vert rouge. toile de 30 carrée

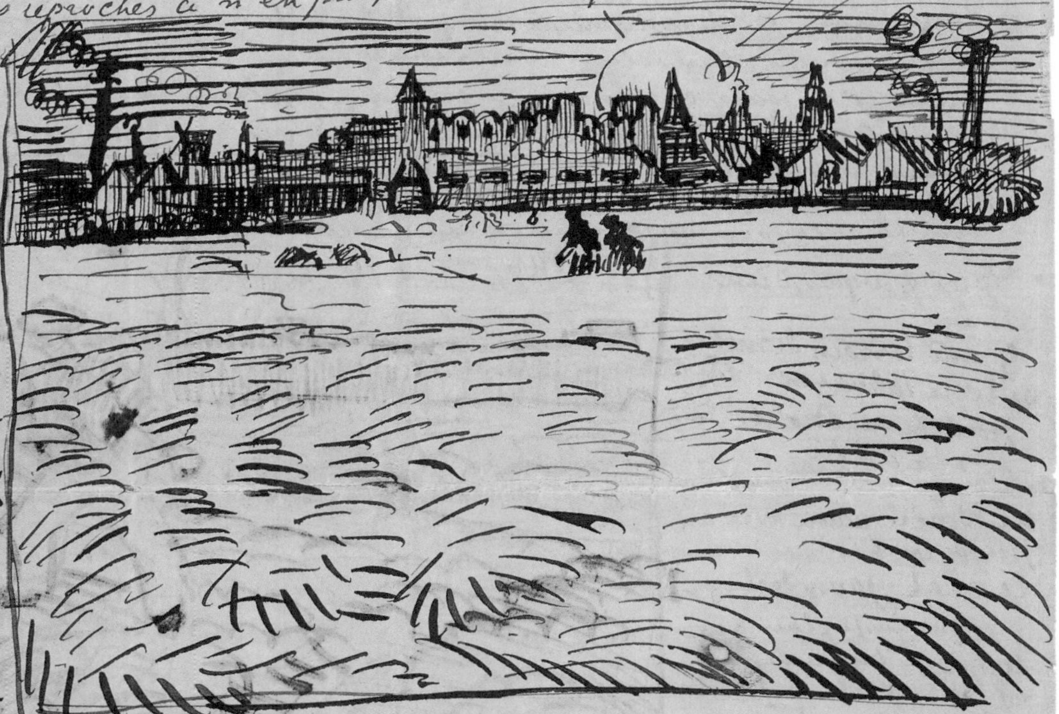
Sketch 2

je l'ai peint en plein mistral. mon chevalet était fixé en terre avec
des piquets de fer procédé que je te recommande
on enfouit les pieds du chevalet et puis on enfonce
à côté un piquet de fer long de 50 centimètres on attache le tout avec des cordes
vous pouvez ainsi travailler dans le vent

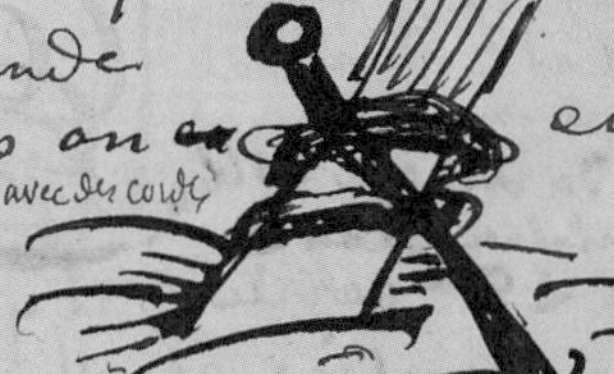
Sketch 3

Voici ce que j'ai voulu dire pour le blanc et le noir
prenons le Semeur le tableau est coupé en deux
une moitié est jaune, le haut, le bas est violet.
eh bien le pantalon blanc repose l'oeil
et le distrait au moment où le contraste simultané
excessif de jaune et de violet l'agacerait. Voilà
ce que j'ai voulu dire

1v:2 (reduced to 85 percent of actual size)

Je connais ici un sous lieutenant des zouaves nommé Milliet. je lui donne des leçons de dessin – avec mon cadre perspectif – et il commence à faire des dessins – ma foi j'en ai vu bien pire que ça et il a du zèle pour apprendre a été au Tonkin &c. Celui là va partir mois d'octobre pour l'afrique Si tu étais dans les zouaves il te prendrait avec lui et te garantirait une large marge de liberté relative pour faire de la peinture si toutefois tu l'aiderais un peu dans ses manigances artistiques à lui. Cela peut il t'être de quelqu'utilité. En cas qu'oui fais le moi savoir aussitôt possible

Une raison de travailler c'est que les toiles valent de l'argent tu me diras que d'abord cette raison est bien prosaïque puis que tu doutes que cela soit vrai. C'est pourtant vrai
Une raison de ne pas travailler c'est que les toiles & couleurs ~~nous~~ ne font que nous coûter des sous en attendant
Les dessins cependant ne nous coûtent pas cher.
Gauguin s'embête aussi à Pont Aven se plaint comme toi de l'isolement. Si tu allais le voir – mais je n'en sais rien s'il y restera et suis porté à croire qu'il a l'intention d'aller à Paris. Il dit qu'il croyait que tu serais venu à Pont Aven.
Mon dieu si nous étions ici tous les trois Tu me diras que c'est trop loin. Bon, mais en hiver ~~est ce qu'on ne~~ puisqu'ici on peut travailler dehors toute l'année. – Voilà ma raison pour aimer ce pays ci d'avoir moins à redouter le froid qui en empêchant mon sang de circuler m'empêche de penser de faire quoi que ce soit. Tu pourras en juger lorsque tu seras soldat – Ta mélancolie s'en ira laquelle pourrait rudement bien venir de ce que tu as trop peu de sang – ou le sang vicié ce que je ne pense pourtant pas. C'est ce sacré sale vin de paris et la sale graisse des biftecks qui vous fait cela. mon dieu j'étais arrivé à un état de choses que chez moi le sang ne marchait plus du tout mais ce qu'on appelle point du tout à la lettre. Seulement au bout de 4 semaines d'ici cela s'est remis en marche mais mon cher copain à cette même époque j'ai eu une attaque de mélancolie comme la tienne de laquelle j'eusse autant souffert que toi si ce n'était que je la saluais avec grand plaisir comme ~~présage~~ signe que j'allais guérir – ce qui est aussi arrivé.

2r:3 (reduced to 85 percent of actual size)

Au lieu donc de retourner à Paris restes en pleine campagne car tu as besoin de forces pour sortir comme il faut de cette épreuve d'aller en Afrique. Or plus que tu te fais du sang et du bon sang avant mieux c'est car là bas dans la chaleur on s'en fabrique peutêtre plus difficilement. Faire de la peinture et baiser beaucoup est pas compatible le cerveau s'en affaiblit voilà ce qui est bien emmerdant

Le symbole de Saint Luc le patron des peintres est comme tu sais un boeuf ~~il~~ il faut donc être patient comme un boeuf si l'on veut labourer dans le champ artistique. Mais les taureaux sont bien heureux de ne pas avoir à travailler dans la sale peinture

Mais ce que je voulais dire est ceci après la période de mélancolie tu seras ~~plus beau~~ plus fort qu'auparavant la santé reprendra et tu trouveras la nature environnante tellement belle que tu n'auras plus d'autre désir que de faire de la peinture

Je crois que ta poésie changera encore aussi dans le même sens qu'en peinture. tu es après des choses excentriques arrivé à en faire qui ont un calme egyptien et une grande simplicité.

~~Est ce que la nourriture est mangeable là bas??~~

"Que l'heure est donc brève
Qu'on passe en aimant-
C'est moins qu'un instant-
Un peu plus qu'un rêve-:
Le temps nous enlève
notre enchantement."-

C'est pas du Baudelaire cela je ne sais même pas de qui c'est ce sont les paroles d'une chanson dans le nabab de Daudet voilà où je l'ai pris - mais est ce que cela ne dit pas la chose comme un haussement d'épaule de vraie Dame

J'ai lu de ces jours ci Madame Chrysanthème de Pierre Loti cela donne des notes intéressantes sur le Japon. Mon frère a dans ce moment une exposition de Claude Monet je voudrais bien les voir - Entre autres Guy de Maupassant y était venu et a dit que dorénavant il reviendrait souvent au Boulevard Montmartre.

Je dois aller peindre donc je finis. probablement je t'écrirai de nouveau sous peu. Je te demande mille pardons de n'avoir pas suffisamment affranchi la lettre je l'avais pourtant affranchie à la poste et ce n'est pas la première fois que cela m'arrive ici d'avoir en demandant à la poste même en cas de doute été trompé en affranchissant. Tu ne te fais pas d'idée du laisser aller de la nonchalance des gens ici Enfin tu verras sous peu tout cela de tes propres yeux en afrique. Merci de ta lettre j'espère t'écrire bientôt à un moment où je serai moins pressé. Poignée de main

t à t

Vincent

2v:4 (reduced to 85 percent of actual size)

1888

Mon cher Bernard, tu fais très bien de lire la bible — je commence par
là parceque je me suis toujours abstenu de te recommander cela
involontairement en lisant les citations multiples de moïse de St Luc &c
tiens, me dis je — il ne lui manquait plus que ça ça y est maintenant
en plein — — — . . . . la névrose artistique.
Car l'étude du christ la donne inévitablement surtout dans mon cas
où c'est compliqué par le calottage de pipes nombrables. —
La bible — c'est le christ car l'ancien testament tend vers ce sommet
St Paul et les évangélistes occupent l'autre pente de la montagne
sacrée. —
Que c'est petit cette histoire! mon dieu voilà — il n'y a donc que
ces juifs au monde! qui commencent par déclarer tout ce qui n'est
pas eux impur.
Les autres peuples sous le grand soleil de là-bas les égyptiens les indiens
les éthiopiens Babylone Ninive. Que n'ont ils leurs annales
écrites avec le même soin. Enfin — l'étude de cela c'est beau et enfin
savoir tout lire équivaudrait presque à ne pas savoir lire du tout
Mais la consolation de cette bible si attristante qui soulève
notre désespoir et notre indignation — nous navre pour de
bon tout outré par sa petitesse et sa folie contagieuse.
la consolation qu'elle contient comme un noyau dans une
écorce dure une pulpe amère — c'est le christ. —
La figure du christ n'a été peint — comme je le sens — que par Delacroix et par
Rembrandt — — — — — — — — et puis millet a ~~été~~ peint . . . la
doctrine du christ. —
Le reste me fait un peu sourire — le reste de la peinture religieuse — au
point de vue religieux — non pas au point de vue de la peinture. —
Et les primitifs italiens (Botticelli disons) les primitifs flamands allemands (V Eyck Cranach) . . . .
ce sont des payens et m'intéressent qu'au même titre que les
Grecs que Velasquez que tant d'autres naturalistes
Le christ — seul — entre tous les philosophes, magiciens, &c
a affirmé comme certitude principale la vie éternelle
l'infini du temps le néant ~~[illegible]~~ de la mort — la nécessité et la raison d'être de la sérénité et du dévouement
a vécu sereinement en artiste plus grand que tous les
artistes — ~~[illegible]~~ dédaignant et le marbre et
l'argile et la couleur ~~[illegible]~~ — travaillant en
chair vivante. c. à. d. — cet artiste inouï et à
peine concevable avec l'instrument obtus de nos cerveaux modernes
nerveux et abrutis ne faisait pas de statues ni des tableaux ni
même des livres . . . . . il l'affirme hautement . . il faisait
. . des hommes vivants ~~[illegible]~~ des immortels —
C'est grave ça, — surtout parceque c'est la verité

Les sommets sont bien — c. à. d. — la couleur en est belle, — Le dessin est moins fort plutôt moins sûr de lui
Ce dessin en hésite encore, je sais pas comment dire — Le tout ne m'en est pas clair

1r:1 (reduced to 85 percent of actual size)

Ce grand artiste n'a pas non plus fait des livres
— la littérature chrétienne ~~certes~~ dans son ensemble certes l'indignerait
et bien rares sont dans celle là les produits littéraires qui
à coté de l'évangile de Luc des épitres de Paul – si simples dans
leur forme dure ou guerrière – puissent trouver grâce.
Ce grand artiste – le Christ – s'il dédaignait écrire des livres sur
des idées & sensations – a certes bien moins dédaigné la
parole parlée – la parabole surtout (Quel semeur quelle moisson
quel figuier &c.)
Et qui nous oserait dire quil en aie menti le jour
où prédisant avec mépris la chute des contructions
Romaines il affirma „quand bien même ciel et
terre passeront mes paroles ne passeront point".–
Ces paroles parlées qu'en grand seigneur prodigue il
ne daigna même pas écrire sont un des plus hauts le plus haut sommet
atteint par l'art qui y devient force créatrice puissance créatrice pure
Ces considérations, mon cher copain Bernard – nous
mènent bien loin – bien loin – nous élevant au dessus de l'art même
Elles nous font entrevoir — l'art de faire la vie
l'art d'être immortel – vivant —
Ont elles des rapports avec la peinture
Le patron des peintres – St Luc – médecin peintre
évangeliste – ayant pour symbole hélas – rien que
le boeuf – est là pour nous donner l'espérance
Pourtant – notre vie propre et vraie – est bien
humble – celle de nous autres peintres.
végétant sous le joug abrutissant des difficultés d'un
métier presque pas praticable sur cette si ingrate
planète sur la surface de laquelle, „l'amour de l'art ~~fait~~ fait perdre l'amour vrai".
Puisque pourtant rien ne s'y oppose – à la supposition
que dans les autres innombrables planètes et soleils
il y ait également et des lignes et des formes et
des couleurs – il nous demeure loisible –
de garder une sérénité relative quant aux possibilités
de faire de la peinture dans des conditions
supérieures et changées d'existence – par un phénomène (existence changée)
peutêtre pas plus malin et pas plus surprenant
que la transformation de la chenille en papillon en hanneton du ver blanc
Laquelle existence de peintre papillon aurait
pour champ d'action ~~un~~ des innombrables astres

1v:2 (reduced to 85 percent of actual size)

qui après la mort ne nous seraient peutêtre pas d'avantage
~~inapprochables~~ inaccessibles que les points ~~noirs~~ qui sur la carte
géographique nous symbolisent villes & villages
ne nous le soient dans notre vie terrestre.
La science – le raisonnement scientifique me parait être un instrument
~~qui~~ qui ira bien loin dans la suite.
Car voici – on a supposé la terre plate. c'était vrai – elle l'est encore
aujourd'hui – de Paris à Asnières par exemple –
Seulement n'empêchait que la science prouva que la terre est surtout ronde
Ce qu'actuellement personne ne conteste –
Or actuellement on en est malgré ça encore à croire que la vie est plate
et va de la naissance à la mort
Seulement elle la vie aussi est probablement ronde et très supérieure
en étendue et capacités ~~en~~ à l'hemisphère unique qui nous
en est à présent connu.
Des générations futures – c'est probable – nous éclairciront à ce sujet
si intéressant – et alors la science elle même – pourrait – ne lui
déplaise – arriver à des conclusions plus ou moins paralèles aux
dictons du Christ relatives à l'autre moitié de l'existence.
Quoi qu'il en soit – le fait est que nous sommes des peintres
dans la vie réelle et qu'il s'agit de souffler de son souffle
tant qu'on a le souffle.
Ah – le beau tableau d'Eug Delacroix –
la barque du Christ sur la mer de Génésareth
lui – avec son auréole d'un pale citron – dormant
lumineux – dans la tâche de violet dramatique
de bleu sombre de rouge sang du groupe des
disciples ahuris – sur la terrible mer
d'émeraude ~~et de~~ montant montant jusqu'à
tout en haut du cadre. Ah – la géniale esquisse
Je te ferais des croquis si ce n'était qu'ayant dessiné et peint
depuis trois ou quatre jours avec un modèle – un
zouave – je n'en peux plus – au contraire cela me repose
et me distrait d'écrire
c'est très laid ce que j'ai foutu un dessin du zouave
assis ~~de croquis~~ une esquisse peinte du zouave contre
un mur tout blanc et enfin son portrait contre
une porte verte et quelques briques orangées d'un mur.
C'est dur et enfin laid et mal foutu – Pourtant
puisque c'est de la vraie difficulté attaquée ça peut aplanir
la route dans l'avenir. La figure que je fais est presque
toujours détestable pour mes propres yeux et les yeux des autres
à plus forte raison – pourtant c'est l'étude de la figure qui
fortifie le plus si on la fait d'une autre façon qu'on ne
nous l'enseigne chez monsieur benjamin constant par exemple.

2r:3 (reduced to 85 percent of actual size)

(10) Ta lettre m'a fait bien plaisir — le croquis est très très intéressant
et je t'en remercie bien; je t'enverrai de ces jours ci un dessin de mon
côté — ce soir je suis trop éreinté de ce côté là mes yeux sont fatigués si
ma cervelle ne l'est pas.
Dis donc — te rappelles tu du Jean Baptiste de Puvis. — moi je trouve cela
épatant et aussi magicien qu'engène delacroix
Le passage que tu as déniché dans l'evangile concernant Jean Baptiste
est absolument ce que tu y as vu … des gens qui se pressent autour
de quelqu'un — es tu le christ, es tu élie — comme serait de nos jours
de demander à l'impressionisme ou à un de ses représentants
chercheurs : as tu trouvé. C'est bien ça.
Mon frère a dans ce moment une exposition de Claude Monet — 10 tableaux
faits de février à Mai à Antibes. C'est fort beau paraît-il.
As tu lu jamais la vie de Luther — car Cranach Durer Holbein
lui appartiennent. c'est lui — sa personalité — qui est la haute
lumière du moyen âge. —
moi je n'aime pas plus que toi le roi soleil — éteignoir il
me semble plutôt — ce louis quatorze. mon dieu quel
emmerdeur en tout cet espèce de salomon methodiste
je n'aime pas non plus salomon et aussi pas du tout
les méthodistes. — Salomon me semble un payen
hypocrite je n'ai vraiment pas de respect pour son architecture
imitation d'autre styles et pas non plus pour ses ecrits que les
payens ont bien mieux faits.
Dis moi un peu où tu en es pour ce qui regarde ton
service militaire faut il oui ou non parler a ce sous-
lieutenant zouaves vas tu en afrique ou pas. Est ce que
les années comptent double dans ton cas en afrique ou non.
Surtout cherche à te faire du sang — avec l'anémie on
n'avance guère. la peinture va lentement — faudrait tacher
de se faire tempérament dur à cuire — tempérament
à vivre vieux — faudrait vivre comme un moine qui
va au bordel une fois par quinzaine — cela je le fais
c'est pas très poétique — mais enfin — je sens que mon
devoir est de subordonner ma vie à la peinture
Si j'étais au Louvre avec toi je voudrais bien voir les
primitifs avec toi
au Louvre moi je vais toujours encore avec grand amour
aux hollandais Rembrandt en tête. Rembrandt que j'ai tant étudié
autrefois — puis Potter par exemple — qui vous fait — sur un panneau
de 4 ou de 6 un étalon blanc seul dans une prairie ~~[illegible]~~
~~4~~ un étalon qui hennit et bande — ~~désolé avec~~
Désolé sous un ciel gros d'orage — navré dans l'immensité vert
tendre d'une prairie humide. enfin il y a des merveilles dans les vieux
hollandais n'ayant aucun rapport avec n'importe quoi. Poignée de main
et encore une fois merci de ta lettre et de ton croquis t à t Vincent

2v:4 (reduced to 85 percent of actual size)

2 Mon cher Bernard – je ne sais ce que j'ai fourré dans ma lettre
d'hier à la place du feuillet ci-inclus ayant rapport à ton
dernier sonnet. Le cas est que je suis si éreinté par le travail
que le soir quoique cela me repose d'écrire – je suis comme une
machine détraquée tellement la journée en plein soleil
m'a fatigué d'un autre côté. et c'est pourquoi j'ai fourré dans la lettre un autre feuillet à la place de celui-ci.
En relisant le feuillet d'hier – ma foi je te l'envoie tel quel
pour moi en le relisant il me semble lisible et donc
je te l'envoie.
Aujourd'hui encore journée raide de travail.
Si tu voyais mes toiles qu'en dirais-tu – tu n'y
trouverais pas le coup le brosse presque timide et
consciencieux de Cézanne –
Mais puisqu'actuellement je peins la même campagne
de la Crau & Camargue – quoiqu'à un endroit un
peu divergent – toutefois il pourrait y demeurer
certains rapports de couleur – Qu'en sais-je –
involontairement j'ai de temps en temps pensé à
Cézanne justement lorsque je me suis rendu compte
de sa touche si malhabile dans certaines études – passe-moi
le mot malhabile – vu qu'il a exécuté les d. des études
probablement lorsque le mistral soufflait
Ayant à faire à la même difficulté la moitié du temps
je m'explique la raison pourquoi la touche de Cézanne est
tantôt très sûre et tantôt paraît maladroite
C'est son chevalet qui branle.
J'ai quelquefois travaillé excessivement vite est ce
un défaut? je n'y peux rien
Ainsi une toile de 30 – le soir d'été – je l'ai peinte
dans une seule séance –
Y revenir est pas possible – la détruire – pourquoi puisque
je suis sorti dehors en plein mistral exprès pour faire
cela –
N'est-ce pas plutôt l'intensité de la pensée que le calme
de la touche que nous recherchons – et dans la circonstance
donnée de travail primesautier sur place et sur nature
la touche calme et bien réglée est-elle toujours possible?
ma foi – il me semble – pas plus que l'escrime à
l'assaut.

1r:1 (reduced to 85 percent of actual size)

J'ai envoyé ton dessin du bordel à mon père et j'ai
sollicité de te faire un achat
Si mon père peut il le fera car il sait bien que je
dois avoir le désir de te faire vendre quelque chôse
Si tu voulais je destinerais à un échange avec toi
la tête de zouave que j'ai peinte
Seulement je n'en parlerai qu'en cas que je puisse
en même temps te faire vendre quelque chôse
Ce serait en réponse de ton esquisse de bordel — Si à nous deux
nous exécutions un bordel je suis sur que comme
caractère nous y emploierions l'étude du zouave —
Ah si plusieurs peintres étaient d'accord pour
collaborer a de grandes chôses —
L'art de l'avenir pourrait nous montrer des exemples de
cela — Les tableaux nécessaires maintenant c'est qu'il
faudrait être à plusieurs pour en supporter les difficultés
matérielles. Enfin — hélas — nous n'en sommes pas là —
l'art de la peinture ne va pas aussi vite que la littérature
Je t'écris cette fois ci ainsi qu'hier bien à la hâte
bien éreinté. et ~~aujourd'hui~~ à ce moment aussi je ne suis pas capable
de dessiner la matinée dans les champs m'a complètement
fatiguée dans cette capacité là.
C'est que ça fatigue ce soleil d'ici — Je suis de même
entièrement incapable de juger mon propre travail
je ne puis pas voir si les études soient bonnes ou mauvaises
J'ai sept études des blés malheureusement
toutes bien contre mon gré rien que des paysages.
Des paysages jaunes vieil or — faits vite vite
vite et pressé comme le moissonneur qui se tait sous
le soleil ardent se concentrant pour en abattre
Je me dis que tu dois peut-être être surpris de voir
combien peu moi j'aime la bible laquelle pourtant
j'ai souvent cherché a étudier un peu — il n'y a que ce
noyau le christ — qui au point de vue de l'art me
semble superieur — dans tous les cas autre chôse que
l'antiquité grecque Indienne Egyptienne Persane
lesquelles ont été si loin. Or je le repète — le christ
est plus artiste que les artistes — il travaille en esprit
et chair vivants il fait des hommes au lieu de statues
alors .... je me sens bien être boeuf —
étant peintre ... et j'admire le taureau
l'aigle l'homme avec une vénération — qui —
m'empêchera d'être un ambitieux
Poignée de main t à t Vincent

1v:2 (reduced to 85 percent of actual size)

5
J'ajoute pour ces sonnets explication
de ce que j'entends par – le dessin n'en est
pas bien sûr de soi :
Tu fais la morale à la fin –
tu dis à la société qu'elle est infâme
parceque la putain nous fait penser
à la viande à la halle –
Très bien cela la putain est comme
la viande chez le charcutier –
moi, abruti, je comprends je sens cela
je retrouve une sensation de ma vie
à moi je dis : c'est bien parlé
car le rythme sonore des mots colorés
m'évoque la réalité brutale du bouge
avec une grande intensité
Mais les reproches adressées à la
fin à "la société". pour moi abruti
mot "creux" comme "le bon dieu"
ne me font plus d'effet –
Ca n'y est pas dis-je et je ~~me~~
retombe dans mon abrutissement
j'oublie la poésie forte assez d'abord
pour dissiper mon hébétude
Est ce vrai ou non.
Constater des faits comme tu
commences à le faire c'est donner
des coups de bistouri de chirurgien
qui explique une anatomie.

2r:3

j'écoute recueilli et interessé je regarde
mais si après le chirurgien anatomiste
va me faire de la morale comme ça
je trouve que cette derniere tirade n'a
pas la même valeur que la démonstration
anatomique cela dit
étudier analyser la société ~~ces~~
toujours plus que moraliser
Rien ne me ~~serait~~ semblerait plus
curieux que de dire par exemple pourtant:
voilà cette viande de la halle remarque
combien tout de même malgré tout
elle reste électrisable momentanément
par le stimulus d'un amour plus raffiné
& inattendu.
Ainsi que la chenille repue qui ne
mange plus qui rampe sur un mur au lieu
de ramper sur une feuille de choux cette
femelle repue ne peut plus aimer quand
bien même qu'elle s'y met – elle cherche
cherche cherche sait-elle elle
même quoi? Elle est consciencieuse
vivante sensible ~~mais impuissante~~ galvanisée rajeunie momentanément
Elle aime encore pourtant – donc sa vie y est –
pas à tortiller – malgré qu'elle soit finie
et mourante en tant que bête terrestre
le papillon en éclot – et le papillon
de cette chenille repue – le hanneton,
~~De ce~~, blanc ver ——. ——
voilà d'ailleurs où j'en suis en tant qu'études
de vieilles putains —— je voudrais bien aussi
approximativement savoir de quoi moi-même je suis
peut-être la larve.

18 1889

Mon cher copain Bernard. peutêtre seras tu
enclin à m'excuser de n'avoir pas incontinent
repondu à ta lettre voyant qu'à celle ci
je joins un petit envoi de croquis
. Dans le croquis le jardin il y a peutêtre
quelque chose comme „ des tapis velus de
fleurs et de verdure tissus – de Crivelli ou Virelli peu importe Enfin – tout
cas à tes citations j'ai voulu répondre
avec la plume ~~pl~~ mais pas en écrivant
des paroles. Aujourdhui aussi j'ai peu la
tête à la discussion je suis dans le travail
jusqu'à par dessus les oreilles.
Ai fait de grands dessins à la plume – 2 –
une immense campagne plate – vue
à vol d'oiseau du haut d'une colline –
des vignes, des champs de blé moissonné.
Tout cela multiplié à l'infini s'étalant
comme la surface d'une mer
vers l'horizon borné par les ~~petits~~
monticules de la Crau.
Ça n'a pas l'air japonais et c'est
la chose la plus japonaise réellement
que j'aie faite

1r:1

un personnage ~~[illegible]~~ microscopique
de laboureur un petit train qui passe
dans les blés, voila tout. la vie qu'il y
a la dedans. Ecoutez j'ai passé les
premiers jours de mon arrivee - à cet
endroit là avec un ami peintre.
Voila ce qui serait embêtant à faire dit-il
moi je ne dis rien mais je trouvais cela
tellement épatant que je n'avais pas
meme la force d'engueuler cet idiot
J'y reviens reviens reviens encore - bon
j'ai fait deux dessins de ca - de ce
paysage plat ou il n'y avait rien que
. . . . l'infini . . .
l'éternité . .
Bon - survient pendant que je dessine
un coco qui n'est pas peintre mais soldat
j'y dis „est ce que ca t'epate que moi je
trouve cela aussi beau que la mer"?
Or il connaissait la mer - lui.
Non - cela ne m'épate pas - dit-il -
que tu trouves cela aussi beau que la
mer - mais moi je trouve cela

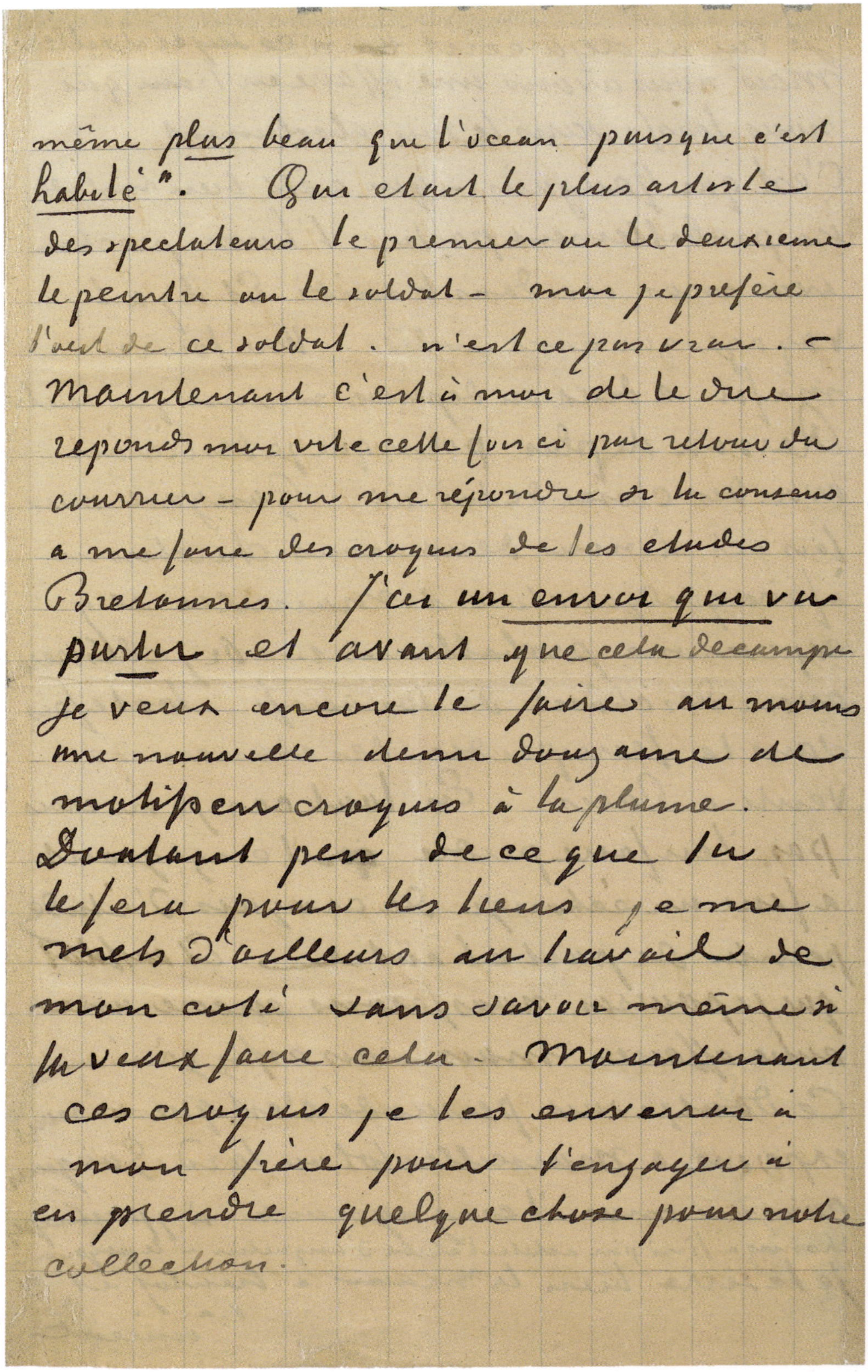
même *plus* beau que l'ocean puisque c'est
habité". Qui était le plus artiste
des spectateurs le premier ou le deuxième
le peintre ou le soldat - moi je préfère
l'oeil de ce soldat. n'est ce pas vrai. -
Maintenant c'est à moi de le dire
reponds moi vite cette fois ci par retour du
courrier - pour me répondre si tu consens
a me faire des croquis de tes etudes
Bretonnes. J'ai *un envoi qui va*
partir et avant que cela decampe
je veux encore te faire au moins
une nouvelle demi douzaine de
motifs en croquis à la plume.
Doutant peu de ce que tu
le fera pour les tiens je me
mets d'ailleurs au travail de
mon coté sans savoir même si
tu veux faire cela - Maintenant
ces croquis je les enverrai à
mon frère pour l'engager à
en prendre quelque chose pour notre
collection.

1v:3

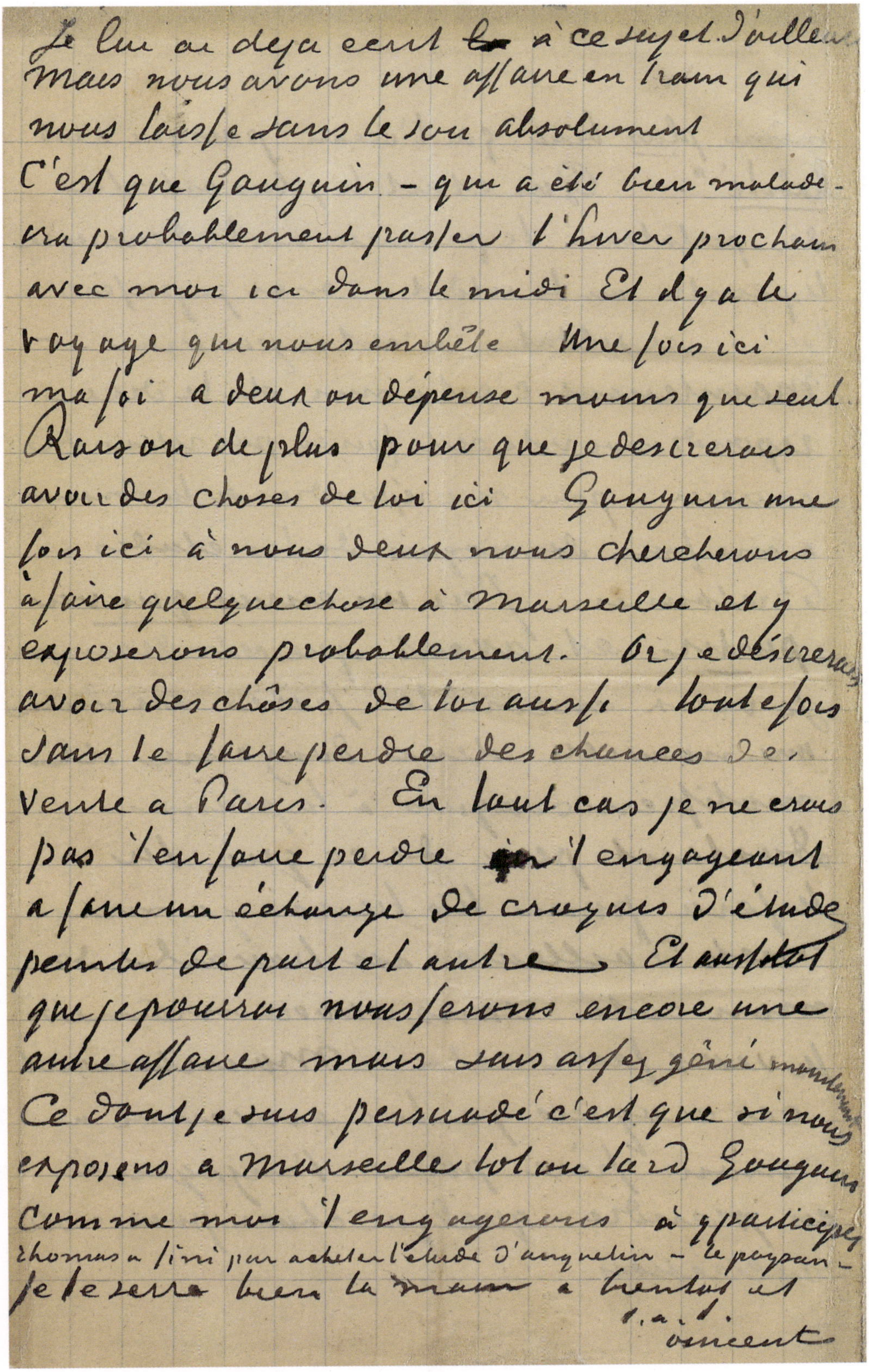

Je lui ai deja écrit à ce sujet d'ailleurs
mais nous avons une affaire en train qui
nous laisse sans le sou absolument
C'est que Gauguin – qui a été bien malade –
va probablement passer l'hiver prochain
avec moi ici dans le midi Et il y a le
voyage qui nous embête Une fois ici
ma foi à deux on dépense moins que seul
Raison de plus pour que je desirerais
avoir des choses de toi ici Gauguin une
fois ici à nous deux nous chercherons
à faire quelque chose à Marseille et y
exposerons probablement. Or je désirerais
avoir des choses de toi aussi toutefois
sans te faire perdre des chances de
vente a Paris. En tout cas je ne crois
pas t'en faire perdre en t'engageant
a faire un échange de croquis d'étude
peints de part et autre Et aussitot
que je pourrai nous ferons encore une
autre affaire mais suis assez géné momentanément
Ce dont je suis persuadé c'est que si nous
exposons a Marseille tot ou tard Gauguin
comme moi t'engagerons à y participer
Thomas a fini par acheter l'étude d'Anquetin – le paysan –
Je te serre bien la main a bientot et
t. à t.
Vincent

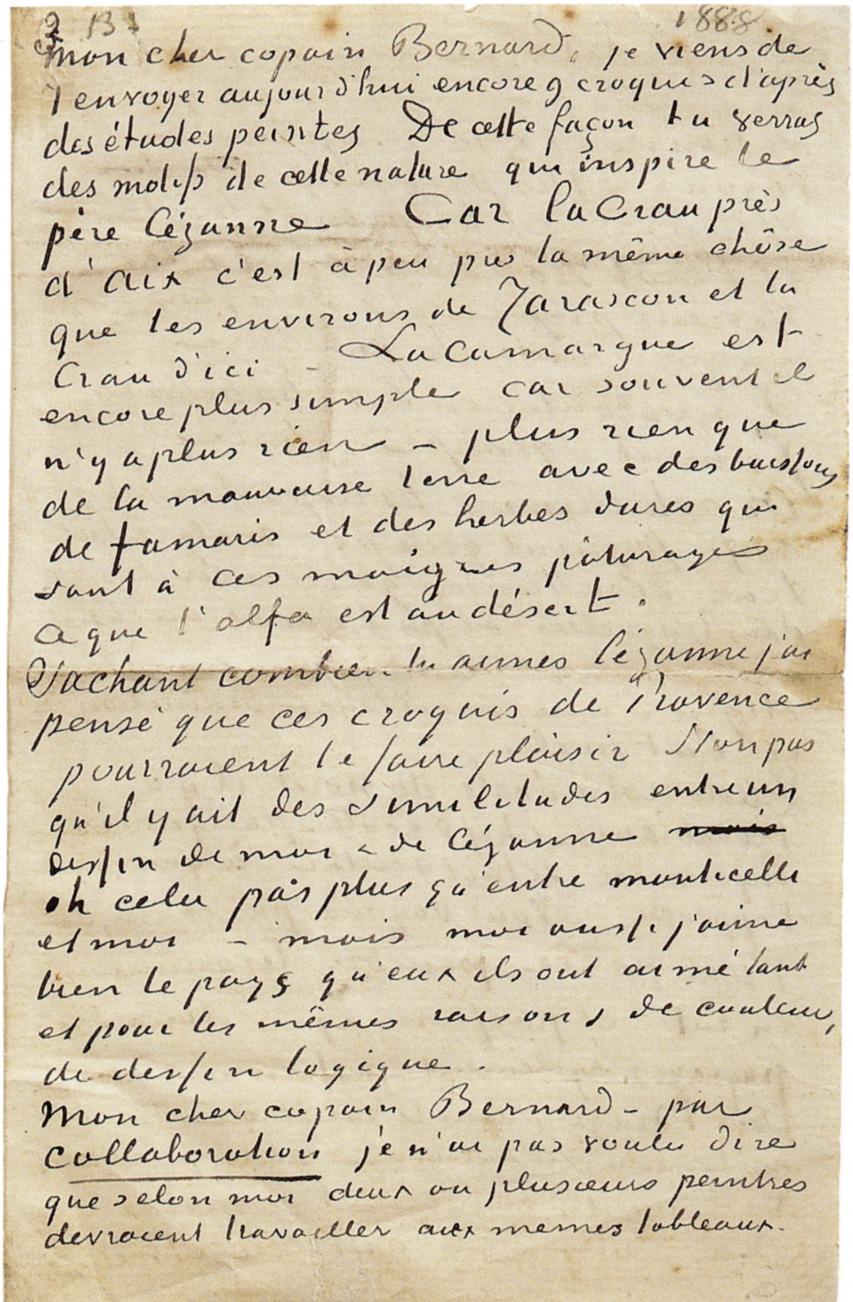
2 B7 1888
Mon cher copain Bernard, je viens de
t'envoyer aujourd'hui encore 9 croquis d'après
des études peintes De cette façon tu verras
des motifs de cette nature qui inspire le
père Cézanne Car la Crau près
d'Aix c'est à peu près la même chose
que les environs de Tarascon et la
Crau d'ici – La Camargue est
encore plus simple car souvent il
n'y a plus rien – plus rien que
de la mauvaise terre avec des buissons
de tamaris et des herbes dures qui
sont à ces maigres pâturages
ce que l'alfa est au désert.
Sachant combien tu aimes Cézanne j'ai
pensé que ces croquis de Provence
pourraient te faire plaisir Non pas
qu'il y ait des similitudes entre un
dessin de moi et de Cézanne ~~mais~~
oh cela pas plus qu'entre Monticelli
et moi – mais moi aussi j'aime
bien le pays qu'eux ils ont aimé tant
et pour les mêmes raisons, de couleur,
de dessin logique.
Mon cher copain Bernard – par
collaboration je n'ai pas voulu dire
que selon moi deux ou plusieurs peintres
devraient travailler aux mêmes tableaux.

1r:1

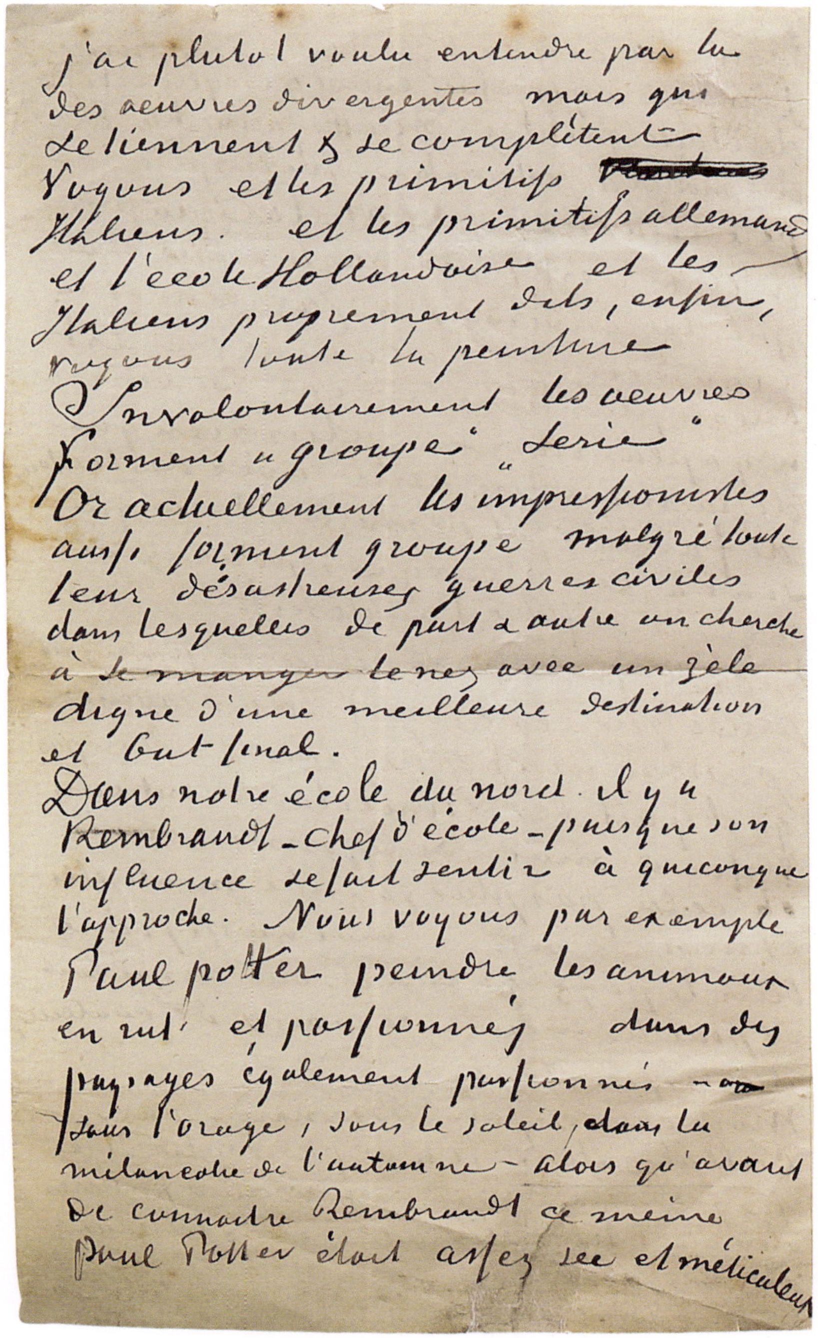

j'ai plutot voulu entendre par là
des oeuvres divergentes mais qui
se tiennent & se complètent
Voyons et les primitifs ~~[illegible]~~
Italiens. et les primitifs allemands
et l'école Hollandaise et les
Italiens proprement dits, enfin,
voyons toute la peinture
Involontairement les oeuvres
forment un groupe "série"
Or actuellement les impressionnistes
aussi forment groupe malgré toute
leur désastreuses guerres civiles
dans lesquelles de part & autre on cherche
à se manger le nez avec un zèle
digne d'une meilleure destination
et but final.
Dans notre école du nord il y a
Rembrandt – chef d'école – puisque son
influence se fait sentir à quiconque
l'approche. Nous voyons par exemple
Paul potter peindre les animaux
en rut et passionnés dans des
paysages également passionnés ~~[illegible]~~
sous l'orage, sous le soleil, dans la
mélancolie de l'automne – alors qu'avant
de connaître Rembrandt ce même
Paul Potter était assez sec et méticuleux

1v:2

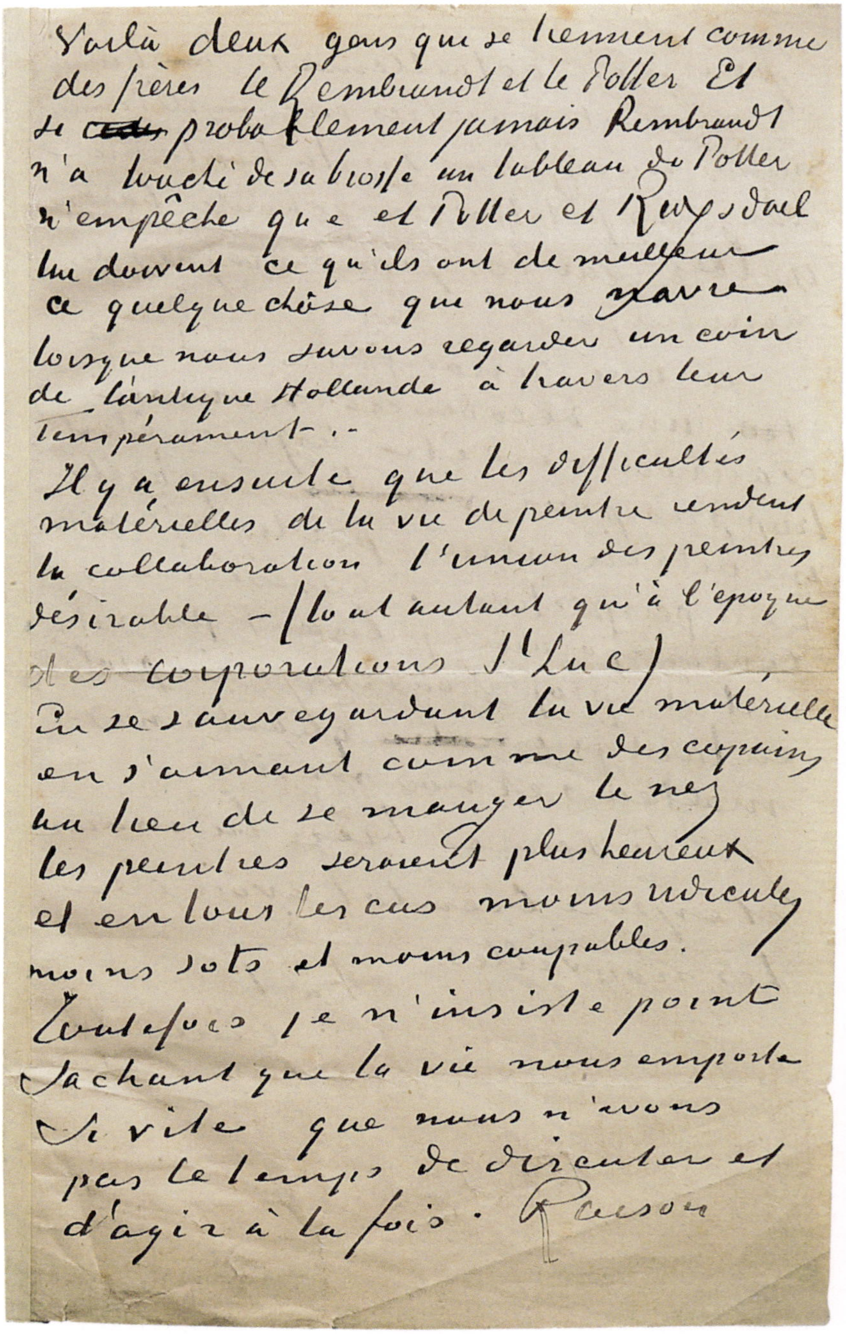
Voilà deux gens qui se tiennent comme
des frères le Rembrandt et le Potter Et
si ~~ceux~~ probablement jamais Rembrandt
n'a touché de sa brosse un tableau de Potter
n'empêche que et Potter et Ruysdael
lui doivent ce qu'ils ont de meilleur
ce quelque chose qui nous navre
lorsque nous savons regarder un coin
de l'antique Hollande à travers leur
tempérament. –
Il y a ensuite que les difficultés
matérielles de la vie de peintre rendent
la collaboration l'union des peintres
désirable – (tout autant qu'à l'époque
des corporations St Luc)
En se sauvegardant la vie matérielle
en s'aimant comme des copains
au lieu de se manger le nez
les peintres seraient plus heureux
et en tous les cas moins ridicules
moins sots et moins coupables.
Toutefois je n'insiste point
Sachant que la vie nous emporte
si vite que nous n'avons
pas le temps de discuter et
d'agir à la fois. Raison

1v:3

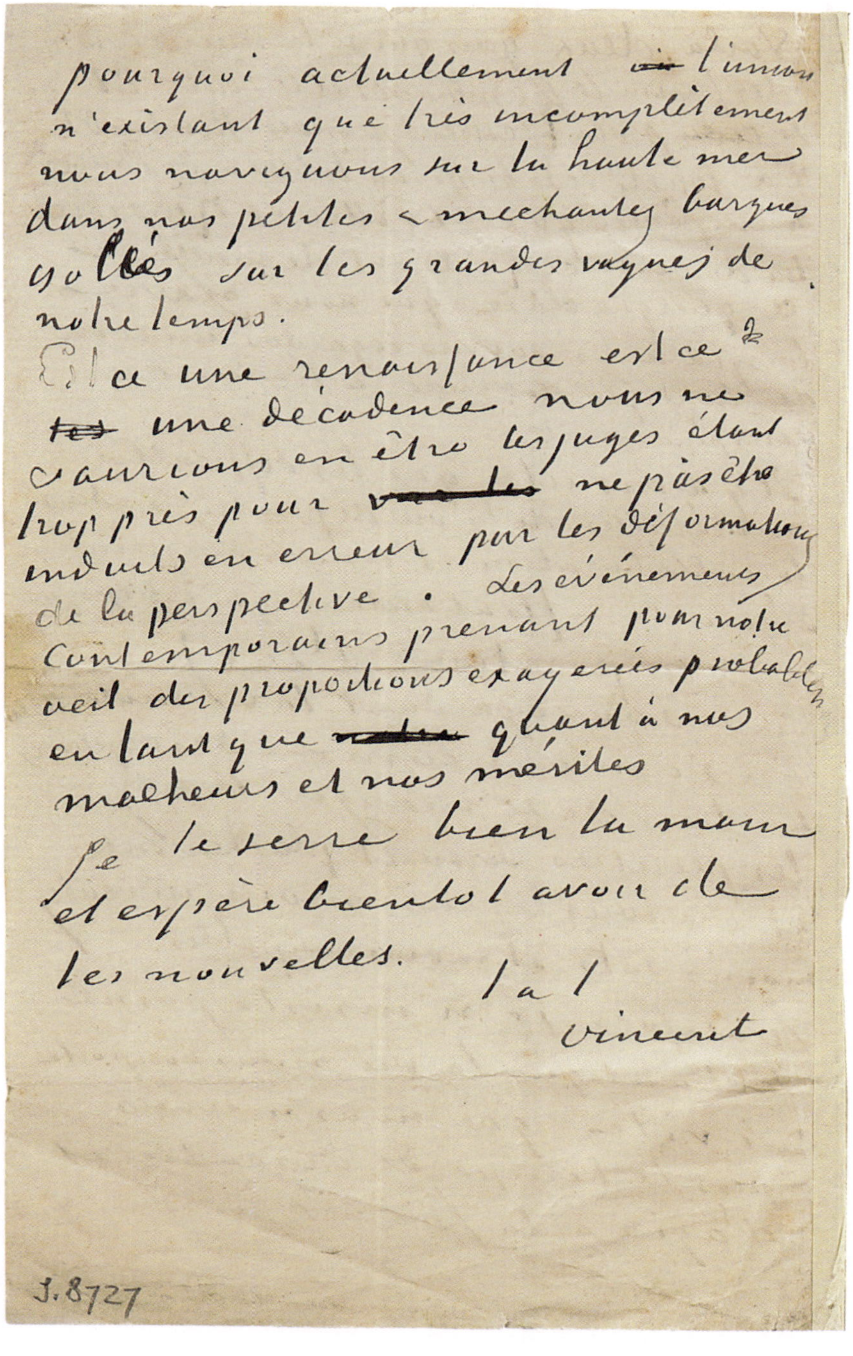
pourquoi actuellement l'union
n'existant que très incomplètement
nous naviguons sur la haute mer
dans nos petites & mechantes barques
jollées sur les grandes vagues de
notre temps.
Est ce une renaissance est ce
une décadence nous ne
saurions en être les juges étant
trop près pour ne pas être
induits en erreur par les déformations
de la perspective. Les événements
contemporains prenant pour notre
oeil des proportions exagerées probablement
en tant que quant à nos
malheurs et nos mérites
Je te serre bien la main
et espère bientot avoir de
tes nouvelles.
t à t
Vincent

J.8727

1r:4

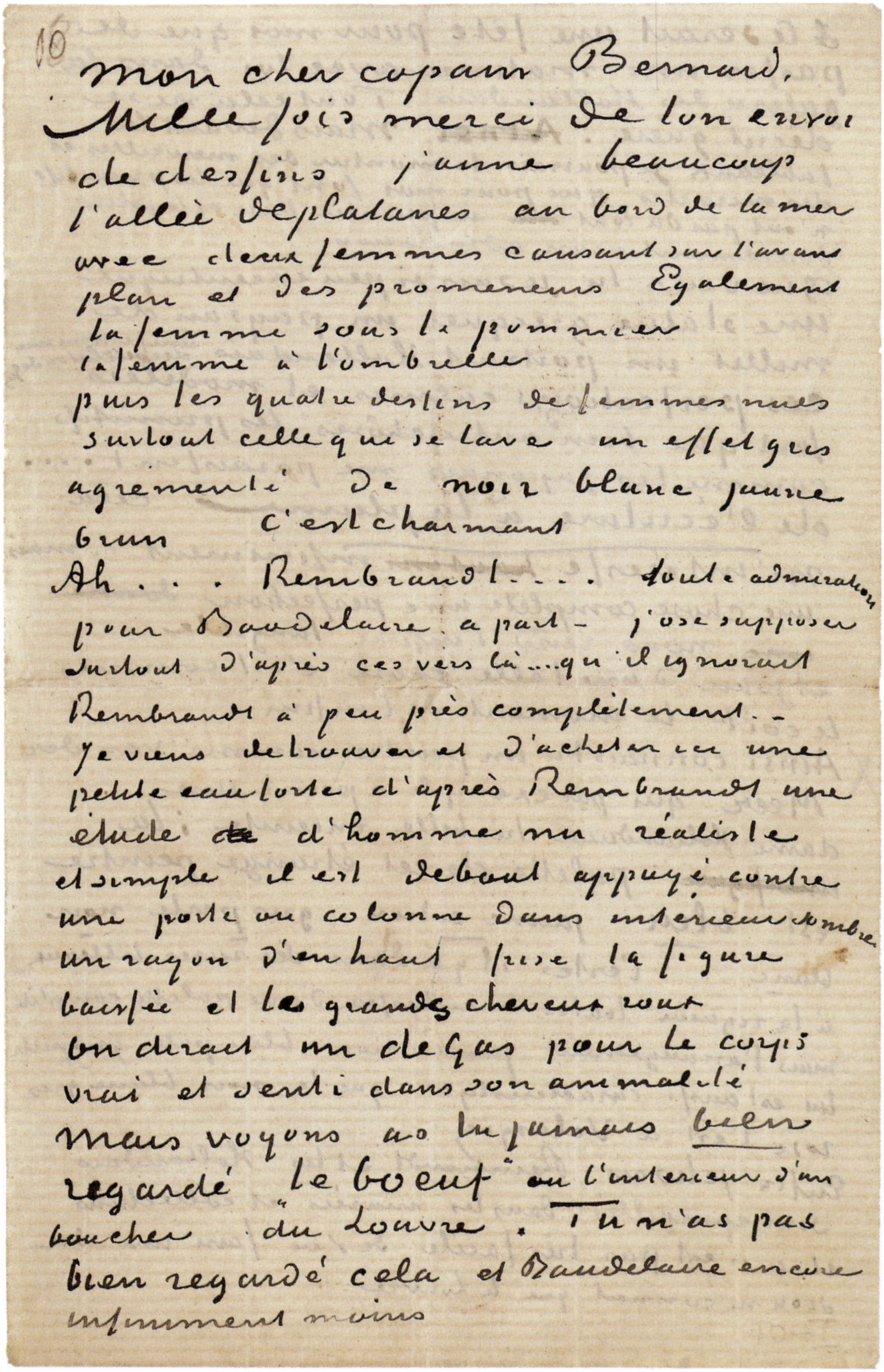
10

Mon cher copain Bernard.
Mille fois merci de ton envoi
de dessins j'aime beaucoup
l'allée de platanes au bord de la mer
avec deux femmes causant sur l'avant
plan et des promeneurs Egalement
la femme sous le pommier
la femme à l'ombrelle
puis les quatre dessins de femmes nues
surtout celle qui se lave un effet gris
agrementé de noir blanc jaune
brun c'est charmant
Ah... Rembrandt... toute admiration
pour Baudelaire à part – j'ose supposer
surtout d'après ces vers là... qu'il ignorait
Rembrandt à peu près complètement. –
Je viens de trouver et d'acheter ici une
petite eauforte d'après Rembrandt une
étude ~~de~~ d'homme nu réaliste
et simple il est debout appuyé contre
une porte ou colonne dans interieur sombre
un rayon d'en haut frise la figure
baissée et les grands cheveux roux
On dirait un Degas pour le corps
vrai et senti dans son animalité
Mais voyons as tu jamais bien
regardé "le boeuf" ou l'interieur d'un
boucher du Louvre. Tu n'as pas
bien regardé cela et Baudelaire encore
infiniment moins

1r:1

Ce serait une fête pour moi que de passer une matinee avec toi dans la galerie des Hollandais Tout cela ne se décrit guère. ~~Ainsi~~ Mais devant les tableaux je pourrais te montrer des merveilles et des miracles qui pour moi font que les primitifs n'ont pas du tout en premier lieu et le plus directement mon admiration

Que veux tu je suis si peu excentrique une statue grecque un paysan de millet un portrait Hollandais une femme nue de Courbet ou de Degas ces perfections calmes et modelées font que bien d'autres choses les primitifs comme les japonais me paraissent.... de l'écriture à la plume cela m'intéresse infiniment mais une chose complète une perfection nous rend l'infini tangible et jouir d'une telle chose c'est comme le coit le moment de l'infini

X Ainsi connais tu un peintre nommé van der Meer qui par exemple a peint une dame Hollandaise très belle enceinte; la palette de cet étrange peintre est bleu jaune citron gris perle noir blanc Certes il y a dans ses rares tableaux à la rigueur toutes les richesses d'une palette complète mais l'arrangement jaune citron bleu pale gris perle lui est aussi caracteristique que le noir blanc gris rose l'est a Velasquez

Enfin je le sais Rembrandt et les Hollandais sont eparpillés dans les musées et collections et ce n'est pas très facile de s'en faire une idee si on ne connait que le Louvre.

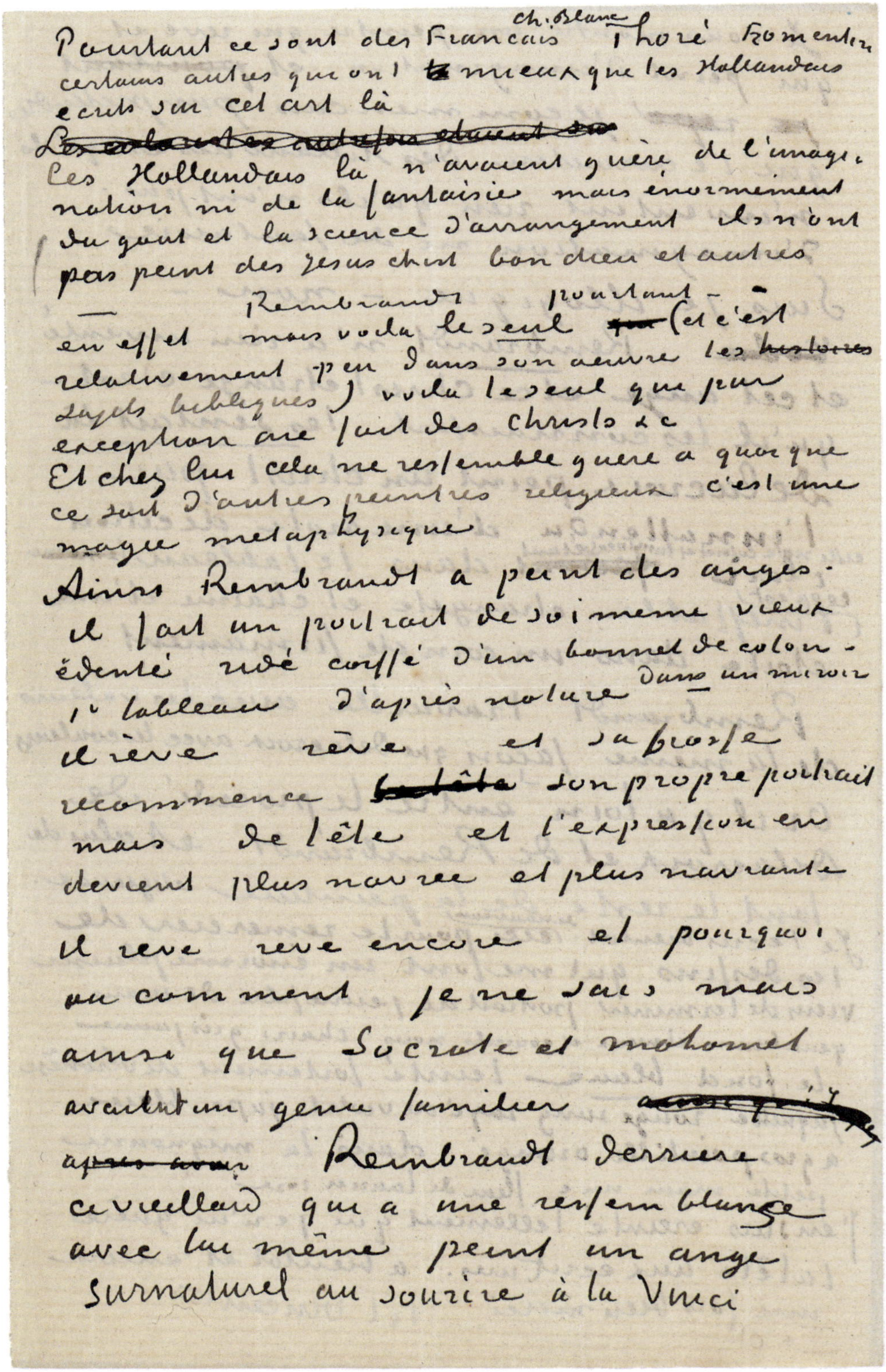
Pourtant ce sont des Francais Ch. Blanc Thoré Fromentin
certains autres qui ont ~~t~~ mieux que les Hollandais
écrits sur cet art là
~~Les [illegible]~~
Les Hollandais là n'avaient guère de l'imagination ni de la fantaisie mais énormément du gout et la science d'arrangement ils n'ont pas peint des Jesus christ bon dieu et autres
— Rembrandt pourtant —
en effet mais voila le seul ~~qu~~ (et c'est relativement peu dans son oeuvre les ~~histoires~~ sujets bibliques) voila le seul qui par exception ait fait des Christs &c
Et chez lui cela ne ressemble guère a quoi que ce soit d'autres peintres religieux c'est une magie metaphysique
Ainsi Rembrandt a peint des anges.
il fait un portrait de soi meme vieux édenté ridé coiffé d'un bonnet de coton.
1r tableau d'après nature dans un miroir
il rêve rêve et sa prose
recommence ~~la tête~~ son propre portrait
mais de tête et l'expression en
devient plus navrée et plus navrante
il reve reve encore et pourquoi
ou comment je ne sais mais
ainsi que Socrate et Mahomet
avaitent un genie familier ~~[illegible]~~
~~apres avoir~~ Rembrandt derriere
ce vieillard qui a une ressemblance
avec lui même peint un ange
surnaturel au sourire à la Vinci

1v:3

Je vous montre un peintre qui reve et
qui peint d'imagination et ~~pourtant~~
~~je~~ ~~[illegible]~~ je commencais par pretendre
que le caractere des Hollandais est qu'ils
n'inventent rien qu'ils n'ont pas.
d'imagination ni de fantaisie
Suis je illogique – non –
~~[illegible]~~ Rembrandt n'a rien inventé
et cet ange et ce christ etrange c'est –
qu'il les connaissait les sentait là
Delacroix peint un christ par
l'innattendu d'une note de citron
clair cette note colorée et lumineuse étant ~~[illegible]~~ dans le tableau ~~[illegible]~~
ce qu'est l'ineffable etrangeté et charme d'une
etoile dans un coin de firmament
Rembrandt travaille avec les valeurs
de la même façon que Delacroix avec les couleurs
Or il y a loin entre le procedé de
Delacroix et de Rembrandt et celui de
tout le reste de la peinture religieuse.
Je t'ecris bientot de nouveau ceci pour te remercier de
tes dessins qui me font un énorme plaisir
viens de terminer portrait de jeune fille de 12 ans
yeux bruns cheveux et sourcils noirs chairs gris jaune
le fond blanc teinté fortement de véronèse
jaquette rouge sang rayé de violet jupe bleue
à gros pointillé orangé dans la mignonne
petite main une fleur de laurier rose
J'en suis éreinté tellement que je n'ai guère
la tête aux ecritures. a bientot et encore
une fois bien merci t. à t. Vincent

1r:4

8

Mon cher ~~copain~~ Bernard. Tu admettras, j'en doute aucunement, que ni toi ni moi ne pourrions avoir de Velasquez et de Goya une idée complète de ce qu'ils étaient comme homme et comme peintres car ni toi ni moi n'avons vu l'espagne leur pays et tant de belles choses qui sont restées dans le midi. N'empêche que ce que l'on en connait c'est déjà quelque chose.

Va sans dire que pour les gens du nord Rembrandt en tête il est excessivement désirable de connaître en jugeant ~~leur~~ ces peintres et leur oeuvre dans toute son étendue et leur pays et l'histoire un peu intime et serrée de l'époque et des moeurs de l'ancien pays.

J'y tiens à te répéter que ni Baudelaire ni toi ont une nette idée suffisamment ~~dans cett~~ en tant que Rembrandt.

Et en tant que quant à toi je ne saurais trop t'encourager à regarder longtemps grands et petits hollandais ~~avant~~ ici avant de t'arrêter une opinion. Ici il s'agit non seulement de pierres précieuses étranges mais il s'agit de démêler des merveilles dans des merveilles.

Puis pas mal de strass dans les diamants. Ainsi pour moi qui ~~depuis~~ 10 ans déjà durant étudie l'école de mon pays la plupart des cas je ne répondrais même pas s'il en était question tellement en général j'entends parler à côté de la question lorsqu'on discute les peintres du nord.

Ainsi à toi je n'ai qu'à répondre Bah, regarde donc un peu mieux que ça vraiment ça en vaut mille fois la peine.

Or si par exemple je prétends que ~~la~~ l'Ostade du Louvre qui représente la famille du peintre l'homme la femme la dizaine de gosses est un tableau infiniment digne d'étude et de réflexion ainsi que la paix de Munster de Terburg Si dans la galerie du Louvre les tableaux que personnellement je préfère et trouve les plus étonnants sont ~~quelq~~ très souvent oubliés par les artistes même qui vont voir les Hollandais alors je n'en suis tout peu étonné sachant que mon choix à moi dans cette galerie là est fondé sur des connaissances en cette matière que la plupart des français ne sauraient avoir.

Je n'aime pas autant que les autres ton dessin Lubricité. J'aime l'arbre cependant il a beaucoup d'allure

1r:1 (reduced to 85 percent of actual size)

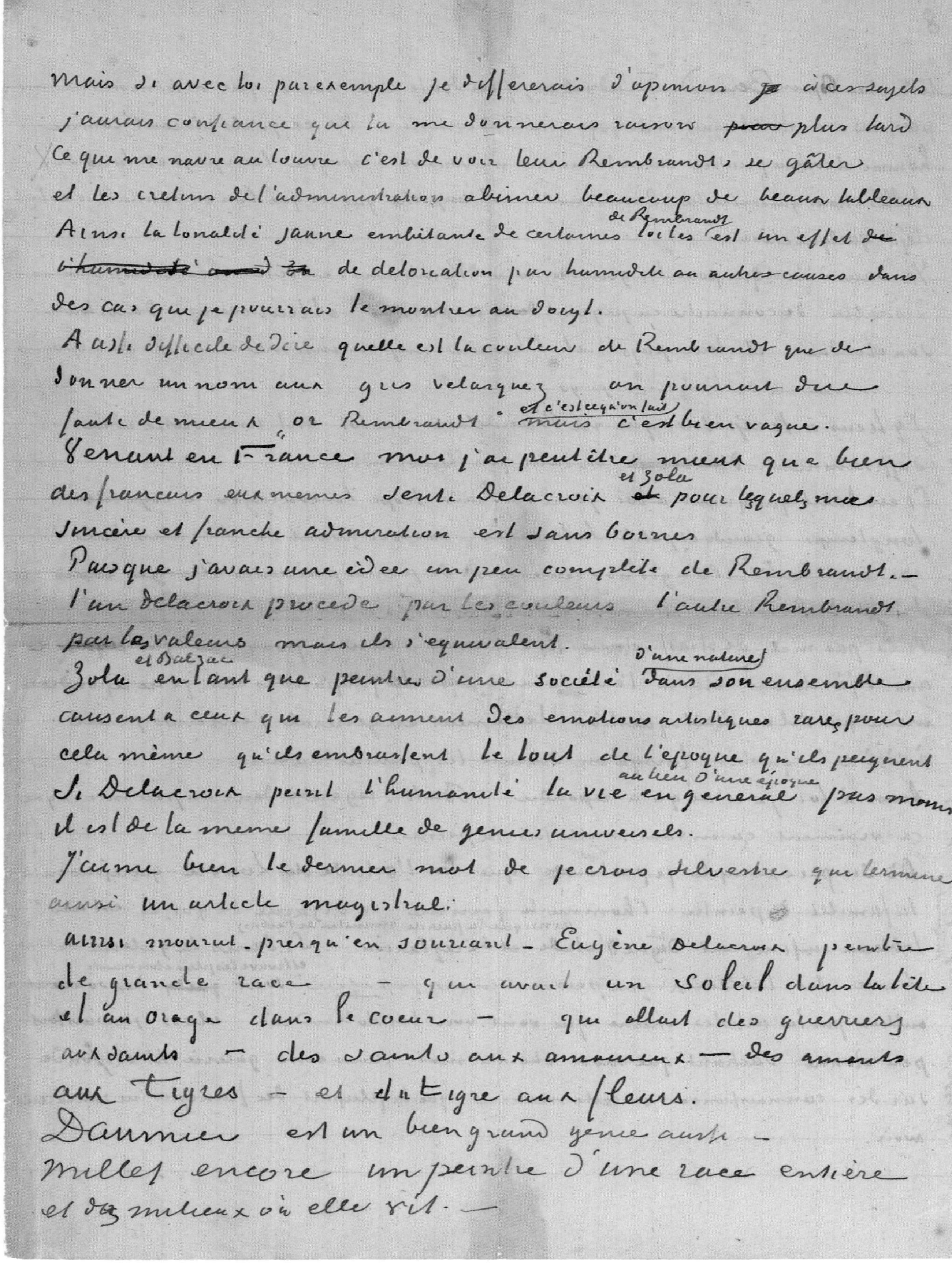

Mais si avec toi par exemple je differerais d'opinion ~~je~~ à ces sujets
j'aurais confiance que tu me donnerais raison ~~pour~~ plus tard
Ce qui me navre au louvre c'est de voir leur Rembrandts se gâter
et les cretins de l'administration abimer beaucoup de beaux tableaux
Ainsi la tonalité jaune embêtante de certaines toiles de Rembrandt est un effet ~~de~~
~~d'humidité ou~~ ~~ou~~ de detoriation par humidité ou autres causes dans
des cas que je pourrais te montrer au doigt.
Aussi difficile de dire quelle est la couleur de Rembrandt que de
donner un nom aux gris Velasquez on pourrait dire
faute de mieux, or Rembrandt ~~mais~~ et c'est ce qu'on fait c'est bien vague.
Venant en France moi j'ai peutêtre mieux que bien
des francais eux mêmes senti Delacroix ~~et~~ et Zola pour lequels ma
sincère et franche admiration est sans bornes
Puisque j'avais une idée un peu complète de Rembrandt. —
l'un Delacroix procède par les couleurs l'autre Rembrandt.
par les valeurs mais ils s'equivalent.
Zola et Balzac en tant que peintres d'une société d'une nature dans son ensemble
causent à ceux qui les aiment des emotions artistiques rares pour
cela même qu'ils embrassent le tout de l'époque qu'ils peignent
Si Delacroix peint l'humanité la vie en general au lieu d'une époque pas moins
il est de la même famille de genies universels.
J'aime bien le dernier mot de je crois Silvestre qui termine
ainsi un article magistral:
ainsi mourut presqu'en souriant — Eugène Delacroix peintre
de grande race — qui avait un soleil dans la tête
et un orage dans le coeur — qui allait des guerriers
aux saints — des saints aux amoureux — des amants
aux tigres — et du tigre aux fleurs.
Daumier est un bien grand genie aussi —
Millet encore un peintre d'une race entière
et des milieux où elle vit. —

1v:2 (reduced to 85 percent of actual size)

possible que ces grands genies ne soient que des toqués et que pour avoir
foi et admiration sans bornes pour eux il faille egalement etre toqué
cela serait — je préfererais ma folie a la sagesse des autres.
Aller indirectement à Rembrandt est peutetre le chemin le plus
direct. Parlons de frans Hals. jamais il n'a peint des christs
des annonciations aux bergers des anges ou des crucifixions et
resurrections jamais il n'a peint des femmes nues voluptueuses
et bestiales —
il a fait des portraits rien rien rien que cela.
Portraits de soldats réunions d'officiers portraits de magistrats
assemblés pour les affaires de la republique portraits de matrones à
peau rose ou jaune de blancs bonnets coiffés de laine et de
satin noir habillées ~~assemblées~~ discutant le budget d'un orphelinat
ou d'un hospice il a fait le portrait de bons bourgeois
en famille l'homme la femme l'enfant il a peint le
buveur gris ~~et ombles~~ la vieille ~~ma~~ marchande de poisson
en hilarité de sorcière la belle putain bohémienne
les bebes au maillot le crâne gentilhomme bonvivant moustachu
botté et éperonné ~~il a peint~~ il s'est peint lui et sa femme
jeunes amoureux dans un jardin sur un banc de gazon
après la premiere nuit de noce. il a peint les voyous
et les gamins riants il a peint les musiciens et
il a peint une grosse cuisinière
Il n'en sait pas plus long que cela mais cela
vaut bien le paradis du Dante
et les michel ange et les rafael et les grecs
même C'est beau comme zola et plus sain et plus
gai mais aussi vivant, parceque son epoque etait plus saine et moins triste
maintenant qu'est ce que Rembrandt. — la meme chose
absolument un peintre de portraits Voila d'abord l'idee saine large claire
qu'il s'agit d'avoir des deux sommités hollandaises qui
s'equivalent. avant d'entrer plus loin en matière.

1v:3 (reduced to 85 percent of actual size)

représentée par ces deux féconds portraitistes
Cela bien compris Toute cette glorieuse republique
reconstituée en grands traits nous conservons tres
amples marges pour les paysages les scenes d'interieur
les animaux les sujets philosophiques
Mais je t'en supplie suis bien ce raisonnement droit que
je m'efforce de te présenter d'une façon fort fort simple
Fourre toi dans la tete ce maitre Frans Hals peintre
de portraits divers de toute une republique crane et vivante et
immortelle Fourre toi dans la tete le non moins grand
et universel maitre peintre de portraits de la republique
Hollandaise Rembrandt Harmensz van Ryn
homme large et naturaliste et sain autant que Hals
lui même Et après nous verrons de cette source
Rembrandt ecouler les eleves directs et vrais Van der
meer de delft Fabritius Nicolaes Maes Pieter de Hooch Bol et les
influencés par lui Potter Ruysdael Ostade Terburg
Je te nomme la Fabritius duquel nous ne connaissons que
— deux toiles — je ne nomme pas un tas de bons
peintres et surtout pas le strass de ces diamants
assez bien introduit dans les cranes francais vulgaires ce strass
Dis-je mon cher copain Bernard très incompré-
hensible cette fois-ci je cherche a te faire voir
la grande chose simple la peinture de l'humanité
de toute une republique disons plutôt par le simple
moyen du portrait Cela d'abord et avant tout
plus tard ... si au sujet de rembrandt nous aurons
a faire un peu à de la magie a des christs et des femmes
nues c'est fort interessant — mais c'est pas le principal
Baudelaire qu'il taise son bec sur ce terrain-la c'est
des mots sonores et puis d'un creux!!! Prenons Baudelaire pour
ce qu'il est poete moderne ainsi que Musset en est un autre
mais qu'il nous fichent la paix quand nous parlons peinture Poignée de main
t. t. Vincent

1r:4 (reduced to 85 percent of actual size)

9

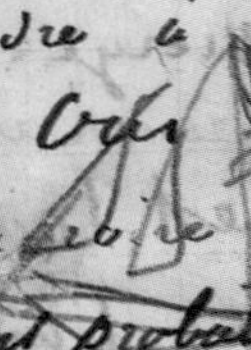

Mon cher copain Bernard je m'aperçois que j'ai oublié de répondre à
la question si ~~G~~ Gauguin est toujours encore à Pont Aven Oui
il y est encore et si tu as envie de lui écrire suis porté à croire
que cela lui fera plaisir. Il demeure jusqu'à présent ~~probable~~
qu'il me rejoindra ici sous peu aussitôt que de part ou d'autre
nous puissions trouver les frais de voyage.
Je ne ~~compte~~ crois pas que cette question des hollandais ~~doit~~
laquelle nous traitons de ces jours ci soit sans intérêt
Lorsqu'il est question de virilité d'originalité de naturalisme
quelconque il est bien interessant de les consulter.
Il faut d'abord que je te reparle de toi de deux natures
mortes ~~que tu as faites~~ et des deux portraits de ta
grand mère. As tu jamais fait mieux as tu jamais
d'avantage été toi et quelqu'un. Pas à mon avis
l'étude profonde de la première chose tombant sous la main de
la première personne venue ~~et~~ ~~tout~~ suffisait pour créer
réellement Sais tu ce qui me faisait tant aimer ces 3 ou 4
études : ~~un~~ je ne sais quoi de volontaire de très sage ~~et~~ je ne sais quoi
de fixe et ferme et sûr de soi + dont ils faisaient preuve
Jamais tu n'as été plus près de Rembrandt mon cher qu'alors
Dans l'atelier de Rembrandt l'incomparable sphinx
Van der Meer de Delft a trouvé cette ~~[illegible]~~
technique excessivement solide qui n'a pas été surpassée
Qu'actuellement .... on brûle ... de trouver
Oh je sais que nous autres travaillons ~~et~~ et raisonnons
Couleur comme eux clair obscur valeur
Qu'importent ces différences alors qu'il s'agit en somme
de s'exprimer fortement

et allemands primitifs

Actuellement ..... tu es en train de scruter les procédés italiens
la signification symbolique que peut contenir le dessin abstrait
et mystique des italiens — Fais le

1r:1 (reduced to 85 percent of actual size)

j'aime assez moi cette anecdote relative à Giotto – il y avait un
concours ~~—~~ pour exécuter je ne sais quel tableau représentant une
vierge. Un tas de projets sont envoyés à l'administration des
beaux arts de ce temps là – Un de ces projets ~~—~~ signé Giotto
est tout simplement – un ovale – 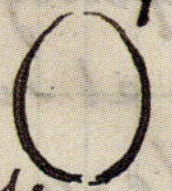 une forme d'oeuf
– l'administration intriguée ~~—~~ et confiante – ~~—~~ confie
la vierge en question – à Giotto – Est ce vrai ou non
je l'ignore mais j'aime assez l'anecdote.
Pourtant retournons à Daumier et à la
grand mère Quand est ce que tu nous en remontreras
d'études de cette solidité là – Je t'y engage tout en ne
méprisant aucunement les recherches relatives aux propriétés
des lignes à mouvement opposé – n'étant point indifferent
je l'espère aux contrastes simultanés ~~—~~ des
lignes des formes. Le mal est vois tu mon cher copain
Bernard que Giotto Cimabue ~~—~~ aussi que Holbein et v Eyck
vivaient dans une société obeliscale passe moi donc le mot
~~—~~ échafaudée construite architecturalement où chaque
individu était une pierre, toutes se tenant et formant société monumentale
Cette société lorsque les socialistes construiront – ce dont
ils sont passablement éloigné – logiquement leur édifice
social on en reverra je n'en doute point une incarnation
Mais tu sais nous sommes en plein laisser aller
et anarchie
nous artistes amoureux de ~~—~~ l'ordre et de la symetrie
nous nous isolons et travaillons à définir une seule
chôse.
Puvis sait bien cela et lorsque lui ~~—~~ si sage et si juste
a voulu oubliant ses champs elysées descendre
aimablement jusqu'à ~~—~~ l'intimité de notre époque
même – il a fait un bien beau portrait
le vieillard serein dans son clair intérieur bleu lisant le roman
a couverture jaune – un verre d'eau dans lequel un pinceau
pour l'aquarelle et une rose – a coté de lui Aussi une dame
du monde telle qu'en ont portraicturé les de Goncourt

1v:2 (reduced to 85 percent of actual size)

Or les Hollandais nous les voyons peindre des choses
telles quelles ~~apparamment sans raisonner~~ comme Courbet peignait ses belles femmes nues
Ils font des portraits paysages natures mortes
On peut être plus bête que ça et faire de plus grandes
folies.

Si nous ne savons que faire mon cher copain
Bernard alors faisons comme eux si ce n'était que
pour ne pas ~~perdre~~ laisser évaporer notre rare force
cérébrale en de stériles méditations métaphysiques ~~ou~~
~~tout~~ ~~mais~~ qui ne sauraient mettre en bocal le chaos
lequel est chaotique pour cela même qu'il ne tient dans
aucun verre ~~[illegible]~~ de notre calibre.
Nous pouvons — et voilà ce que faisaient ces hollandais
désespérément malins pour les gens à système — nous
pouvons peindre un atome du chaos. Un cheval
un portrait — ta grand mère les pommes un
paysage.

Pourquoi dis tu que Degas bande mal. Degas vit comme un
petit notaire et n'aime pas les femmes sachant que s'il les aimait
et les baisait beaucoup cérébralement malade il deviendrait ~~trop~~ inepte
en peinture. La peinture de Degas est virile et impersonnelle
justement parceque il a accepté de n'être personellement
qu'un petit notaire ayant en horreur de faire la noce. Il regarde
des animaux humains plus fort que lui bander et baiser
et il les peint bien justement parcequ'il n'a pas tellement que ça la prétention de bander
Rubens ah voilà il était bel homme et bon baiseur
Courbet aussi. leur santé leur permettait de boire manger baiser
Pour toi mon pauvre cher copain Bernard je te l'ai
déjà prédit ce printemps. Mangé bien fais bien
l'exercice militaire baise pas trop fort la peinture
en ne baisant pas trop fort n'en sera que plus couillarde

1v:3 (reduced to 85 percent of actual size)

Ah Balzac ce grand et puissant artiste nous l'a bien
dit que pour les artistes modernes la chasteté relative
les fortifiait.
Les hollandais étaient gens mariés faisant des enfants
beau bien beau métier bien dans la nature
Une seule hirondelle n'amène pas le printemps. Je ne dis
pas que dans les nouvelles études bretonnes il n'y ait [on]
pas de viriles ~~[illegible]~~ et fermes mais je ne les ai pas encore vues
donc ne saurais en parler. Mais j'ai vu ces choses viriles
le portrait de la grandmère et les natures mortes — d'après les
dessins j'en doute vaguement de ce que les nouvelles études
auraient une égale force juste au point de vue viril
Ces études ~~la~~ [dont je parle en premier lieu] la voici c'est l'hirondelle première de ~~tout~~
ton printemps d'artiste ~~[illegible]~~ Si nous voulons
nous bien bander [pour notre oeuvre] ~~nous devons~~ [quelquefois nous resigner à] peu baiser et pour le
reste être selon que notre tempérament le requiert ~~ou~~ soldats
ou ~~[illegible]~~ moines. Les hollandais encore une fois
avaient des moeurs et une vie paisible calme reglée.
Delacroix ah celui là — "j'ai — dit — il — trouvé
"la peinture lorsque je n'avais plus ni dents ni souffle.
Et ceux qui ont vu peindre cet illustre artiste disaient — quand
Delacroix peint c'est comme le lion qui dévore
le morceau) Lui ne baisait que peu et ne ~~b~~ faisait
que les amours faciles pour ne pas dérober du temps ~~[illegible]~~ consacré
à son oeuvre. Si dans cette lettre, plus incohérente en
apparence et considérée en soi sans ses rapports avec la correspond.
et surtout l'amitié precedente, que je ne la désirais — Si [en tout cas sollicitude]
dans cette lettre tu découvres que j'ai quelques inquiétudes
pour ta santé ~~[illegible]~~ prévoyant la dure épreuve que tu auras à
traverser en faisant ton service obligatoire, hélas, — alors
tu la liras bien. Je sais que l'étude des Hollandais ne
saurait que te faire du bien leurs oeuvres étant
si viriles & si couillardes & si saines.

1r:4 (reduced to 85 percent of actual size)

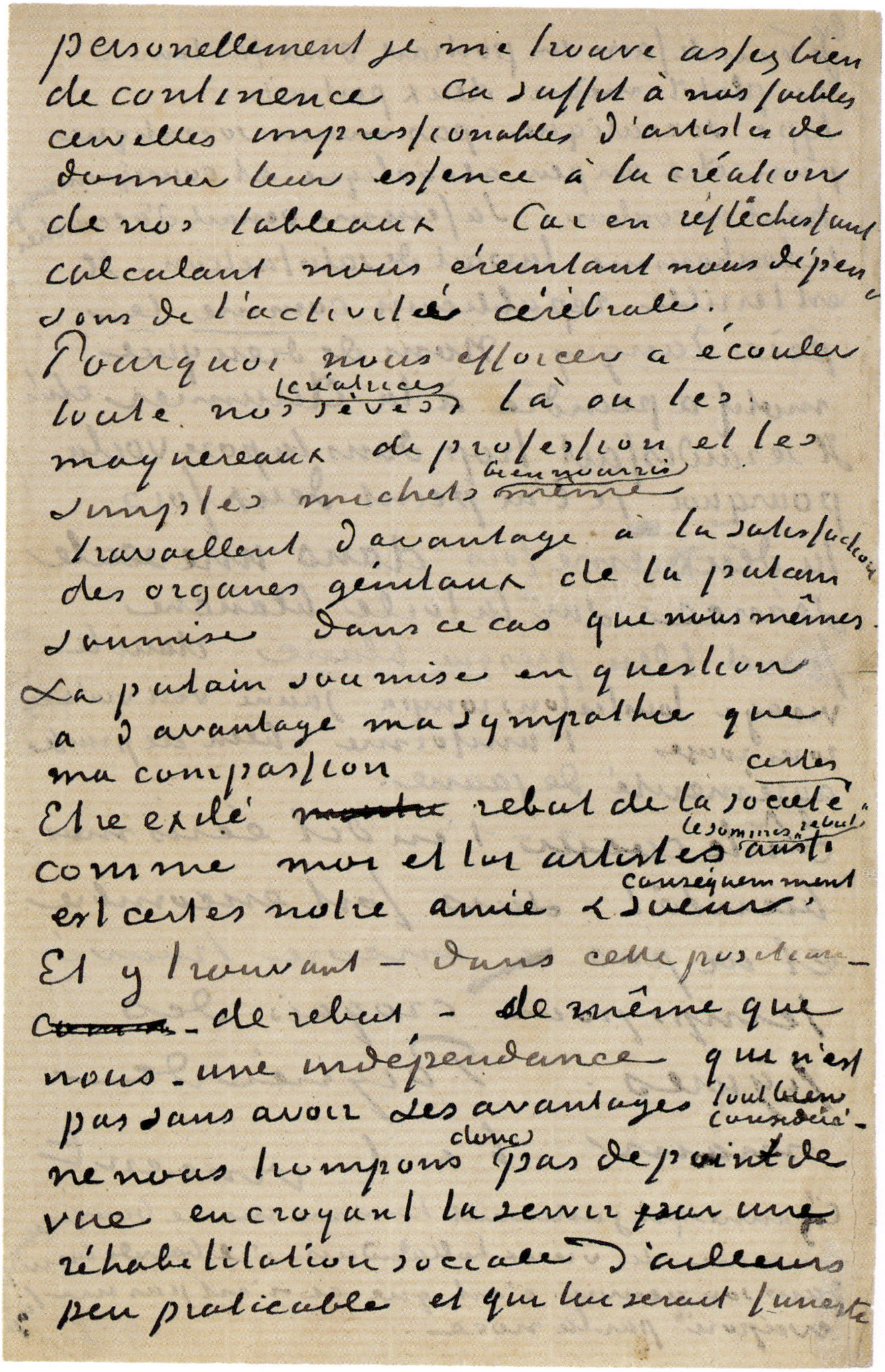

personellement je me trouve assez bien
de continence ça suffit à nos faibles
cervelles impressionables d'artistes de
donner leur essence à la création
de nos tableaux Car en réfléchissant
calculant nous éreintant nous dépen
sons de l'activité cérébrale.
Pourquoi nous efforcer à écouler
toute nos ~~sèves~~ créatrices là ou les
maquereaux de profession et les
simples michets ~~même~~ bien nourris
travaillent davantage à la satisfaction
des organes génitaux de la putain
soumise dans ce cas que nous mêmes.
La putain soumise en question
a davantage ma sympathie que
ma compassion
Etre exilé ~~[illegible]~~ certes rebut de la société
comme moi et les artistes le sommes rebut aussi.
est certes notre amie & sœur conséquemment.
Et y trouvant — dans cette position
~~comme~~ — de rebut — de même que
nous — une indépendance qui n'est
pas sans avoir des avantages tout bien considéré
ne nous trompons donc pas de point de
vue en croyant la servir par une
réhabilitation sociale d'ailleurs
peu praticable et qui lui serait funeste

2r:5

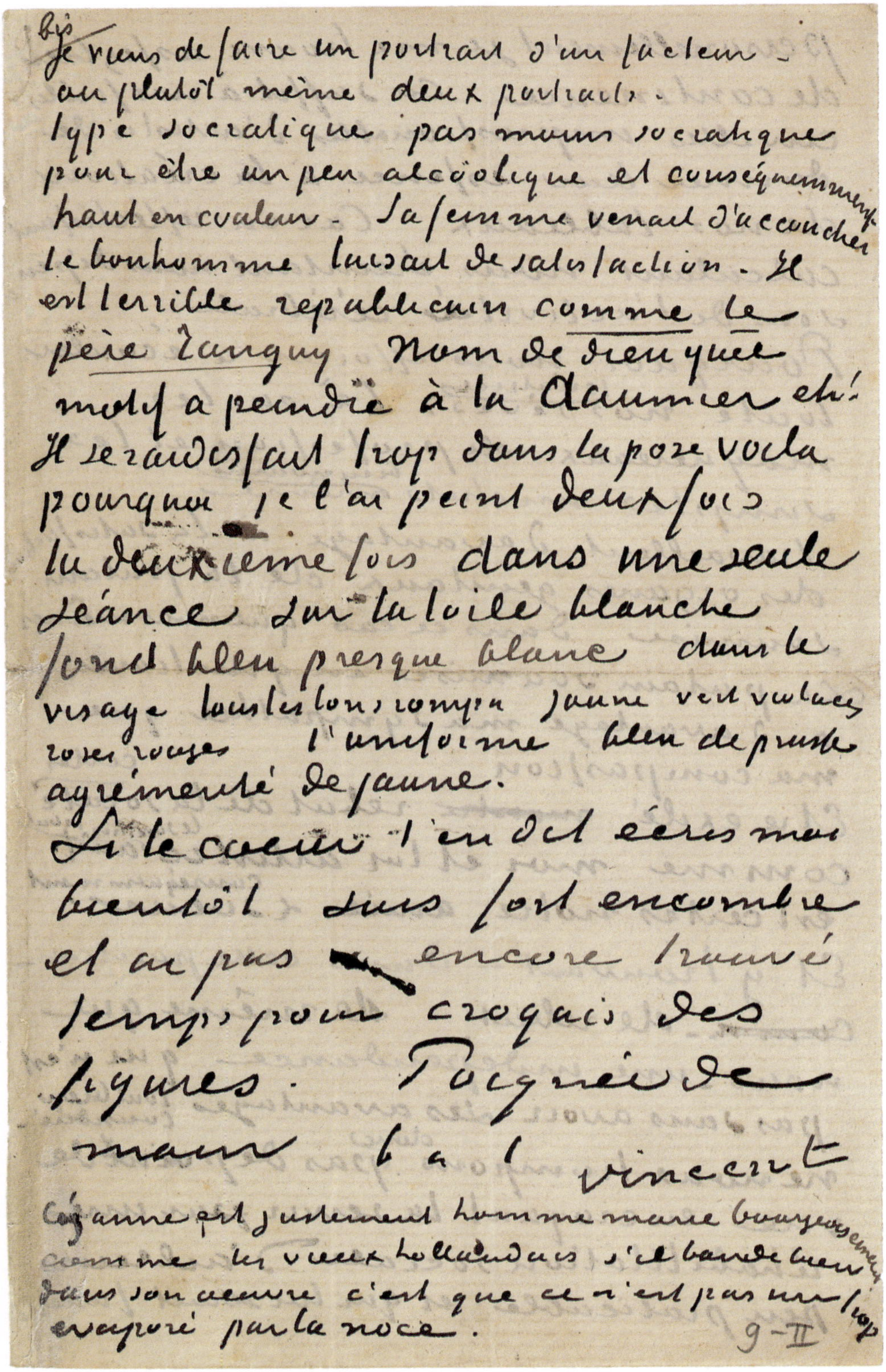

bis
Je viens de faire un portrait d'un facteur –
ou plutôt même deux portraits.
type socratique pas moins socratique
pour être un peu alcoolique et conséquemment
haut en couleur. Sa femme venait d'accoucher
le bonhomme luisait de satisfaction. Il
est terrible républicain comme le
père Tanguy. Nom de dieu quel
motif à peindre à la Daumier eh!
Il se raidissait trop dans la pose voila
pourquoi je l'ai peint deux fois
la deuxième fois dans une seule
séance sur la toile blanche
fond bleu presque blanc dans le
visage tous les tons rompus jaune vert violacés
roses rouges l'uniforme bleu de prusse
agrémenté de jaune.
Si le coeur t'en dit écris moi
bientôt suis fort encombré
et ai pas encore trouvé
temps pour croquis des
figures. Poignée de
main bàt Vincent
Cézanne est justement homme marié bourgeoisement
comme les vieux hollandais s'il bande bien
dans son oeuvre c'est que ce n'est pas un trop
évaporé par la noce.
9-II

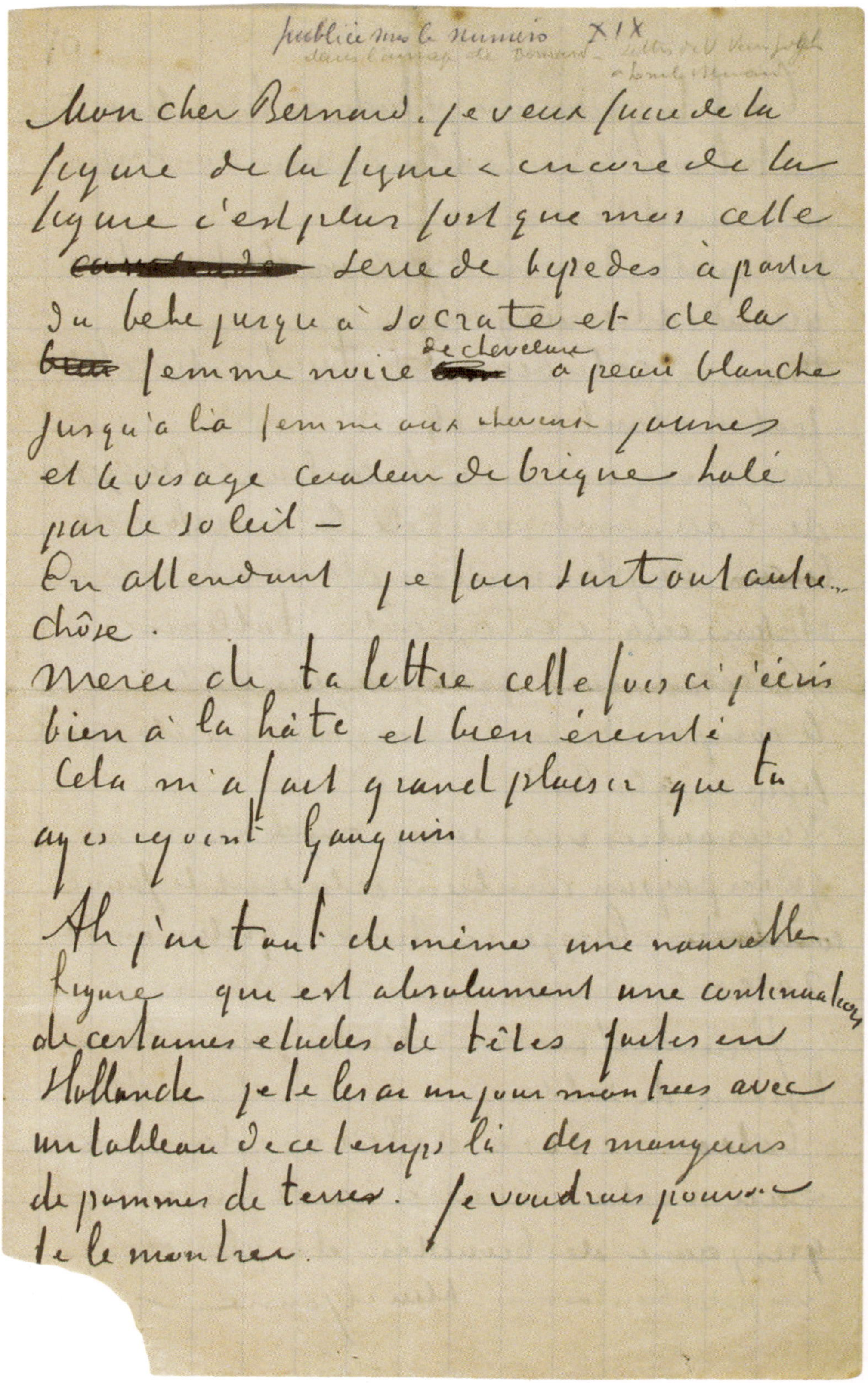

publiée sur le numero XIX dans l'ouvrage de Bernard — lettres de V. van Gogh à Emile Bernard

Mon cher Bernard, je veux faire de la
figure de la figure & encore de la
figure c'est plus fort que moi cette
serie de bipèdes à partir
du bébé jusqu'à Socrate et de la
femme noire de chevelure à peau blanche
jusqu'à la femme aux cheveux jaunes
et le visage couleur de brique hâlé
par le soleil —
En attendant je fais surtout autre
chose.
Merci de ta lettre cette fois ci j'écris
bien à la hâte et bien éreinté.
Cela m'a fait grand plaisir que tu
ayes rejoint Gauguin
Ah j'ai tout de même une nouvelle
figure qui est absolument une continuation
de certaines études de têtes faites en
Hollande je te les ai un jour montrées avec
un tableau de ce temps là des mangeurs
de pommes de terres. Je voudrais pouvoir
te le montrer.

1r:1

C'est toujours une étude où la couleur joue
un tel rôle que le blanc & noir du dessin
ne saurait le rendre
j'ai voulu t'en envoyer un dessin très
grand et très soigné
Bon – cela devenait *tout* autre chose
tout en étant correct.
Car encore une fois la couleur est suggestive
de l'air embrasé de la moisson de
~~la cam~~ du plein midi en pleine canicule
et sans cela c'est un autre tableau.
J'oserais croire que Gauguin et toi
le comprendraient mais comme ils vont
trouver cela laid.
Vous autres vous savez ~~quoi~~ ce que c'est
qu'un paysan combien cela sent le fauve
~~combien~~ lorsqu'on trouve quelqu'un de
race

J'ai aussi un déchargeur d'un
bateau de sable. c.a.d. il y a deux
bateaux rose violacé dans une
eau vert véronèse avec du sable
gris jaune des brouettes des planches
un petit bonhomme bleu et jaune –

1v:2

Tout cela vu d'en haut d'un quai
surplombant le tout à vol d'oiseau
Pas de ciel. Ce n'est qu'une esquisse
ou plutôt une pochade faite en plein mistral.
Ensuite je cherche des chardons
poussiéreux avec grand essaim
de papillons tourbillonnant dessus.
Oh le beau soleil d'ici en plein été
cela tape à la tête et je ne doute
aucunement qu'on en devienne toqué
Or l'étant déjà auparavant je ne fais qu'en jouir
J'y songe de décorer mon atelier
d'une demi douzaine de tableaux
de Tournesols
Une décoration où les chromes crus ou rompus
éclateront sur des fonds divers bleus
depuis le véronèse le plus pâle
jusqu'au bleu de roi encadrés
de minces lattes ~~mi~~ peintes en
mine orange.
Des espèces d'effets de Vitraux
d'église gothique.

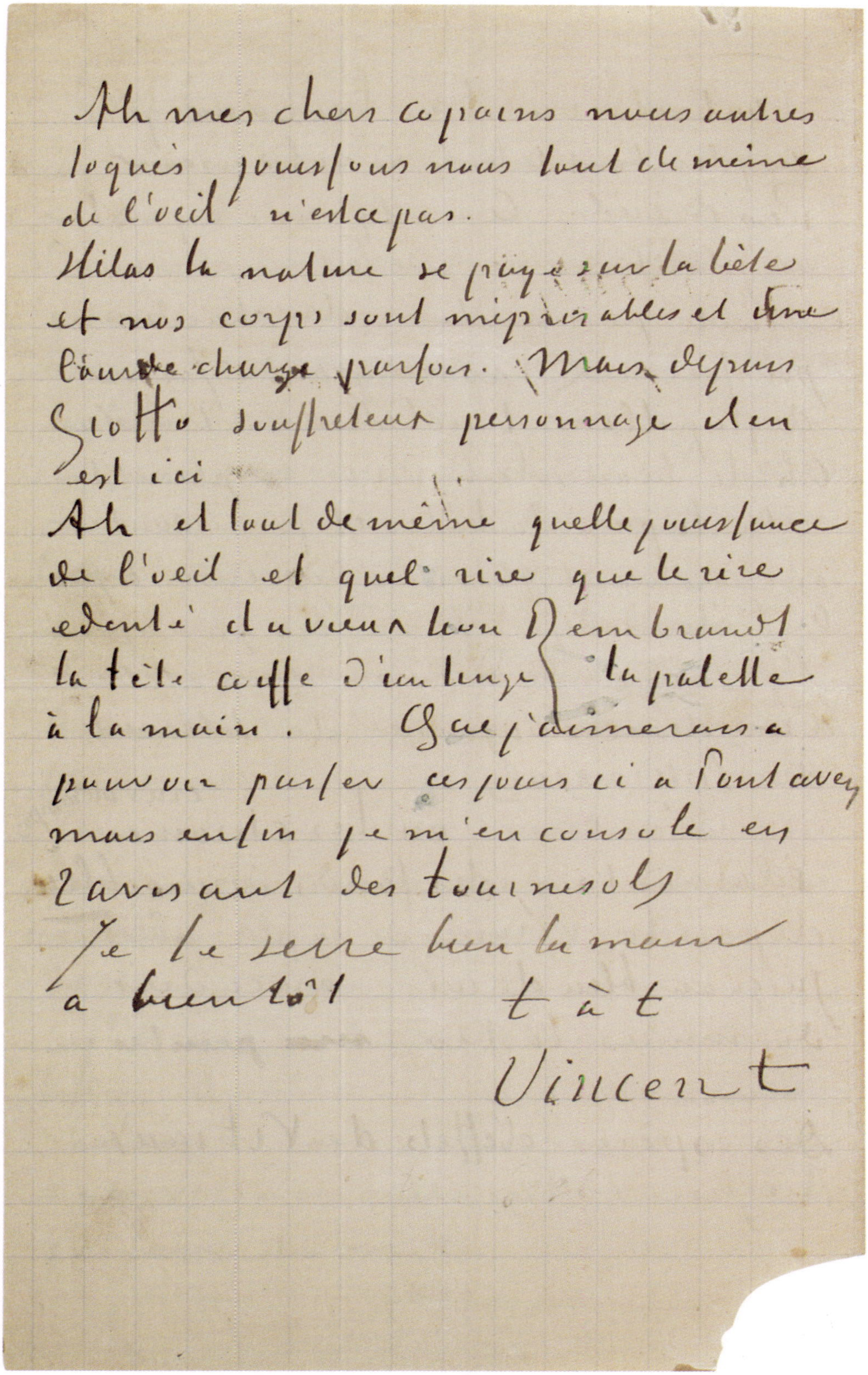
Ah mes chers copains nous autres
loqués jouissons nous tout de même
de l'oeil n'est ce pas.
Hélas la nature se paye sur la bête
et nos corps sont méprisables et une
lourde charge parfois. Mais depuis
Giotto souffreteux personnage c'en
est ici
Ah et tout de même quelle jouissance
de l'oeil et quel rire que le rire
edenté du vieux lion Rembrandt
la tête coiffé d'un linge la palette
à la main. Que j'aimerais à
pouvoir passer ces jours ci à Pont aven
mais enfin je m'en console en
travaillant des tournesols
Je te serre bien la main
à bientôt t à t
Vincent

1r:4

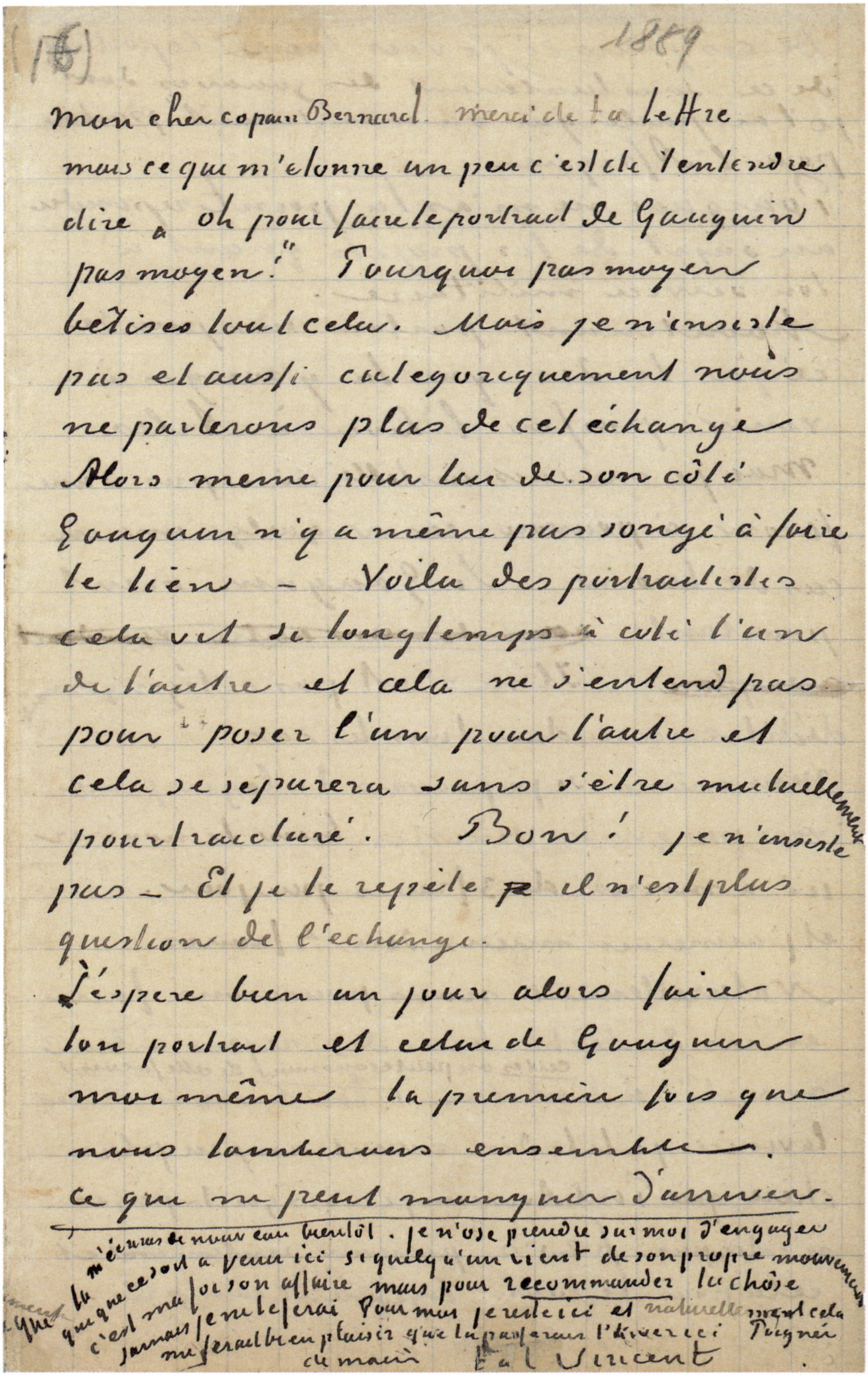
(16) 1889

mon cher copain Bernard merci de ta lettre
mais ce qui m'étonne un peu c'est de t'entendre
dire „ oh pour faire le portrait de Gauguin
pas moyen!" Pourquoi pas moyen
bêtises tout cela. Mais je n'insiste
pas et aussi catégoriquement nous
ne parlerons plus de cet échange
Alors même pour lui de son côté
Gauguin n'y a même pas songé à faire
le sien — Voila des portraitistes
cela vit si longtemps à côté l'un
de l'autre et cela ne s'entend pas
pour poser l'un pour l'autre et
cela se separera sans s'être mutuellement
pourtraicturé. Bon! je n'insiste
pas — Et je le repète il n'est plus
question de l'échange.
J'espere bien un jour alors faire
ton portrait et celui de Gauguin
moi même la premiere fois que
nous tomberons ensemble.
ce qui ne peut manquer d'arriver.

m'écrivas de nouveau bientôt. je n'ose prendre sur moi d'engager
qui que ce soit a venir ici si quelqu'un vient de son propre mouvement
c'est ma foi son affaire mais pour recommander la chose
jamais je ne le ferai Pour moi je reste ici et naturellement cela
me ferait bien plaisir que tu passerais l'hiver ici Poignée
de main t. à t. Vincent.

1r:1

De ces jours ci je vais faire le portrait
de ce sous lieutenant des zouaves dont
je t'ai parlé qui va maintenant partir
pour l'Afrique.
Pourquoi ne m'as tu point repondu
au sujet de tes projets quant a
ton service militaire.
Maintenant parlons un peu de
ce que tu dis que tu songes à
venir passer l'hiver à Arles.
Moi je me suis installé ici expres d'une
façon à pouvoir caser quelqu'un en
cas de besoin Si Gauguin vient
pourtant ~~ou si un autre viendrait~~
~~à sa place~~ Il ne s'est pas catégoriquement
décidé encore dans tous les cas.
Mais même si je pouvais te loger je ne
vois pas que tu puisses bien te nourrir
ici à moins de 3 francs par jour.
et j'aimerais mieux dire 4 francs.
Naturellement nous pourrions faire
en cas de dèche bien des repas à bon
marché à l'atelier certes on peut economiser de cette façon tout de même
la vie ici je te le dis revient un peu plus
chère que Pont Aven où je crois que tu payes
n'est ce pas fr 2.50 par jour seulement et
cela pour le tout. logement compris.

1v:2

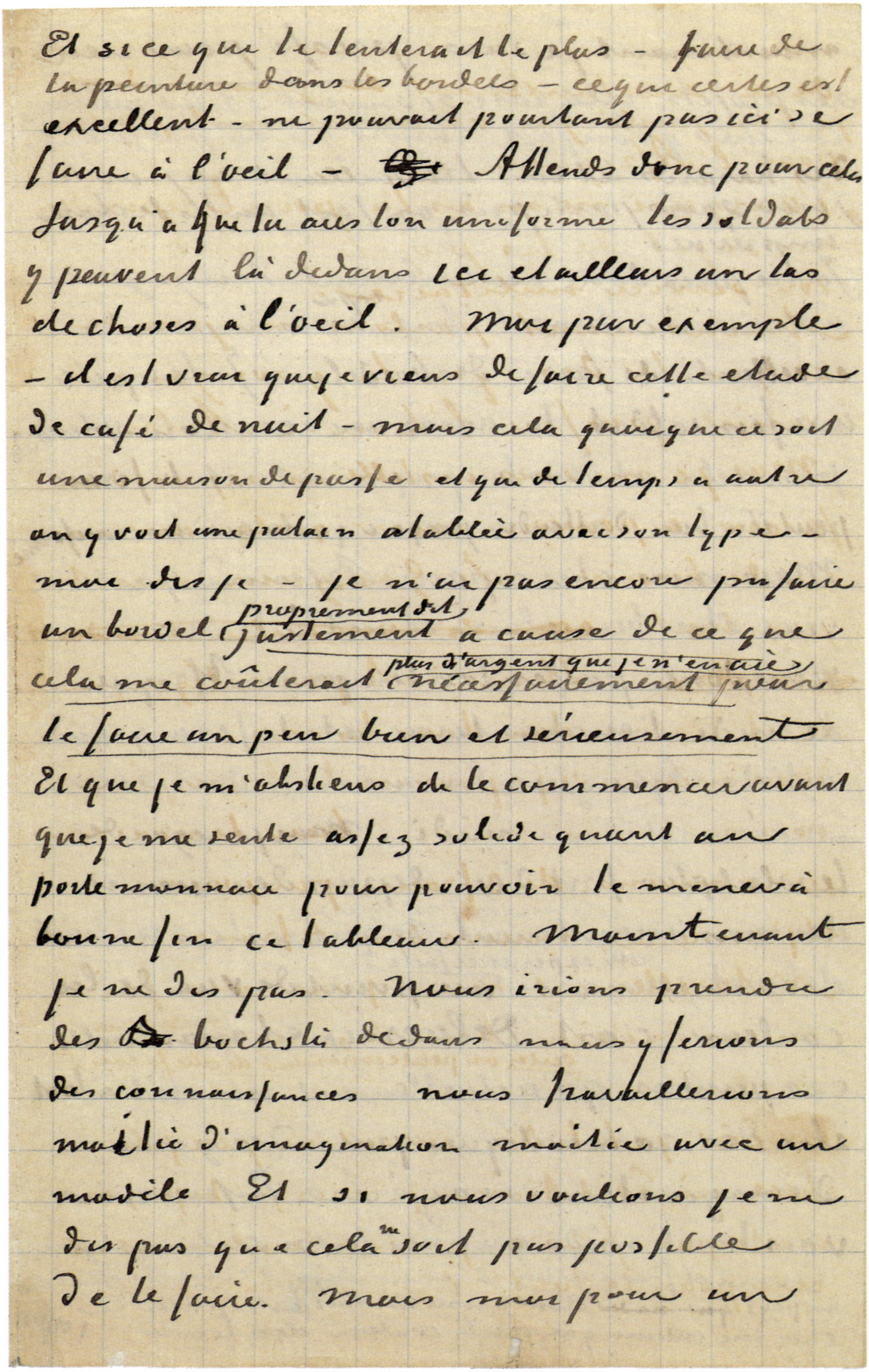
Et si ce que te tenterait le plus – faire de
la peinture dans les bordels – ce qui certes est
excellent – ne pouvait pourtant pas ici se
faire à l'oeil – Attends donc pour cela
jusqu'à que tu aies ton uniforme les soldats
y peuvent là dedans ici et ailleurs un tas
de choses à l'oeil. Moi par exemple
– il est vrai que je viens de faire cette étude
de café de nuit – mais cela quoique ce soit
une maison de passe et qu'de temps à autre
on y voit une putain attablée avec son type –
moi dis-je – je n'ai pas encore pu faire
un bordel [proprement dit] ~~justement~~ à cause de ce que
cela me coûterait [plus d'argent que je n'en aie] ~~nécessairement~~ pour
le faire un peu bien et sérieusement
Et que je m'abstiens de le commencer avant
que je me sente assez solide quant au
porte monnaie pour pouvoir le mener à
bonne fin ce tableau. Maintenant
je ne dis pas. Nous irions prendre
des bochsli dedans nous y ferions
des connaissances nous travaillerons
moitié d'imagination moitié avec un
modèle Et si nous voulions je ne
dis pas qu'à cela ne soit pas possible
de le faire. Mais moi pour un

1v:3

maintenant je suis pressé pour rien
Les projets cela rate si souvent et les meilleurs
calculs qu'on fait tandis qu'en profitant
des hasards et en travaillant au jour le
jour sans parti pris on fait un tas de choses
imprévues
Je ne peux donc aucunement t'engager
a venir ici dans le but – [expe] sans aucun doute
excellent – de faire des bordels. Je le répète
une fois soldat tu auras une occasion splendide
pour cela et dans ton propre interêt tu ferais
peutêtre bien d'attendre jusqu'à quand tu aies ton uniforme
Mais mon cher copain Bernard je
veux être bien clair et net à te dire
viens donc passer ton temps en Afrique
Le midi t'enchantera et te fera grand
artiste Gauguin lui même doit sa
supériorité au midi. Moi je regarde
le soleil plus fort d'ici depuis des mois et
des mois maintenant [et le resultat est que] ce qui reste surtout
debout pour moi [cette experience faite] au point de vue de la
couleur c'est Delacroix et Monticelli
ces peintres qu'actuellement on dit à tort
être des romantiques puis des gens
d'imagination exagérée Enfin mais
vois tu le midi qu'a été fait si sèchement par
Gerome et Fromentin a peint déjà d'ici est essentiellement
un pays ~~qui ne se~~ dont on ne saurait interpreter le
charme intime que par la couleur decolorée T'espere

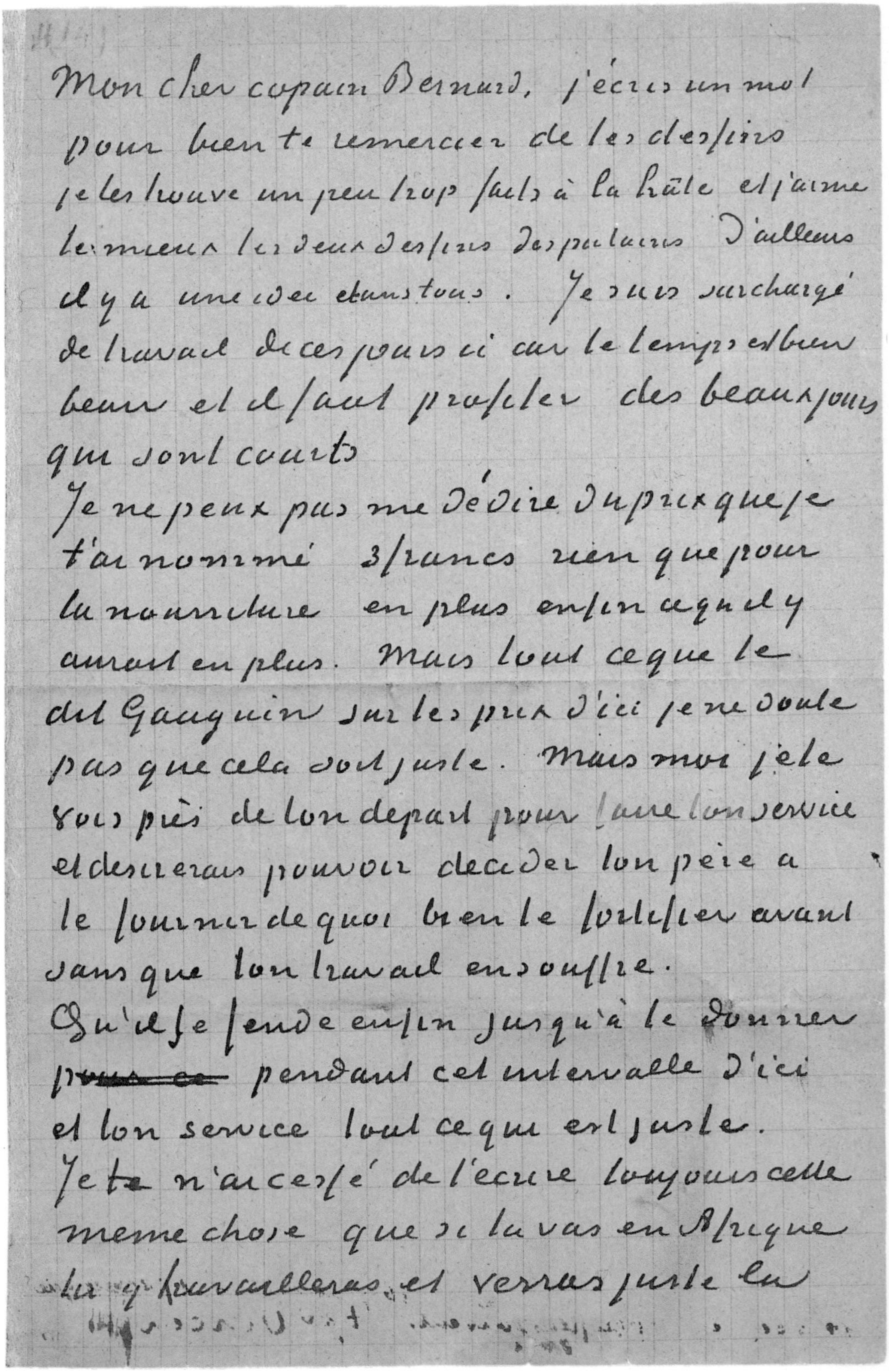
Mon cher copain Bernard, j'écris un mot
pour bien te remercier de tes dessins
je les trouve un peu trop faits à la hâte et j'aime
le mieux les deux dessins des putains D'ailleurs
il y a une idée dans tous. Je suis surchargé
de travail de ces jours ci car le temps est bien
beau et il faut profiter des beaux jours
qui sont courts
Je ne peux pas me dédire du prix que je
t'ai nommé 3 francs rien que pour
la nourriture en plus enfin ce qu'il y
aurait en plus. Mais tout ce que te
dit Gauguin sur les prix d'ici je ne doute
pas que cela soit juste. Mais moi je te
vois près de ton depart pour faire ton service
et desirerais pouvoir decider ton père à
te fournir de quoi bien te fortifier avant
sans que ton travail en souffre.
Qu'il se fende enfin jusqu'à te donner
~~pour ce~~ pendant cet intervalle d'ici
et ton service tout ce qui est juste.
Je ~~te~~ n'ai cessé de t'écrire toujours cette
même chose que si tu vas en Afrique
tu y travailleras et verras juste la

1r:1

nature qu'il faut voir pour developper
dans toute son etendue ton talent
de peintre et de coloriste. Mais
cela ne peut pas se faire qu'au ~~grand~~ d
detriment de ta pauvre carcasse si
ton père ne te met pas en mesure d'eviter
de devenir anémique ou d'attrapper
de la dysenterie débilitante par manque
d'une nourriture fortifiante avant
cette epreuve Africaine
Se faire des forces là bas c'est guère
possible et si on va dans un climat
chaud je suis loin de dire qu'il faille
s'engraisser avant mais je dis
qu'il faut soigner sa nourriture quelque temps d'avance
Et je ne sors pas de là m'étant
trouvé bien ici de ce régime et
la chaleur en Afrique est encore autre chose
que celle d'Arles.
Tu sortiras de cette épreuve de ton
service beaucoup plus fort et fort
assez pour toute une carrière d'artiste
ou — carfé

1v:2

Quoi qu'il en soit j'aimerais énormément que tu
viennes et si Gauguin vient aussi il ne nous
restera à regretter seulement que ce soit l'hiver
et non la belle saison. De plus en plus je
commence à croire que la cuisine a quelque
chose à faire avec ~~notre~~ notre faculté de penser
et de faire des tableaux moi pour un celui ne
contribue pas à la réussite de mon travail si mon
estomac me gêne. Enfin je crois que si ton
père ~~tz~~ veut tranquillement garder les tableaux
et te faire un crédit un peu généreux au bout du
compte il y perdra moins qu'en faisant
autrement. Dans le midi les sens
s'exaltent la main devient plus agile l'oeil
plus vif le cerveau plus clair à une condition
pourtant que la dysenterie ou autre chose
ne vous gâte pas tout cela en vous débilitant trop.
Là dessus j'ose bien me fonder pour croire
que celui qui ~~[illegible]~~ aime
le travail artistique verra dans le midi
ses capacités productrices ~~[illegible]~~ se développer
mais gare au sang et gare ~~a~~ à tout
le reste.

1v:3

Et maintenant tu vas peutêtre me
dire que je t'emmerde bien avec tout
cela
Que tu veux aller au bordel et que tu te
fous du reste. Ma foi cela depend
mais je ne peux pas parler autrement
que ~~ca~~ comme cela. L'art est long et la
vie est courte et il nous faut patienter
en cherchant à vendre cher notre peau
Je voudrais bien moi avoir ton âge et partir
avec ce que je saurais faire mon service
en Afrique. Mais par exemple je me
ferais un meilleur corps que celui que
j'ai. Si Gauguin et moi sommes ici comme il est
probable ensemble ici alors certes nous ferons tout notre
possible pour t'eviter des depenses mais de son côté
ton père devrait bien faire son possible aussi
~~Cet~~ et avoir confiance en nous que nous ne cherchons
pas à lui tirer des carottes inutiles. Mais pour faire
du bon travail il faut bien manger être bien logé
tirer son coup de temps en temps fumer sa pipe
et boire son café en paix. Je ne dis pas que le reste
ne vaut rien & laisse à chacun sa liberté de faire comme il
l'entend mais je dis que ce système me semble préferable
à bien d'autres. bonne poignée de main t à t
Vincent

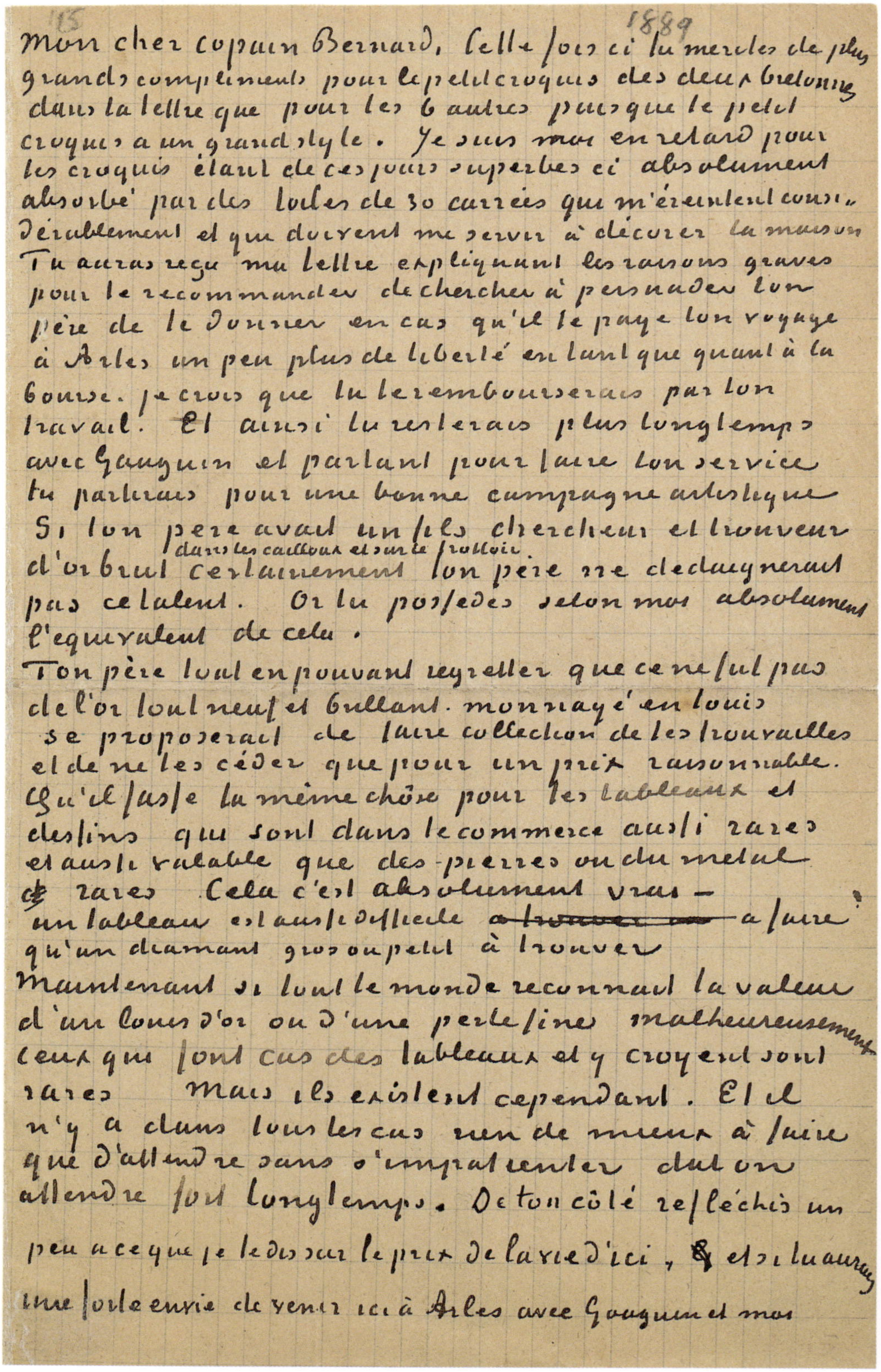

115 1889

Mon cher copain Bernard, Cette fois ci tu merites de plus
grands compliments pour le petit croquis des deux bretonnes
dans la lettre que pour les 6 autres puisque le petit
croquis a un grand style. Je suis moi en retard pour
les croquis étant de ces jours superbes ci absolument
absorbé par des toiles de 30 carrées qui m'éreintent consi-
dérablement et qui doivent me servir à décorer la maison
Tu auras reçu ma lettre expliquant les raisons graves
pour te recommander de chercher à persuader ton
père de te donner en cas qu'il te paye ton voyage
à Arles un peu plus de liberté en tant que quant à la
bourse. je crois que tu le rembourserais par ton
travail. Et ainsi tu resterais plus longtemps
avec Gauguin et partant pour faire ton service
tu partirais pour une bonne campagne artistique
Si ton pere avait un fils chercheur et trouveur
d'or brut dans les cailloux et sur le trottoir certainement ton père ne dedaignerait
pas ce talent. Or tu possedes selon moi absolument
l'equivalent de cela.
Ton père tout en pouvant regretter que ce ne fut pas
de l'or tout neuf et brillant. monnayé en louis
se proposerait de faire collection de tes trouvailles
et de ne les céder que pour un prix raisonnable.
Qu'il fasse la même chose pour tes tableaux et
dessins qui sont dans le commerce aussi rares
et aussi valable que des pierres ou du metal
de rares Cela c'est absolument vrai —
un tableau est aussi difficile ~~a trouver~~ a faire
qu'un diamant gros ou petit à trouver
Maintenant si tout le monde reconnait la valeur
d'un louis d'or ou d'une perle fine malheureusement
ceux qui font cas des tableaux et y croyent sont
rares Mais ils existent cependant. Et il
n'y a dans tous les cas rien de mieux à faire
que d'attendre sans s'impatienter dut on
attendre fort longtemps. De ton côté reflechis un
peu a ce que je te dis sur le prix de la vie d'ici, & et si tu aurais
une forte envie de venir ici à Arles avec Gauguin et moi

1r:1

dis bien à ton père ~~que ni Gauguin ni moi~~ qu'avec
un peu plus d'argent tu ferais de bien meilleurs
tableaux.
L'idée de faire une sorte de franc-maçonnerie
de peintres ne me plaît pas énormément je méprise
profondément les règlements les institutions &c
enfin je cherche autre chose que les dogmes
qui bien loin de régler les choses ne font
que causer les disputes sans fin.
C'est signe de décadence Or une union des
peintres ~~n'étant~~ n'existant pas encore qu'à
l'état d'esquisse vague mais fort large
laissons donc tranquillement arriver ce
qui doit arriver
Ce sera plus beau si cela se cristalize
naturellement plus on en cause moins
cela se fait Si tu veux aider à cela tu
n'as qu'à continuer avec Gauguin
et moi. cela est en train ne parlons plus
si cela doit venir cela se fera sans grands
pourparlers mais par des actions tranquilles
et réfléchies
Pour les échanges c'est bien justement parceque
j'ai souvent dans les lettres eu occasion d'entendre
parler de Laval Moret et l'autre jeune j'ai grand désir de
les connaître Mais - je n'ai pas 5
études - de sèches faudra que j'ajoute au moins
deux essais de tableaux un peu plus graves
un portrait de moi et un paysage
en colère de mistral méchant
Puis j'aurais une étude de petit jardin
de fleurs ~~[illegible]~~ multicolores
Une étude de chardons gris et poussiéreux

et finalement une nature morte de vieux
souliers de paysan. Et un petit paysage
de rien du tout où il n'y a qu'un peu d'étendue
Si maintenant ces études ne plairaient pas et
que l'un ou l'autre préférerait s'abstenir
il n'y a qu'à garder celles dont on voudra et à retourner
avec les échanges celles dont on ne voudra pas.
Rien ne nous presse et dans des échanges il vaut
mieux de part et d'autre chercher à donner
du bon.
J'ajouterais en cas qu'exposé demain au
soleil il devienne sec assez pour le rouler
un paysage de déchargeurs de sable
également ~~[illegible]~~ un projet et essai de tableau
où il y a une plus mûre volonté
Je ne peux pas envoyer encore une répétition
du café de nuit puisqu'elle n'est même
pas commencée mais je veux très volontiers
te la faire pour toi mais encore une fois
il vaut mieux de part et d'autre chercher
à échanger de bonnes choses que de les faire
~~[illegible]~~ trop à la hâte. (qui était dans la lettre)
Le monsieur artistique qui me ressemble ~~[illegible]~~
~~[illegible]~~ cela est-il moi ou un autre.
Cela a bien l'air d'être moi en tant que quant
au visage mais d'abord moi je fume toujours
des pipes et ensuite moi j'ai toujours ~~[illegible]~~ en
horreur innommable de m'asseoir comme cela
sur des rochers ~~[illegible]~~ à pic au bord de la mer
ayant le vertige. Je proteste donc si cela
doit ~~[illegible]~~ être mon portrait contre les ~~[illegible]~~
invraisemblabilités ~~[illegible]~~ ci dessus
mentionnées. —

1v:3

La décoration de la maison m'absorbe terriblement. J'ose croire que ce serait assez de ton goût quoique ce soit certes très différent de ce que tu fais. Mais ainsi tu m'as parlé dans le temps de tableaux qui représenteraient l'un *les fleurs* l'autre *les arbres* l'autre *les champs*

Eh bien j'ai moi *le jardin du poète* (2 toiles) (dans les croquis tu en as la première idée d'après une étude peinte plus petite qui est déjà chez mon frère). puis *la nuit étoilée* puis *la vigne* puis *les sillons* puis la vue de la maison pourrait s'appeler *la rue* ainsi involontairement il y a une certaine suite

Eh bien je serai fort fort curieux de voir des études de Pont aven. mais pour toi donnes moi une chose un peu travaillée. Enfin cela s'arrangera toujours car j'aime tant ton talent que je voudrais bien peu a peu faire une petite collection de tes oeuvres.

J'ai depuis longtemps été touché de ce que les artistes Japonais ont pratiqué très souvent l'échange entre eux. Cela prouve bien qu'ils s'aimaient et se tenaient et qu'il y regnait une certaine harmonie entre eux et qu'ils vivaient justement dans une sorte de vie fraternelle naturellement et non pas dans les intrigues. Plus nous leur ressemblerons sous ce respect là mieux d'on s'en trouvera. Il paraît aussi que ces japonais gagnaient très peu d'argent et vivaient comme de simples ouvriers. J'ai la reproduction (publication Bing) d'un dessin Japonais : Un seul brin d'herbe. Quel exemple de conscience tu le verras un jour. Je te serre bien la main

t à t Vincent.

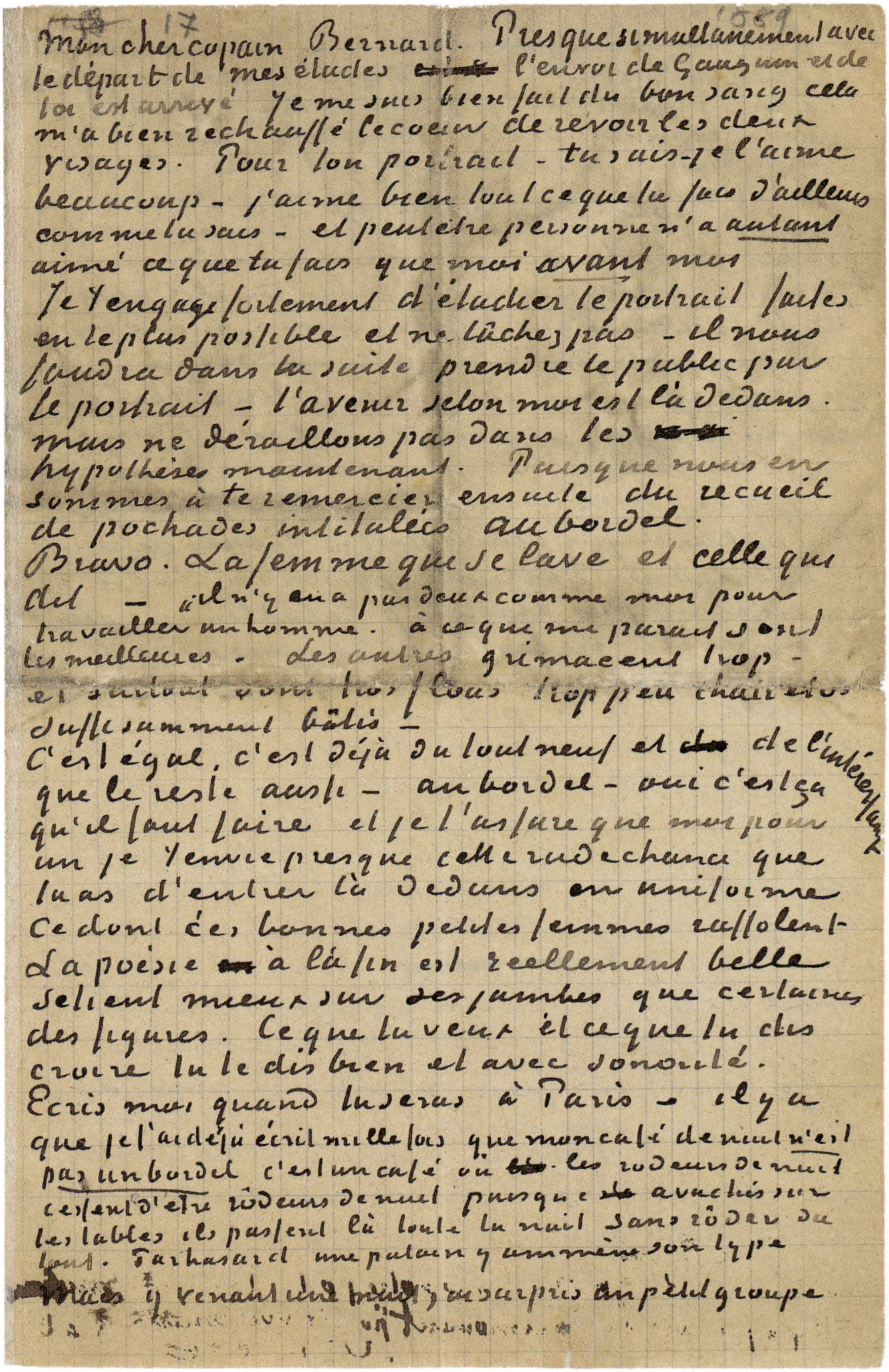

Mon cher copain Bernard. Presque simultanément avec
le départ de mes études l'envoi de Gauguin et de
toi est arrivé. Je me suis bien fait du bon sang cela
m'a bien réchauffé le coeur de revoir les deux
visages. Pour ton portrait – tu sais – je l'aime
beaucoup – j'aime bien tout ce que tu fais d'ailleurs
comme tu sais – et peutêtre personne n'a autant
aimé ce que tu fais que moi avant moi
Je t'engage fortement d'étudier le portrait faites
en le plus possible et ne lâches pas – il nous
faudra dans la suite prendre le public par
le portrait – l'avenir selon moi est là dedans.
mais ne déraillons pas dans les
hypothèses maintenant. Puisque nous en
sommes à te remercier ensuite du recueil
de pochades intitulées au bordel.
Bravo. La femme qui se lave et celle qui
dit – il n'y en a pas deux comme moi pour
travailler un homme. à ce que me parait sont
les meilleures. Les autres grimacent trop –
et surtout sont trop flous trop peu chair et os
suffisamment bâtis –
C'est égal, c'est déjà du tout neuf et de l'intéressant
que le reste aussi – au bordel – oui c'est ça
qu'il faut faire et je t'assure que moi pour
un je t'envie presque cette rude chance que
tu as d'entrer là dedans en uniforme
ce dont ces bonnes petites femmes raffolent.
La poésie à la fin est réellement belle
se tient mieux sur ses jambes que certaines
des figures. Ce que tu veux et ce que tu dis
croire tu le dis bien et avec sonorité.
Ecris moi quand tu seras à Paris – il y a
que je t'ai déjà écrit mille fois que mon café de nuit n'est
pas un bordel c'est un café où les rodeurs de nuit
cessent d'être rodeurs de nuit puisque avachis sur
les tables ils passent là toute la nuit sans rôder du
tout. Par hasard une putain y amène son type
Mais y venant une fois j'ai surpris un petit groupe

1r:1

d'un maquereau et d'une putain qui se raccomodaient
après une brouille la femme faisant l'indifférente
et la superbe l'homme était calin. Je m'étais
mis à le peindre de tête pour toi – sur une
petite toile de 4 ou de 6 – or si tu pars vite –
je te l'enverrai à Paris si tu restes encore dès
joindre à l'envoi c'était pas du tout sec assez.
le je te l'enverrai à Pont Aven. je ne pourrais pas le
Mais je ne ~~te~~ veux signer cette étude car
je ne travaille jamais de tête – il y aura
de la couleur qui t'ira mais encore une
fois je fais là pour toi une étude que
je préférerais ne pas faire. Une toile
importante – un christ avec l'ange
en Getsemané – une autre représentant
le poète avec un ciel étoilé – malgré
la couleur qui était juste je les ai sans
misericorde détruites parceque la forme
n'en était pas étudiée préalablement sur
le modèle nécessaire dans ces cas là.
L'étude que je t'envoie en échange
si elle ne te va pas tu n'as qu'à la
regarder un peu plus longtemps. –
J'ai eu un mal du diable pour la faire avec
un mistral agaçant (comme l'étude en
rouge et vert aussi) Eh bien malgré qu'elle
ne soit pas aussi couramment peinte que le
vieux moulin – elle est plus fine et plus intime
Tu vois que ~~[illegible]~~ tout cela n'est
peutêtre pas du tout – impressioniste –
ma foi tant pis je n'y peux rien –
Mais ~~te~~ je fais ce que je fais avec un abandon
à la nature sans songer à ceci ou à cela
Va sans dire que si tu préférais dans l'envoi
une autre étude aux Déchargeurs de sable tu pourrais
la prendre et effacer ma dédicace si un autre en
veut. Mais je crois que celle là t'ira une fois que tu
l'auras regardée un peu plus longtemps.

Si Laval Moret et l'autre veulent bien
me faire des échanges parfait mais
surtout je serais satisfait de mon côté
s'ils voulaient me faire leurs portraits.
Tu sais Bernard il me semble toujours
que si je veux faire des études de bordels
il me faudrait plus d'argent que je n'en aie
je suis pas jeune et chair
à femme assez pour qu'elles posent pour moi
à l'oeil Et je ne peux pas travailler sans modèle
Je ne dis pas que je ne tourne pas carrément
le dos à la nature pour transformer une
étude en tableau – en arrangeant la
couleur en agrandissant en simplifiant –
mais j'ai tant peur de m'écarter du
possible et du juste en tant que quant à la
forme.
Plus tard après encore dix ans d'études
je ne dis pas mais vrai de vrai j'ai tant
de curiosité du possible et du réellement
existant que j'ai si peu le désir et le courage
de chercher l'idéal en tant que pouvant résulter
de <u>mes</u> études abstraites.
D'autres peuvent avoir pour les études
abstraites plus de lucidité que moi – et certes
tu pourrais être du nombre ainsi que
Gauguin… et peut être moi même quand
je serai vieux
mais en attendant je mange toujours
de la nature. J'exagère je change
parfois au motif mais enfin je n'invente
pas le tout du tableau je le trouve au
contraire tout fait – mais à démêler dans la nature

1v:3

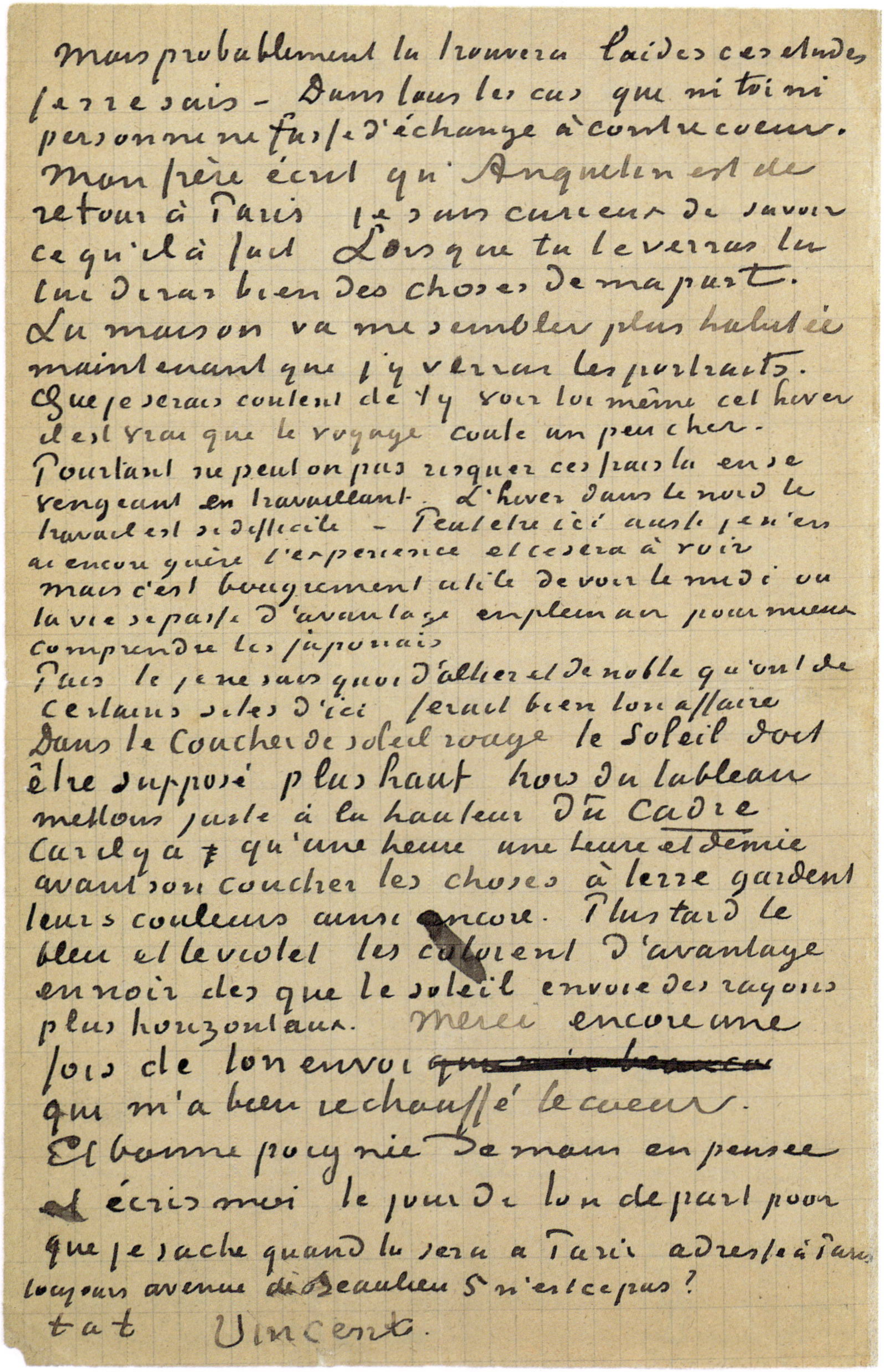
mais probablement la trouvera laides ces études
je le sais — Dans tous les cas que ni toi ni
personne ne fasse d'échange à contre coeur.
Mon frère écrit qu'Anquetin est de
retour à Paris je suis curieux de savoir
ce qu'il a fait Lorsque tu le verras tu
lui diras bien des choses de ma part.
La maison va me sembler plus habitée
maintenant que j'y verrai les portraits.
Que je serais content de t'y voir toi même cet hiver
il est vrai que le voyage coute un peu cher.
Pourtant ne peut on pas risquer ces frais la en se
vengeant en travaillant. L'hiver dans le nord le
travail est si difficile — Peutetre ici aussi je n'en
ai encore guère l'experience et ce sera à voir
mais c'est bougrement utile de voir le midi ou
la vie se passe d'avantage en plein air pour mieux
comprendre les japonais
Puis le je ne sais quoi d'altier et de noble qu'ont de
certains sites d'ici ferait bien ton affaire
Dans le Coucher de soleil rouge le Soleil doit
être supposé plus haut hors du tableau
mettons juste à la hauteur du Cadre
car il y a qu'une heure une heure et demie
avant son coucher les choses à terre gardent
leurs couleurs ainsi encore. Plus tard le
bleu et le violet les colorent d'avantage
en noir dès que le soleil envoie des rayons
plus horizontaux. Merci encore une
fois de ton envoi ~~qui m'a bien~~
qui m'a bien rechauffé le coeur.
Et bonne poignée de main en pensée
écris moi le jour de ton depart pour
que je sache quand tu sera a Paris adresse à Paris
toujours avenue de Beaulieu 5 n'est ce pas?
t à t Vincent.

1r:4

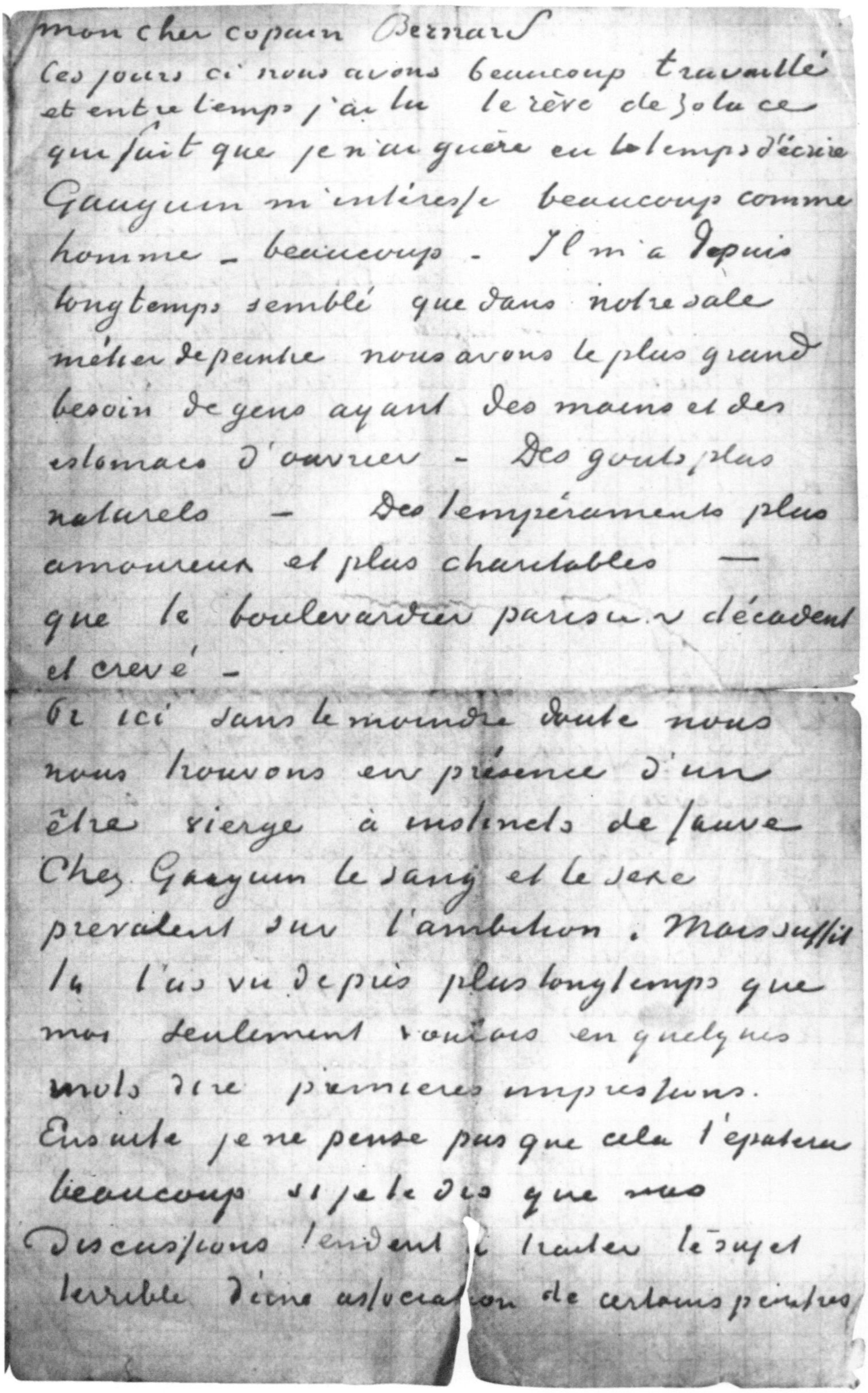

mon cher copain Bernard
Ces jours ci nous avons beaucoup travaillé
et entretemps j'ai lu le rêve de Zola ce
qui fait que je n'ai guère eu le temps d'écrire
Gauguin m'intéresse beaucoup comme
homme – beaucoup – Il m'a depuis
longtemps semblé que dans notre sale
métier de peintre nous avons le plus grand
besoin de gens ayant des mains et des
estomacs d'ouvrier – Des gouts plus
naturels – Des tempéraments plus
amoureux et plus charitables —
que le boulevardier parisien décadent
et crevé –
Or ici sans le moindre doute nous
nous trouvons en présence d'un
être vierge à instincts de fauve
Chez Gauguin le sang et le sexe
prevalent sur l'ambition. Mais suffit
tu l'as vu depuis plus longtemps que
moi seulement voulais en quelques
mots dire premieres impressions.
Ensuite je ne pense pas que cela t'epatera
beaucoup si je te dis que nos
Discussions tendent à traiter le sujet
terrible d'une association de certains peintres,

1r:1

Cette association doit ou peut elle avoir
oui ou non un caractère commercial
Nous ne sommes encore arrivé à
aucun resultat et n'avons point encore
mis le pied sur un continent nouveau
Or moi qui ~~j~~ ai un presentiment
d'un nouveau monde qui crois certes
à la possibilité d'une immense renaissance
de l'art. Qui crois que cet art nouveau
aura les tropiques pour patrie
Il me semble que nous mêmes ne servons
que d'intermédiaires Et que ce ne sera
qu'une génération suivante qui réussira
à vivre en paix. Enfin tout cela
nos devoirs et nos possibilités d'action
ne sauraient nous devenir plus clairs
que par l'expérience même.
J'ai été un peu surpris de ne pas
encore avoir reçu les études promises
en échange des miennes.
Maintenant ce qui t'interessera – nous
avons fait quelques excursions dans les
bordels et il est probable que nous finirons
par aller souvent travailler là. Gauguin
a dans ce moment en train une toile du même

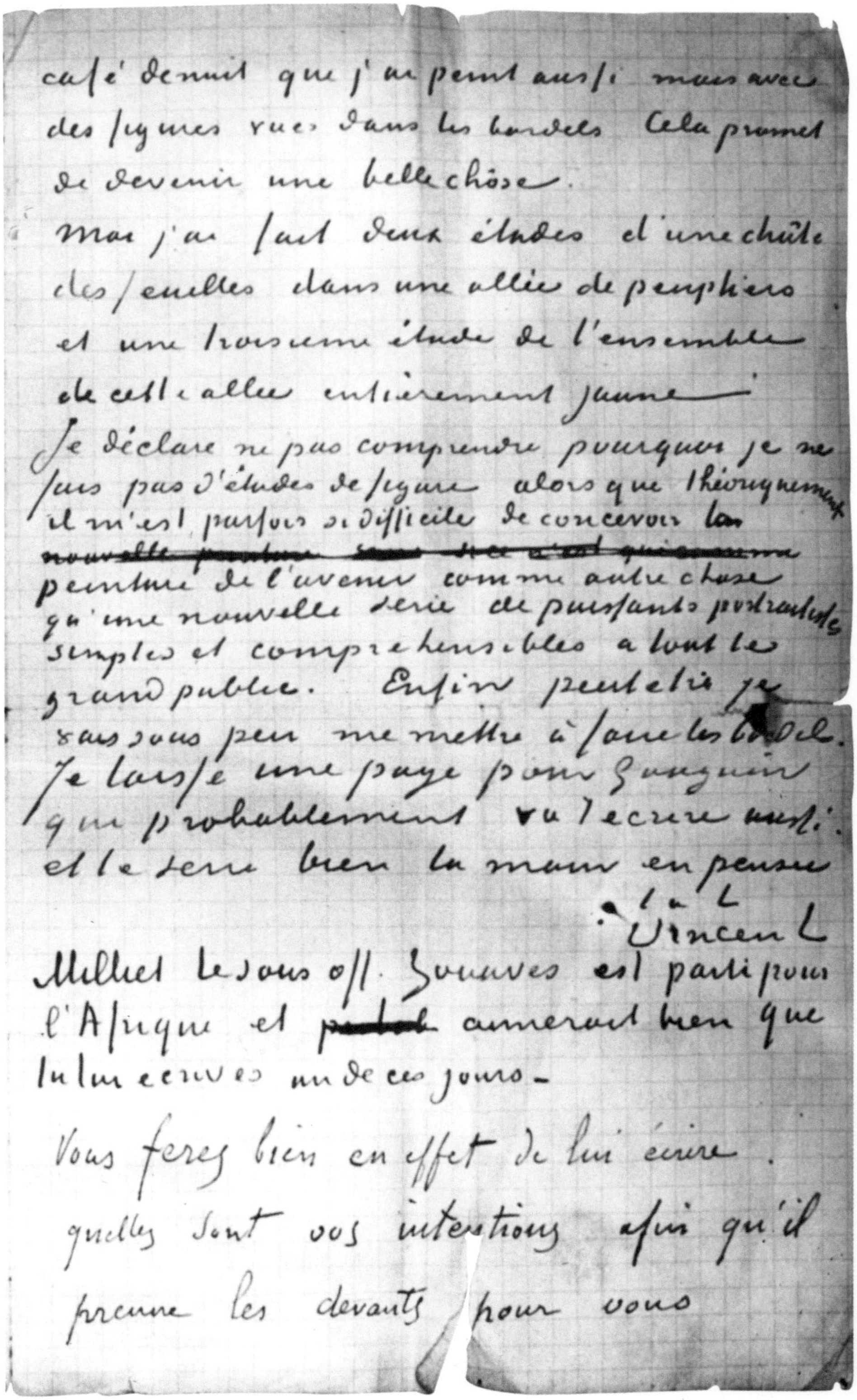

café de nuit que j'ai peint aussi mais avec
des figures vues dans les bordels Cela promet
de devenir une belle chose.
Mais j'ai fait deux études d'une chûte
des feuilles dans une allée de peupliers
et une troisième étude de l'ensemble
de cette allée entièrement jaune.
Je déclare ne pas comprendre pourquoi je ne
fais pas d'études de figure alors que théoriquement
il m'est parfois si difficile de concevoir ~~la~~
~~nouvelle peinture~~ [illegible]
peinture de l'avenir comme autre chose
qu'une nouvelle série de puissants portraitistes
simples et compréhensibles à tout le
grand public. Enfin peutêtre je
sais sous peu me mettre à faire les bordels.
Je laisse une page pour Gauguin
qui probablement va t'écrire aussi.
et te serre bien la main en pensée
t à t
Vincent
Milliet le sous off. zouaves est parti pour
l'Afrique et ~~perait~~ aimerait bien que
tu lui écrives un de ces jours.

Vous ferez bien en effet de lui écrire
quelles sont vos intentions afin qu'il
prenne les devants pour vous

1v:3

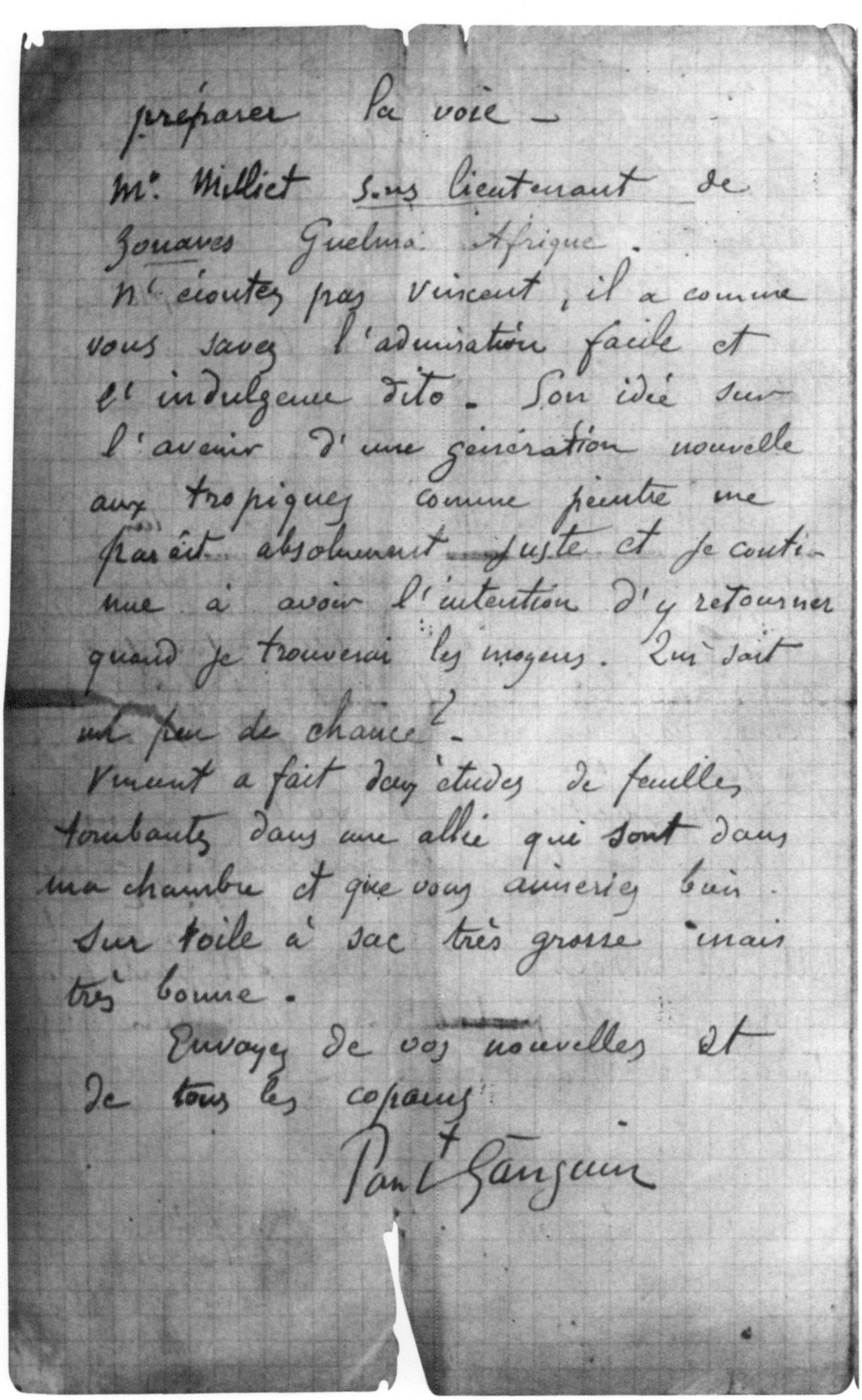

préparer la voie —
Mr Milliet sous lieutenant de
Zouaves Guelma Afrique.
N'écoutez pas Vincent, il a comme
vous savez l'admiration facile et
l'indulgence dito. Son idée sur
l'avenir d'une génération nouvelle
aux tropiques comme peintre me
paraît absolument juste et je conti-
nue à avoir l'intention d'y retourner
quand je trouverai les moyens. Qui sait
un peu de chance?
Vincent a fait deux études de feuilles
tombantes dans une allée qui sont dans
ma chambre et que vous aimeriez bien.
Sur toile à sac très grosse mais
très bonne.
Envoyez de vos nouvelles et
de tous les copains
Paul Gauguin

1r:4

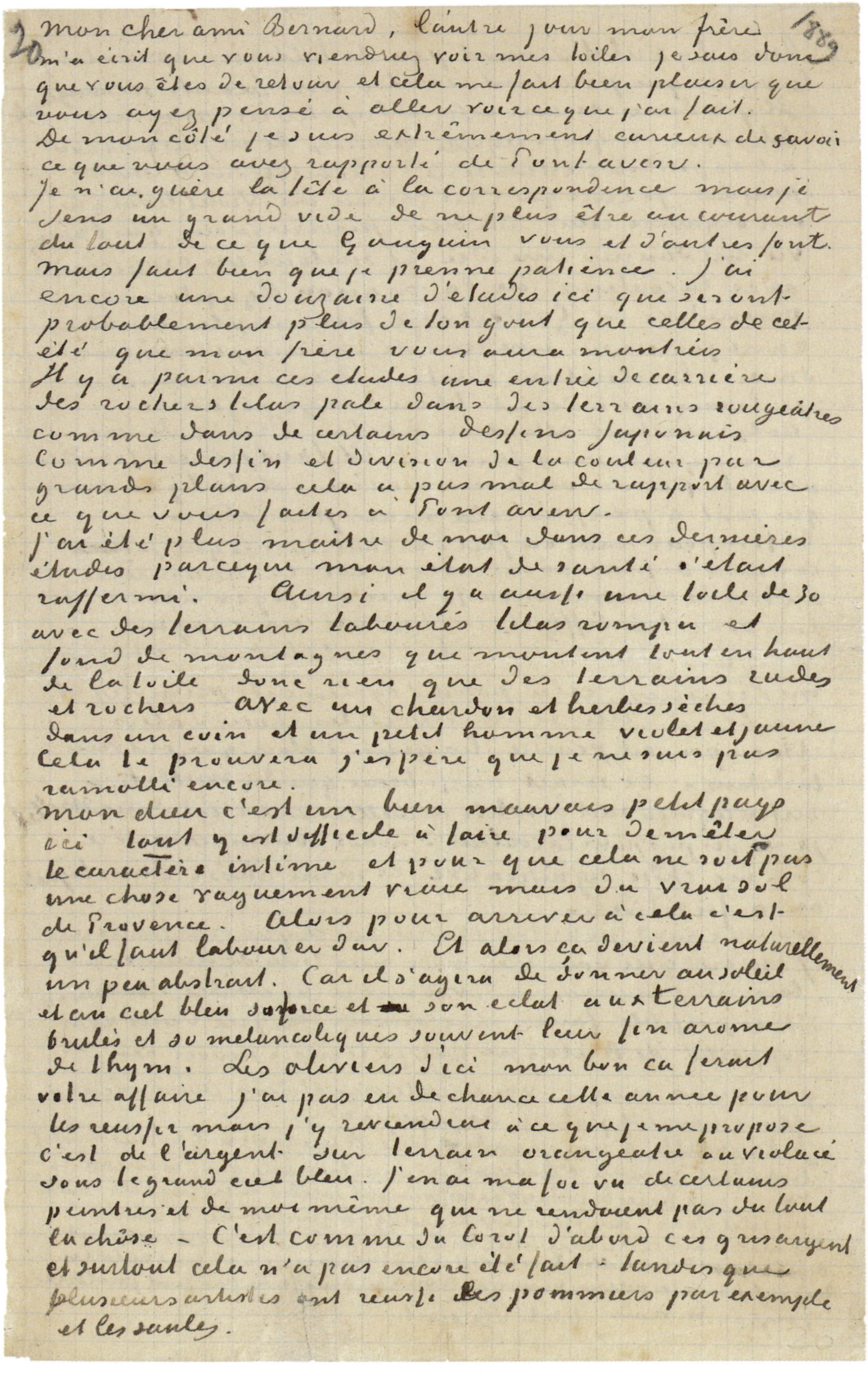
2 Mon cher ami Bernard, l'autre jour mon frère 1889
m'a écrit que vous viendriez voir mes toiles je sais donc
que vous êtes de retour et cela me fait bien plaisir que
vous ayez pensé à aller voir ce que j'ai fait.
De mon côté je suis extrêmement curieux de savoir
ce que vous avez rapporté de Pont Aven.
Je n'ai guère la tête à la correspondance mais je
sens un grand vide de ne plus être au courant
du tout de ce que Gauguin vous et d'autres font.
Mais faut bien que je prenne patience. J'ai
encore une douzaine d'études ici qui seront
probablement plus de ton goût que celles de cet
été que mon frère vous aura montrées
Il y a parmi ces études une entrée de carrière
des rochers lilas pâle dans des terrains rougeâtres
comme dans de certains dessins japonais
Comme dessin et division de la couleur par
grands plans cela a pas mal de rapport avec
ce que vous faites à Pont Aven.
J'ai été plus maître de moi dans ces dernières
études parceque mon état de santé s'était
raffermi. Ainsi il y a aussi une toile de 30
avec des terrains labourés lilas rompu et
fond de montagnes qui montent tout en haut
de la toile donc rien que des terrains rudes
et rochers avec un chardon et herbes sèches
dans un coin et un petit homme violet et jaune
Cela te prouvera j'espère que je ne suis pas
ramolli encore.
Mon dieu c'est un bien mauvais petit pays
ici tout y est difficile à faire pour démêler
le caractère intime et pour que cela ne soit pas
une chose vaguement vécue mais du vrai sol
de Provence. Alors pour arriver à cela c'est
qu'il faut labourer dur. Et alors ça devient naturellement
un peu abstrait. Car il s'agira de donner au soleil
et au ciel bleu sa force et son éclat aux terrains
brulés et so melancoliques souvent leur fin arome
de thym. Les oliviers d'ici mon bon ça serait
votre affaire j'ai pas eu de chance cette année pour
les réussir mais j'y reviendrai à ce que je me propose
c'est de l'argent sur terrain orangeâtre au violacé
sous le grand ciel bleu. J'en ai ma foi vu de certains
peintres et de moi même qui ne rendaient pas du tout
la chose – C'est comme du Corot d'abord ces gris argent
et surtout cela n'a pas encore été fait – tandis que
plusieurs artistes ont réussi les pommiers par exemple
et les saules.

1r:1

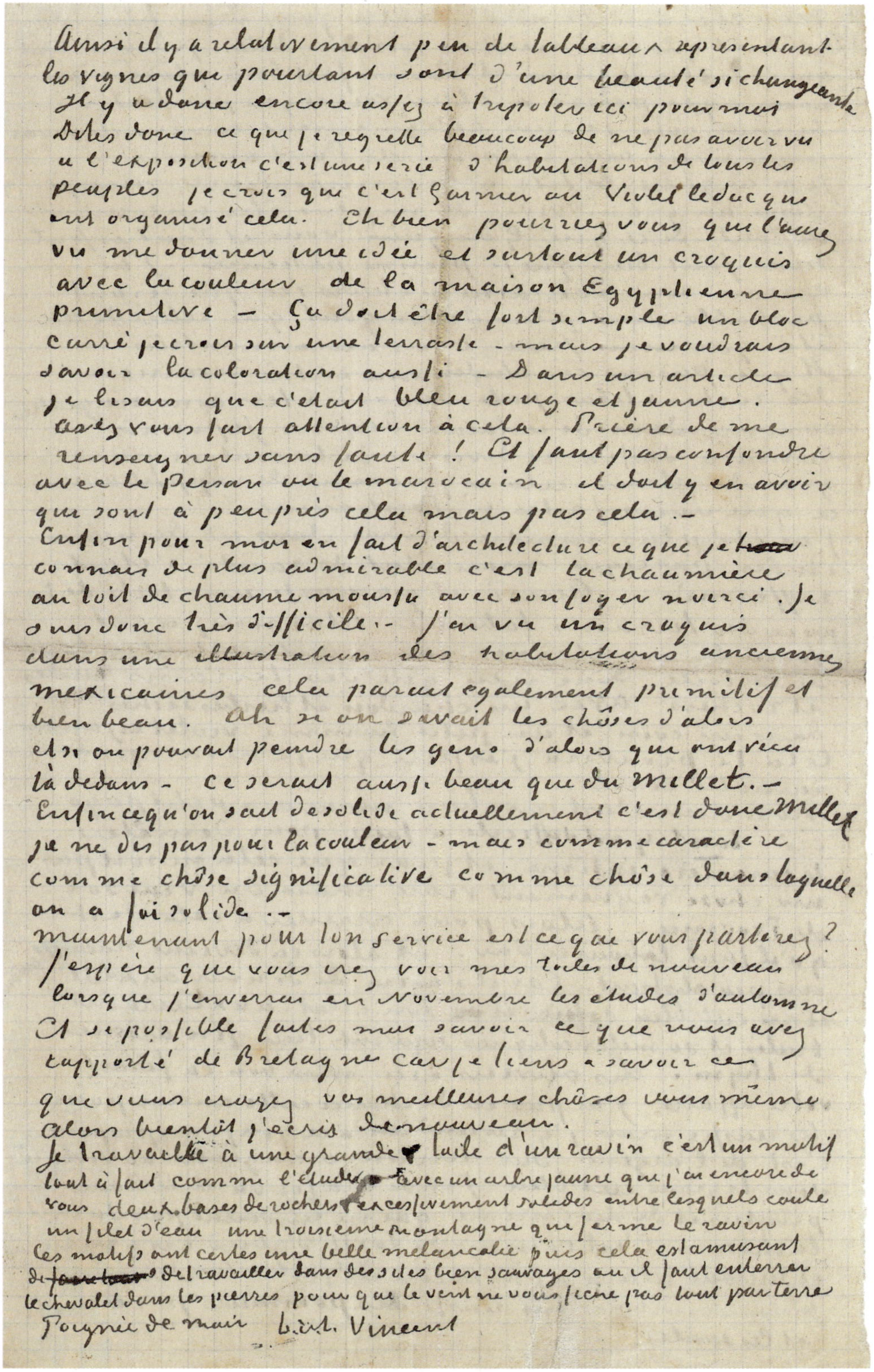
Ainsi il y a relativement peu de tableaux représentant
les vignes qui pourtant sont d'une beauté si changeante
Il y a donc encore assez à tripoter ici pour moi
Dites donc ce que je regrette beaucoup de ne pas avoir vu
à l'exposition c'est une série d'habitations de tous les
peuples je crois que c'est Garnier ou Viollet le duc qui
ont organisé cela. Eh bien pourriez vous qui l'avez
vu me donner une idée et surtout un croquis
avec la couleur de la maison Egyptienne
primitive — Ça doit être fort simple un bloc
carré je crois sur une terrasse — mais je voudrais
savoir la coloration aussi — Dans un article
je lisais que c'était bleu rouge et jaune.
Avez vous fait attention à cela. Prière de me
renseigner sans faute ! Il faut pas confondre
avec le Persan ou le marocain il doit y en avoir
qui sont à peu près cela mais pas cela.—
Enfin pour moi en fait d'architecture ce que je
connais de plus admirable c'est la chaumière
au toit de chaume moussu avec son foyer noirci. Je
suis donc très difficile.— J'ai vu un croquis
dans une illustration des habitations anciennes
mexicaines cela paraît également primitif et
bien beau. Ah si on savait les choses d'alors
et si on pouvait peindre les gens d'alors qui ont vécu
là dedans — ce serait aussi beau que du Millet.—
Enfin ce qu'on sait de solide actuellement c'est donc Millet
je ne dis pas pour la couleur — mais comme caractère
comme chose significative comme chose dans laquelle
on a foi solide.—
maintenant pour ton service est ce que vous partirez?
j'espère que vous irez voir mes toiles de nouveau
lorsque j'enverrai en Novembre les études d'automne
Et si possible faites moi savoir ce que vous avez
rapporté de Bretagne car je tiens à savoir ce
que vous croyez vos meilleures choses vous même
alors bientôt j'écris de nouveau.
Je travaille à une grande toile d'un ravin c'est un motif
tout à fait comme l'étude avec un arbre jaune que j'ai encore de
vous deux bases de roches excessivement solides entre lesquels coule
un filet d'eau une troisième montagne qui ferme le ravin
Ces motifs ont certes une belle mélancolie puis cela est amusant
de travailler dans des sites bien sauvages où il faut enterrer
le chevalet dans les pierres pour que le vent ne vous fiche pas tout par terre
Poignée de main t.à t. Vincent

1v:2

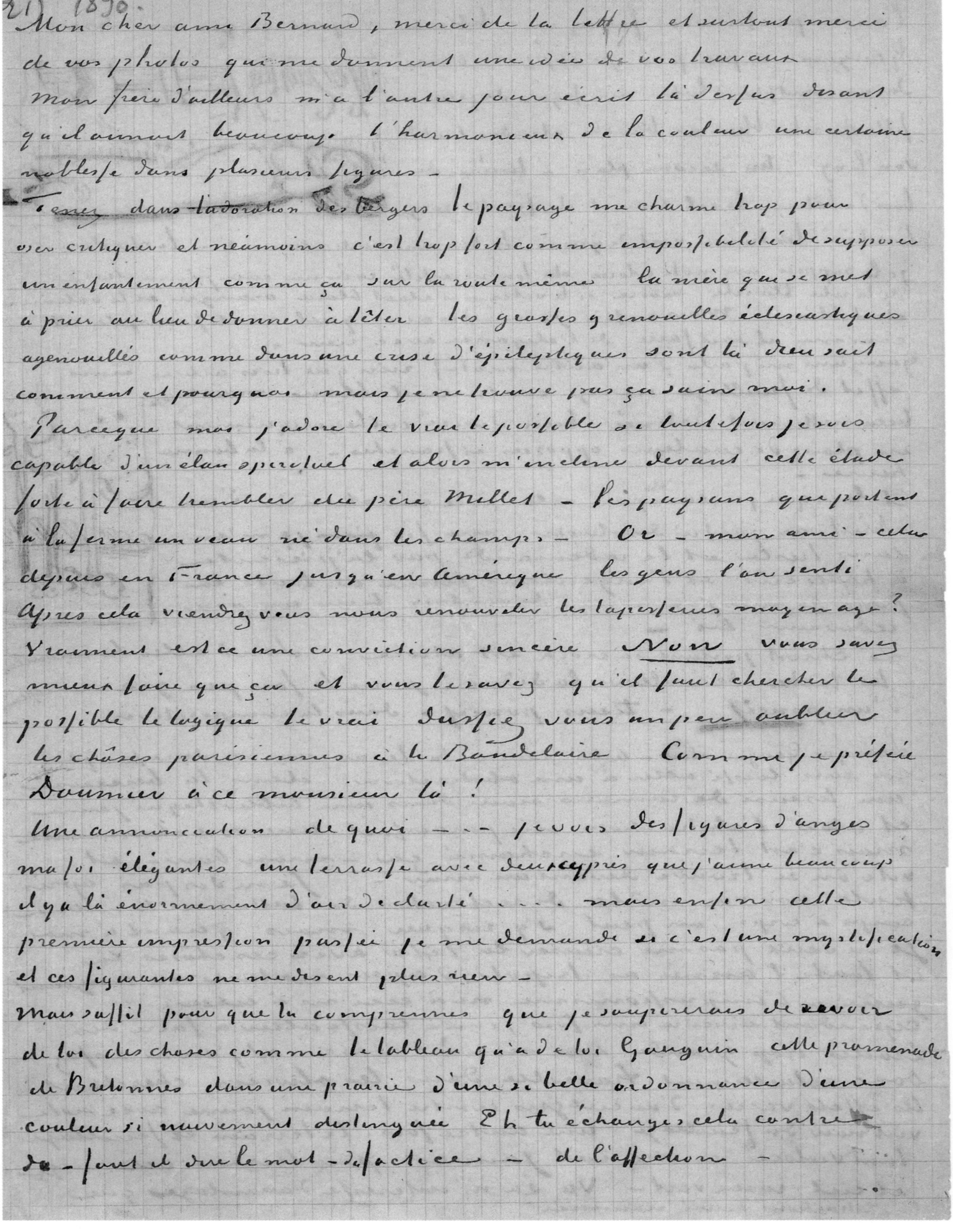
21) 1890.
Mon cher ami Bernard, merci de la lettre et surtout merci
de vos photos qui me donnent une idée de vos travaux
Mon frère d'ailleurs m'a l'autre jour écrit là dessus disant
qu'il aimait beaucoup l'harmonieux de la couleur une certaine
noblesse dans plusieurs figures -
Tenez dans l'adoration des bergers le paysage me charme trop pour
oser critiquer et néanmoins c'est trop fort comme impossibilité de supposer
un enfantement comme ça sur la route même la mère qui se met
à prier au lieu de donner à téter les grosses grenouilles ecclésiastiques
agenouillés comme dans une crise d'épileptiques sont là dieu sait
comment et pourquoi mais je ne trouve pas ça sain moi.
Parceque moi j'adore le vrai le possible si toutefois je suis
capable d'un élan spirituel et alors m'incline devant cette étude
forte à faire trembler du père Millet - les paysans qui portent
à la ferme un veau né dans les champs - Or - mon ami - cela
depuis en France jusqu'en Amérique les gens l'ont senti
Après cela viendrez vous nous renouveler les tapisseries moyen age?
Vraiment est ce une conviction sincère Non vous savez
mieux faire que ça et vous le savez qu'il faut chercher le
possible le logique le vrai dussiez vous un peu oublier
les choses parisiennes à la Baudelaire Combien je préfère
Daumier à ce monsieur là!
Une annonciation de quoi - - je vois des figures d'anges
ma foi élégantes une terrasse avec deux cyprès que j'aime beaucoup
il y a là énormement d'air de clarté . . . mais enfin cette
première impression passée je me demande si c'est une mystification
et ces figurantes ne me disent plus rien -
Mais suffit pour que tu comprennes que je soupirerais de revoir
de toi des choses comme le tableau qu'a de toi Gauguin cette promenade
de Bretonnes dans une prairie d'une si belle ordonnance d'une
couleur si naïvement distinguée Et tu échanges cela contre
de - faut il dire le mot - du factice - de l'affecté -

1r:1 (reduced to 85 percent of actual size)

l'année passée vous faisiez un tableau d'après ce que me disait
Gauguin à peu près je suppose ainsi:
Sur un avant plan d'herbe une figure de jeune
fille en robe bleue ou blanche étendue tout de
son long Un second plan – lisière de
bois de hêtre le sol couvert de feuilles rouges

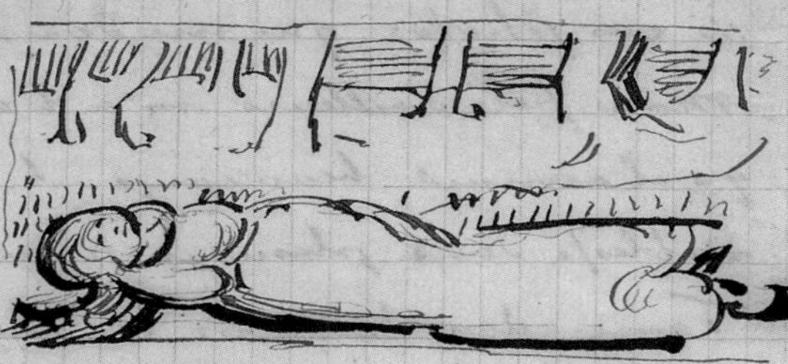

Sketch 1

tombées les troncs vert de grisés le barrant verticalement – La chevelure
je la suppose une note colorée du ton nécessité comme complémentaire
de la robe blanche noire si le vêtement était blanc orangée si le vêtement
était bleu – Mais enfin je me disais quel motif simple et
comme il sait faire de l'élégance avec rien –
Gauguin me parla d'un autre motif rien que trois arbres ainsi
effet de feuillage orangé contre ciel bleu mais encore
bien nettement délinée bien divisé cathegoriquement
en plans de couleurs opposées et franches – à la bonne
heure –

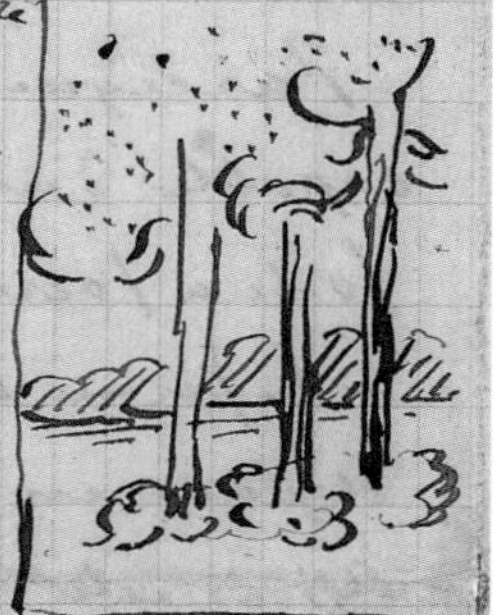

Sketch 2

Et lorsque je compare cela à ce cauchemar d'un
Christ au jardin des oliviers ma foi ~~j'en~~ je m'en
suis triste et te redemande par la présente
à hauts cris et t'engeulant ferme de toute la
force de mes poumons de vouloir bien un peu
redevenir toi –
Le christ portant sa croix est atroce Sont elles harmonieuses
les tâches de couleur là dedans? je ne te fais pas grâce cependant
d'un poncif – tiens poncif – dans la composition
Lorsque Gauguin était à Arles comme tu le sais une ou deux fois je
me suis laissé aller à une abstraction dans la berceuse
une liseuse de romans noire dans une bibliothèque jaune
et alors l'abstraction me paraissait une voie charmante
mais c'est terrain enchanté ça – mon bon – et
vite on se trouve devant un mur – Je ne dis pas après
toute une vie mâle de recherches de lutte avec la nature
corps à corps on peut s'y risquer mais quant à moi
je ne veux pas me creuser la tête avec ces chôses là
Et toute l'année ai tripoté d'après nature ne songeant
guère à l'impressionisme ni à ceci ni à cela.
Cependant encore une fois je me laisse aller à faire des
étoiles trop grandes & nouvel échec et j'en ai assez
Donc actuellement travaille dans les oliviers cherchant
les effets variés d'un ciel gris contre terrain jaune avec note
vert noir du feuillage une autre fois le terrain et feuillage
tout violacé contre ciel jaune puis terrain ocre rouge
et ciel rose et vert – Va ça m'interesse d'avantage que
les abstractions ainsi nommées

1v:2 (reduced to 85 percent of actual size)

Et si je n'ai pas écrit depuis longtemps c'est qu'ayant
à lutter contre ma maladie et à calmer ma tête je
ne me sentais guère envie de discuter et trouvais
du danger à ces abstractions. Et en travaillant tout
tranquillement les beaux sujets viendront tout seuls il s'agit
vraiment surtout de bien se retremper dans la réalité sans
plan conçu d'avance sans parti pris parisien Suis d'ailleurs
fort mécontent de cette année mais peut-être prouvera-t-elle
un fondement solide pour la prochaine je me suis bien
laissé pénétrer par l'air des petites montagnes et des
vergers – avec ça je verrai. Mon ambition se borne bien
à quelques mottes de terre du blé qui germe un verger
d'oliviers un cyprès le dernier par exemple pas
commode à faire. Toi qui aimes les primitifs qui les étudies je te
le demande pourquoi tu sembles ne pas connaître Giotto – Gauguin et moi avons encore vu
un tout petit panneau de lui à Montpellier la mort d'une bonne sainte femme quelconque
là les expressions de douleur et d'extase sont humains à tel point que tout dixneuvième
siècle qu'on soit on s'y sent – et croit avoir été là présent tant on partage l'émotion. Si je
voyais les toiles mêmes je crois que néanmoins la couleur pourrait me passionner –
mais alors tu parles de portraits que tu as fait et serré de près voilà ce qui sera bien
et où tu auras été toi.
Voici description d'une toile que j'ai devant moi dans ce moment. Une vue du parc de la
maison de santé où je suis à droite une terrasse grise un pan de maison quelques buissons
de roses défleuris à gauche le terrain du parc – ocre rouge – terrain brûlé par le soleil couvert de
brindilles de pin tombées Cette lisière de parc est planté de grands pins aux troncs & branches
ocre rouge au feuillage vert attristé par un mélange de noir Ces hauts arbres se
détachent sur un ciel du soir strié de violet sur fond jaune le jaune tourne dans
le haut au rose tourne au vert Une muraille – ocre rouge encore barre la vue
et n'est dépassé que par une colline violette et ocre jaune – Or le premier arbre
est un tronc énorme mais frappé par la foudre et scié Une branche latérale
cependant s'élance très haute et retombe en avalanche de brindilles vert sombre
Ce géant sombre – comme un orgueilleux défait – contraste en tant que considéré
comme caractère d'être vivant avec le sourire pâle d'une dernière rose sur
le buisson qui se fane en face de lui Sous les arbres des bancs de pierre vide
du buis sombre le ciel se reflète jaune après la pluie dans une flaque. Tu
~~qui ne~~ as Un rayon de soleil – le dernier reflet – exalte jusqu'à l'orangé l'ocre
sombre – des figurines noires rodent çà et là entre les troncs
Tu comprendras que cette combinaison d'ocre rouge de vert
attristé de gris des traits noirs qui cernent les contours cela produit un peu la
sensation d'angoisse dont souffrent souvent certains de mes compagnons
d'infortune qu'on appelle „voir rouge". et d'ailleurs le motif du grand arbre
frappé par l'éclair le sourire maladif vert et rose de la dernière fleur d'automne vient
confirmer cette idée. – Une autre toile représente un soleil levant sur un
champ de jeune blé. – Des lignes fuyantes des sillons montent haut dans la toile
vers une muraille et une rangée de collines lilas Le champ est violet et jaune vert
Le soleil blanc est entouré d'une grande auréole jaune Là-dedans j'ai par contraste à
l'autre toile cherché à exprimer du calme une grande paix.

1v:3 (reduced to 85 percent of actual size)

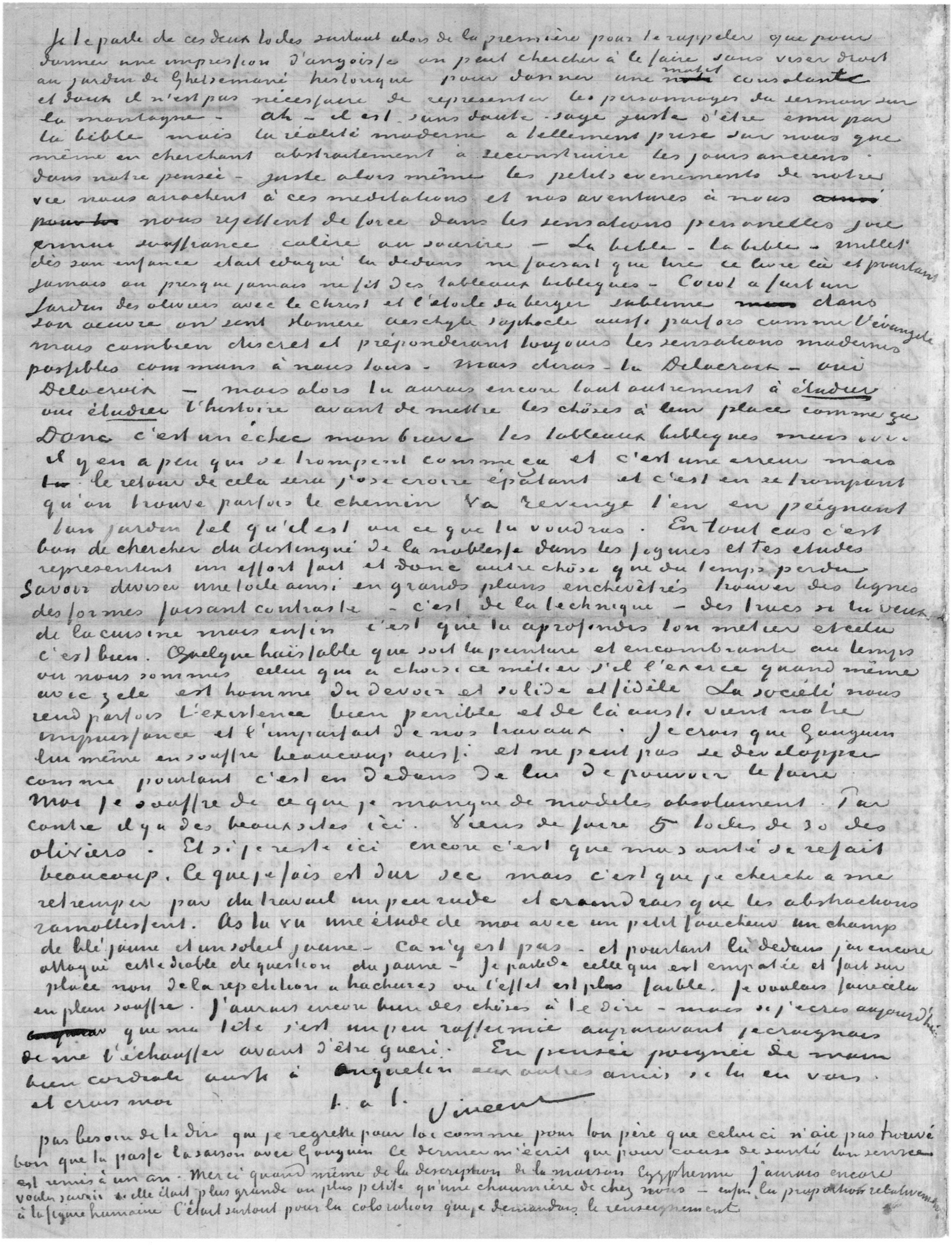
Je te parle de ces deux toiles surtout alors de la première pour te rappeler que pour donner une impression d'angoisse on peut chercher à le faire sans viser droit au jardin de Gethsemané historique pour donner une ~~note~~ motif consolante et douce il n'est pas nécessaire de representer les personnages du sermon sur la montagne — ah — il est sans doute sage juste d'être ému par la bible mais la réalité moderne a tellement prise sur nous que même en cherchant abstraitement à reconstruire les jours anciens dans notre pensée — juste alors même les petits evenements de notre vie nous arrachent à ces meditations et nos aventures à nous ~~ainsi~~ ~~pour tous~~ nous rejettent de force dans les sensations personelles joie ennui souffrance colère ou sourire — La bible — la bible — millet dès son enfance était elevé là dedans ne faisait que lire ce livre là et pourtant jamais ou presque jamais ne fit des tableaux bibliques — Corot a fait un jardin des oliviers avec le christ et l'étoile du berger sublime ~~mais~~ dans son oeuvre on sent Homère Aeschyle Sophocle aussi parfois comme l'évangile mais combien discret et préponderant toujours les sensations modernes possibles communs à nous tous — Mais diras — tu Delacroix — oui Delacroix — mais alors tu auras encore tout autrement à étudier oui étudier l'histoire avant de mettre les choses à leur place comme ça Donc c'est un échec mon brave tes tableaux bibliques mais ... il y en a peu qui se trompent comme ça et c'est une erreur mais ~~tu~~ le retour de cela sera j'ose croire épatant et c'est en se trompant qu'on trouve parfois le chemin Va revenge t'en en peignant ton jardin tel qu'il est ou ce que tu voudras. En tout cas c'est bon de chercher du distingué de la noblesse dans les figures et tes études representent un effort fait et donc autre chose que du temps perdu. Savoir diviser une toile ainsi en grands plans enchevêtrés trouver des lignes des formes faisant contraste — c'est de la technique — des trucs si tu veux de la cuisine mais enfin c'est que tu approfondis ton metier et cela c'est bien. Quelque haissable que soit la peinture et encombrante au temps où nous sommes celui qui a choisi ce métier s'il l'exerce quand même avec zèle est homme du devoir et solide et fidèle. La société nous rend parfois l'existence bien penible et de là aussi vient notre impuissance et l'imparfait de nos travaux. Je crois que Gauguin lui même en souffre beaucoup aussi et ne peut pas se developper comme pourtant c'est en dedans de lui de pouvoir le faire. Moi je souffre de ce que je manque de modèles absolument. Par contre il y a des beaux sites ici. Viens de faire 5 toiles de 30 des oliviers. Et si je reste ici encore c'est que ma santé se refait beaucoup. Ce que je fais est dur sec mais c'est que je cherche à me retremper par du travail un peu rude et craindrais que les abstractions ramollissent. As tu vu une étude de moi avec un petit faucheur un champ de blé jaune et un soleil jaune — Ca n'y est pas — et pourtant là dedans j'ai encore attaqué cette diable de question du jaune — Je parle de celle qui est empatée et fait sur place non de la repetition à hachures où l'effet est plus faible. Je voulais faire cela en plein soufre. J'aurais encore bien des choses à te dire — mais si j'écris aujourd'hui ~~[illegible]~~ que ma tête s'est un peu raffermie auparavant je craignais de me l'échauffer avant d'être guéri. En pensée poignée de main bien cordiale aussi à Anquetin aux autres amis si tu en vois. et crois moi

t. à t.

Vincent

pas besoin de te dire que je regrette pour toi comme pour ton père que celui ci n'aie pas trouvé bon que tu passe la saison avec Gauguin. Ce dernier m'écrit que pour cause de santé ton service est remis à un an. Merci quand même de la description de la maison Egyptienne. J'aurais encore voulu savoir si elle était plus grande ou plus petite qu'une chaumière de chez nous — enfin la proportion relativement à la figure humaine. C'était surtout pour la coloration que je demandais le renseignement.

1r:4 (reduced to 85 percent of actual size)

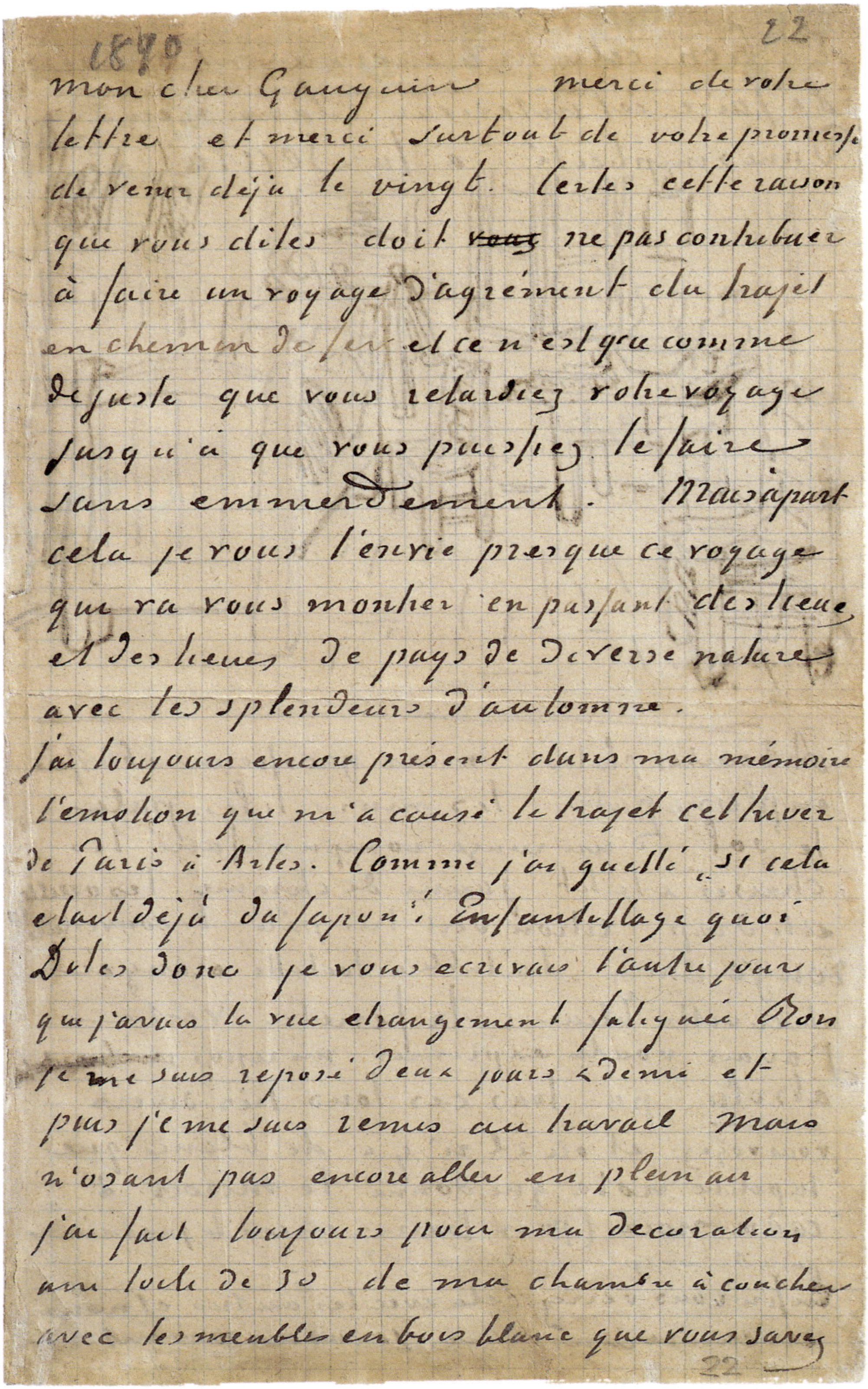
1880 22

mon cher Gauguin merci de votre
lettre et merci surtout de votre promesse
de venir deja le vingt. Certes cette raison
que vous dites doit ~~vous~~ ne pas contribuer
à faire un voyage d'agrément du trajet
en chemin de fer et ce n'est que comme
de juste que vous retardiez votre voyage
jusqu'à ce que vous puissiez le faire
sans emmerdement. Mais à part
cela je vous l'envie presque ce voyage
qui va vous montrer en passant des lieues
et des lieues de pays de diverse nature
avec les splendeurs d'automne.
J'ai toujours encore présent dans ma mémoire
l'emotion que m'a causé le trajet cet hiver
de Paris à Arles. Comme j'ai guetté si cela
etait deja du Japon! Enfantillage quoi
Dites donc je vous ecrivais l'autre jour
que j'avais la vue etrangement fatiguée Bon
je me suis reposé deux jours & demi et
puis je me suis remis au travail Mais
n'osant pas encore aller en plein air
j'ai fait toujours pour ma decoration
une toile de 30 de ma chambre à coucher
avec les meubles en bois blanc que vous savez
22

1r:1

Eh bien cela m'a enormement amusé
de faire cet interieur sans rien.
D'une simplicité à la Seurat

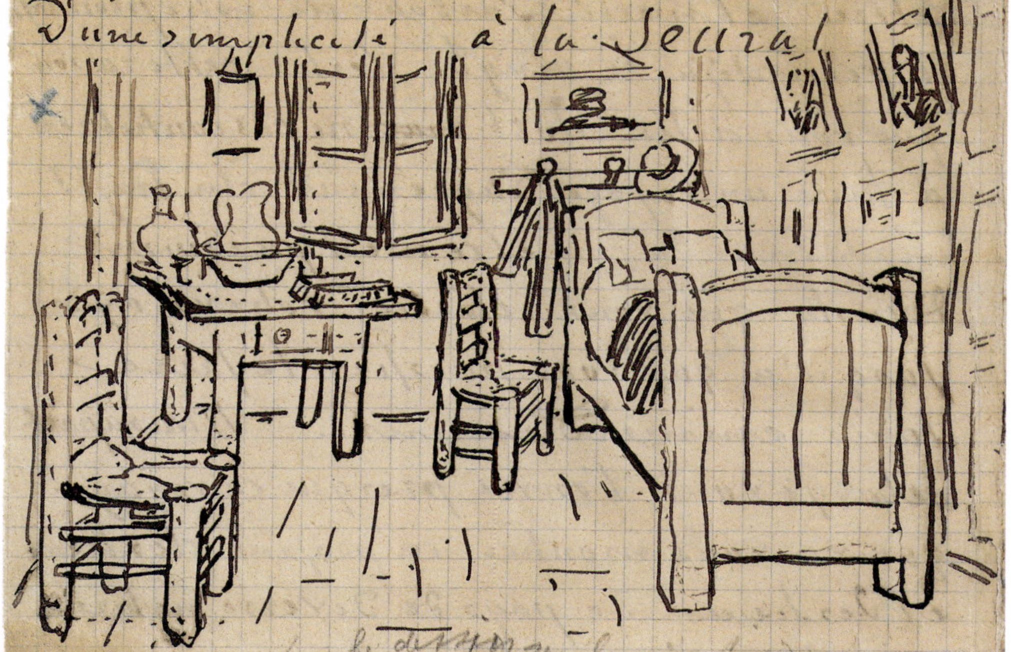

A teintes plates mais grossièrement brossées
en pleine pâte les murs lilas pâle
le sol d'un rouge rompu et fané les
chaises et le lit jaune de chrome les oreillers
et le drap citron vert très pâle la couverture
rouge sang la table à toilette orangée
la cuvette bleue la fenêtre verte
J'avais voulu exprimer un repos
absolu par tous ces tons très divers
vous voyez et où il n'y a de blanc que
la petite note que donne le miroir à
cadre noir (pour fourrer encore la quatrième
paire de complementaires dedans)
Enfin vous verrez cela avec les autres et nous
en causerons car je ne sais souvent

1v:2

par ce que je fais travaillant presqu'en
somnambule.
Il commence à faire froid surtout les
jours de mistral.
J'ai fait mettre le gaz dans l'atelier
pour que nous ayons une bonne
lumière en hiver.
Peutêtre serez vous desenchanté d'Arles
si vous y venez par un temps de mistral
mais attendez... C'est à la longue que
la poésie d'ici pénètre
Vous ne trouverez pas encore la maison
aussi comfortable que peu à peu nous
chercherons à la rendre. Il y a tant de
depenses et cela ne peut pas se
faire d'une seule haleine. Enfin
je crois qu'une fois ici vous allez comme
moi être pris d'une rage de peindre
dans les intervalles du mistral les effets
d'automne. et que vous comprendrez que
j'ai insisté pour que vous veniez ~~avant~~
maintenant qu'il y a de bien beaux
jours. allons au revoir
t à v
Vincent

1v:3

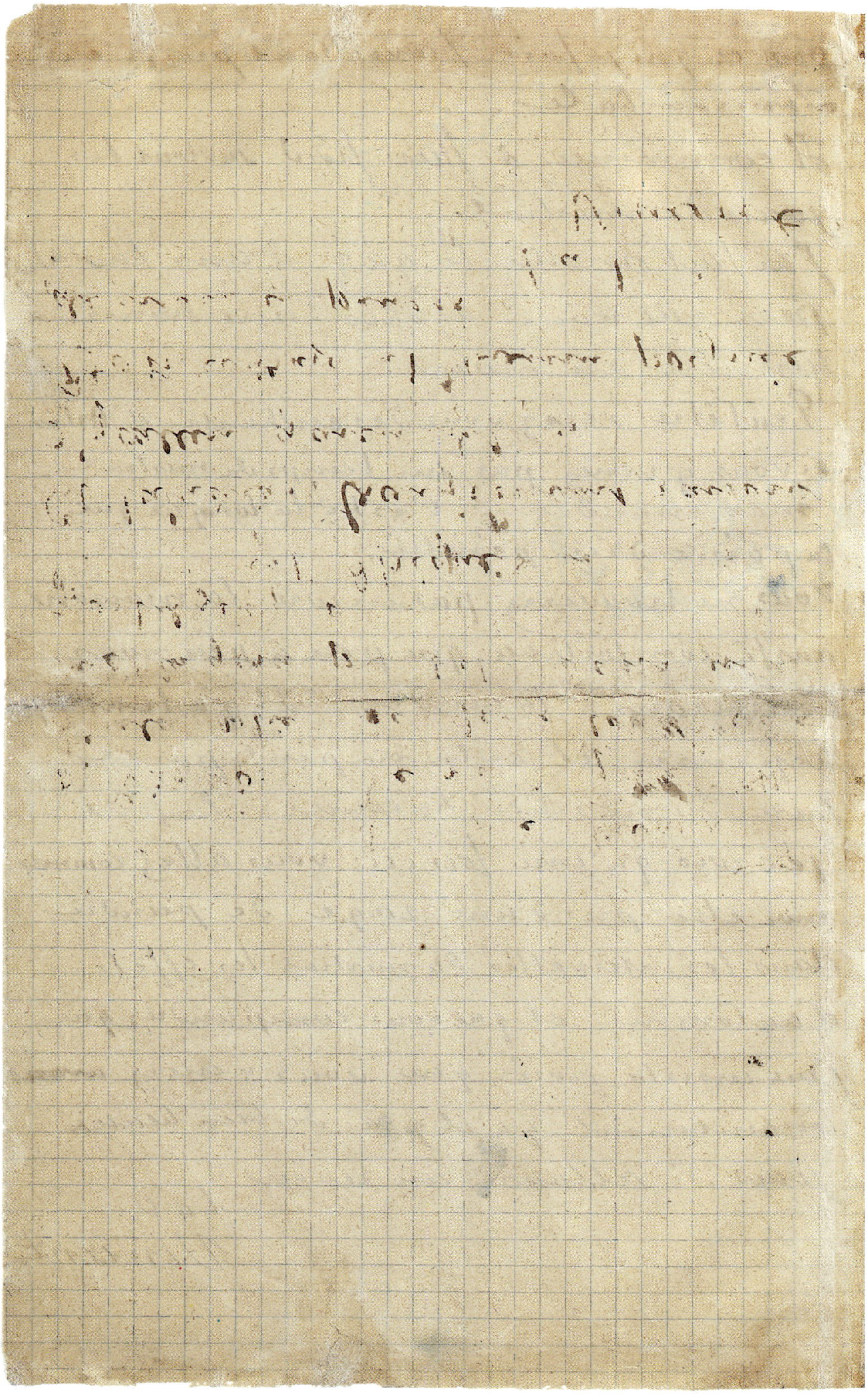

1r:4

Letter 1

Paris, ca. December 1887

Source
Original manuscript

Location
New York, Thaw Collection, The Morgan Library & Museum

Date
Van Gogh organized an exhibition that was held in November or December 1887. The statement "I'll gladly do all I can to make a success of what was started in the dining room" seems to imply that the exhibition had closed, which is why the letter has been dated ca. December 1887.

The correspondence opens with a letter written while van Gogh was still in Paris. One day in December 1887, he and Bernard must have had a heated discussion about a subject close to their hearts: the need to explore new paths in painting. Van Gogh felt that the painters of the "petit boulevard" (see p. 10) should form a group and work together ("united we stand" is a recurring phrase in his letters). Bernard, though, evidently found that unity less important than his own principles, and van Gogh, who took him to task, subsequently wrote this letter to apologize for his outburst. The conciliatory tone, however, is leavened with a lecture. Eating humble pie was just not van Gogh's style.

The fact that the letter dates from the Paris period explains why it deals with matters of the moment. Van Gogh did not need to tell Bernard what he was working on, because Bernard could have seen it for himself in the studio. "Work in progress" became one of the stock topics of the later letters, all of which were written in the south of France.

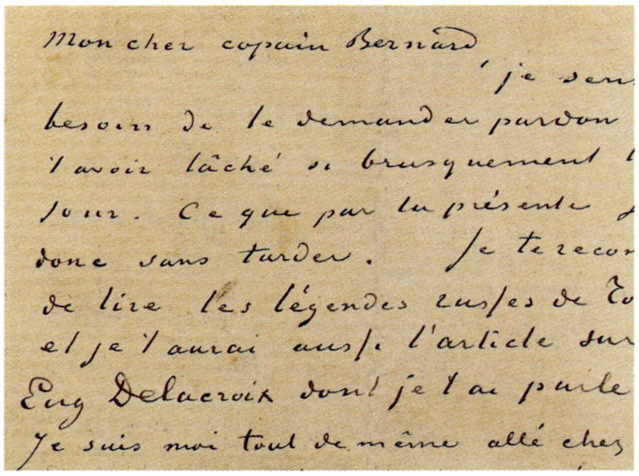
Mon cher copain Bernard,
je sens
besoin de te demander pardon
t'avoir lâché si brusquement
jour. Ce que par la présente
donc sans tarder. Je te recom
de lire les légendes russes de E
et je t'aurai aussi l'article sur
Eug Delacroix dont je t'ai parlé
Je suis moi tout de même allé chez

Translation of Letter 1 / Paris, ca. December 1887

54 rue Lepic.[1]

My dear old Bernard,

I feel the need to beg your pardon for leaving you so abruptly the other day.[2] Which I therefore do herewith, without delay. I recommend that you read Tolstoy's Les Légendes Russes,[3] and I'll also let you have the article on E. Delacroix that I've spoken to you about.[4]

I, for my part, did go to Guillaumin's anyway, but in the evening, and I thought that perhaps you didn't know his address, which is 13 quai d'Anjou.[5] I believe that, as a man, Guillaumin has sounder ideas than the others, and that if we were all like him we'd produce more good things and would have less time and inclination to be at each other's throats.

I persist in believing that—not because I gave you a rocket but because it will become your own conviction—I persist in believing that you'll realize that in the studios not only does one not learn very much as far as painting goes, but not much that's good in terms of *savoir vivre*, either. And that one finds oneself obliged to learn to live, as one does to paint, without resorting to the old tricks and trompe l'oeil of schemers.

I don't think your portrait of yourself will be your last, or your best[6]—although all in all it is frightfully you.

Look here—briefly, what I was trying to explain to you the other day comes down to this. In order to avoid generalities, let me take an example from life.

If you've fallen out with a painter, with Signac, for example, and if as a result you say:

Transcription of Letter 1 / Paris, ca. December 1887

54 Rue Lepic.[1]

Mon cher copain Bernard,

je sens le besoin de te demander pardon de t'avoir lâché si brusquement l'autre jour.[2] *Ce que par la présen-te je fais donc sans tarder. Je te recommande de lire les légendes russes de Tolstoï*[3] *et je t'aurai aussi l'article sur Eug. Delacroix dont je t'ai parlé.*[4]

Je suis moi tout de même allé chez Guillaumin, mais dans la soirée, et j'ai pensé que peut-être toi ne sais pas son adresse qui est 13 Quai d'Anjou.[5] *Je crois que comme homme Guillaumin a les idées mieux en place que les autres et que si tous étaient comme lui on produirait davantage de bonnes choses et aurait moins de temps et d'envie de se manger le nez.*

Je persiste à croire que, non pas parceque moi je t'ai engueulé mais parceque cela deviendra ta propre conviction, je persiste à croire que tu t'apercevras que dans les ateliers non seulement on n'apprend pas grand chose quant à la peinture mais encore pas grand chôse de bien en tant que savoir vivre. Et qu'on se trouve obligé d'apprendre à vivre comme à peindre sans avoir recours aux vieux trucs et trompe l'oeil d'intrigants.

Je ne pense pas que ton portrait de toi-meme sera ton dernier ni ton meilleur[6]*—quoique en somme ce soit terriblement toi.*

Dites donc—en somme ce que je cherchais l'autre jour à t'expliquer revient à ceci.—Pour eviter les généralités permets moi de prendre un exemple sur le vif.—

Si tu es brouillé avec un peintre, par exemple avec Signac et qu'en consequence de cela tu dis—si

I'll withdraw my canvases if Signac exhibits where I exhibit—and if you run him down, then it seems to me that you are not behaving as well as you could.[7]

Because it's better to take a long look at it before judging so categorically and to reflect, reflection making us see in ourselves, when there's a falling out, as many faults on our own side as in our adversary, and in him as many justifications as we might desire for ourselves.

If, therefore, you have already considered that Signac and the others who are doing pointillism often make very beautiful things with it—

Instead of running those things down, one should respect them and speak of them sympathetically, especially when there's a falling out.

Otherwise one becomes a narrow sectarian oneself and the equivalent of those who think nothing of others and believe themselves to be the only righteous ones.

This extends even to the academicians, because take, for example, a painting by Fantin-Latour—and above all his entire oeuvre. Well then—there's someone who hasn't rebelled, and does that prevent him, that indefinable calm and righteousness that he has, being one of the most independent characters in existence?

I also wanted to say a word to you about the military service that you will be required to do.[8] You must absolutely see to that now.

Directly, in order to inform yourself properly about what one can do in such an event; first to retain the right to work, to be able to choose a garrison, etc. But indirectly, by taking care of your health. You mustn't arrive there too anemic or too agitated if you want to emerge from it stronger.

I do not see it as a very great misfortune for you that you have to join the army but as a very grave ordeal, from which, if you emerge from it, you'll emerge a very great artist. Until then, do all you can to build yourself up, because you'll need quite a bit of spirit. If you work hard that year, I believe that you may well succeed in having a fair stock of canvases, some of which we'll try to sell for you, knowing that you'll need pocket money to pay for models.

I'll gladly do all I can to make a success of what was started in the dining room,[9] but I believe that the first condition for success is to put aside petty jealousies; it's only unity that makes strength. It's well worth sacrificing selfishness, the "each man for himself," in the common interest.

I shake your hand firmly.

Vincent

Signac expose là où j'expose je retire mes toiles—et si tu le dénigres, alors il me semble que tu agis pas aussi bien que tu pourrais agir.[7]

Car il est mieux d'y regarder longtemps avant de juger si categoriquement et de refléchir, la réflection nous faisant apercevoir à nous-même, en cas de brouille, pour notre propre compte autant de torts que notre adversaire et à celui ci autant de raison d'être que nous puissions en desirer pour nous.—

Si donc tu as deja réflechi que Signac et les autres qui font du pointillé font avec cela assez souvent de très belles choses—

Au lieu de dénigrer celles-là il faut surtout en cas de brouille les estimer et en parler avec sympathie.

Sans cela on devient sectaire étroit soi-même et l'équivalent de ceux qui n'estiment pour rien les autres et se croient les seuls justes.—

Ceci s'étend même aux académiciens car prends par exemple un tableau de Fantin Latour—surtout l'ensemble de son oeuvre.—Eh bien—voila quelqu'un qui ne s'est pas insurgé et est-ce que cela l'empêche, ce je ne sais quoi de calme et de juste qu'il a, d'etre un des caracteres les plus indépendants existants?

Je voulais encore te dire un mot pour ce qui regarde le service militaire que tu seras obligé de faire.—[8] *Il faut absolument que tu t'occupes dès à présent de cela.—*

Directement pour bien t'informer de ce que l'on peut faire en pareil cas, pour garder le droit de travailler d'abord, pour pouvoir choisir une garnison &c. Mais indirectement en soignant ta santé. il ne faut pas y arriver trop anémique ni trop énervé si tu y tiens à sortir de là plus fort.—

Je ne considère pas cela comme un tres grand malheur pour toi que tu sois obligé de partir soldat mais comme une épreuve très grave de laquelle si tu en sors tu en sortiras un très grand artiste. D'ici là fais tout ce que tu peux pour te fortifier car il te faudra joliment du nerf. Si pendant cette année tu travailles beaucoup je crois que tu peux bien arriver à avoir un certain stock de toiles, desquelles on cherchera à t'en vendre, sachant que tu auras besoin d'argent de poche pour te payer des modèles.

Volontiers je ferai mon possible pour faire que ce que l'on a commencé dans la salle reussisse[9] *mais je crois que la premiere condition pour reussir c'est de laisser là les petites jalousies, il n'y a que l'union qui fait la force. L'interêt commun vaut bien qu'on y sacrifie l'égoisme, le chacun*[a] *pour soi.*

Je te serre bien la main.

Vincent

Annotations to Letter 1

Paris, ca. December 1887

Textual Note
a. le chacun < chacun

1. Theo and Vincent had been living at this address in Montmartre since June 1886. Vincent had his studio there.

2. Further in the letter it is revealed that van Gogh and Bernard had had a difference of opinion about the usefulness of studio training for a painter (van Gogh felt that there was little an artist could learn in those surroundings), and about Bernard's attitude toward the neo-impressionist Paul Signac. Bernard did not want to exhibit with Signac. Van Gogh, however, was concerned with a more "common interest."

3. Léon Tolstoï, *A la recherche du bonheur,* traduit et précédé d'une préface par M. E. Halpérine. Paris 1886 (second edition 1887). A letter of Monday, 25 April, 1887, from Theo to his sister Willemien, discloses that Tolstoy's work had been sent to him and Vincent from Holland. Theo said that he found it "magnifique" and that Vincent had also enjoyed it very much (Van Gogh Museum, inv. no. b911). The anthology contains a series of folktales about divine omniscience and human virtues and vices, among them readiness to forgive, compassion, and greed. Some of the stories are like fairy tales (with apparitions, an angel, and talking animals), while others are realistic (featuring farm laborers and craftsmen).

4. This was probably Théophile Silvestre's *Eugène Delacroix. Documents nouveaux* (1864), which van Gogh also referred to as an article elsewhere (Letter 13). It is known that on one occasion he lent it to Bernard (*CL* 570).

5. That was indeed Armand Guillaumin's address. It had previously been the studio of the painter Charles Daubigny.

6. It is not known to which of Bernard's self-portraits he was referring.

7. Bernard had rejected the neo-impressionism of Seurat and Signac over the course of 1887; see Introduction, p. 10. Van Gogh, on the other hand, wanted to involve them with the group of artists that had exhibited in the Restaurant du Chalet: "This group, to which he wished to introduce Seurat and Signac, was not to survive; its life was therefore limited to this single presentation" *(Ce groupe auquel il voulait rattacher Seurat et Signac, ne devait pas vivre; son existence se borna donc à cette unique présentation.).* See Bernard 1994, vol. 1, pp. 241–42. The exhibition in the Restaurant du Chalet is mentioned later in the letter (see n. 9).

8. Bernard's obligatory military service was a regular topic of conversation. In 1888 it was thought he would do it in Algeria, but in the end he was not called.

9. In November–December 1887, van Gogh organized an exhibition of painters of the "petit boulevard"—Louis Anquetin, Bernard, Arnold Koning, Henri de Toulouse-Lautrec, and himself—in Grand Bouillon, Restaurant du Chalet, 43, avenue de Clichy. See Paris 1988, p. 33. For the "petit boulevard" see Introduction, p. 10. According to Bernard, the show was "an endeavor on Van Gogh's part alone" *(une tentative de Van Gogh seul).* See Bernard 1994, vol. 1, p. 242. Bernard wrote about the room: "The room referred to here is the dining room of a working-class restaurant on the avenue de Clichy, whose owner Vincent had won over, and which he had turned into an exhibition of our paintings. Unfortunately, this socialist exhibition of our inflammatory canvases came to a rather sorry end. There was a violent altercation between the owner and Vincent, which made Vincent decide to take a handbarrow without delay and cart the whole exhibition to his studio in rue Lepic. Obviously, the art of the petit boulevard had not been understood by its Barnum." *(La salle dont il est question ici est celle d'un restaurant populaire de l'avenue de Clichy dont Vincent avait conquis le patron et qu'il avait transformée en exposition de nos tableaux. Par malheur, cette exhibition socialiste de nos toiles incendiaires se termina assez piteusement. Il y eut une altercation violente entre le patron et Vincent, ce qui décida ce dernier à prendre sans retard une charette à bras et à porter toute l'exposition à son atelier de la rue Lepic. Evidemment l'art du petit boulevard n'avait pas été compris de son barnum).* See *Lettres à Bernard* 1911, p. 75.

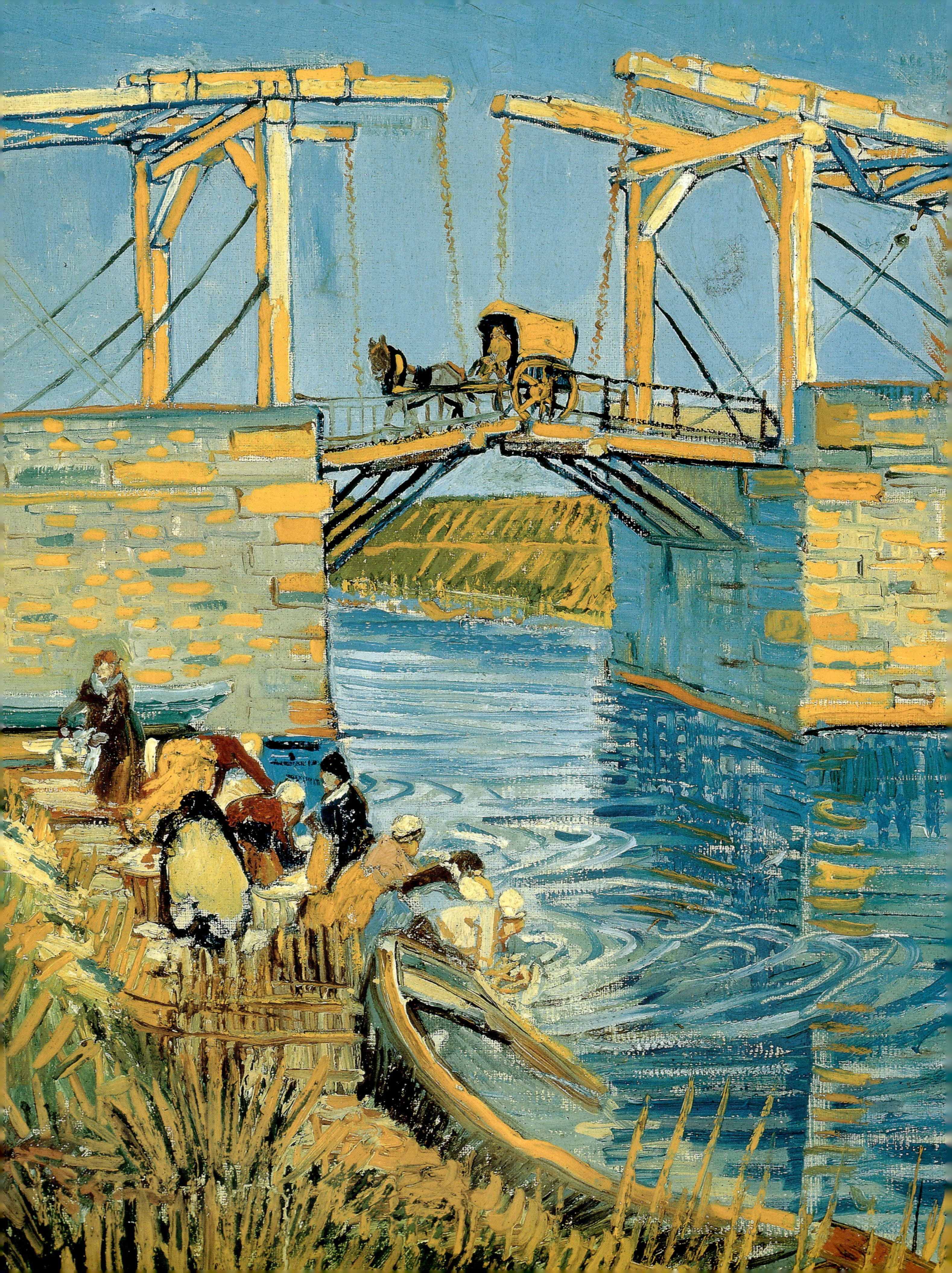

Letter 2

Arles, Sunday, 18 March, 1888

Source
Original manuscript

Location
New York, Thaw Collection, The Morgan Library & Museum

Date
Vincent sent this letter off with one to Theo dating from Wednesday, 21, or Thursday, 22 March (*CL* 470). In letter *CL* 469 of 17 March van Gogh mentioned that he planned to write the present letter the following Sunday, the day that he often set aside for correspondence. Since there is no reason to believe that he deviated from that plan, and lacking any other clues, we have dated the letter Sunday, 18 March, 1888.

Sketch
Drawbridge with Walking Couple (F - / JH 1370), letter sketch. Color notations: above the sun, *jaune* (yellow); on the walls under the bridge, *lilas* (lilac) twice; on the path, *rose* (pink) three times; on the water, *emeraude* (emerald); on the far bank, *vert* (green); on the grass in the foreground, *vert*; to the left of the man of the couple by the bridge, *ocre jaune* (yellow ocher); to the right of that couple, *rose* and *noir* (black); above the hat of the man in the foreground, *jaune*; beside his arm, *bleu* (blue); on his trousers, *ocre-jaune*; beside the woman's head, *orangé* (orange); on her blouse, *rouge* (red); and on her skirt, *carmin* (carmine).

Van Gogh had been living in Arles since 20 February 1888. He left for the south of France because he was not feeling well after several years in Paris, which he found debilitating and exhausting, not just as a result of too much bad wine and tobacco but also because of disagreements among the resident artists. Life, he expected, would be cheaper in the south, and he hoped to discover new subjects and brighter colors. His choice must have been influenced by his great role models, Eugène Delacroix and Adolphe Monticelli, who had struck out on new coloristic paths in Africa and Provence, respectively. Japanese art was also running through his mind, and he later wrote to Gauguin that on the train to Arles he was constantly looking to see whether the landscape was beginning to look Japanese.

The move south may have been prompted in part by artist friends like Signac and Toulouse-Lautrec, who knew the region well. Reading contemporary literatûre about Provence, such as the novels of Alphonse Daudet, of whom van Gogh was a great admirer, may have made it even more attractive. It was not certain from the outset that van Gogh would stay in Arles. It seems at first he regarded the small town as a stopover on the way to Marseille.

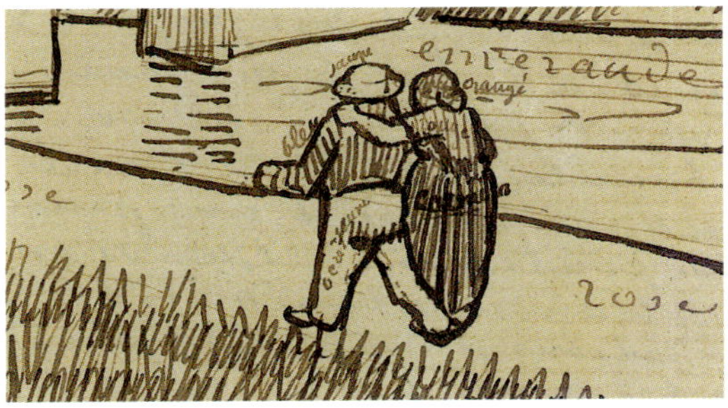

Soon after his arrival van Gogh met the Danish painter Christian Mourier-Petersen, whom he saw regularly until the latter's departure for Paris in May 1888. He was not very impressed by Mourier's work, but he was happy that he had someone intelligent to talk to about impressionism. Bernard, however, was the main person with whom he discussed color and technique during this period. The moment that the latter received van Gogh's letter, he was planning to visit Saint-Briac in Brittany for several months, as he had in previous years.

Detail of Fig. 11.

Translation of Letter 2 / Arles, Sunday, 18 March, 1888

[sketch]

My dear Bernard,
Having promised to write to you,[1] I want to begin by telling you that this part of the world seems to me as beautiful as Japan for the limpidity of the atmosphere and the gay color effects. The stretches of water[2] make patches of a beautiful emerald and a rich blue in the landscapes, as we see it in the Japanese prints.[3] Pale orange sunsets making the fields look blue—glorious yellow suns. So far, however, I've hardly seen this part of the world in its usual summer splendor. The women's costume is pretty, and especially on the boulevard on Sunday you see some very naive and well-chosen arrangements of color.[4] And that, too, will doubtless get even livelier in summer.

I regret that living here isn't as cheap as I'd hoped, and until now I haven't found a way of getting by as easily as one could in Pont-Aven.[5] I started out paying 5 francs and now I'm on 4 francs a day.[6] One would need to know the local patois, and know how to eat bouillabaisse and aioli, then one would surely find an inexpensive family boardinghouse. Then if there were several of us, I'm inclined to believe we would get more favorable terms. Perhaps there would be a real advantage in emigrating to the south for many artists in love with sunshine and color. The Japanese may not be making progress in their country, but there is no doubt that their art is being carried on in France. At the top of this letter I am sending you a little sketch of a study that is preoccupying me as to how to make something of it—sailors coming back with their sweethearts toward the town, which projects the strange silhouette of its drawbridge against a huge yellow sun.[7]

I have another study of the same drawbridge with a group of washerwomen.[8] Shall be happy to have a line from you to know what you're doing and where you're going to go. A very warm handshake to you and the friends.

Yours,
Vincent

Transcription of Letter 2 / Arles, Sunday, 18 March, 1888

[sketch]

Mon cher Bernard,
ayant promis de t'écrire[1] je veux commencer par te dire que le pays me parait aussi beau que le Japon pour la limpidité de l'atmosphère et les effets de couleur gaie. Les eaux[2] font des taches d'un bel éméraude et d'un riche bleu dans les paysages ainsi que nous le voyons dans les crepons.[3] Des couchers de soleil orangé pâle faisant paraître bleu les terrains—des soleils jaunes splendides. Cependant je n'ai encore guère vu le pays dans sa splendeur habituelle d'été. Le costume des femmes est joli et le dimanche surtout on voit sur le boulevard des arrangements de couleur très-naïfs et bien trouvés.[4] Et cela aussi sans doute s'égayera encore en été.

Je regrette que la vie ici n'est pas à si bon marché que je l'avais espéré et je n'ai pas trouvé moyen jusqu'à présent de m'en tirer à aussi bon compte qu'on pourrait le faire à Pont Aven.[5] J'ai commencé par payer 5 fr. et maintenant je suis à 4 francs par jour.[6] Il faudrait savoir le patois d'ici et savoir manger de la bouillabaisse et de l'aïoli, alors on trouverait surement une pension bourgeoise peu coûteuse. Puis si on était à plusieurs on obtiendrait, je suis porté à le croire, des conditions plus avantageuses.—Il y aurait peut-être un réel avantage pour bien des artistes amoureux de soleil et de couleur d'émigrer dans le midi. Si les Japonais ne sont pas en progrès dans leur pays il est indubitable que leur art se continue en France. En tête de cette lettre je t'envoie un petit croquis d'une étude qui me préoccupe pour en faire quelque chôse—des matelots qui remontent avec leurs amoureuses vers la ville qui profile l'étrange silhouette de son pont levis sur un énorme soleil jaune.[7]

J'ai une autre étude du même pont levis avec un groupe de laveuses.[8] Serai content d'un mot de toi pour savoir ce que tu fais et où tu iras.—Poignée de main bien cordiale à toi-même et aux amis.

bien à toi
Vincent

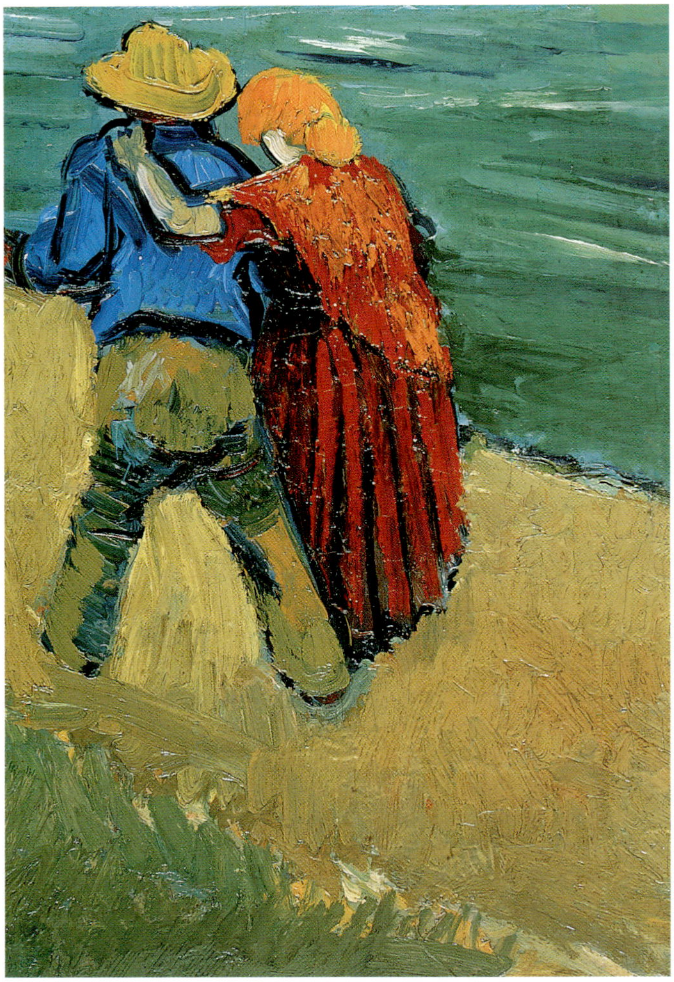

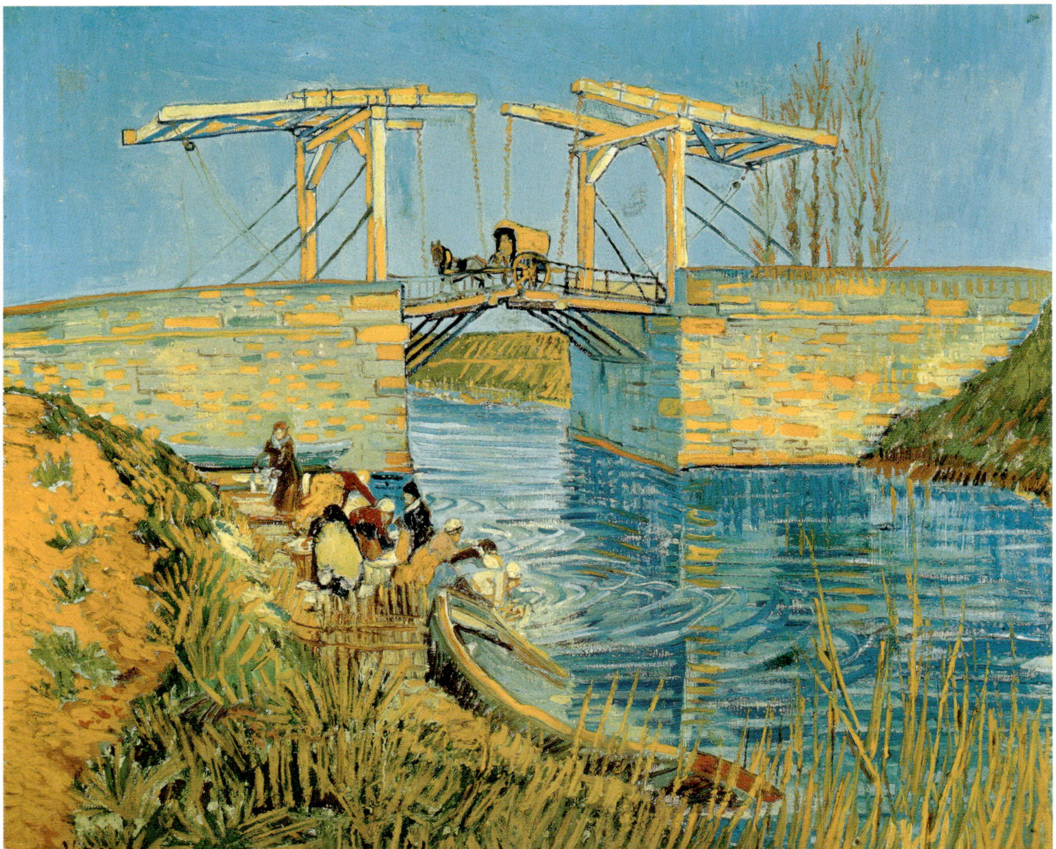

Annotations to Letter 2

Arles, Sunday, 18 March, 1888

1. In his letter of ca. 24 February, Vincent had asked Theo to tell Bernard that he would shortly let him know about the cost of living in Provence (*CL* 464). Here he made good on his promise, which makes it apparent that, even before van Gogh left for Arles, they had discussed the idea of Bernard joining him in the south of France. That idea, however, was overshadowed when the brothers approached Gauguin about a possible collaboration (Letter 10).

2. Arles is situated on the Rhône. There are also several canals in and outside the town, including the Arles-Bouc, which is shown in the letter sketch. It is also depicted in the paintings of the Langlois Bridge subsequently mentioned in the letter.

3. Although a *crépon* is, strictly speaking, a woodcut printed on crepe paper or fabric, van Gogh used the term for Japanese prints in general, which he also called *japonaiseries*.

4. The legendary beauty of the women of Arles was a popular topic in nineteenth-century painting, literature, and theater. They wore the traditional costume of the region. See Arles 1999–2000 and Dorn 1990, p. 152.

5. Pont-Aven, a small village in Brittany in western France, was discovered by painters around 1865 and grew to become a well-known artists' colony. Bernard had gone there in August 1886 and met Paul Gauguin. The latter was there again since January 1888, as he had told van Gogh (GAC 28); Bernard undoubtedly knew that as well. The group of artists who worked in Gauguin's style there is known as the school of Pont-Aven. See Paris and Quimper 2003.

6. Between the end of February and the beginning of May, van Gogh rented a room in the northern part of town at the Hotel-Restaurant Carrel, 30 rue Amédée-Pichot. The hotel was a "two-story house, small roof terrace on top and balcony on the first floor" (*maison à deux étages, petite terrasse au-dessus et balcon au premier*). See Coquiot 1923, p. 161.

7. Only the fragment *Walking Couple* (F 544 / JH 1369; Fig. 10) of this study has survived; the complete study is reproduced in the letter sketch *Drawbridge with Walking Couple* (F - / JH 1370). In letter *CL* 471, van Gogh told Theo that he had ruined the painting.

8. *Drawbridge with Carriage* (F 397 / JH 1368; Fig. 11). Van Gogh painted a second version a few weeks later: *Drawbridge with Carriage* (F 571 / JH 1392; private collection).

---

10. Vincent van Gogh, *Walking Couple (fragment)*, 1888 (F 544 / JH 1369). Private collection.
11. Vincent van Gogh, *Drawbridge with Carriage*, 1888 (F 397 / JH 1368). Otterlo, Kröller-Müller Museum.

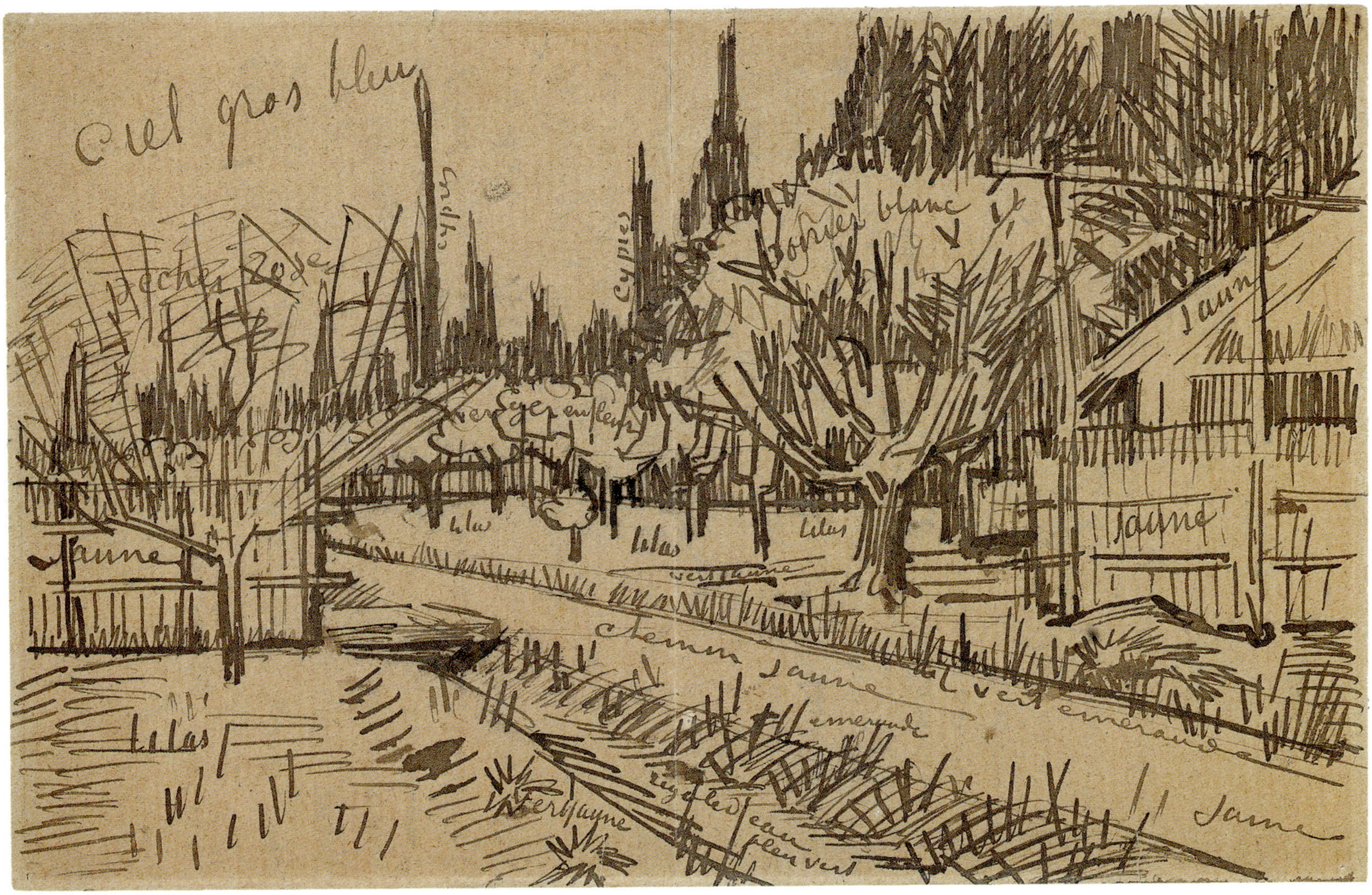
Ciel gros bleu
Cypres
jaune
lilas
chemin jaune
vert emeraude
jaune

Letter 3

Arles, ca. Thursday, 12 April, 1888

Source
Original manuscript

Location
New York, Thaw Collection, The Morgan Library & Museum

Date
This letter followed one to Theo of about 11 April (*CL* 476), in which van Gogh made no mention of the subject of the fenced orchard with pear and peach trees, which seems to indicate that it preceded this letter to Bernard, in which he does describe the orchard. Furthermore, the present letter precedes the one to Theo of about 13 April (*CL* 477), in which several canvases of orchards in blossom are described to have been further developed than when van Gogh wrote this letter, which we have therefore dated ca. Thursday, 12 April, 1888.

Sketch
Orchard Surrounded by Cypresses (F - / JH 1390), letter sketch. Color notations: at top left, *Ciel gros bleu* (Big blue sky); in the left-hand tree, *pecher rose* (pink peach tree); in the center background, twice beside the treetops and once in the group of trees at the same height as the word *blanc* (white), *cypres* (cypress); in the right-hand tree, *poirier blanc* (white pear tree); in the trees in the center, *verger en fleur* (orchard in blossom); on the ground under the trees, *lilas* (lilac), three times; on the path under the trees, *vert jaune* (green yellow); on the fences at left and right, and on the roof on the right, *jaune,* three times; on the path, *chemin jaune* (yellow path) and *jaune*; by the upper strip beside the path, *ail vert emeraude* (emerald-green garlic); by the lower strip, *emeraude*; on the strip in the foreground, beside the path, *rigole d'eau bleu vert* (blue-green ditch with water); on the patch of land in the left foreground, *lilas*; and on the patch in the foreground, *vertjaune* (green yellow).

The opening paragraph of this letter tells us that Bernard had sent van Gogh a batch of drawings and had written about working from the imagination. This subject was not only important in the correspondence between Bernard and Gauguin but also in their collaboration in Pont-Aven and then between van Gogh and Gauguin in Arles. Here van Gogh adopted a rather ambivalent position, for on the one hand he recognized the desirability and potential benefits of that approach but at the same time stated that he did not want to abandon reality as his point of departure. He was also ambivalent about what he was working on. According to him, it was executed very freely yet still satisfied several criteria of cloisonism.

In the meantime, the fourth exhibition of the Société des Artistes Indépendants had opened in Paris on 22 March. Van Gogh was represented by three paintings: *The Gardens of Montmartre* (Amsterdam, Van Gogh Museum; F 316 / JH 1246), *Vegetable Gardens in Montmartre* (Amsterdam, Stedelijk Museum; F 350 / JH 1245) and *Piles of French Novels and a Glass with a Rose* (Perth, Robert Holmes à Court Collection; F 359 / JH 1332). Bernard had been to the exhibition but felt that the three works did not really reveal van Gogh's potential (see Appendix 2). It is not known whether he told his friend this.

During his first few months in Provence, van Gogh explored the possibilities of publicizing the work of the impressionists, and of the painters of the "petit boulevard" in particular. The letters to Theo show that he was toying with the idea of looking for exhibition space in Marseille for himself and his Paris colleagues. The brothers considered dealing in impressionist work in England; they also tried to promote it through H. G. Tersteeg in The Hague, their former superior at the branch of the Goupil Gallery there. Theo sent Tersteeg a painting by Vincent as well as works by Degas, Monet, Sisley, Pissarro, Guillaumin, Gauguin, Toulouse-Lautrec, and Monticelli. This did not prove successful; only a single work by Monticelli was sold. Vincent had asked his brother to include Bernard's "little head of a Breton woman,"[1] but Theo decided against it. Bernard was not apprised of these efforts to proselytize the new art.

Detail of Letter 3.

Translation of Letter 3 / Arles, ca. Thursday, 12 April, 1888

My dear old Bernard,
Thanks for your kind letter and the sketch of your decoration included with it, which I find really amusing.[1] I sometimes regret that I can't decide to work more at home and from the imagination. Certainly—imagination is a capacity that must be developed, and only that enables us to create a more exalting and consoling nature than what just a glance at reality (which we perceive changing, passing quickly like lightning) allows us to perceive.

A starry sky, for example, well—it's a thing that I should like to try to do, just as in the daytime I'll try to paint a green meadow studded with dandelions.

But how to arrive at that unless I decide to work at home and from the imagination? This, then, to criticize myself and to praise you.

At present I am busy with the fruit trees in blossom: pink peach trees, yellow-white pear trees.[2]

I follow no system of brushwork at all, I hit the canvas with irregular strokes, which I leave as they are, impastos, uncovered spots of canvas—corners here and there left inevitably unfinished—reworkings, roughnesses; well, I'm inclined to think that the result is sufficiently worrying and annoying not to please people with preconceived ideas about technique.

Here's a sketch, by the way, the entrance to a Provençal orchard with its yellow reed fences, with its shelter (against the mistral), black cypresses, with its typical vegetables of various greens, yellow lettuces, onions and garlic and emerald leeks.[3]

Transcription of Letter 3 / Arles, ca. Thursday, 12 April, 1888

Mon cher copain Bernard
merci de ta bonne lettre et des croquis y–inclus de ta décoration que je trouve bien drôle.—[1] *Je regrette parfois de ne pas pouvoir me résoudre à travailler davantage chez moi et de fantaisie. Certainement—l'imagination est une capacité qu'il faut developper et elle seule peut nous faire arriver à créer une nature plus exaltante & plus consolatrice que ce que le clin d'oeil seul sur la realité (que nous apercevons changeante, passant vite comme l'éclair) nous fasse apercevoir.—*

Un ciel étoilé par exemple, tiens—c'est une chôse que je voudrais essayer à faire de même que le jour j'essayerai à peindre une verte prairie etoilée de pissenlits.

Comment pourtant y arriver à moins de me résoudre à travailler chez moi et d'imagination?—Ceci donc à ma critique et à ta louange.

Actuellement je suis pris par les arbres fruitiers en fleur, pêchers roses, poiriers blancs-jaunes.[2]

Ne suis aucun système de touche, je tape sur la toile à coups irréguliers que je laisse tels quels, des empâtements, des endroits de toile pas couvertes—par ci par là des coins laissés fatalement inachevés[a]*—des reprises, des brutalités, enfin le résultat est, je suis porté à le croire, assez inquietant et agaçant pour que ca ne fasse pas le bonheur des gens à idées arrêtées d'avance sur la technique.—*

Voici d'ailleurs un croquis, l'entrée d'un verger de Provence avec ses clotures jaunes de roseaux, avec son abri (contre le mistral), des cypres noirs, avec ses legumes caracteristiques[b] *de verts variés, salades jaunes, oignons & ail & poireaux émeraudes.*[3]

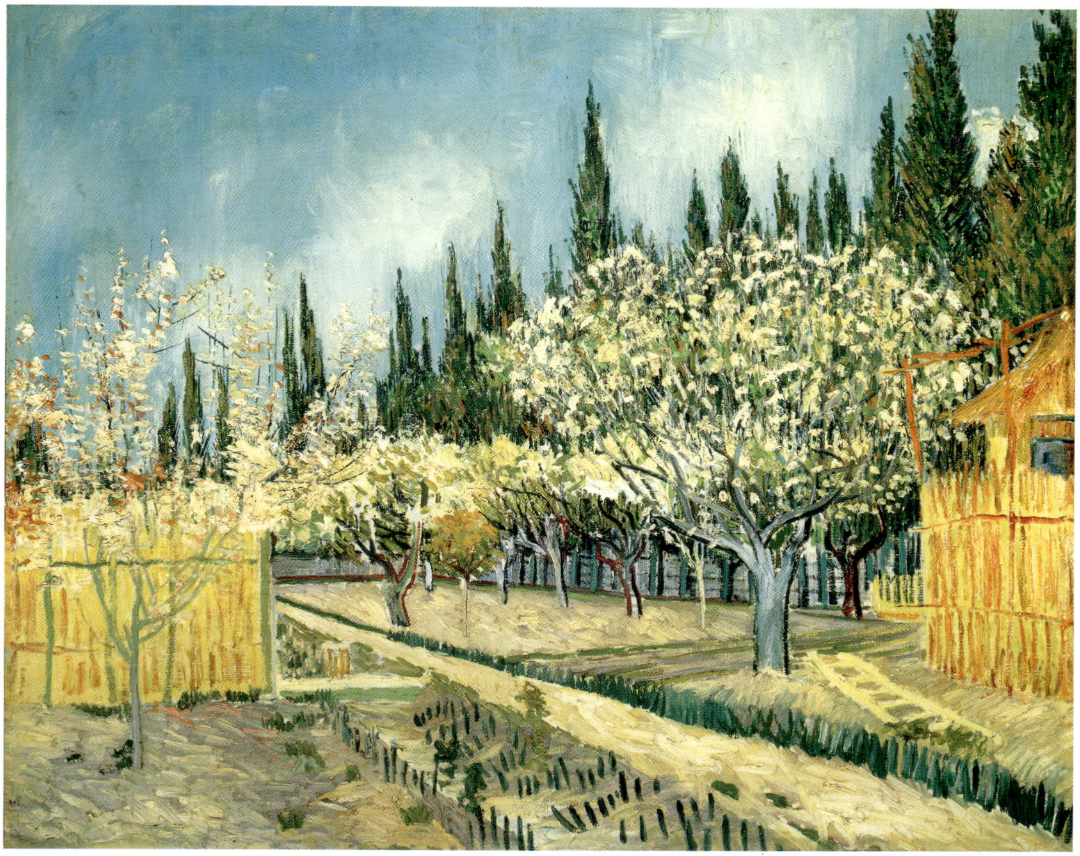

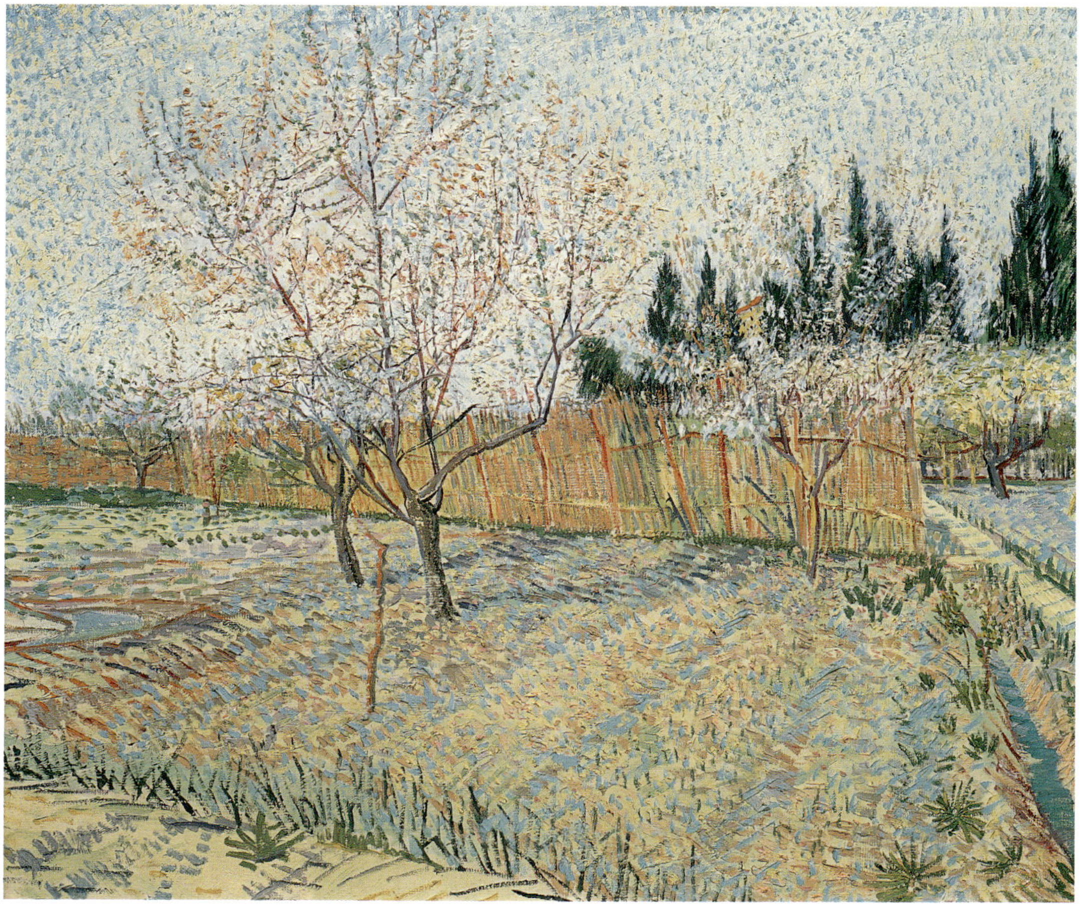

12. Vincent van Gogh, *Orchard Surrounded by Cypresses*, 1888 (F 513 / JH 1389). Otterlo, Kröller-Müller Museum.
13. Vincent van Gogh, *Orchard with Cypresses*, 1888 (F 551 / JH 1396). Private collection.

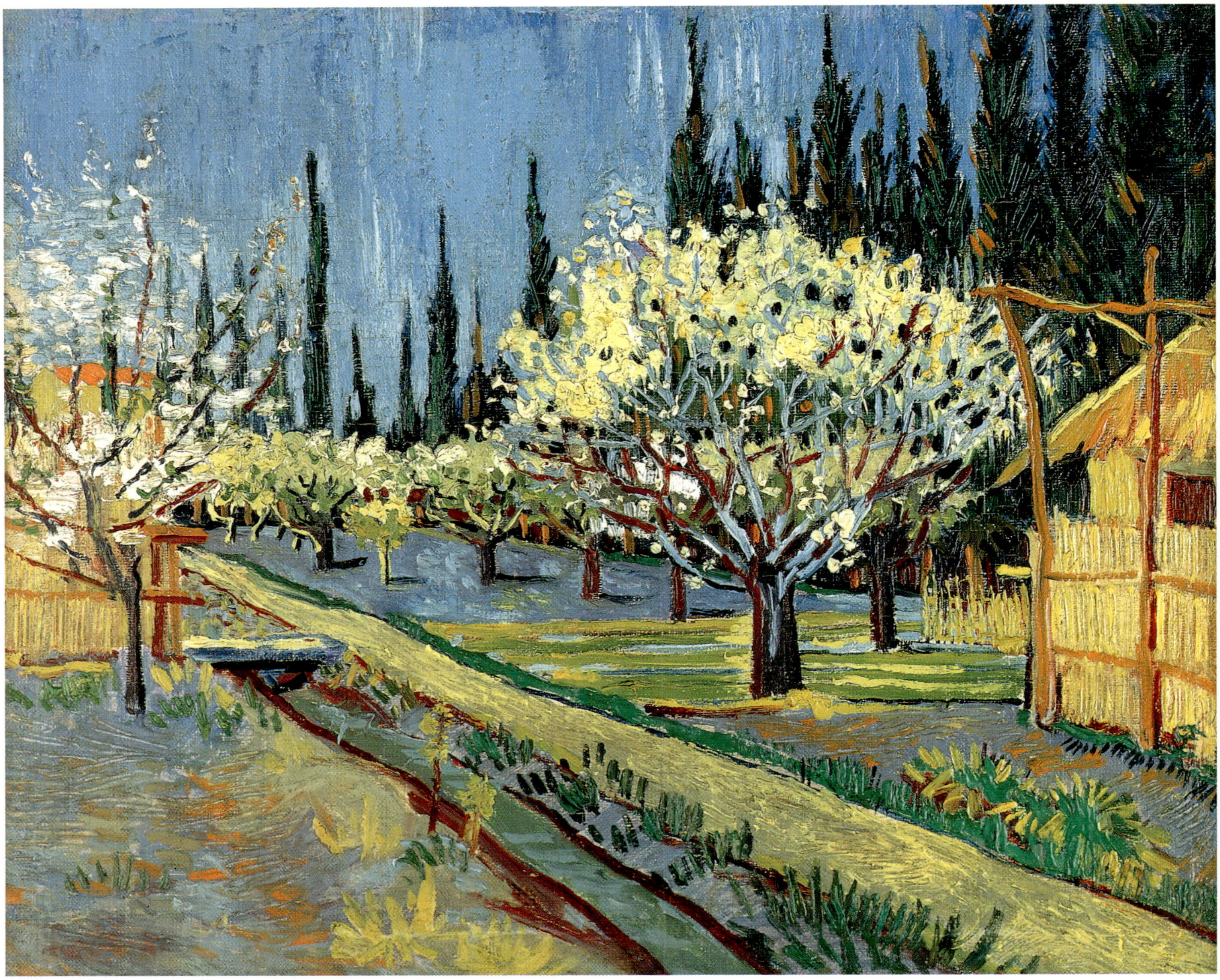

While always working directly on the spot, I try to capture the essence in the drawing—then I fill the spaces demarcated by the outlines (expressed or not) but felt in every case, likewise with simplified tints, in the sense that everything *[sketch]* that will be earth will share the same purplish tint, that the whole sky will have a blue tonality, that the greenery will either be blue greens or yellow greens, deliberately exaggerating the yellow or blue values in that case.[4] Anyway, my dear pal, no trompe l'oeil in any case. As for going to visit Aix, Marseille, Tangier, no fear; if I were to go there, however, it would be in search of cheaper lodgings, etc. Otherwise, I'm convinced that if I worked my whole life, couldn't do as much as half of all that is characteristic of this town alone.

By the way, have seen bullfights in the arenas,[5] or rather, simulated fights, seeing that the bulls were numerous but nobody was fighting them. But the crowd was magnificent, great multicolored crowds. One on top of the other on two, three tiers, with the effect of sun and shade and the shadow of the immense circle. Wish you bon voyage[6]—handshake in thought, your friend

Vincent

Tout en travaillant toujours directement sur place je cherche à saisir dans le dessin ce qui est essentiel—puis les espaces limitées par des contours (exprimés ou non) mais sentis dans tous les cas, je les remplis des tons simplifiés egalement, dans ce sens que tout [sketch] *ce qui sera terrain participera d'un même ton violacé, que tout le ciel aura une tonalité bleue, que les verdures seront ou bien des verts bleus ou bien des verts jaunes, exagérant à dessein les qualites jaunes ou bleues dans ce cas.[4] Enfin mon cher copain—pas du trompe l'oeil en tout cas.—Pour ce qui est d'aller visiter Aix, Marseille, Tanger, pas de danger, si c'est que pourtant j'y aille[c] ce serait en quête de logement à meilleur compte &c. Sans cela, je suis persuadé que travaillant toute ma vie pourrais pas à moitié près faire tout ce qui est caractéristique de cette ville seule.—*

à propos ai vu des combats de taureaux dans les arênes[5] ou plutôt des simulacres de combats vu que les taureaux étaient nombreux mais que personne ne les combattait.—Seulement la foule etait magnifique, les grandes foules bariolées. Superposées à 2, 3 étages de gradins avec l'effet de soleil et d'ombre et d'ombre portée de l'immense cercle.—Te souhaite bon voyage[6]—poignee de main en pensée, ton ami

Vincent

---

14. Vincent van Gogh, *Orchard Surrounded by Cypresses*, 1888 (F 554 / JH 1388). Private collection.

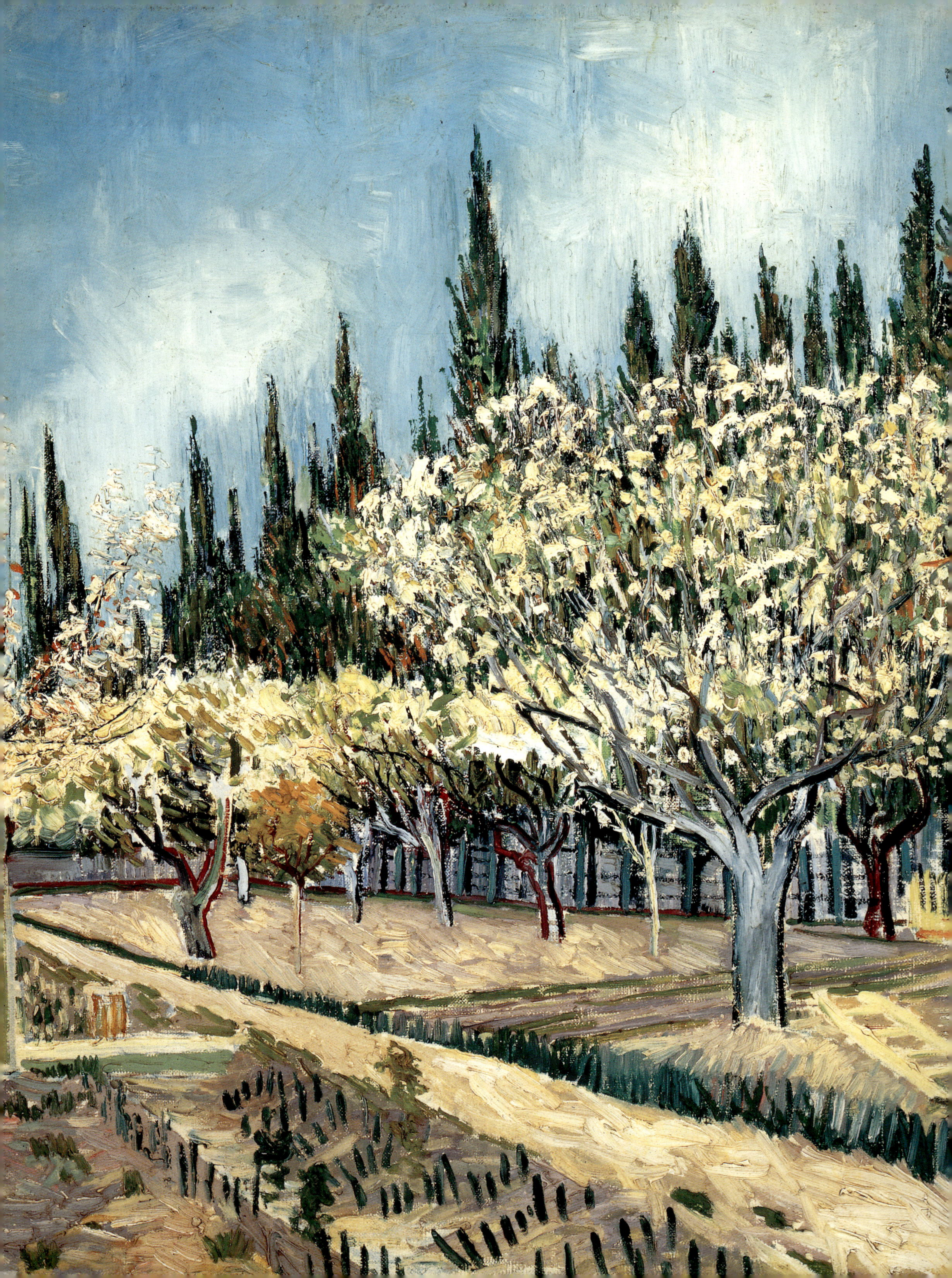

Annotations to Letter 3

Arles, ca. Thursday, 12 April, 1888

Textual Notes
a. inachevés— < inachevés
b. caracteristiques < carateristiques
c. This should be read as *si j'y vais tout de même.*

1. No such sketches are known. They would have been for the decoration of the wooden studio that had been built for Bernard in his parents' garden in Asnières. There may be a connection with the paintings of "flowers, [. . .] trees, [. . .] fields" mentioned by van Gogh in Letter 18. With thanks to Fred Leeman.

2. Van Gogh was working on two paintings of peach trees and pear trees: *Orchard Surrounded by Cypresses* (F 513 / JH 1389; Fig. 12) and *Orchard with Cypresses* (F 551 / JH 1396; Fig. 13).

3. The altered ductus at this point on the page indicates that Van Gogh first made the sketch *Orchard Surrounded by Cypresses* (F - / JH 1390) on the facing page before returning to the letter. He made two paintings of the subject: *Orchard Surrounded by Cypresses* (F 554 / JH 1388; Fig. 14) and *Orchard Surrounded by Cypresses* (F 513 / JH 1389; Fig. 12); the first, smaller work probably preceding the second. Judging from the composition and the color notations on the sketch, the latter probably was made after the first painting.

4. Van Gogh was suggesting that his style is in line with the cloisonism of Bernard and Anquetin (see Introduction, p. 10). The object of this tactical remark was to stress that they were all following the same path, whereas in fact he worked differently in several important respects, namely, out of doors and employing a coarse, visible brushstroke. Bernard painted in the studio and avoided impasto.

5. Vincent described this visit to the Roman arena in the center of the town in a letter to Theo written a few days earlier. "Yesterday I saw a bullfight where 5 men were working the ox with banderillas and rosettes. A toreador crushed one of his balls jumping over the barrier. He was a blond man with gray eyes and a lot of sangfroid, they said he'd feel it for a long time. He was dressed in sky blue and gold, just like the little horseman in our Monticelli with the 3 figures in a wood. The bullring looks so beautiful when there's sunshine and a crowd." (*Hier j'ai encore vu un combat de taureaux où 5 hommes travaillaient le boeuf avec des banderilles et des cocardes. Un toreador s'est écrasé une couille en sautant la barricade. C'était un homme blond aux yeux gris qui avait beaucoup de sang froid, ils disaient qu'il en aurait pour longtemps. Il était habillé en bleu céleste et or, absolument comme le petit cavalier dans notre Monticelli à 3 figures dans un bois. Les arènes sont fort belles lorsqu'il y a soleil et foule; CL* 474.)

6. Bernard had spent the summers of 1886 and 1887 in Brittany, mainly in Saint-Briac, and was preparing to go there again. He left for Saint-Briac on 23 April 1888. See Harscoët-Maire 1997, p. 162.

Detail of Fig. 12.

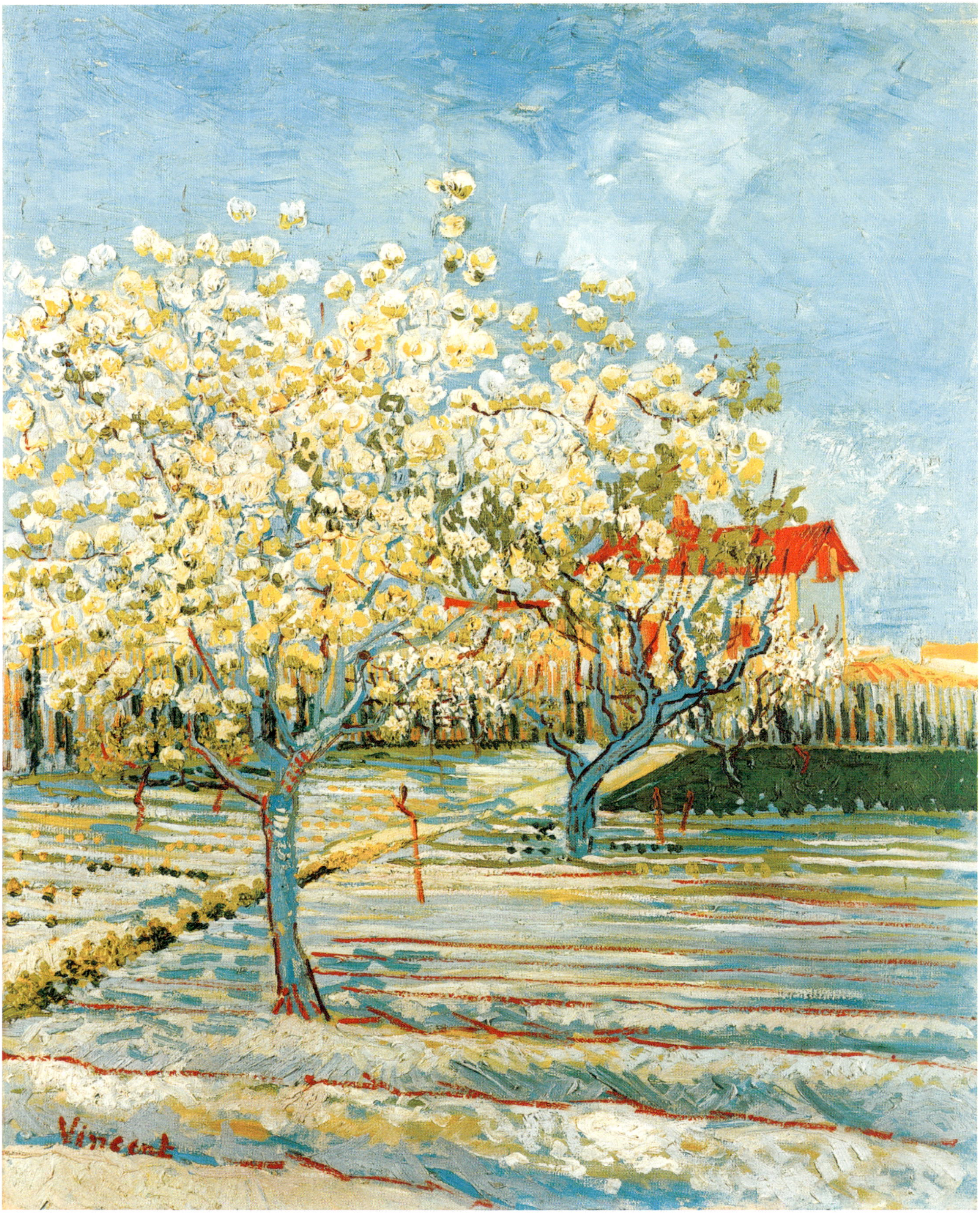
Vincent

Letter 4

Arles, Thursday, 19 April, 1888

Source
Original manuscript

Location
New York, Thaw Collection, The Morgan Library & Museum

Date
Van Gogh wrote: "Unfortunately there's rain today." The weather reports record that it rained heavily on Thursday, 19 April (*Météo-France*), so we have assigned this letter to that date.

Sketch
Orchard and House with Orange Roof (F - / JH 1401), letter sketch. Color notations: in the sky, *Bleu* (blue); beside the second tree, *arbre vert* (green tree); among the blossoms on the first tree, *Blanc* (white); on the patch of land in the foreground, *lilas* (lilac); beside the roof, *toit orangé* (orange roof); on the ground in front of the house, *vert* (green).

Bernard must have sounded rather depressed in his letter to which this is the reply, for van Gogh did everything he could to cheer him up. It is apparent from Bernard's correspondence with his family that on 11 April, shortly before his departure for Brittany, he had engaged in a furious row with his mother, the consequences of which must have echoed in his letter to van Gogh. The latter consequently paid him all kinds of compliments, applauded his intention of doing his military service in Algeria, and assured him that there was not a trace of spleen in the south. His praise of the sonnets might have had more weight had he repeated the words he had written to Theo: "I've had a letter from Bernard with some Sonnets that he's made, some of which are successful; he'll succeed in making a good sonnet, which I almost envy him."[1] He did not say that in this letter, but he did urge Bernard to carry on writing poetry.

At the time he wrote the letter he was completely immersed in painting orchards in blossom, as is shown by the letter sketch. The fact that he was thinking of using them for a "decoration," or a series to be hung in a room in a private house or an institution, may have been prompted in part by his friend, who had sent drawings of a decoration of his own (see Letter 3).

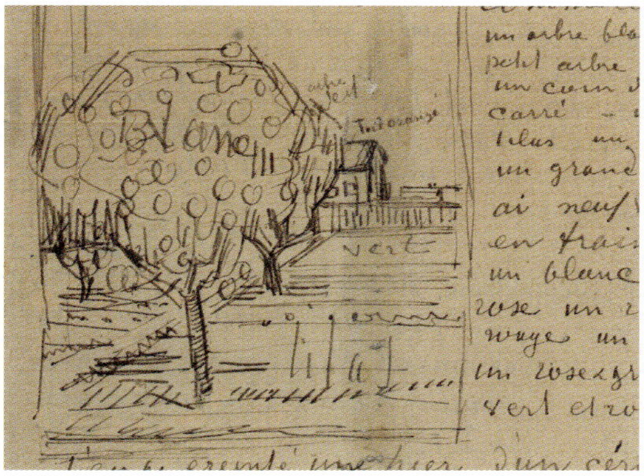

He was in good spirits and "enraptured by the scenery here," as he wrote the same day to the Australian painter John Peter Russell (*CL* 477a).

Bernard found van Gogh's encouraging letter waiting for him when he arrived in Saint-Briac on 24 April, where, until August 1888, he lived in a little house beside the inn run by Madame Lemasson. During the period he most likely got to know the writer and critic Albert Aurier, who was staying in nearby Saint-Enogat. Aurier wrote about modern art; together with Bernard, he was to become one of the early champions of van Gogh's work.

15. Vincent van Gogh, *Orchard and House with Orange Roof,* 1888 (F 406 / JH 1399). Private collection.

Translation of Letter 4 / Arles, Thursday, 19 April, 1888

My dear old Bernard,

Many thanks for sending your sonnets.[1] For form and sonority I very much like the first one, "Under the sleeping canopies of the gigantic trees." Now for idea and sentiment it's perhaps the last one that I prefer: "For hope has poured its nervousness into my breast," but it seems to me that what you want to evoke isn't stated clearly enough: the certainty that we seem to have and which anyway we can prove, of nothingness, of emptiness, of the treachery of desirable, good, or beautiful things, and despite this knowledge we forever allow ourselves to be deceived by the spell that external life, things outside ourselves, cast over our six senses, as though we knew nothing, and especially not the difference between objective and subjective. And fortunately for us, in that way we remain ignorant and hopeful. Now I also like "In winter, have neither a sou nor a flower,"[2] and "Contempt." "Corner of a chapel" and "Drawing by Albrecht Dürer" I find less clear. For example, precisely which drawing by Albrecht Dürer is it? But excellent passages in it nevertheless. "Having come from the blue plains, Made pale by the long miles" is a jolly good rendering of the landscapes bristling with blue rocks between which the roads wind in the backgrounds of Cranach and Van Eyck.

Twisted on his cross *in a spiral* is a very, very good rendering of the exaggerated thinness of the mystical Christs; why not add to it that the anguished expression of the martyr is like the eye of a brokenhearted cab horse?[3] That way it would be more utterly Parisian, where you see looks like that, either in the drivers of the little carriages or in poets and artists. But all in all it's not as good as your painting yet. Never mind. It'll come, and you must certainly continue doing sonnets.

Transcription of Letter 4 / Arles, Thursday, 19 April, 1888

Mon cher copain Bernard

merci beaucoup de ton envoi de sonnets.[1] j'aime beaucoup comme forme & sonorité le premier, "Sous les dômes dormeurs des arbres gigantesques." Maintenant comme idée & sentiment c'est peutêtre le dernier que je préfère: Car l'espoir dans mon sein a versé sa névrose, mais il me semble que c'est pas assez clairement dit, ce que tu veux donner à sentir: la certitude qu'on semble avoir et qu'on peut en tout cas prouver, du néant, du vide, de la trahison des chôses désirables, bonnes ou belles, et malgré cette science on se laisse duper éternellement par le charme qu'exercent sur nos 6 sens la vie exterieure, les choses en dehors de nous comme si l'on ne savait rien et surtout pas la différence entre objectif et subjectif. et heureusement pour nous nous restons bêtes et espérants ainsi. maintenant j'aime aussi "l'hyver n'avoir ni sou ni fleurs"[2] et Mépris. Coin de chapelle & Dessin d'Albert Durer, je les trouve moins clairs, par exemple, quel est le dessin d'Albert Durer au juste? mais là-dedans des passages excellents neamoins. "Venus des plaines bleues, Blémis par la longueur des lieues" rend joliment bien les paysages hérissés de rocs bleus entre lesquels serpentent des chemins des fonds de Cranach & de v. Eyck.

Tordu sur sa croix en spirale *rend fort fort bien la maigreur exagerée des Christs mystiques, pourquoi pas y ajouter que le regard angoissé du martyr est comme l'oeil d'un cheval de fiacre navré,[3] ce serait ainsi plus parisien de Paris où on voit des regards comme ca soit chez les pensionaires des petites voitures soit chez les poètes & artistes. Mais en somme c'est pas si bien que ta peinture encore. n'importe. ça viendra et faut surement continuer les sonnets.*

There are so many people, especially among our pals, who imagine that words are nothing. On the contrary, don't you think, it's as interesting and as difficult to say a thing well as to paint a thing. There's the art of lines and colors, but there's the art of words that will last just the same.[4] *[sketch]* Here's a new orchard, quite simple in composition: a white tree, a small green tree, a square corner of greenery—a lilac field, an orange roof, a big blue sky.[5] Have nine orchards in progress; one white, one pink, one almost red pink, one white and blue, one pink and gray, one green and pink.[6]

I worked one to death yesterday, of a cherry tree against blue sky, the young shoots of the leaves were orange and gold, the clusters of flowers white. That, against the blue green of the sky, was darned glorious. Unfortunately there's rain today, which prevents me going back on the attack.

Saw a brothel here on Sunday (not to mention the other days), a large room tinged with a bluish limewash—like a village school—a good fifty or so red soldiers and black civilians, with faces of a magnificent yellow or orange (what tones in the faces down here), the women in sky blue, in vermilion, everything that's of the purest and gaudiest. All of it in yellow light. Far less gloomy than the establishments of the same kind in Paris. Spleen is not in the air down here. At present I'm still keeping very quiet and very calm, because first I have to get over a stomach ailment of which I am the happy owner, but afterwards I'll have to make a lot of noise, because I aspire to share the renown of the immortal Tartarin de Tarascon.[7]

It interested me enormously that you intend spending your time in Algeria. That's perfect and a hell of a long way from being a misfortune. Truly, I congratulate you on it. We'll see each other in Marseille in any case.

Il y a tant de gens surtout dans les copains qui s'imaginent que les paroles ne sont rien. Au contraire n'est ce pas, c'est aussi intéressant & aussi difficile de bien dire une chôse que de peindre une chôse. Il y a l'art des lignes & couleurs mais l'art des paroles y est et y restera pas moins.[4] [sketch] *Voici un nouveau verger, assez simple comme composition, un arbre blanc, un petit arbre vert, un coin de verdure carré—un terrain lilas, un toit orangé, un grand ciel bleu.*[5] *ai neuf vergers en train, un blanc, un rose, un rose presque rouge, un blanc & bleu, un rose & gris, un vert et rose.*[6]

J'en ai ereinté une hier d'un cérisier contre ciel bleu, les jeunes pousses des feuilles étaient de l'orangé et de l'or, les touffes de fleurs blanches. Cela contre le bleu vert du ciel était rudement glorieux. Malheureusement voilà la pluie aujourd'hui qui m'empêche de revenir à la charge.

Ai vu un bordel ici le dimanche (sans compter les autres jours), une grande salle teinte à la chaux bleuie—comme une ecole de village—une bonne cinquantaine de militaires rouges et de bourgeois noirs aux visages d'un magnifique jaune ou orangé (quels tons dans les visages d'ici), les femmes en bleu céleste, en vermillon, tout ce qu'il y a de plus entier & de plus criard.—Tout cela eclairé de jaune. Bien moins lugubre que les administrations du même genre à Paris. Le spleen n'est pas dans l'air d'ici. Actuellement je me tiens encore très coit[a] *et très-tranquille puisque je dois d'abord guérir un dérangement d'estomac dont je suis l'heureux propriétaire mais après il faudra faire beaucoup de bruit car j'y aspire à partager la gloire de l'immortel Tartarin de Tarascon.*[7]

Cela m'a énormément intéressé que tu aies l'intention de passer ton temps en Algérie.—C'est parfait et rudement loin d'être un malheur. Vraiment je t'en félicite. Nous nous verrons dans tous les cas à Marseille.

You'll find that you'll enjoy seeing the blue down here and feeling the sun.

I now have a terrace for a studio.[8]

I really intend to go and do seascapes, too, in Marseille, and I don't pine here for the gray sea of the north. If you see Gauguin, greet him warmly for me; I must write to him in a moment.[9]

My dear old Bernard, don't despair and above all, don't be downhearted, my good fellow, because with your talent and your stay in Algeria, you'll be a hell of a good artist. True—you'll be a southerner, too. If I have a piece of advice to give you, it's to build yourself up by eating healthy and simple things for a year beforehand, *yes*. Starting now. Because it's better not to come here with a ruined stomach or spoiled blood. That was the case with me, and although I'm recovering, I'm recovering slowly, and I regret not having been a little more prudent beforehand. But who can do anything in a bloody winter like this one, because it was a preternatural winter. So see that your blood's good beforehand; with the bad food here it's difficult to regain that, but once you're healthy it's less difficult to stay that way than in Paris.

Write to me soon, still same address, Restaurant Carrel, Arles. Handshake.

Ever yours,
Vincent

Tu verras que cela te fera du plaisir de voir le bleu d'ici et de sentir le soleil.

J'ai pour atelier maintenant une terrasse.[8]

J'ai bien l'intention d'aller faire des marines aussi à Marseille et je ne languis pas ici d'après la mer grise du Nord. Si tu vois Gauguin dis lui bien le bonjour pour moi, je dois justement lui écrire.[9]

Mon cher copain Bernard, ne désespères pas et n'aies surtout pas le spleen, mon bon, car avec ton talent et ton séjour en Algérie tu seras un rudement bon artiste. Vrai—Tu seras aussi du Midi. Si j'ai un conseil à te donner c'est de te fortifier de manger des chôses saines et simples un an d'avance, oui.—*Dès maintenant. Parceque il vaut mieux ne pas venir ici l'estomac délabré ou le sang vicié. Moi j'étais dans ce cas et quoique je guéris je guéris lentement et je regrette de ne pas avoir été un peu plus prudent d'avance. Mais par un sacré hiver comme celui ci qui est-ce qui y peut rien puisque c'etait un hiver surhumain. Fais toi donc du bon sang*[b] *d'avance, ici avec la mauvaise nourriture c'est difficile de s'en refaire mais une fois qu'on est sain il est moins difficile qu'à Paris de le rester.*

Ecris moi bientôt, toujours même adresse, Restaurant Carrel Arles. Poignée de main.

t. à t.
Vincent

Annotations to Letter 4

Arles, Thursday, 19 April, 1888

Textual Notes

a. This should be read as *coi*. The slip of the pen may have been due to the context; *coït* means "intercourse."
b. The expression *se faire du bon sang* means "to enjoy oneself," but van Gogh used it literally here as a bit of wordplay, because he was well aware of the figurative sense (*CL* 462).

1. None of these sonnets is now known, except for "L'hiver" (see n. 2).

2. Bernard included the sonnet *"A feu Joseph Delorme"* (1887) in *Le Voyage de l'être. Poèmes d'évolution*:

In winter, have neither a sou nor a flower,	*L'hiver, n'avoir ni sou, ni fleurs,*
To freeze under the roof, on the sixth floor;	*Glacer sous le toit, au sixième;*
To drown your pillow in your tears	*Noyer son oreiller de pleurs*
While crying that you suffer and you love.	*En criant qu'on souffre et qu'on aime.*
Never to see her: as you burn,	*Ne la voir jamais: plein d'ardeurs*
To long for her with love's keenest desire,	*La désirer d'amour extrême,*
Resigned to decent stratagems	*Et se résoudre à des pudeurs*
To bring the problem to an end.	*Pour la conclusion du problème.*
To stay within doors, closely penned up, alone;	*Rester chez-soi, bien claustré, seul;*
To waste, to die, to turn a deathly pale . . .	*Maigrir, mourir, devenir blême . . .*
Or see the snow, that dismal sign,	*Ou voir la neige, sombre emblême,*
Cast o'er the earth a shroud;	*Jeter sur la terre un linceul;*
To muse that it's for you, perhaps . . .	*Songer qu'il est pour soi, peut-être . . .*
—'Twere better had you not been born.	*—Mieux aurait valu ne pas naître.*

See Bernard 1898, p. 36.

3. Van Gogh repeatedly used the image of a worn-out coach horse as a metaphor for man's arduous life. On 17 March 1888, for instance, he had written to Theo about "poor Paris cab horses like yourself and several of our friends, the poor impressionists" (*les pauvres chevaux de fiacre de Paris qui sont toi-meme et plusieurs de nos amis, les impressionistes pauvres; CL* 469). Back in Holland he had read the poetry of François Coppée, who had dealt with the subject in his "Cheval de Renfort" (in the collection *Le Cahier Rouge*). See *Poésies de François Coppée*. Paris 1880, p. 163.

4. Bernard paraphrased these words of van Gogh's in a letter to his parents of Thursday, 26 April, 1888. He used van Gogh's reaction as an argument for continuing with his poetic aspirations. See Introduction, p. 13. According to Gauguin, one of van Gogh's favorite sayings was "stone will perish, the word will remain" (*la pierre périra, la parole restera*). See Pickvance 1992, p. 133.

5. This letter sketch (Vincent also sent one to Theo in letter *CL* 478) is based on *Orchard and House with Orange Roof* (F 406 / JH 1399; Fig. 15).

6. In a letter to Theo written about a week earlier (*CL* 477), Vincent gave more details about this series of nine orchards, making sketches of the first three and of the central scene of the second triad, supplying a more precise description. This makes it possible to identify those four works with absolute certainty. They are *Orchard with Blossoming Apricot Trees* (F 555 / JH 1380; Amsterdam, Van Gogh Museum), *Pink Peach Trees* (F 404 / JH 1391; Amsterdam, Van Gogh Museum), *Orchard with Blossoming Plum Trees (The White Orchard;* F 403 / JH 1378; Amsterdam, Van Gogh Museum) and *Little Blossoming Pear Tree* (F 405 / JH 1394; Fig. 16). It is also clear from the same letter that the last work was flanked by two horizontal canvases, probably *Orchard with Blossoming Plum Trees and Factory* (F 553 / JH 1387; Edinburgh, National Gallery of Scotland) and *Orchard with Blossoming Plum Trees* (F 556 / JH 1383; private collection). The third triad was only in a preparatory stage. It certainly contained *Orchard Surrounded by Cypresses* (F 513 / JH 1389; Fig. 12), *Orchard with Cypresses* (F 551 / JH 1396; Fig. 13), and probably also the study of the cherry tree that van Gogh reported in this letter as having been ruined. The ninth work must therefore be the new painting, *Orchard and House with Orange Roof* (F 406 / JH 1399; Fig. 15).

7. "Make a lot of noise" *(Faire beaucoup de bruit)* is an allusion to the Provençal battle cry that features several times in Alphonse Daudet's *Tartarin sur les Alpes* (1885). It first appears in Chapter 7: "That terrible war cry in the Tarascon dialect: 'Fen dé brut! . . . let's make a noise . . . .'" (*Ce terrible cri de guerre en patois tarasconnais: "Fen dé brut! . . . faisons du bruit . . .* "). See Daudet 1986–94, vol. 3, pp. 614 (quotation), 626 (Chapter 8), and 635 (Chapter 10).

Like the first volume in the series, *Tartarin de Tarascon* (1872), this satirical novel pokes fun at the people of the south of France, particularly the inhabitants of Tarascon. The protagonist, Tartarin, a self-styled lion hunter and chairman of the Alpine Club of Tarascon (the members of which have never gone beyond the hills of the nearby Alpilles), sets out for Switzerland in order to conquer the highest peaks in the Alps and strengthen his position for the forthcoming election of a new chairman. Tartarin is a windbag who tries to extricate himself without loss of face from difficult situations that he has created himself.

8. The covered roof terrace that van Gogh used as a studio was that of Hotel-Restaurant Carrel, where he was living. See Letter 2, n. 6. He told Theo that he dried his paintings there (*CL* 478).

9. Gauguin was in Pont-Aven in Brittany from the end of January until his departure for Arles on 21 October. He stayed in the boardinghouse run by Marie Jeanne Gloanec-Morvan, which was popular with other impoverished artists.

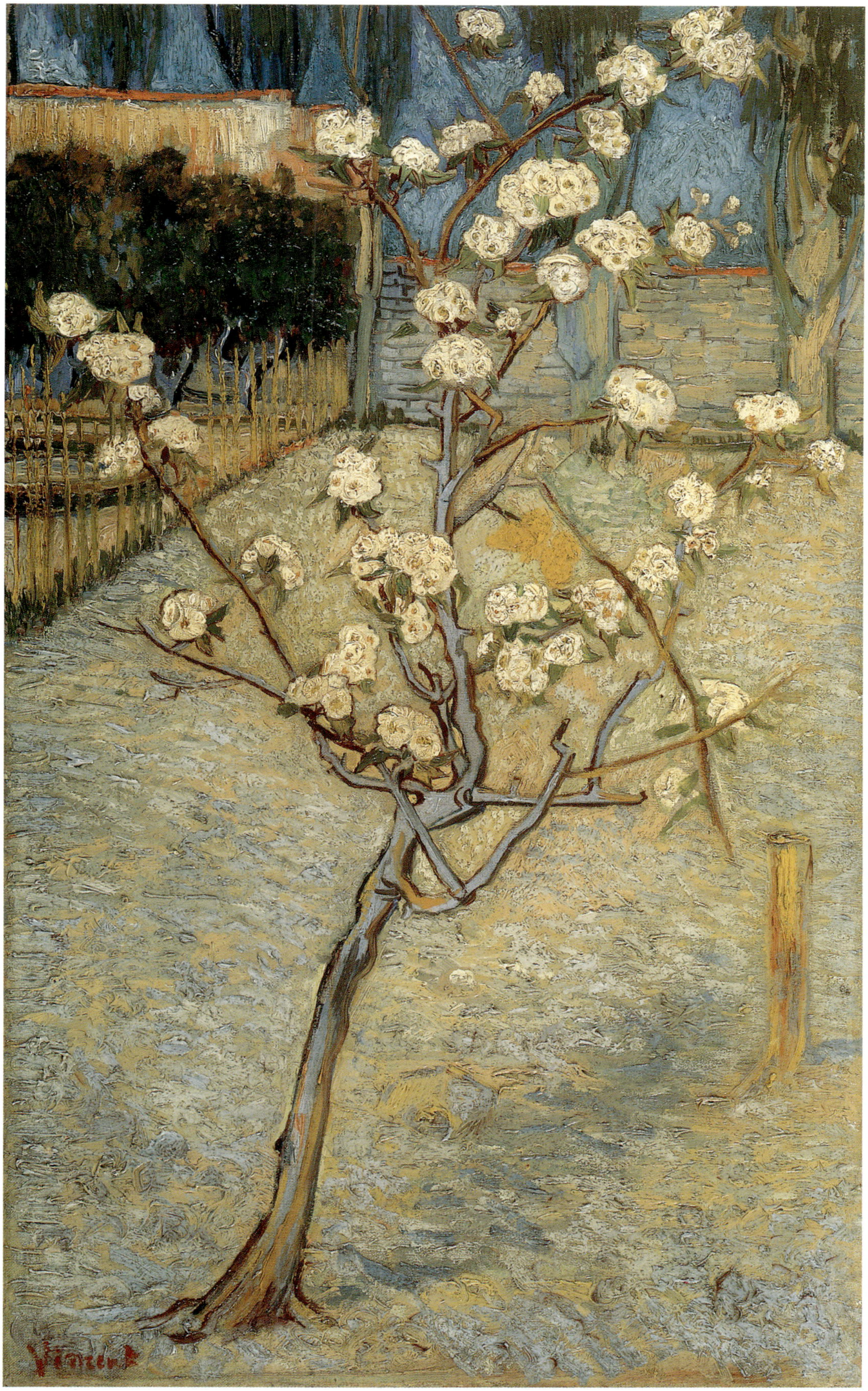

16. Vincent van Gogh, *Little Blossoming Pear Tree,* 1888 (F 405 / JH 1394). Amsterdam, Van Gogh Museum (Vincent van Gogh Foundation).

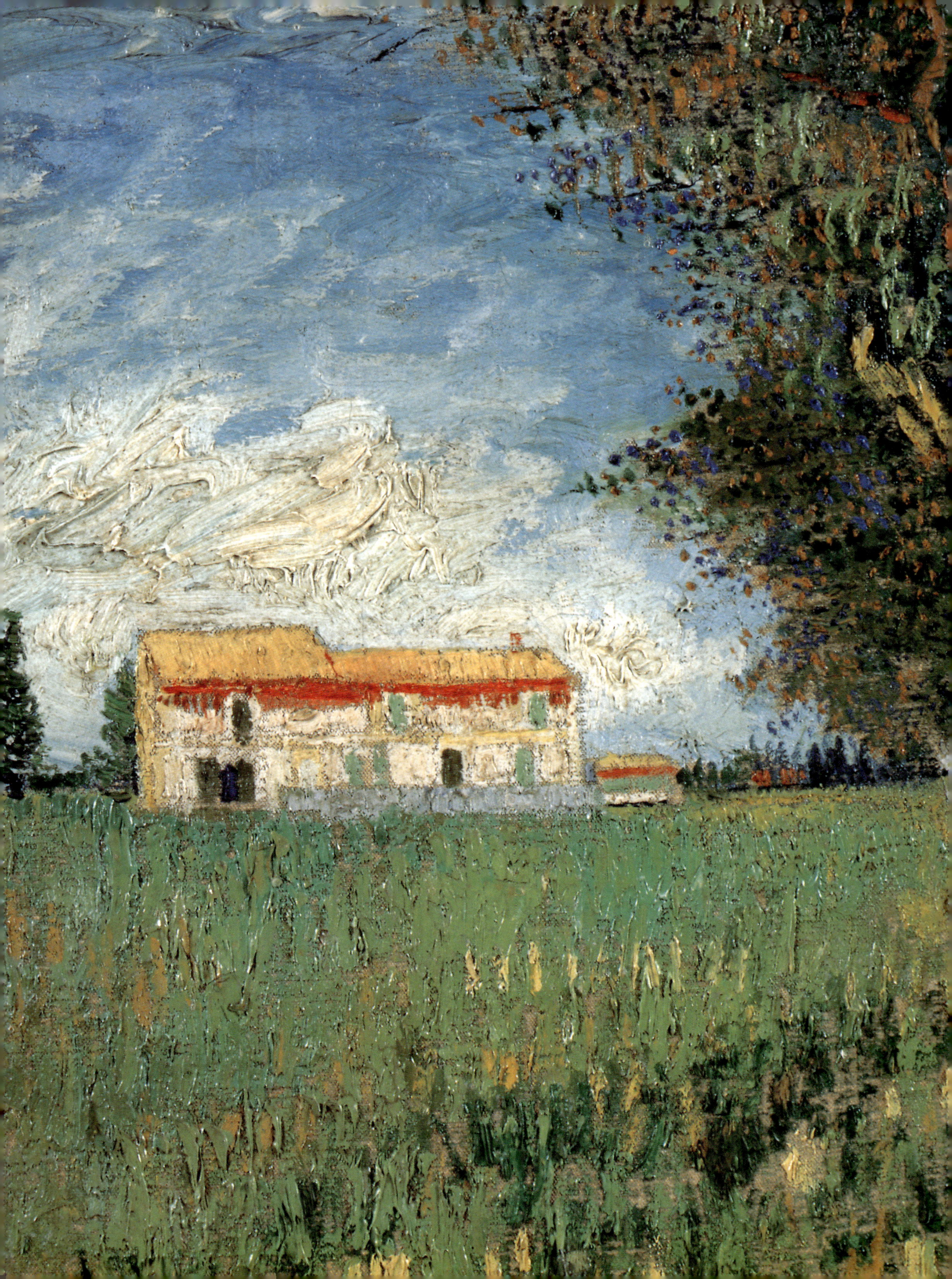

Letter 5

Arles, ca. Tuesday, 22 May, 1888

Source
Original manuscript

Location
New York, Thaw Collection, The Morgan Library & Museum

Date
Van Gogh described the same works as those in letter *CL* 489 of about 20 May to Theo, and mentioned a new still life, so this letter would have been written not long after that one. He had evidently not started on the drawings that he sent to Theo around 26 May (letter *CL* 490), for he made no mention of them here. It is for these reasons that we have dated the letter ca. Tuesday, 22 May, 1888.

Arrangement
It is suggested in *De brieven* 1990 that the sketch *Still Life with Coffeepot* (F - / JH 1428) belonged with this letter. That is incorrect; it was in fact sent with Letter 6.

Additional details
Bernard told his parents about this letter on Monday, 28 May, 1888: "Vincent has written me a very nice letter. He has rented a house in Arles. What appealed to him was that it's yellow, with all the walls whitewashed. . . . He's not in very good health, he says. Let's hope it won't be serious. . . . He's an excellent friend." (*Vincent m'a écrit une très jolie lettre. Il a loué une maison à Arles. Ce qui l'a séduit c'est qu'elle est jaune, avec tous les murs peints à la chaux. . . . Il n'est pas très bien portant, dit-il. Espérons que cela sera pas grave. . . . C'est un excellent ami*). See Harscoët-Maire 1997, p. 171.

It was a month before van Gogh wrote to Bernard again; his excuses suggest that the latter had recently pleaded for a sign of life. One important event of the preceding month was van Gogh's renting the Yellow House in Arles. He could now concentrate on his dream of a studio that he would share with other artists, where they could work together and exchange ideas. Not the least attractive aspect of the plan was that it would reduce living expenses. Vincent first mentioned the possibility of sharing the studio with Gauguin in a letter to Theo of 1 May.

Bernard was so hard at work that he barely had time "to commit the follies that go with my age," as he put it to his family.[1] Here he was trying to make it appear that he was not distracted by his love for Marie Lemasson, the daughter of the innkeeper with whom he was lodging. He wrote to his mother on 4 May to tell her that he was making a large painting of a procession. "I'm going to do a kind of set of portraits of all the people of the area; the Lemasson family will appear in this painting, as well as several others whom you do not know."[2] He was still working on the painting, which is now lost, on 16

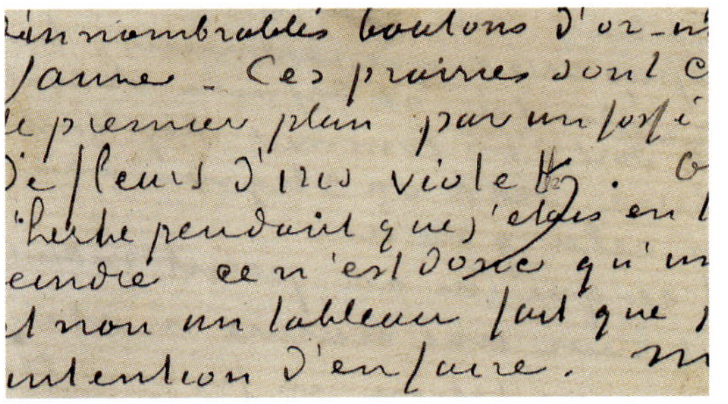
innombrables boutons d'or
jaune. Ces prairies sont
le premier plan par un fossé
de fleurs d'iris violettes.
l'herbe pendant que j'étais en
peindre ce n'est donc qu'un
et non un tableau fait que
intention d'en faire.

May, and reported that he had other studies as well: " . . . one, among others, very large, showing Saint-Briac in blossom. It's raining, snowing from fruit trees, apple trees, apricot trees, pear trees, cherry trees in blossom; orchard walls, meadows, wild trees, and groups of houses appear here and there."[3]

Detail of Fig. 23.

Translation of Letter 5 / Arles, ca. Tuesday, 22 May, 1888

My dear Bernard,

I've just received your last letter—you're quite right to see that those negresses[1] were heartrending—you're quite right not to find it innocent.

I've just read a book—not beautiful and not well written, by the way—on the *Marquesas Islands,*[2] but very heartrending in its description of the extermination of an entire tribe of natives—cannibals in the sense that let's say an individual was eaten once a month, and what of that?

The whites, very Christian, etc., to put an end to this barbarity? REALLY NOT VERY SAVAGE. . . . could think of nothing better than to exterminate both the tribe of cannibal natives and the tribe with which the former was at war (in order to obtain the requisite edible prisoners of war on both sides). Then the two islands were annexed, and did they become dismal!!! Those tattooed races, those negroes, those Indians, everything, everything, everything disappears or is corrupted. And the frightful white man, with his bottle of alcohol, his wallet and his pox, when will we have seen enough of him! The frightful white man, with his hypocrisy, his greed and his sterility! And those savages were so gentle and so loving.

Ah, you do darned well to think of Gauguin—they're high poetry, his negresses—and everything his hand makes has a sweet, heartrending, astonishing character. People don't understand him yet, and he suffers greatly from not selling, like other true poets.[3]

My dear pal, I would have written to you sooner, only have had quite a few things on my hands; I've sent a first batch of studies to my brother is one,[4] I've had trouble with my health is two, and

---

Transcription of Letter 5 / Arles, ca. Tuesday, 22 May, 1888

Mon cher Bernard,

je viens de recevoir ta dernière lettre—tu as bien raison de voir que ces négresses[1] *étaient navrantes—tu as bien raison de ne pas trouver cela innocent.*

Je viens de lire un livre—pas beau et pas bien écrit d'ailleurs—sur les Iles Marquises,[2] *mais bien navrant lorsqu'il raconte l'extermination de toute une tribu d'indigènes—antropophages dans ce sens que disons une fois par mois on mangeait un individu, qu'est ce que ça fait?*

Les blancs, très crétiens, etc., pour mettre fin à cette barbarie? RÉELLEMENT PEU FÉROCE. . . . *n'ont pas trouvé mieux que d'exterminer*[a] *et la tribu des indigenes antropophages et la tribu avec laquelle la première guerroyait (pour se procurer ainsi de part et d'autre les prisonniers de guerre mangeables nécessaires). Ensuite on a annexé les deux îles, qui sont devenus d'un lugubre!!! Ces races tatouées, ces nègres, ces indiens, tout tout tout disparaît ou se vicie. Et l'affreux blanc avec sa bouteille d'alcool, son porte-monnaie et sa vérole, quand donc l'aura-t on assez vu! L'affreux blanc avec son hypocrisie, son avarice et sa stérilité. Et ces sauvages etaient si doux et si amoureux.*

Ah tu fais rudement bien de penser à Gauguin—c'est de la haute poesie ses négresses—et tout ce que fait sa main a un caractère doux navré étonnant. On ne le comprend pas encore et lui souffre beaucoup de ne pas vendre, comme d'autres vrais poètes.[3]

Mon cher copain je t'aurais déjà écrit plus tôt,[b] *seulement ai eu pas mal de chôses sur les bras, j'ai expedié un premier envoi d'études à mon frère*[4] *et d'un, j'ai eu du mal avec ma santé et de deux, et de trois j'ai loué une maison peint en jaune en dehors, blanchie à la chaux en dedans, en plein soleil (4 pieces).*[5]

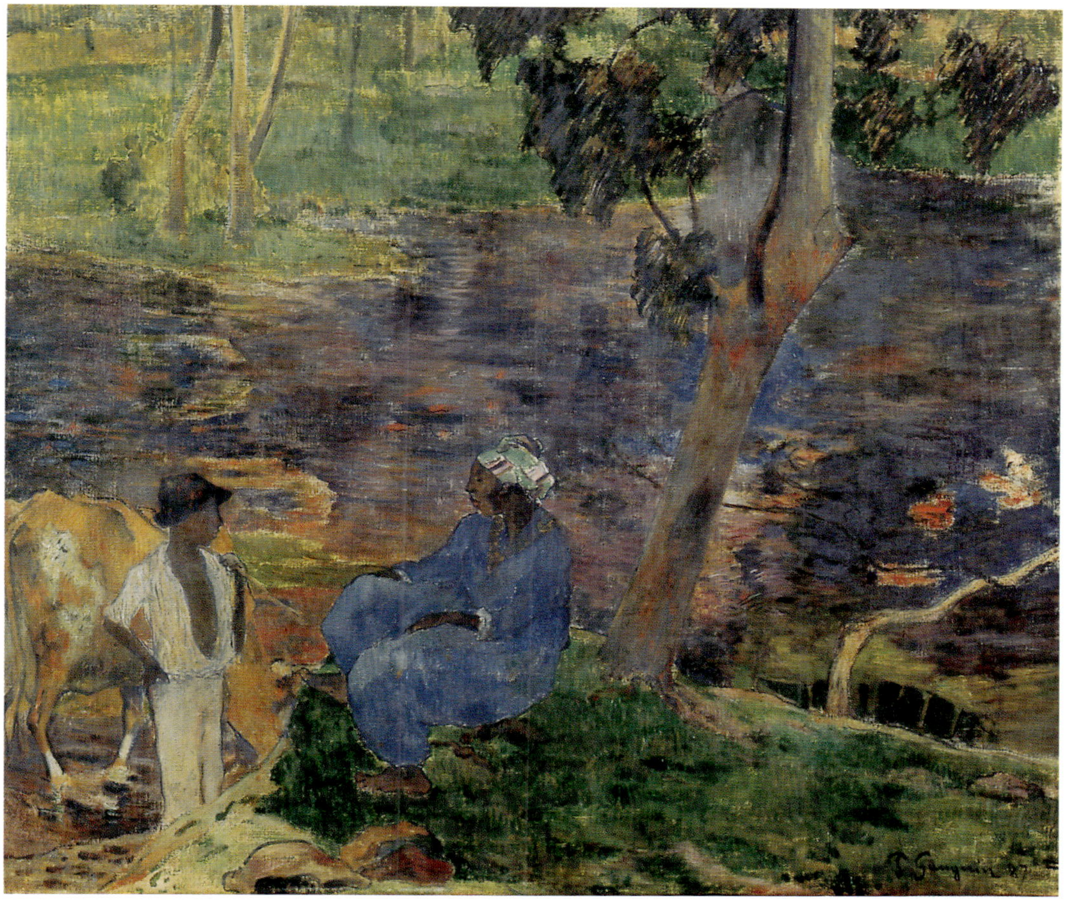

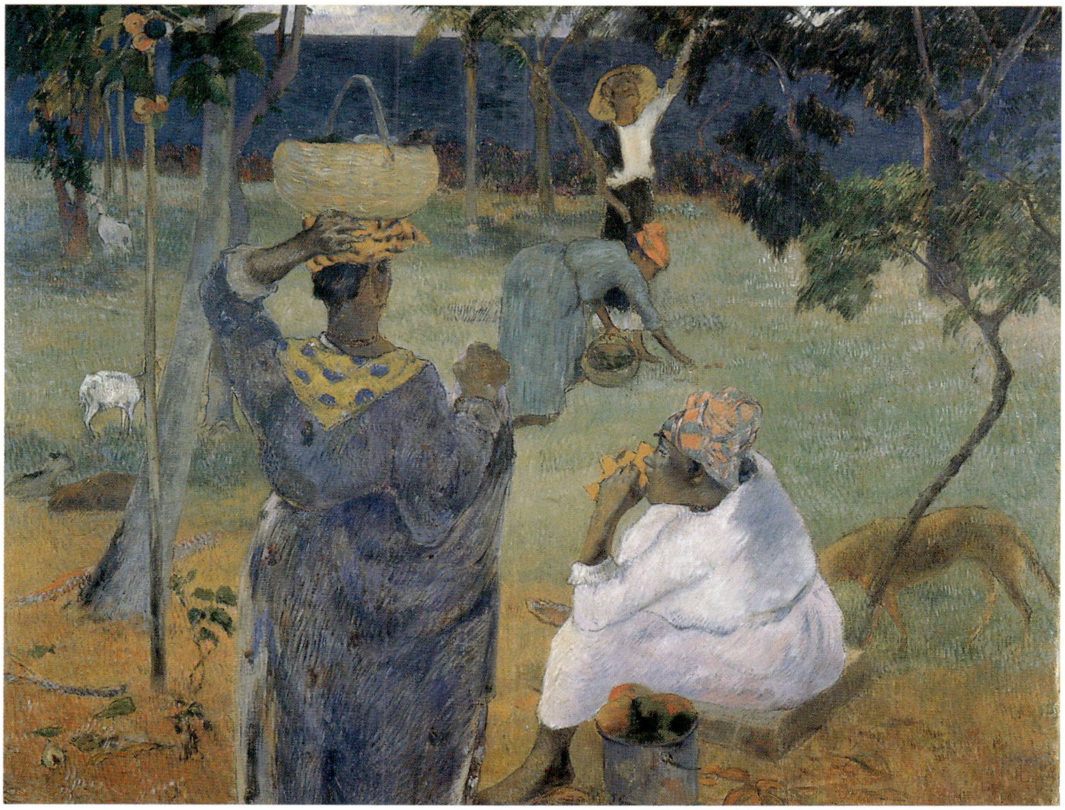

17. Paul Gauguin, *On the Shore of the Lake, Martinique*, 1887 (W252/W222). Amsterdam, Van Gogh Museum (Vincent van Gogh Foundation).

18. Paul Gauguin, *Among the Mangoes*, 1887 (W250/W224). Amsterdam, Van Gogh Museum (Vincent van Gogh Foundation).

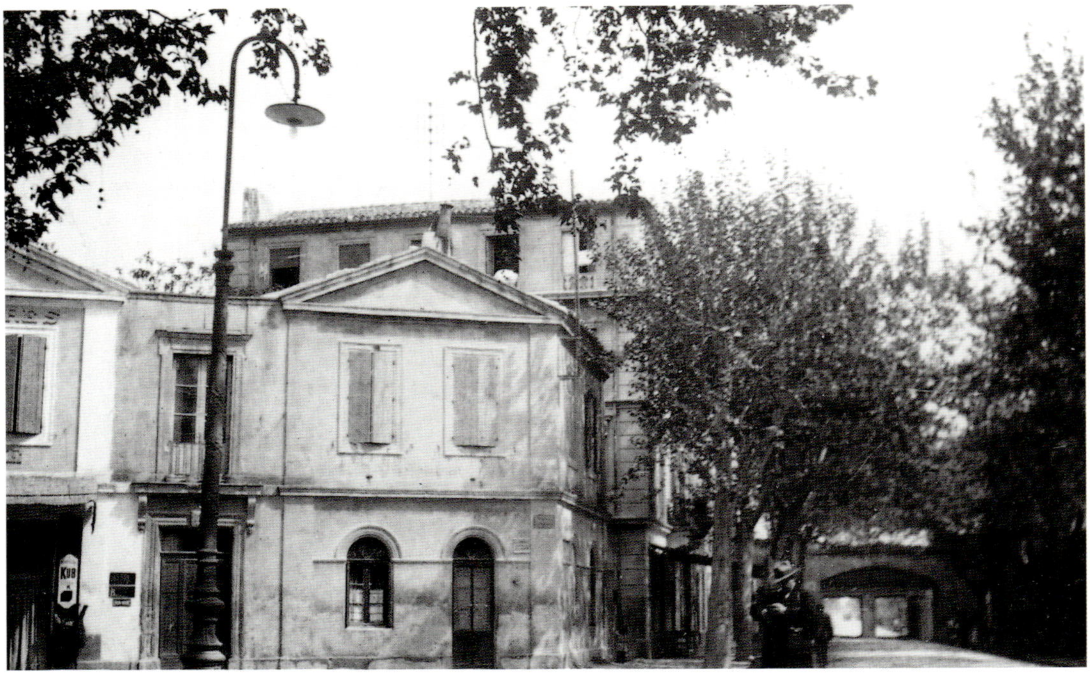

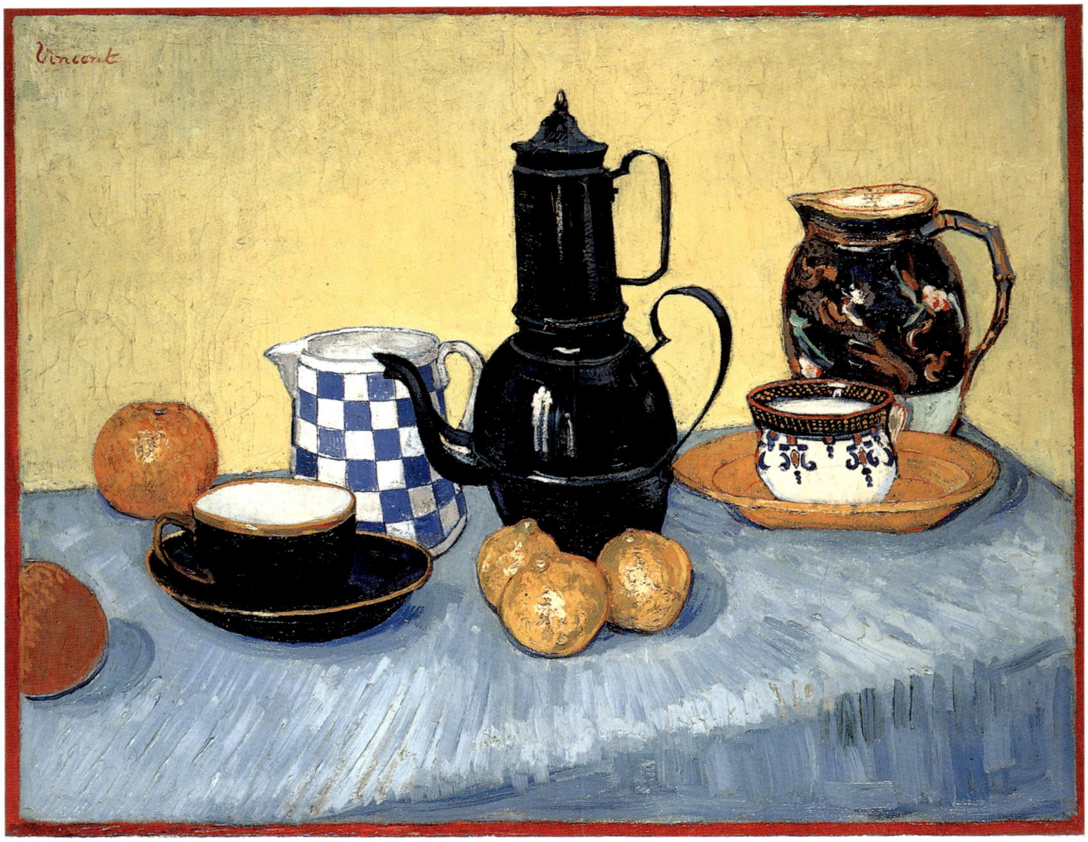

19. *The Yellow House, Place Lamartine, Arles.* Photographed by John Rewald. Amsterdam, Van Gogh Museum (Documentation).
20. Vincent van Gogh, *Still Life with Coffeepot,* 1888 (F 410 / JH 1426). Private collection.

three is that I've rented a house painted yellow outside, whitewashed inside, in the full sun (four rooms).[5]

With all that, new studies in progress. And in the evening I was often too numbed to write.

That's why my reply was delayed.

Listen, the sonnet about the women of the boulevard has some good things, but it isn't there yet—the end's banal.

A "sublime" woman, I don't know what you mean by that, nor do you in this case.

Then

"Hunting among the clan of old and young
Those whom she'll take to bed late at night."[6]

Something like that—It's not characteristic, because the women of our boulevard—*le petit*[7]—usually sleep *alone* at night because they screw five or six times during the day or the evening and—late at night it's that honorable carnivore, their pimp, who comes to collect them and take them home; yes, but he doesn't sleep with them (only rarely). The worn-out and haggard woman usually goes to bed alone and sleeps a leaden sleep. But with two or three lines redone, it'll be there.

What have you painted now? I myself have done a still life with—a coffeepot in blue enameled iron—a royal blue cup and saucer, a milk jug with pale cobalt and white checks, a cup with orange and blue designs on a white background, a blue majolica jug with green, brown, pink flowers and foliage, all of it on a blue tablecloth against a yellow background. With these pieces of crockery,

---

Avec tout cela de nouvelles études en train.—Et le soir j'étais souvent trop abruti pour écrire.

Voila pourquoi ma réponse a tardé.

Ecoute, le sonnet des femmes du boulevard a du bon mais n'y est pas—la fin est banale.

une femme "sublime," je ne sais pas ce que tu entends par là ni toi non plus dans ce cas.

Ensuite

"dans le clan des vieux et des jeunes maraude
Ceux qu'elle emmenera coucher le soir très tard."[6]

quelque chôse comme ca—c'est pas caractéristique car les femmes de notre boulevard—du petit[7]*—d'habitude couchent* seules *la nuit car elles tirent 5 ou 6 coups dans la journee ou le soir et—très tard c'est cet honorable carnivore, leur maquereau, qui vient les chercher et les reconduire, oui, mais il ne couche pas avec (que rarement). la femme éreintée et defaite se couche seule d'habitude et dort d'un sommeil de plomb. Mais avec deux ou 3 lignes de refaites cela y sera.*

Qu'est ce que tu as peint maintenant? J'ai fait moi une nature morte avec—une cafetière en fer emaillé bleu—une tasse & soucoupe bleu de roi, un pot au lait carrelé cobalt pâle et blanc, une tasse avec dessins orangés et bleus sur fond blanc, un pot en majolique bleu avec fleurs & feuillages verts, bruns, roses, tout cela sur une nappe bleue sur un fond jaune. Avec ces poteries 2 oranges & trois citrons.[8] *C'est donc une variation de bleus égayée par une serie de jaunes qui vont jusqu'à l'orangé.*

Puis j'ai une autre nature morte, des citrons dans un panier sur fond jaune.[9]

Puis une vue d'Arles—de la ville on n'apercoit que quelques toits rouges et une tour, le reste est cachée par de la verdure de figuiers &c.

two oranges, and three lemons.[8] It's thus a variation of blues enlivened by a series of yellows ranging all the way to orange.

Then I have another still life, some lemons in a basket against a yellow background.[9]

Then a view of Arles—of the town you see only a few red roofs and a tower, the rest's hidden by the foliage of fig trees, etc.

All that far off in the background and a narrow strip of blue sky above. The town is surrounded by vast meadows decked with innumerable buttercups—a yellow sea. These meadows are intersected in the foreground by a ditch full of purple irises.[10] They cut the grass while I was painting, so it's only a study and not a finished painting, which I intended to make of it. But what a subject—eh—that sea of yellow flowers with a line of purple irises and in the background the neat little town of pretty women. Then two studies of roadsides—afterwards—done out in the mistral.[11]

If you were not expecting my reply right away, I'd make sketches. Courage, good luck, handshake. I'm worn out this evening.

I'll write to you again one of these days, more at my ease.

Vincent

P.S. The sketch of the woman in the last letter but one is really pretty.[12]
My address:
Place Lamartine 2
Arles

Cela tout au fond et une bande étroite de ciel bleu dessus. La ville est entourée d'immenses prairies toutes fleuries d'innombrables boutons d'or—une mer jaune.—Ces prairies sont coupés sur le premier plan par un fossé rempli de fleurs d'iris violettes.[10] *On a coupé l'herbe pendant que j'etais en train de peindre, ce n'est donc qu'une étude et non un tableau fait que j'avais l'intention d'en faire. Mais quel motif—hein—cette mer de fleurs jaunes avec une barre d'iris violets et au fond la coquette petite ville aux jolies femmes. Puis deux études de bords de route—après—faites en plein mistral.*[11]

Si tu n'attendais pas ma réponse de suite je ferais croquis. Bon courage, bonne chance, poignée de main. Je suis ereinté ce soir.

Je t'écris de nouveau de ces jours ci plus à mon aise.

Vincent

P.S. le croquis de femme dans l'avant-dernière lettre est bien joli.[12]
Mon adresse:
Place Lamartine 2
Arles

---

21. Vincent van Gogh, *Basket with Lemons,* 1888 (F 384 / JH 1425). Otterlo, Kröller-Müller Museum.
22. Vincent van Gogh, *Field with Flowers,* 1888 (F 409 / JH 1416). Amsterdam, Van Gogh Museum (Vincent van Gogh Foundation).

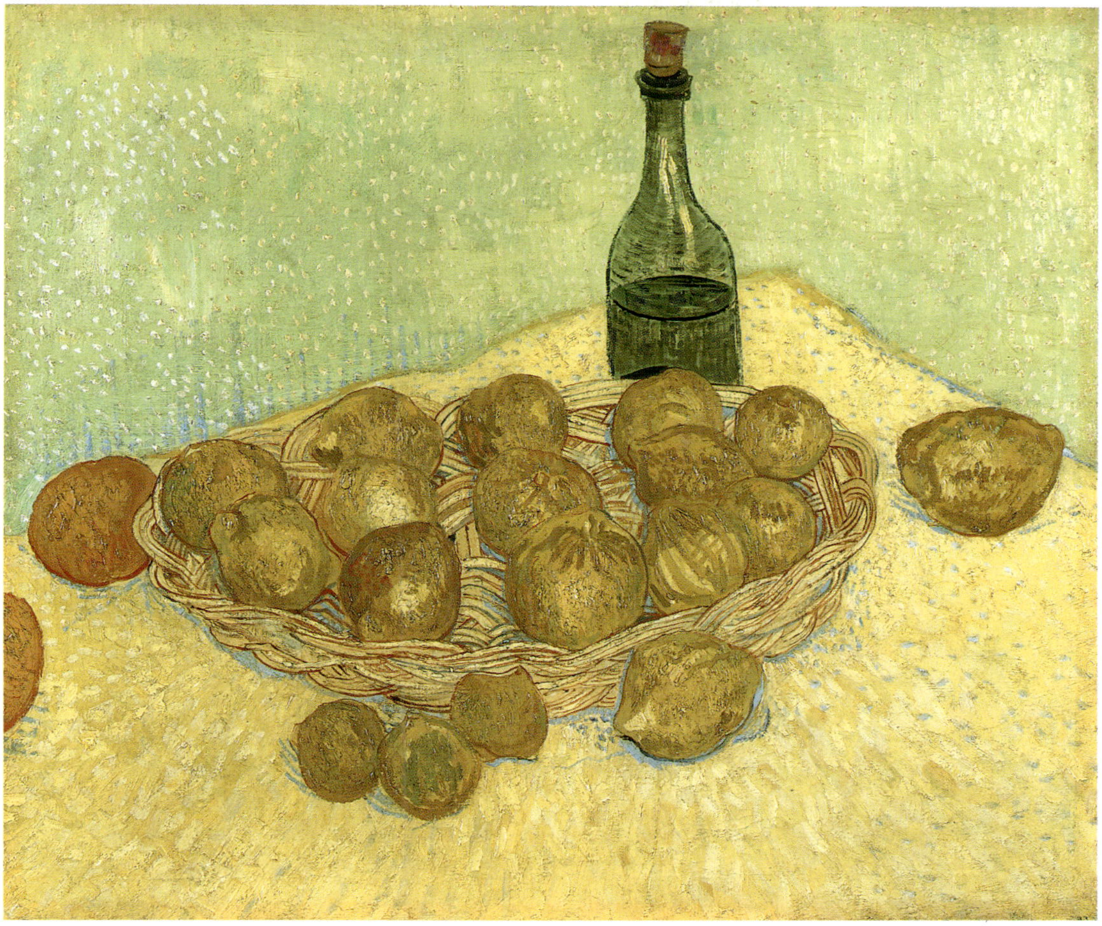

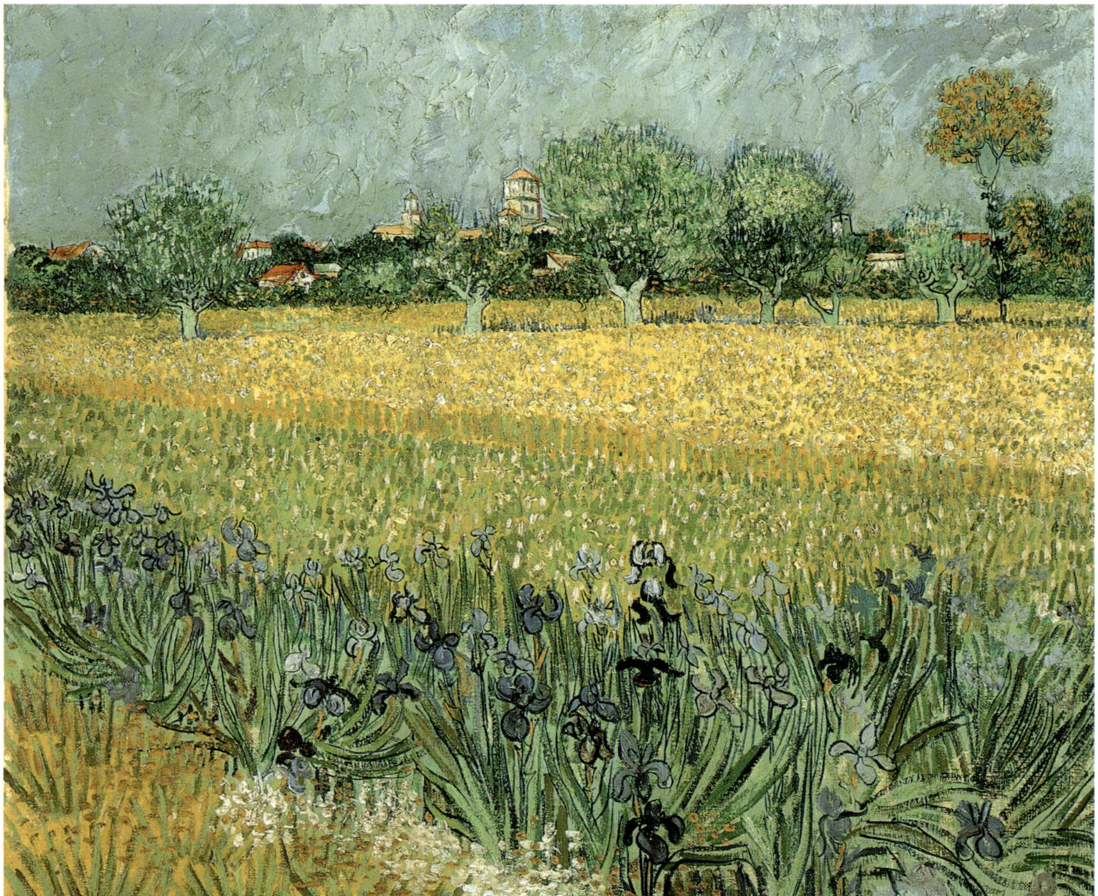

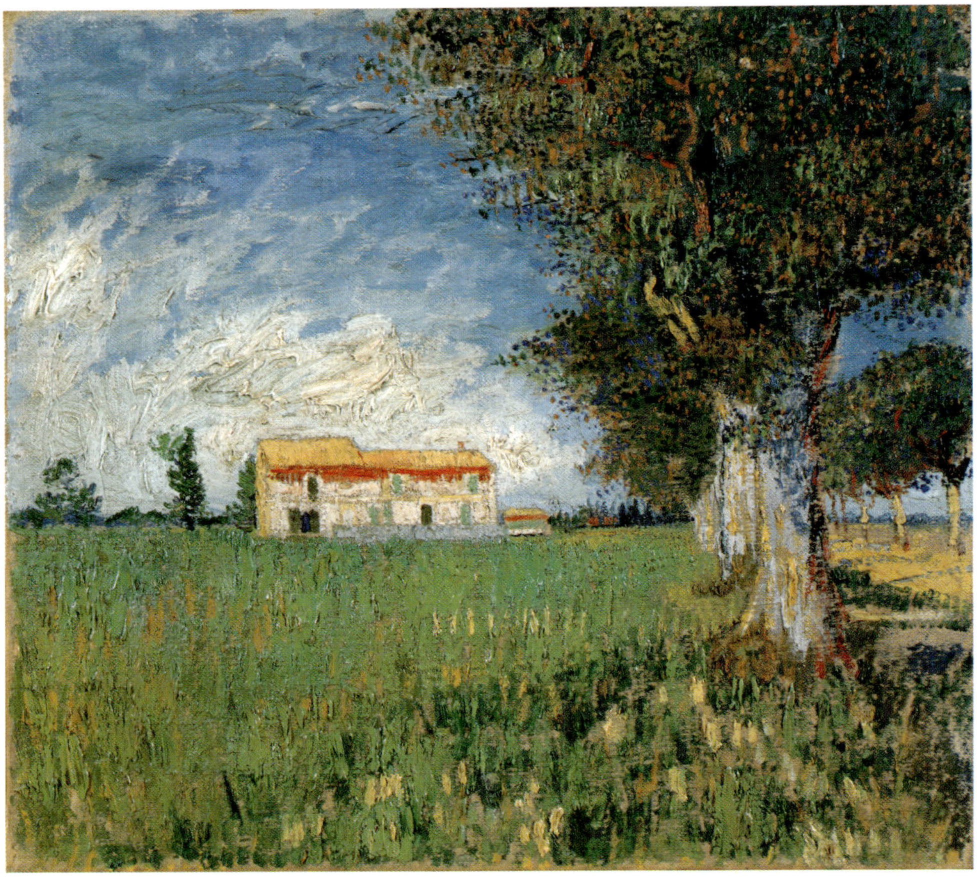

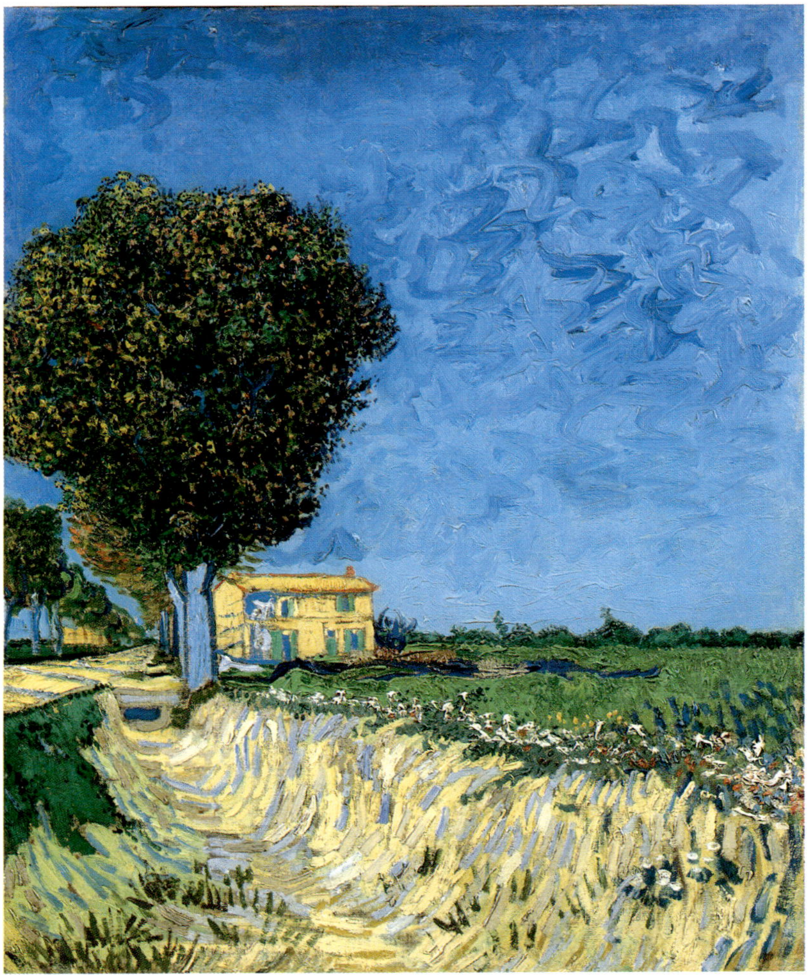

Annotations to Letter 5

Arles, ca. Tuesday, 22 May, 1888

TEXTUAL NOTES
a. d'exterminer < d'exterminér
b. plus tôt, < plutôt

1. It is revealed later in the letter that van Gogh was talking about the negresses in the paintings that Paul Gauguin had painted in Martinique between May and October 1887. Bernard certainly knew the two paintings that Theo and Vincent had in their collection: *On the Shore of the Lake, Martinique* (W252/W222; Fig. 17) and *Among the Mangoes* (W250/W224; Fig. 18). That he saw these works is documented in his 1904 article "Concernant Paul Gauguin," in which he gave a detailed description of *Among the Mangoes* and remarked: "This work, with its qualities of style and color, with its characteristic drawing, is the best that Gauguin painted during that period" (*Cette oeuvre par ses qualités de style et de couleur, par son dessin caractéristique, est la meilleure que Gauguin ait peinte à cette époque*). See Bernard 1994, vol. 1, p. 77.

2. The Marquesas are in French Polynesia (Oceania) and have been French colonies since 1842. We have been unable to discover which book van Gogh is speaking of. Merlhès suggested that it was Max Radiguet, *Les Derniers sauvages. Souvenirs de l'occupation française aux îles Marquises: 1842–1859* (1861). See Merlhès 1989, p. 189 (n. 3). The events as described by van Gogh, however, are not found in that book. The conflict to which he referred was probably the war that took place between the islands of Hivaoa and Tahuata at the time the French assumed power there.

3. Theo had paid Gauguin 400 francs for *Among the Mangoes;* see *Gauguin lettres* 1983, p. 33.

4. Around 10 May, Vincent had sent off all the studies he had done so far in Arles, some twenty-six paintings in all.

5. The owner of the Hotel-Restaurant Carrel, where van Gogh was staying, felt that his paintings were taking up too much space, so from 1 May van Gogh rented the right half of a building that has become known as the Yellow House. It was at 2 place Lamartine, in the northern part of town (Fig. 19). Van Gogh installed his studio there but only started living in the house in September. He officially registered there on 16 October 1888 (Van Gogh Museum, inv. no. b2949). For a floor plan of 1922 see Dorn 1990, fig. 6.

23. VINCENT VAN GOGH, *Farmhouse with Wheat Field Along a Road*, 1888 (F 408 / JH 1417). Amsterdam, Van Gogh Museum (Vincent van Gogh Foundation).
24. VINCENT VAN GOGH, *Landscape with the Edge of a Road*, 1888 (F 567 / JH 1419). Greifswald, Pommersches Landesmuseum.

6. This is a reference to and quotation from the poem "La Prostitution" by Bernard, who wrote in his 1911 publication: "It will perhaps not be without interest that I publish here the sonnet criticized by Vincent, not for the sake of my lines, which are bad, but because of his opinion itself:

PROSTITUTION
To Vincent

Prostitution sallies forth, her face all paint and rouge;
Along the brightly lit boulevard she prowls
Hunting among the clan of old and young,
Those whom she'll take to bed, tonight, very late.

In beauty though she be no match for Aude,
Her charms are not a jot the less, because
What's beauty, if the female's hot
And of love's arts has perfect mastery?

My friend, let's go attend her dismal rites,
I love her shameless nakedness by candlelight;
Let's go and strip her of her bodice and her hose.

And when we've set her, naked, on our lap,
When paint and rouge are gone, what stranger
May emerge, who's more sublime . . . who knows?

October 1887

I add the date in order to excuse these follies."

Il ne sera pas sans intérêt peut-être que je publie ici le sonnet critiqué par Vincent, non à cause de mes vers, qui sont mauvais, mais à cause de son opinion même:

LA PROSTITUTION
A Vincent

La Prostitution sort couverte de fard,
Le long du boulevard lumineux elle rôde
Et dans le clan des vieux et des jeunes maraude
Ceux qu'elle emmènera coucher ce soir, très tard.

Certes, si sa beauté n'est exquise comme Aude
Elle n'en est pas moins très séduisante, car
Qu'importe la beauté si la femelle est chaude
Et connaît cet amour dont elle-même est l'art!

Allons tous deux, ami, vers sa funèbre orgie,
J'aime sa nudité flambant sous la bougie;
Allons pour lui ravir ses bas et son corset.

Et, quand sur nos genoux nous l'aurons mise nue,
Que le fard tombera, quelque femme inconnue
Surgira, qui sera plus sublime . . . qui sait?

Octobre 1887

Je mets la date pour excuser ces folies.

See *Lettres à Bernard* 1911, pp. 84–85. See also New Brunswick 1988, p. 23.

7. For the painters of the "petit boulevard," see Introduction, p. 10.

8. *Still Life with Coffeepot* (F 410 / JH 1426; Fig. 20). Van Gogh sent Bernard a sketch of this painting with his next letter.

9. *Basket with Lemons* (F 384 / JH 1425; Fig. 21).

10. *Field with Flowers* (F 409 / JH 1416; Fig. 22).

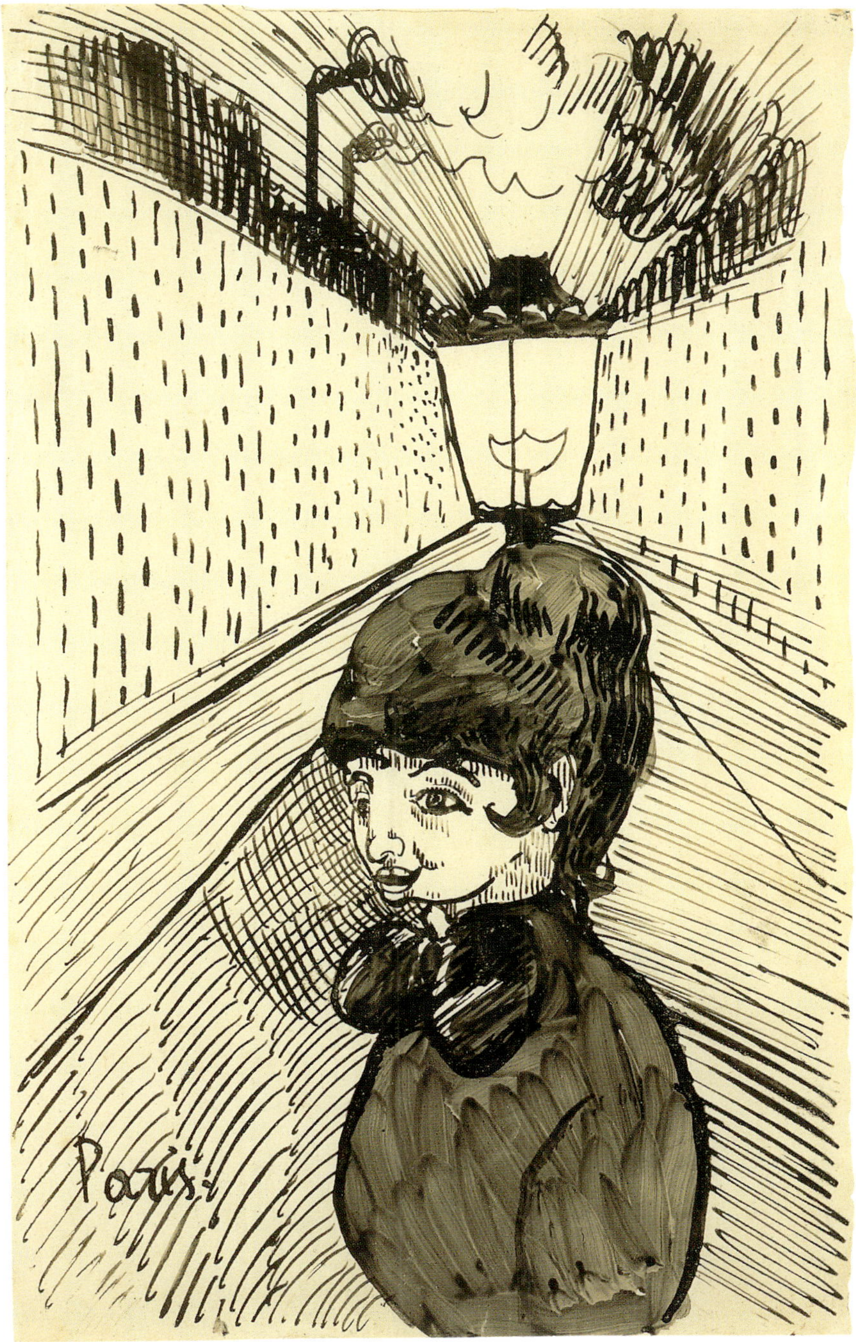

11. *Farmhouse with Wheat Field Along a Road* (F 408 / JH 1417; Fig. 23) and *Landscape with the Edge of a Road* (F 567 / JH 1419; Fig. 24). The mistral blew on 11 and 12 May (*Météo-France*).

12. This was probably the drawing *Girl in a Paris Street* (Fig. 25), which the van Gogh brothers had in their collection.

25. Émile Bernard, *Girl in a Paris Street,* 1888. Amsterdam, Van Gogh Museum (Vincent van Gogh Foundation).

Letter 6

Arles, ca. Thursday, 7 June, 1888

Source
Original manuscript

Location
New York, Thaw Collection, The Morgan Library & Museum

Date
Van Gogh wrote this letter after his return from Saintes-Maries-de-la-Mer around 5 June (see n. 10). Since he said he was working up the drawings that he had made there, it must have been written not long afterward. It must also be dated a few days before Tuesday, 12 June (letter *CL* 496), for then he was working on his harvest landscapes, of which there is no mention here (there is in Letter 7). It is on these grounds that we have dated this letter ca. Thursday, 7 June, 1888.

Arrangement
The sketches sent with this letter included *Still Life with Coffeepot* (F - / JH 1428), which was formerly placed with Letter 5.

Sketches
1. *Cabane in Saintes-Maries* (F - / JH -), letter sketch. Color notations: in the sky, *bleu* (blue), twice; on the ground, *orange* and *orangé* (orange).
2. *Woman with a Parasol* (F - / JH -), letter sketch. Color notations: in the sky, *bleu* (blue); on the ground, *orangé* (orange).
3. *Street in Saintes-Maries* (F - / JH 1463), enclosed sketch. Color notations: in the sky, *Citron vert pale* (pale lemon green); on the roof of the house in the left foreground, *bleu & orangé* (blue and orange); on the lower edge of the house, *cobalt tres clair* (very light cobalt); on the side of the second house, *chrome 2*; on the chimney and the lower edge of the house, *blanc* (white), twice; on the roof, *violet*; on the side of the third house, *chrome 2*; on the house in the left background, *émeraude* (emerald); on the front of the house second from left in the background, *blanc*; on the roof of that house, *violet*; on the third house in the background, *orangé* and *chrome 3*; on the surface of the street, *rose*; below the poppies beside the street, *coquelicots rouge* (red poppies); on the vegetation on the right: *Vert* (green).
4. *Fishing Boats at Sea* (F - / JH 1464), enclosed sketch; two landscapes on the right, here numbered 5 and 6 (F - / JH 1464). Color notations: on the sail of the first boat, *jaune* (yellow); on the sail of the second boat, *blanc* (white); on the hull of the first boat, *vert* (green); on the hull of the second boat, *rouge* (red); in the water in front of these boats, *bleu* (blue); a little lower down, *vert & blanc*; on the shoreline, *blanc*; on the beach, *vert & blanc rosé* (green and pinkish white); in the water in front of the central boats, *violet vert* (violet green).
5. *Landscape with the Edge of a Road* (F - / JH 1464), enclosed sketch. Color notations: in the sky, *Bleu* (blue); beside the leaves of the tree, *vert* (green); beside the house in the background, *orangé & jaune* (orange and yellow); below that, *ciel bleu* (blue sky); on the ground in front of the house, *Vert* (green); in the foreground, *jaune & bleu* (yellow and blue).
6. *Farm Along a Road* (F - / JH 1464), enclosed sketch. Color notations: *maison rose* (pink house); below that, *ciel bleu* (blue sky); on the right, *champ de blé / vert* (wheat field / green); below that, *route bordé / d'arbres / aux troncs violets* (road lined / with trees / with violet trunks).
7. *Fishing Boats on the Beach* (F - / JH 1461), enclosed sketch.
8. *Still Life with Coffeepot* (F - / JH 1428), enclosed sketch. Color notations: in the background, *Citron vert pale* (pale lemon green); on the orange in the left foreground, *mine orange* (orange lead); below the cup and saucer on the left, *tasse bleu de roi / or & blanc* (royal blue/ gold and white cup); on the orange in the left background, *chrome 3*; above the milk jug on the left, *carrelé / bleu & cobalt* (blue and cobalt check); on the tablecloth, center foreground, *bleu myosotys* (forget-me-not blue); on the foremost of the three lemons, *chrome / N° 1*; on the two other lemons, the numeral *1* (for chrome 1); beside the coffee pot in the middle, *émaillé / bleu* (blue enamel); on the edge of the saucer on the right, *chrome 2*; beside the cup on the right, *tasse blanche / dessins bleu / orangé* (white cup / patterns blue / orange); beside the jug on the right, *pot en majolique / bleu à flammes / brunes à fleurs / roses and vertes* (blue majolica jug / with wavy / brown decoration with / pink and green flowers).

Van Gogh wrote this letter soon after returning from a visit to Saintes-Maries-de-la-Mer. As he told Theo, "The Mediterranean—has a color like mackerel, in other words, variable—you don't always know if it's green or violet—you don't always know if it's blue—because a second later its shimmering surface has taken on a pink or gray hue."[1] He sent Bernard several beautiful sketches in order to give him an idea of what the trip had yielded in the way of work. After his stay by the sea, he wanted to further intensify his colors, as he had with the still life he had described in his previous letter, of which he now included a sketch. Bernard would have noticed that it bore a marked resemblance to a still life he himself had made six months previously, which van Gogh liked very much indeed (see Letter 14).

The care he took with the sketches shows that van Gogh was looking for an artistic exchange and a discussion. It is from that same, deeply felt need that he asked Bernard to react to his remarks about pure black and pure white. Another subject that came up is the simplification of colors in imitation of Japanese prints, which was an artistic challenge that also preoccupied Bernard in his experiments.

Van Gogh felt that the future of the new kind of art still lay in the south, but that it should be a collective effort. Seeking solidarity and mutual support among artists, he took up the cause of Gauguin, who had

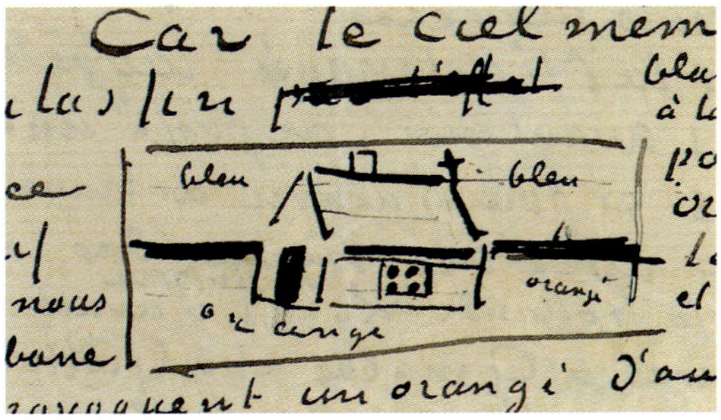

been living on credit in Pont-Aven for three months and had appealed to Theo for help. Vincent knew of his plight and now tried to get Russell, who had already bought work by Guillaumin and Bernard, to add a Gauguin to his collection. And in the meantime he daydreamed, "If Gauguin came here, he and I could perhaps accompany Bernard to Africa when he goes there to do his service."[2]

Bernard was still working on his painting of the procession at the beginning of June and complained to his father about the models he was using. "All the same, it's very annoying, a large canvas done in such conditions as mine, the models are erratic, pose badly, are not dressed as they ought to be, and although they demonstrate their good will, they're not short of bad will."[3] He had hung his canvases in a café popular with tourists but doubted whether that exhibition would be a success.

Translation of Letter 6 / Arles, ca. Thursday, 7 June, 1888

My dear old Bernard,

More and more it seems to me that the paintings that *ought to be made,* the paintings that are necessary, indispensable for painting today to be fully itself and to rise to a level equivalent to the serene peaks achieved by the Greek sculptors, the German musicians,[1] the French writers of novels,[2] exceed the power of an isolated individual, and will therefore probably be created by groups of men combining to carry out a shared idea.

One has a superb orchestration of colors[3] and lacks ideas.

The other overflows with new, harrowing or charming conceptions but is unable to express them in a way that is sufficiently sonorous, given the timidity of a limited palette.

Very good reason to regret the lack of an esprit de corps among artists, who criticize each other, persecute each other, while fortunately not succeeding in canceling each other out.

You'll say that this whole argument is a banality. So be it—but the thing itself—the existence of a Renaissance—that fact is certainly not a banality.

A technical question. Do give me your opinion in next letter.

I'm going to put the *black* and the *white* boldly on my palette, just the way the colorman sells them to us, and use them as they are.

When—and note that I'm talking about the simplification of color in the Japanese manner—when I see in a green park with pink paths a gentleman who is dressed in black, and a justice of the peace by profession (the Arab Jew in Daudet's Tartarin calls this honorable official "shustish of the

---

Transcription of Letter 6 / Arles, ca. Thursday, 7 June, 1888

Mon cher copain Bernard,

*il me semble toujours de plus en plus que les tableaux qu'*il faudrait faire, *les tableaux nécessaires, indispensables pour que la peinture actuelle soit entièrement elle et monte à une hauteure équivalente aux cimes sereines qu'atteignirent les sculpteurs grecs, les musiciens allemands,*[1] *les ecrivains de romans*[2] *français, dépassent la puissance d'un individu isolé, seront donc créées probablement par des groupes d'hommes se combinant pour executer une idée commune.—*

Tel a une orchestration superbe des couleurs[3] *et manque d'idées.*

Tel surabonde en conceptions neuves navrantes ou charmantes mais ne sait les exprimer d'une façon suffisamment sonore, donné la timidite d'une palette bornée.

Grande raison pour regretter le manque d'esprit de corps dans les artistes, lesquels se critiquent, se persécutent, tout en ne parvenant heureusement point à s'annuler.

Tu diras que tout ce raisonnement est une banalité.—Que soit—la chôse elle-même pourtant—l'existence d'une Renaissance—ce fait-là certes n'en est pas une, de banalites.

Une question technique. Dis moi un peu ton opinion dans prochaine lettre.

le noir *et le* blanc *tel que le marchand nous les vend tout simplement, je vais le mettre sur ma palette hardiment et les employer tels quels.*

lorsque—et remarquez que je parle de la simplification de la couleur à la Japonaise—lorsque je vois dans un parc vert aux sentiers roses un monsieur qui est habillé de noir et juge de paix de son métier (le juif arabe dans Tartarin de Daudet appelle cet honorable fonctionnaire zouge de paix),[4]

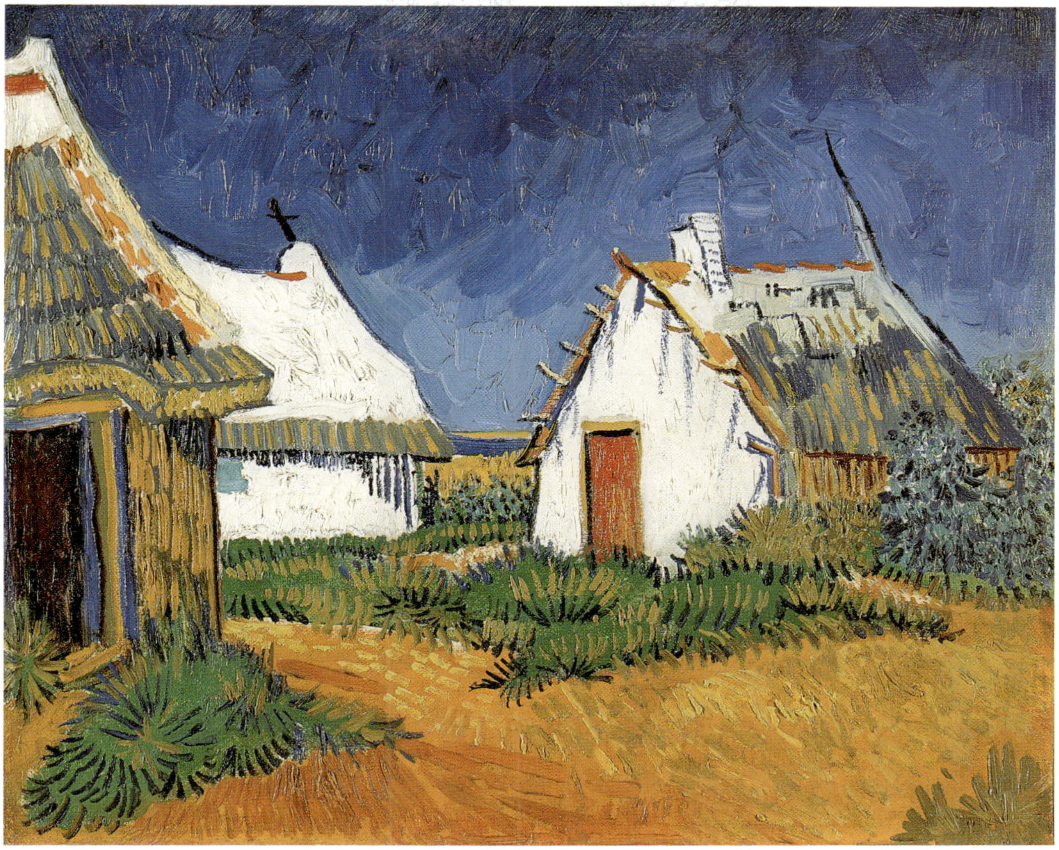

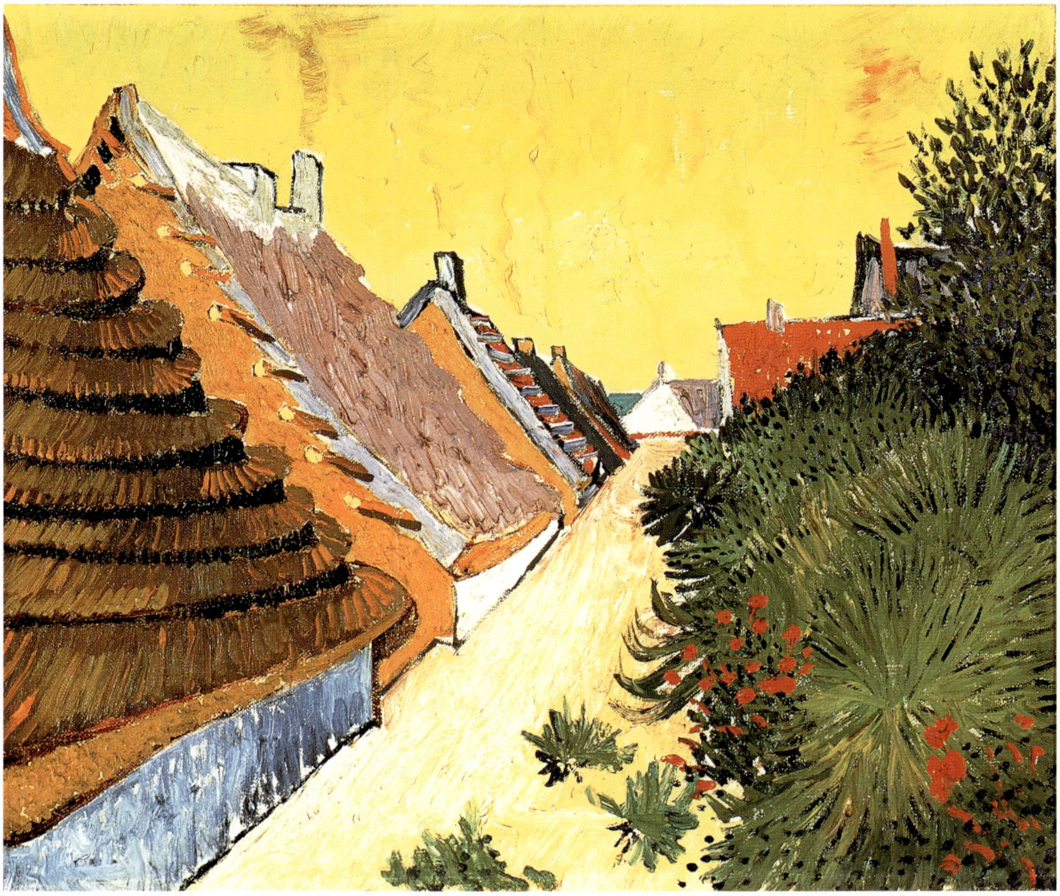

26. Vincent van Gogh, *Three Cottages in Saintes-Maries,* 1888 (F 419 / JH 1465). Kunsthaus Zürich.

27. Vincent van Gogh, *Street in Saintes-Maries,* 1888 (F 420 / JH 1462). Private collection.

beace"),[4] who's reading L'Intransigeant.[5]

Above him and the park a sky of a simple cobalt.

Then why not paint the said shustish of the beace with simple bone black and L'Intransigeant with simple, very harsh white?

Because the Japanese disregards reflection, placing his solid tints one beside the other—characteristic lines naively marking off movements or shapes.[6]

In another category of ideas, when you compose a color motif expressing, for example, a yellow evening sky.

The harsh, hard white of a white wall against the sky can be expressed, at a pinch and in a strange way, by harsh white and by that same white softened by a neutral tone. Because the sky itself colors it with a delicate lilac hue. *[sketch]* Again, in this very naive landscape, which is meant to show us a hut, whitewashed overall (the roof, too), placed in an orange field, of course, because the sky in the south and the blue Mediterranean produce an orange that is all the more intense the higher in tint the range of blues.

The black note of the door, of the windowpanes, of the little cross on the rooftop creates a simultaneous contrast[7] of white and black *[sketch]* just as pleasing to the eye as that of the blue with the orange.[8]

To take a more entertaining subject, let's imagine a woman dressed in a black and white checked dress, in the same primitive landscape of a blue sky and an orange earth—that would be quite amusing to see, I imagine. In fact, in Arles they often do wear white and black checks.[9]

In short, black and white are colors too, or rather, in many cases may be considered colors,

---

lequel lit l'Intransigeant.[5]

Au dessus de lui & du parc un ciel d'un simple cobalt.

Alors pourquoi pas peindre le dit zouge de paix avec du simple noir d'os et l'Intransigeant avec du simple blanc tout cru?

Car le japonais fait abstraction du reflet posant ses teintes plates l'une à côté de l'autre—des traits caractéristiques arrêtant naivement des mouvements ou des formes.[6]

Dans une autre catégorie d'idées, lorsqu'on compose un motif de couleur exprimant par exemple un ciel jaune du soir.

le blanc cru et dur d'un mur blanc contre le ciel à la rigueur s'exprime, et d'une façon etrange, par le blanc cru et ce même blanc rabattu par un ton neutre. Car le ciel même le colore d'un ton lilas fin. [sketch] *Encore dans ce paysage si naif, lequel est censé*[a] *nous représenter une cabane blanchie entièrment à la chaux (le toit aussi), posée sur un terrain orangé certes, car le ciel du midi et la mediterranée bleue provoquent un orangé d'autant plus intense que la gamme des bleus est plus montée de ton,*

la note noire de la porte, des vitres, de la petite croix sur la faîte font qu'il y ait un contraste simultané[7] *de blanc & noir* [sketch] *agréable à l'oeil tout autant que celui du bleu avec l'orange.—*[8]

Pour prendre un motif plus amusant supposons une femme habillée d'une robe carrelée noir & blanc dans le même paysage primitif d'un ciel bleu & d'une terre orangée—ce serait assez drôle à voir je m'imagine. Justement à Arles on porte souvent du carrelé blanc & noir.[9]

Suffit que le noir et le blanc sont des couleurs aussi, plutôt dans bien des cas peuvent être considerés comme couleurs car leur contraste simultané est aussi piquant que celui du vert & du rouge par exemple.

Les Japonais s'en servent d'ailleurs—ils expriment merveilleusement bien le teint mat & pâle d'une

since their simultaneous contrast is as sharp as that of green and red, for example.

The Japanese use it too, by the way—they express a young girl's matte and pale complexion, and its sharp contrast with her black hair wonderfully well with white paper and four strokes of the pen. Not to mention their black thornbushes, studded with a thousand white flowers.

I've finally seen the Mediterranean, which you will probably cross before I do. Spent a week in Saintes-Maries,[10] and to get there crossed the Camargue[11] in a diligence, with vineyards, heaths, fields as flat as Holland. There, at Saintes-Maries, there were girls who made one think of Cimabue and Giotto: slim, straight, a little sad and mystical.[12] On the completely flat, sandy beach, little green, red, blue boats, so pretty in shape and color that one thought of flowers; one man boards them, these boats hardly go on the high sea—they dash off when there's no wind and come back to land if there's a bit too much. It appears that Gauguin is still ill.[13] I'm quite curious to know what you've done lately; I'm still doing landscapes, sketch enclosed.[14] I'd very much like to see Africa too, but I hardly make any firm plans for the future, it will depend on circumstances. What I should like to know is the effect of a more intense blue in the sky. Fromentin and Gérôme[15] see the earth in the south as colorless, and a whole lot of people saw it that way. My God, yes, if you take dry sand in your hand and if you look at it closely. Water, too, air, too, considered this way, are colorless. No BLUE WITHOUT YELLOW and WITHOUT ORANGE, and if you do blue, then do yellow and orange as well, surely. Ah well, you'll tell me that I write you nothing but banalities. Handshake in thought,

Ever yours,
Vincent

---

jeune fille et le contraste piquant de la chevelure noire avec du papier blanc et 4 traits de plume. Sans compter leurs buissons d'epines noires étoilés de mille fleurs blanches.

J'ai enfin vu la Méditerranée, laquelle il est probable tu franchiras avant moi. ai passé une semaine à Saintes Maries[10] et pour y arriver ai traversé en diligence la Camargue[11] avec des vignes, des landes, des terrains plats comme la Hollande. Là, à Stes Maries, il y avait des filles qui faisaient penser à Cimabue et à Giotto, minces, droites, un peu tristes & mystiques.[12] Sur la plage toute plate, sablonneuse, de petits bateaux verts, rouges, bleus tellement jolis comme forme & couleur qu'on pensait à des fleurs, un seul homme les monte, ces barques-là ne vont guère sur la haute mer—ils fichent le camp lorsqu'il n'y a pas de vent et reviennent à terre s'il en fait un peu trop. Il parait que Gauguin est toujours encore malade.[13] Je suis bien curieux de savoir ce que tu as fait dernierement, moi je fais toujours encore du paysage, ci inclus croquis.[14] J'aurais bien envie de voir l'Afrique aussi mais je ne fais guère de plan fixe pour l'avenir, cela dépendra des circonstances. Ce que je voulais savoir c'est l'effet d'un bleu plus intense dans le ciel. Fromentin et Gerome[15] voient le terrain du midi incolore et un tas de gens le voiaient tel. Mon dieu oui si vous prenez du sable sec dans votre main & si vous allez regarder cela de près. l'eau aussi, l'air aussi, considerée de cette façon, est incolore. PAS DE BLEU SANS JAUNE ET SANS ORANGÉ *et si vous faites le bleu faites donc le jaune & l'orangé aussi, n'est ce pas. Enfin tu vas me dire que je ne t'écris que des banalités. Poignée de main en pensée.*

t. à t.
Vincent

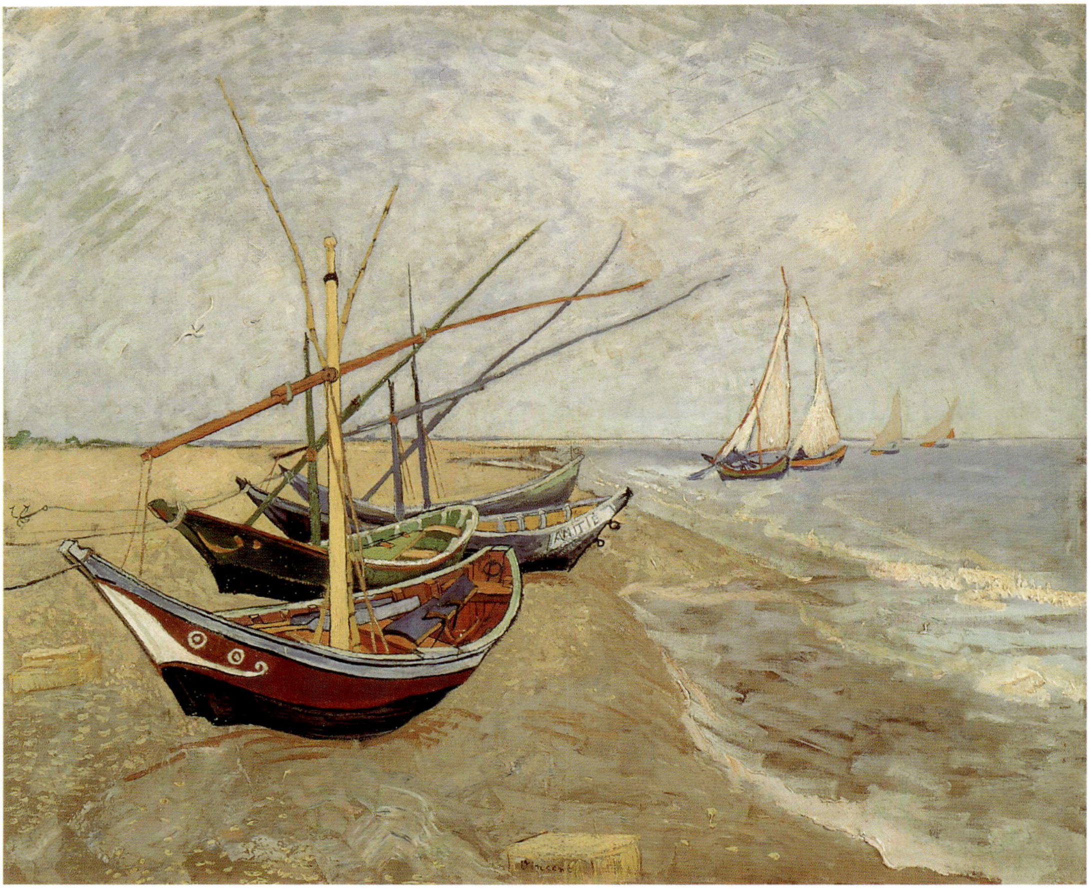

28. Vincent van Gogh, *Fishing Boats on the Beach,* 1888 (F 413 / JH 1460). Amsterdam, Van Gogh Museum (Vincent van Gogh Foundation).

Annotations to Letter 6

Arles, ca. Thursday, 7 June, 1888

Textual Note
a. censé < sensé

1. Van Gogh would have been thinking first and foremost of Richard Wagner, about whom he had written to Theo a few days previously, "I'm reading a book about Wagner which I'll send you later—what an artist—one like that in painting, now that would be something" (*Je lis un livre sur Wagner que je t'enverrai après—quel artiste—un comme ca dans la peinture, voila ce qui serait chic*; *CL* 494).

2. Van Gogh added *de romans* (of novels) later.

3. Van Gogh had spoken of "symphonies of color" back in October 1885, possibly basing this on Charles Blanc, who wrote about "the orchestration of colors" in *Les artistes de mon temps* (Paris 1876, p. 28). The same phrase is found in Blanc's *Grammaire des arts du dessin* (Paris 1870, p. 607). Van Gogh's reading about Wagner may also have prompted this choice of words (see n. 1).

4. A reference to Alphonse Daudet's *Aventures prodigieuses de Tartarin de Tarascon*, in which an Arab Jew with a heavy accent cries out: *"Au zouge de paix! Au zouge de paix!"* See Daudet 1986–94, vol. 2, p. 537 (3rd episode, chapter 3).

5. The political daily *L'Intransigeant*, founded in 1880 by Henri Rochefort, had been the mouthpiece of General Georges Boulanger's radical nationalist party since 1887.

6. This characterization of Japanese prints also applies to cloisonism, the style in which Bernard and Anquetin worked (see Introduction, p. 10). Van Gogh felt that, "in the Japanese style, young Bernard has perhaps gone further than Anquetin" (*dans la japonaiserie le petit Bernard a été plus loin peut etre qu'Anquetin*; *CL* 500).

7. "The law of the simultaneous contrast of colors" is what the physicist Michel Eugène Chevreul called the phenomenon of complementary colors reinforcing each other when placed side by side. He discussed it at length in his book *De la loi du contraste simultané des couleurs* (1839). Van Gogh knew of it from Charles Blanc's essay on Delacroix in *Les artistes de mon temps* (he quoted the relevant passage on color theory in letter *CL* 401) and from Blanc's *Grammaire des arts du dessin*.

   Félix Bracquemond also mentioned the "contraste simultané" in *Du dessin et de la couleur* (Paris 1885, pp. 241–45), which, in September 1885, van Gogh said he had read "more than once." He reread it in February 1886. See letters *CL* 424 and *CL* 456.

8. These descriptions match the paintings *Three Cottages in Saintes-Maries* (F 419 / JH 1465; Fig. 26) and *Street in Saintes-Maries* (F 420 / JH 1462; Fig. 27).

9. No clear-cut examples of the fabrics described by van Gogh have been found. He may have been referring to the summer clothing worn on feast days, which consisted of a dress of black cotton or satin worn beneath a skirt of violet lace. The lace allowed the underlying dark color to show through, creating the optical effect of a checked dress. With thanks to Dominique Séréna of the Museon Arlaten in Arles.

10. Various proposals have been put forward for the sequence and dating of the letters that van Gogh wrote in late May and early June 1888. The key point in the discussion is the precise date of his visit to Saintes-Maries-de-la-Mer, a small seaside town by the Mediterranean, some 40 km south of Arles. A summary of the views of Jan Hulsker, Ronald Pickvance, Victor Merlhès, the editors of *De brieven* 1990, and Roland Dorn will be found in Dorn 1998, p. 25. Dorn is the only one who believes that van Gogh was in Saintes-Maries in the week of 10 to 16 June 1888. We are not convinced by his main argument, which is that when van Gogh wrote *refile* (return to) in letter *CL* 494 of ca. 5 June, he really meant *file* (go to), and had thus not yet been there. In this we subscribe to the criticism in Hulsker 1999 and van der Veen 2002, p. 73.

Van Gogh said that he spent a week in Saintes-Maries. This must be read as a rough approximation, since on 29 or 30 May, he wrote to Theo from Arles, telling him that he would leave the following day (*CL* 495), and he must have been back in Arles around Tuesday, 5 June (*CL* 500). We therefore date his departure to Wednesday, 30, or Thursday, 31 May, 1888.

11. The Camargue is the marshy region in the Rhône delta between Arles and Saintes-Maries populated with flamingos, wild horses, and bulls.

12. Bernard wrote to his parents about this passage on 11 June 1888: "Vincent writes to me. He's enjoying himself very much in Arles, he went to the Camargue recently, where he saw the Mystic girls, who made him think of Cimabue and Giotto" (*Vincent m'écrit. Il se plaît beaucoup à Arles, il est allé ces derniers temps en Camargue où il a vu des filles Mystiques, qui l'ont fait penser à Cimabuë et Giotto*). See Harscoët-Maire 1997, p. 174.

13. Gauguin had been ill for some time. Vincent had written to Theo as long ago as ca. 3 March 1888: "I've had a letter here from Gauguin, who says he's been ill in bed for a fortnight" (*J'ai reçu ici une lettre de Gauguin qui dit qu'il a été malade au lit durant 15 jours*; *CL* 466). He was suffering from the aftereffects of the malaria and dysentery he had caught on his journey to Panama and Martinique with the painter Charles Laval from April to November 1887. See Washington and elsewhere 1988–89, p. 45.

14. These rough sketches of landscapes were *Street in Saintes-Maries* (F - / JH 1463), *Fishing Boats on the Beach* (F - / JH 1461), *Fishing Boats at Sea*, *Landscape with the Edge of a Road* and *Farm Along a Road* (all F - / JH 1464). They were made after the following paintings: *Street in Saintes-Maries* (Fig. 27); *Fishing Boats on the Beach* (F 413 / JH 1460; Fig. 28); *Fishing Boats at Sea* (F 417 / JH 1453; Fig. 29); *Landscape with the Edge of the Road* (F 567 / JH 1419; Fig. 24); and *Farmhouse with Wheat Field Along a Road* (F 408 / JH 1417; Fig. 23). Van Gogh also sent the sketch *Still Life with Coffeepot* (F - / JH 1428) after the painting *Still Life with Coffeepot* (F 410 / JH 1426; Fig. 20).

15. Eugène Fromentin had painted in Algeria; Jean-Léon Gérôme in Turkey, Greece, and Egypt.

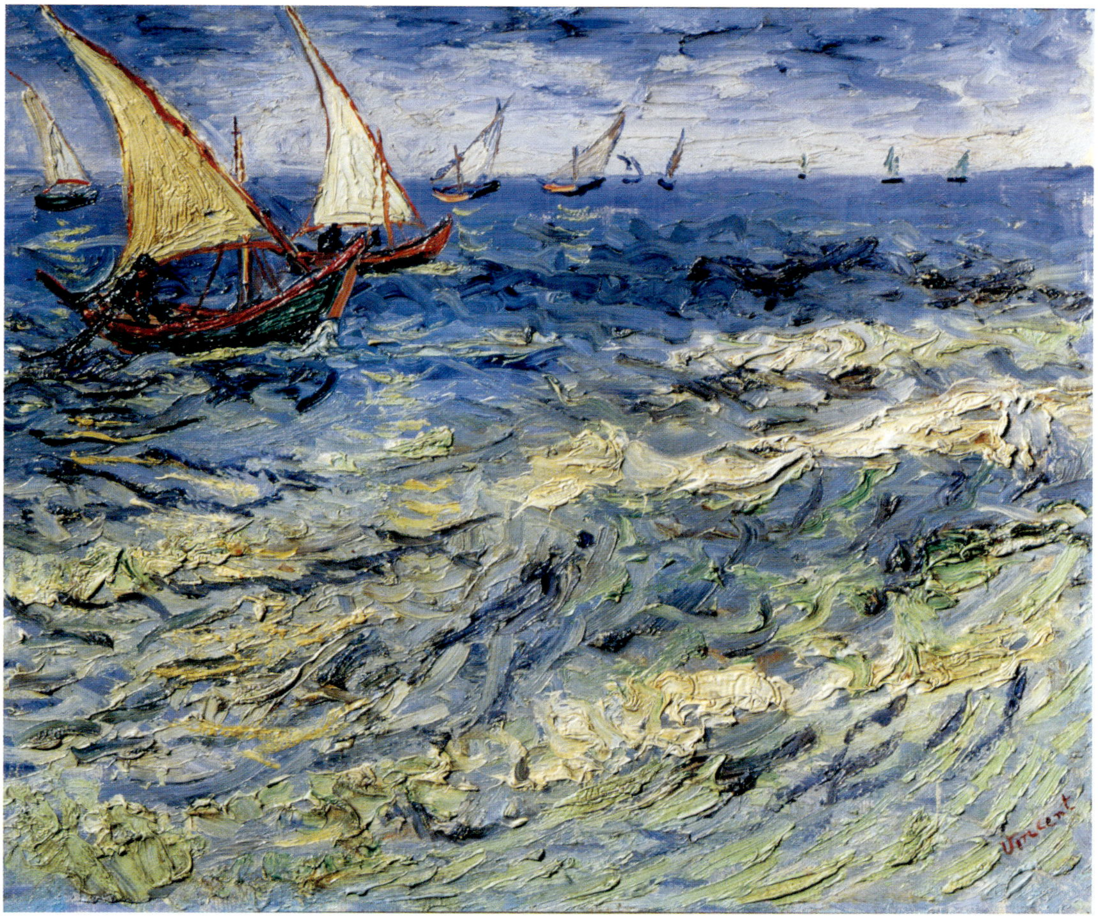

29. Vincent van Gogh, *Fishing Boats at Sea,* 1888 (F 417 / JH 1453). Moscow, Pushkin State Museum of Fine Arts.

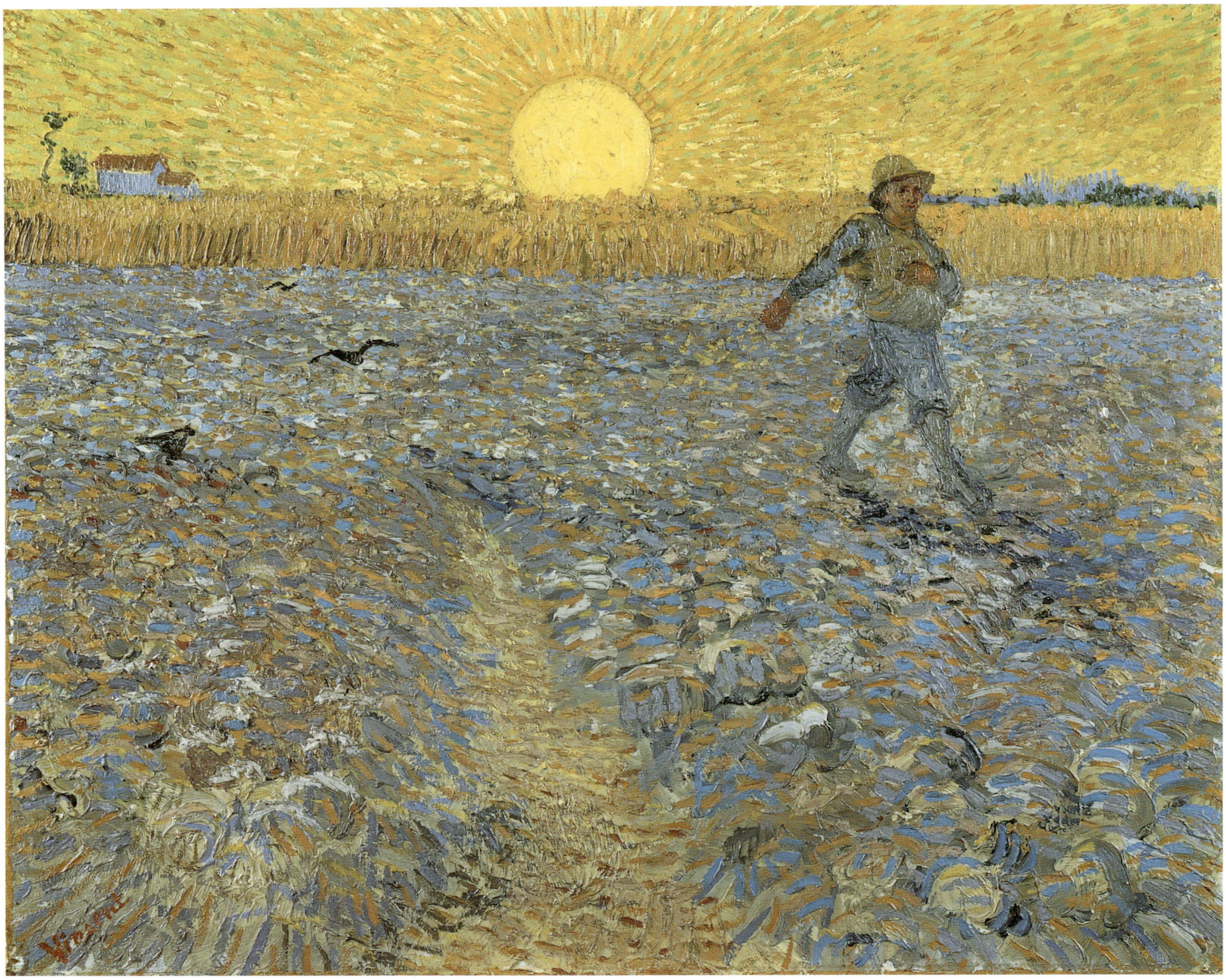
Vincent

Letter 7

Arles, ca. Tuesday, 19 June, 1888

Source
Original manuscript

Location
New York, Thaw Collection, The Morgan Library & Museum

Date
Vincent told Theo on 21 June that he had received a letter from Bernard (letter *CL* 501). Because he said in the present letter that he was replying immediately, it must precede the one to Theo. He had also progressed further with *Sower with Setting Sun* than he could report in letter *CL* 501a, which was written around 17 June, and he mentioned a new wheat field. This suggests that a few days had passed since he wrote that letter, so we have dated the present one around 19 June 1888.

Sketches
1. *Sower with Setting Sun* (F - / JH 1472), letter sketch. Color notations: in the sky on the left, *Jaune* (yellow); in the sun, *jaune*; in the sky on the right, *jaune*; on the sower's trousers, *blanc* (white); on his smock, *bleu* (blue); outside the border on the left, in line with the land in the background, in a box, *jaune / rompu /* vieil or (yellow / broken / *old gold*); diagonally in the foreground below the sower, in very large letters, *Violet.*
2. *Wheat Field with Setting Sun* (F - / JH 1474), letter sketch
3. *Leg of an Easel with a Ground Spike* (F - / JH -), letter sketch

This letter was written in a hurry, because work called. Van Gogh had been working like a man possessed in the wheat fields, under the full heat of the sun, for a week. The fruits of his labors were seven studies of wheat fields and one of a sower. He told both Bernard and Russell about the latter, illustrating it in both cases with a rapid letter sketch. The studies include the masterly *Harvest Landscape* (Amsterdam, Van Gogh Museum; F 412 / JH 1440), with which van Gogh was very pleased, and *Haystacks Near a Farm* (Otterlo, Kröller-Müller Museum; F 425 / JH 1442), which he regarded as its companion piece.

Vincent was answering a letter he had just received from Bernard, and part of his reply is clarified by what he wrote to Theo about Bernard's letter. "I've had a letter from Bernard, who says he feels very isolated but works all the same—and has written a new poem about himself in which he rather touchingly makes fun of himself. And he asks 'what's the use of working?' But he asks that *while working*, he tells himself that work's of no use whatsoever, *while working*—which is not at all the same as saying it while not working. I'd very much like to see what he's

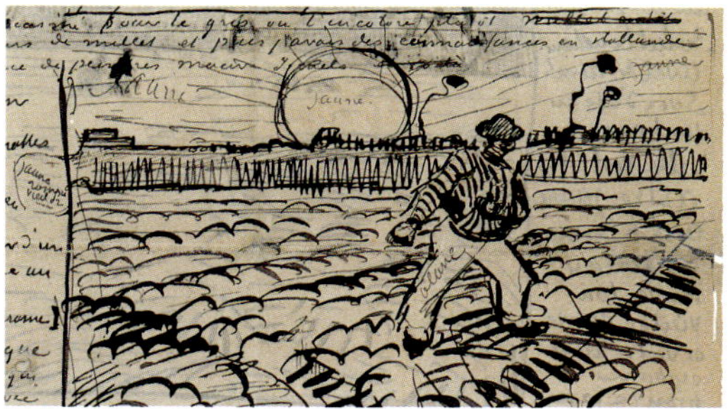

doing. I'm curious to know what Gauguin will do, and if Bernard will not go to join him at Pont-Aven; I already gave each of them the other's address, because they could need one another."[1]

Van Gogh was constantly thinking about all the potential benefits of collaborating with Gauguin. The brothers had asked Gauguin to go to Arles and had proposed a scheme whereby Theo would get a painting from him each month in exchange for his financial support. The main obstacles were Gauguin's poor health and lack of money. It is revealing that van Gogh told Bernard about the plans involving Gauguin only after the latter had agreed to go to Arles (see Letter 10).

30. Vincent van Gogh, *Sower with Setting Sun,* 1888 (F 422 / JH 1470). Otterlo, Kröller-Müller Museum.

Translation of Letter 7 / Arles, ca. Tuesday, 19 June, 1888

My dear Bernard,
Forgive me if I write in great haste; I fear that my letter won't be at all legible, but I want to reply to you right away.

Do you know that we've been very foolish, Gauguin, you, and I, in not all going to the same place? But when Gauguin left, I wasn't yet sure of being able to leave. And when you left, there was that dreadful money for the fare, and the bad news I had to give about the expenses here, which prevented it.[1] If we had all left for here together it wouldn't have been so foolish, because the three of us would have done our own housekeeping. And now that I've found my bearings a little more, I'm beginning to see the advantages here. For myself, I'm in better health here than in the north—I even work in the wheat fields at midday, in the full heat of the sun, without any shade whatever, and there you are, I revel in it like a cicada. My God, if only I had known this country at twenty-five, instead of coming here at thirty-five—In those days I was enthusiastic about gray, or rather, absence of color. I was always dreaming about Millet,[2] and then I had acquaintances in the category of painters like Mauve, Israëls.[3] *[sketch]* Here's sketch of a sower.[4]

Large field with clods of plowed earth, mostly downright violet.

Field of ripe wheat in a yellow ocher tone with a little crimson.

The chrome yellow 1 sky almost as bright as the sun itself, which is chrome yellow 1 with a little white, while the rest of the sky is chrome yellow 1 and 2 mixed, very yellow, then.

The sower's smock is blue, and his trousers white. Square no. 25 canvas.[5] There are many

---

Transcription of Letter 7 / Arles, ca. Tuesday, 19 June, 1888

mon cher Bernard
Pardonne moi si j'écris bien à la hâte, je crains que ma lettre ne sera point lisible mais je veux te répondre tout de suite.

Sais tu que nous avons été très bêtes, Gauguin, toi et moi, de ne pas aller dans un même endroit? Mais lorsque Gauguin est parti moi j'etais pas encore sûr de pouvoir partir. Et lorsque toi tu es parti il y avait cet affreux argent du voyage et les mauvaises nouvelles que j'avais à donner des frais ici qui l'ont empeché.[1] *Si nous étions parti tous ensemble vers ici ce n'aurait pas été si bête car à trois nous eussions fait le ménage chez nous. Et maintenant que je suis un peu mieux orienté je commence à entrevoir des avantages ici. Pour moi, je me porte mieux ici que dans le nord—je travaille même en plein midi en plein soleil sans ombre aucune dans les champs de blé et voilà, j'en jouis comme une cigale. Mon dieu si à 25 ans j'eusse connu ce pays au lieu d'y venir à 35—à cette epoque j'etais enthousiasmé pour le gris ou l'incolore plutôt. Je revais toujours de Millet*[2] *et puis j'avais des connaissances en Hollande dans la catégorie de peintres Mauve, Israels.*[3] [sketch] *Voici croquis d'un semeur.*[4]

Grand terrain de mottes de terre labourés, franchement violet en grande partie.

Champ de blé mûr d'un ton d'ocre jaune avec un peu de carmin.

Le ciel jaune de chrome I presque aussi clair que le soleil lui-meme qui est jaune de chrome I avec un peu de blanc tandis que le reste du ciel est jaune de chrome 1 et 2 melangés, très jaune donc.

la blouse du semeur est bleue et son pantalon blanc. toile de 25 carrée.[5] *il y a bien des rappels de jaune dans le terrain, des tons neutres, résultantes du mélange du violet avec le jaune, mais je me suis*

repetitions of yellow in the earth, neutral tones, resulting from the mixing of violet with yellow, but I could hardly give a damn about the *veracity* of the color. Better to make naive almanac pictures—old country almanacs, where hail, snow, rain, fine weather are represented in an utterly primitive way. The way *Anquetin* got his Harvest so well.[6]

I don't hide from you that I don't detest the countryside—having been brought up there, snatches of memories from past times, yearnings for that infinite of which the sower, the sheaf, are the symbols, still enchant me as before.[7]

But when will I do the starry sky, then, that painting that's always on my mind?[8] Alas, alas, it's just as our excellent pal Cyprien says, in "En ménage" by *J. K. Huysmans,* the most beautiful paintings are those one dreams of while smoking a pipe in one's bed but which one doesn't make.[9] But it's a matter of attacking them nevertheless, however incompetent one may feel vis-à-vis the ineffable perfections of nature's glorious splendors.

But how I should like to see the study you did at the brothel.[10] I reproach myself endlessly for not having done figures here yet. *[sketch]* Here's another landscape.[11] Setting sun? Moonrise? Summer evening, at any rate.

Town violet, star yellow, sky blue green; the wheat fields have all the tones: old gold, copper, green gold, red gold, yellow gold, green, red and yellow bronze. Square no. 30 canvas.[12]

I painted it out in the mistral. My easel was fixed in the ground with iron pegs, a method that I recommend to you. *[sketch]* You shove the feet of the easel in and then you push a 50-centimeter-long iron peg in beside them. You tie everything together with ropes; that way you can work in the wind.

Here's what I wanted to say about the white and the black.[13] Let's take the Sower. The painting is

---

un peu foutu de la vérité *de la couleur. faire des images naives d'almanach plutôt—de vieil almanach de campagne où la grêle, la neige, la pluie, le beau temps sont représentés d'une façon tout à fait primitive. ainsi qu'*Anquetin *avait si bien trouvé sa moisson.*[6]

Je ne te cache pas que je ne déteste pas la campagne—y ayant été elevé, des bouffées de souvenirs d'autrefois, des aspirations vers cet infini dont le Semeur, la gerbe sont les symboles, m'enchantent encore comme autrefois.[7]

Mais quand donc ferai je le ciel étoilé, ce tableau qui toujours me préoccupe?[8]*—helas, helas, c'est bien comme dit l'excellent copain Cyprien dans "en ménage" de* J. K. Huysmans: *les plus beaux tableaux sont ceux que l'on rêve en fumant des pipes dans son lit mais qu'on ne fait pas.*[9] *S'agit pourtant de les attaquer quelqu'incompétent qu'on se sente vis à vis des ineffables perfections*[a] *de splendeurs glorieuses de la nature.*

Mais comme je voudrais voir l'étude que tu as fait au bordel.[10] *je me fais des reproches à n'en pas finir de ne pas encore avoir fait de figures ici.* [sketch] *Voici encore un paysage.*[11] *Soleil couchant? lever de lune? Soir d'eté en tout cas.*

Ville violette, astre jaune, ciel bleu vert, les blés ont tous les tons: vieil or, cuivre, or vert, or rouge, or jaune, bronze jaune, vert, rouge. toile de 30 carrée.[12]

je l'ai peint en plein mistral. mon chevalet etait fixé en terre avec des piquets de fer, procédé que je te recommande. [sketch] *On enfouit les pieds du chevalet et puis on enfonce à coté un piquet de fer long de 50 centimètres. on attache le tout avec des cordes, vous pouvez ainsi travailler dans le vent.*

Voici ce que j'ai voulu dire pour le blanc et le noir.[13] *prenons le Semeur. le tableau est coupé en deux, une moitie est jaune, le haut, le bas est violet. eh bien le pantalon blanc repose l'oeil et*

divided into two; one half is yellow, the top; the bottom is violet. Well, the white trousers rest the eye and distract it[14] just when the excessive simultaneous contrast[15] of yellow and violet would annoy it. That's what I wanted to say.

I know a second lieutenant of Zouaves here called Milliet. I give him drawing lessons—with my perspective frame[16]—and he's beginning to make drawings—my word, I've seen a lot worse than that, and he's eager to learn; has been to Tonkin, etc. He's leaving for Africa in October.[17] If you were in the Zouaves, he'd take you with him and would guarantee you a wide margin of relative freedom to paint, provided you helped him a little with his own artistic schemes. Could this be of some use to you? If so, LET ME KNOW AS SOON AS POSSIBLE.[18]

One reason for working is that canvases are worth money. You'll tell me that first of all this reason is very prosaic, then that you doubt that it's true. But it's true. A reason for not working is that in the meantime canvases and paints only cost us money. Drawings, though, don't cost us much.

Gauguin's bored too in Pont-Aven; complains about isolation, like you. If you went to see him—but I have no idea if he'll stay there, and am inclined to think that he intends to go to Paris. He said that he thought you would have come to Pont-Aven.

My God, if all three of us were here! You'll tell me it's too far away. Fine, *but in winter*—because here one can work outside all year round. That's my reason for loving this part of the world, not having to dread the cold so much, which by preventing my blood from circulating prevents me from thinking, from doing anything at all. You can judge that for yourself when you're a soldier. Your

---

le distrait[14] *au moment où le contraste simultané*[15] *excessif de jaune et de violet l'agacerait. Voilà ce que j'ai voulu dire.*

Je connais ici un sous-lieutenant des zouaves nommé Milliet. je lui donne des leçons de dessin—avec mon cadre perspectif[16]*—et il commence à faire des dessins—ma foi j'ai vu bien pire que ça et il a du zèle pour apprendre, a été au Tonkin &c. Celui-là va partir mois d'octobre pour l'Afrique.*[17] *Si tu étais dans les zouaves il te prendrait avec lui et te garantirait une large marge de liberté relative pour faire de la peinture si toutefois tu l'aiderais un peu dans ses manigences artistiques à lui. Cela peut il t'être de quelqu'utilité. En cas qu'oui* FAIS LE MOI SAVOIR AUSSITÔT POSSIBLE.[18]

Une raison de travailler c'est que les toiles valent de l'argent. tu me diras que d'abord cette raison est bien prosaïque, puis que tu doutes que cela soit vrai. C'est pourtant vrai. Une raison de ne pas travailler c'est que les toiles & couleurs ne font que nous coûter des sous en attendant. Les dessins cependant ne nous coûtent pas cher.

Gauguin s'embête aussi à Pont Aven, se plaint comme toi de l'isolement. Si tu allais le voir—mais je n'en sais rien s'il y restera et suis porté à croire qu'il a l'intention d'aller à Paris. il dit qu'il croyait que tu serais venu à Pont Aven.

Mon dieu si nous étions ici tous les trois. Tu me diras que c'est trop loin. Bon, mais en hiver *puisqu'ici on peut travailler dehors toute l'année.—Voilà ma raison pour aimer ce pays ci, d'avoir moins à redouter le froid, qui en empêchant mon sang de circuler m'empêche de penser, de faire quoi que ce soit. Tu pourras en juger lorsque tu seras soldat.—Ta mélancolie s'en ira, laquelle pourrait rude-*

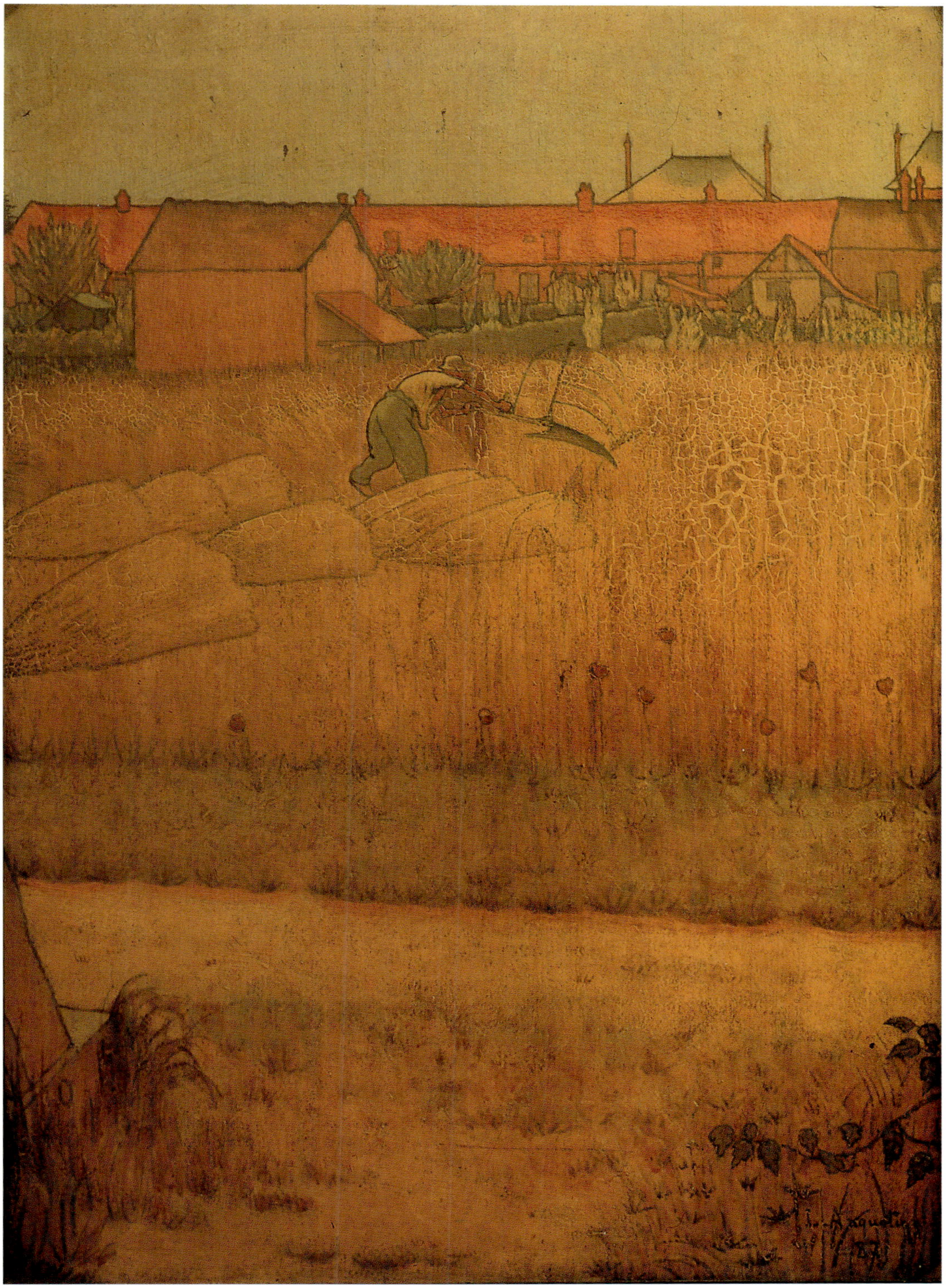

31. LOUIS ANQUETIN, *The Mower at Noon*, 1887. Private collection.

melancholy will go away, which may darned well come from the fact that you have too little blood—or spoiled blood, which I don't think, however. It's that bloody filthy Paris wine and the filthy fat of the steaks that do that to you—dear God, I had come to a state in which my own blood was no longer working at all, but literally not at all, as they say. But after 4 weeks down here it got moving again, but, my dear pal, at that same time I had an attack of melancholy like yours, from which I would have suffered as much as you were it not that I welcomed it with great pleasure as a sign that I was going to recover—which happened too.

Instead of going back to Paris, then, stay out in the country, because you need strength to get through this ordeal of going to Africa properly. Now the more blood, and good blood, that you make yourself beforehand, the better, because over there in the heat it's perhaps harder to produce it. Painting and fucking a lot are not compatible; it weakens the brain, and that's what's really damned annoying.[19]

The symbol of Saint Luke, the patron of painters, is, as you know, an *ox*; we must therefore be as patient as an ox[20] if we wish to labor in the artistic field. But bulls are pretty glad not having to work in the filthy business of painting. But what I wanted to say is this. After the period of melancholy you'll be[21] stronger than before, your health will pick up—and you'll find the surrounding nature so beautiful that you'll have no other desire than to paint. I believe that your poetry will also change, in the same way as your painting. After some eccentric things you have succeeded in making some that have an *Egyptian* calm and a great simplicity.[22]

How short is the hour
We spend loving—

---

ment bien venir de ce que tu as trop peu de sang—ou le sang vicié, ce que je ne pense pourtant pas. C'est ce sacré sale vin de Paris et la sale graisse des biftecks qui vous font cela—mon dieu j'etais arrivé à un etat de chôses que chez moi le sang ne marchait plus du tout, mais ce qu'on appelle point du tout à la lettre. Seulement, au bout de 4 semaines d'ici[b] *cela s'est remis en marche, mais mon cher copain à cette même époque j'ai eu une attaque de mélancolie comme la tienne, de laquelle j'eusse autant souffert que toi si ce n'etait que je la saluais avec grand plaisir comme signe que j'allais guerir—ce qui est aussi arrivé.*

Au lieu donc de retourner à Paris, restes en pleine campagne car tu as besoin de forces pour sortir comme il faut de cette épreuve d'aller en Afrique. Or plus que tu te fais du sang et du bon sang avant, mieux c'est car là-bas dans la chaleur on s'en fabrique peutêtre plus difficilement. Faire de la peinture et baiser beaucoup est pas compatible, le cerveau s'en affaiblit, voilà ce qui est bien emmerdant.[19]

Le symbole de Saint Luc, le patron des peintres, est comme tu sais un boeuf, *il faut donc être patient comme un boeuf*[20] *si l'on veut labourer dans le champ artistique. Mais les taureaux sont bien heureux de ne pas avoir à travailler dans la sale peinture. Mais ce que je voulais dire est ceci. après la période de mélancolie tu seras*[21] *plus fort qu'auparavant, ta santé reprendra—et tu trouveras la nature environnante tellement belle que tu n'auras plus d'autre désir que de faire de la peinture. Je crois que ta poesie changera encore aussi dans le même sens qu'en peinture. tu es après des choses excentriques arrivé à en faire qui ont un calme* egyptien *et une grande simplicité.*[22]

Que l'heure est donc brève
Qu'on passe en aimant—

—It's less than an instant—
—A little more than a dream—:
—Time takes away
—Our spell.

That's not Baudelaire,[23] I don't even know who it's by, they're the words of a song in Daudet's Le Nabab,[24] that's where I took it from—but doesn't it say the thing *like a real Lady's shrug of her shoulder*?

These last few days I read Pierre *Loti's* Madame Chrysanthème; it provides interesting remarks about Japan.[25] At the moment my brother has an exhibition of Claude Monet,[26] I'd very much like to see them. Guy de Maupassant,[27] among others, had been there, and said that from now on he would often revisit the boulevard Montmartre.

I have to go and paint, so I'll finish—I'll probably write to you again before long. I beg a thousand pardons for not having put enough stamps on the letter, and yet I did stamp it AT THE POST OFFICE *and this isn't the first time that it's happened here*, that when in doubt, and asking *at the post office itself*, I've been misled about the postage.

You can't imagine the carelessness, the nonchalance of the people here. Anyway, you'll see that shortly with your own eyes in Africa. Thanks for your letter, I hope to write to you soon at a moment when I'm in less of a hurry. Handshake,

Ever yours,
Vincent

—C'est moins qu'un instant—
—Un peu plus qu'un rêve—:
—Le temps nous enlève
—notre enchantement.

C'est pas du Baudelaire[23] *cela, je ne sais même pas de qui c'est, ce sont les paroles d'une chanson dans le Nabab de Daudet,*[24] *voilà où je l'ai pris—mais est-ce que cela ne dit pas la chôse* comme un haussement d'épaule *de* vraie Dame.

J'ai lu de ces jours ci Madame Chrysantème de Pierre Loti, *cela donne des notes intéressantes sur le Japon.*[25] *Mon frère a dans ce moment une exposition de Claude Monet,*[26] *je voudrais bien les voir. Entre autres Guy de Maupassant*[27] *y était venu et a dit que dorénavant il reviendrait souvent au Boulevard Montmartre.*

Je dois aller peindre donc je finis—probablement je t'écrirai de nouveau sous peu. Je te demande mille pardons de n'avoir pas suffisamment affranchi la lettre, je l'avais pourtant affranchie À LA POSTE et ce n'est pas la première fois que cela m'arrive ici *d'avoir, en demandant* à la poste même, *en cas de doute,*[c] *été trompé en affranchissant.*

Tu ne te fais pas d'idée du laisser aller, de la nonchalance des gens ici. Enfin, tu verras sous peu tout cela de tes propres yeux en Afrique. merci de ta lettre, j'espère t'écrire bientôt à un moment où je serai moins pressé. Poignée de main.

t. à t.
Vincent

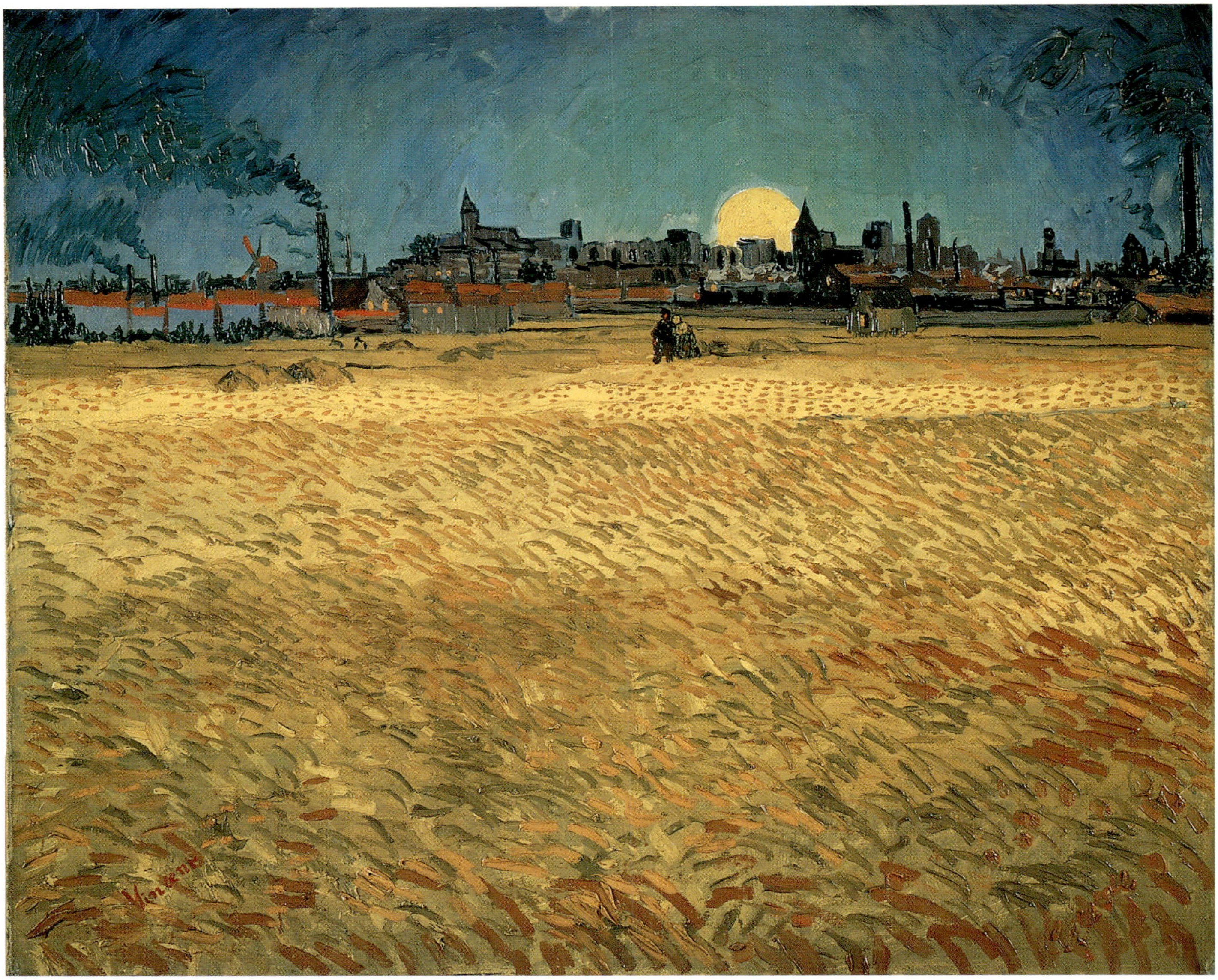

Annotations to Letter 7

Arles, ca. Tuesday, 19 June, 1888

Textual Notes
a. perfections < pecfections
b. This should be read as *ici.*
c. This should be read as *ayant un doute.*

1. A reference to Letter 2, in which van Gogh wrote about the cost of living in Arles.

2. Van Gogh wrote with great admiration about the life and work of Jean-François Millet. His knowledge about the artist came mainly from the biography by Alfred Sensier, *La vie et l'oeuvre de J.-F. Millet* (1881). Millet was van Gogh's guiding light in art and life during his Dutch period, and the latter depicted the life of peasants in imitation of the Frenchman.

3. Anton Mauve, who was married to Ariëtte (Jet) Sophia Jeanette Carbentus—a cousin of Vincent and Theo—had introduced van Gogh to the basic principles of painting in 1881–82. Mauve and Israëls were members of the so-called Hague school, and van Gogh often mentioned them in the same breath. He regarded the work of Jozef Israëls as the counterpart to that of Millet (Barbizon school). Nothing is known about any contacts between van Gogh and Israëls, although he very likely met him when he was working in the Goupil gallery in The Hague.

4. The letter sketch was done after the painting *Sower with Setting Sun* (F 422 / JH 1470; Fig. 30). Van Gogh described and sketched it when it was in an earlier state, for he worked on it again later (*CL* 503).

5. By "square no. 25 canvas" van Gogh meant the squarest variant of that size of canvas, which was known as "*toile de 25 figure*" (31⅞ x 25⅝ in.; 81 x 65 cm).

6. Louis Anquetin, *The Mower at Noon* (Fig. 31). Bernard described it as one of Anquetin's "Japanese abstractions" (*abstractions Japonaises*) and regarded it as one of the first experiments with cloisonism. The painting hung in the exhibition organized by van Gogh in the Restaurant du Chalet and in the offices of the *Revue Indépendante* in January 1888. See Bernard 1994, vol. 1, pp. 64, 241, and Letter 1, n. 9. Van Gogh's *Wheat Field with Sheaves and Arles in the Background* (F 545 / JH 1477; Paris, Musée Rodin) followed the precedent set by Anquetin's work.

   Van Gogh likened Anquetin's painting to "naive almanac pictures—old country almanacs." The critic Édouard Dujardin had made a similar assocation between Anquetin's work and the "*images d'Epinal*" (cheap, colored, popular prints) in his article "Aux XX et aux Indépendants.

32. Vincent van Gogh, *Wheat Field with Setting Sun,* 1888 (F 465 / JH 1473). Winterthur, Kunstmuseum.

Le cloisonisme," *La Revue Indépendante* 6 (March 1888), no. 17, pp. 487–92. Van Gogh had not read the article but had heard what it was about (*CL* 500), possibly from Bernard. Rewald believes that Bernard, who was not mentioned in Dujardin's article, had complained about that in a letter to van Gogh. See Rewald 1978, pp. 176–77.

7. Van Gogh was referring to his Nuenen period, from late 1883 to late 1885, when he tried to express the symbolism of the countryside and peasant life.

8. Van Gogh had already written to Bernard about this subject (see Letter 3).

9. The character Cyprien remarks in *En ménage* (1881) by Joris Karl Huysmans, "—And what about the paintings?—The painter scratched his beard with his long fingers. The paintings, pah, he said, it's sometimes good to muse about those you will never do, in bed, of an evening, when you're not asleep!" (*Alors les tableaux?—Le peintre se frotta la barbe de ses longs doigts. Les tableaux, peuh, dit-il, c'est quelquefois bon de songer à ceux qu'on ne fera jamais, au lit, le soir, quand on ne dort pas!*). See 3rd ed., Paris 1881, chapter 16, p. 346. The novel is set in an artistic milieu, and centers around a broken marriage, the day-to-day worries of an old bachelor, the loneliness of the search for love and the need for a woman. See Sund 1992, p. 253 (n. 27).

10. Bernard sent him a drawing of a brothel soon afterward, which Vincent sent on to Theo, saying, "he probably has a more finished painted study of it" (*il est probable qu'il en a une etude peinte plus faite; CL* 502). It is likely, then, that Bernard's drawing *Brothel Scene* (see letter 8, n. 16) was based on that study of a brothel. No such painted version is known today, however.

11. *Wheat Field with Setting Sun* (F 465 / JH 1473; Fig. 32).

12. By "square no. 30 canvas" van Gogh meant a no. 30 "*figure*" (36¼ x 28¾ in.; 92 x 73 cm). See n. 5.

13. This is a subject that van Gogh had raised in his previous letter, and presumably Bernard had asked him to explain it in more detail.

14. This formulation is similar to that used by Charles Blanc in his *Grammaire des arts du dessin* when he wrote that, when using bold colors, white can serve "to rest the eye, to refresh it, by moderating the dazzling brilliance of the whole spectacle" (*à reposer l'oeil, à le rafraîchir, en modérant l'éblouissant éclat du spectacle entier*). See the Paris 1870 edition, p. 609. Van Gogh later made the trousers blue.

15. See Letter 6, n. 7, for the concept of simultaneous contrast.

16. Van Gogh used a wooden frame with wires stretched on it to form a grid. He looked at the subject through the frame in order to study and depict the proportions and perspectival distortion better. See van Heugten 1996, pp. 18–25, and Amsterdam and New York 2005, pp. 8–10.

17. Paul Eugène Milliet, second lieutenant in the 3rd Zouave Regiment, garrisoned in Arles, was leaving for Guelma in Algeria on 1 November 1888.

18. Van Gogh drew a box around *Je connais [. . .] possible.*

19. Van Gogh was preoccupied with the relationship between social or artistic ambitions and creativity on the one hand, and sexual activity and procreation on the other. He admired men who were very active sexually or who had children but personally felt that such pursuits would get in the way of his art.

20. It is known from letter *CL* 336 that the observation that a painter had to have the patience of an ox was based on an (unsourced) saying of Gustave Doré.

21. Van Gogh originally wrote *plus boeuf* (more of an ox) after *seras.*

22. The paragraph originally continued with the words *Est ce que la nourriture est mangeable là bas??* (Is the food edible over there??), which van Gogh then deleted.

23. Van Gogh mentioned the poet and art critic Charles Baudelaire because he knew that he was an important figure for Bernard, with his poetic aspirations. Bernard's veneration of Baudelaire, which van Gogh did not share, is very apparent in his correspondence with his mother, who also wrote poetry. With thanks to Fred Leeman.

24. Taken from Alphonse Daudet, *Le nabab,* where it is described as "a melancholy Lied" (*un lied mélancolique*). Van Gogh wrote "*un instant*" where Daudet had "*un moment.*" Daudet took the lines from a poem by Armand Silvestre that Jules Massenet set to music in his cycle *Poème d'avril* (1866). See Daudet 1986–94, vol. 2, chapter 22, pp. 804, 1395.

25. Pierre Loti's novel *Madame Chrysanthème* (1888) is set in Nagasaki. A French officer marries the Japanese Kikou-san, or Madame Chrysanthème. In reality the marriage is a paid, temporary concubinage. The Frenchman has no real feelings of love for her, he is more taken with her doll-like qualities. Loti describes the setting and the customs. The underlying message is that it is difficult for Europeans to penetrate the mysterious closed nature and morals of the Japanese or the artificial refinement of objects. Van Gogh probably read an illustrated version that he borrowed from Milliet, for the way in which he portrayed himself in *Self-Portrait* (F 476 / JH 1581) could derive from an illustration of bonzes in the edition of *Madame Chrysanthème* published in Paris in 1888 by Calmann-Lévy. See Kōdera 1990, p. 56. It is known from letter *CL* 561 that Milliet gave Gauguin this copy of the book in November 1888 in exchange for a drawing.

26. In June 1888 Theo van Gogh organized an exhibition of ten landscapes that Monet had painted that spring in Antibes, near Cannes, on the Mediterranean. See Amsterdam and Paris 1999–2000, p. 111, and Wildenstein 1996, vol. 1, pp. 241–44.

27. Theo had written to tell Vincent about his meeting with the writer Guy de Maupassant (letter *CL* 498).

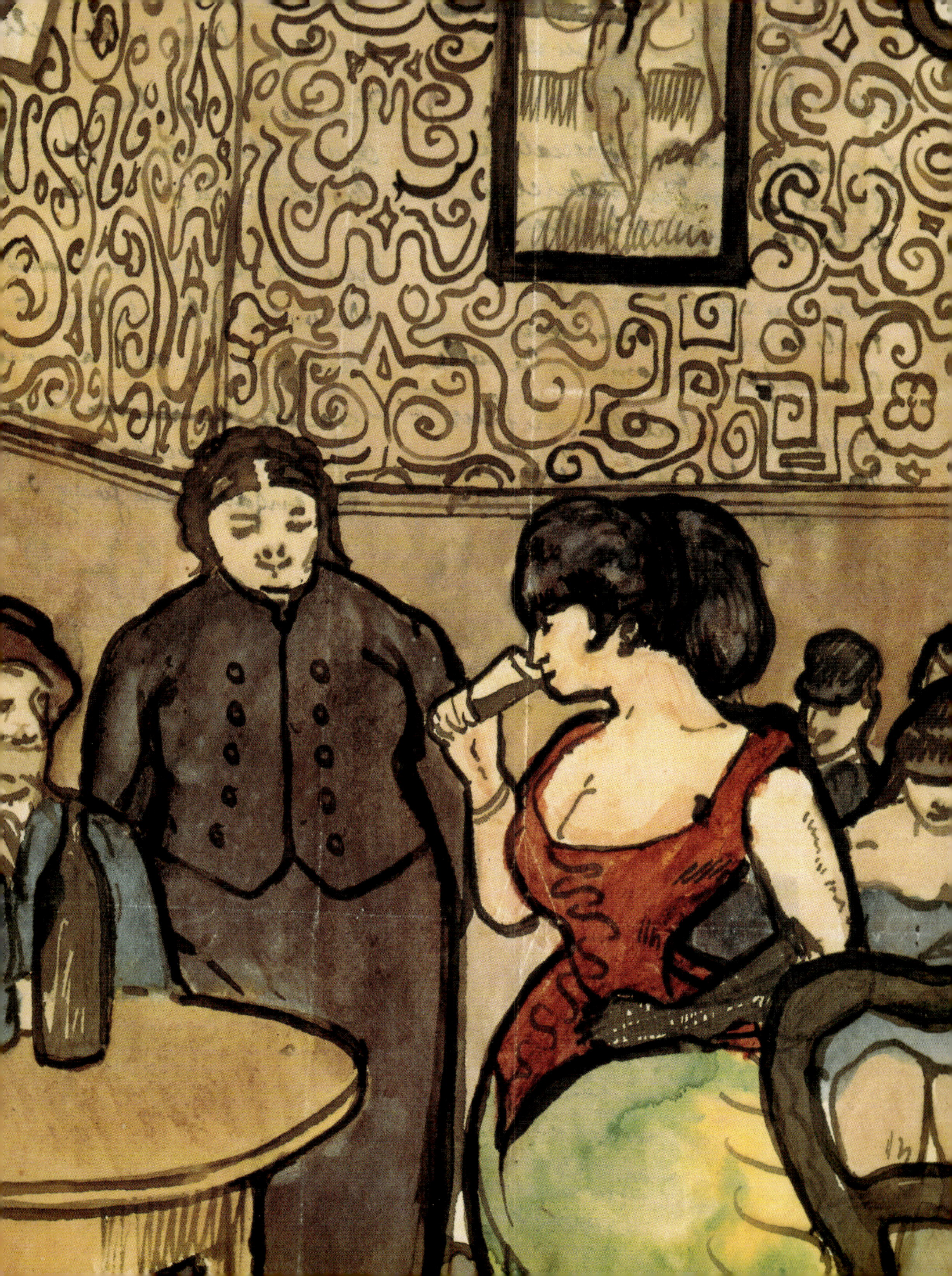

Letter 8

~

Arles, Tuesday, 26 June, 1888

Source
Original manuscript

Location
New York, Thaw Collection, The Morgan Library & Museum

Date
This letter was written one day before Letter 9, as is clear from the latter's opening words. Since Letter 9 dates from Wednesday, 27 June, we have dated this one Tuesday, 26 June, 1888.

Additional details
Van Gogh revised this letter heavily, as is shown by the many additions. Originally there was also a postscript, but he forgot to enclose it. See the beginning of Letter 9, with which it was sent.

On 23 June van Gogh had received a letter from Bernard and the drawing *Brothel Scene*, with two poems on the back, which he sent to Theo the same day "to pin up next to the acrobats by him that you have." He was referring to Bernard's *Acrobats* (Montevideo, Uruguay, Museo Nacional de Bellas Artes). Van Gogh had himself just painted his first serious figure studies in Arles, *Zouave, Half-Length* (F 423 / JH 1486; Fig. 36) and *Zouave Sitting, Full-Length* (F 424 / JH 1488; Fig. 35). He was convinced that painting figures was the quickest route to producing something worthwhile, and added, "Bernard's in the same position."[1] He felt that his friend might exchange a painted study for the portrait of the Zouave but thought it better if Theo bought something from him.

Van Gogh replied to Bernard's letter three days later. The latter's many quotations from the Bible prompted him to embark on an unconventional argument concerning the possibility of life after death. Here van Gogh expressed some of the ideas that formed the core of his philosophy, which is why this exceptional letter is one of the most quoted in the entire correspondence. He then went on to the subject of depicting biblical scenes. This would recur regularly in later letters, and the two friends' differing views about it eventually contributed to the termination of their correspondence.

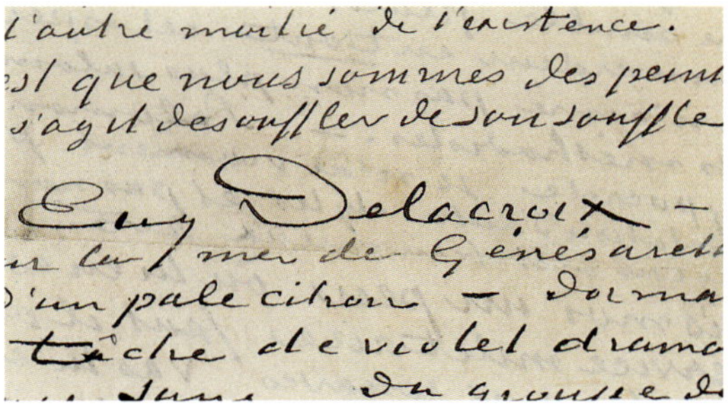
l'autre moitié de l'existence.
que nous sommes des peint
s'agit de souffler de son souffle
Eug Delacroix –
la mer de Génésareth
d'un pale citron – dorma
tache de violet dramat

Van Gogh discussed Bernard's poems on a separate sheet, which he then forgot to put in the envelope, rectifying his mistake the following day (Letter 9). Bernard also sent poems to his parents during this period—not about prostitutes, like the ones to van Gogh, but about a child's funeral and a cortege in the snow.[2] His paintings also deal with those contrasting subjects, for after his large canvas of the procession he painted a brothel scene (see Letter 7).

Detail of Fig. 38.

Translation of Letter 8 / Arles, Tuesday, 26 June, 1888

My dear Bernard,
You do very well to read the Bible—I start there because I've always refrained from recommending it to you.

When reading your many quotations from Moses, from St. Luke,[1] etc., I can't help saying to myself—well, well—that's all he needed. There it is now, full-blown—. . . the artist's neurosis.

Because the study of Christ inevitably brings it on, especially in my case, where it's complicated by the seasoning of innumerable pipes.

The Bible—that's Christ, because the Old Testament leads toward that summit; St. Paul and the evangelists occupy the other slope of the holy mountain.

How petty that story is! My God, are there only these Jews in the world, then? Who start out by declaring that everything that isn't themselves is impure?

The other peoples under the great sun over there—the Egyptians, the Indians, the Ethiopians, Babylon, Nineveh. Why didn't they write their annals with the same care? Still, the study of it is beautiful, and anyway, to be able to read everything would be almost the equivalent of not being able to read at all. But the consolation of this so saddening Bible, which stirs up our despair and our indignation—thoroughly upsets us, completely outraged[2] by its pettiness and its contagious folly—the consolation it contains, like a kernel inside a hard husk, a bitter pulp—is Christ. The figure of Christ has been painted—as I feel it—only by Delacroix and by Rembrandt . . . And then Millet has painted . . . Christ's doctrine.[3]

Transcription of Letter 8 / Arles, Tuesday, 26 June, 1888

Mon cher Bernard,
tu fais très bien de lire la bible—je commence par là parceque je me suis toujours abstenu de te recommander cela.

involontairement en lisant tes citations multiples de Moïse, de st. Luc[1] &c., tiens—me dis je—il ne lui manquait plus que ça, ça y est maintenant en plein— . . . la névrose artistique.

Car l'étude du christ la donne inévitablement, surtout dans mon cas où c'est compliqué par le culottage de pipes inombrables.—

La bible—c'est le christ car l'ancien testament tend vers ce sommet, st. Paul et les évangélistes occupent l'autre pente de la montagne sacrée.—

Que c'est petit cette histoire! mon dieu voilà—il n'y a donc que ces juifs au monde! qui commencent par déclarer tout ce qui n'est pas eux impur?

Les autres peuples sous le grand soleil de là-bas, les égyptiens, les indiens, les éthiopiens, Babylone, Ninive. Que n'ont ils leurs annales écrites avec le même soin? Enfin—l'étude de cela c'est beau et enfin savoir tout lire équivaudrait presque à ne pas savoir lire du tout.

Mais la consolation de cette bible si attristante, qui soulève notre désespoir et notre indignation —nous navre pour de bon, tout outré[2] par sa petitesse et sa folie contagieuse—la consolation qu'elle contient comme un noyau dans une ecorce dure, une pulpe amère—c'est le christ.—La figure du christ n'a été peinte[a]—comme je la sens—que par Delacroix et par Rembrandt . . . et puis Millet a peint . . . la doctrine[b] du christ.—[3]

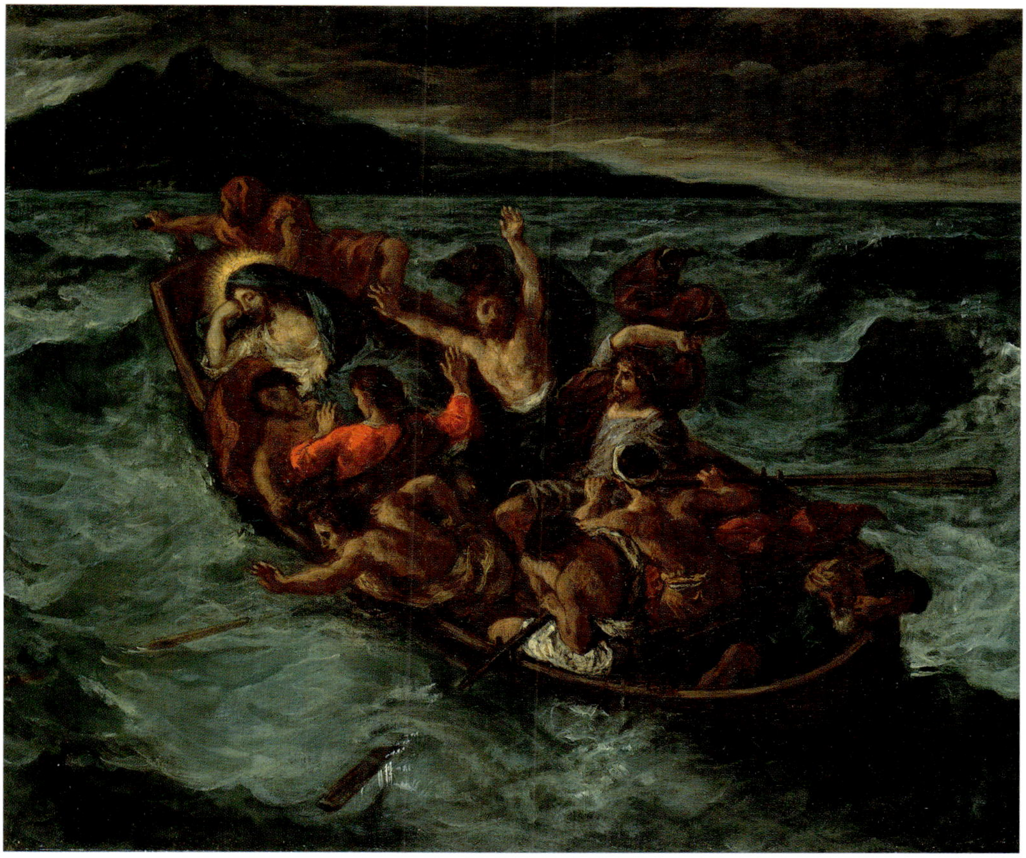

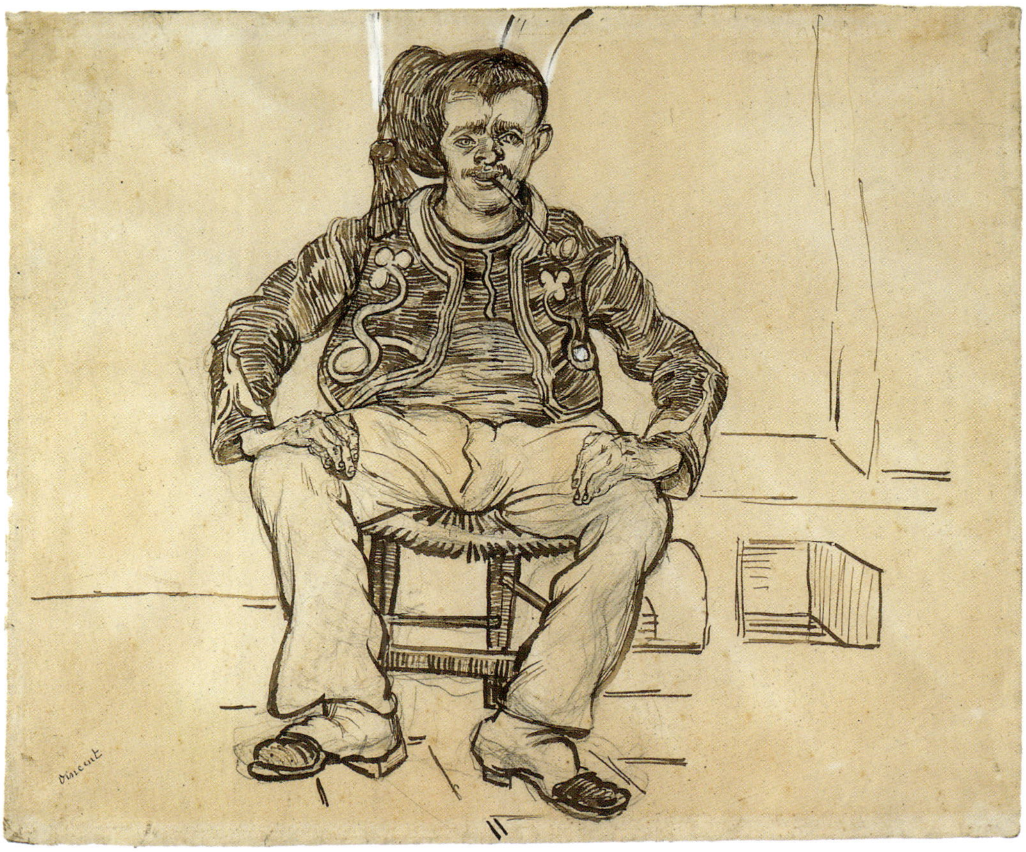

33. Eugène Delacroix, *Christ Asleep During the Tempest,* ca. 1853. New York, The Metropolitan Museum of Art.

34. Vincent van Gogh, *Zouave Sitting, Full-Length,* 1888 (F 1443 / JH 1485). Amsterdam, Van Gogh Museum.

The rest makes me smile a little—the rest of religious painting—from the religious point of view—not from the point of view of painting. And the Italian primitives (Botticelli, say), the Flemish, German primitives (V. Eyck, & Cranach) . . . They're pagans, and only interest me for the same reason as the Greeks do, and Velázquez, and so many other naturalists. Christ—alone—among all the philosophers, magicians, etc., declared eternal life—the endlessness of time, the nonexistence of death—to be the principal certainty. The necessity and the raison d'être of serenity and devotion.

Lived serenely as *an artist greater than all artists—disdaining marble and clay and paint—working in* LIVING FLESH.[4] I.e.—this extraordinary artist, hardly conceivable with the obtuse instrument of our nervous and stupefied modern brains, made neither statues nor paintings nor even books . . . he states it loud and clear . . . he made . . . LIVING men, immortals.[5]

That's serious, you know, especially because it's the truth.

That great artist didn't make books, either—Christian literature as a whole would certainly infuriate him, and its literary products that could find favor beside Luke's gospel, Paul's epistles—so simple in their hard or warlike form—are few and far between. This great artist—Christ—although he disdained writing books on ideas & feelings—was certainly much less disdainful of the spoken word—THE PARABLE above all. (What a sower, what a harvest, what a fig-tree, etc.)[6]

And who would dare tell us that he lied, the day when, scornfully predicting the fall of the buildings of the Romans, he stated, "heaven and earth shall pass away, but my words shall not pass away?"[7]

Those spoken words, which as a prodigal, great lord he did not even deign to write down, are one of the highest, the highest summit attained by art, which in them becomes a creative force, a pure creative power.

Le reste me fait un peu sourire—le reste de la peinture religieuse—au point de vue religieux—non pas au point de vue de la peinture.—Et les primitifs italiens (Botticelli disons)[c] *les primitifs flamands, allemands (v. Eyck, & Cranach)*[d] *. . . ce sont des payens et m'intéressent qu'au même titre que les Grecs, que Velasquez, que tant d'autres naturalistes. Le christ—seul—entre tous les philosophes, magiciens, &c. a affirmé comme certitude principale la vie éternelle, l'infini du temps, le néant de la mort. la nécessité et la raison d'être de la sérénité et du devouement.*

a vecu séreinement en artiste plus grand que tous les artistes—dédaignant et le marbre et l'argile et la couleur—travaillant en *CHAIR VIVANTE.*[4] *c. à. d.—cet artiste inoui, et à peine concevable avec l'instrument obtus de nos cerveaux modernes nerveux et abrutis, ne faisait pas de statues ni des tableaux ni même des livres . . . il l'affirme hautement . . . il faisait . . . des hommes* VIVANTS, *des immortels.*—[5]

C'est grave ça, surtout parce que c'est la verité.

Ce grand artiste n'a pas non plus fait des livres—la littérature chrétienne certes dans son ensemble l'indignerait et bien rares sont dans celle là les produits littéraires qui à coté de l'évangile de Luc, des épitres de Paul—si simples dans leur forme dure ou guerrière—puissent trouver grâce. Ce grand artiste—le christ—s'il dédaignait écrire des livres sur des idees & sensations—a certes bien moins dedaigné[e] *la parole parlée—*LA PARABOLE *surtout. (Quel semeur, quelle moisson, quel figuier &c.)*[6]

Et qui nous oserait dire qu'il en aie menti le jour où prédisant avec mépris la chûte des constructions romaines il affirma "quand bien même ciel et terre passeront mes paroles ne passeront point".—[7]

ces paroles parlées qu'en grand seigneur prodigue il ne daigna même pas ecrire sont un des plus hauts, le plus haut sommet atteint par l'art, qui y devient force créatrice, puissance créatrice pure.

These reflections, my dear old Bernard—take us a very long way—a very long way—*raising us above art itself.* They enable us to glimpse—the art of making life, the art of being immortal—alive.

Do they have connections with painting? The patron of painters—St. Luke—physician, painter, evangelist—having for his symbol—alas—nothing but the ox—is there to give us hope.[8]

Nevertheless—our own real life—is humble indeed—our life as painters.

Stagnating under the stupefying yoke of the difficulties of a craft almost impossible to practice on this so hostile planet, on the surface of which "love of art makes one lose real love."[9]

Since, however, nothing stands in the way—of the supposition that on the other innumerable planets and suns there may also be lines and shapes and colors—we are still at liberty—to retain a relative serenity as to the possibilities of doing painting in better and changed conditions of existence—an existence changed by a phenomenon perhaps no cleverer and no more surprising than the transformation of the caterpillar into a butterfly, of the white grub into a cockchafer.

That existence of painter as butterfly would have for its field of action one of the innumerable stars, which, after death, would perhaps be no more unapproachable, inaccessible to us than the black dots that symbolize towns and villages on the map in our earthly life. Science—scientific reasoning—seems to me to be an instrument that will go a very long way in the future.

Because, look—it was thought that the earth was *flat*—that was true—it still is today—from Paris to Asnières, for example.

But that didn't prevent science proving that the earth is above all round. Which nobody disputes nowadays.

---

*Ces considérations, mon cher copain Bernard—nous mènent bien loin—bien loin—*nous élevant au-dessus de l'art même.

Elles nous font entrevoir—l'art de faire la vie, l'art d'être immortel—vivant.—

Ont elles des rapports avec la peinture? le patron des peintres—St Luc—médecin, peintre, évangeliste—ayant pour symbole—hélas—rien que le boeuf—est là pour nous donner l'espérance.[8]

Pourtant—notre vie propre et vraie—est bien humble—celle de nous autres peintres.

Végétant sous le joug abrutissant des difficultés d'un métier presque pas praticable sur cette si ingrate planète, sur la surface de laquelle "l'amour de l'art fait perdre l'amour vrai".[9]

Puisque pourtant rien ne s'y oppose—à la supposition: que dans les autres inombrables planètes et soleils il y ait également et des lignes et des formes et des couleurs—il nous demeure loisible—de garder une serénité relative quant aux possibilités de faire de la peinture dans des conditions supérieures et changées d'existence—existence changée par un phenomène peutêtre pas plus malin et pas plus surprenant que la transformation de la chenille en papillon, du ver blanc en hanneton.

Laquelle existence de peintre papillon aurait pour champ d'action un des inombrables[f] *astres, qui après la mort ne nous seraient peutêtre pas davantage inaprochables, inaccessibles, que les points noirs qui sur la carte géographique nous symbolisent villes & villages ne nous le soient dans notre vie terrestre. La science—le raisonnement scientifique me parait être un instrument qui ira bien loin dans la suite.*

Car voici—on a supposé la terre plate*—c'était vrai—elle l'est encore aujourd'hui—de Paris à Asnières par exemple.—*

Seulement n'empêchait que la science prouva que la terre est surtout ronde. Ce qu'actuellement personne ne conteste.—

Now at present, despite that, we're still in the position of believing that *life* is *flat* and goes from birth to death.

But life too is probably round, and far superior in extent and potentialities to the single hemisphere that is known to us at present.

Future generations—probably—will enlighten us on this subject that is so interesting—and then science itself—could—with all due respect—reach conclusions more or less parallel to Christ's words concerning the other half of existence.

Whatever the case—the fact is that we are painters in real life, and it's a matter of breathing one's breath as long as one has breath.[10]

Ah—E. DELACROIX's beautiful painting—Christ's boat on the sea of Gennesaret, he—with his pale lemon halo—sleeping, luminous—within the dramatic violet, dark blue, blood-red patch of the group of stunned disciples. On the terrifying emerald sea, rising, rising all the way up to the top of the frame. Ah—the brilliant sketch.[11]

I would make you some sketches were it not that having drawn and painted for three or four days with a model—a Zouave—I'm exhausted—on the contrary, writing is restful and diverting.

What I've done is bloody ugly: a drawing of the Zouave, seated,[12] a painted sketch of the Zouave against an all-white wall[13] and lastly his portrait against a green door and some orange bricks of a wall.[14] It's harsh and, well, *ugly* and badly done. However, since that's the real difficulty attacked, it may smooth the way in the future. The figures that I do are almost always detestable in my own eyes, and all the more so in others' eyes—nevertheless, it's the study of the figure that strengthens us the most, if we do it in a different way than we're taught at Monsieur Benjamin Constant's, for example.[15]

Or actuellement on en est malgré-ça encore à croire que la vie *est* plate *et va de la naissance à la mort.*

Seulement elle aussi, la vie, est probablement ronde et très supérieure en étendue et capacités à l'hemisphère unique qui nous en est à présent connu.

Des générations futures—il est probable—nous éclairciront à ce sujet si intéressant—et alors la science elle-même—pourrait—ne lui déplaise—arriver à des conclusions plus ou moins paralèles aux dictions du christ relatives à l'autre moitié de l'existence.

Quoi qu'il en soit—le fait est que nous sommes des peintres dans la vie réelle et qu'il s'agit de souffler de son souffle tant qu'on a le souffle.[10]

*Ah—le beau tableau d'*EUG. DELACROIX*—la barque du Christ sur la mer de Génésareth, lui—avec son auréole d'un pale citron—dormant, lumineux—dans la tache de violet dramatique, de bleu sombre, de rouge sang, du groupe des disciples ahuris.—Sur la terrible mer d'émeraude montant, montant jusqu'à tout en haut du cadre. Ah—la géniale esquisse.*[11]

Je te ferais des croquis si ce n'était qu'ayant dessiné et peint depuis trois ou quatre jours avec un modèle—un zouave—je n'en peux plus—au contraire cela me repose et me distrait d'écrire.

C'est très laid ce que j'ai foutu, un dessin du zouave assis,[12] *une esquisse peinte du zouave contre un mur tout blanc*[13] *et enfin son portrait contre une porte verte et quelques briques orangées d'un mur.*[14] *C'est dur et enfin* laid *et mal foutu.—Pourtant puisque c'est de la vraie difficulté attaquée ça peut aplanir la route dans l'avenir. La figure que je fais est presque toujours détestable pour mes propres yeux et les yeux des autres à plus forte raison—pourtant c'est l'etude de la figure qui fortifie le plus si on la fait d'une autre façon qu'on ne nous l'enseigne chez monsieur Benjamin Constant par exemple.*[15]

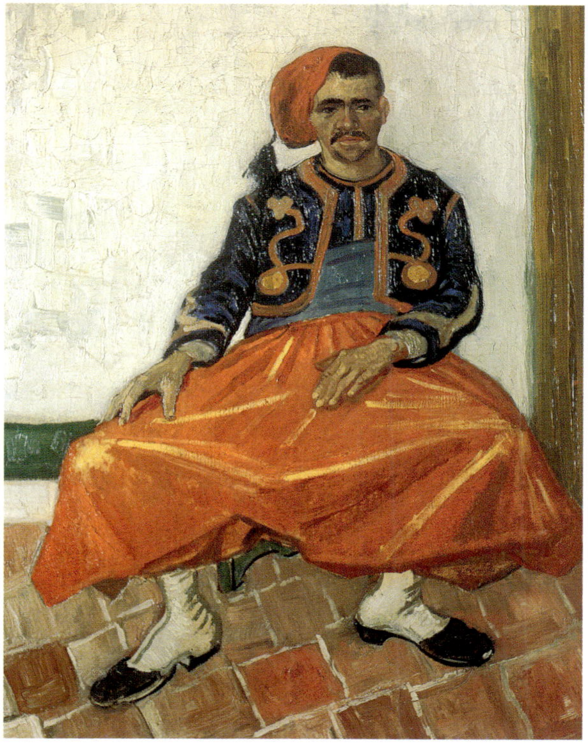

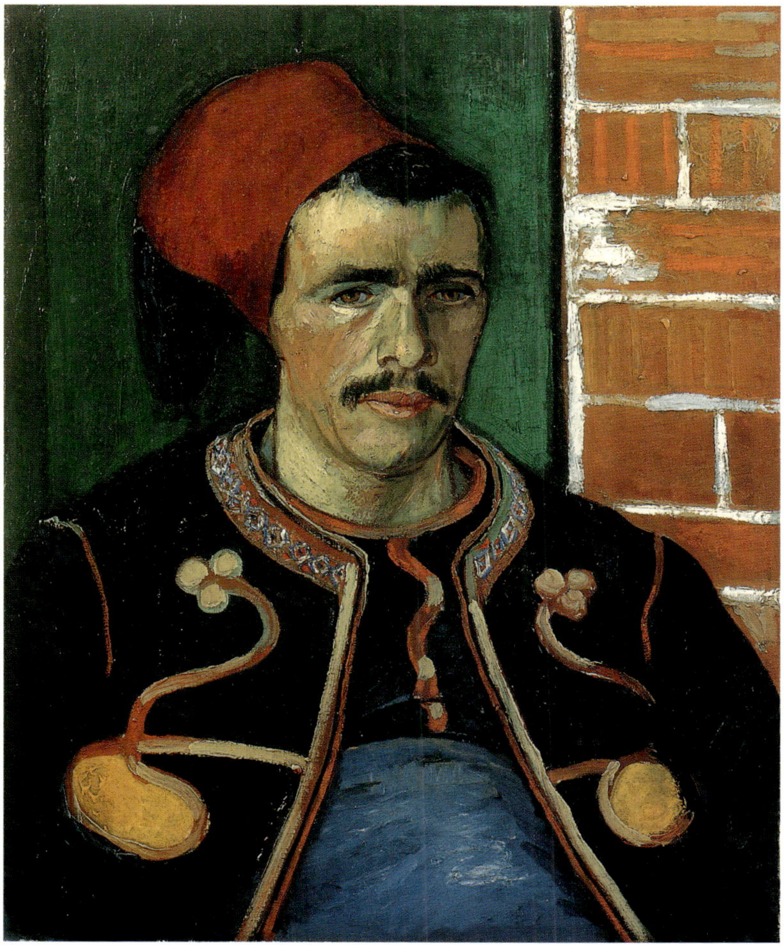

35. Vincent van Gogh, *Zouave Sitting, Full-Length,* 1888 (F 424 / JH 1488). Private collection.
36. Vincent van Gogh, *Zouave, Half-Length,* 1888 (F 423 / JH 1486). Amsterdam, Van Gogh Museum (Vincent van Gogh Foundation).

Your letter gave me great pleasure—the SKETCH IS VERY VERY INTERESTING[16] and I do thank you for it—for my part I'll send you a drawing one of these days—this evening I'm too worn out in that respect; my eyes are tired, not to mention my brain.

Listen—do you remember *John the Baptist by Puvis*?[17] I find it marvelous and as much the MAGICIAN[18] as Eugène Delacroix.

The passage about John the Baptist that you dug out of the gospel is absolutely what you saw in it . . . People pressing around somebody—art thou Christ, art thou Elias?[19] As it would be in our day to ask impressionism or one of its searcher-representatives,[20] "have you found it?"[21] That's just it.

At the moment my brother has an exhibition of Claude Monet—10 paintings done in Antibes from February to May.[22] It seems it's very beautiful.

Have you ever read the life of Luther? Because Cranach, Dürer, Holbein belong to *him*—it's he—*his personality*—that's the lofty light of the Middle Ages.[23]

I like the Sun King no more than you do—extinguisher of light[24] it rather seems to me—that Louis XIV—my God, what a pain, *in every way*, that Methodist Solomon. I don't like Solomon either, and the Methodists not at all, as well. Solomon seems a hypocritical pagan to me; I really have no respect for his architecture, an imitation of other styles, nor for his writings, which the pagans have done much better.[25]

Tell me a bit about where you stand as far as your military service is concerned; should I talk to that second lieutenant of Zouaves or not?[26] Are you going to Africa or not? In your case, do the years count double in Africa or not? Most of all, see that your blood's in order—you don't get very far with anemia—painting goes slowly—better try to make your constitution as tough as old boots,

---

Ta lettre m'a fait bien plaisir—le CROQUIS EST TRÈS TRÈS INTÉRESSANT[16] et je t'en remercie bien—je t'enverrai de ces jours ci un dessin de mon côté—ce soir je suis trop éreinté de ce côté-là, mes yeux sont fatigués, si ma cervelle ne l'est pas.

Dis donc—te rappelles tu du Jean Baptiste de Puvis?—[17] *Moi je trouve cela épatant et aussi MAGICIEN[18] qu'Eugène Delacroix.*

Le passage que tu as deniché dans l'evangile concernant Jean Baptiste est absolument ce que tu y a vu . . . des gens qui se pressent autour quelqu'un—es tu le christ, es tu Elie?—[19] Comme serait de nos jours de demander à l'impressionisme ou à un de ses représentants chercheurs[20] "as tu trouvé"?[21] C'est bien ça.

Mon frère a dans ce moment une exposition de Claude Monet—10 tableaux faits de février à Mai à Antibes.[22] c'est fort beau paraît-il.

As-tu lu jamais la vie de Luther?—car Cranach, Durer, Holbein lui *appartiennent—c'est lui—sa* personalité—*qui est la haute lumière du moyen âge.—[23]*

Moi je n'aime pas plus que toi le roi soleil—éteignoir[24] il me semble plutôt—ce Louis quatorze—mon dieu quel emmerdeur en tout *cet espèce de Salomon methodiste. je n'aime pas non plus Salomon et aussi pas du tout les méthodistes.—Salomon me semble un payen hypocrite, je n'ai vraiment pas de respect pour son architecture, imitation d'autre styles et pas non plus pour ses ecrits que les payens ont bien mieux faits.[25]*

Dis moi un peu où tu en es pour ce qui regarde ton service militaire, faut il oui ou non parler à ce sous-lieutenant zouaves?[26] Vas tu en Afrique ou pas? Est ce que les années comptent double dans ton cas en Afrique ou non? Surtout cherche à te faire du sang—avec l'anémie on n'avance guère—la peinture

a constitution to make old bones—better live like a monk who goes to the brothel once a fortnight—I do that, it's not very poetical—but anyway—I feel that my duty is to subordinate my life to painting.

If I was in the Louvre with you, I'd really like to see the primitives with you.

In the Louvre, I still return with great love to the Dutch, Rembrandt first and foremost—Rembrandt whom I once studied so thoroughly—then Potter, for example—who makes—on a no. 4 or no. 6 panel,[27] a white stallion alone in a meadow, a stallion neighing, and with a hard-on—forlorn under a sky brewing up a thunderstorm—heartbroken in the tender green immensity of a wet meadow[28]—ah well, there are wonderful things in the old Dutchmen having no connection with anything at all. Handshake, and thank you again for your letter and for your sketch.

Ever yours,
Vincent

The sonnets are going well[29]—i.e.—the color in them is good—the design isn't as strong, less sure of itself, rather; the conception's still hesitant, I don't know how to put it—its moral purpose isn't clear.

---

va lentement—faudrait tâcher de se faire tempérament dur à cuire—temperament à vivre vieux—faudrait vivre comme un moine qui va au bordel une fois par quinzaine—cela je le fais, c'est pas très poétique—mais enfin—je sens que mon devoir est de subordonner ma vie à la peinture.

Si j'étais au Louvre avec toi je voudrais bien voir les primitifs avec toi.

au Louvre, moi je vais toujours encore avec grand amour aux hollandais, Rembrandt en tête—Rembrandt que j'ai tant étudié autrefois—puis Potter par exemple—qui vous fait—sur un panneau de 4 ou de 6,[27] un étalon blanc seul dans une prairie, un étalon qui hennit et bande—désolé sous un ciel gros d'orage—navré dans l'immensite verte tendre d'une prairie humide[28]—enfin il y a des merveilles dans les vieux hollandais n'ayant aucun rapport avec n'importe quoi.[g] Poignée de main et encore une fois merci de ta lettre et de ton croquis.

t. à t.
Vincent

Les sonnets vont bien[29]—c.à.d.—la couleur en est belle—le dessin est moins fort, plutot moins sûr de soi, le dessin en hésite encore, je sais pas comment dire—le but moral n'en est pas clair.

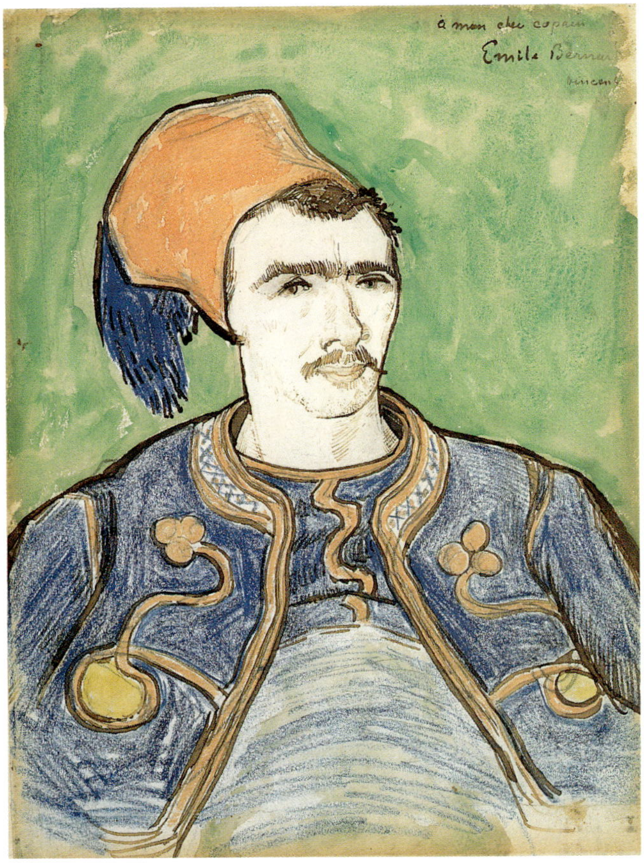
à mon cher copain
Emile
Vincent

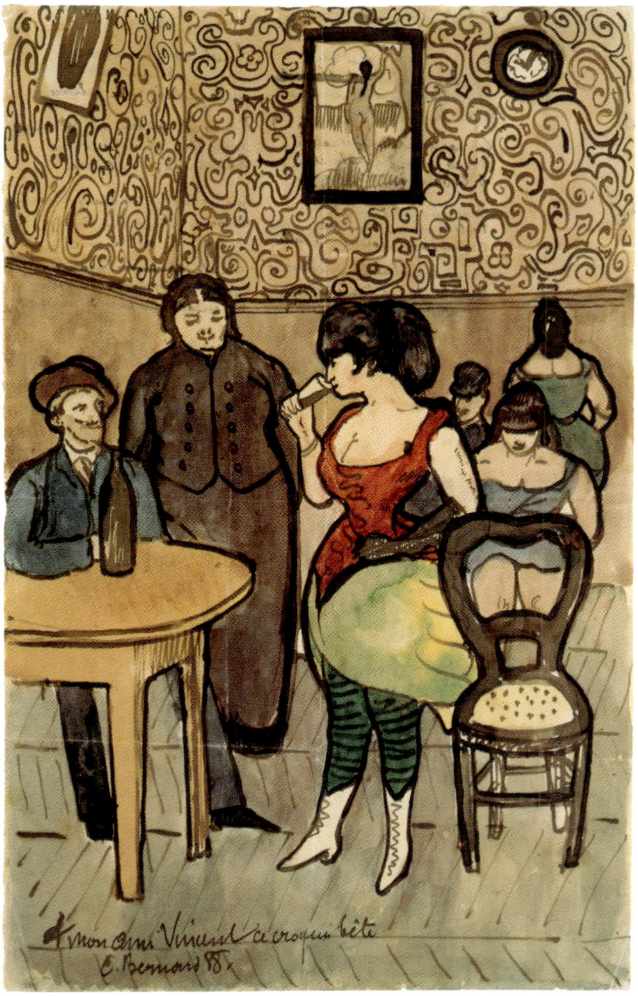
A mon ami Vincent ce croquis bête
E. Bernard 88

Annotations to Letter 8

Arles, Tuesday, 26 June, 1888

Textual Notes

a. La *[. . .]* peinte < Le *[. . .]* peint *(Van Gogh added the word* figure, *but forgot to change the gender of the definite article.)*

b. doctrine < doctine

c. (Botticelli disons) < *Added later; parentheses added by the authors.*

d. (v. Eyck, & Cranach) < *Added later; parentheses added by the authors. Van Gogh incorrectly placed the insertion mark before* allemands.

e. dedaigné < dedaingé

f. inombrables < inombrabes

g. This should be read as *quoi que ce soit.*

1. References to the Book of Exodus and the Gospel of St. Luke.

2. Van Gogh wrote either *outre* or *autre,* but neither reading is entirely clear. The version printed here corresponds with the one in *Lettres à Bernard* 1911, p. 109. The alternative would be: "*Mais la consolation [. . .] nous navre pour de bon tout autre par [. . .]*" (But the consolation [. . .] thorougly spoils everything else for us by [. . .]).

3. Van Gogh was thinking mainly of Delacroix's painting *Christ Asleep During the Tempest,* which he discussed later in this letter. The Rembrandts would have been above all the print *The Agony in the Garden* (B75) and the painting *The Supper at Emmaus* (Paris, Musée du Louvre). When van Gogh said that Millet had painted Christ's doctrine he meant that the painter was truly interested in what animated people, in what life is all about.

4. Whether he knew it or not, van Gogh's ideas tied in with the Renaissance view that Christ was an artist, with visual artists in turn being compared to him. See Kris and Kurz 1979, esp. pp. 64–86 *("Deus artifex—Divino artista"),* and Greer 2000.

5. See John 5:21, Rom. 8:11, and 1 Cor. 15:22.

6. For the parable of the sower and the seed, see Matt. 13:3–23, Mark 4:3–29, and Luke 8:5–15; and for that of the fig tree, Matt. 21:19–22, Mark 11:12–26, and Luke 13:6–9.

7. Matt. 24:35. The prediction about the destruction of the buildings is from Matt. 24:2.

8. St. Luke was also associated with van Gogh's ideal of collaboration among artists; see Letter 11.

9. In one of his earlier letters (*CL* 462), van Gogh attributed this maxim to Jean Auguste Jules Richepin. The precise source has not been identified.

37. Vincent van Gogh, *Zouave, Half-Length,* 1888 (F 1482 / JH 1487). New York, The Metropolitan Museum of Art.

38. Émile Bernard, *Brothel Scene,* 1888. Amsterdam, Van Gogh Museum (Vincent van Gogh Foundation).

10. There is a good chance that van Gogh was paraphrasing what Silvestre said about Delacroix—*ni dents, ni souffle* (no teeth nor breath)—which van Gogh quoted on several occasions; see Letter 14.

11. Eugène Delacroix, *Christ Asleep During the Tempest* (Fig. 33). It is clear that this is the version of the painting he is referring to (Delacroix painted several) from the fact that elsewhere Vincent wrote that he and Theo had seen it at the commercial exhibition of John Saulnier's collection (letter *CL* 533). That sale, at Drouot's, was held on 5 June 1886, with the viewing days on 2 and 4 June. See Lugt 1938–87, no. 48531; Paris 1886; and Johnson 1981–89, vol. 3, pp. 232–38.

The phrase "the terrifying emerald sea" echoes what Paul Mantz had written about the painting in his article "La collection John Saulnier" in *Le Temps* of Thursday, 3 June, 1886: "We did not know, before seeing this picture, that it was possible to achieve so terrifying an effect with blue" (*Nous ne savions pas, avant d'avoir vu ce tableau, qu'il fût possible d'arriver à un effet aussi terrible avec du bleu*). Van Gogh paraphrased those words in letter *CL* 533 to Theo.

12. *Zouave Sitting, Full-Length* (F 1443 / JH 1485; Fig. 34).

13. *Zouave Sitting, Full-Length* (F 424 / JH 1488; Fig. 35).

14. *Zouave, Half-Length* (F 423 / JH 1486; Fig. 36). Van Gogh made a drawing after this painting and added the dedication "*A mon cher copain Bernard. Vincent*": *Zouave, Half-Length* (F 1482 / JH 1487; Fig. 37), which he sent to Bernard in mid-July. See Letter 10, n. 1.

15. Benjamin-Constant, who enjoyed great success with his portraits of prominent and aristocratic figures, was one of the targets of van Gogh's criticism of academic realism. Benjamin Constant had a studio in the impasse Hélène in Montmartre. See Milner 1988, pp. 22–23.

16. Émile Bernard, *Brothel Scene* (Fig. 38). That this is the drawing he is speaking of can be deduced from letter *CL* 502. Bernard wrote the following on the back:

I	*I*
It's in a faraway corner, A dark tavern saddened By the feeble light of a closed shutter.	*C'est dans un coin très retiré* *Un cabaret sombre qu'attriste* *Le jour bas d'un volet tiré.*
The landlady's a specialist And sells, as in a quite open trade, Both drink and flesh . . .	*La marchande est specialiste* *Et vend comme, en un débit clair,* *De la boisson et de la chair . . .*
With a look that displays All of a heart's wretchedness, Each woman, as if at market,	*Avec un regard où s'étale* *Toute la misère d'un cœur,* *Chaque femme, comme à la halle,*
Meat dressed with a flower, Decked out in silk and gold, Sells her poor resigned soul.	*La viande qu'habille une fleur.* *Dans la soie et l'or bien peignée,* *Vend sa pauvre âme résignée.*

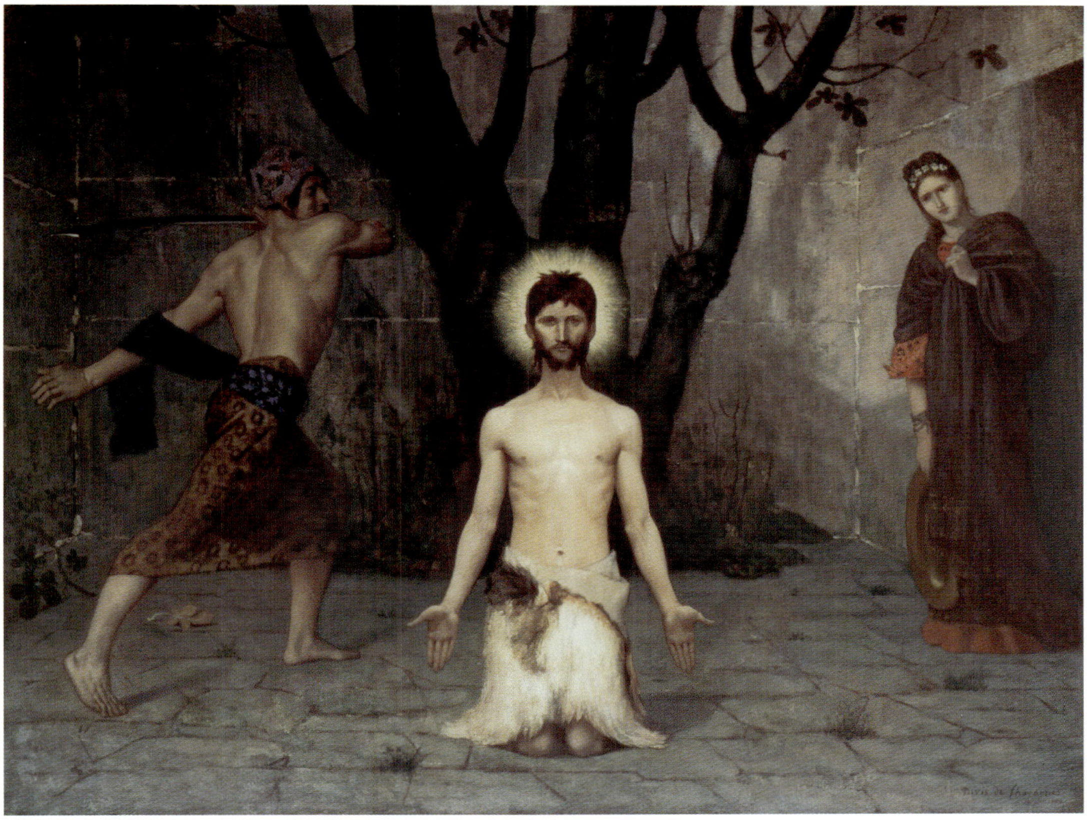

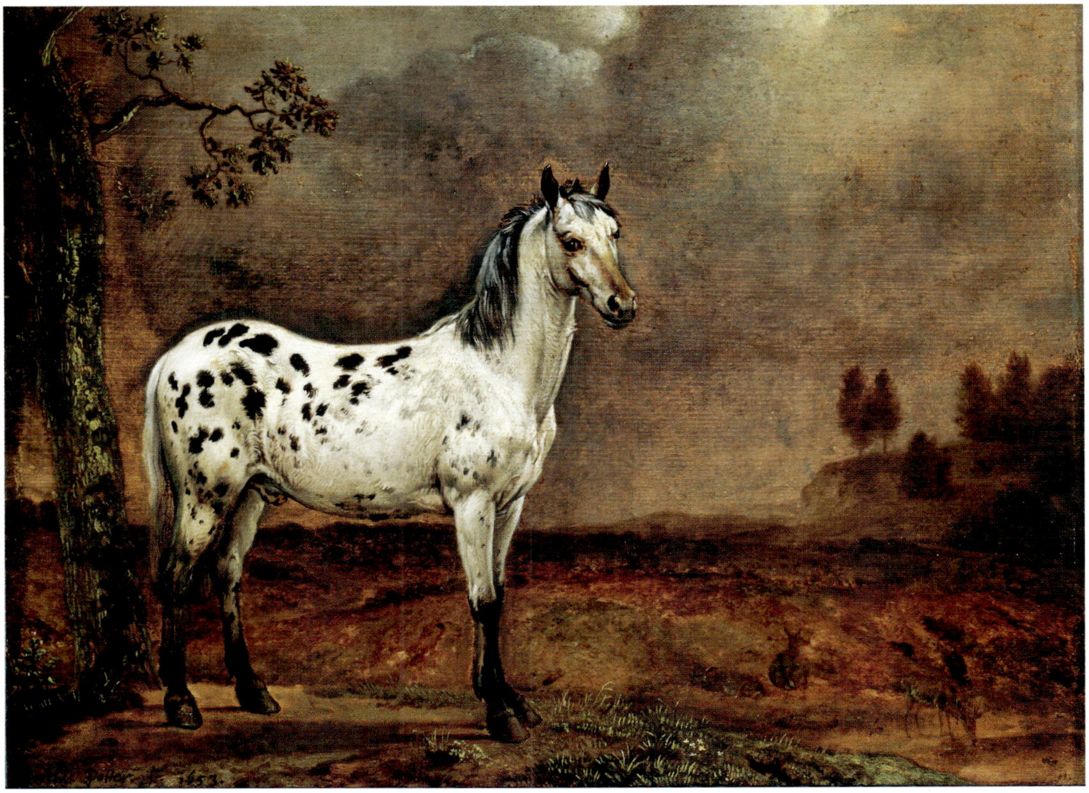

39. Pierre Puvis de Chavannes, *The Beheading of St. John the Baptist,* 1869. Birmingham, The University of Birmingham, The Barber Institute of Fine Arts.

40. Paulus Potter, *The Piebald Horse,* 1653. Paris, Musée du Louvre.

II
Society, behold your crime . . .
Man, cast a lenient glance
Upon the whore, this victim.

Woman, who knows full well that everything is a lie,
Longing for nothing now,
Not even the end of life,

Who sees only a great emptiness
Round all her being and her soul,
Love's sad victim!

—Society, you are wicked
When, for your own Desire, you force
Children under Pleasure's yoke.

19 June 1888

II
Société voici ton crime . . .
Homme jette un regard clément
Sur la putain, cette victime.

Femme, qui sait bien que tout ment,
A qui plus rien ne fait envie,
Pas même la fin de la vie,

Qui ne voit qu'un grand vide autour
De tout son être et de son âme,
Triste victime de l'amour!

—Société tu es infâme
Quand, tu courbes, pour ton Désir
Des enfants au joug du Plaisir.

19 Juin 1888

Some missing accents have been inserted.

17. Pierre Puvis de Chavannes, *The Beheading of Saint John the Baptist* (Fig. 39). Van Gogh had seen the painting at an exhibition at Durand-Ruel (20 November–20 December 1887), during the period when he and Bernard were keeping company in Paris. See Amsterdam 1994, pp. 127–29, no. 57.

18. Van Gogh had earlier applied the term *magician* to Rembrandt. He had borrowed it from Jules Michelet, *L'amour* (book 5, chapter 4, "*Il n'y a point de vieille femme*"), in which Michelet spoke of "the powerful magician Rembrandt" (*le puissant magicien Rembrandt*). Ed. Paris n.d., p. 382.

19. John the Baptist bearing witness is from John 1:19–34. The quotation is from John 1:20–25.

20. Van Gogh used the term *impressionism* very broadly for all forms of modern painting, not just for "traditional" impressionism but also for what are now known as neoimpressionism, synthetism, cloisonism, and so on.

21. Possibly an allusion to 1 Kings 21:20.

22. Van Gogh had already written about the Monet exhibition in Letter 7.

23. Lucas Cranach, Albrecht Dürer, and Hans Holbein were Protestant artists in Martin Luther's circle. See also Introduction, p. 19.

24. Although Bernard evidently shared van Gogh's opinion of King Louis XIV at the time, he later noted against this passage (and the one about Luther): "so many ideas that I do not share, despite my great friendship for Vincent" *(autant d'idées que je ne partage pas, malgré ma grande amitié pour Vincent).* See *Lettres à Bernard* 1911, p. 113.

25. A reference to the glorious Temple of Solomon on Moriah in Jerusalem. The biblical books of Proverbs, Ecclesiastes, and The Song of Songs are attributed to Solomon, the third king of Israel, who reigned from 993 to 953 B.C.

Van Gogh's characterization of Louis XIV and Solomon, the fact that he speaks of them in the same breath, and his disapproval of Solomon's writings display remarkable parallels with some passages in Ernest Renan's *Règne de Salomon.* Strangely enough, though, to the best of our knowledge, that article was first published in *Revue des Deux Mondes* 58 (1 August 1888), 3rd series, vol. 88, pp. 536–70 (esp. 539–40, 547, 565), in other words, two months after van Gogh wrote his letter. It is not impossible, however, that the passages in question appeared in an earlier publication.

Van Gogh wrote *"quel emmerdeur en* tout, *cet espèce de Salomon méthodiste."* Gauguin used precisely the same phrase, *"quel emmerdeur de Salomon,"* in a letter to Émile Schuffenecker dated to the last ten days of August 1888, so Bernard must have shown him van Gogh's letter. See *Correspondance Gauguin* 1984, pp. 216, 498–99 (n. 272), and Merlhès 1989, pp. 87–89.

26. Paul Eugène Milliet.

27. The no. 4 size measured 13 x 9½ in. (33 x 24 cm), and the no. 6, 16⅛ x 13 in. (41 x 33 cm). Potter's painting measures 16⅛ x 11⅞ in. (41 x 30 cm), which is as large as a no. 6 canvas.

28. Paulus Potter, *The Piebald Horse* (Fig. 40). The animal is not as aroused as van Gogh makes out; he evidently took pleasure in laying it on a bit for Bernard.

29. Here he was referring to the poems on the back of the drawing *Brothel Scene* (see n. 16). He discussed them at greater length in the postscript to Letter 9, which was actually intended for the present letter.

Letter 9

Arles, Wednesday, 27 June, 1888

Source
Original manuscript

Location
New York, Thaw Collection, The Morgan Library & Museum

Date
Van Gogh said that he was tired *again* after working out in the sun, which means that there must have been at least two days of good weather after the rainy period, which ended on 25 June (*Météo-France*). Since he would immediately have seized the chance to work outdoors again, we have dated this letter to Wednesday, 27 June, 1888.

The immediate reason for this letter was that van Gogh had forgotten to enclose a sheet with his previous one, detailing his reactions to Bernard's poetry, which he now included. He was absentminded during this period and had mistakenly sent the letter enclosing Bernard's drawing *Brothel Scene* to Theo's old address. It was returned to him, but the drawing must have raised some eyebrows among the post office staff, to van Gogh's amusement: "So when they returned the letter to me opened, the people at the post office had the pleasure of being able to edify themselves by contemplating Bernard's brothel."[1]

Van Gogh attributed his absentmindedness to all the work he was doing. It was around this time that he returned to *Sower with Setting Sun* (F 422 / JH 1470; Fig. 30), with the result that the study was "completely reworked."[2] The work was an attempt to paint Millet's *Sower* in the contrasting colors of Delacroix, which could speak a symbolic language. His symbolism, in other words, lay in the way he depicted observed reality and not, as Gauguin and Bernard interpreted it, in the scene itself.

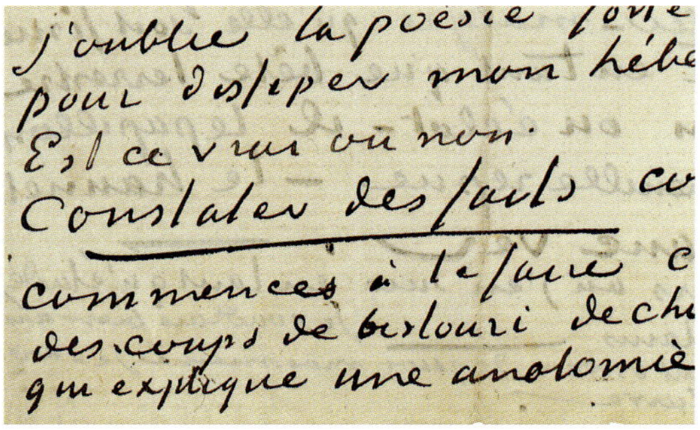
j'oublie la poesie
pour dissiper mon
Est ce vrai ou non.
Constater des faits
commencés à le faire
des coups de bistouri
qui explique une anatomie

The discussion of Bernard's poems is interesting in that it provides an insight into van Gogh's approach to literature. He believed that it was the poet's task to give an arresting picture of the modern age. Realism and probability count for a great deal, and the poet must make what he writes palpable to his readers, which is only possible if they also recognize it.

Translation of Letter 9 / Arles, Wednesday, 27 June, 1888

My dear Bernard—
I don't know what I stuck into my letter of yesterday instead of the enclosed sheet on the subject of your last sonnet. The fact is that I am so worn out by work that in the evening—although writing is restful for me—I'm like a broken-down machine, so much has the day in the full sun tired me otherwise. And that's why I stuck another sheet into your letter instead of this one.

On rereading yesterday's sheet—well, I'm sending you it as it is; on rereading it, it seems legible to me and so I'm sending you it.

Another hard day's work today.

If you saw my canvases, what would you say about them—you wouldn't find Cézanne's almost diffident and conscientious brushstroke there.

But since at present I am painting the same countryside of La Crau and the Camargue[1]—although in a slightly different place—nevertheless, certain color relationships could remain. What do I know about it—from time to time I couldn't help thinking of Cézanne, particularly when I realized that his touch is so clumsy in certain studies—disregard the word clumsy—seeing that he probably executed those studies when the mistral was blowing.

Having to deal with the same difficulty half the time, I can explain why Cézanne's touch is sometimes so sure and sometimes seems awkward. It's his easel that's wobbling.

I have sometimes worked excessively fast; is that a fault? I can't help it.

For example I've painted a no. 30 canvas—the summer evening[2]—at a single sitting.

Transcription of Letter 9 / Arles, Wednesday, 27 June, 1888

Mon cher Bernard—
je ne sais ce que j'ai fourré dans ma lettre d'hier à la place du feuillet ci-inclus ayant rapport à ton dernier sonnet. Le cas est que je suis si éreinté par le travail que le soir—quoique cela me repose d'écrire—je suis comme une machine détraquée, tellement la journée en plein soleil m'a fatigué d'un autre côté. et c'est pourquoi j'ai fourré dans la lettre un autre feuillet à la place de celui-ci.

En relisant le feuillet d'hier—ma foi je te l'envoie tel quel, pour moi en le relisant il me semble lisible et donc je te l'envoie.

Aujourd'hui encore journée raide de travail.

Si tu voyais mes toiles qu'en dirais-tu—tu n'y trouverais pas le coup de brosse[a] presque timide et consciencieux de Cezanne.—

Mais puisqu'actuellement je peins la même campagne de la Crau & Camargue[1]—quoiqu'à un endroit un peu divergent—toutefois il pourrait y demeurer certains rapports de couleur.—Qu'en sais-je—involontairement j'ai de temps en temps pensé à Cezanne, justement lorsque je me suis rendu compte de sa touche si malhabile dans certaines etudes—passe moi le mot malhabile—vu qu'il a exécuté les dites études probablement lorsque le mistral soufflait.

Ayant affaire[b] à la même difficulté la moitié du temps, je m'explique la raison pourquoi la touche de Cezanne est tantôt très sûre et tantôt parait maladroite. C'est son chevalet qui branle.

J'ai quelquefois travaillé excessivement vite, est ce un defaut? je n'y peux rien.

Ainsi une toile de 30—le soir d'eté[2]—je l'ai peinte dans une seule seance.—

It's not possible to rework it; to destroy it—why, because I deliberately went outside to make it, out in the mistral.

Isn't it rather intensity of thought than calmness of touch that we're looking for—and in the given circumstances of impulsive work on the spot and from life, is a calm and controlled touch always possible? Well—it seems to me—no more than fencing moves during an attack.

I have sent your drawing of the brothel[3] to my brother, and I've asked him to buy something of yours.

If my brother *can*, he'll do it, because he knows very well that I must want to have you sell something.

If you wished, I would earmark for an exchange with you the head of a Zouave that I've painted.[4]

But I won't speak about it unless I can have you sell something at the same time.

That would be in response to your attempt at a brothel. If we executed a brothel *together*, I'm sure we would use the study of the Zouave as a character type in it. Ah, if several painters agreed to collaborate on great things.

The art of the future might be able to show us examples of that. The thing is, for the paintings that are *needed* now there would have to be several of us in order to cope with the material difficulties. Well—alas—we're not at that point—the art of painting doesn't move as fast as literature.

Like yesterday, I'm writing to you this time in great haste, really worn out. And at this moment, too, I'm not capable of drawing; the morning in the fields has tired me out completely in that capacity.

The thing is, it's tiring, the sun down here. I'm also utterly incapable of judging my own work. I can't see whether the studies are good or bad. I have *seven studies of wheat fields,*[5] unfortunately all of them nothing but landscapes, much against my will. Old gold yellow landscapes—done quick quick quick and in a hurry, like the reaper who is silent under the blazing sun, concentrating on getting the job done.

Y revenir est pas possible—la détruire—pourquoi, puisque je suis sorti dehors en plein mistral exprès pour faire cela.—

N'est-ce pas plutôt l'intensité de la pensée que le calme de la touche que nous recherchons—et dans la circonstance donnée de travail primesautier sur place et sur nature, la touche calme et bien reglée est-elle toujours possible? Ma foi—il me semble—pas plus que l'escrime à l'assaut.

J'ai envoyé ton dessin du bordel[3] *à mon frère et j'ai sollicité de te faire un achat.*

Si mon frère peut, *il le fera, car il sait bien que je dois avoir le désir de te faire vendre quelque chôse.*

Si tu voulais je destinerais à un échange avec toi la tête de zouave que j'ai peinte.[4]

Seulement je n'en parlerai qu'en cas que je puisse en même temps te faire vendre quelque chôse.

Ce serait en réponse de ton essai de bordel.—Si à nous deux *nous exécutions un bordel je suis sûr que comme caractère nous y employerions l'étude du zouave.—Ah si plusieurs peintres étaient d'accord pour collaborer à de grandes chôses.—*

L'art de l'avenir pourrait nous montrer des exemples de cela.—Les tableaux nécessaires *maintenant, c'est qu'il faudrait être à plusieurs pour en supporter les difficultés matérielles. Enfin—hélas—nous n'en sommes pas là—l'art de la peinture ne va pas aussi vite que la littérature.*

Je t'écris cette fois ci ainsi qu'hier bien à la hâte, bien éreinté. et à ce moment aussi je ne suis pas capable de dessiner, la matinée dans les champs m'a complètement fatiguée dans cette capacité là.

C'est que çà fatigue, ce soleil d'ici.—Je suis de même entièrement incapable de juger mon propre travail. Je ne puis pas voir si les études soient bonnes ou mauvaises. J'ai sept études des blés,[5] *malheureusement toutes bien contre mon gré rien que des paysages.—Des paysages jaunes vieil or—faits vite vite vite et pressé comme le moissonneur qui se tait sous le soleil ardent, se concentrant pour en abattre.*

I tell myself that you may perhaps—be surprised to see how little I love the Bible myself, which I have nevertheless often tried to study a little—there is only this kernel, Christ—who, from the point of view of art, seems superior to me—at any rate *something other*—than Greek, Indian, Egyptian, Persian antiquity, which went so far. Now I say it again—this Christ is more of an artist than the artists—he works in living spirit and flesh, he makes men instead of statues, so . . . as a painter I feel good being an ox . . . and I admire the bull, the eagle, the man,[6] with a veneration—which—will prevent my being a man of ambition.[7]

Handshake.

Ever yours,
Vincent

I add about these sonnets[8] explanation of what I understand by—their design is not really sure of itself:

You moralize at the end.

You tell society that it is squalid because the whore makes us think of meat, of the market.

Very good, that, the whore is like meat at the butcher's.

For myself—numbed—I understand, I feel that, I recognize a sensation from my own life, I say: that's well said.

Because the sonorous rhythm of the colorful words suggests to me the brutal reality of the dive with great intensity.

But the reproofs addressed at the end to "society." *As for me, numbed,* hollow words like "the

---

Je me dis que tu dois peut-être—être surpris de voir combien peu moi j'aime la bible laquelle pourtant j'ai souvent cherché à etudier un peu—il n'y a que ce noyau, le christ—qui au point de vue de l'art me semble superieur—dans tous les cas autre chôse—*que l'antiquité Grecque, Indienne, Egyptienne, Persane, lesquelles ont été si loin. Or je le repète—ce Christ est plus artiste que les artistes—il travaille en esprit et chair vivants, il fait des hommes au lieu de statues alors . . . je me sens bien être boeuf—etant peintre . . . et j'admire le taureau, l'aigle, l'homme,*[6] *avec une vénération—qui—m'empêchera d'être un ambitieux.*[7]

Poignée de main.

t. à t.
Vincent

j'ajoute pour ces sonnets[8] *explication de ce que j'entends par—le dessin n'en est pas bien sûr de soi:*

Tu fais la morale à la fin.—

tu dis à la société qu'elle est infâme parceque la putain nous fait penser à la viande, à la halle.—

Très bien cela, la putain est comme la viande chez le charcutier.—

Moi, abruti, je comprends, je sens cela, je retrouve une sensation de ma vie à moi, je dis: c'est bien parlé.

car le rythme sonore des mots colorés m'évoque la réalité brutale du bouge avec une grande intensité.

Mais les reproches adressées à la fin à "la societe". pour moi abruti, *mot creux comme "le bon dieu", ne me font plus d'effet.—*

Ca n'y est pas, dis-je, et je retombe dans mon abrutissement, j'oublie la poésie forte assez d'abord[c] *pour dissiper mon hébétude.*

good Lord" no longer have any effect on me.

It isn't there, I say, and I sink into my numbness again; I forget the poem, at first strong enough to dispel my lethargy.

Is that true or not?

To report the facts, as you do at the beginning, is to wield the lancet like a surgeon explaining anatomy.

I listen, meditative and interested; I watch, but if, later, the surgeon-anatomist is going to moralize at me like that, I find that that last tirade does not have the same value as the anatomy demonstration.

To study, to analyze society, that always says more than moralizing.

Nothing would seem more curious to me, however, than to say, for example: "see that meat from the market, notice how, all the same, despite everything, it can still be electrified for a moment by the stimulus of a love more refined and unexpected."

Like the sated caterpillar that no longer eats, that crawls on a wall instead of crawling on a cabbage leaf, this sated female can no longer love, either, even though she goes about it—she seeks, seeks, seeks, does she herself know what for? She's conscientious, alive, responsive, galvanized, rejuvenated for a moment, but powerless. Yet she still loves—her life's there, then—*make no bones about it*—despite the fact that she's finished and dying as an earthly creature. The butterfly, where does the butterfly emerge, from that sated caterpillar—the cockchafer from that white grub?

Here, by the way, is where I am in terms of studies of old whores———I would also very much like to know roughly what I am the larva of myself, perhaps.

Est ce vrai ou non?

Constater des faits *comme tu commences à le faire c'est donner des coups de bistouri de chirurgien qui explique une anatomie.*

j'écoute recueilli et interessé, je regarde mais si après le chirurgien anatomiste va me faire de la morale comme ça, je trouve que cette derniere tirade n'a pas la même valeur que la démonstration anatomique.

étudier, analyser la société, cela dit toujours plus que moraliser.

Rien ne me semblerait plus curieux que de dire par exemple pourtant: "voilà cette viande de la halle, remarquez combien tout de même, malgré tout, elle reste électrisable momentanément par le stimulus d'un amour plus raffiné & inattendu."

*Ainsi que la chenille repue qui ne mange plus, qui rampe sur un mur au lieu de ramper sur une feuille de choux, cette femelle repue ne peut plus aimer quand bien même qu'elle s'y met—elle cherche, cherche, cherche, sait-elle elle-même quoi? Elle est conscientieuse, vivante, sensible, galvanisée, rajeunie momentanément, mais impuissante. Elle aime encore pourtant—donc sa vie y est—*pas à tortiller—*malgré qu'elle soit finie et mourante en tant que bête terrestre. le papillon, où éclot-il le papillon, de cette chenille repue—le hanneton de ce blanc ver?——*

Voilà d'ailleurs où j'en suis en tant qu'études de vieilles putains———je voudrais bien aussi aproximativement savoir de quoi moi-même je suis peutêtre la larve.

Annotations to Letter 9

Arles, Wednesday, 27 June, 1888

TEXTUAL NOTES
a. de brosse < le brosse
b. affaire < à faire
c. Read *suffisamment forte en premier lieu.*

1. Paul Cézanne, whom Bernard greatly admired, lived in Aix-en-Provence. La Crau is a vast plain in the Rhône valley, southeast of Arles. Cézanne painted at various places in the region. See Rewald 1986, pp. 267–69. For the Camargue, see Letter 6.

2. Fig. 32, which measures 29 1/8 x 35 7/8 in. (74 x 91 cm), making it a no. 30 canvas.

3. Fig. 38.

4. Fig. 36. Bernard never got this painting.

5. These seven studies are *Wheat Field with Setting Sun* (F 465 / JH 1473; Fig. 32), *Wheat Field* (F 411 / JH 1476; Amsterdam, Van Gogh Museum), *Wheat Field with Sheaves and Arles in the Background* (F 545 / JH 1477; Paris, Musée Rodin), *Wheat Field with Sheaves* (F 561 / JH 1480; Honolulu Academy of Arts), *Wheat Field with Sheaves* (F 558 / JH 1481; Jerusalem, Israel Museum), *Haystacks Near a Farm* (F 425 / JH 1442; Otterlo, Kröller-Müller Museum) and *Sower with Setting Sun* (F 422 / JH 1470; Fig. 30).

6. In his Vollard edition of the letters, Bernard felt that he had to correct van Gogh about the animals symbolizing the evangelists: "He ought to have said *lion* instead of *bull*, the ox having already been mentioned for Saint Luke, patron of painters, to whom Vincent dedicates himself" *(Il eut fallu dire le* lion *au lieu du* taureau, *le boeuf étant déjà cité pour Saint Luc, patron des peintres, auquel Vincent se voue.).* See *Lettres à Bernard* 1911, p. 117. The crux of the passage, however, is not so much iconographical accuracy or completeness as van Gogh's view that one must accept one's humble place in the face of the very great. See also Chicago and Amsterdam 2001–2, p. 122.

7. Van Gogh was referring to his earlier remarks about Christ as an artist (Letter 8) and about creativity as opposed to sexual activity (Letter 7).

8. These were the poems on the back of the drawing *Brothel Scene;* see Letter 8, n. 16. Although van Gogh called them sonnets, strictly speaking they are not.

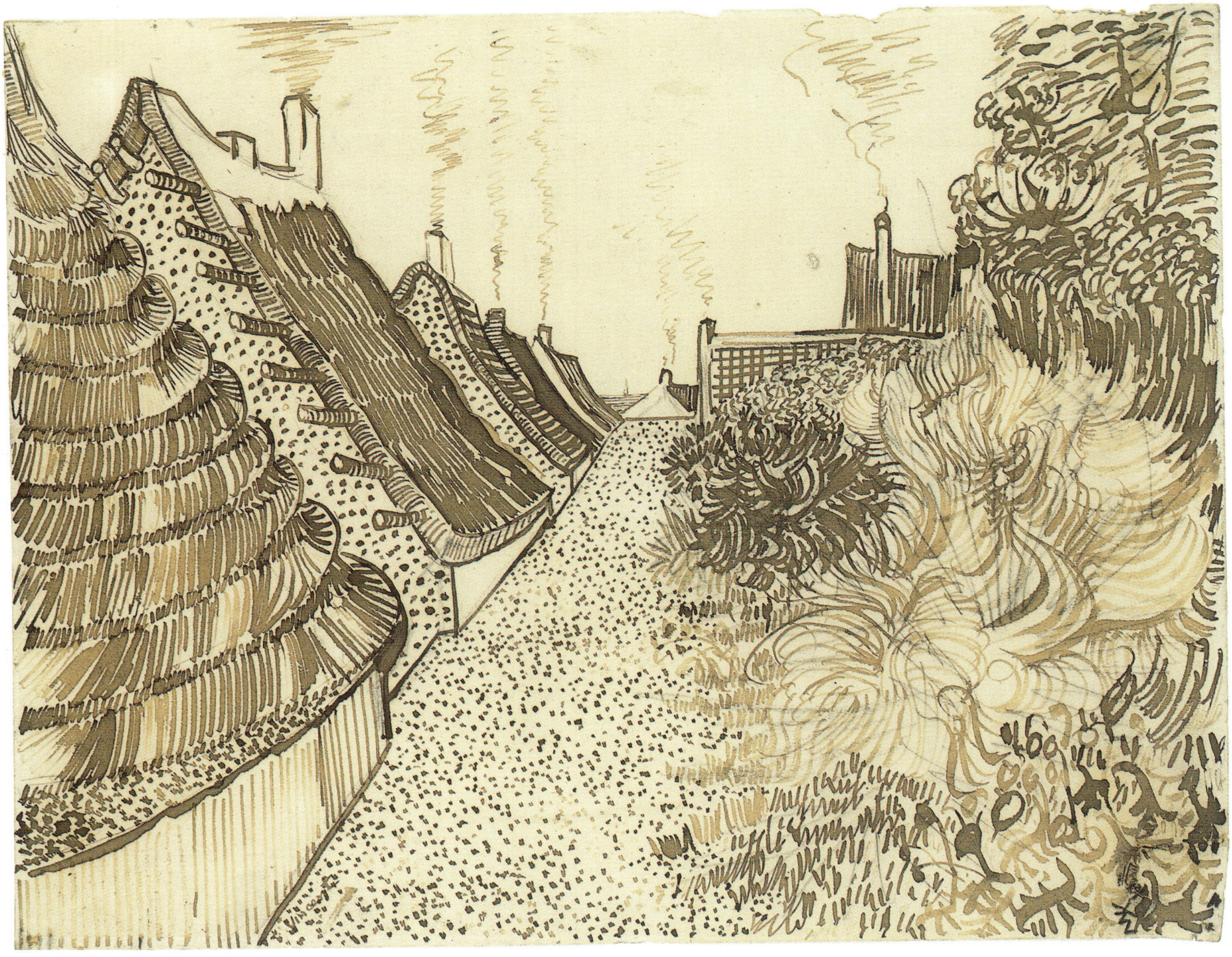

Letter 10

Arles, Sunday, 15 July, 1888

Source
Original manuscript

Location
New York, Thaw Collection, The Morgan Library & Museum

Date
Van Gogh wrote that he had drawings ready to send to Bernard. In a letter to Theo of Sunday, 15 July, he said that he had sent them "today" and that he had also written to Bernard that Sunday (letter *CL* 511). The present letter is accordingly dated Sunday, 15 July, 1888.

Van Gogh had made a series of large drawings on Montmajour, near Arles, and in this letter he said that two of them were the most "Japanese" he had ever produced. He also wrote to Theo, telling him that these drawings should be viewed in a bare room, just like japonaiseries, an idea that he got from Pierre Loti's novel *Madame Chrysanthème*. Van Gogh's studio, too, was "a bare interior, 4 white walls and red tiles on the floor."[1] He had started on a series of drawings after his recent paintings for Bernard, in the hope that his friend would also send him sketches of his own paintings. Van Gogh enclosed six drawings with this letter, in which he told Bernard for the first time about his plans for working with Gauguin, who had accepted his invitation to Arles.

Bernard was now thinking of leaving Saint-Briac. Shortly after receiving van Gogh's letter, he told his parents that his love affair with Marie, the daughter of Madame Lemasson, was over, and that he intended to go on 1 August. He was thinking of moving to nearby Saint-Jacut and suggested that his mother and his sister Madeleine visit him. There was no hint of his departure on 4 July, when he wrote enthusiastically about a mural he was painting. "I'm doing a decoration 4 meters wide by 2 meters high. I've chosen a religious subject, *The Adoration of the Shepherds*, as I write to you there are about twenty figures, twice life-size, I'm working at full stretch, because I haven't

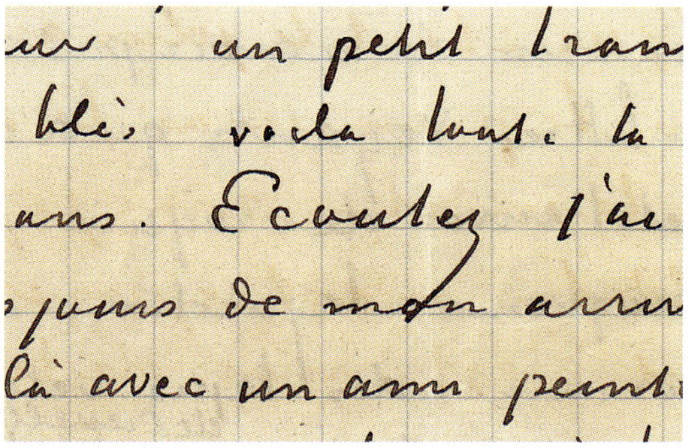
un petit tram
blé; voilà tout. La
ans. Ecoutez j'ai
jours de mon arriv
là avec un ami peint

budged from it for two days. The paint is the paint used on buildings. I do it with three: blue, white, red, and I achieve some interesting things in tones. I've never felt as bold as since I started it. It's an excellent exercise for me, and I believe I've never done better, either."[2]

41. Vincent van Gogh, *Street in Saintes-Maries*, 1888 (F 1435 / JH 1506). New York, The Metropolitan Museum of Art.

Translation of Letter 10 / Arles, Sunday, 15 July, 1888

My dear old Bernard.

Perhaps you will be disposed to forgive me for not having replied to your letter straightaway, seeing that I'm attaching a small batch of sketches to this one.[1]

In the sketch The Garden, there is perhaps something like "the shaggy carpets of flowers and woven greenery"[2] of Crivelli or Virelli,[3] doesn't much matter. Ah, well—in any case I wanted to reply to your quotations with my pen, but not by writing words. Today, too, I don't have much of a head for discussion; I'm up to my ears in work.

Have made large pen drawings—*2*—an immense flat expanse of country—seen in bird's-eye view from the top of a hill—vineyards, reaped fields of wheat, all of it multiplied endlessly, streaming away like the surface of a sea toward the horizon bounded by the hillocks of La Crau.[4]

It *does* NOT look Japanese, and it's *actually* the most Japanese thing that I've done.

A microscopic figure of a plowman, a little train passing through the wheat fields; that's the only life there is in it. Listen, I passed—a few days after my arrival—that place with a painter friend.[5]

There's something that would be boring to do, he said. I said nothing myself, but I found that so astonishing that I didn't even have the strength to give that idiot a piece of my mind. I go back there, go back, go back again—well, I've done two drawings of it—of that flat landscape in which there was *nothing* but . . . the infinite . . . eternity.

Well—while I'm drawing along comes a chap who isn't a painter but a soldier.[6] I say, "Does it astonish you that I find that as beautiful as the sea?" Now he knew the sea—that one. "No—it doesn't astonish me"—he says—"that you find that as beautiful as the sea—but I find it even *more* beautiful than the ocean because it's *inhabited*." Which of the spectators was more the artist, the first or the second, the painter or the soldier—I myself prefer that soldier's eye. Isn't that true?

Now it's my turn to say to you, reply to me quickly this time by return of post—to let me know if you agree to make me some sketches of your Breton studies. I have *a consignment that's about to go off*,[7] and before it clears off I want to do at least another half a dozen subjects in pen sketches for you. Having few doubts that you will do it for yours, I'm getting down to work on my side, anyway, without even knowing if you want to do that. Now, I'll send these sketches to my brother, to urge him to take something from them for our collection.

I've already written to him about that, anyway. But we're working on something that leaves us absolutely without a sou.

The fact is that Gauguin—who has been very ill—is probably going to spend the coming winter with me here in the south. And there's the fare, which is worrying us. Once here, well, two together spend less than one alone. All the more reason why I should like to have some things by you here. Once Gauguin's here, we'll try to do something together in Marseille, and will probably exhibit there. Now I'd like to have some things by you, too, although without making you lose opportunities for selling in Paris. In any case, I don't believe I'm making you lose them by encouraging you to exchange sketches of painted studies between us. And as soon as I can, we'll do another piece of business as well, but am quite hard up now. What I'm convinced of is that if we exhibit in Marseille, sooner or later Gauguin and I will encourage you to join us.

Thomas[8] bought Anquetin's study in the end—the peasant.[9]

I shake your hand firmly, so long, and

Ever yours,
Vincent

Transcription of Letter 10 / Arles, Sunday, 15 July, 1888

Mon cher copain Bernard.
peut être seras tu enclin à m'excuser de n'avoir pas incontinent repondu à ta lettre, voyant qu'à celle ci je joins un petit envoi de croquis.[1]

Dans le croquis le jardin il y a peutêtre quelque chose comme "des tapis velus de fleurs et de verdure tissus"[2] *de Crevelli ou Virelli,*[3] *peu importe.—Enfin—en*[a] *tout cas à tes citations j'ai voulu répondre avec la plume mais pas en écrivant des paroles. Aujourd'hui aussi j'ai peu la tête à la discussion, je suis dans le travail jusqu'à par-dessus les oreilles.*

Ai fait de grands dessins à la plume—2—une immense campagne plate—vue à vol d'oiseau d'en haut d'une colline—des vignes, des champs de blé moissonnés, tout cela multiplié à l'infini, détalant comme la surface d'une mer vers l'horizon borné par les monticules de la Crau.[4]

Ca n'a PAS *l'air japonais et c'est la chôse la plus japonaise* reellement *que j'aie faite.*

un personnage microscopique de laboureur, un petit train qui passe dans les blés, voila toute la vie qu'il y a là-dedans. Ecoutez j'ai passé—les premiers jours de mon arrivee—à cet endroit-là avec un ami peintre.—[5]

Voila ce qui serait embêtant à faire, dit-il. moi je ne dis rien mais je trouvais cela tellement épatant que je n'avais pas même la force d'engueuler cet idiot. J'y reviens, reviens, reviens encore—bon, j'ai fait deux dessins de ca—de ce paysage plat où il n'y avait rien *que . . . l'infini . . . l'éternité.*

Bon—survient pendant que je dessine un coco qui n'est pas peintre mais soldat.[6] *j'y dis "est ce que ca t'epate que moi je trouve cela aussi beau que la mer"? Or il connaissait la mer—lui. "Non—cela ne m'épate pas—dit-il—que tu trouves cela aussi beau que la mer—mais moi je trouve cela même* plus *beau que l'ocean puisque c'est* habité.*" Qui etait le plus artiste des spectateurs, le premier ou le deuxieme, le peintre ou le soldat—moi je prefère l'oeil de ce soldat. n'est ce pas vrai?—*

Maintenant c'est à moi de te dire, réponds moi vite cette fois ci par retour du courrier—pour me répondre si tu consens à me faire des croquis de tes etudes Bretonnes. J'ai un envoi qui va partir[7] *et avant que cela décampe je veux encore te faire au moins une nouvelle demi douzaine de motifs en croquis à la plume. Doutant peu de ce que tu le fera pour les tiens, je me mets d'ailleurs au travail de mon côté sans savoir même si tu veux faire cela. Maintenant ces croquis je les enverrai à mon frère pour l'engager à en prendre quelque chose pour notre collection.*

Je lui ai deja ecrit à ce sujet d'ailleurs. Mais nous avons une affaire en train qui nous laisse sans le sou absolument.

C'est que Gauguin—qui a été bien malade—ira probablement passer l'hiver prochain avec moi ici dans le midi. Et il y a le voyage qui nous embête. Une fois ici, ma foi, à deux on dépense moins que seul. Raison de plus pour que je desirerais avoir des choses de toi ici. Gauguin une fois ici, à nous deux nous chercherons à faire quelquechose à Marseille et y exposerons probablement. Or je désirerais avoir des chôses de toi aussi, toutefois sans te faire perdre des chances de vente à Paris. En tous cas je ne crois pas t'en faire perdre en t'engageant à faire un échange de croquis d'études peintes de part et autre. Et aussitot que je pourrai nous ferons encore une autre affaire mais suis assez gêné maintenant. Ce dont je suis persuadé c'est que si nous exposons à Marseille tot ou tard Gauguin comme moi t'engagerons à y participer.

Thomas[8] *a fini par acheter l'etude d'Anquetin—le paysan.—*[9]

Je te serre bien la main, à bientot et

t. à. t.
Vincent

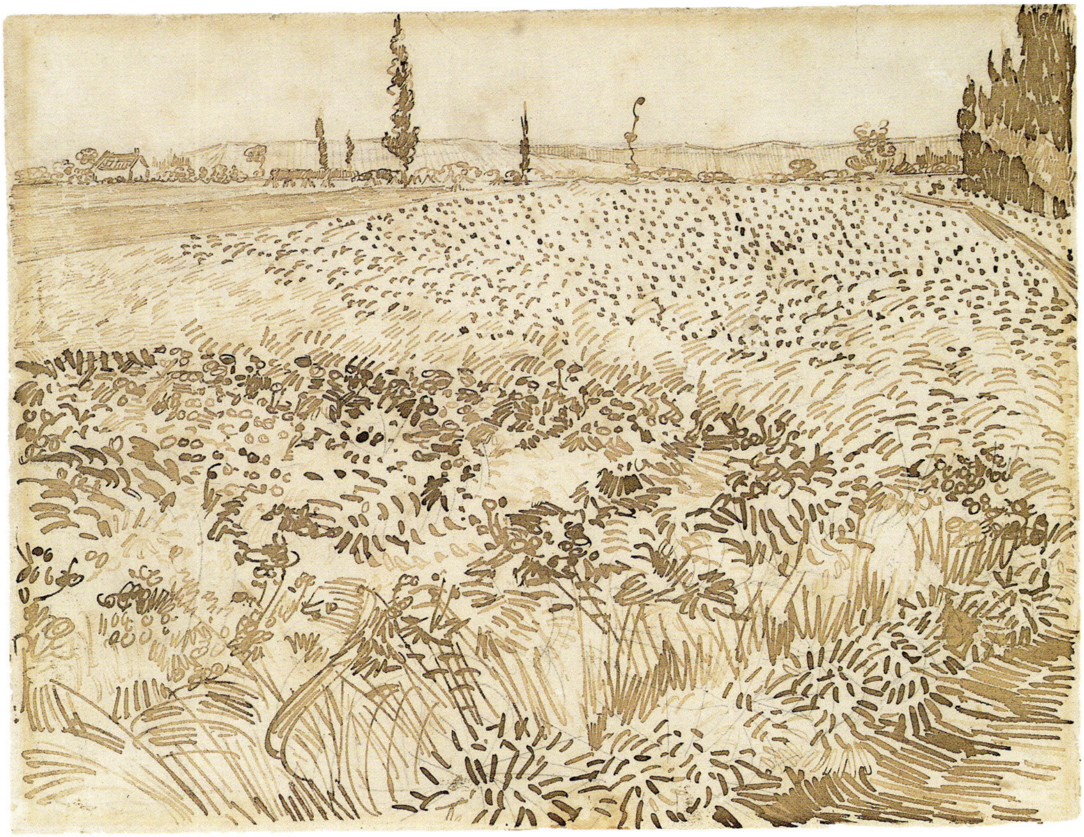

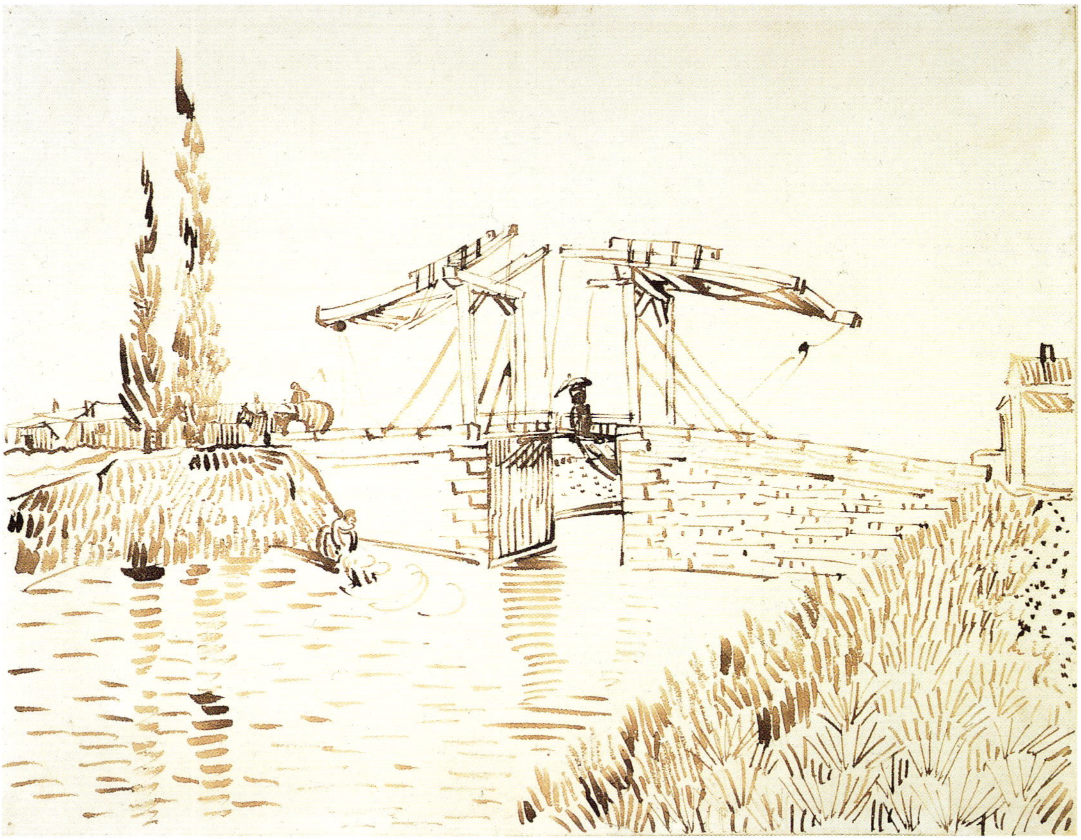

42. Vincent van Gogh, *Wheat Field*, 1888 (F 1481 / JH 1515). New York, The Metropolitan Museum of Art.

43. Vincent van Gogh, *Drawbridge with a Lady with a Parasol*, 1888 (F 1471 / JH 1420). Los Angeles County Museum of Art.

Annotations to Letter 10

Arles, Sunday, 15 July, 1888

TEXTUAL NOTE
a. Enfin—en < Enfin—

1. Vincent sent six drawings, going by what he wrote to Theo later that day (letter *CL* 511) and what Bernard wrote to his parents in July. He spoke of receiving a packet with "six truly remarkable pen drawings. There's a head of a Zouave that amazes me. Vincent's becoming very good. At the same time that he's an excellent artist, he's a thinker, because every one of his works contains an idea that flashes on the eye of the man who looks for it. And his literature keeps me excited, too, it's so vivid" *(six dessins à la plume vraiment remarquables. Il y a une tête de zouave qui m'a étonné. Vincent devient très fort. En même temps que c'est un excellent artiste, c'est un penseur car chacune de ses oeuvres contient une idée qui éclate à l'oeil de celui qui la cherche. De plus sa littérature me tient en émoi tant elle est vibrante).* He then quoted from Vincent's letter, with such asides as "Ah! Just like him! I understand him" *(ah! comme c'est lui, je l'entends).* He ended with the words: "This passage of the letter is absolutely remarkable, it would make Hugo go wild with excitement." *(Ce passage de la lettre est absolument remarquable, il ferait délirer Hugo).* See Harscoët-Maire 1997, pp. 177–78.

It is not entirely certain which six sketches made up the batch. It is known from Bernard's letter to his parents that there was the head of a Zouave (Fig. 37), with the dedication *A mon cher copain Bernard; Vincent.* Later in the present letter van Gogh mentioned one of a garden, which must have been *Newly Mown Lawn with Weeping Tree* (F 1450 / JH 1509; private collection), as also emerges from Letter 18.

A few days later van Gogh sent Bernard nine more sketches (see Letter 11). Roskill has identified a further eleven drawings in addition to the two listed above, but it is impossible to say what was in which batch: *Fishing Boats at Sea* (F 1430 / JH 1505; Berlin, Nationalgalerie), *Street in Saintes-Maries* (F 1435 / JH 1506; Fig. 41), *Sower with Setting Sun* (F 1442 / JH 1508; private collection), *Canal with Women Washing* (F 1444 / JH 1507; Otterlo, Kröller-Müller Museum), *Harvest Landscape* (F 1485 / JH 1540; Berlin, Nationalgalerie), *Wheat Field* (F 1481 / JH 1515; Fig. 42), *Wheat Field with Sheaves* (F 1488 / JH 1517; Berlin, Nationalgalerie), *View of a River, Quay and Bridge* (F 1507 / JH 1469; private collection), *Rocks with a Tree* (F 1554 / JH 1518; private collection), *Haystacks Near a Farm* (F 1426 / JH 1514; Budapest, Szépmüvészeti Museum), *Wheat Field with Sheaves and Arles in the Background* (F 1491 / JH 1516; Washington, National Gallery of Art). See Roskill 1971, pp. 142–55.

Drawbridge with a Lady with a Parasol (F 1471 / JH 1420; Fig. 43) and *Wheat Field with Setting Sun* (F 1514 / JH 1546; Winterthur, Kunstmuseum) also belonged to Bernard and were probably sent in one of the July batches. See Amsterdam 2005, pp. 204, 250, 269–72.

Roskill also mentioned *Mousmé, Sitting in a Cane Chair, Half Length* (F 1504 / JH 1520; Moscow, Pushkin State Museum of Fine Arts), which belonged to Bernard (see Roskill 1971, p. 174), but according to Pickvance—and we agree—van Gogh only made this drawing later, after

finishing the painting. That is also clear from Letter 14 of ca. 5 August, in which van Gogh reported, "have not yet found time for figure sketches."

On the basis of Letter 15, Pickvance believed that van Gogh sent Bernard *Mousmé* and *Joseph Roulin, Sitting in a Cane Chair* (F 1723 / JH 1523; private collection) during the first half of August 1888. There is, however, no evidence that Bernard ever had the latter drawing.

The illustrations of drawings published with the excerpts from the letters in *Mercure de France* and in the illustrations section of the Vollard edition of the letters to Bernard are of no assistance in fleshing out the above information.

2. This is derived from the first two verses of the thirtieth rondeau, "*Les fourriers d'Esté sont venus,*" by Charles d'Orléans (see d'Orléans 1923–27, vol. 2, p. 307):

The harbingers of summer have arrived	*Les fourriers d'Esté sont venus*
To dress his dwelling place,	*Pour appareiller son logis,*
And have had his carpets spread,	*Et ont fait tendre ses tappis,*
Of flowers and verdure wove.	*De fleurs et verdure tissus.*
Spreading shaggy carpets out	*En estendant tappis velus,*
Of green grass o'er the land,	*De vert herbe par le païs,*
The harbingers [of summer have arrived.]	*Les fourriers [d'Esté sont venus.]*
Hearts weary and dejected once,	*Cueurs d'ennuy pieça morfondus,*
Thanks be to God, are healthy now and blithe,	*Dieu mercy, sont sains et jolis;*
Away with you, be gone,	*Alez vous ent, prenez païs,*
Winter, you'll stay no more;	*Yver, vous ne demourrés plus;*
The harbingers [of summer have arrived!]	*Les fourriers [d'Esté sont venus!]*

3. Since Bernard often mentioned Crivelli in his correspondence, it is likely that van Gogh was reacting here to something Bernard had written. He may also have cited the preceding quotation. Carlo Crivelli mainly painted biblical scenes, often with detailed flowers in the foreground. This, however, might also be a reference to Vittore Crivelli, a maker of religious paintings and very probably Carlo's brother. See Bovero 1961 and Provvido 1972.

4. *La Crau, Seen from Montmajour* (F 1420 / JH 1501; Fig. 44) and *Landscape Near Montmajour with Train* (F 1424 / JH 1502; Fig. 45). The drawings measure roughly 19 x 23⅞ in. (48.5 x 60.5 cm).

5. This was probably the Danish painter Christian Vilhelm Mourier-Petersen, who was in Arles from ca. 10 October 1887 to ca. 22 May 1888, apart from a brief excursion to Martigues at the end of March. He wrote on 16 March 1888 about his acquaintance with van Gogh: "Initially I considered him to be mad, but by and by I note that there is method in it. He knows the friends of Jastrau: MacKnight, Russell etc.—but at the moment I can't remember his name: van Prut or something of the kind." See Larsson 1993, pp. 14, 26.

---

44. Vincent van Gogh, *La Crau, Seen from Montmajour,* 1888 (F 1420 / JH 1501). Amsterdam, Van Gogh Museum (Vincent van Gogh Foundation).

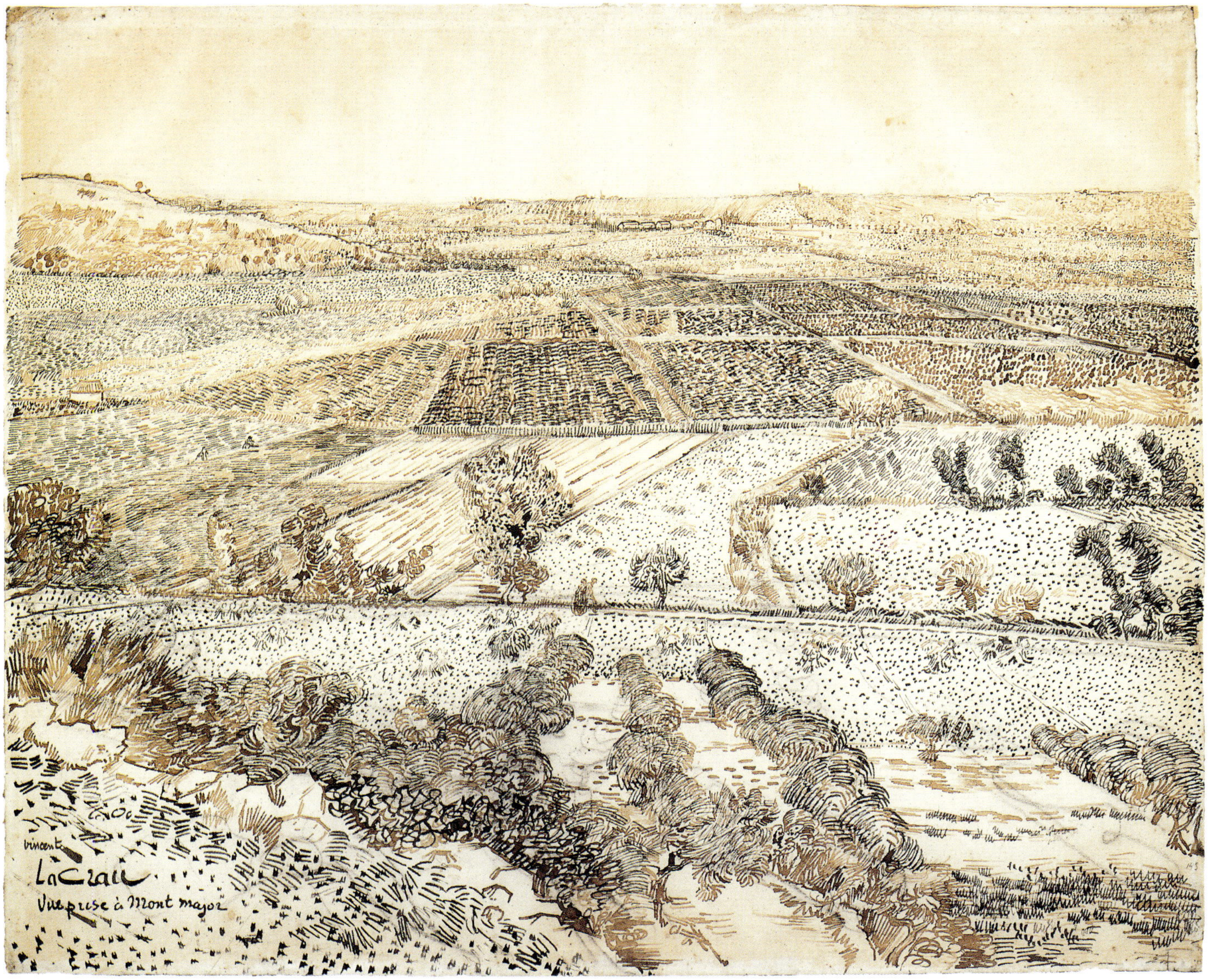
vincent
La Crau
Vue prise à Mont major

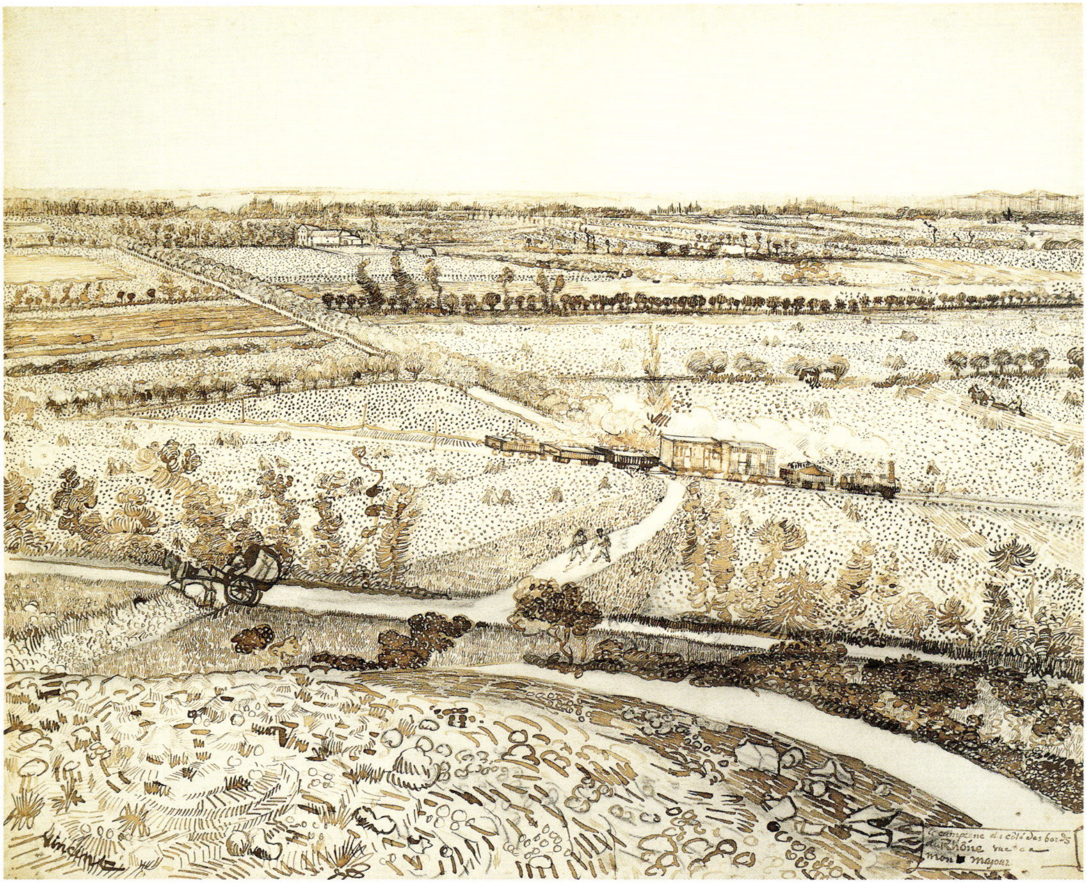

6. He is referring to the Zouave lieutenant Paul Eugène Milliet; see Letter 7, n. 17. He had spent a day with him on Montmajour shortly before.

7. These must be the paintings that Milliet was to take to Paris in mid-August; see letter *CL* 524.

8. Georges Thomas, called "le père Thomas," was known among a small circle as a dealer who championed the cause of the most contemporary art. He sold one of Toulouse-Lautrec's first paintings and exhibited work by van Gogh. His gallery at the time was at 43, boulevard Malesherbes. See Paris 1988, p. 342. Vincent repeatedly speaks of Thomas in his letters to Theo.

9. Probably Louis Anquetin, *Old Peasant* (Fig. 46).

---

45. Vincent van Gogh, *Landscape Near Montmajour with Train,* 1888 (F 1424 / JH 1502). London, The British Museum.
46. Louis Anquetin, *Old Peasant,* 1886. Amsterdam, Van Gogh Museum.

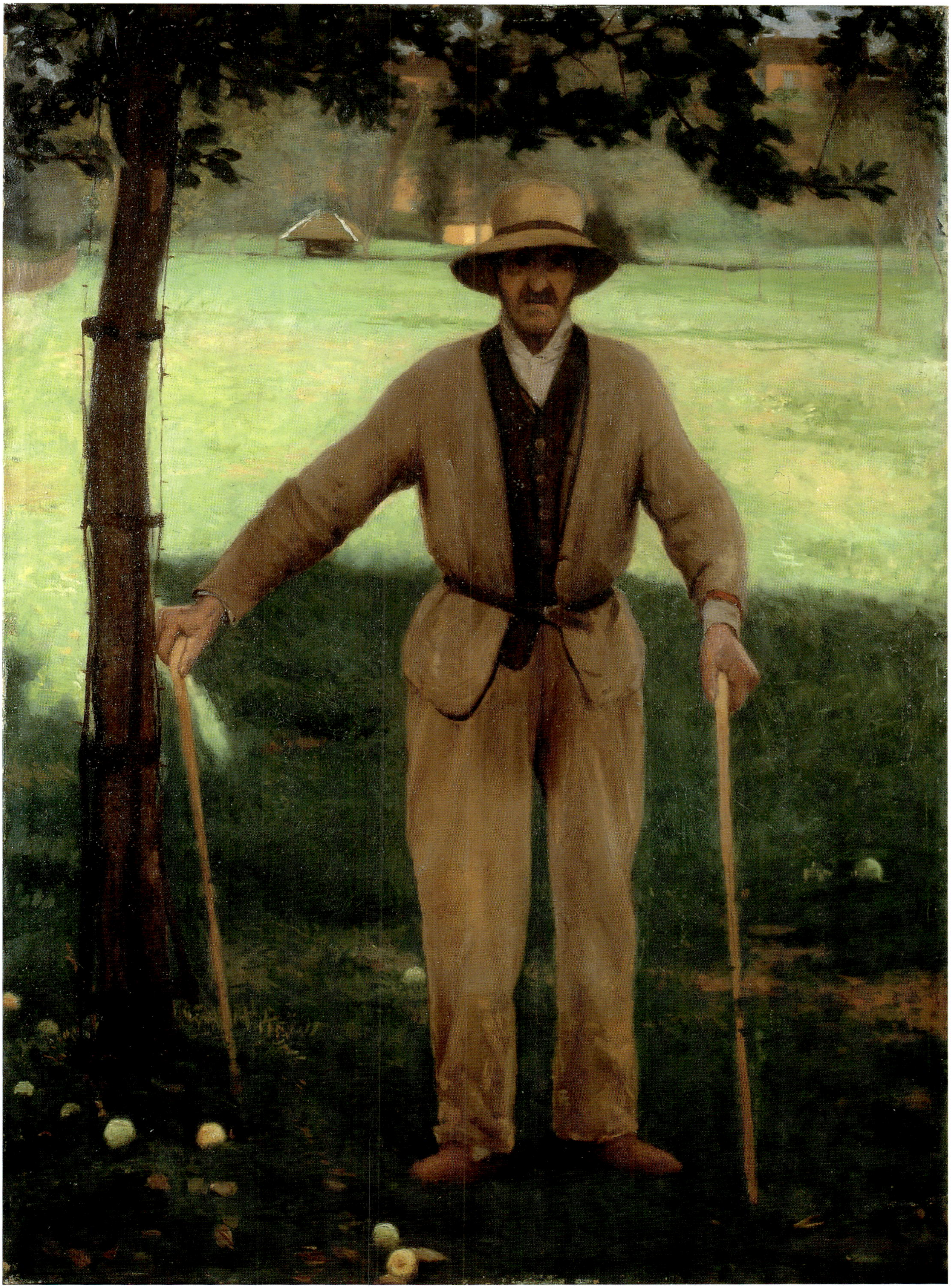

Letter 11

Arles, between Tuesday, 17, and Friday, 20 July, 1888

Source
Original manuscript

Location
Paris, Institut Néerlandais (Fondation Custodia)

Date
Van Gogh had just sent Bernard the drawings he had promised in Letter 10, of 15 July. The choice of words he used in that letter to announce the new "half a dozen" shows that he was planning to start on them almost right away, connecting them with the six sent with Letter 10. This ties in with his usual practice, which was to work in "campaigns" in which he set himself a single artistic task, so it is unlikely that he would needlessly have interrupted the continuity of the series of drawings for Bernard. That being said, it is not impossible that he waited a day before starting on the second series. This letter would therefore have been written a few days after the one of 15 July, but it is difficult to say precisely how many days he would have needed to complete the nine drawings that were ultimately sent. With the proviso that the second date, in particular, is a little arbitrary, we date this letter between Tuesday, 17, and Friday, 20 July, 1888.

Additional details
Roskill thought that this letter might have been written after Letter 12. He based this on the drawing *Mousmé* (F 1504 / JH 1520) in Bernard's collection, which Roskill believed was sent with the *second* batch of drawings and was made after the almost finished painting F 431 (letter *CL* 514). See Letter 10, n. 1.

Van Gogh sent Bernard a second batch of drawings after painted studies. As he did in letters to other correspondents, he utilized Bernard's own frame of reference by making a connection between his own landscape drawings and the work of Cézanne, whom Bernard and Gauguin greatly admired. By establishing this link he was trying to play down the differences among artists, in line with his ideal of unity. That is why he also returned to the subject of collaboration, which he considered so important.

It is understandable, then, that he was impatient to hear when Gauguin would be coming to Arles. He wrote to Theo, saying that he found it odd that Gauguin had not yet let him know, and thought that he must be "ill and discouraged."[1] He even toyed with the idea of going to Brittany himself if the journey was too expensive for Gauguin and life was cheaper there.

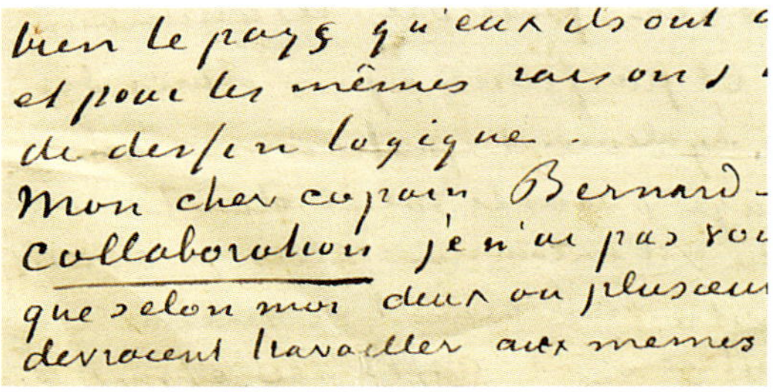
bien le pays qu'eux ils ont
et pour les mêmes raisons
de dessin logique.
Mon cher copain Bernard -
collaboration je n'ai pas
que selon moi deux ou plusieurs
devraient travailler aux mêmes

In the meantime, Bernard was planning to go to Pont-Aven. On 29 July he wrote to his sister Madeleine that he was glad the decision had been made "that you are going to come with me to Pont-Aven, you and Mother."[2] He intended to leave on 8 or 10 August.

Translation of Letter 11 / Arles, between Tuesday, 17, and Friday, 20 July, 1888

My dear old Bernard,

Today I have just sent you another nine sketches after painted studies.[1] In this way you'll see some of the subjects from this nature that inspires *père* Cézanne. Because La Crau near Aix is roughly the same as the surroundings of Tarascon and La Crau here. The Camargue is even simpler, because often there's nothing left—nothing but poor soil with tamarisk bushes and the coarse kinds of grass that are to these scanty pastures what alfa grass is to the desert.

Knowing how much you love Cézanne, I thought these sketches of Provence might please you. Not that there are similarities between a drawing by me and by Cézanne; oh, no, no more than between Monticelli and me—but I too love the region that they have loved so much, and for the same reasons of color, of logical design.

My dear old Bernard—by *collaboration*[2] I didn't mean that in my view two or more painters should work on the same paintings. By that I meant, rather, works that are divergent but go together and complement each other. Let's look at the Italian primitives and the German primitives and the Dutch school and the Italians proper, in a word, let's look at painting in its entirety.

Works unintentionally form a "group," a "series." Now then, at present the impressionists, too, form a group, in spite of all their disastrous civil wars, in which people on both sides try to get at each others' throats with a zeal worthy of a better destination and final goal.

In our northern school there's Rembrandt—head of the school—since his influence is felt by anyone who comes close to him. We see, for example, Paulus Potter painting animals rutting and impassioned[3] in landscapes that are also impassioned—in a thunderstorm, in sunshine, in the melancholy of autumn—whereas before knowing Rembrandt this same Paulus Potter was rather dry and meticulous. There you have two people who go together like brothers, Rembrandt and Potter. And while Rembrandt probably never touched a painting by Potter with his brush, that doesn't alter the fact that both Potter and *Ruisdael* owe to him what's best in them, that something that affects us deeply when we know how to look at a corner of old Holland through their temperament.[4]

And then there is the fact that the material difficulties of the painter's life make collaboration, union among painters, desirable—(just as much as in the days of the guilds of St. Luke).[5]

By safeguarding their material life, by liking each other as pals instead of getting at each others' throats, painters would be happier and anyway less ridiculous, less foolish, and less guilty.

However, I don't insist, knowing that life carries us along so fast that we don't have the time to discuss and act simultaneously. That's why at present, while the union exists only very incompletely, we're sailing on the high seas in our small and wretched boats, isolated on the great waves of our time.

Is it renaissance, is it decline? We have no way of judging that, for we're too close to avoid being led into error by distortions of perspective. For contemporary events, in our eyes, take on proportions that are probably exaggerated as regards our misfortunes and our merits.

I shake your hand firmly and hope to have news from you soon.

Ever yours,
Vincent

Transcription of Letter 11 / Arles, between Tuesday, 17, and Friday, 20 July, 1888

Mon cher copain Bernard,

je viens de t'envoyer aujourd'hui encore 9 croquis d'après des études peintes.[1] *De cette façon tu verras des motifs de cette nature qui inspire le père Cézanne. Car la Crau près d'Aix c'est à peu près la même chôse que les environs de Tarascon et la Crau d'ici.—La Camargue est encore plus simple car souvent il n'y a plus rien—plus rien que de la mauvaise terre avec des buissons de tamaris et des herbes dures qui sont à ces maigres pâturages ce que l'alfa est au désert.*

Sachant combien tu aimes Cézanne j'ai pensé que ces croquis de Provence pourraient te faire plaisir. Non pas qu'il y ait des similitudes entre un dessin de moi & de Cézanne, oh cela pas plus qu'entre Monticelli et moi—mais moi aussi j'aime bien le pays qu'eux ils ont aimé tant et pour les mêmes raisons de couleur, de dessin logique.

Mon cher copain Bernard—par collaboration[2] *je n'ai pas voulu dire que selon moi deux ou plusieurs peintres devraient travailler aux memes tableaux. j'ai plutot voulu entendre par là des oeuvres divergentes mais qui se tiennent & se complètent. Voyons et les primitifs Italiens et les primitifs allemands et l'ecole Hollandaise et les Italiens proprement dits, enfin, voyons toute la peinture.*

Involontairement les oeuvres forment "groupe", "serie". Or actuellement les impressionistes aussi forment groupe malgré toute leur désastreuses guerres civiles dans lesquelles de part & autre on cherche à se manger le nez avec un zèle digne d'une meilleure destination et but final.

Dans notre école du nord il y a Rembrandt—chef d'école—puisque son influence se fait sentir à quiconque l'approche. Nous voyons par exemple Paul Potter peindre les animaux en rut et passionnés[3] *dans des paysages également passionnés—sous l'orage, sous le soleil, dans la mélancolie de l'automne—alors qu'avant de connaitre Rembrandt ce même Paul Potter était assez sec et méticuleux. Voilà deux gens qui se tiennent comme des frères, le Rembrandt et le Potter. Et si probablement jamais Rembrandt n'a touché de sa brosse un tableau de Potter, n'empêche que et Potter et* Ruysdael *lui doivent ce qu'ils ont de meilleur, ce quelque chôse qui nous navre lorsque nous savons regarder un coin de l'antique Hollande à travers leur tempérament.—*[4]

Il y a ensuite que les difficultés matérielles de la vie de peintre rendent la collaboration, l'union des peintres désirable—(tout autant qu'à l'epoque des corporations St Luc).[5]

En se sauvegardant la vie matérielle, en s'aimant comme des copains au lieu de se manger le nez, les peintres seraient plus heureux et en tous les cas moins ridicules, moins sots et moins coupables.

Toutefois je n'insiste point, sachant que la vie nous emporte si vite que nous n'avons pas le temps de discuter et d'agir à la fois. Raison pourquoi actuellement, l'union n'existant que très incomplètement, nous naviguons sur la haute mer dans nos petites & mechantes barques isolées sur les grandes vagues de notre temps.

Est ce une renaissance, est ce une décadence, nous ne saurions en être les juges étant trop près pour ne pas être induits en erreur par les déformations de la perspective. Les événements contemporains prenant pour notre oeil des proportions exagerées probablement en tant que quant à nos malheurs et nos mérites.

Je te serre bien la main et espère bientot avoir de tes nouvelles.

t. à t.
Vincent

Annotations to Letter 11

Arles, between Tuesday, 17, and Friday, 20 July, 1888

1. Van Gogh had sent six drawings shortly before. For the drawings in the two batches see Letter 10, n. 1.

2. Bernard must have reacted to what van Gogh had written two letters previously: "Ah, if several painters agreed to collaborate on great things" (Letter 9).

3. There are not many "rutting and impassioned" animals to be found in Potter's oeuvre, at most a bull mounting a cow or a quadruped urinating.

4. This is in accordance with Émile Zola's dictum regarding the naturalistic approach to art. In *Mes haines* he described a good work of art as "a corner of creation seen through a temperament" *(un coin de la création vu à travers un tempérament).* See Zola 1966–70, vol. 10, p. 38.

5. Luke the evangelist was the patron saint of painters. The guilds of St. Luke, which emerged during the fifteenth century, drew up statutes in consultation with the local authority that closely regulated the training and defined the rights and duties of painters. The guilds had to guarantee that apprentices received a proper training, and they were obliged to look after the welfare of their members. See Hoogewerff 1947.

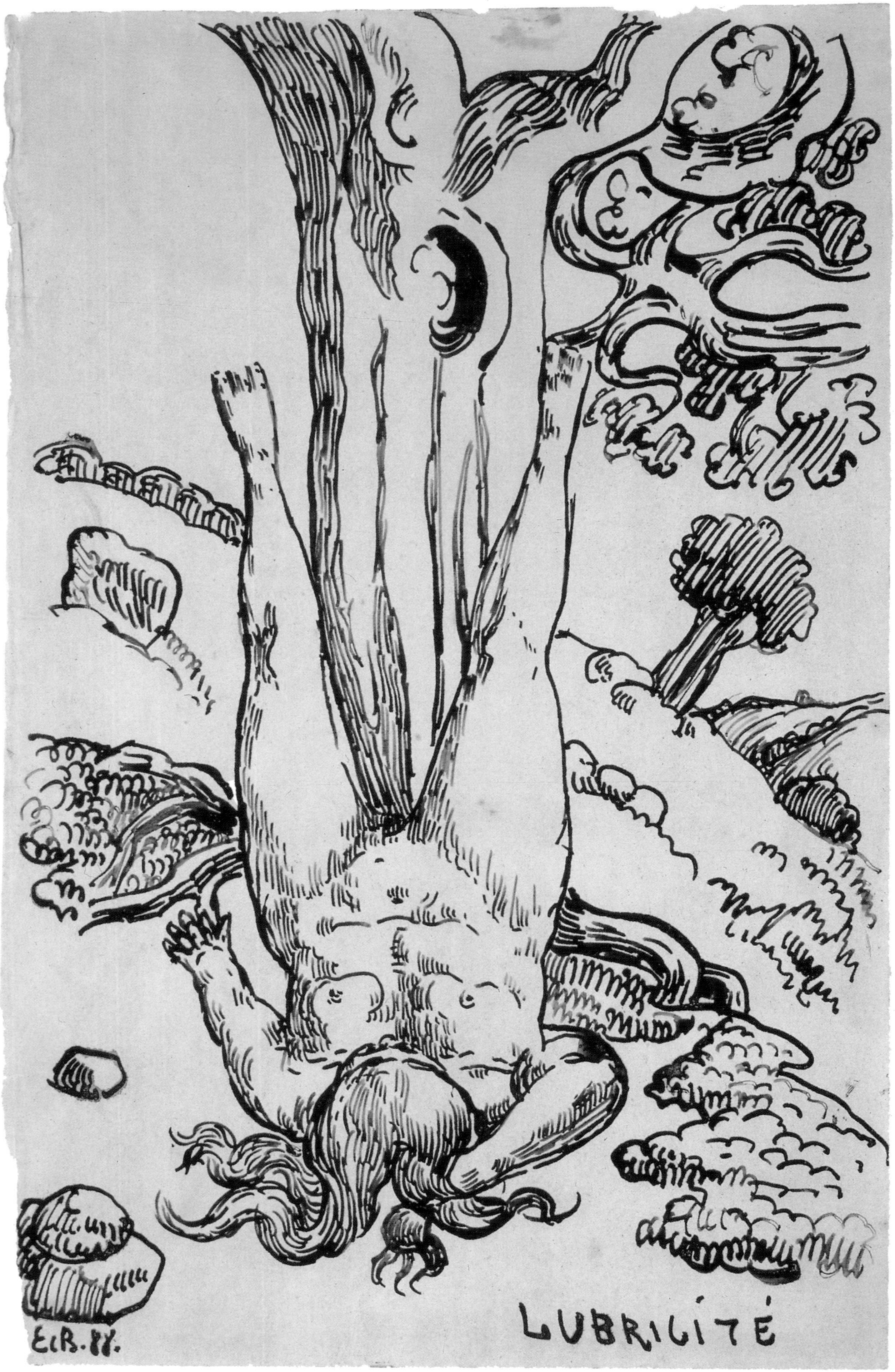
E.B. 88.
LUBRICITÉ

Letter 12

Arles, Sunday, 29 July, 1888

Source
Original manuscript

Location
New York, Thaw Collection, The Morgan Library & Museum

Date
Van Gogh thanked Bernard for the drawings he had sent, which shows that this letter follows Letter 11, in which van Gogh was still waiting for news from Bernard. The letter must have been written at the end of the week, because he had just finished the painting *La Mousmé*. He mentions its completion in similar terms in letter *CL* 514 of 29 July. We have therefore dated this letter, too, to Sunday, 29 July, 1888.

Additional details
Druick and Zegers believe that *Mousmé, Sitting in a Cane Chair* (F 1504 / JH 1520), the drawing after the painting mentioned here, was sent with this letter. See Chicago and Amsterdam 2001, pp. 126–27. There are no firm indications, however, that this was the case; it is more likely that van Gogh only sent the drawing later. See Letter 10, n. 1.

Bernard had, in turn, sent van Gogh some drawings, and van Gogh liked them very much. He wrote glowingly about them to Theo and immediately sent them on to Paris. "I have received ten sketches from Bernard like his brothel; there are three of them that are in the style of Redon; the enthusiasm he has for that, I don't much share myself. But there is a woman washing herself, very Rembrandtesque or in the style of Goya, and a very strange landscape with figures. He expressly forbids me to send them to you, but you'll receive them by the same post."[1]

Here, as elsewhere, it is clear that van Gogh actively supported his fellow artists by telling others about their work and praising it. In this period he was still trying to get Russell to buy something by Gauguin, and Gauguin, trying to find the money to go to Arles, still hoped that something would come of it. He wrote to van Gogh that he had heard "that Russell had great admiration for me and that he had to go to Belle-Île. I don't quite understand why a rich man doesn't buy what he admires. Anyway, let's hope."[2] As it happened, Russell wrote to van Gogh on 22 July from Belle-Île, the island off the southern coast of Brittany where he had recently gone to live, inviting him to come and work with him there for a

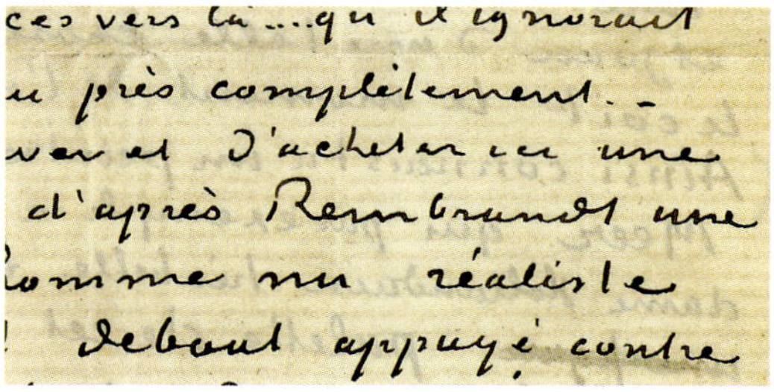
ces vers là ...qu'il ignorait
u près complètement. -
ver et d'acheter ici une
d'après Rembrandt une
comme un réaliste
debout appuyé contre

while. Russell told him that Bernard, with whom he also corresponded, was having trouble with his work because of the bad weather in Saint-Briac (*CL* 501b). So, despite the distances separating the artists who knew each other from Paris, they still managed to keep in touch.

At this time, van Gogh was in the habit of reflecting upon what he had achieved. Although he was only thirty-five, he felt that his body was failing and that his mind had taken a severe knock from a life that was overwhelming him. But his "painter's fingers" were "loosening up." He was throwing himself into his work, and when the inner storm became too fierce, he drank "a glass too many to deaden myself."[3] Bernard's youth and the opportunities that were still open to him countered such thoughts.

47. Émile Bernard, *Lubricity,* 1888. Amsterdam, Van Gogh Museum (Vincent van Gogh Foundation).

Translation of Letter 12 / Arles, Sunday, 29 July, 1888

My dear old Bernard,
A thousand thanks for sending your drawings;[1] I very much like the avenue of plane trees beside the sea with two women chatting in the foreground and the promenaders.[2] Also

the woman under the apple tree[3]
the woman with the parasol[4]

then the four drawings of nude women, especially the one washing herself, a gray effect embellished with black, white, yellow, brown. It's charming.[5]

Ah . . . Rembrandt . . . all admiration for Baudelaire aside—I venture to assume, especially on the basis of those verses . . . that he knew more or less nothing about Rembrandt.[6] I have just found and bought here a little etching after Rembrandt, a study of a nude man, realistic and simple; he's standing, leaning against a door or column in a dark interior. A ray of light from above skims his downturned face and the bushy red hair.[7]

You'd think it a Degas for the body, true and felt in its animality.

But see, have you ever looked *closely* at "The Ox" or the *Interior of a Butcher's Shop* in the Louvre?[8] You haven't looked closely at them, and Baudelaire infinitely less so.

It would be a treat for me to spend a morning with you in the Dutch gallery. All that is barely describable. But in front of the paintings I could show you marvels and miracles that are the reason that, for me, the primitives really don't have my admiration first and foremost and most directly.[9]

Transcription of Letter 12 / Arles, Sunday, 29 July, 1888

Mon cher copain Bernard,
Mille fois merci de ton envoi de dessins,[1] *j'aime beaucoup l'allée de platanes au bord de la mer avec deux femmes causant sur l'avant-plan et des promeneurs.*[2] *Egalement*

la femme sous le pommier[3]
la femme à l'ombrelle[4]

puis les quatre dessins de femmes nues, surtout celle qui se lave, un effet gris agrémenté de noir, blanc, jaune, brun. C'est charmant.[5]

Ah . . . Rembrandt . . . toute admiration pour Baudelaire à part—j'ose supposer surtout d'après ces vers-là . . . qu'il ignorait Rembrandt à peu près complètement.—[6] *Je viens de trouver et d'acheter ici une petite eauforte d'après Rembrandt, une étude d'homme nu réaliste et simple, il est debout appuyé contre une porte ou colonne dans intérieur sombre. Un rayon d'en haut frise la figure baissée et les grands cheveux roux.*[7]

On dirait un de Gas pour le corps vrai et senti dans son animalité.

Mais voyons, as tu jamais bien *regardé* "le boeuf" *ou l'interieur d'un boucher du Louvre?*[8] *Tu n'as pas bien regardé cela et Baudelaire encore infiniment moins.*

Ce serait une fête pour moi que de passer une matinee avec toi dans la galerie des Hollandais. Tout cela ne se décrit guère. Mais devant les tableaux je pourrais te montrer des merveilles et des miracles qui pour moi font que les primitifs n'ont pas du tout en premier lieu et le plus directement mon admiration.[9]

But there you are; I'm so far from eccentric. A Greek statue, a peasant by Millet, a Dutch portrait, a nude woman by Courbet or Degas, these calm and modeled perfections are the reason that many other things, the primitives as well as the Japanese, seem to me . . . like WRITING WITH A PEN;[10] they interest me infinitely . . . but something complete, a perfection, makes the infinite tangible to us.

And to enjoy such a thing is like coitus, the moment of the infinite.

For instance, do you know a painter called Vermeer, who, for example, painted a very beautiful Dutch lady, pregnant? This strange painter's palette is *blue, lemon yellow, pearl gray, black, white.*[11] Of course, in his few paintings[12] there are, if it comes to it, all the riches of a complete palette, but the arrangement of lemon yellow, pale blue, pearl gray is as characteristic of him as the black, white, gray, pink is of Velázquez.

Anyway, I know, Rembrandt and the Dutch are scattered around museums and collections, and it's not very easy to form an idea of them if you only know the Louvre.

However, it's Frenchmen, C. Blanc, Thoré, Fromentin,[13] certain others who have written better than the Dutch on that art.

Those Dutchmen had scarcely any imagination or fantasy but great taste and the art of arrangement; they did not paint Jesus Christs, the Good Lord and others. Rembrandt though—indeed, but he's the *only one* (and there are relatively few biblical subjects in his oeuvre),[14] he's the only one who, as an exception, did Christs, etc.

And in his case, they hardly resemble anything by other religious painters; it's a metaphysical magic.

So, Rembrandt painted angels—he makes a portrait of himself as an old man, toothless, wrinkled, wearing a cotton cap—first, painting from life in a mirror[15]—he dreams, dreams, and his brush

---

Que veux tu, je suis si peu excentrique. Une statue grecque, un paysan de Millet, un portrait Hollandais, une femme nue de Courbet ou de de Gas, ces perfections calmes et modelees font que bien d'autres choses, les primitifs comme les japonais me paraissent . . . de L'ÉCRITURE À LA PLUME,[10] cela m'intéresse infiniment . . . mais une chose complète, une perfection nous rend l'infini tangible.

et jouir d'une telle chose c'est comme le coït, le moment de l'infini.

Ainsi connais tu un peintre nommé Van der Meer qui par exemple a peint une dame Hollandaise très belle, enceinte; la palette de cet étrange peintre est bleu, jaune citron, gris perle, noir, blanc.[11] *Certes, il y a dans ses rares tableaux[12] à la rigueur toutes les richesses d'une palette complète mais l'arrangement jaune citron, bleu pâle, gris perle lui est aussi caracteristique que le noir, blanc, gris, rose l'est à Vélasquez.*

Enfin, je le sais, Rembrandt et les Hollandais sont eparpillés dans les musées et collections et ce n'est pas très facile de s'en faire une idee si on ne connaît que le Louvre.

Pourtant ce sont des Français, Ch. Blanc, Thoré, Fromentin,[13] certains autres qui ont mieux que les Hollandais ecrits sur cet art-là.

Ces Hollandais-là n'avaient guère de l'imagination ni de la fantaisie, mais énormément du gout et la science d'arrangement, ils n'ont pas peint des Jesus christ, bon dieu et autres.—Rembrandt pourtant—en effet, mais voila le seul *(et c'est relativement peu dans son oeuvre, les sujets bibliques)[14] voila le seul qui par exception aie fait des christs &c.*

Et chez lui cela ne ressemble guere à quoi que ce soit d'autres peintres religieux, c'est une magie metaphysique.

Ainsi Rembrandt a peint des anges—il fait un portrait de soi-meme vieux, édenté, ridé, coiffé d'un bonnet de coton—1° tableau d'après nature dans un miroir[15]—il rêve, rêve et sa brosse recommence son

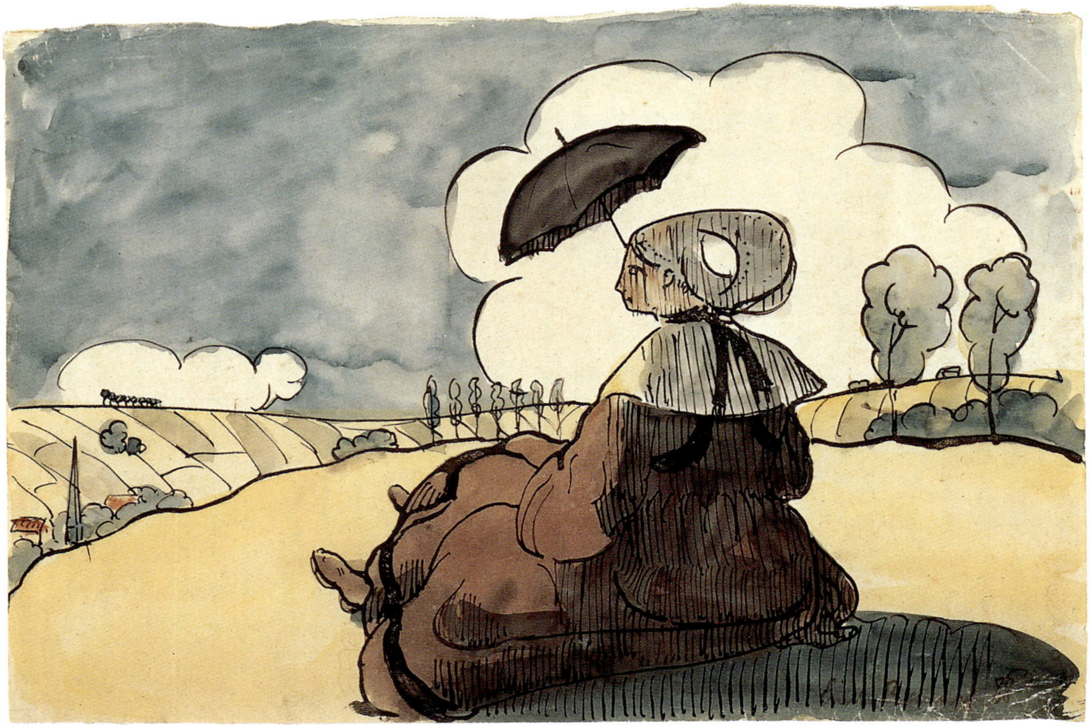

begins his own portrait again, but from memory, and its expression becomes sadder and more saddening; he dreams, dreams on, and why or how I do not know, but just as Socrates and Mohammed had a familiar genie,[16] Rembrandt, behind this old man who bears a resemblance to himself, paints a supernatural angel with a da Vinci smile.[17]

I'm showing you a painter who dreams and who paints from the imagination, and I started off by claiming that the character of the Dutch is that they invent nothing, that they have neither imagination nor fantasy.

Am I illogical? No. *Rembrandt* invented nothing, and that angel and that strange Christ; it's—that he knew them, *felt* them there.

Delacroix paints a Christ using an unexpected light lemon note, this colorful and luminous note in the painting being what the ineffable strangeness and charm of a star is in a corner of the firmament.[18]

Rembrandt works with values in the same way as Delacroix with colors.

Now, there's a gulf between the method of Delacroix and Rembrandt and that of all the rest of religious painting.

I'll write to you again soon. This to thank you for your drawings, which give me enormous pleasure. Have just finished portrait of young girl of twelve, brown eyes, black hair and eyebrows, flesh yellow gray, the background *white*, strongly tinged with veronese, jacket blood-red with violet stripes, skirt blue with large orange spots, an oleander flower in her sweet little hand.[19]

I'm so worn out from it that I hardly have a head for writing.[20] So long, and again, many thanks.

Ever yours,
Vincent

48. Émile Bernard, *Breton Woman with an Umbrella,* 1888. Amsterdam, Van Gogh Museum (Vincent van Gogh Foundation).

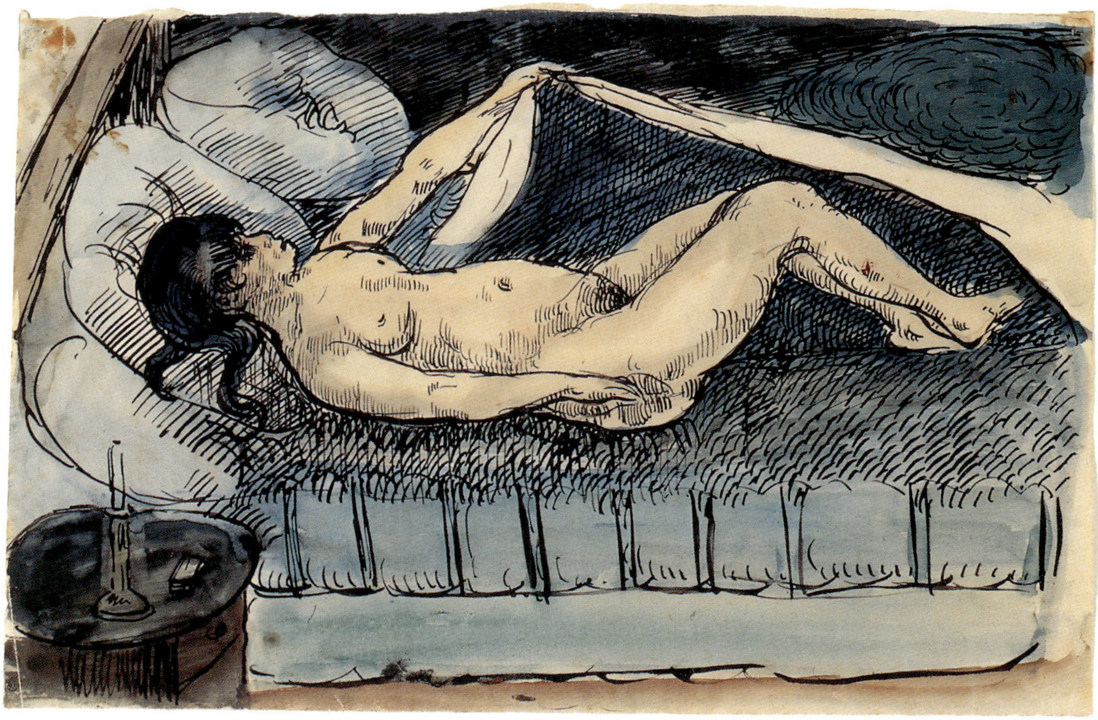

propre portrait mais de tête, et l'expression en devient plus navree et plus navrante, il rêve, rêve encore et pourquoi ou comment, je ne sais, mais ainsi que Socrate et Mahomet avaient un genie familier,[16] Rembrandt, derriere ce vieillard qui a une ressemblanse avec lui-même, peint un ange surnaturel au sourire à la Vinci.[17]

Je vous montre un peintre qui rêve et qui peint d'imagination et je commencais par pretendre que le caractere des Hollandais est qu'ils n'inventent rien, qu'ils n'ont pas d'imagination ni de fantaisie.

Suis je illogique—non.—Rembrandt n'a rien inventé et cet ange et ce Christ etrange, c'est—qu'il les connaissait, les sentait là.

Delacroix peint un christ par l'innattendu d'une note de citron clair, cette note colorée et lumineuse étant dans le tableau ce qu'est l'ineffable etrangete et charme d'une étoile dans un coin de firmament.[18]

Rembrandt travaille avec les valeurs de la même façon que Delacroix avec les couleurs.

Or il y a loin entre le procedé de Delacroix et de Rembrandt et celui de tout le reste de la peinture religieuse.

Je t'ecris bientot de nouveau. ceci pour te remercier de tes dessins qui me font un énorme plaisir.

viens de terminer portrait de jeune fille de 12 ans, yeux bruns, cheveux et sourcils noirs, chairs gris jaune, le fond blanc teinté fortement de véronèse, jaquette rouge sang rayé de violet, jupe bleue à gros pointillé orangé, dans la mignonne petite main une fleur de laurier rose.[19]

J'en suis éreinté tellement que je n'ai guère la tête aux ecritures.[20] à bientot et encore une fois bien merci.

t. à t.
Vincent

49. Émile Bernard, *Female Nude Reclining on a Bed*, 1888. Amsterdam, Van Gogh Museum (Vincent van Gogh Foundation).

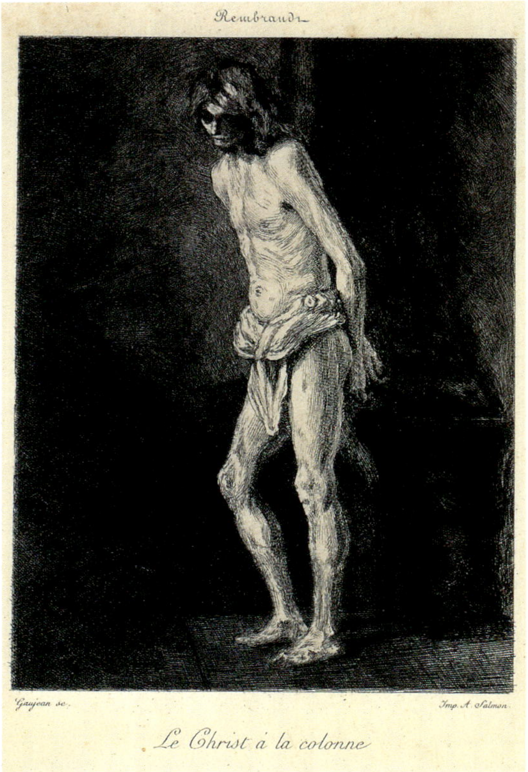

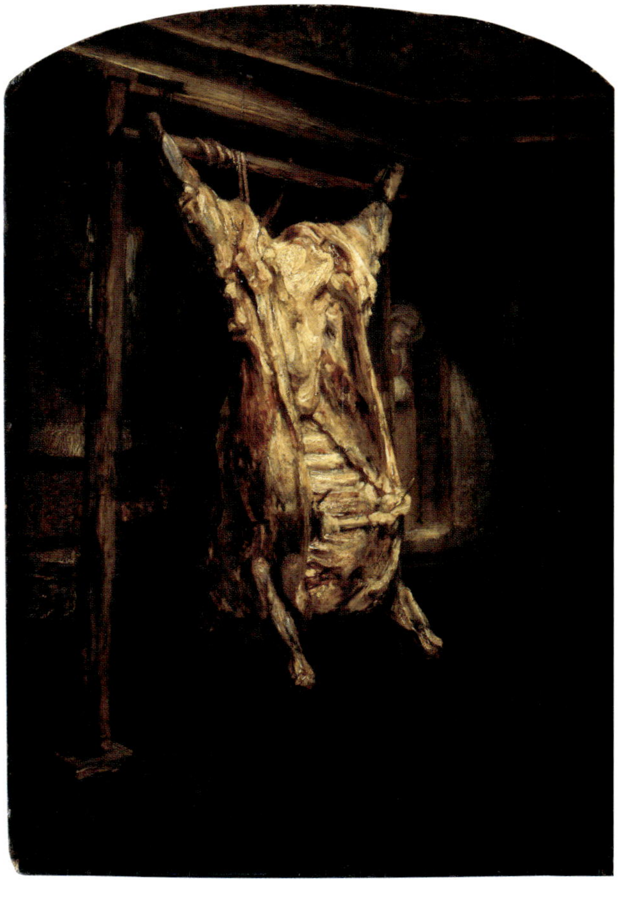

50. Rembrandt van Rijn, *Christ at the Column.* Etching by Eugène Gaujean. Amsterdam, Van Gogh Museum (Vincent van Gogh Foundation).

51. Rembrandt van Rijn, *The Slaughtered Ox,* 1655. Paris, Musée du Louvre.

Annotations to Letter 12

Arles, Sunday, 29 July, 1888

1. Bernard probably sent those drawings in response to van Gogh's request in Letter 10. In his next letter to Theo (*CL* 514) Vincent said that there were ten drawings. Seven are listed below. The other three were *Breton Woman in a Chapel*, *Breton Woman,* and *Lubricity* (Fig. 47). All ten are from the collection of the van Gogh brothers (now Amsterdam, Van Gogh Museum). See also Roskill 1970, pp. 219–20.

2. Émile Bernard, *Lane in Brittany with Figures.*

3. Émile Bernard, *Breton Woman in an Orchard.*

4. Émile Bernard, *Breton Woman with an Umbrella* (Fig. 48).

5. The batch included five drawings of nude women. In Letter 13 van Gogh said that he did not like *Lubricity* as much as the others, so that could not be the one he was talking about here. The four drawings he was referring to are *Women Bathing* and the brothel scenes *Female Nude Reclining on a Bed* (Fig. 49), *Female Nude Seated on a Bed,* and *A Woman Washing Herself,* the latter being the one van Gogh called "the one washing herself."

6. Émile Bernard added an annotation in his 1911 edition of the letters that is worth including here (in that edition it was placed with Letter 13, which at the time preceded the present one, and van Gogh criticized Baudelaire in both letters): "All this prompted by an admiring quotation on my part of the beautiful quatrain from *Phares,* by Charles Baudelaire:

   > Rembrandt—sad hospital filled full with murmurings,
   > decorated only by an immense crucifix,
   > where the stone tearfully exhales filth
   > and is rudely traversed by a ray of winter."

   (*Tout ceci provoqué par une citation admirative de ma part du beau quatrain des* Phares, *de Charles Baudelaire:*

   > *Rembrandt triste hôpital tout rempli de murmures*
   > *Et d'un grand crucifix décoré seulement,*
   > *D'où la prière en pleurs s'exhale des ordures*
   > *Et d'un rayon d'hiver traversé brusquement.*)

   See *Lettres à Bernard* 1911, p. 99 (English translation by Douglas Cooper). The famous poem praising several artists is from Baudelaire's *Les fleurs du mal* (1857).

7. There is a good chance that van Gogh bought the etching *Christ at the Column,* which was made by Eugène Gaujean. This print after an oil sketch attributed to Rembrandt (now in Cologne, Wallraf-Richartz-Museum; Bredius 1969, no. 591), was included in *Catalogue des tableaux anciens de toutes les écoles composant la très importante collection de M. Le Baron de Beurnonville,* Paris 1881, lot 435, facing p. 264 (Fig. 50). The print was in the van Gogh estate (Amsterdam, Van Gogh Museum). Van Gogh may have known that Christ has red hair in the painting.

8. Rembrandt van Rijn, *The Slaughtered Ox* (Fig. 51).

9. Bernard defended the style of the primitives, as is clear from his introduction to the 1911 edition, where he spoke of "my preoccupations with the methods of the Italian and German primitives; with the symbolic meaning of line and color, which preoccupied me, and which van Gogh disapproved of, putting to me the contrasting case of Dutch naturalism" (*mes préoccupations des procédés italiens et allemands primitifs; du sens symbolique de la ligne et de la couleur, qui me préoccupait, et que van Gogh désapprouvait en m'opposant le naturalisme hollandais*). See *Lettres à Bernard* 1911, p. 35.

10. Here van Gogh associated writing with drawing (and painting). His ideal was to make drawing as automatic and as natural a means of expression as writing was for him.

11. Johannes Vermeer was often called "Van der Meer" or "Van der Meer of Delft" during the nineteenth century. The painting is *Woman in Blue Reading a Letter,* which van Gogh had seen in the Rijksmuseum in Amsterdam (Fig. 52).

12. At present, depending on attributions and deattributions, there are some thirty known paintings by Vermeer. The French writer and critic E. J. T. Thoré (who wrote under the pseudonym of W. Bürger), whose *Musées de la Hollande* (1858–60) was an important source for van Gogh's taste and art-historical knowledge, assumed that there were between two and three dozen Vermeers. See Thoré 1858–1860, vol. 2, p. 88.

13. Charles Blanc wrote about Dutch art mainly in his *École Hollandaise* (1861), which is part of the series *Histoire des peintres de toutes les écoles* (Paris 1861–76). See n. 12 for Thoré, who described collections in the Netherlands. Eugène Fromentin wrote *Les maîtres d'autrefois* (1876), a survey of old Dutch and Flemish masters. Fromentin, who was an artist himself, approached them with a painter's eye, and dealt at length with technique, composition, use of color and the like. The painter Anthon van Rappard had sent this book to van Gogh to read in 1885.

14. Contrary to what van Gogh asserted, biblical scenes make up an important part of Rembrandt's oeuvre. In a footnote against this remark in the 1911 edition Bernard wrote: "Strange assertion! . . . The Pilgrims of Emmaus or the Good Samaritan, not much in Rembrandt's oeuvre! . . . " (*Etrange assertion! . . . Les Pèlerins d'Emmaüs ou le Bon Samaritain, peu de chose dans l'oeuvre de Rembrandt! . . .*). See *Lettres à Bernard* 1911, p. 107. For Rembrandt's figure of Christ, see also Letter 8, n. 3.

---

52. Johannes Vermeer, *Woman in Blue Reading a Letter,* ca. 1663–64. Amsterdam, Rijksmuseum.

53. Rembrandt van Rijn, *Self-Portrait at the Easel,* 1660(?). Paris, Musée du Louvre.

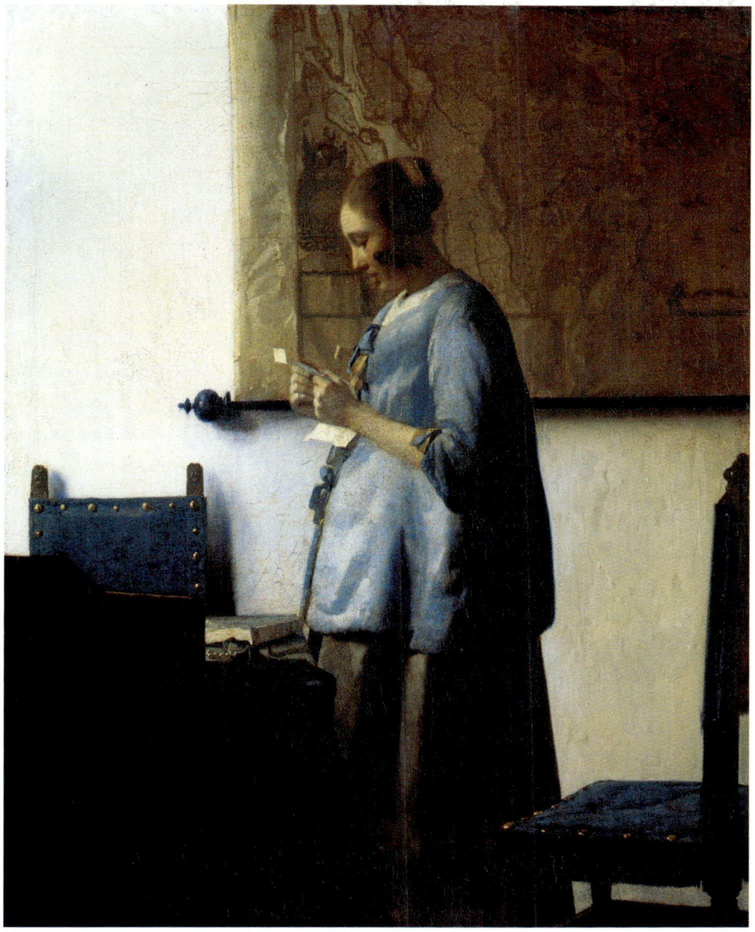

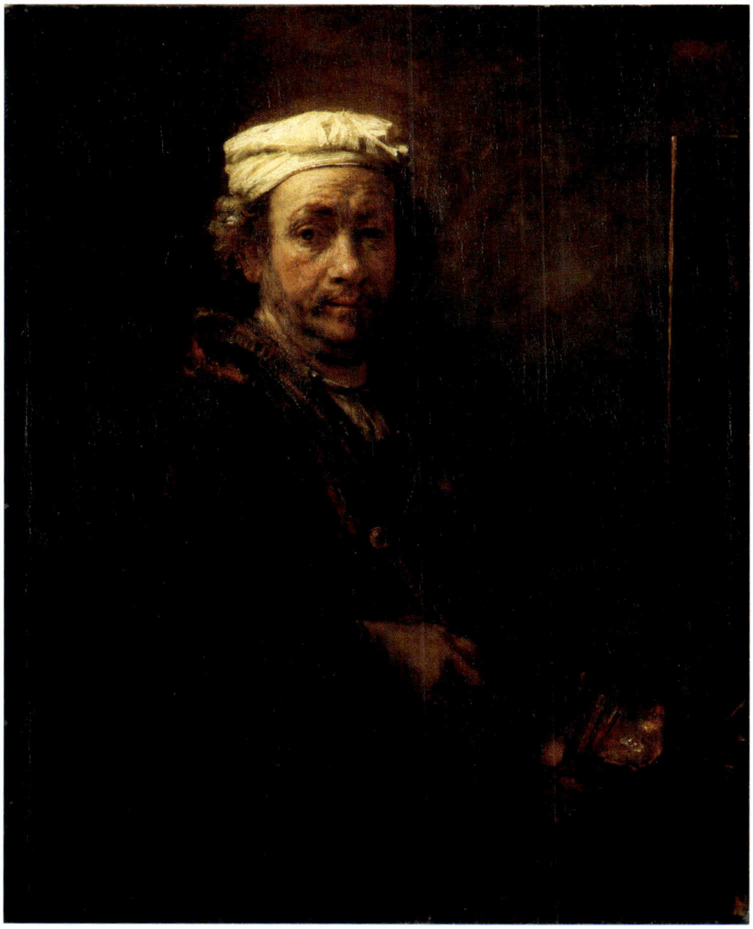

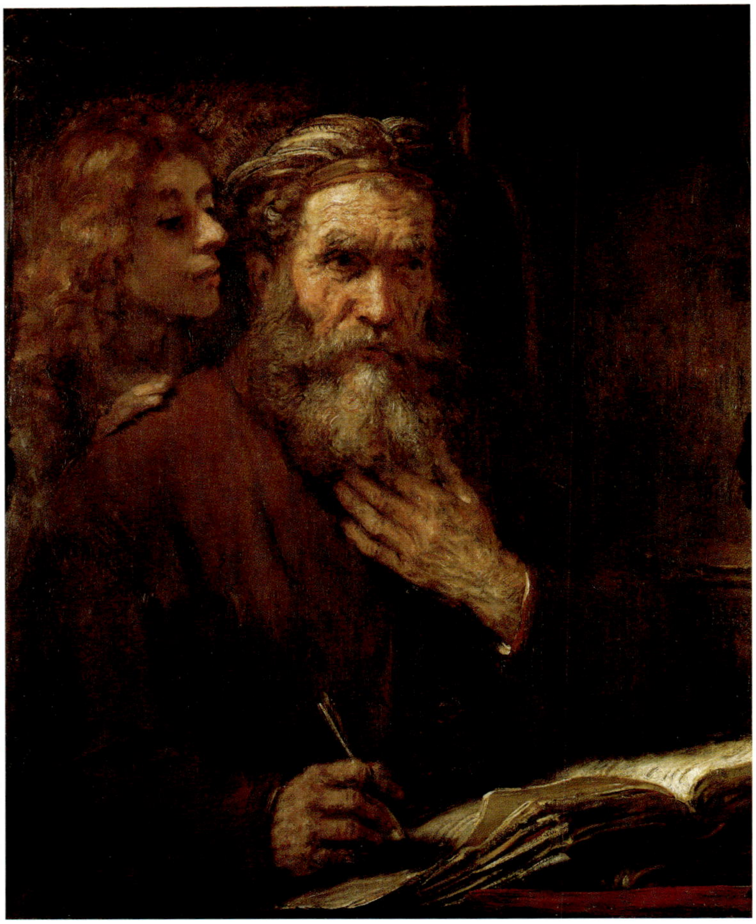

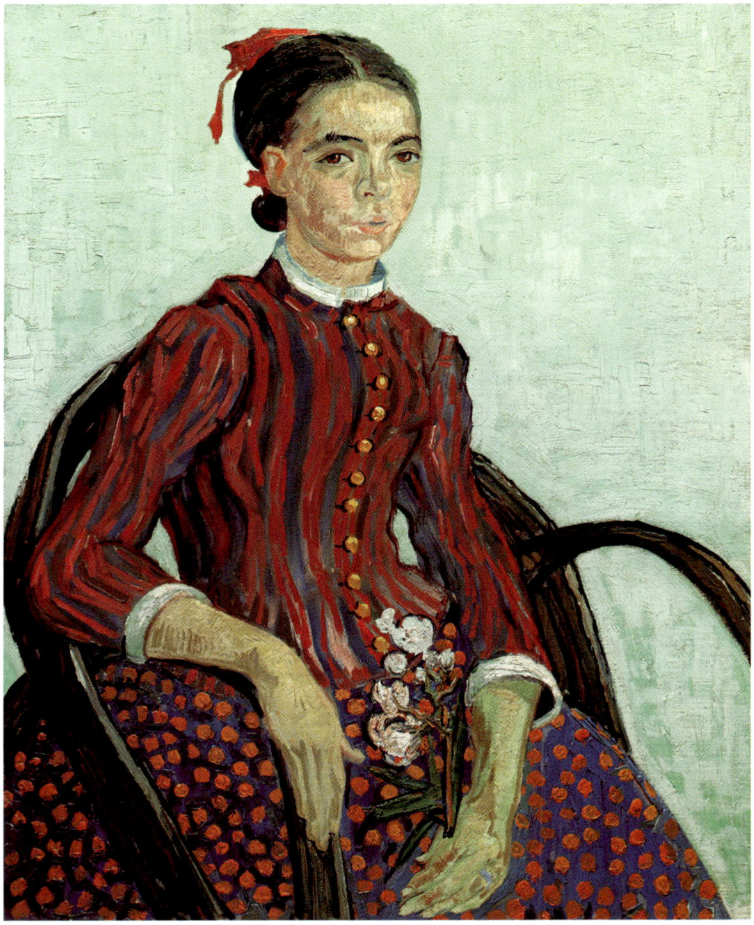

15. Given the very similar wording in Letter 15 (*le rire edenté du vieux lion Rembrandt, la tête coiffé d'un linge, la palette à la main*), which was also written to Bernard, who was familiar with the collection in the Louvre, it is most likely that he is talking about *Self-Portrait at the Easel* (Fig. 53). However, he also could have been thinking of the *Self-Portrait as Zeuxis* of ca. 1669 (Cologne, Wallraf-Richartz-Museum).

Van Gogh's description displays similarities with that of Fromentin, who remarked in *Les maîtres d'autrefois* that in his days of difficulty Rembrandt depicted himself in "graver, more modest, more veracious garb, in dark garments with a handkerchief around his head, his face saddened, wrinkled, emaciated, his palette in his rugged hands"; see Fromentin 1981, p. 224 (*tenues plus graves, plus modestes, plus véridiques [. . .] en vestes sobres, avec un mouchoir en serre-tête, le visage attristé, ridé, macéré, la palette entre ses rudes mains*; see Fromentin 1902, chapter 16, p. 399).

16. After *familier* van Gogh deleted the words *ainsi qu'Ingres* (as did Ingres).

17. Van Gogh was imagining the creation of Rembrandt's *The Evangelist Matthew Inspired by an Angel* (Fig. 54).

18. Van Gogh was probably thinking of Delacroix's *Christ Asleep During the Tempest*, which he had also written about in Letter 8 (Fig. 33).

19. *Mousmé, Sitting in a Cane Chair* (F 431 / JH 1519; Fig. 55). Vincent told Theo that he had been inspired by Loti's *Madame Chrysanthème* for this portrait of *une mousmé:* "A mousmé is a Japanese girl—a Provençale in this case—aged between 12 and 14" (*Une mousmé est une fille Japonaise—provencale dans ce cas—de 12 à 14 ans; CL* 514).

20. Van Gogh actually wrote *ecritures,* which means "the Scriptures." The mistake can probably be put down to the weariness he mentioned earlier in the sentence.

---

54. Rembrandt van Rijn, *The Evangelist Matthew Inspired by an Angel,* 1661. Paris, Musée du Louvre.

55. Vincent van Gogh, *Mousmé, Sitting in a Cane Chair,* 1888 (F 431 / JH 1519). Washington, National Gallery of Art, Chester Dale Collection.

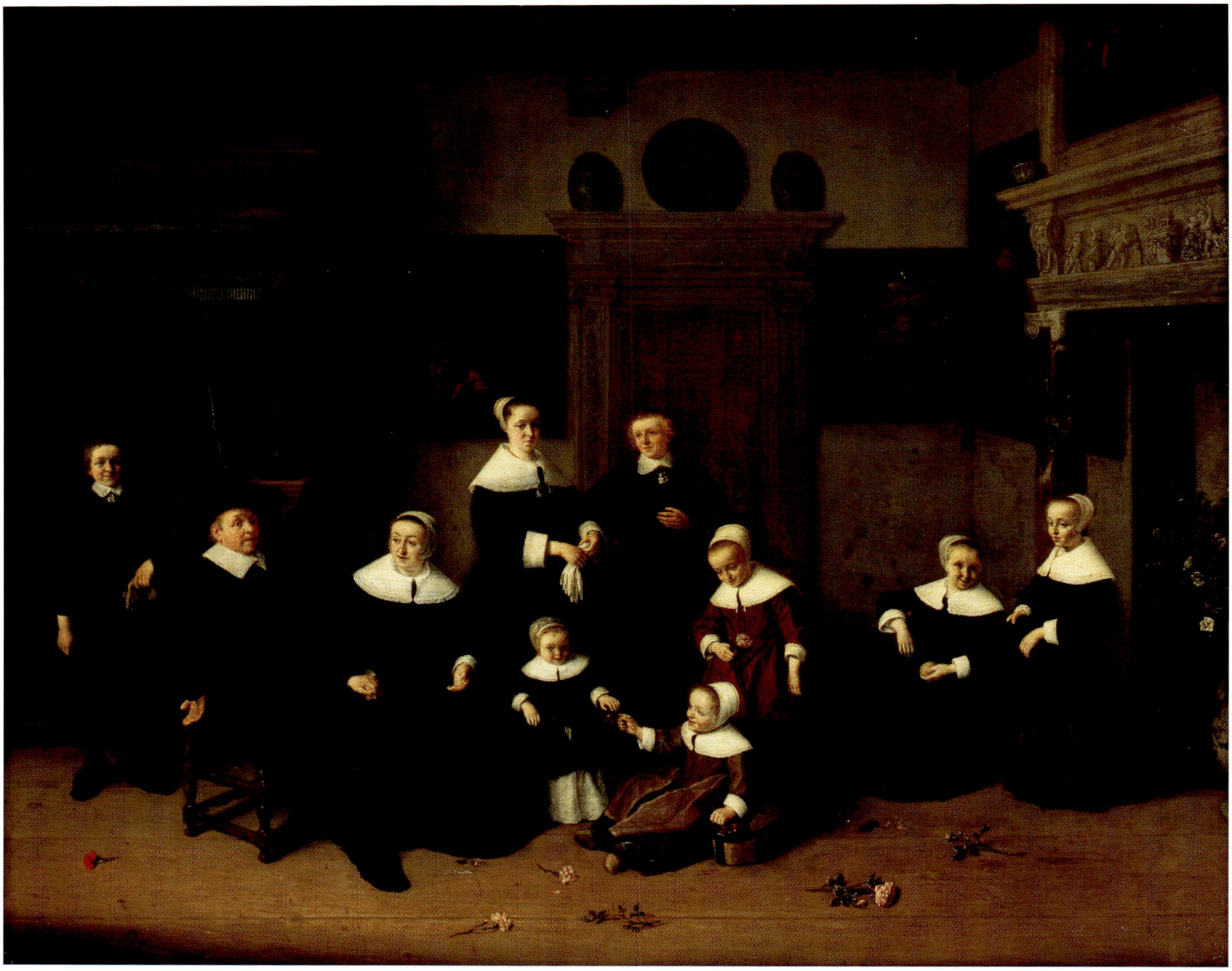

Letter 13

Arles, Monday, 30 July, 1888

Source
Original manuscript

Location
New York, Thaw Collection, The Morgan Library & Museum

Date
Assuming that van Gogh honored his promise to write again soon, the present letter dates from shortly after the previous one to Bernard (Letter 12, 29 July). The opening words accordingly appear to be an immediate continuation of their discussion about painting, while the drawings that Bernard had sent were examined at the end. Van Gogh's new model, Joseph Roulin, who posed for him on 31 July, is not mentioned, despite the fact that the importance of painting portraits is stressed in this letter. On the assumption that he would have told Bernard about Roulin's portrait if he had already painted it, as he did Theo and Willemien in letters *CL* 516 and *CL* W5, both of 31 July, we have dated this letter Monday, 30 July, 1888.

A day after writing to Bernard, van Gogh picked up his pen again to continue the discussion about Dutch painting. He also returned to the subject of the drawings Bernard had sent him.

Gauguin, whose health was improving, had written around 22 July to say that he hoped to proceed with his trip to Provence. He agreed with van Gogh that verisimilitude in art was of little importance. "Art is an abstraction; unfortunately we are becoming increasingly misunderstood." He had just completed his *Young Wrestlers* (private collection; W298/W273). He sent a letter sketch of the painting, which he was sure van Gogh would like, with its lawn of pure veronese green shading into chrome yellow, "*with no execution*, like Japanese prints."[1] So he, too, was consciously relating to Japanese art.

Van Gogh continued to think about growing older and recognized the feeling of emptiness about which Theo had written. In his eyes, a champion of the new art, like Theo, had as difficult a time of it as the modern artist himself. "If a painter ruins his character by working hard at painting, which makes him sterile

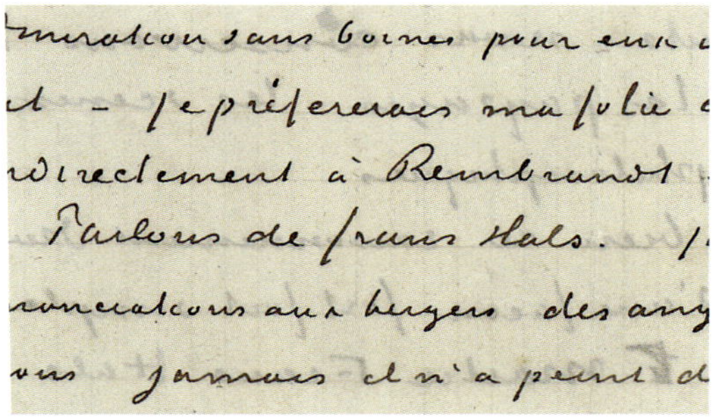
miration sans bornes pour eux
t – je préférerais ma folie
directement à Rembrandt
Parlons de Frans Hals.
nonciations aux bergers des ang
vus jamais il n'a peint d

for many things, for family life, etc., etc. If as a consequence he paints not only with paint but with self-denial and with self-abnegation and a broken heart. Not only are you not paid for your own work either, but it costs you exactly the same as this effacement of personality, half deliberate, half accidental, costs a painter." He had shaved off his beard but said that he was still looking unkempt.[2]

56. Adriaan van Ostade, *Portrait of a Family,* 1654. Paris, Musée du Louvre.

Translation of Letter 13 / Arles, Monday, 30 July, 1888

My dear old Bernard.
You'll agree, I've no doubt at all, that neither you nor I can have a full idea of what Velázquez and Goya were like as men and as painters, because neither you nor I have seen Spain, their country, and so many fine things that have remained in the south. Even so, what we know of them does count for something in itself.[1]

It goes without saying that for the northerners, Rembrandt first and foremost, it is extremely desirable, when judging these painters, to know both their work in its full extent and their country, and the rather intimate and hidden history of those days, and of the customs of the ancient country.

I want to repeat to you that neither Baudelaire nor you has a sufficiently clear idea when it comes to Rembrandt.

And when it comes to you, I could not encourage you enough to take a long look at major and minor Dutchmen before arriving at an opinion. Here it's not just a matter of strange precious stones, but it's a matter of sorting out marvels from among marvels.

And a fair amount of paste from among the diamonds. Thus for myself, having been studying my country's school for twenty years now, in most cases I wouldn't even reply if the subject came up, so much do I generally hear people talk beside the point when the painters of the north are being discussed.

So to you I can only reply, come on, just look a little more closely than that; really, it's worth the effort a thousand times over.

Transcription of Letter 13 / Arles, Monday, 30 July, 1888

Mon cher copain Bernard.
Tu admettras, j'en doute aucunement, que ni toi ni moi ne puissions avoir de Velasquez et de Goya une idée complète de ce qu'ils etaient comme homme et comme peintres, car ni toi ni moi n'avons vu l'Espagne, leur pays et tant de belles choses qui sont restées dans le midi. N'empêche que ce que l'on en connait c'est déjà quelque chôse.[1]

Va sans dire que pour les gens du nord, Rembrandt en tête, il est excessivement désirable de connaître, en jugeant ces peintres, et leur oeuvre dans toute son étendue, et leur pays et l'histoire un peu intime et serrée de l'époque et des moeurs de l'antique pays.

J'y tiens à te répéter que ni Baudelaire ni toi ont une nette idée suffisamment en tant que Rembrandt.

Et en tant que quant à toi je ne saurais trop t'encourager à regarder longtemps grands et petits hollandais avant de t'arreter une opinion. Ici il s'agit non seulement de pierres precieuses étranges mais il s'agit de démeler des merveilles dans des merveilles.

Puis pas mal de strass dans les diamants. Ainsi pour moi qui 20 ans déjà durant étudie l'ecole de mon pays, la plupart des cas je ne répondrais même pas s'il en était question, tellement en général j'entends parler à côté de la question lorsqu'on discute les peintres du nord.

Ainsi à toi je n'ai qu'à répondre, Bah, regarde donc un peu mieux que ça, vraiment ça en vaut mille fois la peine.

Or si par exemple je pretends que l'Ostade du Louvre qui réprésente la famille du peintre,

Now if, for example, I claim that the van Ostade in the Louvre, which shows the painter's family, the man, the wife, the ten or so kids, is a painting infinitely deserving of study and thought,[2] just like ter Borch's Peace of Münster.[3] If the paintings in the gallery in the Louvre that I personally *prefer* and find the most astonishing are very often forgotten by the very artists who go to see the Dutchmen, then I'm not in the least surprised, knowing that my own choice in that gallery is based on a knowledge of this subject that most of the French could not have.

But if, for example, my opinion differed from yours on those subjects, I'm confident that you would agree with me later. What grieves me at the Louvre is to see their Rembrandts getting spoiled and the cretins in the administration damaging many beautiful paintings. Thus the annoying yellow tonality of certain canvases by Rembrandt is an effect of deterioration through humidity or other causes, instances of which I could point out to you.

As difficult to say what Rembrandt's color is as to give a name to the Velázquez grays; we could say, for want of something better, "Rembrandt gold," and that's what we do, but that's quite vague.

Having come to France I have, perhaps better than many Frenchmen themselves, felt Delacroix and Zola, for whom my sincere and frank admiration is boundless.

Since I had a fairly complete idea of Rembrandt. One, Delacroix, proceeds by way of colors, the other, Rembrandt, by values, but they are on a par.

Zola and Balzac, as painters of a society, of reality as a whole, arouse rare artistic emotions in those who love them, for the very reason that they embrace the whole epoch that they paint. When Delacroix paints humanity, life in general instead of an epoch, he belongs to the same family of universal geniuses all the same.

---

l'homme, la femme, la dizaine de gosses, est un tableau infiniment digne d'etude et de reflexion,[2] *ainsi que la paix de Munster de Terburg.*[3] *Si dans la galerie du Louvre les tableaux que personellement je* prefère *et trouve les plus etonnants, sont très souvent oubliés par les artistes mêmes*[a] *qui vont voir les Hollandais, alors j'en suis fort peu étonné, sachant que mon choix à moi dans cette galerie-là est fondé sur des connaissances en cette matière que la plupart des français ne sauraient avoir.*

Mais si avec toi par exemple je differerais d'opinion à ces sujets, j'aurais confiance que tu me donnerais raison plus tard. Ce qui me navre au Louvre c'est de voir leur Rembrandts se gâter et les cretins de l'administration abîmer beaucoup de beaux tableaux. Ainsi la tonalité jaune embêtante de certaines toiles de Rembrandt est un effet de detoriation par humidite ou autres causes dans des cas que je pourrais te montrer au doigt.

Aussi difficile de dire quelle est la couleur de Rembrandt que de donner un nom aux gris Velasquez, on pourrait dire faute de mieux "or Rembrandt" et c'est ce qu'on fait, mais c'est bien vague.

Venant en France, moi j'ai peutêtre mieux que bien des francais eux memes senti Delacroix et Zola pour lesquels ma sincère et franche admiration est sans bornes.

Puisque j'avais une idee un peu complète de Rembrandt.—l'un, Delacroix, procède par les couleurs, l'autre, Rembrandt, par les valeurs mais ils s'equivalent.

Zola et Balzac en tant que peintres d'une société, d'une nature dans son ensemble, causent à ceux qui les aiment des emotions artistiques rares pour cela même qu'ils embrassent le tout de l'epoque qu'ils peignent. Si Delacroix peint l'humanité, la vie en general au lieu d'une époque, pas moins il est de la même famille de genies universels.

J'aime bien le dernier mot de je crois Silvestre, qui termine ainsi un article magistral:

I love the closing words of Silvestre, I think it was, who ends a masterly article like this:

Thus died—almost smiling—Eugène Delacroix, a painter of high breeding—who had a sun in his head and a thunderstorm in his heart—who went from warriors to saints—from saints to lovers—from lovers to tigers—and from the tiger to flowers.[4]

Daumier is also a really great genius.

Millet, another painter of an entire race and the settings in which it lives.

Possible that these great geniuses are no more than loonies, and that to have faith and boundless admiration for them you'd have to be a loony too. That may well be—I would prefer my madness to other people's wisdom.

To go to Rembrandt indirectly is perhaps the most direct route. Let's talk about Frans Hals.[5] Never did he paint Christs, annunciations to shepherds, angels or crucifixions and resurrections; never did he paint voluptuous and bestial naked women.[6]

He painted portraits; nothing nothing nothing but that.

Portraits of soldiers,[7] gatherings of officers,[8] portraits of magistrates assembled for the business of the republic,[9] portraits of matrons with pink or yellow skin, wearing white bonnets, dressed in wool and black satin, discussing the budget of an orphanage or an almshouse;[10] he did portraits of good citizens with their families, the man, his wife, his child;[11] he painted the sozzled drinker,[12] the old fishwife full of a witch's mirth,[13] the beautiful gypsy whore,[14] babies in swaddling clothes,[15] the gallant, bon vivant gentleman, mustachioed, booted and spurred;[16] he painted himself and his wife as young lovers on a turf bench in a garden, after their first wedding night.[17] He painted guttersnipes and laughing urchins,[18] he painted musicians[19] and he painted a fat cook.[20]

---

ainsi mourut—presqu'en souriant—Eugène Delacroix, peintre de grande race—qui avait un soleil dans la tête et un orage dans le coeur—qui allait des guerriers aux saints—des saints aux amoureux—des amants aux tigres—et du tigre aux fleurs.[4]

Daumier est un bien grand genie aussi.—

Millet, encore un peintre d'une race entière et des milieux où elle vit.—

Possible que ces grands genies ne soient que des toqués et que pour avoir foi et admiration sans bornes pour eux il faille egalement etre toqué. Cela serait—je préfererais ma folie à la sagesse des autres.

Aller indirectement à Rembrandt est peutetre le chemin le plus direct. Parlons de Frans Hals.[5] *jamais il n'a peint des christs, des annonciations aux bergers, des anges ou des crucifixions et resurrections, jamais il n'a peint des femmes nues voluptueuses et bestiales.—*[6]

il a fait des portraits, rien rien rien que cela.

Portraits de soldats,[7] *réunions d'officiers,*[8] *portraits de magistrats assemblés pour les affaires de la republique,*[9] *portraits de matrones à peau rose ou jaune, de blancs bonnets coiffés, de laine et de satin noir habillées, discutant le budget d'un orphelinat ou d'un hospice,*[10] *il a fait le portrait de bons bourgeois en famille, l'homme, la femme, l'enfant,*[11] *il a peint le buveur gris,*[12] *la vieille marchande de poisson en hilarité de sorcière,*[13] *la belle putain bohémienne,*[14] *les bebes au maillot,*[15] *le crane gentilhomme bon vivant, moustachu, botté et éperonné,*[16] *il s'est peint lui et sa femme jeunes amoureux dans un jardin sur un banc de gazon après la premiere nuit de noce.*[17] *il a peint les voyous et les gamins riants,*[18] *il a peint les musiciens*[19] *et il a peint une grosse cuisinière.*[20]

Il n'en sait pas plus long que cela mais cela ———————— vaut bien le paradis du Dante[21] *et*

He doesn't know much more than that, but it's——————well worth Dante's Paradise[21] and the Michelangelos and Raphaels and even the Greeks.[22] It's beautiful like Zola, and healthier and more cheerful, but just as alive, because his epoch was healthier and less sad. Now what is Rembrandt? The same thing entirely—a painter of portraits. That's the healthy, broad, clear idea that one must have first of all of the two eminent Dutchmen, who are on a par, before going into the subject more deeply.

This fully understood, ALL this glorious republic, represented by these two prolific portraitists, re-created in broad strokes, we retain very wide margins for landscapes, interior scenes, animals, philosophical subjects.

But I beg you, carefully follow this straightforward argument, which I am doing my utmost to present to you in a very very simple way.

Get him into your head, this Master Frans Hals, painter of various portraits of a whole self-assured and lively and immortal republic. Get into your head the no less great and universal master portrait painter of the Dutch republic, Rembrandt Harmensz. van Rijn, a broad and naturalistic and healthy man, as much as Hals himself. And after that we'll see flowing from that source, Rembrandt, the direct and true pupils, Vermeer of Delft, Fabritius, Nicolaas Maes, Pieter de Hooch, Bol; and those influenced by him, Potter, Ruisdael, Ostade, ter Borch. I mention Fabritius to you there, by whom we know only—two canvases[23]—I *don't* mention a heap of good painters, and especially not the paste of these diamonds, paste firmly embedded in ordinary French skulls.

Am I, my dear old Bernard, terribly incomprehensible this time? I'm trying to make you see the great simple thing, the painting of humanity, let us rather say of a whole republic, through the

---

les Michel Ange et les Rafael et les grecs même.[22] *C'est beau comme Zola et plus sain et plus gai, mais aussi vivant, parceque son époque etait plus saine et moins triste. Maintenant qu'est ce que Rembrandt?—la même chôse absolument—un peintre de portraits. Voilà d'abord l'idee saine, large, claire qu'il s'agit d'avoir des deux sommites hollandaises qui s'equivalent, avant d'entrer plus loin en matière.*

Cela bien compris, TOUTE *cette glorieuse republique, representée par ces deux féconds portraitistes, reconstituée à grands traits, nous conservons tres amples marges pour les paysages, les scenes d'interieur, les animaux, les sujets philosophiques.*

Mais je t'en supplie, suis bien ce raisonnement droit que je m'efforce de te présenter d'une facon fort fort simple.

Fourre toi dans la tête ce Maître Frans Hals, peintre de portraits divers de toute une republique crane et vivante et immortelle. Fourre toi dans la tete le non moins grand et universel maitre peintre de portraits de la republique Hollandaise, Rembrandt Harmensz van Rijn, homme large et naturaliste et sain autant que Hals lui-même. Et après nous verrons de cette source, Rembrandt, ecouler les élèves directs et vrais, Van der Meer de Delft, Fabritius, Nicolaes Maes, Pieter de Hooch, Bol, et les influencés par lui, Potter, Ruysdael, Ostade, Terburg. Je te nomme là Fabritius, duquel nous ne connaissons que—deux toiles[23]*—je ne nomme* pas *un tas de bons peintres et surtout pas le strass de ces diamants, bien introduit dans les cranes francais vulgaires, ce strass.*

Suis-je, mon cher copain Bernard, très incompréhensible cette fois-ci? Je cherche à te faire voir la grande chose simple, la peinture de l'humanité, de toute une republique disons plutôt, par le simple moyen du portrait. Cela d'abord et avant tout, plus tard———si au sujet de Rembrandt nous aurons affaire[b] *un peu à de la magie, à des christs et des femmes nues,*[24] *c'est fort intéressant—mais c'est pas*

simple medium of the portrait. This first and foremost; later———if, on the subject of Rembrandt, we're dealing to some extent with magic, with Christs and nude women,[24] it's very interesting—but it's not the main thing. Let Baudelaire hold his tongue in this department, they're resounding words, and how hollow!!![25] Let's take Baudelaire for what he is, a modern poet just as Musset is another, but let them leave us alone when we're talking painting.

Handshake.

Ever yours,
Vincent

I *don't* like your drawing Lubricity as much as the others; I like *the tree*, however, it has a great look.[26]

---

le principal. Baudelaire qu'il taise son bec sur ce territoire, c'est des mots sonores et puis d'un creux!!![25] *Prenons Baudelaire pour ce qu'il est, poete moderne ainsi que Musset en est un autre, mais qu'ils nous fichent la paix quand nous parlons peinture.*

Poignee de main.

t. à t.
Vincent

Je n'aime pas *autant que les autres ton dessin lubricité, j'aime* l'arbre *cependant, il a beaucoup d'allure.*[26]

---

57. Gerard ter Borch, *The Swearing of the Oath of Ratification of the Treaty of Münster,* 1648. London, National Gallery.
58. Frans Hals, *The Regents of the Old Men's Alms House,* 1664. Haarlem, Frans Hals Museum.

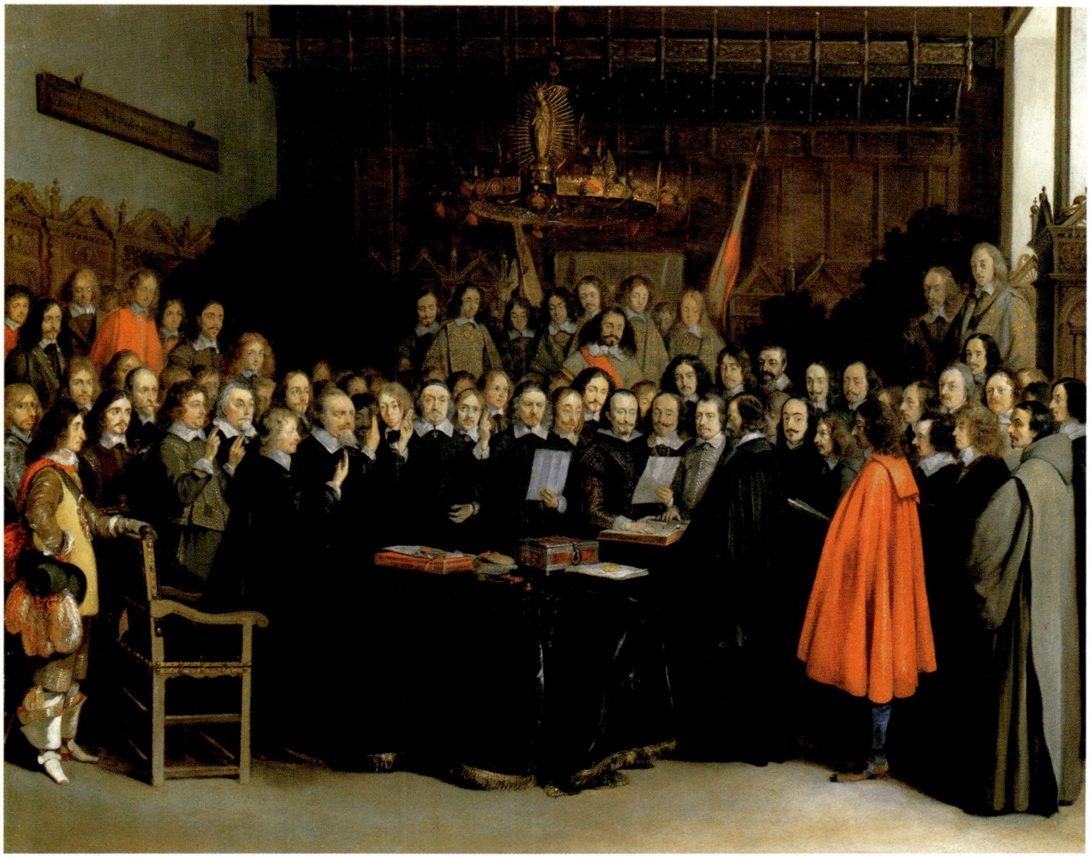

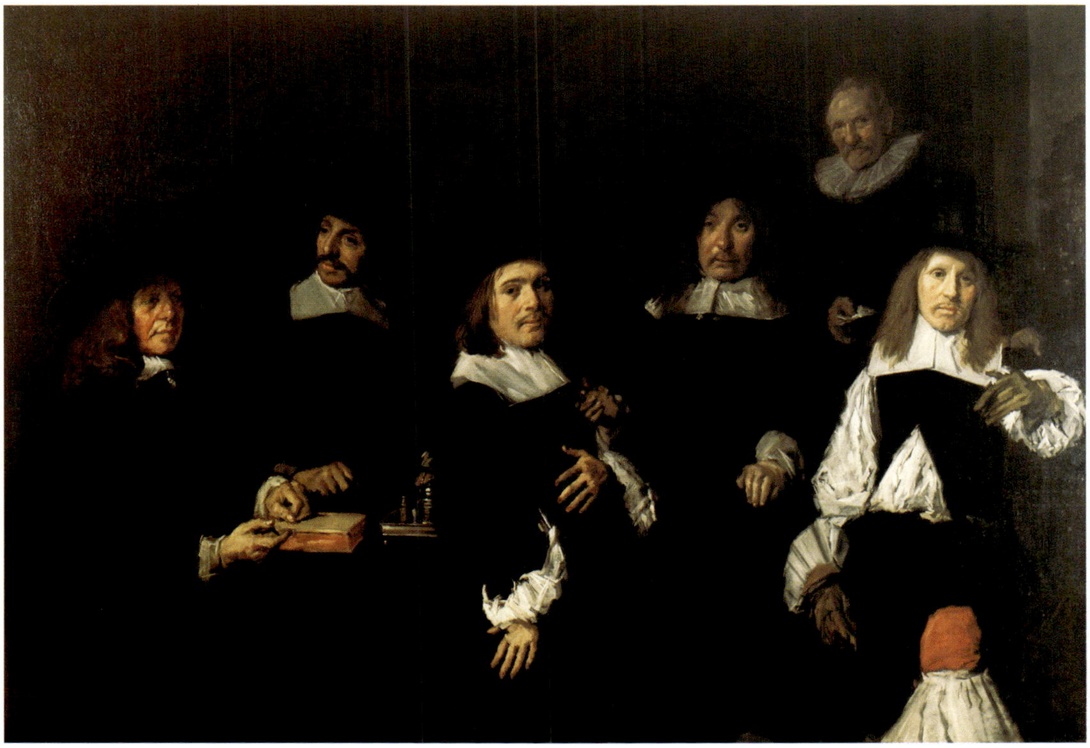

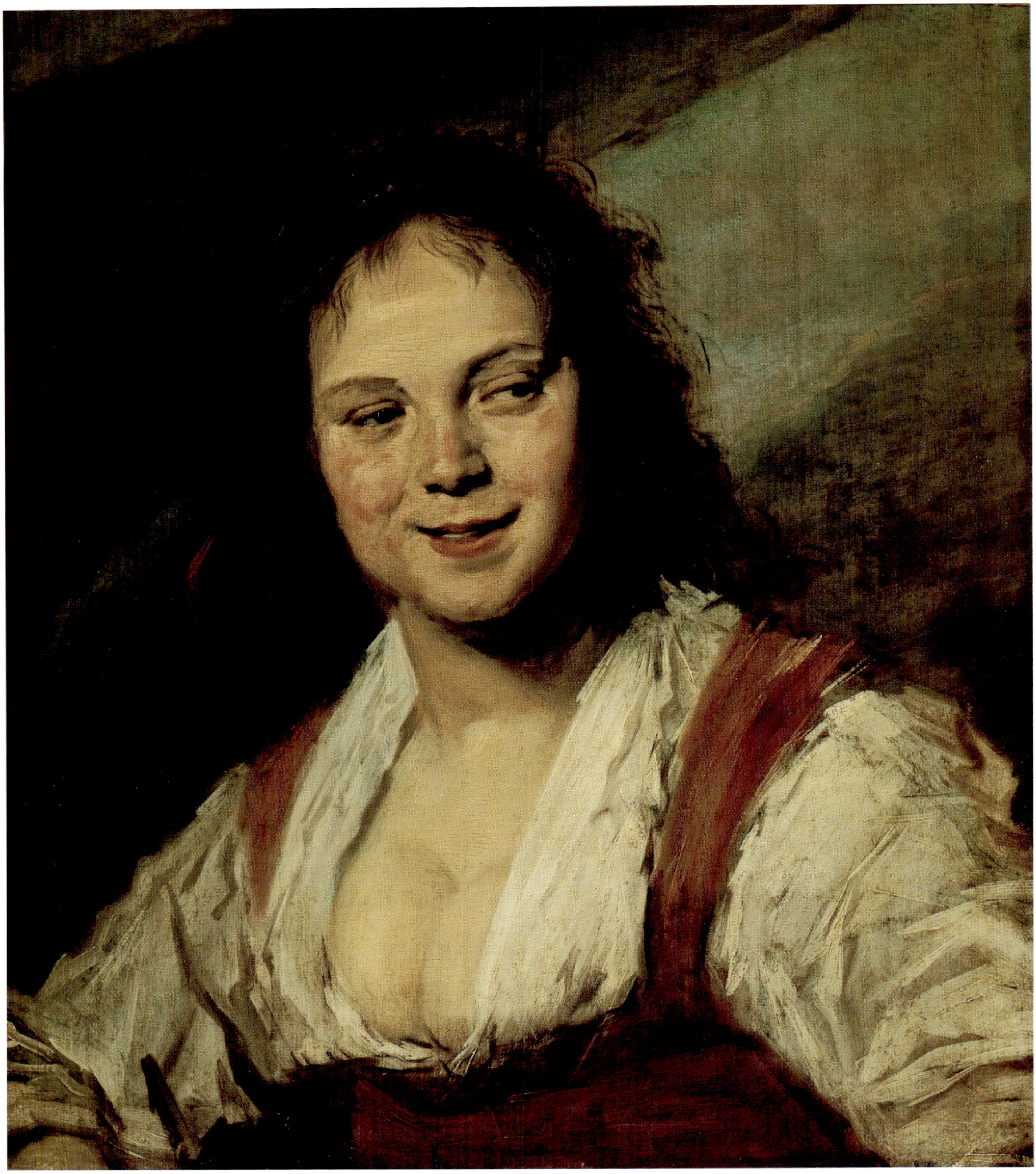

Annotations to Letter 13

Arles, Monday, 30 July, 1888

Textual Notes
a. mêmes < même
b. affaire < a faire

1. Van Gogh was thinking above all of the paintings by Velázquez and Goya in the Louvre, with which he and Bernard were familiar. The ones by Velázquez were *Portrait of the Infanta Maria Margarita, Portrait of the Infanta Maria Theresa, Gathering of Thirteen Characters, Portrait of a Priest of Toledo,* and *Portrait of Philip IV of Spain.* The Goya in the Louvre was the *Portrait of Ferdinand Guillamardet.* See letter *CL* T28 and Baedeker 1889, pp. 113, 129.

2. Adriaan van Ostade, *Portrait of a Family*, formerly known as *The Artist's Family* (Fig. 56).

3. Gerard ter Borch, *The Swearing of the Oath of Ratification of the Treaty of Münster* (Fig. 57).

4. Théophile Silvestre was the compiler of *Eugène Delacroix. Documents nouveaux*. The passage quoted by van Gogh reads in full: "Thus died, almost smiling, 13 August 1863, Ferdinand-Victor-Eugène Delacroix, a painter of high breeding, who had a sun in his head and thunderstorms in his heart, who for 40 years played the whole keyboard of human feeling, and whose imposing, fearsome or mellow brush went from saints to warriors, from warriors to lovers, from lovers to tigers, and from tigers to flowers." (*Ainsi mourut, presque en souriant, le 13 août mil huit cent soixante-trois, Ferdinand-Victor-Eugène Delacroix, peintre de grande race, qui avait un soleil dans la tête et des orages dans le coeur; qui toucha quarante ans tout le clavier des passions humains, et dont le pinceau grandiose, terrible ou suave passait des saints aux guerriers, des guerriers aux amants, des amants aux tigres, et des tigres aux fleurs*). See Silvestre 1864, pp. 63–64. Van Gogh lent this book to Bernard, as mentioned in letter *CL* 570.

5. Van Gogh had got to know quite a few works by Frans Hals from reproductions when he was working at Goupil & Cie as well as from the originals in the museum in Haarlem, the Rijksmuseum in Amsterdam, and the Louvre in Paris.

6. This passage was prompted by van Gogh's objections to Bernard's works with these subjects.

7. Hals made at least one work that can be described as the portrait of a soldier: *Portrait of a Man Wearing a Cuirass*, ca. 1638–40 (Washington, National Gallery of Art, Mellon Collection). It is not certain, however, that this is the one van Gogh meant.

59. Frans Hals, *Gipsy Girl,* 1628–30. Paris, Musée du Louvre.

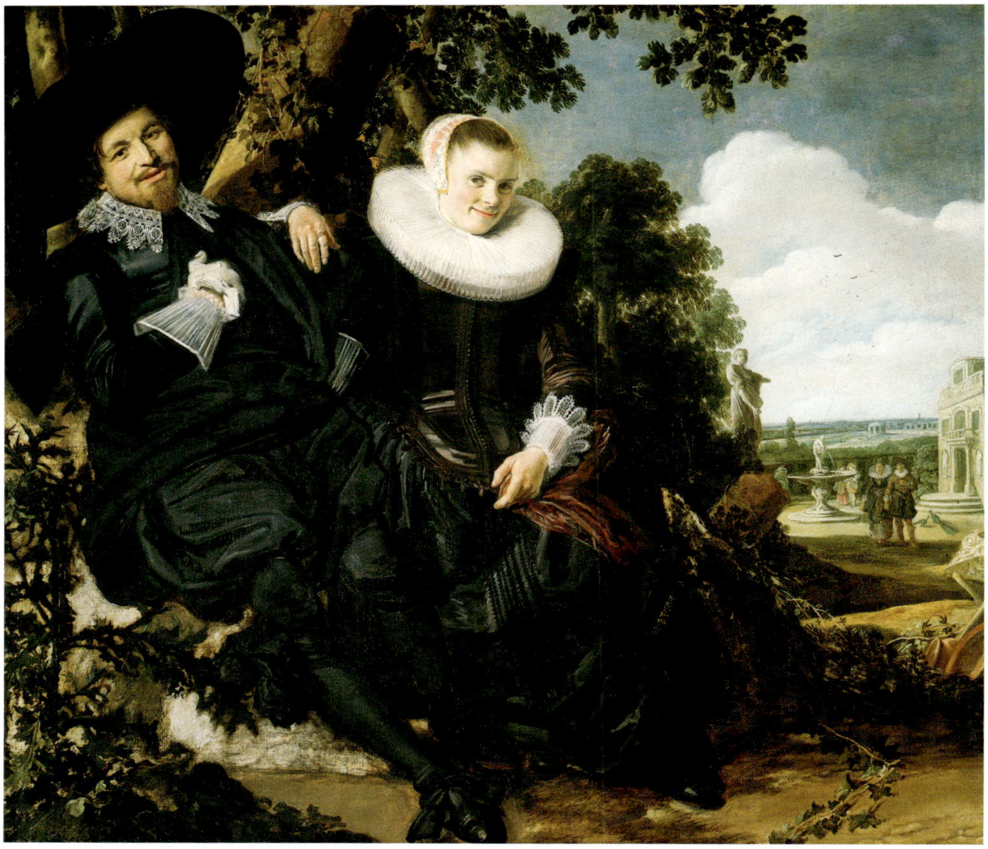

8. Hals painted several group portraits of officers. Van Gogh certainly knew the large canvas painted jointly by Hals and Pieter Codde: *The Company of Captain Reynier Reael and Lieutenant Cornelis Michielsz Blaeuw ("The Meagre Company")* of 1637 (Amsterdam, Rijksmuseum), and was lyrical about it (letter *CL* 426).

9. There are two known group portraits of governors of institutions that fit this description: *The Regents of St. Elizabeth's Hospital*, ca. 1641 (Haarlem, Frans Hals Museum) and *The Regents of the Old Men's Alms House* (Fig. 58).

10. Frans Hals, *The Regentesses of the Old Men's Alms House*, 1664 (Haarlem, Frans Hals Museum).

11. The following are candidates for these family portraits by Hals: *Family Portrait in a Landscape*, ca. 1620 (private collection); *Family Portrait*, ca. 1635 (Cincinnati Art Museum), and *Family Group in a Landscape*, ca. 1648 (Madrid, Thyssen-Bornemisza Collection). See Washington and elsewhere 1989–90, pp. 156–60 (no. 10), 270–72 (no. 49), 317–19 (no. 67).

12. Frans Hals, *The Merry Drinker*, ca. 1628–30 (Amsterdam, Rijksmuseum).

13. Van Gogh was probably thinking of *Malle Babbe and a Smoker,* which was attributed to Hals at the time. It shows the grimacing face of the old woman above a table laden with fish (Dresden, Gemäldegalerie). This work is currently regarded as an anonymous pastiche after Hals.

60. Frans Hals, *Marriage Portrait of Isaac Massa and Beatrix van der Laen*, ca. 1622. Amsterdam, Rijksmuseum.

14. Frans Hals, *Gipsy Girl* (Fig. 59).

15. It is not known to which work or works van Gogh is referring.

16. Frans Hals, *Willem van Heythuysen*, ca. 1638 (Brussels, Musées Royaux des Beaux-Arts).

17. Frans Hals, *Marriage Portrait of Isaac Massa and Beatrix van der Laen* (Fig. 60). During the nineteenth century, this painting was still thought to be a depiction of Frans Hals and his wife Lysbeth Reyniersdr. Compare, for example, Fromentin 1902, chapter 11, pp. 299–300, Fromentin 1981, p. 167, and Washington and elsewhere 1989–90, pp. 162–65, no. 12.

18. Hals painted several "guttersnipes and laughing urchins," but it is impossible to make out whether van Gogh was thinking of any one in particular. Compare Washington and elsewhere 1989–90, pp. 176–77, no. 16.

19. Hals made a number of paintings of musicians, so it is impossible to identify the one van Gogh is referring to. Compare Washington and elsewhere 1989–90, pp. 168–71 (no. 14), 174–75 (no. 15), 202–3 (nos. 25–26), 205–7 (no. 28).

20. It is hard to say which painting of a cook van Gogh meant. Perhaps it was *Young Woman with a Glass and Flagon* (Washington, The Corcoran Gallery of Art). See Slive 1970–74, vol. 3, p. 15, cat. no. 22.

21. "Paradise" is the third and final part of Dante's *Divine Comedy* (1313–21).

22. The adverb *même* (even) can refer to the Greeks but also to "the Michelangelos, Raphaels and the Greeks" as a whole.

23. Today there are only twelve paintings that are attributed to Carel Fabritius, and in van Gogh's day it was known that his oeuvre was small. E. J. T. Thoré (writing under the pseudonym of W. Bürger), who was largely responsible for the rediscovery of Fabritius, attributed nine paintings to him in the second volume of his *Musées de la Hollande*. According to Thoré, incidentally, the brothers Bernart (Barent) and Carel Fabritius were one and the same person. See The Hague and Schwerin 2004–5, and Thoré 1858–60, vol. 2, pp. 170–76. One work that van Gogh certainly knew was the Rotterdam self-portrait. It is possible that he used the word *deux* (two) in the sense of "only a few."

24. Van Gogh would have been referring to the paintings by Rembrandt in the Louvre: the figure of Christ in *The Supper at Emmaus* and the nude women in *Bathsheba Bathing* and *Susanna Bathing* (now regarded as a copy after Rembrandt).

25. Bernard added a note here in his 1911 edition to explain why van Gogh was being so vehement; see Letter 12, n. 6.

26. See Letter 12 for Bernard's *Lubricity*. Although the 1911 edition renders *l'arbre* (the tree) as *l'Arbre,* giving the impression that there was a second drawing, this must simply be a reference to the tree in *Lubricity.* Van Gogh did not use a capital letter.

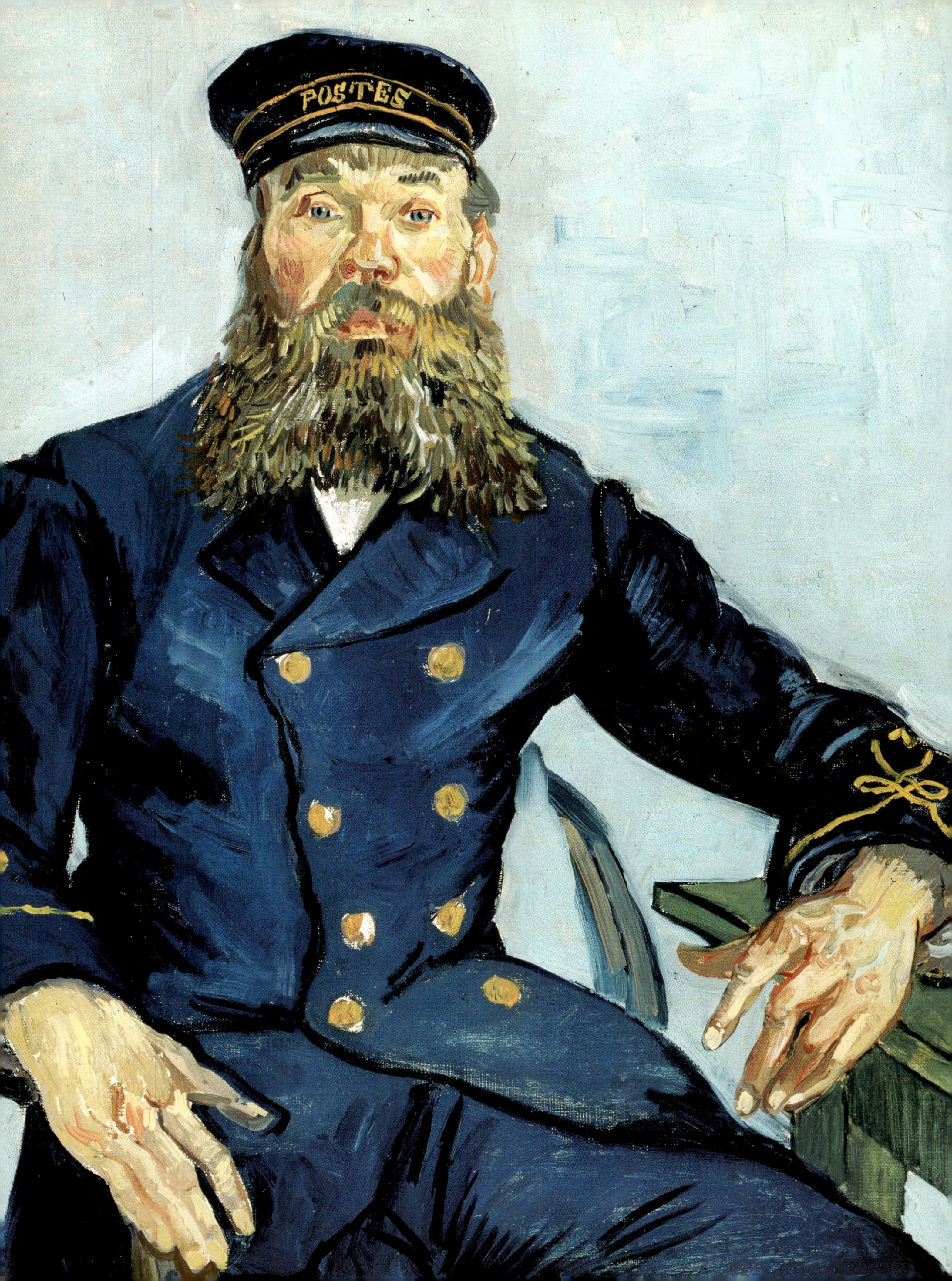
POSTES

Letter 14

Arles, ca. Sunday, 5 August, 1888

Source
Original manuscript

Location
New York, Thaw Collection, The Morgan Library & Museum

Date
In letter *CL* 517 to Theo, which dates from ca. 3 August, van Gogh reported that he was working on two portraits of Roulin the postman. In the present one he said that they were now finished, so it must have been written a few days later. In letter *CL* 519 of 8 August, he wrote that he had started on new work, so we have dated this one ca. Sunday, 5 August, 1888.

Additional details
Someone other than van Gogh made a small sketch of a sailing boat at top right on p. 1; see the facsimile.

Bernard must have dismissed van Gogh's earlier discourse about seventeenth-century Dutch painting as of little importance, for that is the reaction that van Gogh chose as the starting point for this letter. He took the opportunity to go into his ideas about virility, originality, and naturalism at length. Once again, then, this is a letter that succinctly sets out essential aspects of van Gogh's thinking.

The strategy he adopted to get Bernard to change his mind is a shrewd one. He praised several still lifes by Bernard that displayed the requisite qualities, using that as the argument why Bernard should continue on that course. The path followed by the primitives and by symbolistic painting turned out to be the wrong one in the end. Following on naturally from these exhortations he dusted off a few hobbyhorses like the importance of good health and sexual moderation. He also wrote to Theo on these subjects. "What Gruby says—do without women and eat well—it's true that does you good, and if you spend your brains and your marrow working with your mind, it's very logical not to spend yourself making love any more than is necessary."[1]

Van Gogh was now getting opportunities to work in the genre that he preferred: the figure piece or portrait. Joseph Roulin had volunteered to sit for him, and van Gogh was to paint the sturdy postman several times in his blue uniform.

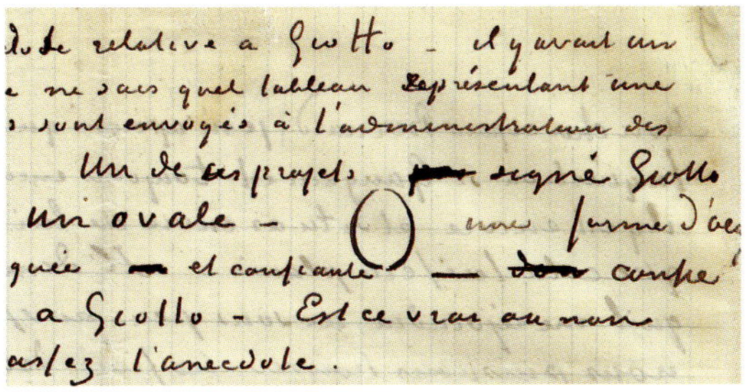
de relative a Giotto - il y avait un
ne sais quel tableau représentant une
sont envoyés à l'administration des
Un de ces projets signé Giotto
un ovale - ( ) une forme d'oe
guée et confiante — confié
a Giotto - Est ce vrai ou non
assez l'anecdote.

In the meantime, van Gogh had eased his isolation to some extent through personal contacts with colleagues. On a few occasions he met Eugène Boch and Dodge MacKnight, who were staying in nearby Fontvieille. At first they cloaked themselves in an "icy silence" about his work, but later he was able to report with satisfaction that MacKnight had praised a few of his studies (*CL* 512 and 516). Van Gogh found Boch a congenial person, in contrast to MacKnight, and hoped to paint his portrait.

The campaign to promote Gauguin's work continued apace. Following the two batches he had sent Bernard, van Gogh now dispatched twelve drawings after painted studies to Russell in order to make him receptive to the idea of buying a work by Gauguin.

Detail of Fig. 67.

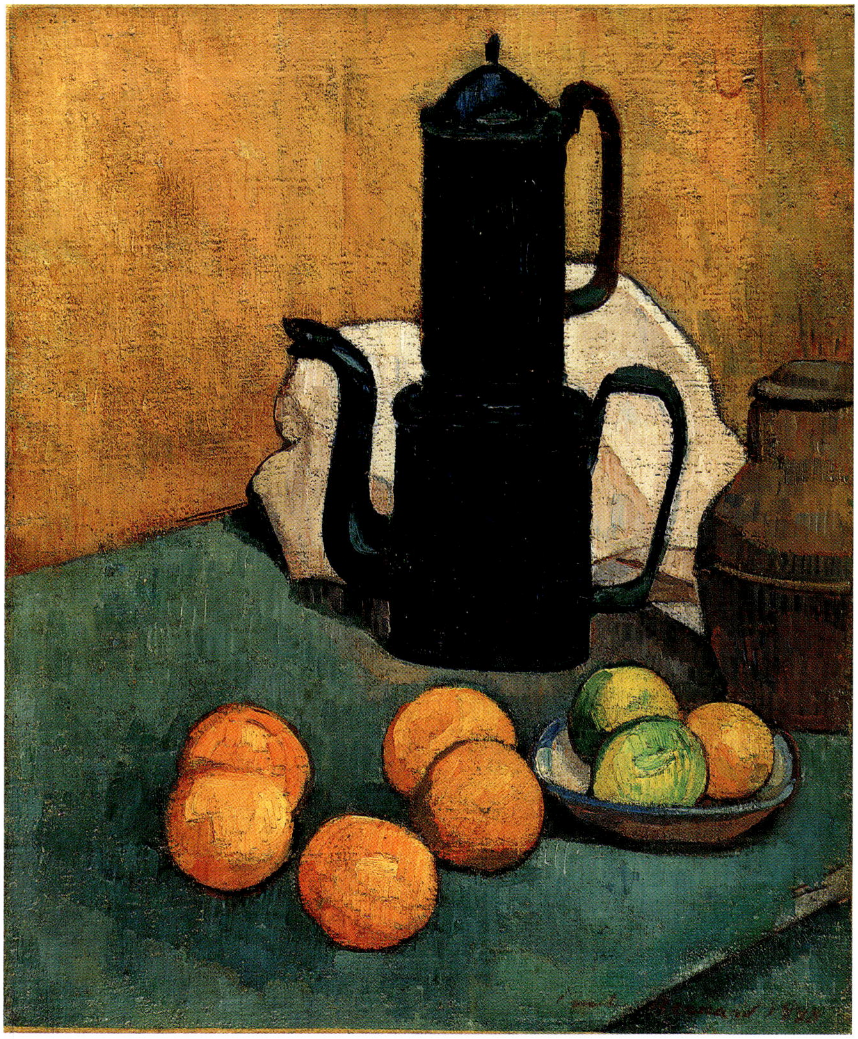

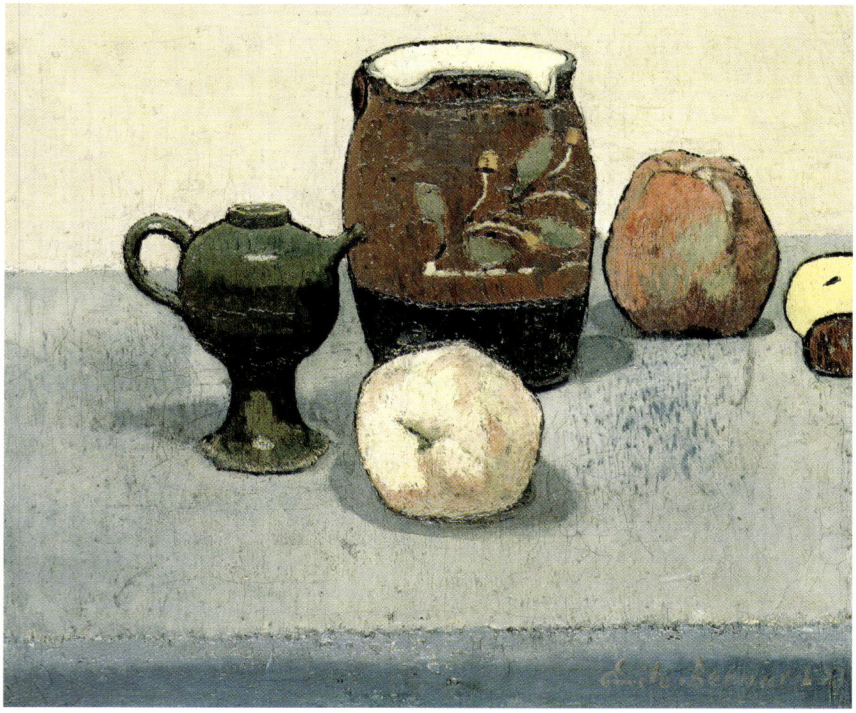

61. Émile Bernard, *Still Life: The Blue Coffeepot,* 1888. Bremen, Kunsthalle.

62. Émile Bernard, *Still Life: Earthenware Pot and Apples,* 1887–88. Paris, Musée d'Orsay.

Translation of Letter 14 / Arles, ca. Sunday, 5 August, 1888

My dear old Bernard,
I realize that I've forgotten to answer your question as to whether Gauguin is still in Pont-Aven. Yes, he's still there, and if you feel like writing to him am inclined to believe that it will please him. It is still likely that he will join me here shortly, as soon as either one of us is able to find the travel expenses.

I do not believe that this question of the Dutchmen, which we're discussing these days, is without interest. It is quite interesting to consult them when it's a matter of any kind of virility, originality, naturalism.

In the first place, I must speak to you again about yourself, about two still lifes that you have done,[1] and about the two portraits of your grandmother.[2] Have you ever done better, have you ever been more *yourself*, and somebody?[3] Not in my opinion. Profound study of the first thing to come to hand, of the first person to come along, was enough to really *create* something. Do you know what made me like these three or four studies so much? That je ne sais quoi of something deliberate, very wise, that je ne sais quoi of something steady and firm and sure of oneself, which they show. You have never been closer to Rembrandt, my dear chap, than then. In Rembrandt's studio, the incomparable sphinx, Vermeer of Delft,[4] found this extremely sound technique that has not been surpassed. Which today . . . we're burning . . . to find. Oh, I know that we are working and arguing COLOR as they did *chiaroscuro, value.*

What do these differences matter when in the end it's a question of expressing oneself powerfully?

Transcription of Letter 14 / Arles, ca. Sunday, 5 August, 1888

Mon cher copain Bernard
je m'aperçois que j'ai oublié de répondre à ta question si Gauguin est toujours encore à Pont Aven. Oui il y est encore et si tu as envie de lui écrire suis porté à croire que cela lui fera plaisir. Il demeure jusqu'à présent probable qu'il me réjoindra ici sous peu, aussitôt que de part ou d'autre nous puissions trouver les frais de voyage.

Je ne crois pas que cette question des hollandais, laquelle nous traitons de ces jours ci, soit sans interêt. Lorsqu'il est question de virilité, d'originalité, de naturalisme quelconques[a] *il est bien interessant de les consulter.*

Il faut d'abord que je te reparle de toi, de deux natures mortes que tu as faites[1] *et des deux portraits de ta grand'mère.*[2] *As tu jamais fait mieux, as tu jamais davantage été* toi *et quelqu'un?*[3] *Pas à mon avis. l'étude profonde de la premiere chôse tombant sous la main, de la première personne venue, suffisait pour* créer *réellement. Sais tu ce qui me faisait tant aimer ces 3 ou 4 études: Le je ne sais quoi de volontaire, de très sage, le je ne sais quoi de fixe et ferme et sûr de soi dont ils faisaient preuve. Jamais tu n'as été plus près de Rembrandt, mon cher, qu'alors. Dans l'atelier de Rembrandt, l'incomparable sphinx van der Meer de Delft*[4] *a trouvé cette technique excessivement solide qui n'a pas été surpassée. Qu'actuellement . . . on brûle . . . de trouver. Oh je sais que nous autres travaillons et raisonnons* COULEUR *comme eux* clair-obscur, valeur.

Qu'importent ces différences alors qu'il s'agit en somme de s'exprimer fortement.

Actuellement . . . tu es en train de scruter les procédés italiens et allemands primitifs, la significa-

At present . . . you're examining primitive Italian and German techniques, the symbolic meaning that the Italians' abstract and mystical drawing may contain. Do so.[5]

I myself rather like this anecdote about Giotto—there was a competition for the execution of some painting or other of a Virgin. Lots of proposals were sent to the fine arts authorities of those days. One of these proposals, signed Giotto, was simply—*an oval*—[sketch] an egg shape—the authorities, intrigued and trusting—entrust the Virgin in question—to Giotto. Whether it's true or not, I don't know, but I rather like the anecdote.[6]

However, let's return to Daumier and to your grandmother. When are you going to show us more of them, studies of that soundness? I urge you to do so, while at the same time in no way belittling your investigations concerning the properties of lines in contrary motion—being not at all indifferent, I hope, to the simultaneous contrasts of lines,[7] of forms. The trouble is, do you see, my dear old Bernard, that Giotto, Cimabue, as well as Holbein and van Eyck, lived in an obeliscal—if you'll pardon the expression—society, layered, architecturally constructed, in which each individual was a stone, all of them holding together and forming a monumental society. I have no doubt that we'll again see an incarnation of this society when the socialists logically build their social edifice[8]—from which they're a fair distance away yet. But you know we're in a state of total laxity and anarchy.

We, artists in love with order and symmetry, isolate ourselves and work to define *one single thing*.

Puvis knows that very well, and when he, so wise and so just, decided to descend good-naturedly into the intimacy of our very own epoch, forgetting his Elysian Fields, he made a

---

*tion symbolique que peut contenir le dessin abstrait et mystique des italiens.—*FAITES.[5]

J'aime assez moi cette anecdote relative à Giotto—il y avait un concours pour exécuter je ne sais quel tableau représentant une Vierge. Un tas de projets sont envoyés à l'administration des beaux arts de ce temps-là.—Un de ces projets signé Giotto est tout simplement—un ovale—[sketch] *une forme d'oeuf.—l'administration intriguée et confiante—confie la Vierge en question—à Giotto.—Est-ce vrai ou non, je l'ignore mais j'aime assez l'anecdote.*[6]

Pourtant retournons à Daumier et à ta grand mère. Quand est-ce que tu nous en remontreras, d'études de cette solidité-là?—Je t'y engage tout en ne méprisant aucunement tes recherches relatives aux propriétes des lignes à mouvement opposé—n'étant point indifferent je l'espère aux contrastes simultanés des lignes,[7] *des formes. le mal est, vois tu mon cher copain Bernard, que Giotto, Cimabue, ainsi que Holbein et v. Eyck vivaient dans une société obeliscale, passe moi donc le mot, echafaudée, construite architecturalement, où chaque individu était une pierre, toutes se tenant et formant societé monumentale. Cette societé, lorsque les socialistes construiront—ce dont ils sont passablement éloigné—logiquement leur édifice social,*[8] *on en reverra, je n'en doute point, une incarnation. Mais tu sais nous sommes en plein laisser aller et anarchie.*

nous artistes amoureux de l'ordre et de la symetrie, nous nous isolons et travaillons à definir une seule chôse.

Puvis sait bien cela et lorsque lui si sage et si juste a voulu, oubliant ses champs elysées, descendre aimablement jusqu'à l'intimité de notre époque même—il a fait un bien beau portrait, le vieillard serein dans son clair intérieur bleu lisant le roman à couverture jaune—un verre d'eau dans lequel un pinceau pour l'aquarelle et une rose—à coté de lui. Aussi une dame du monde telle qu'en ont portraic-

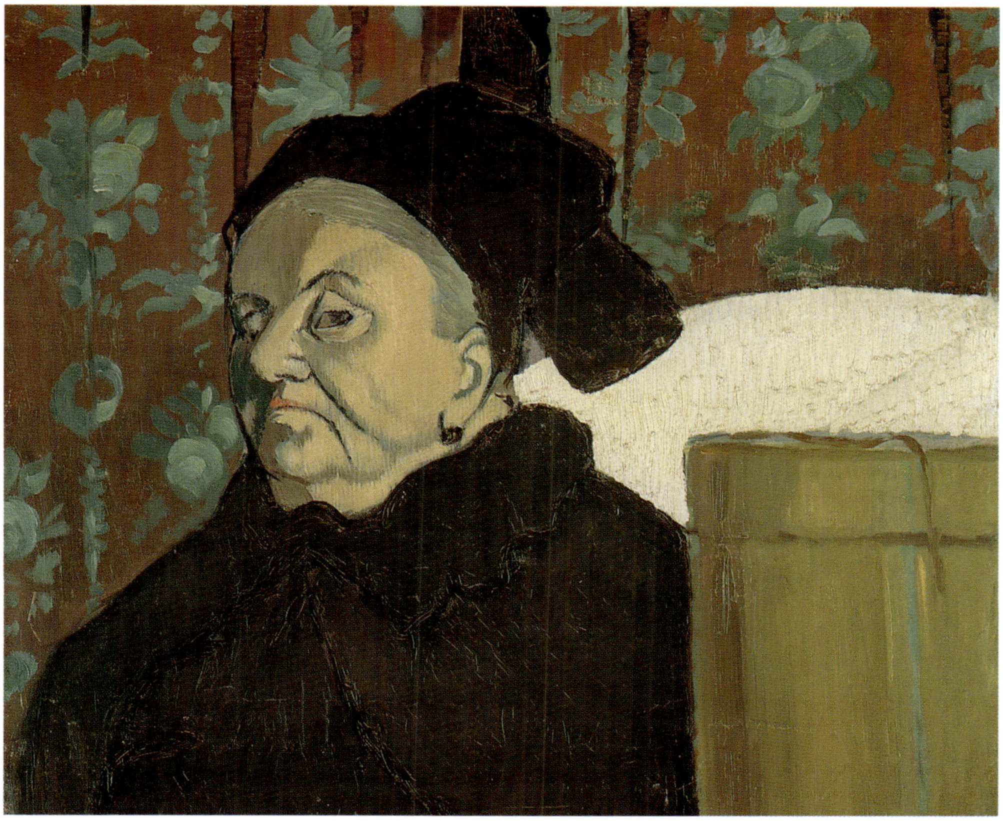

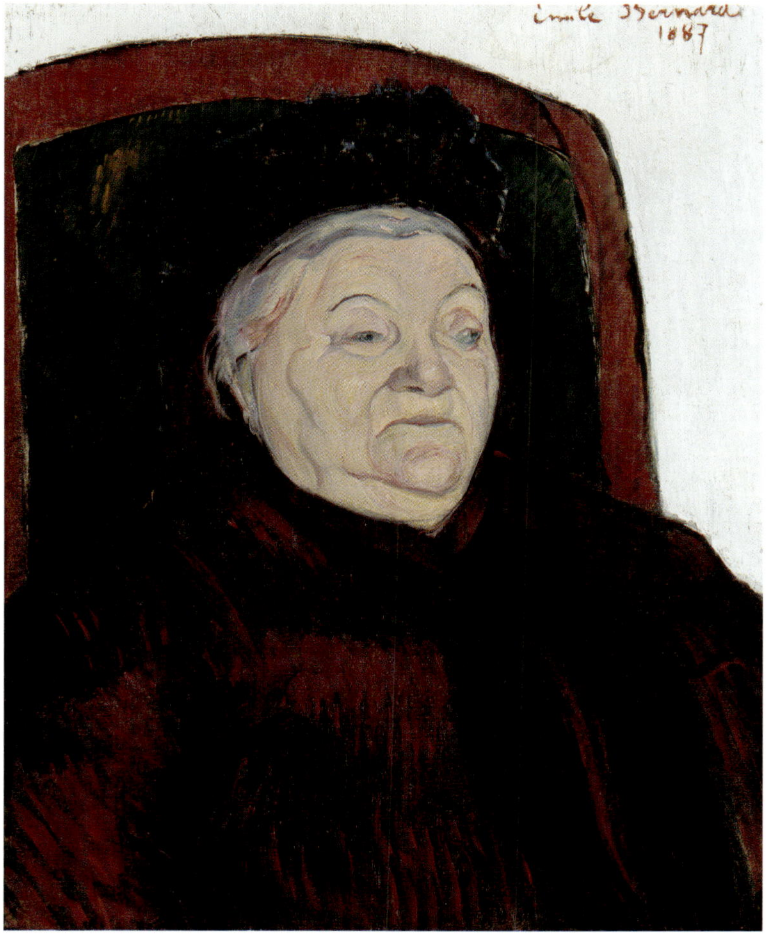

63. Émile Bernard, *Portrait of Bernard's Grandmother,* 1887. Amsterdam, Van Gogh Museum (Vincent van Gogh Foundation).
64. Émile Bernard, *Portrait of Bernard's Grandmother,* 1887. Boston, Museum of Fine Arts.

very fine portrait, the serene old man in his bright, blue interior, reading the novel with a yellow cover—a glass of water beside him, in which a watercolor brush and a rose. And also a society lady, like those the de Goncourts portrayed.[9]

The Dutchmen, now, we see them painting things just as they are, apparently without thought, the way Courbet painted his beautiful naked women.

They make portraits, landscapes, still lifes. One could be stupider than that and commit greater follies.

If we do not know what to do, my dear old Bernard, then let's do the same as they, if only so as not to allow our scarce mental powers to evaporate in sterile metaphysical meditations that aren't up to bottling chaos, which is chaotic for the very reason that it won't fit into any glass of our caliber.

We can—and that's what those Dutchmen did, desperately clever in the eyes of people wedded to system—we can paint an *atom* of chaos. A horse, a portrait, your grandmother, apples, a landscape.

Why do you say that Degas has trouble getting a hard-on? Degas lives like a little lawyer, and he doesn't like women, knowing that if he liked them and fucked them a lot he would become cerebrally ill and hopeless at painting. Degas's painting is virile and impersonal precisely because he has resigned himself to being personally no more than a little lawyer, with a horror of riotous living. He watches human animals stronger than himself getting a hard-on and fucking, and he paints them well, precisely because he doesn't make such great claims about getting a hard-on.[10]

Rubens, ah, there you have it, he was a handsome man and a good fucker,[11] Courbet too;[12]

---

turé les de Goncourt.[9]

Or les Hollandais, nous les voyons peindre des choses telles quelles, aparamment sans raisonner, comme Courbet peignait ses belles femmes nues.

Ils font des portraits, paysages, natures mortes. On peut etre plus bête que ça et faire de plus grandes folies.

Si nous ne savons que faire, *mon cher copain Bernard, alors faisons comme eux, si ce n'était que pour ne pas laisser évaporer notre rare force cérébrale en de stériles méditations métaphysiques qui ne sauraient mettre en bocal le chaos, lequel est chaotique pour cela même qu'il ne tient dans aucun verre de notre calibre.*

Nous pouvons—et voilà ce que faisaient ces hollandais deséspérément malins pour les gens à systeme—nous pouvons peindre un atome *du chaos. Un cheval, un portrait, ta grand mère, les pommes, un paysage.*

Pourquoi dis tu que de Gas bande mal? de Gas vit comme un petit notaire et il n'aime pas les femmes, sachant que s'il les aimait et les baisait beaucoup, cerebralement malade il deviendrait inepte en peinture. La peinture de de Gas est virile et impersonelle justement parceque il a accepté de n'être personellement qu'un petit notaire ayant en horreur de faire la noce. Il regarde des animaux humains plus fort que lui bander et baiser et il les peint bien, justement parcequ'il n'a pas tant que ça la pretention de bander.[10]

Rubens, *ah voilà, il etait bel homme et bon baiseur,*[11] *Courbet aussi,*[12] *leur santé leur permettait de boire, manger, baiser.*

Pour toi, mon pauvre cher copain Bernard, je te l'ai deja prédit ce printemps.[13] *Mange bien, fais*

their health allowed them to drink, eat, fuck.

In your case, my poor dear old Bernard, I already told you last spring.[13] Eat well, do your military drill well, don't fuck too hard; if you don't fuck too hard, your painting will be all the spunkier for it.

Ah, Balzac, that great and powerful artist, already told us very well that for modern artists a certain chastity made them stronger.[14]

The Dutchmen were *married people making children*, a beautiful, very beautiful occupation, very natural.

One swallow doesn't make a summer. I'm not saying that among your new Breton studies there aren't some virile and strong ones, but I haven't seen them yet and so wouldn't be able to talk about them. But—I have seen those virile things, the portrait of your grandmother and the still lifes—judging from your drawings I have vague doubts whether these new studies would have the same vigor, just from the virile point of view.[15]

These studies that I'm talking about first, you see it's the first swallow of your summertime as an artist. If we want, ourselves, to get a hard-on for our work, we must sometimes resign ourselves to fucking only a *little*, and for the rest to be, according as our temperament demands, soldiers or monks. The Dutchmen, once again, had morals, and a quiet, calm, well-ordered life.

Delacroix, ah, him—"I," he said, "found painting when I had no teeth nor breath left."[16] And those who saw this famous artist paint said: when *Delacroix paints it's like the lion devouring his piece of flesh.*[17] He fucked only a little, and had only casual love affairs so as not to filch from the time devoted to his work. If in this letter, on the face of it more incoherent, and taken on its own

---

bien l'exercice militaire, baise pas trop fort, ta peinture en ne baisant pas trop fort n'en sera que plus couillarde.

Ah Balzac, ce grand et puissant artiste nous l'a bien dit que pour les artistes modernes la chastete relative les fortifiait.[14]

Les hollandais étaient gens mariés faisant des enfants, *beau, bien beau metier bien dans la nature.*

Une seule hirondelle n'amene pas le printemps. Je ne dis pas que dans tes nouvelles etudes bretonnes il n'y en ait pas de viriles et fermes mais je ne les ai pas encore vues donc ne saurais en parler. Mais—j'ai vu ces chôses viriles, le portrait de ta grandmère et les natures mortes—d'après tes dessins j'en doute vaguement de ce que tes nouvelles etudes auraient une égale force juste au point de vue viril.[15]

Ces études dont je parle en premier lieu, tu vois c'est l'hirondelle première de ton printemps d'artiste. Si nous voulons, nous, bien bander pour notre oeuvre nous devons quelquefois nous résigner à peu *baiser et pour le reste être, selon que notre temperament le requiert, soldats ou moines. Les hollandais, encore une fois, avaient des moeurs et une vie paisible, calme, reglée.*

Delacroix, ah celui-là—"j'ai"—dit-il—"trouvé la peinture lorsque[b] *je n'avais plus ni dents ni soufle".*[16] *Et ceux qui ont vu peindre cet illustre artiste disaient—quand* Delacroix peint c'est comme le lion qui dévore le morceau.[17] *Lui ne baisait que peu et ne faisait que les amours faciles pour ne pas dérober du temps consacré à son oeuvre. Si dans cette lettre, plus incohérente en aparance, et considérée en soi sans ses rapports avec la correspondance et surtout l'amitié precedente, que je ne la désirais—Si dans cette lettre tu découvres que j'ai quelques inquietudes—en tout cas sollicitudes—pour ta santé,*

without its connections to the previous correspondence and above all, friendship, than I should wish—If in this letter you find that I have some anxieties—concerns in any case—for your health, foreseeing the hard ordeal that you'll have to go through in doing your service, obligatory, alas,—then you will read it correctly. I know that the study of the Dutchmen could only do you good, their works being so virile and so spunky and so healthy.

Personally, I find continence is quite good for me. It's enough for our weak, impressionable artists' brains to give their essence to the creation of our paintings. Because in thinking, calculating, wearing ourselves out, we expend cerebral activity.

Why exert ourselves in spending all our creative juices when those who pimp for a living and even their simple, well-fed clients work more to the satisfaction of the genital organs of the registered whore[18] in this case than we do? The whore in question has my sympathy more than my compassion.

Being exiled, a social outcast, as artists like you and I surely are, also "outcasts," she is surely therefore our friend and sister. And finding—in this position—of outcast—the same as us—an independence that is not without its advantages—all things considered—let's not adopt a false position by believing we're serving her through social rehabilitation, which is in any case impractical and would be fatal for her.

I have just made a portrait of a postman—or rather, two portraits even—Socratic type, no less Socratic for being something of an alcoholic, and with a high color as a result.[19] His wife had just given birth, the good fellow was glowing with satisfaction.[20] He's a fierce republican, *like père Tanguy*. Goddamn, what a subject to paint à la Daumier, eh? He was getting too stiff while posing, and that's why I painted him twice, the second time at a single sitting, on white canvas, background blue, almost white, in the face all the broken tones: yellow, green, purples, pinks, reds, the uniform Prussian blue trimmed with yellow.

Write to me soon if you feel like it; am very encumbered and have not yet found time for figure sketches. Handshake

Yours,
Vincent

Cézanne is as much a respectably married man as the old Dutchmen were. If he has a good hard-on in his work it's because he's not overly dissipated through riotous living.

prévoyant la dure épreuve que tu auras à traverser en faisant ton service, obligatoire, hélas, alors tu la liras bien. Je sais que l'etude des Hollandais ne saurait que te faire du bien, leurs oeuvres etant si viriles & si couillardes & si saines.—

personellement je me trouve assez bien de continence. Ca suffit à nos faibles cervelles impressionables d'artistes de donner leur essence à la création de nos tableaux. Car en réfléchissant, calculant, nous éreintant, nous dépensons de l'activité cérébrale.

Pourquoi nous efforcer à écouler toutes nos sèves créatrices là où les maquereaux de profession et les simples michets bien nourris même, travaillent davantage à la satisfaction des organes génitaux de la putain soumise[18] *dans ce cas, que nous mêmes? La putain soumise en question a davantage ma sympathie que ma compassion.*

Etre exilé, rebut de la societé, certes comme moi et toi artistes le sommes, "rebut" aussi, elle est[c] *certes notre amie & soeur conséquemment. Et y trouvant—dans cette position—de rebut—de même que nous—une indépendance qui n'est pas sans avoir ses avantages—tout bien considéré—ne nous trompons donc pas de point de vue en croyant la servir par une réhabilitation sociale d'ailleurs peu praticable et qui lui serait funeste.*

Je viens de faire un portrait d'un facteur—ou plutôt même deux portraits—type socratique, pas moins socratique pour être un peu alcôolique, et conséquemment haut en couleur.—[19] *Sa femme venait d'accoucher, le bonhomme luisait de satisfaction.*[20] *Il est terrible republicain* comme le père Tanguy. *Nom de dieu quel motif à peindre à la Daumier eh! Il se raidissait trop dans la pose, voila pourquoi je l'ai peint deux fois, la deuxieme fois dans une seule séance sur la toile blanche, fond bleu presque blanc, dans le visage tous les tons rompu, jaune, vert, violaces, roses, rouges, l'uniforme bleu de prusse agrémenté de jaune.*

Si le coeur t'en dit écris moi bientôt, suis fort encombré et ai pas encore trouvé temps pour croquis des figures. Poignée de main.

b. à t.
Vincent

Cézanne est justement homme marié bourgeoisement comme les vieux hollandais. s'il bande bien dans son oeuvre c'est que ce n'est pas un trop evaporé par la noce.

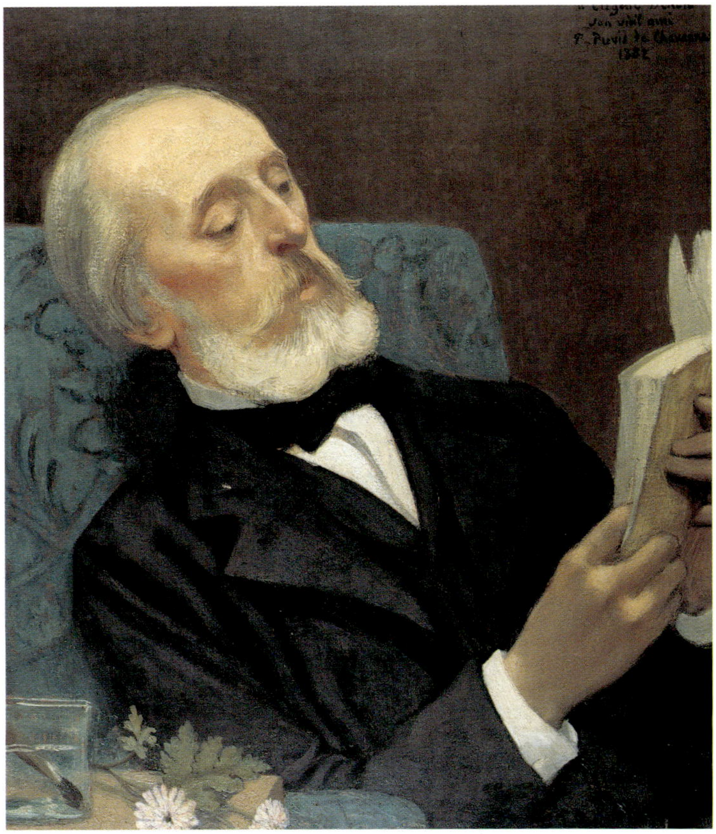
son vieil ami
P. Puvis de Chavannes
1882

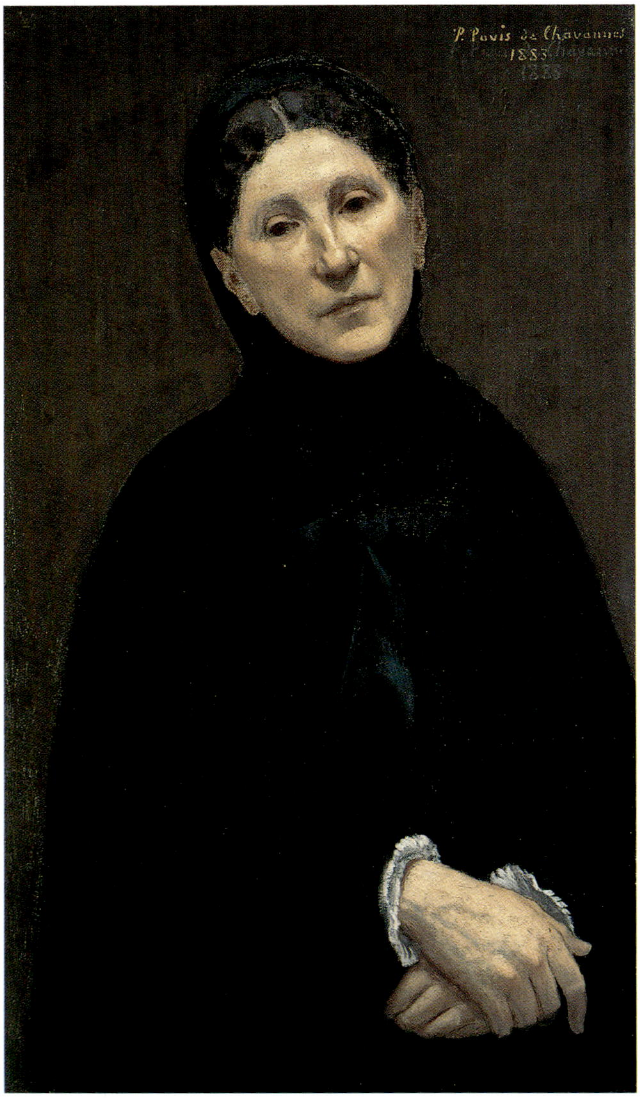
P. Puvis de Chavannes
1883

Annotations to Letter 14

Arles, ca. Sunday, 5 August, 1888

TEXTUAL NOTES
a. quelconques < quelconque
b. lorsque < lorque
c. elle est < est

1. Émile Bernard, *Still Life: The Blue Coffeepot* (Fig. 61) and *Still Life: Earthenware Pot and Apples* (Fig. 62).

2. Émile Bernard, *Portrait of Bernard's Grandmother* (Fig. 63). Bernard gave this painting to van Gogh in Paris in exchange for a self-portrait. The second painting is *Portrait of Bernard's Grandmother* (Fig. 64).

3. Van Gogh probably took this expression from Edmond de Goncourt's foreword to his novel *Chérie* (1884), in which he extolled the years of fruitful collaboration with his brother Jules. They wrote about art and literature and published several novels. Van Gogh read *Chérie* in the autumn of 1885 and spoke enthusiastically of the foreword in various letters to Theo. The expression that one must try to become "somebody" was taken from the following passage: "the search for the *true* in literature, the revival of the art of the 18th century, the triumph of the Japanese style: these are [. . .] the three great literary and artistic movements of the second half of the nineteenth century . . . and we will have led them, these three movements. . . we, poor obscure men. Well! When one has done that . . . it's truly difficult not to be *somebody* in the future." (*la recherche du* vrai *en littérature, la résurrection de l'art du XVIIIe siècle, la victoire du japonisme: ce sont [. . .] les trois grands mouvements littéraires et artistiques de la seconde moitié du XIXe siècle . . . et nous les aurons menés, ces trois mouvements . . . nous, pauvres obscurs. Eh bien! quand on a fait cela . . . c'est vraiment difficile de n'être pas* quelqu'un *dans l'avenir*). See Goncourt 1884, quotation on pp. XV–VI.

4. Van Gogh took this passage about Rembrandt's influence on Vermeer from E. J. T. Thoré (writing under the pseudonym of W. Bürger), *Musées de la Hollande*, who said of Vermeer: "The sphinx again!" (*Encore le sphinx*). And when giving "the biography of the *sphinx*" (*la biographie du* sphinx) wrote: "He comes from Rembrandt [. . .]. The boldness of the pure tones which are combined with virtuoso gradations of chiaroscuro, the deep sincerity of the expressions, the firm placing of the impasto in the light areas, the transparent scumbles in the shadows, it was Rembrandt who taught those secrets." (*Il sort de chez Rembrandt [. . .]. L'audace des tons francs combinés avec des dégradations prodigieuses de clair-obscur, la sincérité profonde des expressions, la pose de la pâte ferme dans les lumières, les frottis transparents dans les ombres, c'était Rembrandt qui enseignait ces secrets-là.*) See Thoré 1858–60, vol. 2, pp. 67, 79–80.

65. PIERRE PUVIS DE CHAVANNES, *Portrait of a Man (Eugène Benon),* 1882. Private collection.
66. PIERRE PUVIS DE CHAVANNES, *Portrait of a Woman (Portrait of Madame M. C. [Maria Cantacuzène]),* 1883. Lyon, Musée des Beaux-Arts.

5. Van Gogh later added this paragraph in the bottom margin.

6. The story is known as "Giotto's O" and originated in Giorgio Vasari's *Vita di Giotto*. The pope was looking for someone to paint scenes in St. Peter's, and various artists had submitted work for approval. Giotto, though, displayed his mastery by drawing a perfect circle freehand. This stunning evidence of his skill resulted in his being summoned to Rome, where he was awarded splendid commissions. See Vasari 1822, vol. 1, pp. 75–78. The tale is also recounted in Karel van Mander, *Het Schilder-boeck,* Haarlem 1604, fol. 96v.

7. Van Gogh first wrote "*des angles droites*" (right angles). The concept of simultaneous contrast, which played an important part in the color theory of the neoimpressionists, was applied to lines and forms by Bernard and Anquetin. They were searching for a natural language of contrasting lines and forms that expressed religiosity of their own accord, and they drew their inspiration from primitive woodcuts and stained glass. With thanks to Fred Leeman.

8. Van Gogh believed in Hippolyte Taine's view that true art was spawned by the society that produced it. Here van Gogh accused Bernard of trying to produce art that belonged centuries in the past even though he was living in an age of industrialization and urbanization in which the relationships among the ranks and classes were changing.

9. The two portraits by Puvis de Chavannes are *Portrait of a Man (Eugène Benon;* Fig. 65) and *Portrait of a Woman (Portrait of Madame M.C. [Maria Cantacuzène];* Fig. 66). Van Gogh saw them in Paris at the *Exposition de tableaux, pastels, dessins par M. Puvis de Chavannes,* in the Galeries Durand-Ruel from 20 November–20 December 1887. See Amsterdam 1994, pp. 171–77, nos. 89, 92.

   Van Gogh was mistaken about the flowers in Benon's portrait. They are chrysanthemums, not roses, and they are lying on the table.

10. Edgar Degas was a bachelor, and on several occasions van Gogh showed that he respected the fact that Degas adapted his way of life to fit his task as an artist. See also Kendall 1999, pp. 38–39.

11. Van Gogh may have deduced that Rubens was virile and sexually active from the fact that in 1630, at the age of fifty-three, he married the sixteen-year-old Hélène Fourment, by whom he had five children in seven years. He made several paintings of his young wife in seductive poses. See de Dijn 2002, p. 208.

12. Van Gogh could have read about Courbet's sex life in Théophile Silvestre's *Histoire des artistes vivants français et étrangers. Études d'après nature* (1853). It contains Courbet's saying: "A man cannot restrict himself to a single woman if he wishes to know woman." (*L'homme ne peut s'en tenir à une seule femme s'il veut connaître la femme.*) Ed. Paris n.d., p. 247.

13. Van Gogh had written about the importance of eating properly in Letter 4, and in Letter 7 he had pointed out to Bernard that "painting and fucking a lot are not compatible."

---

67. Vincent van Gogh, *Joseph Roulin, Sitting in a Cane Chair,* 1888 (F 432 / JH 1522). Boston, Museum of Fine Arts.

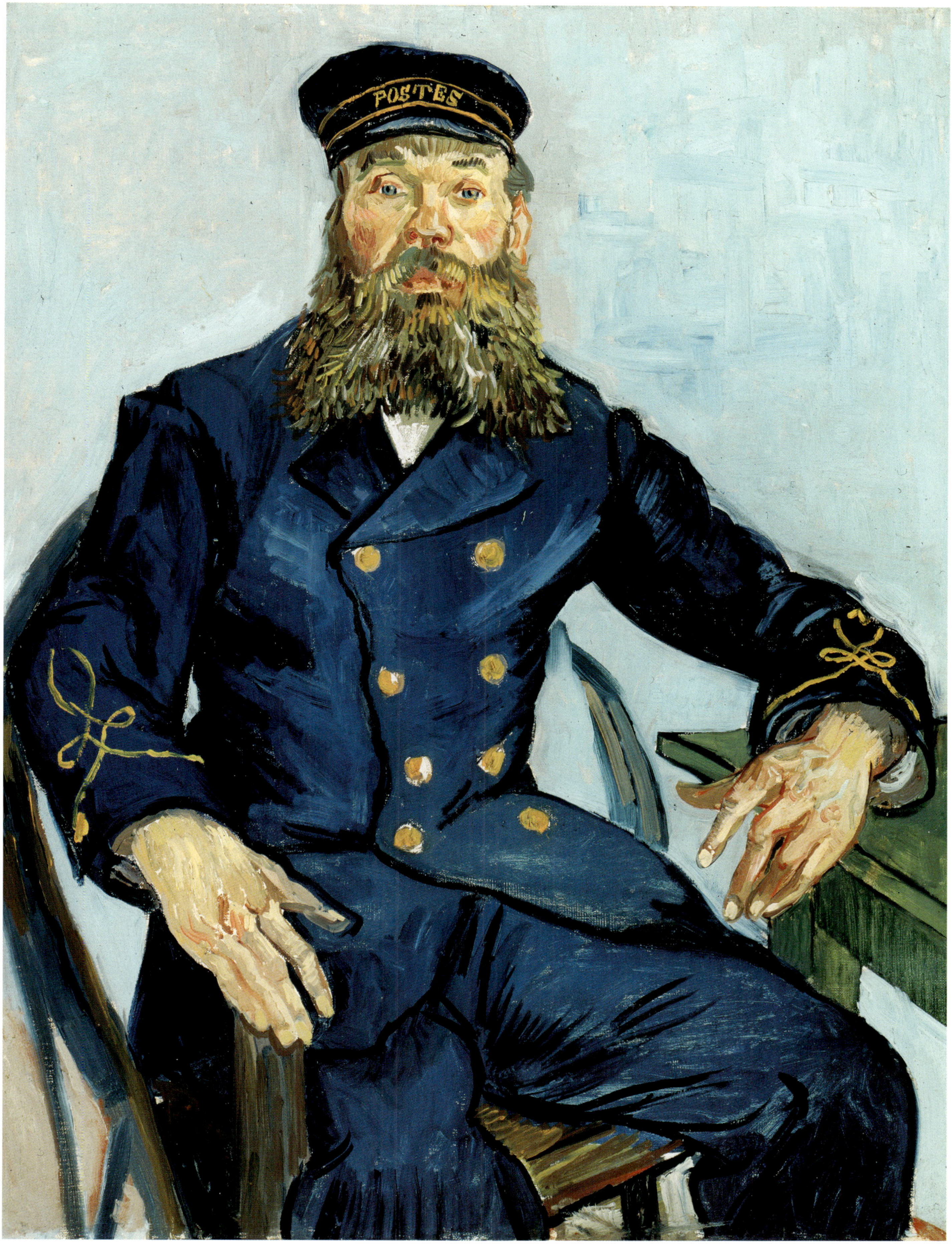
POSTES

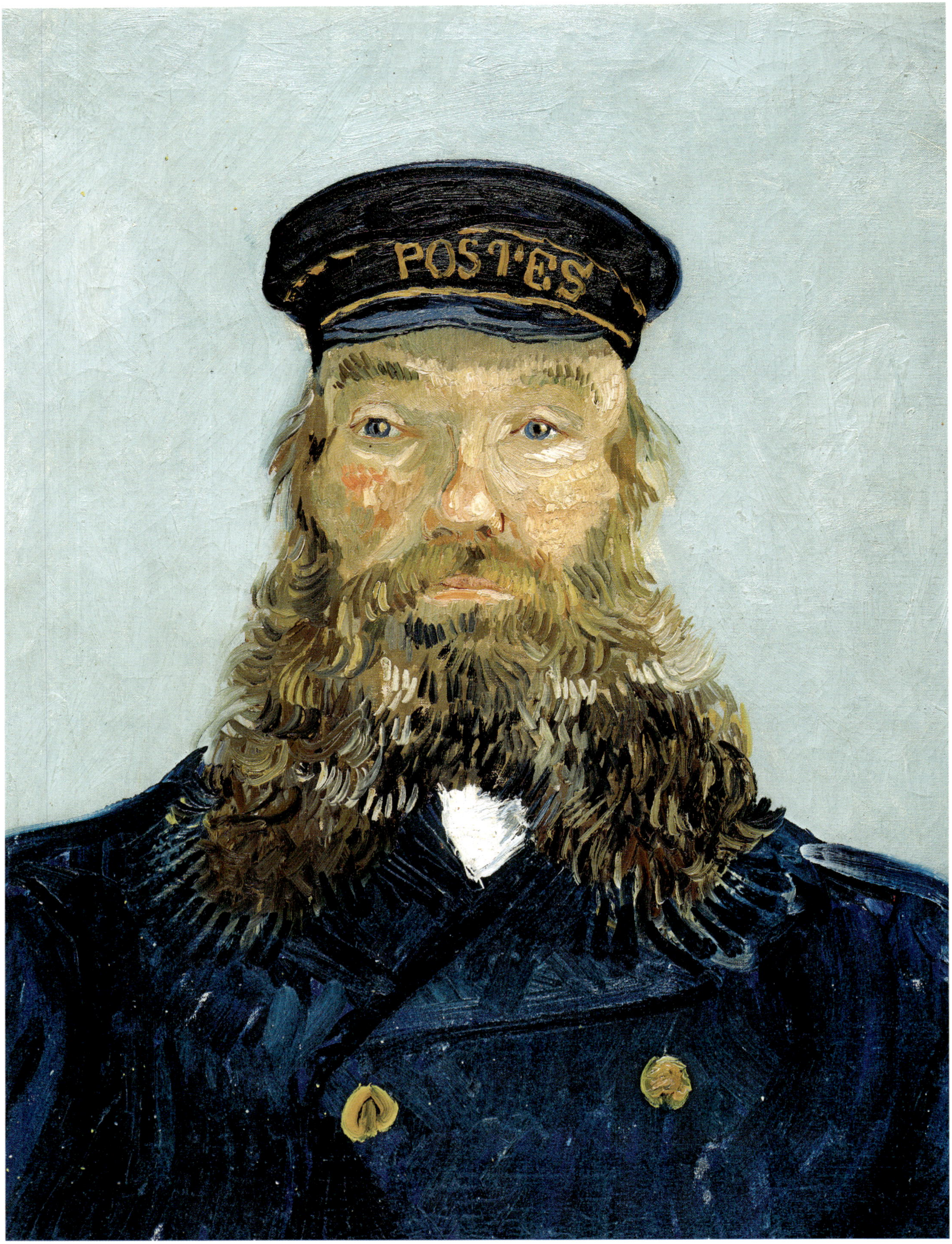
POSTES

14. That an artist should love in moderation and should guard against the constraining influence that marriage can have on his calling—"Artists should never marry" (*Les artistes ne devraient jamais se marier*)—is a recurring refrain in Balzac's work, notably in *La cousine Bette* and *Les illusions perdues*. See Wingfield Scott 1936, pp. 50–55 (quotation on p. 54).

15. Van Gogh must be referring to the drawings mentioned in Letters 12 and 13.

16. The phrase "no teeth nor breath" (*ni dents ni souffle*), which van Gogh works into several of his letters, was taken from what Théophile Silvestre said about Delacroix in *Histoire des artistes vivants français et étrangers. Études d'après nature*: "The very writer who, in all the ardor of youth and emotion, is confused, disorganized, in other words, mediocre and even bad, may become, like wine, excellent as he ages, and find himself at the height of his powers, just at the time when he no longer has either teeth or breath." (*L'écrivain même qui, dans toute l'ardeur de la jeunesse et du sentiment, est confus, désordonné, c'est-à-dire médiocre et même mauvais, peut devenir, comme le vin, excellent en vieillissant, et se trouver dans toute sa puissance, précisément à l'heure où il n'a plus ni dents ni souffle.*) See Paris n.d., p. 43.

17. Van Gogh probably knew this quotation from Jean Gigoux, *Causeries sur les artistes de mon temps*. Gigoux wrote: "When Delacroix paints, he (the sculptor Auguste Préault) used to say, it's like a lion carrying off his piece of flesh!" (*Quand Delacroix peint, disait-il, c'est comme un lion qui emporte le morceau!;* Paris 1885, p. 174).

18. The registered prostitute *(fille soumise)* was tied to her establishment, worked under the supervision of a madam, and was given routine medical checks. A *fille insoumise* was a prostitute working unregulated on the streets. See Thomson 2005, p. 206.

19. At the end of July, van Gogh had resolved to concentrate on the figure. "The change that I'm going to try to make in my paintings will be to do more figures. In the end, it's the only thing in painting that excites me deeply and that gives me a sense of the infinite. More than the rest" (*Le changement que je vais essayer de faire dans mes tableaux sera faire davantage de figures. C'est en somme la seule chose qui m'émotionne jusqu'au fond dans la peinture et qui me fait sentir l'infini. davantage que le reste*; *CL* 516). See also the opening words of Letter 15. The first of the two portraits mentioned here is *Joseph Roulin, Sitting in a Cane Chair* (F 432 / JH 1522; Fig. 67); the second is *Joseph Roulin, Head* (F 433 / JH 1524; Fig. 68). Van Gogh likened Roulin's appearance several times to that of the philosopher Socrates, undoubtedly because of his shaggy beard and republican convictions.

20. Marcelle, the daughter of Joseph and Augustine Roulin, was born on Tuesday, 31 July 1888.

---

68. Vincent van Gogh, *Joseph Roulin, Head*, 1888 (F 433 / JH 1524). The Detroit Institute of Arts.

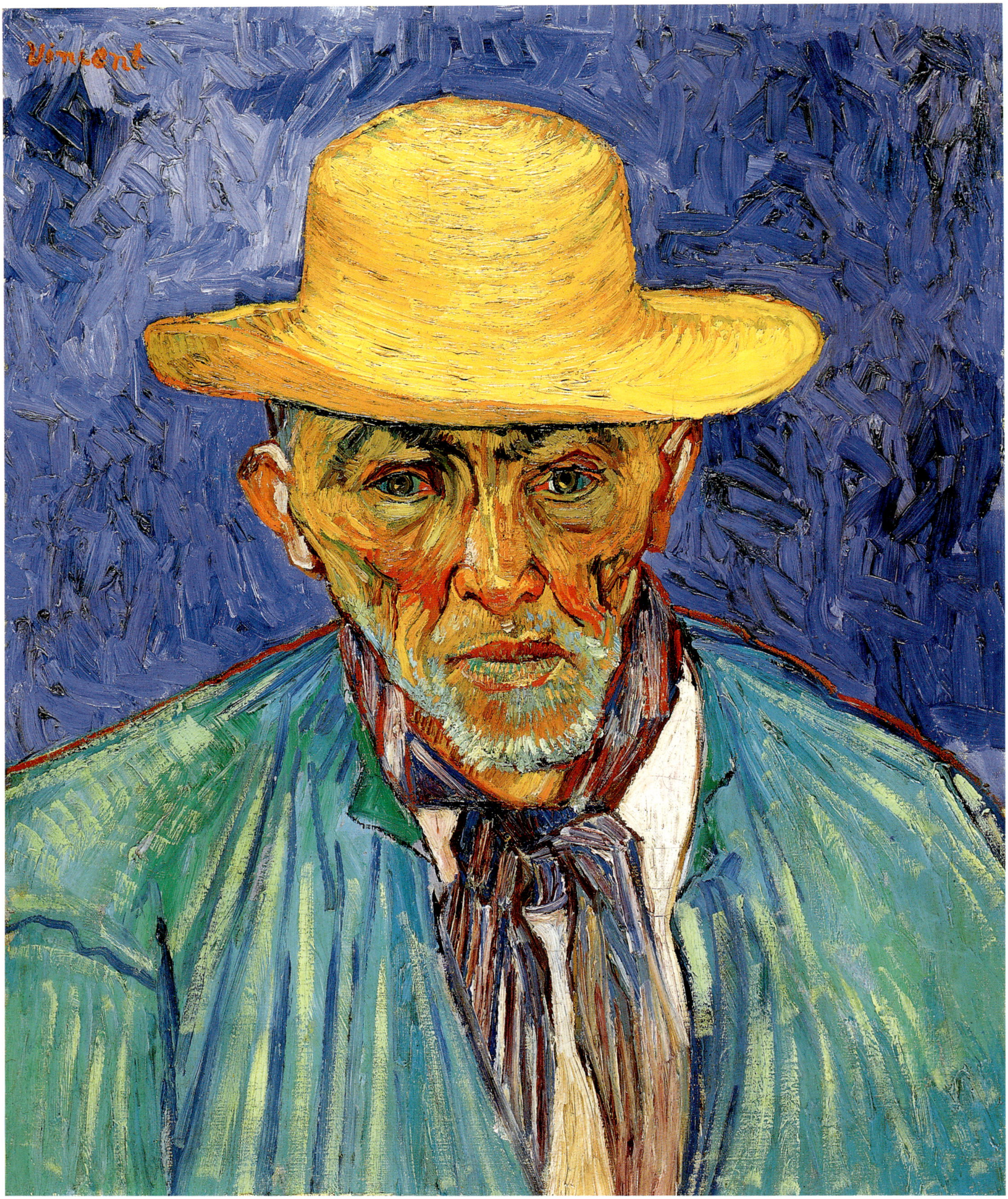
Vincent

Letter 15

Arles, ca. Tuesday, 21 August, 1888

Source
Original manuscript (sale, Paris, Drouot-Montaigne, 3 May 2001, lot 221)

Location
Collection Anne-Marie Springer

Date
This letter was written in reply to one from Bernard that van Gogh mentioned in letter *CL* 523 to Theo of 19 or 20 August. Both letters would have been written at about the same time, but because the one to Theo says nothing about the plan for the sunflower series outlined here, we assume that the letter to Bernard is the later of the two, and we have therefore dated it ca. Tuesday, 21 August, 1888.

Some sixteen days separate this letter to Bernard and the previous one. During that time van Gogh had written several times to Theo, evocatively describing his position as an artist. "While waiting, I am in my skin, and my skin in the gears of the Beaux Arts like the grain between the millstones."[1] He attributed the tempestuousness of the works he had painted out of doors partly to his battle with the mistral. He was now eating better, the sun was doing him good, and he felt his old strength returning. He was pleased with *The Old Peasant Patience Escalier* (F 443 / JH 1548; Fig. 69) because he had been able to express himself forcefully in it; he compared this peasant portrait to his *Potato Eaters* of 1885 (Fig. 70).

Bernard had in the meantime moved from Saint-Briac to Pont-Aven. Van Gogh received a letter from him on 19 or 20 August and wrote to Theo about it. "I've just received a letter from Bernard, who joined Gauguin, Laval and someone else in Pont-Aven a few days ago. In this letter, which is otherwise very kind, there isn't, however, a syllable about whether Gauguin intends joining me, nor another syllable, furthermore, asking me to go there. All the same, the letter was very friendly. From Gauguin himself, not a word for almost a month." The one thing van Gogh knew for certain was that he would not go to Pont-Aven if he had to live in a guesthouse among other artists with whom he would have to hold discussions every evening.[2] To his relief, Gauguin wrote shortly

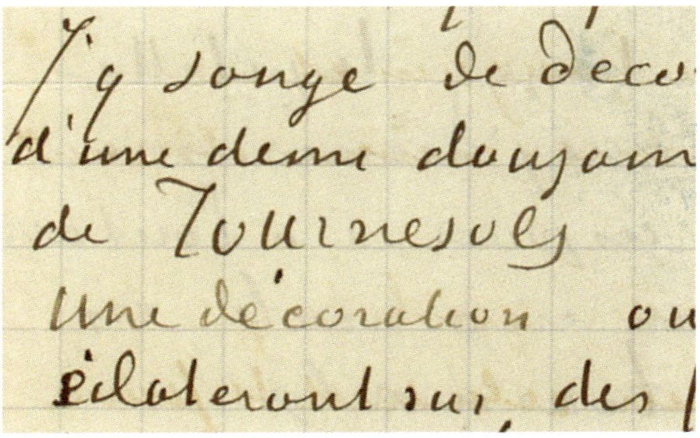
J'y songe de déco
d'une demi douzain
de Tournesols
une décoration ou
éclateront sur des

afterward, saying that he was still planning to come to Arles. This cheered van Gogh up, and he started work on his decorative program of sunflowers. He wrote to Theo about Gauguin's letter: "They're having a fine time, painting, debating, quarreling with the virtuous Englishmen; he says many good things about Bernard's work, and Bernard says many good things about Gauguin's work."[3]

69. Vincent van Gogh, *The Old Peasant Patience Escalier, Head*, 1888 (F 443 / JH 1548). Pasadena, The Norton Simon Museum.

Translation of Letter 15 / Arles, ca. Tuesday, 21 August, 1888

My dear Bernard,

I want to do figures, figures and more figures, it's stronger than me, this series of bipeds from the baby to Socrates[1] and from the black-haired woman with white skin to the woman with yellow hair and a sunburnt face the color of brick.

Meanwhile, I mostly do other things.

Thanks for your letter; this time I'm writing in great haste and really worn out.

I'm very pleased that you have joined Gauguin.[2]

Ah, I do have a new figure all the same,[3] which is absolutely a continuation of certain studies of heads done in Holland; I showed you them once, with a painting from that time, potato eaters.[4] I wish I could show it to you.

Again it's a study in which color plays a role that the black and white of a drawing could not convey.

I wanted to send you a very large and very carefully finished drawing of it.

Well—it turned into something *entirely different*, while still being correct.[5]

Because once again the color suggests the scorched air of harvest time at midday in the blistering heat, and without that it's a different painting. I would dare to believe that you and Gauguin would understand it, but how ugly they'll find it!

You fellows know what a peasant is, how much of the wild animal there is when you come across somebody purebred.[6]

I also have a man unloading a sand boat. That is, there are two boats, purplish pink, in veronese green water, with yellow-gray sand, wheelbarrows, planks, a little blue and yellow man.

All of it seen from the top of a quay overhanging everything in a bird's-eye view. No sky.[7] It's just a sketch, or rather, a rough sketch done out in the mistral.

Next, I'm attempting to do dusty thistles with a great swarm of butterflies swirling above them.[8] Oh, the beautiful sun down here in high summer; it beats down on your head and I have no doubt at all that it drives you loony. Now being that way already, all I do is enjoy it.

I'm thinking of decorating my studio with half a dozen paintings of *Sunflowers*.[9]

A decoration in which harsh or broken yellows will burst against various BLUE backgrounds, from the palest veronese to royal blue, framed with thin laths painted in orange lead.

Sorts of effects of *stained-glass windows* of a Gothic church.[10]

Ah, my dear pals,[11] we loonies, let's anyway enjoy with our eyes, shall we?

Alas, nature takes it out on the beast, and our bodies are despicable and sometimes a heavy burden. But since Giotto, a sickly character,[12] that's the way things are.[13]

Oh, and nevertheless, what delight of the eye and what laughter, the toothless laughter of Rembrandt the old lion, his head covered in a cloth, his palette in his hand.[14] How I should like to spend these present days in Pont-Aven, but anyway, I console myself by reconsidering the sunflowers.

I shake your hand firmly; so long.

Ever yours,
Vincent

Transcription of Letter 15 / Arles, ca. Tuesday, 21 August, 1888

Mon cher Bernard,

je veux faire de la figure, de la figure & encore de la figure, c'est plus fort que moi, cette serie de bipedes à partir du bebe jusqu'à Socrate[1] *et de la femme noire de chevelure à peau blanche jusqu'à la femme aux cheveux jaunes et le visage couleur de brique hâlé par le soleil.—*

En attendant je fais surtout autre chôse.

Merci de ta lettre, cette fois ci j'écris bien à la hâte et bien éreinté.

Cela m'a fait grand plaisir que tu ayes rejoint Gauguin.[2]

Ah j'ai tout de même une nouvelle figure[3] *qui est absolument une continuation de certaines etudes de têtes faites en Hollande, je te les ai un jour montrees avec un tableau de ce temps-là, des mangeurs de pommes de terre.*[4] *Je voudrais pouvoir te le montrer.*

C'est toujours une étude où la couleur joue un tel rôle que le blanc & noir du dessin ne saurait le rendre.

J'ai voulu t'en envoyer un dessin tres grand et très soigné.

Bon—cela devenait tout autre *chôse tout en etant correct.*[5]

Car encore une fois la couleur est suggestive de l'air embrasé de la moisson[a] *du plein midi en pleine canicule et sans cela c'est un autre tableau. J'oserais croire que Gauguin et toi le comprendraient, mais comme ils vont trouver cela laid.*

Vous autres vous savez ce que c'est qu'un paysan, combien cela sent le fauve lorsqu'on trouve quelqu'un de race.[6, b]

J'ai aussi un déchargeur d'un bateau de sable. c.à.d. il y a deux bateaux, rose violacé, dans une eau verte véronese avec du sable gris jaune, des brouettes, des planches, un petit bonhomme bleu et jaune.

Tout cela vu d'en haut d'un quai surplombant le tout à vol d'oiseau. Pas de ciel.[7] *Ce n'est qu'une esquisse ou plutôt une pochade faite en plein mistral.*

Ensuite, je cherche des chardons poussiereux avec grand essaim de papillons tourbillonnant dessus.[8] *Oh le beau soleil d'ici en plein été, cela tape à la tête et je ne doute aucunément qu'on en devienne toqué. Or l'étant déja auparavant je ne fais qu'en jouir.*

J'y songe de decorer mon atelier d'une demi douzaine de tableaux de Tournesols.[9]

Une décoration où les chrômes crûs ou rompus éclateront sur des fonds divers BLEUS *depuis le véronèse le plus pâle jusqu'au bleu de roi, encadrés de minces lattes peintes en mine orange.*

Des espèces d'effets de Vitraux *d'eglise Gothique.*[10]

Ah mes chers copains,[11] *nous autres toqués, jouissons nous tout de même de l'oeil n'est ce pas?*

Hélas la nature se paye sur la bête et nos corps sont méprisables et une lourde charge parfois. Mais depuis Giotto, souffreteux personnage,[12] *il en est ici.*[13]

Ah et tout de même quelle jouissance de l'oeil et quel rire que le rire edenté du vieux lion Rembrandt, la tête coiffé d'un linge, la palette à la main.[14] *Que j'aimerais à pouvoir passer ces jours ci à Pont Aven mais enfin je m'en console en ravisant des tournesols.*

Je te serre bien la main, à bientôt.

t. à t.
Vincent

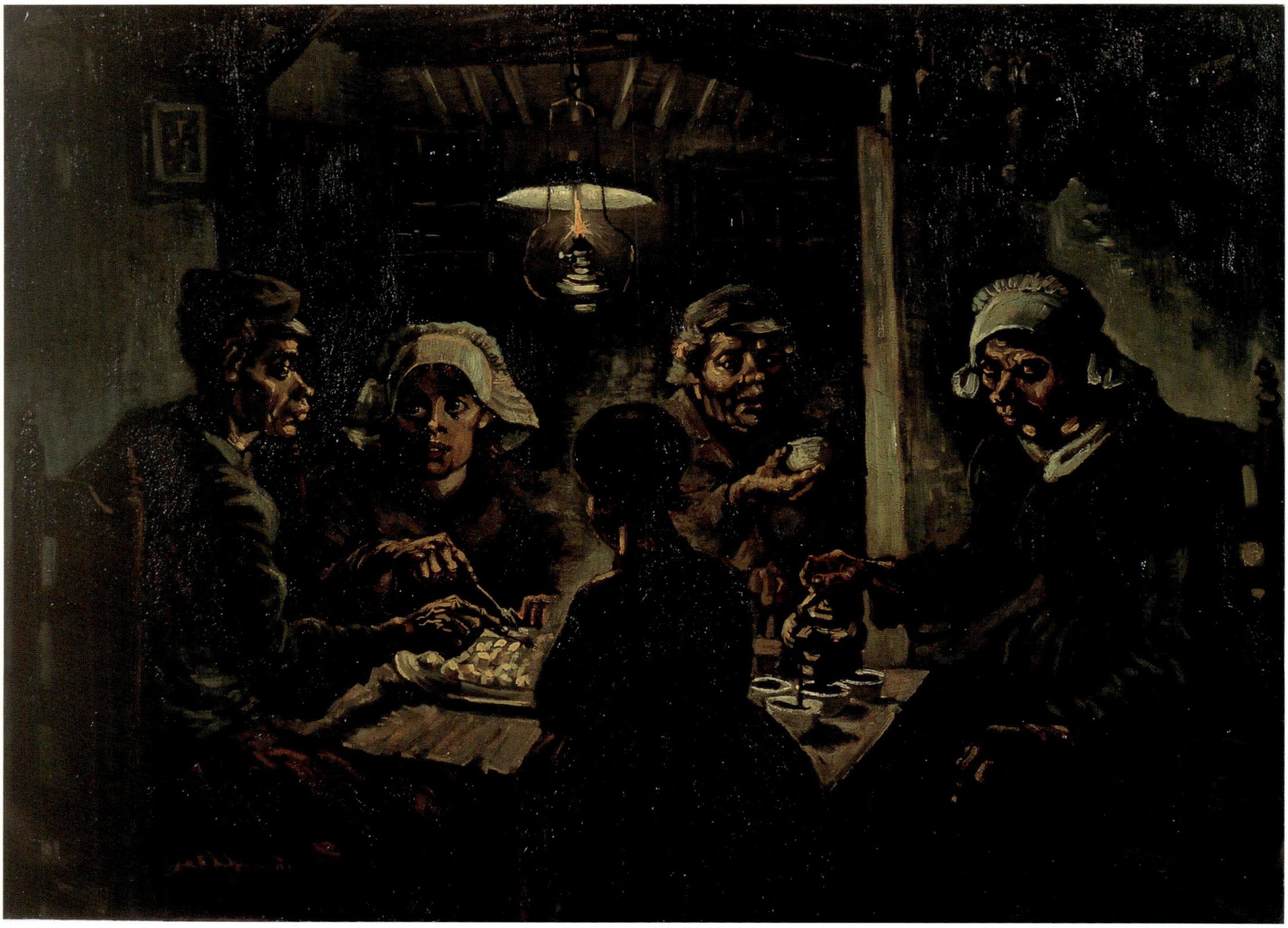

Annotations to Letter 15

Arles, ca. Tuesday, 21 August, 1888

Textual Notes
a. moisson < moisson de
b. race < *(Van Gogh may have meant* racé.*)*

1. Van Gogh was here referring to the type of old man he had recorded in his portraits of the postman Joseph Roulin. For the comparison of Roulin with Socrates, see Letter 14, n. 19. Van Gogh also hoped to paint Roulin's newborn daughter, Marcelle. This passage is probably a reference to the well-known riddle from classical mythology that the sphinx of Thebes posed to Oedipus: "What goes on four feet in the morning, two feet at midday, and three feet in the evening? Man."

2. In Letter 14 of ca. 5 August, van Gogh had confirmed that Gauguin was still in Pont-Aven. Even before receiving it, however, Bernard had decided to go there himself, as he wrote in a letter of 29 July to his sister Madeleine. He planned to arrive there on 8 or 10 August (see Harscoët-Maire 1997, p. 180). Gauguin wrote to Schuffenecker on 14 August 1888, saying: "Young Bernard is here and has brought back interesting things from Saint-Briac" *(Le petit Bernard est ici et a rapporté de St-Briac des choses intéressantes).* See *Correspondance Gauguin* 1984, p. 210. After Gauguin left for Arles, Bernard returned to Paris at the beginning of November. See Mannheim and Amsterdam 1990, p. 98.

3. Van Gogh was referring to the portrait of a gardener that he had painted about a week before, *The Old Peasant Patience Escalier, Head* (F 443 / JH 1548; Fig. 69).

4. In Nuenen in the first months of 1885, van Gogh had drawn and painted dozens of heads of peasants in preparation for what he regarded as his "masterpiece," *The Potato Eaters* (F 82 / JH 764; Fig. 70). See also Introduction, p. 14.

5. If he did send a drawing, it has not survived. The only known drawing after the portrait, *The Old Peasant Patience Escalier, Head* (F 1460 / JH 1549; Fogg Art Museum, Cambridge, MA), had been sent to Theo with letter *CL* 520. Bernard probably did, however, get the drawing *The Old Peasant Patience Escalier with Walking Stick* (F 1461 / JH 1564; private collection), since its provenance goes back to Ambroise Vollard, who bought many works by van Gogh from Bernard between 1894 and 1905. The painting after which that drawing was made (F 444 / JH 1563; private collection), however, dates from later in August (see letter *CL* 529). Pickvance's theory that that drawing was sent with a letter from van Gogh to Bernard that is now lost is therefore plausible. See New York 1984, p. 167.

70. Vincent van Gogh, *The Potato Eaters,* 1885 (F 82 / JH 764). Amsterdam, Van Gogh Museum (Vincent van Gogh Foundation).

6. There is a comparable notion about the similarity between a peasant and a wild animal in Sensier's biography of Millet, which for years had been a touchstone for van Gogh. In connection with Millet's attempts to depict the "type," Sensier wrote: "He was not at all afraid to make room in his rustic compositions for figures that were rough looking, whose individual nature was somewhat crude or at least unpolished, with an expression that seems to admit that the human being is not always so very superior to the animal" (*Il ne craignait point de donner place dans ses compositions rustiques à des figures d'un aspect rude, d'une individualité quelque peu grossière ou du moins mal dégrossie, d'une expression qui semble avouer que l'être humain n'est pas toujours prodigieusement au-dessus de l'animal*). See Sensier 1881, p. 355. See also Paris 1998–99, p. 50.

   Van Gogh wrote *race* without an accent, but he could equally well have meant *racé* (distinguished).

7. This is the painting *Quay with Men Unloading Sand Barges* (F 449 / JH 1558; Fig. 71).

8. This study is not known. It is neither *Thistles* (F 447 / JH 1550; Fig. 79) nor *Thistles* (F 447a / JH 1551; private collection) since neither has "a great swarm of butterflies." There could be a connection with the drawing *Thistles Along the Road* (F 1466 / JH 1552; Amsterdam, Van Gogh Museum), although there is no swarm of butterflies there either. Dorn identified the study described here as *Corner of a Garden with Flowers and Butterflies* (F 460 / JH 1676; private collection); see Dorn 1999, p. 44 (n. 7). There are, however, no thistles in that painting, and van Tilborgh places it in the Paris period. See Hendriks and van Tilborgh 2008.

9. This idea of decoration may have been owed in part to Bernard, who had done something similar in his studio. See Letter 3. Van Gogh worked from mid-August to the end of December 1888 on the decoration of his studio and the other rooms in the Yellow House, starting with a series of canvases of sunflowers. He took account of the fact that this homogeneous series of paintings (which he described as an "ensemble" and "a whole") could also be displayed outside the Yellow House and toyed with the idea of exhibiting them at the Revue Indépendante. See Dorn 1990 for a reconstruction of the project and the possible sources of inspiration for these decorations.

10. Here van Gogh cited one of Bernard's sources of inspiration in order to lend weight to his argument.

11. This form of address indicates that van Gogh counted on Bernard allowing Gauguin (and possibly other people as well) to read this letter. See also Letter 8, n. 25.

12. Van Gogh based his description of Giotto as "a sickly character" on Henry Cochin, "Boccace d'après ses oeuvres et les témoignages contemporains," *Revue des Deux Mondes* 58 (15 July 1888), 3rd series, vol. 88, pp. 373–413. On p. 378 Cochin called Giotto "ugly and sickly" (*laid et chétif*). Letter *CL* 539 to Theo shows that van Gogh knew the article.

13. The sense of this sentence is not entirely clear. It is possible that van Gogh intended to write *ainsi* instead of *ici,* and it is also conceivable that he didn't finish the sentence.

14. See Fig. 53 and Letter 12, n. 15.

---

71. Vincent van Gogh, *Quay with Men Unloading Sand Barges,* 1888 (F 449 / JH 1558). Essen, Museum Folkwang.

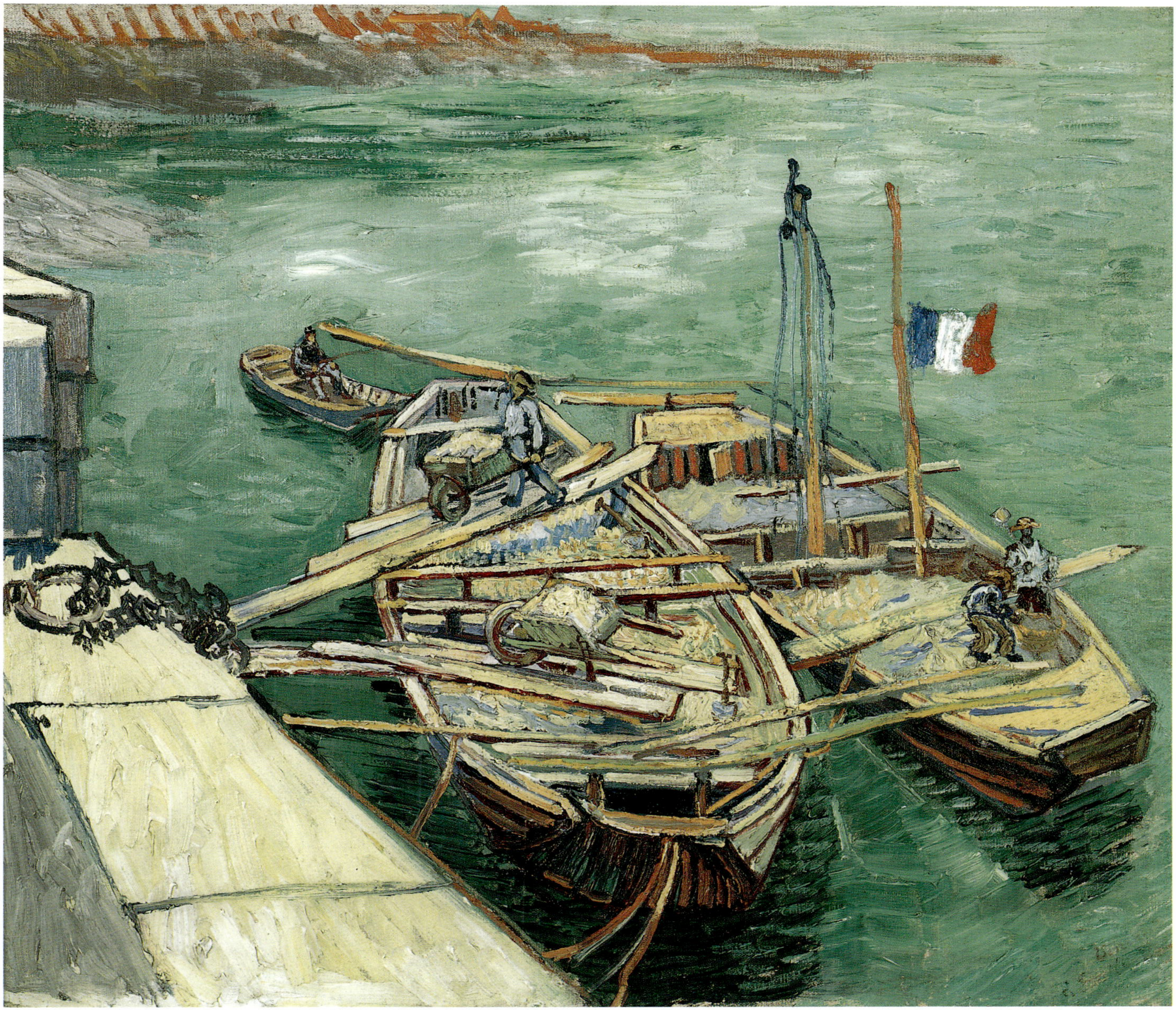

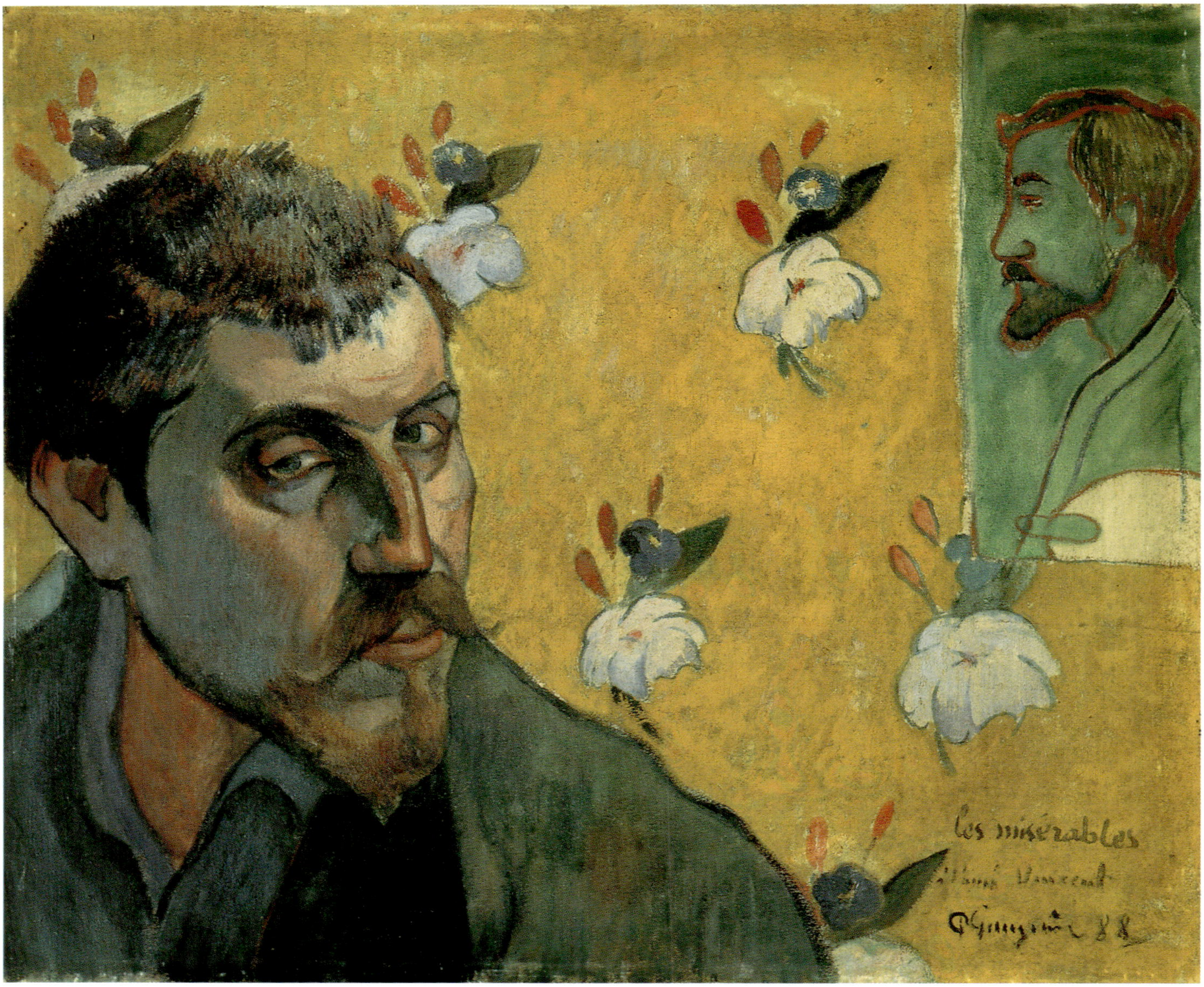
les misérables
PGauguin 88

Letter 16

Arles, between Wednesday, 19, and Tuesday, 25 September, 1888

Source
Original manuscript

Location
New York, Thaw Collection, The Morgan Library & Museum

Date
Vincent told Theo on 18 September about receiving a letter from Bernard (see letters *CL* 538–538a and *CL* 539). Those letters, however, give no indication that he had yet replied, which increases the likelihood that this one had not yet been written. He did tell Theo that he replied in letter *CL* 541a of 25 September. There are no more clues that would narrow the gap between Wednesday, 19, and Tuesday, 25 September, 1888.

Bernard and Gauguin struck up a friendship in Pont-Aven and strongly influenced each other. They told van Gogh that they were "now talking about doing 'children's painting.'"[1] During the two months of their collaboration, from August to October 1888, they pursued the path of painting from the imagination, at the same time simplifying forms and colors. Bernard painted *Breton Women in the Meadow* (Fig. 103), and Gauguin painted *Vision of the Sermon* (W308/W245; Edinburgh, National Gallery of Scotland)—works that would prove to be important milestones in the development of pictorial symbolism. Both artists also painted portraits of Bernard's sister Madeleine.

By this point, therefore, there was a solid triangular relationship. Van Gogh suggested that the two in Pont-Aven paint each other's portrait in return for work by him. What he wrote to Theo about the relationship is revealing. "Today, while actually working, I thought a lot about Bernard. His letter is full of veneration for Gauguin's talent—he says that he finds him so great an artist that it almost frightens him, and he finds everything that he, Bernard, does, bad in comparison with Gauguin. And you know that last winter Bernard was still trying to pick a quarrel with Gauguin. Ah well, whatever the case, and whatever happens, it is very consoling that those artists are our friends, and I dare to say will remain so, no matter how things turn out." He realized that there were unpleasant sides to Bernard's character but admired

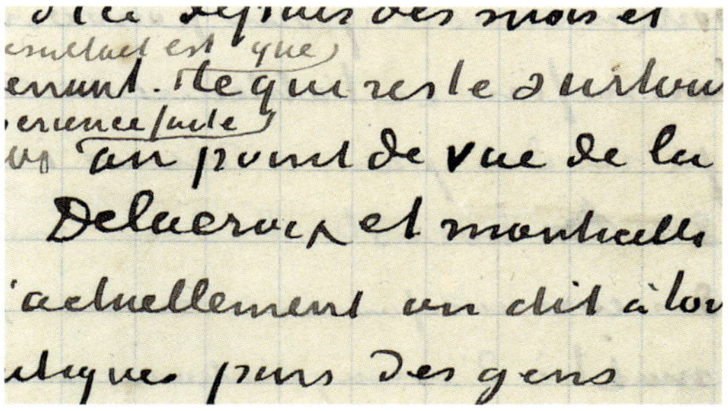
ce qui reste surtout
au point de vue de la
Delacroix et monticelli
actuellement on dit à lo

his forceful personality. "He said he would exchange his portrait for one of my studies. But he said that he *daren't* do Gauguin, as I had asked him, because he feels too shy with Gauguin. Bernard is basically such a temperamental character!! He's sometimes crazy and unpleasant, but I'm certainly not the one who has the right to blame him for that, because I know the same neurosis too much myself, and I know that he wouldn't blame me either."[2]

72. Paul Gauguin, *Self-Portrait with Portrait of Bernard, "Les misérables,"* 1888 (W309/W239). Amsterdam, Van Gogh Museum (Vincent van Gogh Foundation).

Translation of Letter 16 / Arles, between Wednesday, 19, and Tuesday, 25 September, 1888

My dear old Bernard.

Thanks for your letter, but what surprises me a little is to hear you say, "Oh, no way of doing Gauguin's portrait!"[1] Why no way? That's all rubbish. But I'm not pressing the point, and so we categorically won't mention that exchange any more. So even Gauguin, for his own part, hasn't even thought of doing yours. Here you have portraitists, living for so long side by side and they don't agree on posing for each other and they'll separate without having portrayed each other. Well! I'm not pressing the point. And I repeat, there's no longer a question of an exchange.

So I really hope to do your portrait and Gauguin's myself one day, the first time we get together. Which is bound to happen.

One of these days I'm going to do the portrait of that second lieutenant of Zouaves whom I've spoken to you about, who's now on the point of leaving for Africa.[2]

Why have you not replied to me about your plans regarding your military service?

Now let's talk a little about what you say, that you're thinking of coming to spend the winter in Arles.[3] I have deliberately set myself up here in such a way as to be able to fit someone in if necessary. If Gauguin comes, however.[4] He still hasn't categorically said no, in any case.

But even if I could put you up, I don't see that you could feed yourself well here for less than 3 francs a day. And I'd prefer to say 4 francs. Naturally, in the case of being broke, we could make many meals cheaply at the studio, *certainly* we could save that way; all the same, living here, I tell

---

Transcription of Letter 16 / Arles, between Wednesday, 19, and Tuesday, 25 September, 1888

Mon cher copain Bernard.

Merci de ta lettre, mais ce qui m'etonne un peu c'est de t'entendre dire "oh pour faire le portrait de Gauguin pas moyen!"[1] Pourquoi pas moyen, bêtises tout cela. Mais je n'insiste pas et aussi categoriquement nous ne parlerons plus de cet échange. Alors même pour lui de son côté Gauguin n'y a même pas songé à faire le tien.—Voila des portraitistes, cela vit si longtemps à côté l'un de l'autre et cela ne s'entend pas pour poser l'un pour l'autre et cela se separera sans s'être mutuellement pourtraicturé. Bon! je n'insiste pas.—Et je le repète, il n'est plus question de l'echange.

J'espere bien un jour alors faire ton portrait et celui de Gauguin moi-même, la première fois que nous tomberons ensemble. ce qui ne peut manquer d'arriver.

De ces jours ci je vais faire le portrait de ce sous-lieutenant des zouaves dont je t'ai parlé qui va maintenant partir pour l'Afrique.[2]

Pourquoi ne m'as tu point répondu au sujet de tes projets quant à ton service militaire?

Maintenant parlons un peu de ce que tu dis que tu y songes à venir passer l'hiver à Arles.[3] Moi je me suis installé ici expres d'une facon à pouvoir caser quelqu'un en cas de besoin. Si Gauguin vient pourtant.[4] Il ne s'est pas catégoriquement dédit encore, dans tous les cas.

Mais même si je pouvais te loger je ne vois pas que tu puisses bien te nourrir ici à moins de 3 francs par jour. et j'aimerais mieux dire 4 francs. Naturellement nous pourrions faire, en cas de dèche, bien des repas à bon marché à l'atelier, certes *on peut economiser de cette facon, tout de même la vie ici, je*

you, comes a bit dearer than in Pont-Aven, where I believe you're paying, aren't you, only 2.50 francs a day, and that's for everything. Lodging included.

And what if the thing that would tempt you the most—painting in the brothels—which is certainly excellent—could not after all be done here for free? Wait for that until you have your uniform, then; here and elsewhere, soldiers can do a whole lot of things in it for free. I, for example—it's true that I've just done that study of a night café[5]—but that, although it's a house of assignation, and from time to time you see a whore sitting there at a table with her fellow—I myself, I say, I haven't yet been able to do a brothel as such, *precisely because it would cost me more money than I'm forced to have, to do it reasonably well and seriously.* And that I refrain from beginning it before I feel sufficiently sure, as far as the wallet goes, of being able to complete that painting properly. Now, all right. We'd drink some glasses of beer in there, we'd meet people there; we'd work half from the imagination, half with a model.[6] And if we wanted to, I'm not saying that it might not be possible to do it. But I for one, I'm *not in any hurry for anything*, now. Projects so often fall through, and the best calculations you make; while by taking advantage of chance, and working from day to day without bias, you do a whole lot of unforeseen things.

So in no way can I encourage you to come here with the express purpose—excellent, without any doubt—of doing brothels. I repeat, once you're a soldier, you'll have a splendid opportunity for that, and in your own interest you would perhaps do well to wait until you have your uniform.

But, my dear old Bernard, I want to be very clear and plain in saying to you, do come and spend your time in Africa. The south will delight you and make you a great artist; Gauguin himself owes his superiority to the south.[7] I've been looking at the stronger sun down here for months

---

te le dis, revient un peu plus chère qu'à Pont Aven où je crois que tu payes, n'est ce pas, fr. 2.50 par jour seulement et cela pour le tout. logement compris.

Et si ce qui te tenterait le plus—faire de la peinture dans les bordels—ce qui certes est excellent—ne pouvait pourtant pas ici se faire à l'oeil?—Attends donc pour cela jusqu'à que tu aies ton uniforme, les soldats y peuvent là-dedans ici et ailleurs un tas de choses à l'oeil. Moi par exemple—il est vrai que je viens de faire cette etude de café de nuit[5]—mais cela, quoique ce soit une maison de passe et que de temps à autre on y voit une putain attablée avec son type—moi dis je—je n'ai pas encore pu faire un bordel proprement dit justement à cause de ce que cela me coûterait plus d'argent que je n'en aie nécessairement pour le faire un peu bien et sérieusement. *Et que je m'abstiens de le commencer avant que je me sente assez solide quant au porte monnaie pour pouvoir le mener à bonne fin, ce tableau. Maintenant je ne dis pas. Nous irions prendre des bocks[a] là-dedans, nous y ferions des connaissances, nous travaillerions moitié d'imagination, moitie avec un modèle.[6] Et si nous voulions je ne dis pas que cela ne soit pas possible de le faire. Mais moi pour un, maintenant je suis* pressé *pour rien. Les projets cela rate si souvent et les meilleurs calculs qu'on fait; tandis qu'en profitant des hasards et en travaillant au jour le jour sans parti-pris on fait un tas de choses imprévues.*

Je ne peux donc aucunément t'engager à venir ici dans le but expres—sans aucun doute excellent—de faire des bordels. Je le repète, une fois soldat tu auras une occasion splendide pour cela et dans ton propre interêt tu ferais peut être bien d'attendre jusqu'à que tu aies ton uniforme.

Mais mon cher copain Bernard je veux être bien clair et net à te dire, viens donc passer ton temps en Afrique. Le midi t'enchantera et te fera grand artiste, Gauguin lui-même doit sa supériorité au midi.[7] Moi je regarde le soleil plus fort d'ici depuis des mois et des mois maintenant. et le resultact est

and months now. And the result is that, from the point of view of color, what remains more than anything for me, having gained the experience, is Delacroix and Monticelli, those painters who nowadays are wrongly said to be pure romantics, people of exaggerated imagination. But anyway, do you see, the south, that was done so drily by Gérôme and Fromentin, is from this place on essentially a region whose intimate charm could only be interpreted by a colorist's color. I hope that you'll write to me again soon. I daren't take it upon myself to encourage just anyone to come here; if somebody comes of his own accord, well, that's his business, but as far as *advising* the thing, I'll never do it. For myself, I'm staying here, and naturally it would please me greatly if you were to spend the winter here. Handshake.

Ever yours,
Vincent

---

que ce[b] qui reste surtout debout pour moi, cette experience faite, au point de vue de la couleur, c'est Delacroix et Monticelli, ces peintres qu'actuellement on dit à tort être des romantiques purs, des gens d'imagination exagérée. Enfin mais vois tu, le midi qui a été fait si sèchement par Gerome et Fromentin, à partir déjà d'ici est essentiellement un pays dont on ne saurait interpreter le charme intime que par la couleur de coloriste. J'espere que tu m'écriras de nouveau bientôt. je n'ose prendre sur moi d'engager qui que ce soit à venir ici, si quelqu'un vient de son propre mouvement c'est ma foi son affaire mais pour recommander *la chôse, jamais je ne le ferai. Pour moi je reste ici et naturellement cela me ferait bien plaisir que tu passerais l'hiver ici. Poignée de main.*

t. à t.
Vincent

---

73. Émile Bernard, *Self-Portrait with Portrait of Gauguin,* 1888. Amsterdam, Van Gogh Museum (Vincent van Gogh Foundation).
74. Vincent van Gogh, *Self-Portrait,* 1888 (F 476 / JH 1581). Cambridge, MA, Fogg Art Museum.

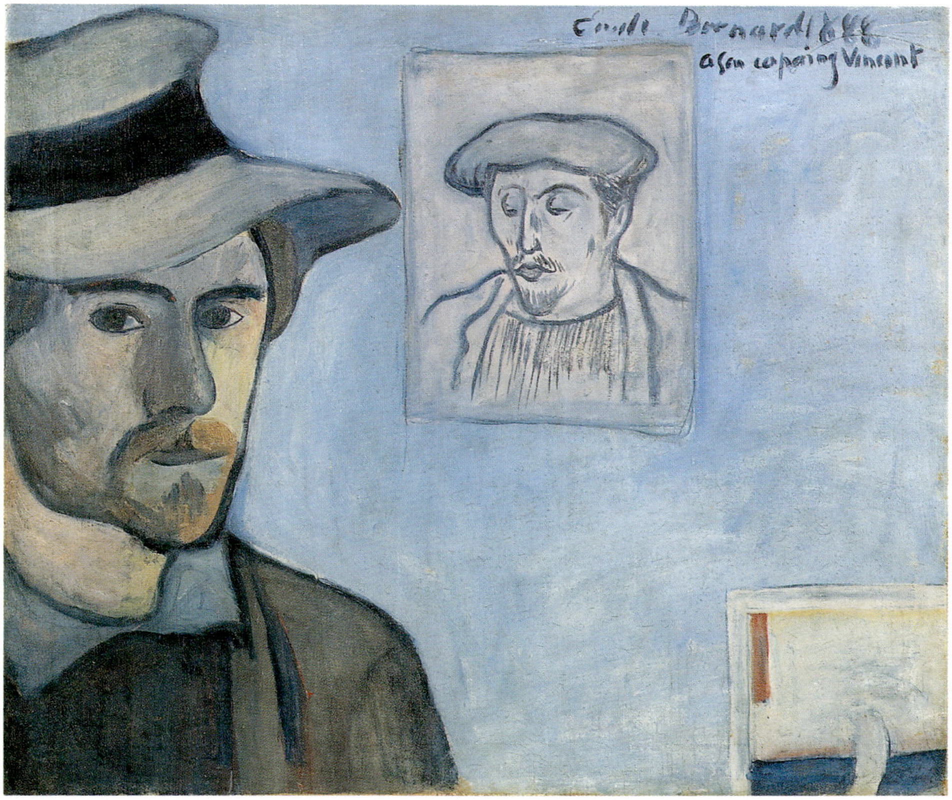
Emile Bernard 1888
a son copaing Vincent

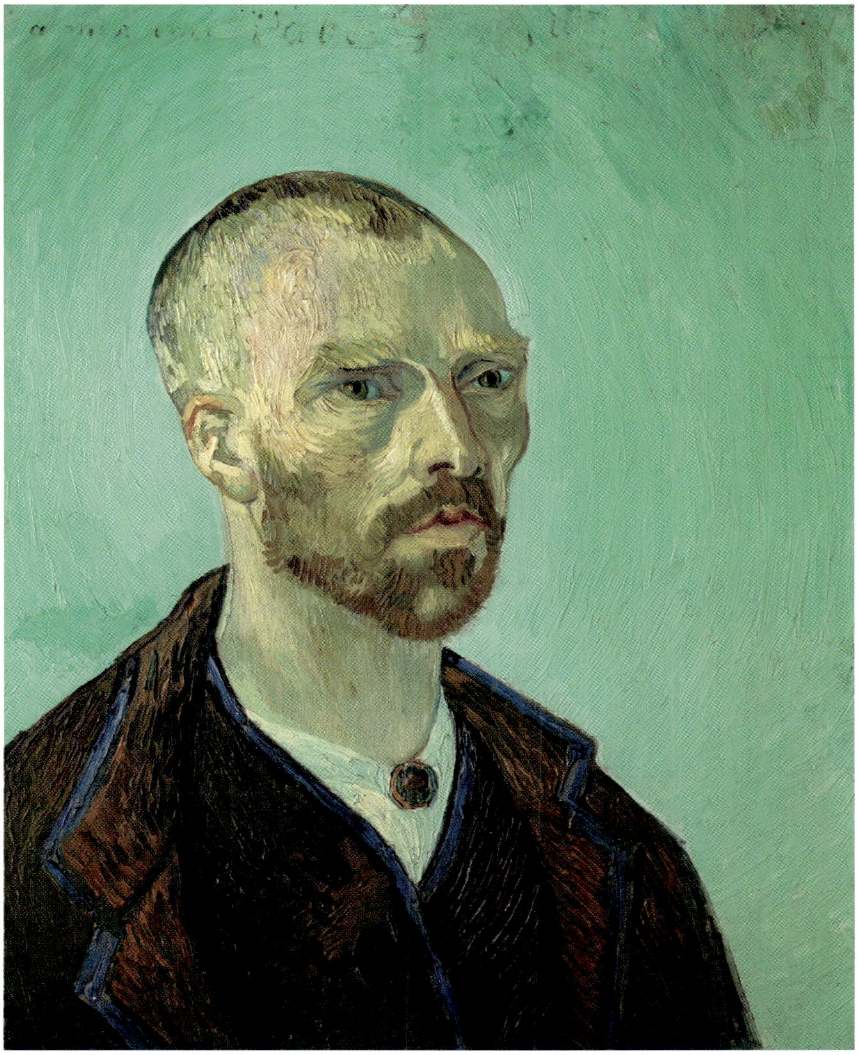

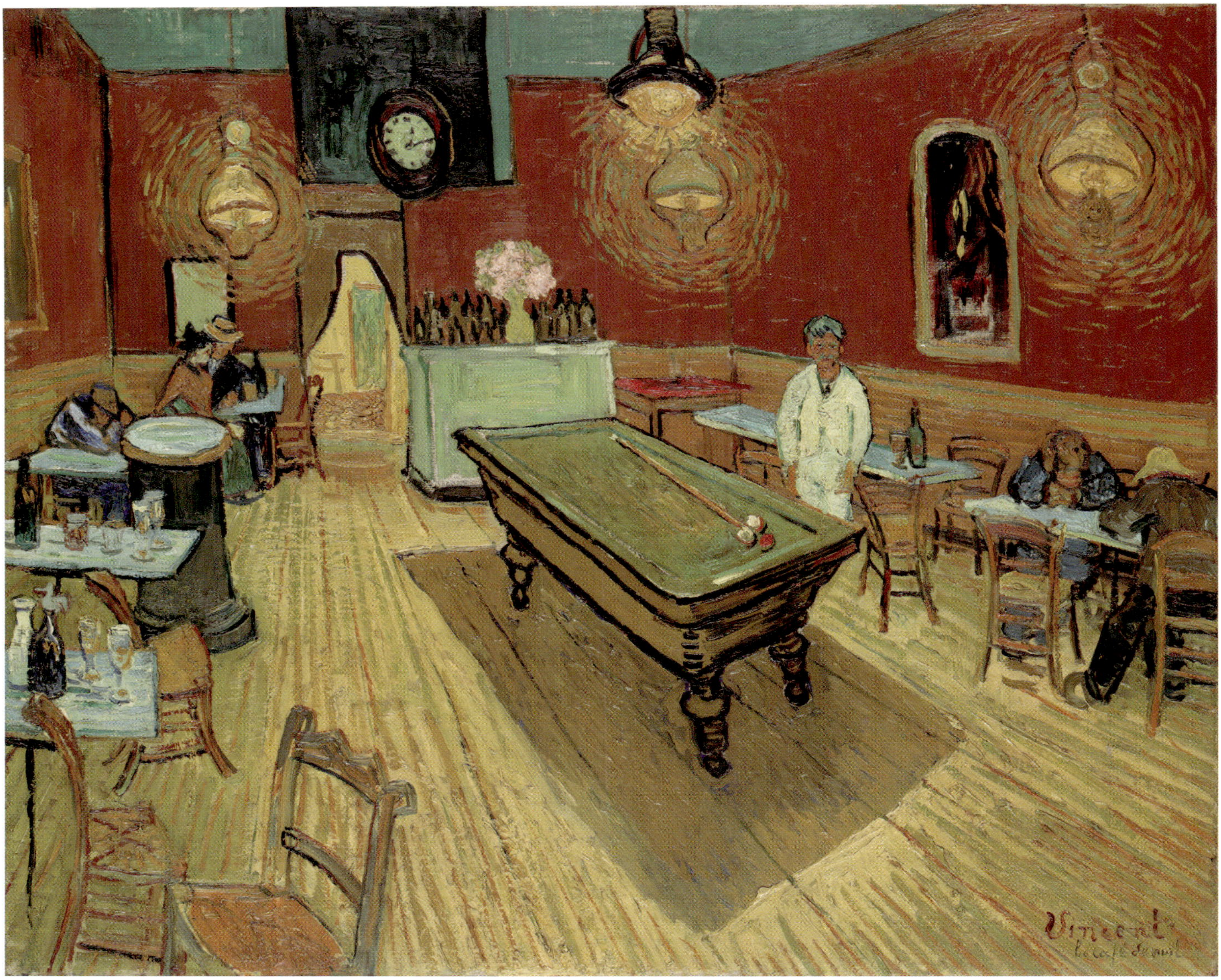
Vincent

Annotations to Letter 16

Arles, between Wednesday, 19, and Tuesday, 25 September, 1888

Textual Notes
a. bocks < bochs
b. ce < Ce

1. A letter to Gauguin and Bernard written between the preceding letter and this one is lost. In it, van Gogh had proposed that the two artists in Pont-Aven paint each other's portraits in exchange for work by him. The exchange is mentioned several times in the next few letters. Gauguin and Bernard acceded to van Gogh's request at the beginning of October, but they opted for self-portraits instead of portraits. Gauguin exchanged *Self-Portrait with Portrait of Bernard, "Les misérables"* (W309/W239; Fig. 72) and Bernard sent *Self-Portrait with Portrait of Gauguin* (Fig. 73). In return, Gauguin got *Self-Portrait* (F 476 / JH 1581; Fig. 74), and Bernard got *Quay with Men Unloading Sand Barges* (F 449 / JH 1558; Fig. 71).

2. Milliet the Zouave was introduced to Bernard in Letter 7. It was around this time that van Gogh painted his portrait *Lieutenant Milliet* (F 473 / JH 1588; Otterlo, Kröller-Müller Museum).

3. Van Gogh suspected that Bernard's plan to come to Arles was a "whim," so he advised Theo not to offer Bernard, who was perhaps thinking of taking Gauguin's place, 150 francs a month for a painting (the sum that had been suggested to Gauguin). He was very firm about this: "But no sort of contract with him. He's too changeable" (*Mais avec lui pas de contrat quelconque, il est trop variable; CL* 538).

4. It looks as if van Gogh did not complete this sentence. After *pourtant* he originally wrote: *ou si un autre viendrait a sa place* (or if someone else were to come in his place), but then crossed it out.

5. This study, which van Gogh painted at the beginning of September, and which, judging by his choice of words, he must have mentioned in the lost letter referred to in n. 1, was *The Night Café* (F 463 / JH 1575; Fig. 75).

6. This passage reflects the ideas of Bernard and Gauguin, who were constantly urging van Gogh to work from memory and the imagination. He followed their advice to the extent of undertaking a few experiments. See Introduction, p. 18.

7. Van Gogh was referring to Gauguin's stay in tropical Martinique between May and October 1887.

75. Vincent van Gogh, *The Night Café*, 1888 (F 463 / JH 1575). New Haven, Yale University Art Gallery.

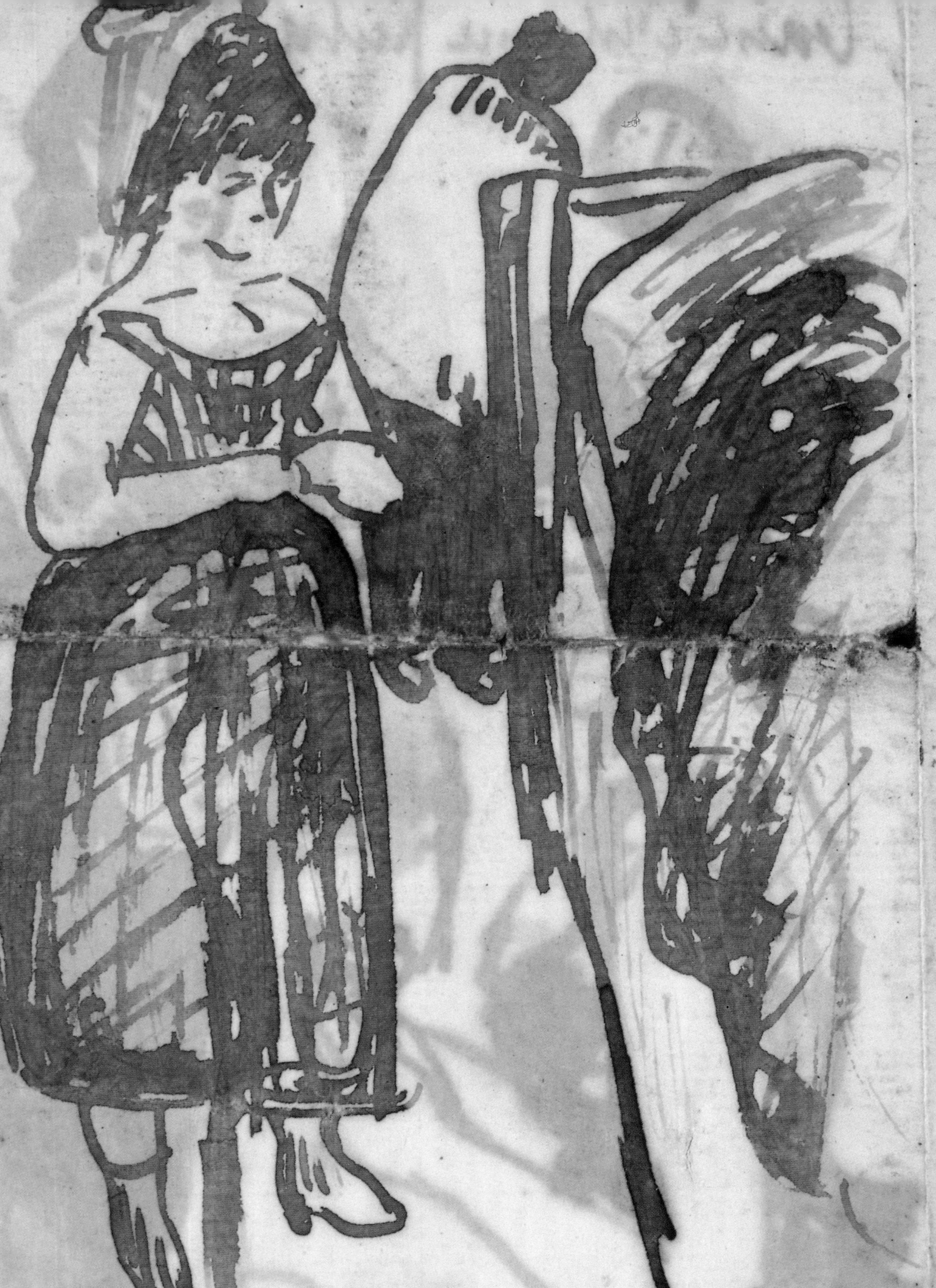

— J'ai jamais pu m'habituer

Letter 17

Arles, between Thursday, 27 September, and Monday, 1 October, 1888

Source
Original manuscript

Location
New York, Thaw Collection, The Morgan Library & Museum

Date
In letter *CL* 541 of Wednesday, 26 September, Vincent told Theo that he was expecting a letter from Bernard at any moment, following up on the sketches that the latter had sent, as reported in letter *CL* 541a of 25 September. Van Gogh had not yet received the letter that he was expecting when he wrote this one. One can assume that he would have reacted not long after receiving Bernard's sketches. Because, moreover, in the present letter he wrote: "the weather's really beautiful" (from Wednesday, 26 September, until 1 October it was dry, with scattered clouds and a temperature of 25ºC), and because on Wednesday, 3 October, he told Theo that he had received Bernard's letter, we have dated this one between Thursday, 27 September, and Monday, 1 October, 1888. Pickvance placed it between letters *CL* 542 and *CL* 541a, but in those van Gogh reported that the weather was autumnal. Compare New York 1984, p. 260.

Additional details
In the bottom margin of p. 1 there is the counterimpression of *t à v Vincent.* We have not been able to find any manuscript from which it could have come. It is possible that it was left by the draft of a letter to Gauguin, a crossed-out fragment of which has been preserved on the back of a sketch sent to Boch on 2 October 1888 (letter *CL* 553b) or by one to Gauguin in reply to letter GAC 32, which may have been enclosed with this one to Bernard. In any event, van Gogh usually signed his letters to Gauguin with *t. à v.*

Autumn had arrived. Van Gogh ordered large quantities of paint and canvas and worked from seven in the morning until six in the evening in the park across from his house. He followed Monticelli's example by using a thick impasto. "The present studies actually consist of a single *layer of impasto.* The brushstroke is not greatly divided, and the tones are often broken. And so, without intending to, I'm forced to lay it on thickly, in the style of Monticelli. Sometimes I really believe I'm following in that man's footsteps, only I haven't yet done people in love, like him."[1] He was certainly working in a very different manner from his friends in Brittany.

Bernard had sent six drawings, which Vincent sent on to Theo as usual, expressing the same negative comments as in this letter to Bernard.[2] Gauguin said that the idea of exchanging portraits appealed to him, but added: "I am not in a fit state to do it, seeing that it's not a copy of a face that you want, but a portrait as I understand the word. I am studying young Bernard, and I don't have him yet. I'll perhaps do it from memory, but in any case it will be an abstraction."

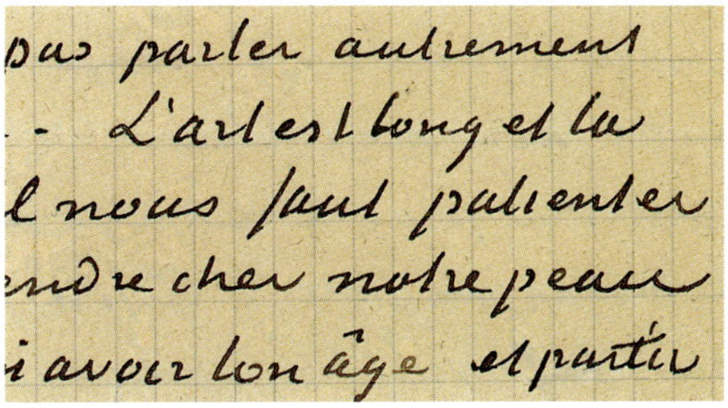
pas parler autrement
. - L'art est long et la
l nous faut patienter
ndre chez notre peau
i avoir bon âge et partir

He went on to say that it was not just Bernard who wanted to come to the south, but Laval as well. "As far as accommodation goes, apart from yours, Laval and Bernard could have a small furnished room nearby. I love the way you picture your house and its arrangement, and my mouth is watering to see it."[3] News of this kind stirred Vincent's imagination, as he wrote to Theo: "How I think of you and of Gauguin and of Bernard, everywhere and at all times. It's so beautiful, and I would so much like to see everyone over here."[4]

Detail of Fig. 77.

Translation of Letter 17 / Arles, between Thursday, 27 September, and Monday, 1 October, 1888

My dear old Bernard,
I'm writing a line to thank you kindly for your drawings; I find them done in a bit too much of a rush, and I like the two drawings of whores the most;[1] but there's an idea in all of them. I've been overloaded with work these past few days, because the weather's really beautiful and you have to make the most of the fine days, which are short.

I can't alter the price that I quoted to you, 3 francs for food alone, and in addition, well, whatever there would be on top of that.[2] But I have no doubt that everything Gauguin tells you about the prices down here is correct. But I see you near your departure to do your service, and would like to be able to persuade your father to supply you with enough to strengthen you thoroughly first, without your work suffering as a result.

Let him stump up at last, to the point of giving you whatever's fair during the interval between now and your service.

I have not ceased writing this same thing to you all the time, that if you go to Africa you'll work there and you'll see just the kind of nature you have to see in order to develop your talent as a painter and colorist to its full extent. But that can be done only to the detriment of your poor carcass, if your father does not make it possible for you to avoid becoming anemic or to catch debilitating dysentery through lack of strengthening food before this African ordeal.

It's scarcely possible to make yourself strong over there, and if you go to a hot climate, I'm far

---

Transcription of Letter 17 / Arles, between Thursday, 27 September, and Monday, 1 October, 1888

Mon cher copain Bernard,
j'écris un mot pour bien te remercier de tes dessins, je les trouve un peu trop faits à la hâte et j'aime le mieux les deux dessins des putains,[1] *d'ailleurs il y a une idee dans tous. Je suis surchargé de travail de ces jours ci car le temps est bien beau et il faut profiter des beaux jours qui sont courts.*

Je ne peux pas me dédire du prix que je t'ai nommé, 3 francs rien que pour la nourriture, en plus enfin ce qu'il y aurait en plus.[2] *Mais tout ce que te dit Gauguin sur les prix d'ici je ne doute pas que cela soit juste. Mais moi je te vois près de ton depart pour faire ton service et desirerais pouvoir decider ton père à te fournir de quoi bien te fortifier avant, sans que ton travail en souffre.*

Qu'il se fende enfin jusqu'à te donner pendant cet intervalle d'ici et ton service tout ce qui est juste.

Je n'ai cessé de t'ecrire toujours cette même chose que si tu vas en Afrique tu y travailleras et verras juste la nature qu'il faut voir pour developper dans toute son etendue ton talent de peintre et de coloriste. Mais cela ne peut[a] *se faire qu'au detriment de ta pauvre carcasse si ton père ne te met pas en mesure d'eviter de devenir anémique ou d'attrapper de la dyssenterie débilitante par manque d'une nourriture fortifiante avant cette epreuve Africaine.*

Se faire des forces là-bas c'est guère possible et si on va dans un climat chaud je suis loin de dire qu'il faille s'engraisser avant mais je dis qu'il faut soigner sa nourriture quelque temps d'avance. Et je

---

76. Émile Bernard, *Figures by the Riverside,* 1888. Amsterdam, Van Gogh Museum (Vincent van Gogh Foundation).

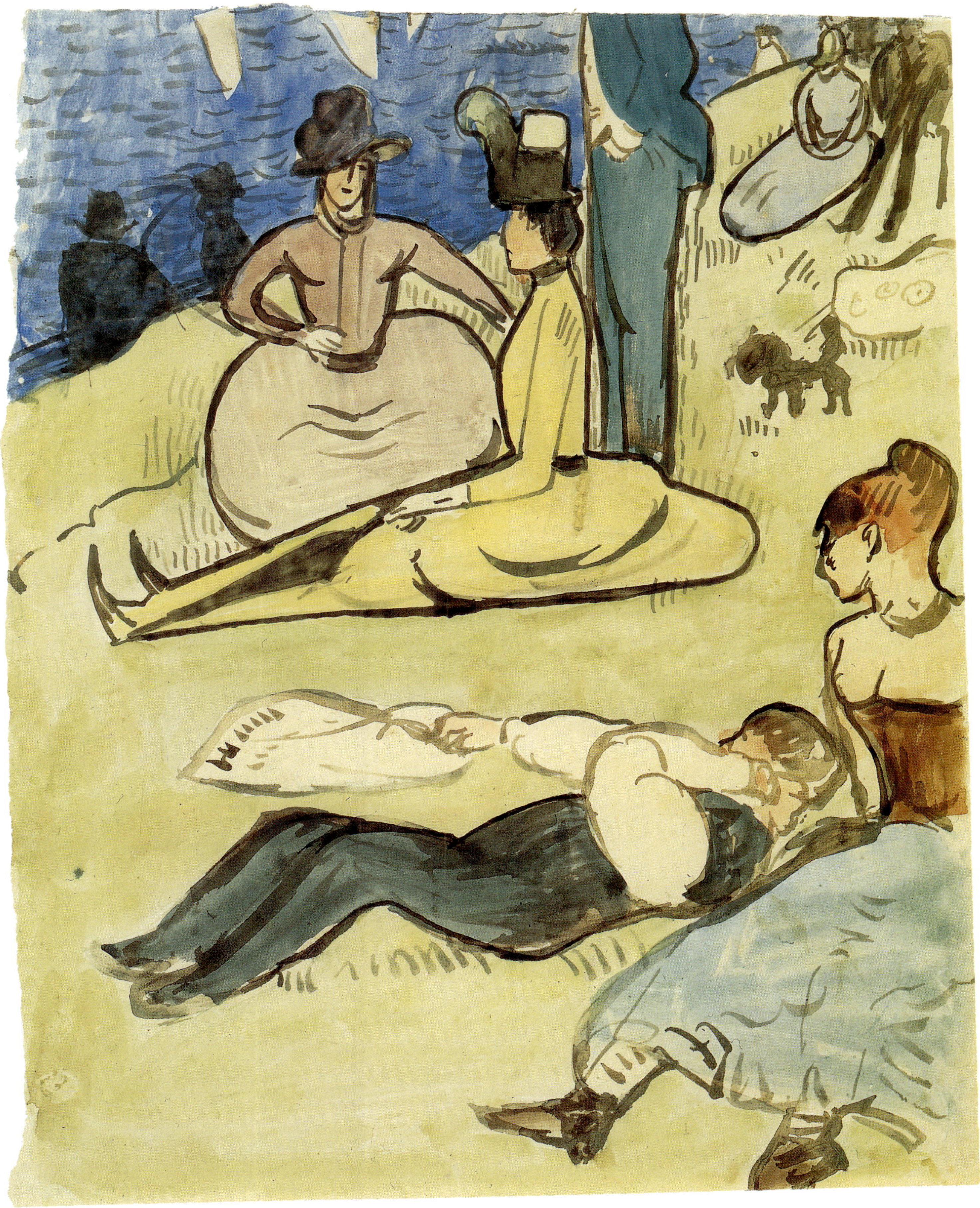

from saying you have to fatten yourself up beforehand, but I do say you have to pay attention to your food for some time in advance. And I'm sticking to that, having found myself doing well here on that regime, and the heat of Africa is something different again from that of Arles.

You'll emerge from this ordeal of your service much stronger, and strong enough for a whole career as an artist or—broken.

In any event, I would like you to come enormously, and if Gauguin comes too, all that will be left for us to regret will be that it's winter and not the warm season. I'm beginning to believe more and more that food has something to do with our power to think and to make paintings; as for me, it doesn't contribute to the success of my work if my stomach's bothering me. Anyway, I believe that if your father wanted quietly to keep your paintings and to fund you fairly generously, on balance he'll lose less than by doing otherwise. In the south, the senses are elated, the hand becomes nimbler, the eye livelier, the brain clearer, on one condition, though: that dysentery or something else does not spoil all that by debilitating you too much. On that point, I really dare to take my stand in believing that he who loves artistic work will see his productive capacities develop in the south, but watch your blood, and watch everything else.

And now you'll perhaps tell me that I'm bloody well getting on your nerves with all that.

That you want to go to the brothel, and that you don't give a damn about all the rest. My word, that depends, but I can't say other than that. Art is long and life is short,[3] and we must wait patiently while trying to sell our skin dearly. Me, I'd really like to be your age and go off with whatever knowledge I had to do my service in Africa. But, for example, I'd surely get myself a better body than the one I have. If Gauguin and I are here, as is probable, together—then here for certain we'll do our level best to spare you expenses. But on his side, your father should certainly do his best too, and have confidence in us that we're not trying to extract money from him pointlessly. But in order to do good work you have to eat well, be well housed, have a screw from time to time, smoke your pipe and drink your coffee in peace. I'm not saying that the rest counts for nothing, and leave everyone free to do as he sees fit, but I do say that this system seems preferable to many others to me. Good handshake.

Ever yours,
Vincent

ne sors pas de là, m'étant trouvé bien ici de ce régime, et la chaleur en Afrique est encore autre chose que celle d'Arles.

Tu sortiras de cette épreuve de ton service beaucoup plus fort et fort assez pour toute une carriere d'artiste ou—cassé.

Quoi qu'il en soit j'aimerais énormement que tu viennes et si Gauguin vient aussi il ne nous restera à regretter seulement que ce soit l'hiver et non la belle saison. De plus en plus je commence à croire que la cuisine a quelque chôse à faire avec notre faculté de penser et de faire des tableaux, moi pour un, cela ne contribue pas à la reussite de mon travail si mon estomac me gène. Enfin je crois que si ton père veut tranquillement garder tes tableaux et te faire un credit un peu genereux, au bout du compte il y perdra moins qu'en faisant autrement. Dans le midi les sens s'exaltent, la main devient plus agile, l'oeil plus vif, le cerveau plus clair, à une condition pourtant que la dyssenterie ou autre chôse ne vous gâte pas tout cela en vous debilitant trop. Là-dessus j'ose bien me fonder pour croire que celui qui aime le travail artistique verra dans le midi ses capacités productrices se developper mais gare au sang et gare à tout le reste.

Et maintenant tu vas peutêtre me dire que je t'emmerde bien avec tout cela.

Que tu veux aller au bordel et que tu te fous du reste.—Ma foi cela depend, mais je ne peux pas parler autrement que comme cela.—L'art est long et la vie est courte[3] *et il nous faut patienter en cherchant à vendre cher notre peau. Je voudrais bien moi avoir ton âge et partir avec ce que je saurais, faire mon service en Afrique. Mais par exemple je me ferais un meilleur corps que celui que j'ai. Si Gauguin et moi sommes ici, comme il est probable, ensemble—ici alors certes, nous ferons tout notre possible pour t'eviter des dépenses. Mais de son côté ton père devrait bien faire son possible aussi et avoir confiance en nous, que nous ne cherchons pas à lui tirer des carottes inutiles. Mais pour faire du bon travail il faut bien manger, etre bien logés, tirer son coup de temps en temps, fumer sa pipe et boire son café en paix. Je ne dis pas que le reste ne vaut rien & laisse à chacun sa liberté de faire comme il l'entend mais je dis que ce système me semble préferable à bien d'autres. bonne poignee de main.*

t. à t.
Vincent

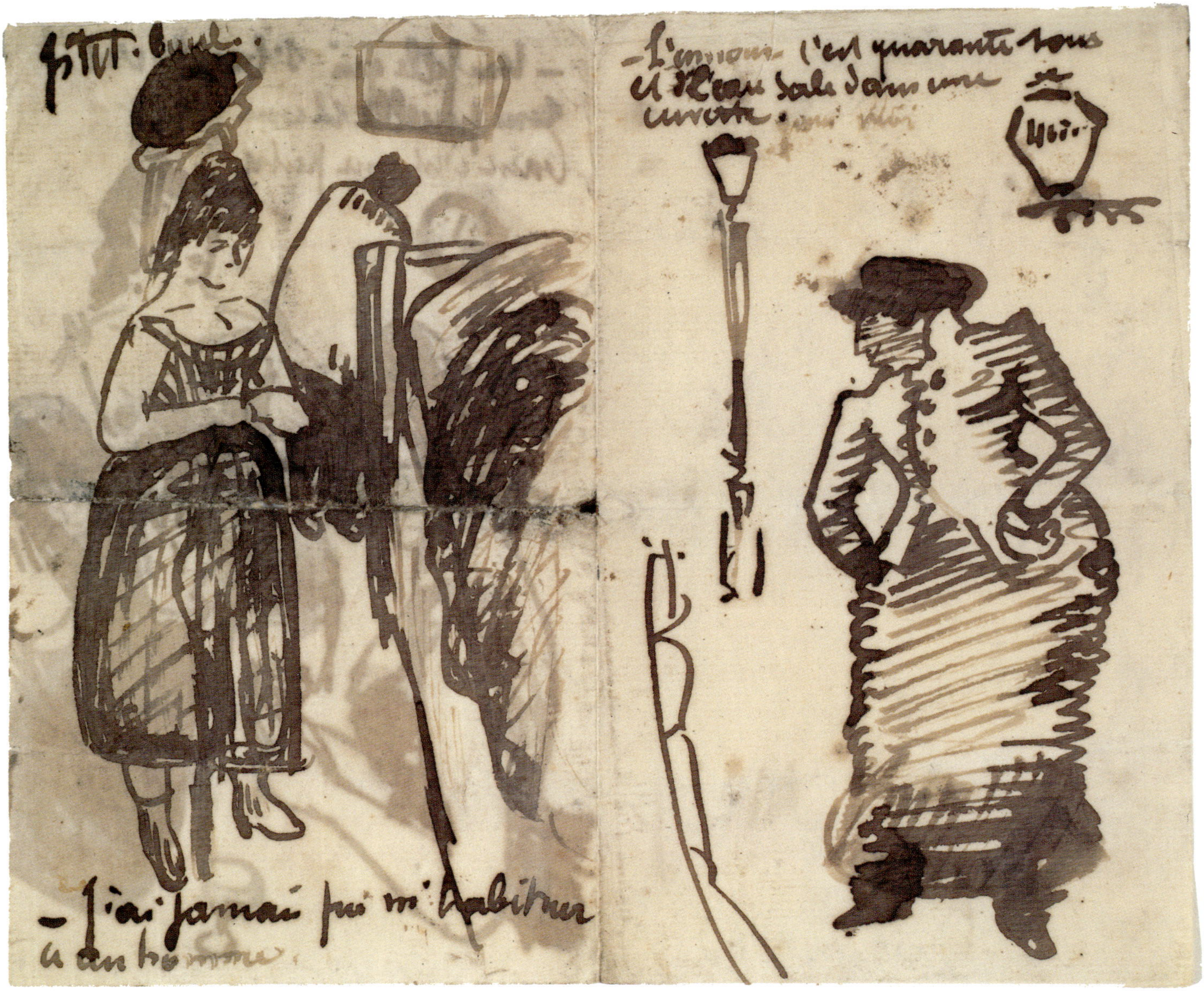
—L'amour c'est quarante sous
et de l'eau sale dans une
cuvette.
—J'ai jamai pu m'habituer
a un homme

Annotations to Letter 17

Arles, between Thursday, 27 September, and Monday, 1 October, 1888

TEXTUAL NOTE
a. peut < peut pas

1. It is known from Letter 18 that Bernard had sent six sketches. They were probably *Meadow with Figures and Animals*, *Idyll at Asnières*, *Figures by the Riverside* (Fig. 76), and a sheet with drawings on both sides, *Brothel Scene and Two Sketches of Prostitutes* (all Amsterdam, Van Gogh Museum). See Roskill 1970, pp. 223–24.

   Van Gogh was discussing the *Two Sketches of Prostitutes* (Fig. 77), which are both on the same side of the sheet. *Brothel Scene* was on the back.

2. Van Gogh had written about the cost of living in Arles in Letter 16.

3. A well-known saying that derives from the first aphorism of Hippocrates. It is known chiefly through Seneca, in the Latin translation *Ars longa, vita brevis* (*De brevitate vitae* 1,1).

77. ÉMILE BERNARD, *Two Sketches of Prostitutes,* 1888. Amsterdam, Van Gogh Museum (Vincent van Gogh Foundation).

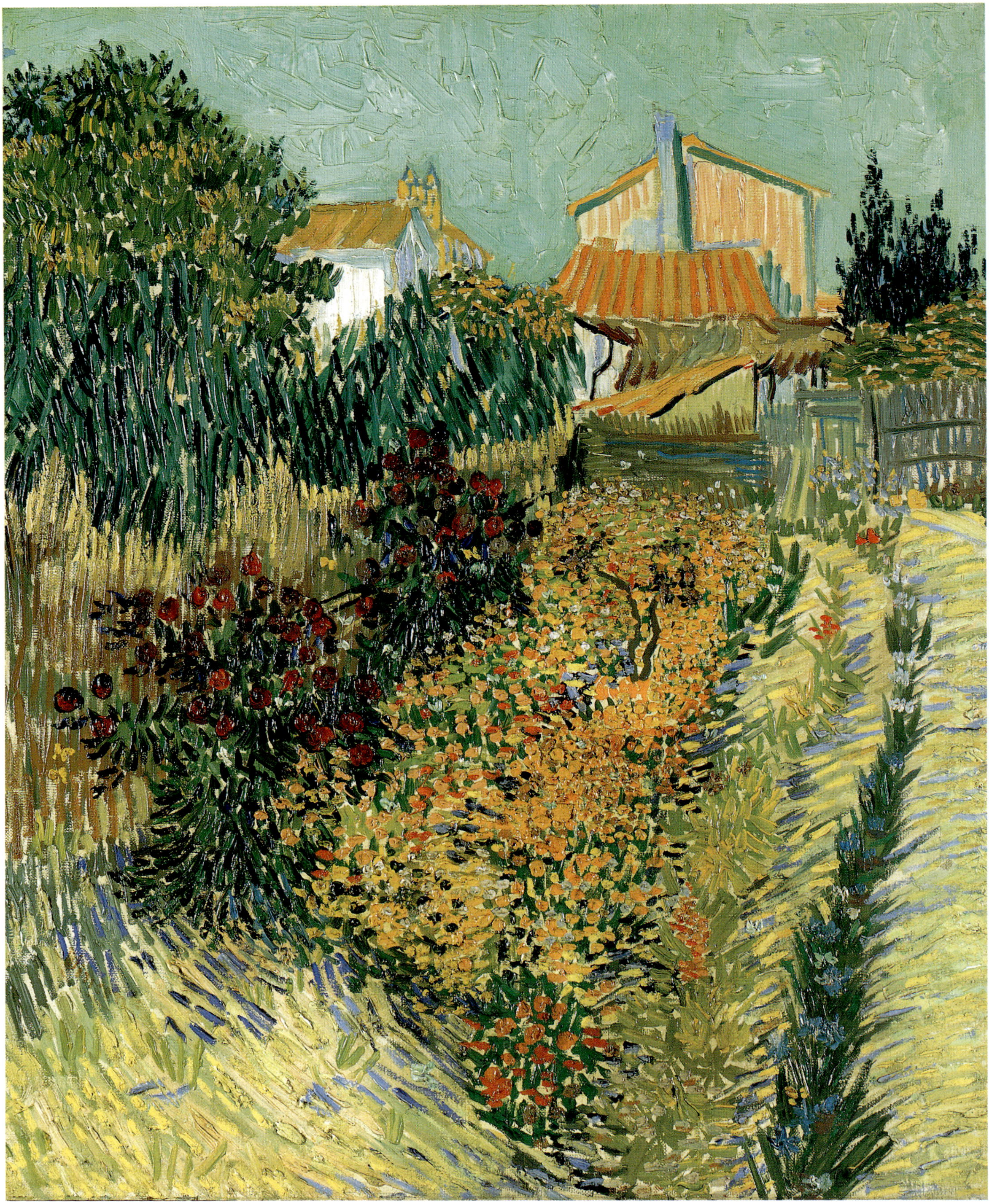

Letter 18

Arles, Wednesday, 3 October, 1888

Source
Original manuscript

Location
New York, Thaw Collection, The Morgan Library & Museum

Date
Van Gogh had planned to write to Gauguin and to Bernard on the same day (see letter *CL* 544). Assuming that he did, so that the letters could be sent off together, this letter is of the same date as that to Gauguin (*CL* 553a): Wednesday, 3 October, 1888.

Because van Gogh sent Bernard several letters in quick succession during this period, some subjects naturally recur. One is Bernard's lack of money and more specifically his father's refusal to increase his allowance. Van Gogh, who once had an argument with Bernard's father (see Introduction p. 10) and was thus not very acceptable as an adviser, had already made up his mind. If Bernard's father would be a little more generous in return for paintings from his son, he might profit in the long run. Theo and Vincent had exactly the same arrangement, on the same uncertain basis. As far as is known, Bernard's father was never tempted to enter into such an agreement.

The friends in Brittany had at last made not each other's portraits but self-portraits painted expressly for the exchange. Gauguin described his *Self-Portrait with Portrait of Bernard, "Les misérables"* (W309/W239; Fig. 72), as "The mask of a thief, badly dressed and powerful like Jean Valjean, who has his nobility and inner gentleness."[1]

That letter from Gauguin arrived on the same day as one from Bernard. As is often the case, a letter to Theo reveals a little more about what Bernard wrote. He repeated that he would love to come to Arles and proposed an exchange with Vincent on behalf of himself, Laval, Henri Moret, and Ernest Ponthier de Chamaillard. "He also says that Laval will come, too, and that those two

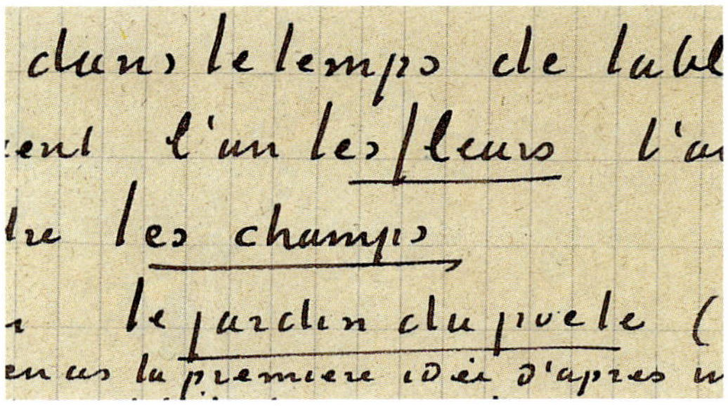
dans le temps de
l'un les fleurs
les champs
le jardin du poete
la premiere idée d'après

others have a wish to come. I couldn't ask for more, but when it's a matter of several painters living communally, I stipulate first and foremost that there would have to be a father superior to impose order, and that naturally that would be Gauguin. One reason why I should wish Gauguin to be here some time before them [. . .]. Bernard's letter is once again full of the conviction that Gauguin is a truly great master, and an absolutely superior man in terms of character and intelligence."[2]

78. Vincent van Gogh, *Garden with Flowers,* 1888 (F 578 / JH 1538). Private collection.

Translation of Letter 18 / Arles, Wednesday, 3 October, 1888

My dear old Bernard,

This time you deserve bigger compliments for the little sketch of the two Breton women in your letter than for the other six, since the little sketch has a great style.[1] I'm behind myself as far as sketches go, being so totally absorbed these recent superb days with square no. 30 canvases, which wear me out considerably and I intend to use to decorate the house.[2]

You will have received my letter explaining the serious reasons for advising you to try to persuade your father to give you a little more freedom as far as your purse is concerned, should he pay your fare to Arles.[3] I believe that you would repay him through your work. And that way you would stay longer with Gauguin, and leaving to do your service, you would leave for a good artistic campaign. If your father had a son who was a prospector and discoverer of raw gold among the pebbles and on the pavement, your father would certainly not look down on that talent. Now in my opinion, you have absolutely the equivalent of that.

Your father, while he might regret that it wasn't shiny new gold, minted in louis,[4] would set out to make a collection of your finds, and to sell them only for a reasonable price. Let him do the same thing for your paintings and drawings, which are as rare and as valuable on the market as rare stones or rare metal. That's absolutely true—a painting is as difficult to make as a large or small diamond is to find.[5]

Now while everyone acknowledges the value of a gold louis or a real pearl, unfortunately those who set store by paintings and believe in them are few and far between. But they do exist. And in

---

Transcription of Letter 18 / Arles, Wednesday, 3 October, 1888

Mon cher copain Bernard,

Cette fois ci tu mérites de plus grands compliments pour le petit croquis des deux bretonnes dans ta lettre que pour les 6 autres puisque le petit croquis a un grand style.[1] *Je suis moi en retard pour les croquis étant de ces jours superbes ci absolument absorbé par des toiles de 30 carrées qui m'éreintent considérablement et qui doivent me servir à décorer la maison.*[2]

Tu auras reçu ma lettre expliquant les raisons graves pour te recommander de chercher à persuader ton père de te donner, en cas qu'il te paye ton voyage à Arles, un peu plus de liberté en tant que quant à la bourse.[3] *je crois que tu le rembourserais par ton travail. Et ainsi tu resterais plus longtemps avec Gauguin, et partant pour faire ton service tu partirais pour une bonne campagne artistique. Si ton pere avait un fils chercheur et trouveur d'or brut dans les cailloux et sur le trottoir, certainement ton père ne dedaignerait pas ce talent. Or tu possèdes selon moi absolument l'equivalent de cela.*

Ton père, tout en pouvant regretter que ce ne fut pas de l'or tout neuf et brillant, monnayé en louis,[4] *se proposerait de faire collection de tes trouvailles et de ne les céder que pour un prix raisonnable. Qu'il fasse la même chôse pour tes tableaux et dessins, qui sont dans le commerce aussi rares et aussi valable que des pierres ou du metal rares. Cela c'est absolument vrai—un tableau est aussi difficile à faire qu'un diamant gros ou petit à trouver.*[5]

Maintenant si tout le monde reconnaît la valeur d'un louis d'or ou d'une perle fine, malheureuse-

---

79. Vincent van Gogh, *Thistles,* 1888 (F 447 / JH 1550). Private collection.

80. Vincent van Gogh, *A Pair of Old Shoes,* 1888 (F 461 / JH 1569). New York, The Metropolitan Museum of Art.

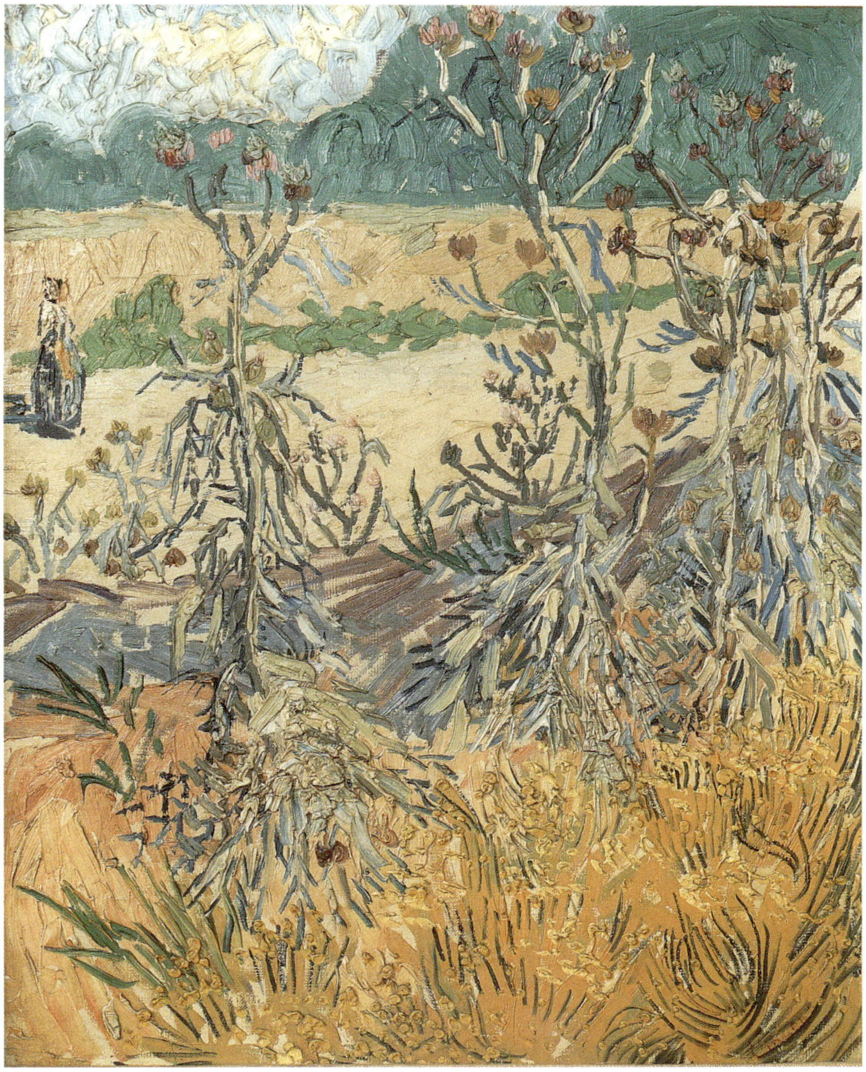

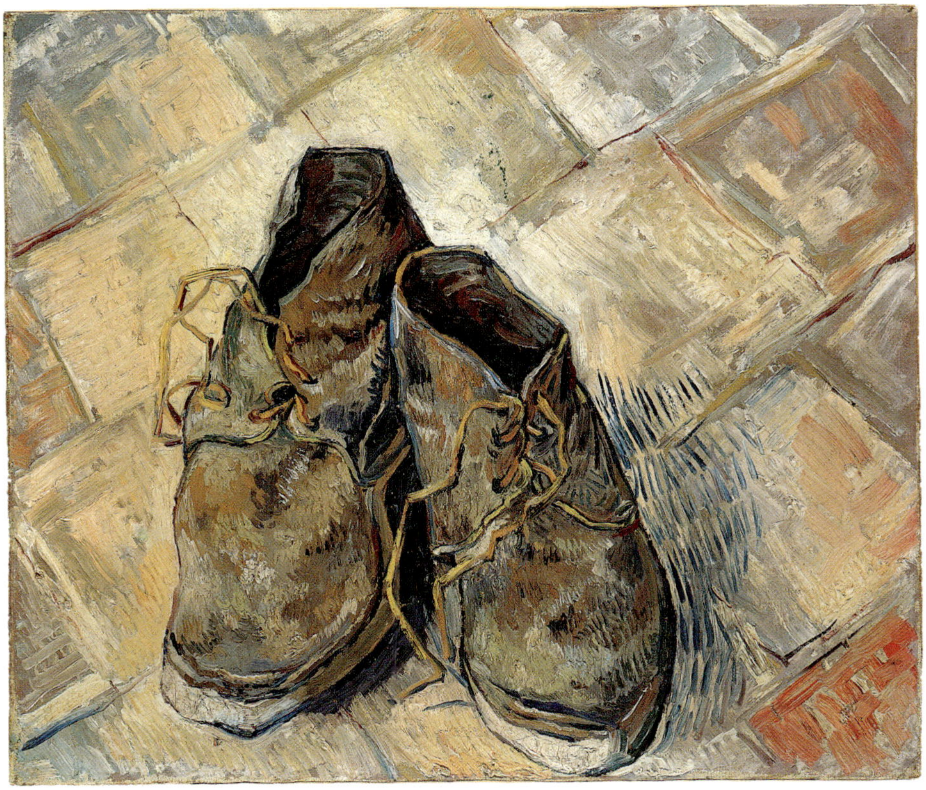

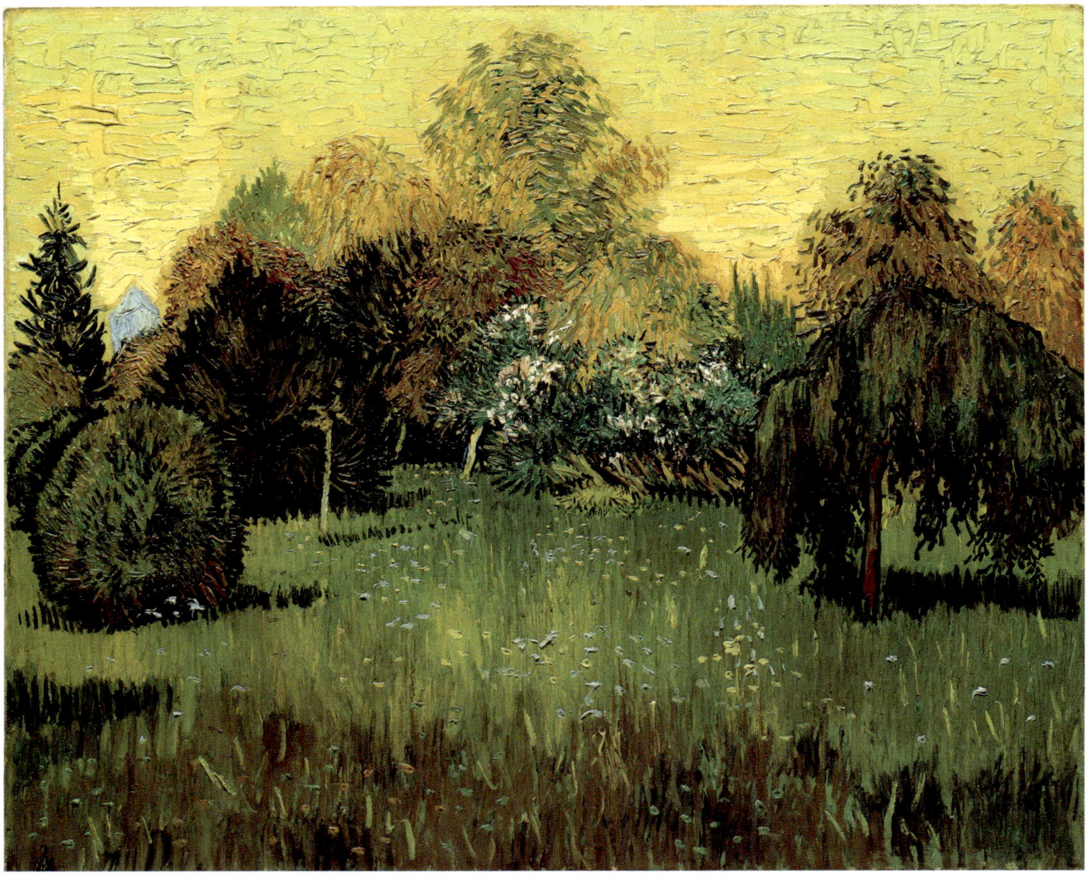

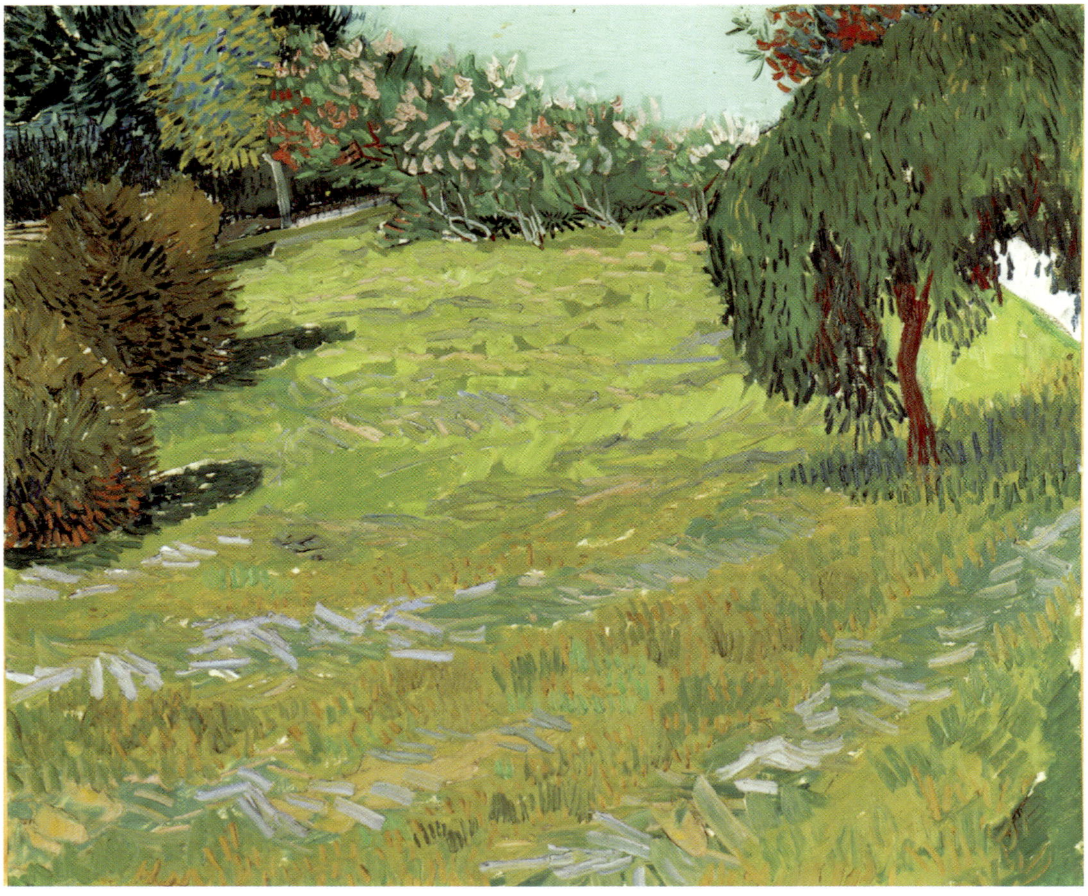

any case, there's nothing better to do than to wait without getting impatient, even if one has to wait for a long time. On your side, think a little about what I'm telling you about the cost of living here,[6] and should you have a strong wish to come to Arles with Gauguin and me, be sure to tell your father that with a little more money you would make much better paintings.

The idea of making a kind of freemasonry of painters does not please me hugely;[7] I deeply despise rules, institutions, etc. In short, I'm looking for something other than dogmas, which, very far from settling things, only cause endless disputes.

It's a sign of decadence. Now, as a union of painters exists so far only in the form of a vague but very broad sketch, then let's calmly allow what must happen to happen.

It will be better if it crystallizes naturally; the more one talks about it, the less it comes about. If you wish to support it, you have only to continue with Gauguin and me. It's in progress, let's not talk any more; if it must come it will come about without big negotiations but through calm and well-thought-out actions.

As regards the exchanges, it's precisely because I have often had occasion to hear mention in your letters of Laval, Moret and the other young man,[8] that I have a great desire to get to know them.[9] But—I don't have five dry studies—will have to add at least two slightly more serious attempts at paintings, a portrait of myself and a landscape angry with a nasty mistral.[10]

Then I would have a study of a little garden of multicolored flowers.[11]

A study of gray and dusty thistles,[12] and lastly a still life of old peasants' shoes.[13] And a small landscape of nothing at all, in which there's nothing but a bit of an expanse.[14] Now, if these studies aren't found pleasing, and if one or other preferred not to take part, all you have to do is keep those

---

ment ceux qui font cas des tableaux et y croyent sont rares. Mais ils existent cependant. Et il n'y a dans tous les cas rien de mieux à faire que d'attendre sans s'impatienter, dut on attendre fort longtemps. De ton côté refléchis un peu à ce que je te dis sur le prix de la vie d'ici,[6] et si tu aurais une forte envie de venir ici à Arles avec Gauguin et moi, dis bien à ton père qu'avec un peu plus d'argent tu ferais de bien meilleurs tableaux.

L'idee de faire une sorte de franc-maçonnerie de peintres ne me plaît pas enormement,[7] je méprise profondement les règlements, les institutions &c. enfin je cherche autrechose que les dogmes qui bien loin de regler les choses ne font que causer les disputes sans fin.

C'est signe de decadence. Or une union des peintres n'existant encore[a] qu'à l'état d'esquisse vague mais fort large, laissons donc tranquillement arriver ce qui doit arriver.

Ce sera plus beau si cela se cristalise naturellement, plus on en cause moins cela se fait. Si tu veux aider à cela tu n'as qu'à continuer avec Gauguin et moi. Cela est en train, ne parlons plus, si cela doit venir cela se fera sans grands pourparlers mais par des actions tranquilles et réflechies.

Pour les échanges c'est bien justement parceque j'ai souvent dans tes lettres eu occasion d'entendre parler de Laval, Moret et l'autre jeune,[8] j'ai grand désir de les connaitre.[9] Mais—je n'ai pas 5 etudes de sèches—faudra que j'ajoute au moins deux essais de tableaux un peu plus graves, un portrait de moi et un paysage en colère de mistral méchant.[10]

---

81. VINCENT VAN GOGH, *Public Garden with Round Clipped Shrub and Weeping Tree,* 1888 (F 468 / JH 1578). The Art Institute of Chicago.

82. VINCENT VAN GOGH, *Newly Mown Lawn with Weeping Tree,* 1888 (F 428 / JH 1499). Private collection.

that are wanted and return with the exchanges those that aren't wanted. We're in no hurry, and in exchanges it's better on both sides to try to give something good.

If it's dry enough to be rolled up after being exposed to the sun tomorrow, I'll add a landscape of men unloading sand,[15] another project and attempt at a painting, in which there is a more fully developed sense of purpose.

I cannot send a repetition of the night café yet because it hasn't even been started, but I'm very willing to do it for you,[16] but once again, it's better on both sides to try to exchange good things than to do them too hastily.

The artistic gentleman who was in your letter, who resembles me—is that me or somebody else?[17]

He certainly looks like me as far as the face is concerned, but in the first place I'm always smoking a pipe, and then, having vertigo, I have an unspeakable horror of sitting like that on sheer crags beside the sea. So if that's meant to be my portrait, I protest against the above-mentioned improbabilities. The decoration of the house absorbs me terribly. I dare to believe that it would be quite to your liking, although it's very different from what you do, of course. But just as you spoke to me in the past about paintings that would depict, one *flowers*, the other *trees*, the other *fields*.[18]

Well, I have the *Poet's Garden* (2 canvases); (among the sketches you have the first idea for it, after a smaller painted study that's already at my brother's).[19]

Then *The Starry Night*,[20] then *The Vineyard*,[21] then *The Furrows*,[22] then the view of the house could be called *The Street*,[23] so unintentionally there's a certain sequence.

Well, I'll be very very curious to see studies of Pont-Aven. But for yourself, give me something fairly worked up. It will work out, anyway, because I like your talent so much that I'd be very pleased to make a small collection of your works, bit by bit.

For a long time I have been touched by the fact that Japanese artists very often made exchanges among themselves.[24] It clearly proves that they liked one another and stuck together, and that there was a certain harmony among them and that they did indeed live in a kind of brotherly life, in a natural way and not in the midst of intrigues. The more we resemble them in that respect, the better it will be for us. It seems also that those Japanese earned very little money and lived like simple laborers.[25] I have the *reproduction* (Bing publication) of a Japanese drawing: a single blade of grass.[26] What an example of *awareness*—you'll see it one day. I shake your hand firmly.

Ever yours,
Vincent

Puis j'aurais une étude de petit jardin de fleurs multicolores.[11]

Une etude de chardons gris et poussiereux[12] *et finalement une nature morte de vieux souliers de paysan.*[13] *Et un petit paysage de rien du tout où il n'y a qu'un peu d'étendue.*[14] *Si maintenant ces études ne plairaient pas et que l'un ou l'autre préférerait s'abstenir, il n'y a qu'à garder celles dont on voudra et à retourner avec les échanges celles dont on ne voudra pas. Rien ne nous presse et dans des échanges il vaut mieux de part et d'autre chercher à donner du bon.*

J'ajouterai, en cas qu'exposé demain au soleil il devienne sec assez pour le rouler, un paysage de déchargeurs de sable,[15] *également un projet et essai de tableau où il y a une plus mûre volonté.*

Je ne peux pas envoyer encore une répétition du café de nuit puisqu'elle n'est même pas commencée mais je veux tres volontiers te la faire pour toi,[16] *mais encore une fois il vaut mieux de part et d'autre chercher à echanger de bonnes chôses que de les faire trop à la hâte.*

Le monsieur artistique qui était dans ta lettre, qui me ressemble, cela est-il moi ou un autre?[17]

Cela a bien l'air d'être moi en tant que quant au visage mais d'abord moi je fume toujours des pipes et ensuite moi j'ai toujours en horreur innommable de m'assoir comme cela sur des rochers à pic au bord de la mer, ayant le vertige. Je proteste donc, si cela doit être mon portrait, contre les invraisemblabilités ci dessus mentionnées.—

La décoration de la maison m'absorbe terriblement. J'ose croire que ce serait assez de ton gout quoique ce soit certes très different de ce que tu fais. Mais ainsi que[b] *tu m'as parlé dans le temps de tableaux qui representeraient l'un* les fleurs, *l'autre* les arbres, *l'autre* les champs.[18]

Eh bien j'ai moi le jardin du poete *(2 toiles) (dans les croquis tu en as la premiere idée d'après une etude peinte plus petite qui est déjà chez mon frère).*[19]

puis la nuit étoilée,[20] *puis* la vigne,[21] *puis* les sillons,[22] *puis la vue de la maison pourrait s'appeler* la rue,[23] *ainsi involontairement il y a une certaine suite.*

Eh bien je serai fort fort curieux de voir des etudes de Pont Aven. Mais pour toi donnes moi une chose un peu travaillée. Enfin cela s'arrangera toujours car j'aime tant ton talent que je voudrais bien peu à peu faire une petite collection de tes oeuvres.

J'ai depuis longtemps été touché de ce que les artistes Japonais ont pratiqué tres souvent l'échange entre eux.[24] *Cela prouve bien qu'ils s'aimaient et se tenaient et qu'il y regnait une certaine harmonie entre eux et qu'ils vivaient justement dans une sorte de vie fraternelle naturellement et non pas dans les intrigues. Plus nous leur ressemblerons sous ce respect-là, mieux l'on s'en trouvera. Il paraît aussi que ces japonais gagnaient tres peu d'argent et vivaient comme de simples ouvriers.*[25] *J'ai la* reproduction *(publication Bing) d'un dessin Japonais: Un seul brin d'herbe.*[26] *Quel exemple de* conscience, *tu le verras un jour. Je te serre bien la main.*

t. à t.
Vincent

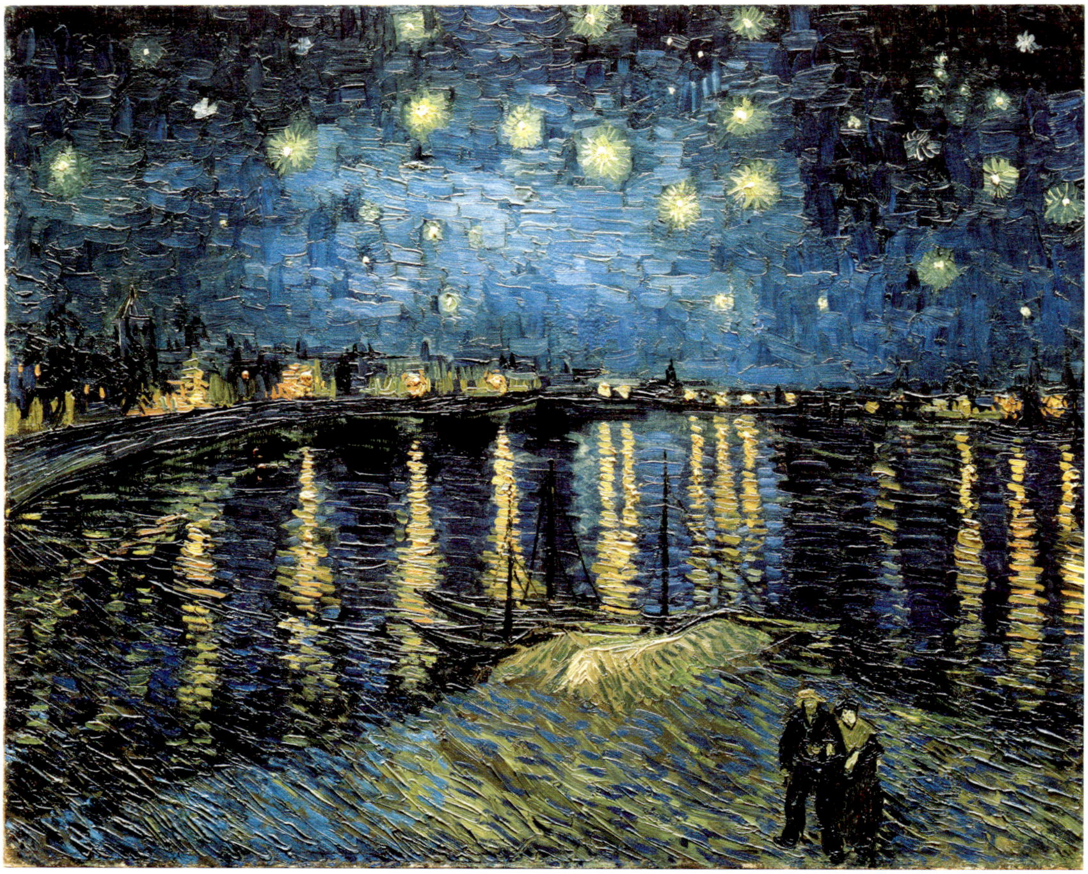

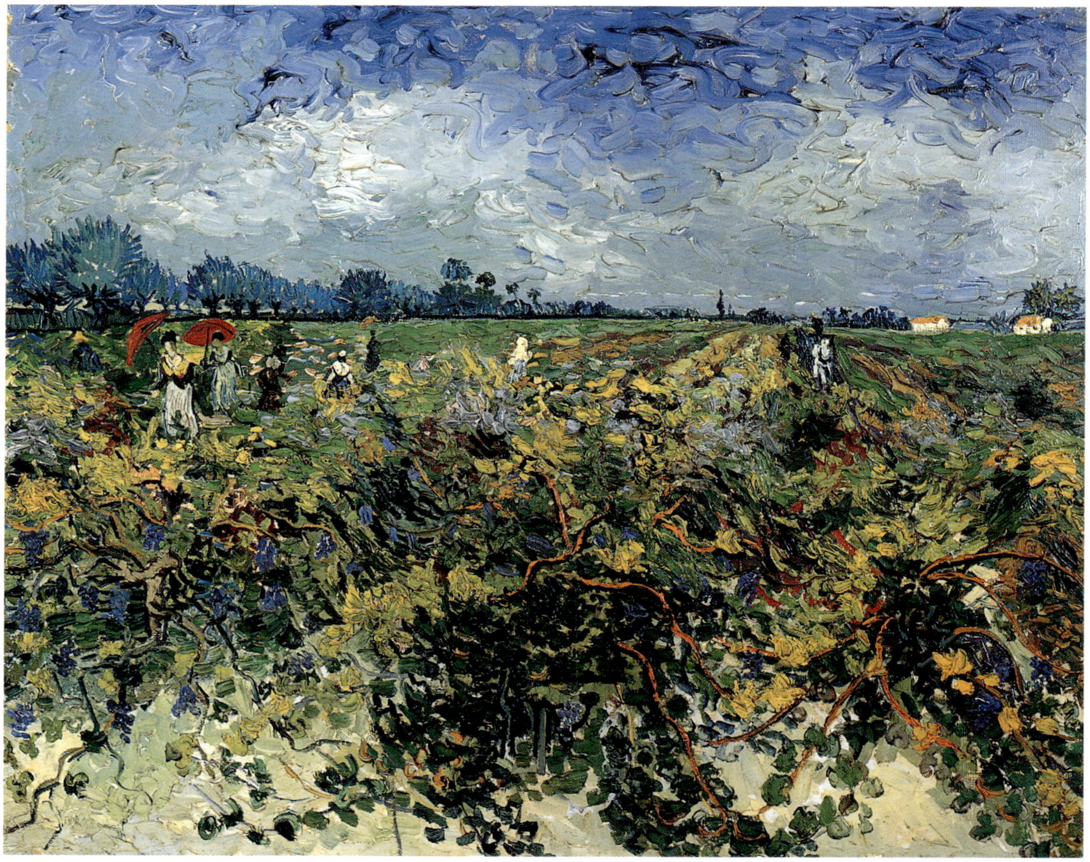

Annotations to Letter 18

Arles, Wednesday, 3 October, 1888

Textual Notes
a. encore < pas encore
b. ainsi que < ainsi

1. Bernard's last letter had evidently contained a small sketch of two Breton women. It is not known today and was probably not on a separate sheet but was an integral part of the letter, which has not survived. By "the other six" van Gogh meant the previous batch of drawings from Bernard discussed in Letter 17.

2. Vincent spoke of ten no. 30 canvases in letter *CL* 544 to Theo. They would have been the following works (some of which are mentioned later in the present letter): *The Night Café* (F 463 / JH 1575), an unknown painting of the park (see n. 19), *Public Garden with Round Clipped Shrub and Weeping Tree* (F 468 / JH 1578), *A Lane in the Public Garden* (F 470 / JH 1582, Otterlo, Kröller-Müller Museum), *Plowed Field* (F 574 / JH 1586), *The Yellow House* (F 464 / JH 1589), *The Starry Night* (F 474 / JH 1592), *The Green Vineyard* (F 475 / JH 1595), *Café Terrace at Night* (F 467 / JH 1580, Otterlo, Kröller-Müller Museum) and possibly *A Lane in the Public Garden* (F 471 / JH 1613; now lost).

3. Van Gogh is referring to Letter 17.

4. A louis was a coin worth 20 francs.

5. This simile had a particular appeal for van Gogh. He had already used it in Letter 13, and he told Theo: "There are no more good paintings than there are diamonds" (*Il n'y a pas plus de bons tableaux que des diamants; CL* 543).

6. Van Gogh had written about the cost of living in Arles in Letters 16 and 17.

7. This idea of a freemasonry of painters must have been suggested by Bernard in his latest letter.

8. The young man in question was Ernest Ponthier de Chamaillard, an amateur painter who joined the group around Gauguin in Pont-Aven. Van Gogh never met him and did not even know his name. See *Lettres à Bernard* 1911, p. 132 and *Correspondance Gauguin* 1984, pp. 502–3.

9. Bernard had proposed an exchange with the group in Pont-Aven. Van Gogh sent seven studies; see Letter 19.

83. Vincent van Gogh, *The Starry Night*, 1888 (F 474 / JH 1592). Paris, Musée d'Orsay.
84. Vincent van Gogh, *The Green Vineyard*, 1888 (F 475 / JH 1595). Otterlo, Kröller-Müller Museum.

10. These were *Self-Portrait* (F 476 / JH 1581, Fig. 74) and an unknown landscape, probably the work that van Gogh had described in letter *CL* 535 to Theo as "a landscape with factory, and an enormous sun in a red sky, above red roofs, in which nature seems to be in a rage, on a day of nasty mistral" *(un paysage avec usine et un soleil enorme dans un ciel rouge au-dessus des toits rouges où la nature semble être en colère un jour de mistral méchant).*

11. *Garden with Flowers* (F 578 / JH 1538; Fig. 78).

12. *Thistles* (F 447 / JH 1550; Fig. 79). This work once belonged to Henri Moret, so it must have been in the batch. See Bernard 1994, vol. 1, p. 307.

13. *A Pair of Old Shoes* (F 461 / JH 1569; Fig. 80).

14. The cursory description makes it impossible to identify this work. According to Roskill it could have been either *Meadow with Poppies* (F 576 / JH 1423, Amsterdam, Van Gogh Museum) or *Landscape with the Edge of a Road* (F 567 / JH 1419; Fig. 24), but their provenance (Jo van Gogh-Bonger) rules out their having been sent to Bernard. See Roskill 1971, p. 161 (n. 105), and *Account Book* 2002, pp. 178–79.

15. *Quay with Men Unloading Sand Barges* (F 449 / JH 1558; Fig. 71). Van Gogh dedicated this painting to Bernard (see Letter 19, n. 11).

16. *The Night Café* (F 463 / JH 1575; Fig. 75). This paragraph seems to imply that Bernard had asked for a repetition of this work, which van Gogh had written about in Letter 16. No repetition was ever made.

17. Bernard added the following note at this point in the Vollard edition: "Allusion to a caricature by Gauguin that showed Vincent sitting on the tip of a rock, drawing the sun." *(Allusion à une caricature de Gauguin qui représentait Vincent assis sur la pointe d'un rocher, en train de dessiner le soleil.)* See *Lettres à Bernard* 1911, p. 126.

18. It is not clear which three paintings by Bernard he meant. There may be a connection with the sketches for the decoration that Bernard had sent van Gogh (see Letter 3, n. 1), or with the landscape studies he had worked on in the spring of 1888. On 16 May he wrote telling his mother about a "very big" study "showing Saint-Briac in bloom" *(très grande [étude] qui représente Saint-Briac en fleurs).* See Harscoët-Maire 1997, p. 168.

Bernard later said that he had given van Gogh the idea of making decorative ensembles: "I explained to him my idea for executing studies in series: the sea, the flowers, the trees, the fields. He agreed with me, and got down to doing just that" *(Je lui exposai mon idée d'exécuter des études par séries: la mer, les fleurs, les arbres, les champs. Il m'approuva et se mit à en faire autant).* See *Gauguin lettres* 1954, pp. 16–17.

---

85. VINCENT VAN GOGH, *Plowed Field,* 1888 (F 574 / JH 1586). Amsterdam, Van Gogh Museum (Vincent van Gogh Foundation).
86. VINCENT VAN GOGH, *The Yellow House,* 1888 (F 464 / JH 1589). Amsterdam, Van Gogh Museum (Vincent van Gogh Foundation).

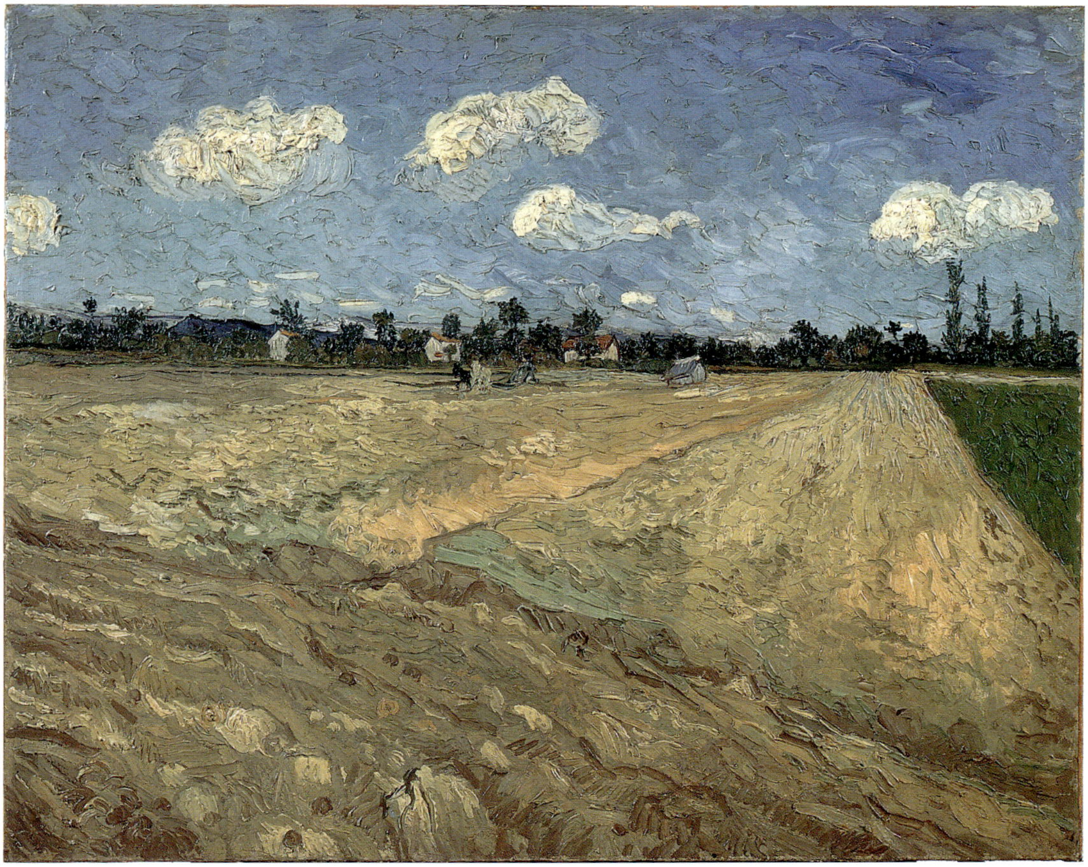

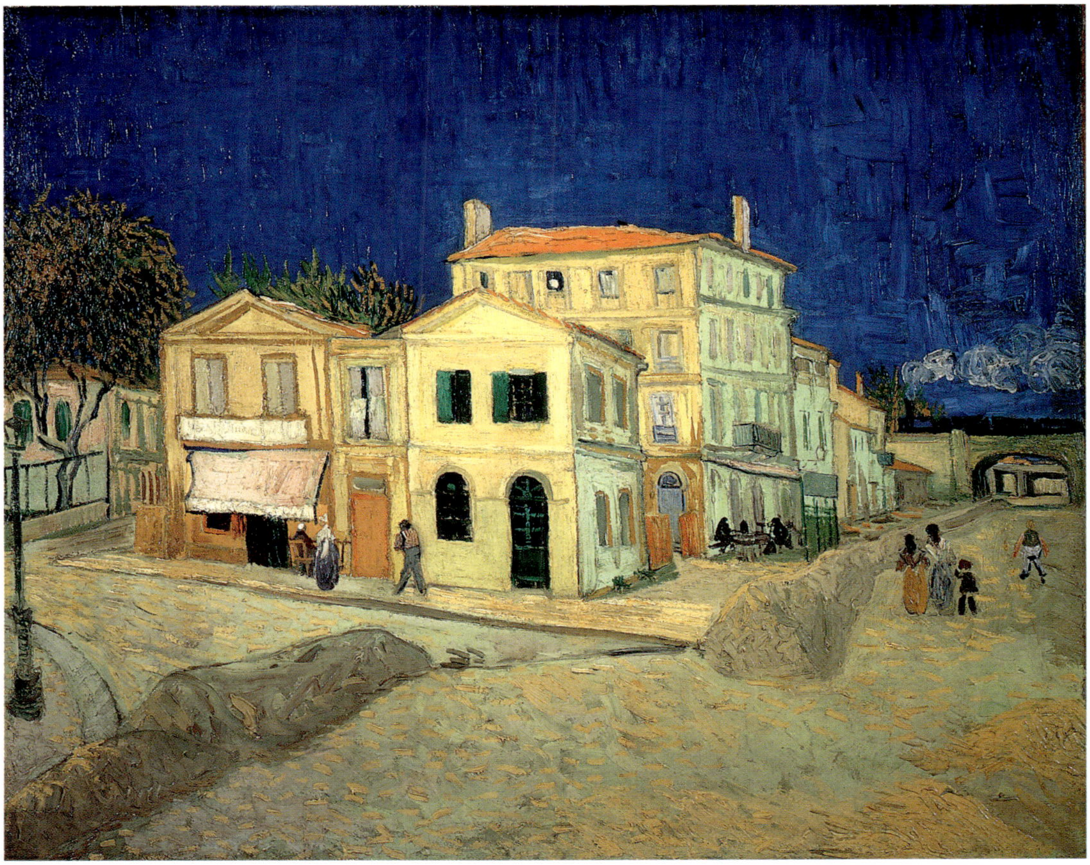

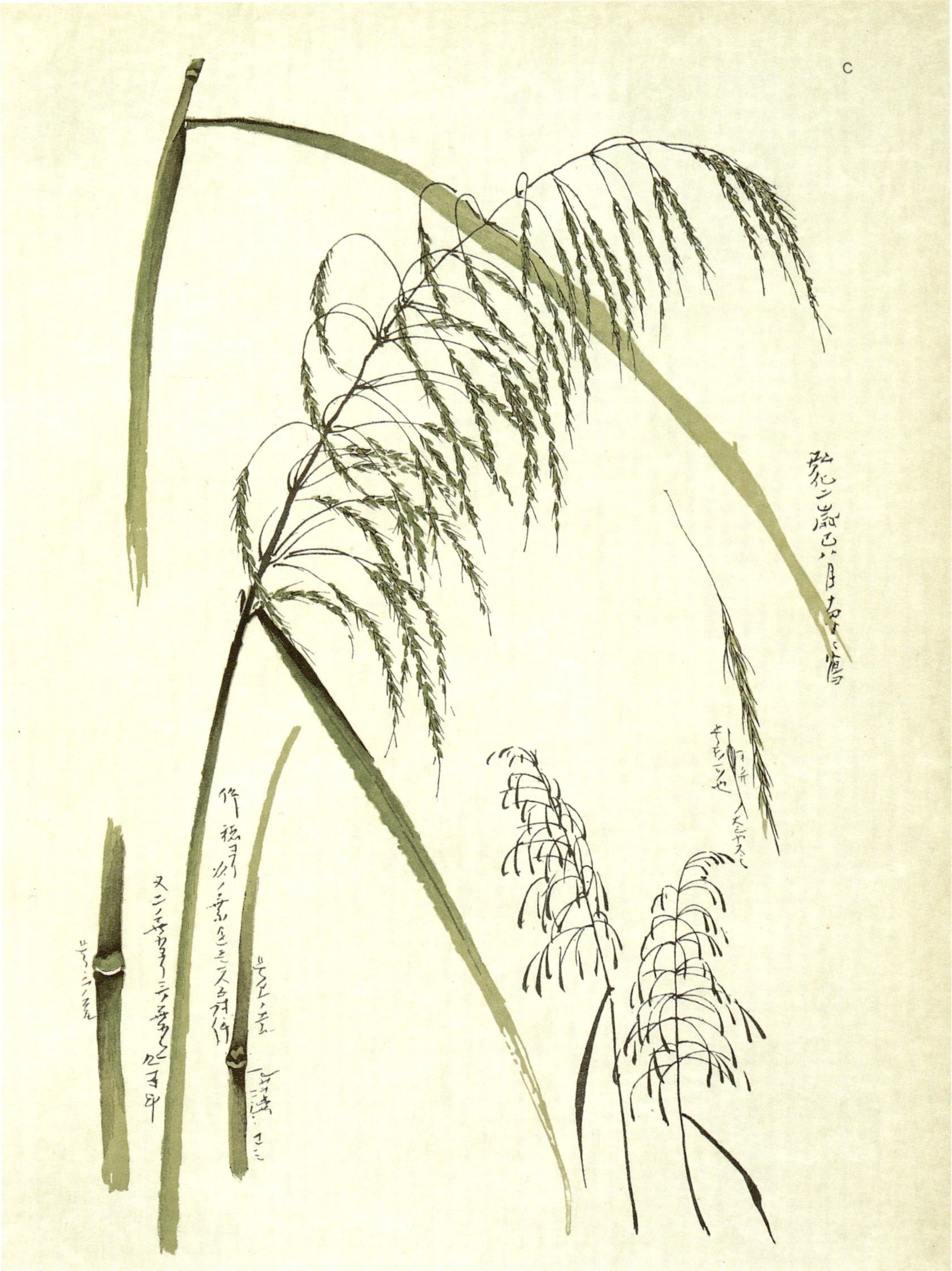

87. *Étude d'herbe*. In: *Le Japon Artistique* 1 (May 1888), no. C. Amsterdam, Van Gogh Museum Library.

19. The two canvases of "the poet's garden" are *Public Garden with Round Clipped Shrub and Weeping Tree* (F 468 / JH 1578; Fig. 81) and the unknown painting of the park, which van Gogh had previously described as "a round cedar or cypress bush" (*un buisson de cèdre ou de cyprès en boule; CL* 541) and as a "garden with the round bush and the oleanders" (*jardin avec le buisson en boule et les lauriers roses; CL* 544). He regarded these two paintings as companion pieces. Compare the letter sketch after this work in letter *CL* 553b and the drawing *Round Clipped Shrub in the Public Garden* (F 1465 / JH 1583, private collection). See also Dorn 1990, pp. 378–82.

Bernard owned the drawing *Newly Mown Lawn with Weeping Tree* (F 1450 / JH 1509; private collection), which shows the same corner of the park; see Letter 10. The painting on which the drawing is based, *Newly Mown Lawn with Weeping Tree* (F 428 / JH 1499; Fig. 82), had been with Theo since mid-August (see letter *CL* 531); it measures 23⅝ x 28⅞ in. (60 x 73.5 cm).

20. *The Starry Night* (F 474 / JH 1592; Fig. 83).

21. *The Green Vineyard* (F 475 / JH 1595; Fig. 84).

22. *Plowed Field* (F 574 / JH 1586; Fig. 85).

23. *The Yellow House* (F 464 / JH 1589; Fig. 86).

24. In his influential book *L'art japonais* (1883), Louis Gonse wrote about the custom among Japanese artists of exchanging prints called *surimonos,* "small sheets, drawn or engraved by members of societies of artists, poets and tea-drinkers, are called *surimonos.* [. . .] At New Year, the members of these societies were normally in the habit of giving each other presents. It was also good manners to make a drawing for the occasion, which one would have engraved and of which one would print a limited number of proofs for selection. These proofs, called *surimonos,* perpetuated the memory of their periodic meetings in the hands of members" (*On appelle* sourimonos, *de petites feuilles dessinées ou gravées par des membres de sociétés d'artistes, de poètes et de buveurs de thé. [. . .] Au retour de la nouvelle année, les membres de ces sociétés avaient généralement l'habitude de s'offrir quelque présent. Il était aussi de bon ton de composer quelque dessin de circonstance que l'on faisait graver et que l'on tirait à un nombre limité d'épreuves de choix. Ces épreuves, dites* sourimonos, *perpétuaient entre les mains des sociétaires le souvenir de leurs réunions périodiques.).* See *L'art japonais,* Paris, 1886, p. 324, and Silverman 2000, pp. 42–43.

25. Kōdera said that van Gogh was projecting his own ideal onto Japanese artists, who generally did not live harmoniously together and, equally, were not simple laborers. See van Rappard-Boon et al. 1991, p. 38.

26. Van Gogh was referring to the illustration *Étude d'herbe*, with its printed note: *of the family of Graminae. Facsimile of a brush sketch. Copied from life, the 14th day of the 8th month, in the 2nd year of Kokwa [1845].* (de la famille des graminées. Fac-similé d'une esquisse au pinceau. Copié d'après nature le 14e jour du 8e mois, dans la 2e année de Kokwa; 1845; Fig. 87). See *Le Japon Artistique* 1 (May 1888), no. C.

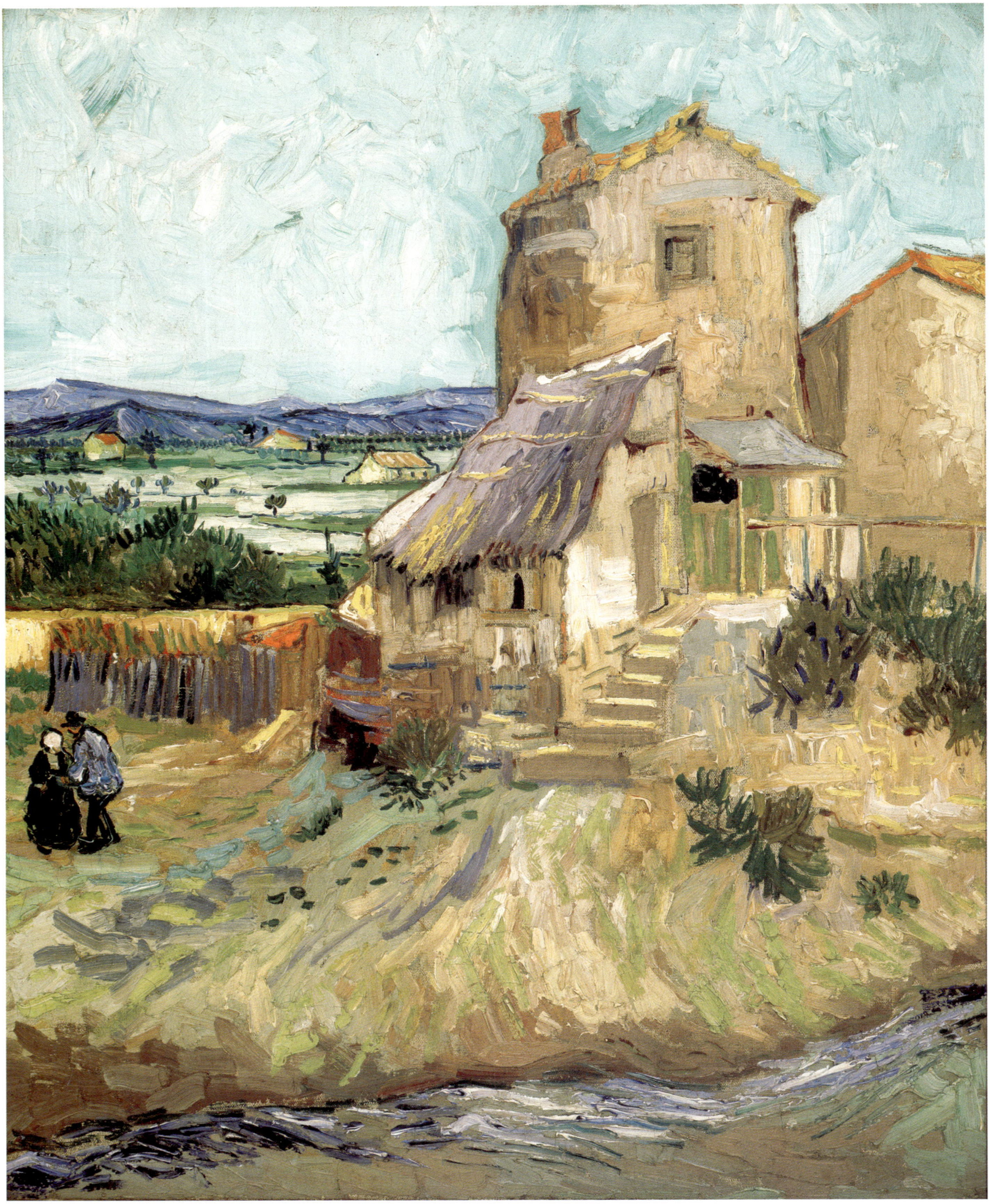

Letter 19

Arles, ca. Friday, 5 October, 1888

Source
Original manuscript

Location
New York, Thaw Collection, The Morgan Library & Museum

Date
In this letter van Gogh spoke of receiving self-portraits from Gauguin and Bernard. They had not yet arrived on 3 October, but they had when he wrote letter *CL* 545. We have therefore dated this letter to around that same day: ca. Friday, 5 October, 1888.

Again, this is an instance of one letter following hard on the heels of another, but the tone is now very different. Bernard and Gauguin had at last sent their works for the exchange, which was something van Gogh regarded as one of the most natural things to do within an artistic collaboration. In addition, Bernard sent ten new drawings, sketches of brothel scenes. Vincent also gave Theo his opinion about the ten drawings and the enclosed poem "Au bordel," which he considered masterful.

The exchanged works were self-portraits, and van Gogh was delighted. "The Gauguin is immediately remarkable, but I myself like Bernard's very much, it's nothing but an idea of a painter, some cursory tones, some blackish lines, but it's as stylish as real, real Manet. The Gauguin is more studied, taken further. [. . .] And now at last I have a chance to compare my painting with that of the pals."[1] That comparison was undoubtedly the implicit reason for his repeated defense of his own way of working, in which he again stressed the primacy of reality over the imagination. His insistence on this point, certainly when seen in retrospect, was a sign that this was becoming a crucial point of disagreement in the three-sided relationship.

Van Gogh sent Bernard and Gauguin paintings in return, adding studies for the exchanges with Bernard, Laval, Moret, and Chamaillard. For Gauguin he chose his *Self-Portrait* (F 476 / JH 1581; Fig. 74), which he believed was as good as Gauguin's. "I wrote

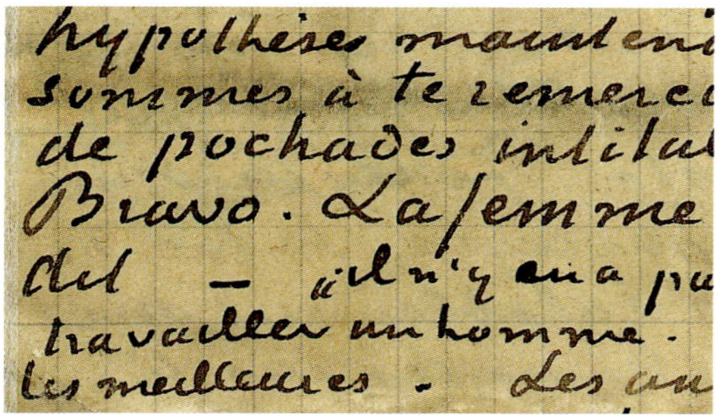
hypothèses maintenant
sommes à te remerci
de pochades intitul
Bravo. La femme
Bel — il n'y en a pa
travailler un homme.
les meilleures - Les au

to Gauguin in reply to his letter that if I too was allowed to enhance my personality in a portrait, I had, trying to show in my portrait not only myself but an impressionist in general, I had conceived this portrait as being that of a bonze, a simple worshiper of the eternal Buddha. And when I put Gauguin's conception and mine side by side, mine is equally serious but less desperate."[2] So along with all the admiration for his friends in Brittany, the confrontation with their recent work helped bolster his self-confidence.

88. Vincent van Gogh, *The Old Mill,* 1888 (F 550 / JH 1577). Buffalo, Albright-Knox Art Gallery.

Translation of Letter 19 / Arles, ca. Friday, 5 October, 1888

My dear old Bernard.
The consignment Gauguin and you sent arrived at almost the same time as my studies went off.[1] I was delighted, it really warmed my heart to see the two faces again. As for your portrait—you know—I like it very much—I actually like everything that you do, as you know—and perhaps nobody *before* me has liked what you do *as much* as I do.

I really urge you to study the portrait; make as many as possible and don't give up—later we'll have to attract the public through portraits—in my view that's where the future lies. But let's not get sidetracked into hypotheses now. Because it's up to us next to thank you for the collection of rough sketches entitled *At the brothel*.[2]

Bravo! The woman washing herself and the one who says "I'm second to none when it comes to taking it out of a man"[3] are the best, it seems to me. The others are grimacing too much—and most of all, are too vague, too little flesh and bone properly built up.

It doesn't matter; it's already something altogether new and interesting, and the rest, too—at the brothel—yes, that's what needs to be done, and I assure you that I for one almost envy you this bloody good opportunity you have to go in there in uniform. Which those good little women adore. The poem at the end is really beautiful; stands up better than some of the figures.[4] What you want, and what you say you believe, you say well and resonantly.

Write to me when you're going to be in Paris—the thing is that I've already written you a thousand times that my night café *is not a brothel*, it's a café where night prowlers cease to be night

---

Transcription of Letter 19 / Arles, ca. Friday, 5 October, 1888

Mon cher copain Bernard.
Presque simultanément avec le départ de mes études l'envoi de Gauguin et de toi est arrivé.[1] *Je me suis bien fait du bon sang, cela m'a bien rechauffé le coeur de revoir les deux visages. Pour ton portrait—tu sais—je l'aime beaucoup—j'aime bien tout ce que tu fais d'ailleurs comme tu sais—et peutêtre personne n'a* autant *aimé ce que tu fais que moi* avant *moi.*

Je t'engage fortement d'étudier le portrait, faites en le plus possible et ne lâchez pas—il nous faudra dans la suite prendre le public par le portrait—l'avenir selon moi est là-dedans. Mais ne déraillons pas dans les hypothèses maintenant. Puisque nous en sommes à te remercier ensuite du recueil de pochades intitulées au bordel.[2]

Bravo. La femme qui se lave et celle qui dit—"il n'y en a pas deux comme moi pour travailler un homme"[3] *à ce qui me paraît sont les meilleures.—Les autres grimacent trop—et surtout sont trop*[a] *flous, trop peu chair et os suffisamment bâtis.—*

C'est égal, c'est déjà du tout neuf et de l'intéressant, que le reste aussi—au bordel—oui c'est ça qu'il faut faire et je t'assure que moi pour un je t'envie presque cette rude chance que tu as d'entrer là-dedans en uniforme. Ce dont ces bonnes petites femmes raffolent. La poésie à la fin est reellement belle, se tient mieux sur ses jambes que certaines des figures.[4] *Ce que tu veux et ce que tu dis croire, tu le dis bien et avec sonorité.*

Ecris moi quand tu seras à Paris—il y a que je t'ai déjà écrit mille fois que mon café de nuit n'est pas un bordel, *c'est un café où les rodeurs de nuit cessent d'etre rôdeurs de nuit, puisque avachis sur les*

prowlers, since, slumped over tables, they spend the whole night there without prowling at all.[5] Occasionally a whore brings her fellow there. But arriving there one night I came across a little group of a pimp and a whore who were making up after a quarrel. The woman was pretending to be indifferent and haughty, the man was tender. I started to paint it for you from memory—on a little no. 4 or no. 6 canvas[6]—now if you're leaving soon—I'll send it to you in Paris; if you're staying longer, say so, I'll send it to you in Pont-Aven. I couldn't add it to the consignment, it was nowhere near dry enough.

But I don't want to sign this study, because I never work from memory—there will be color in it, which will suit you, but to repeat, here I'm doing a study for you that I would prefer not to do. I mercilessly destroyed an important canvas—a Christ with the angel in Gethsemane—as well as another one depicting the poet with a starry sky—because the form hadn't been studied from the model beforehand, necessary in such cases—despite the fact that the color was right.[7]

If the study I'm sending you in exchange doesn't suit you, just look at it a little longer.

I had the devil's own job to do it with an irritating mistral[8] (like the study in red and green, as well).[9] Well, despite the fact that it wasn't painted as fluently as the old mill[10]—it's more delicate and more intimate. You see that all of this is perhaps not at all—impressionist—well, too bad, I can't do anything about it—but I do what I do with an abandonment to reality, without thinking about this or that. Goes without saying that if you preferred another study from the batch to the men unloading sand, you could take it and remove my dedication[11] if someone else wants it. But I believe that that one will suit you once you've looked at it a little longer.

If Laval, Moret and the other one[12] agree to make exchanges with me, perfect, but on my side I

---

tables, ils passent là toute la nuit sans rôder du tout.[5] *Par hasard une putain y ammène son type. Mais y venant une nuit j'ai surpris un petit groupe d'un maquereau et d'une putain qui se raccomodaient après une brouille. La femme faisait l'indifférente et la superbe, l'homme était calin.—Je m'étais mis à le peindre de tête pour toi—sur une petite toile de 4 ou de 6*[6]*—or si tu pars vite—je te l'enverrai à Paris, si tu restes encore, dis le, je te l'enverrai à Pont Aven. je ne pouvais pas le joindre à l'envoi, c'etait pas du tout sec assez.*

Mais je ne veux signer cette etude car je ne travaille jamais de tête—il y aura de la couleur qui t'ira mais encore une fois, je fais là pour toi une etude que je préférerais ne pas faire. Une toile importante—un christ avec l'ange en Getsemané—une autre représentant le poète avec un ciel étoilé—malgré la couleur qui était juste, je les ai sans miséricorde détruites parceque la forme n'en était pas étudiée préalablement sur le modèle, nécessaire dans ces cas-là.—[7]

L'étude que je t'envoie en échange, si elle ne te va pas tu n'as qu'à la regarder un peu plus longtemps.—

J'ai eu un mal du diable pour la faire avec un mistral agaçant[8] *(comme l'etude en rouge et vert aussi).*[9] *Eh bien malgré qu'elle ne soit pas aussi couramment peinte que le vieux moulin*[10]*—elle est plus fine et plus intime. Tu vois que tout cela n'est peut-être pas du tout—impressioniste—ma foi tant pis, je n'y peux rien—mais je fais ce que je fais avec un abandon à la nature sans songer à ceci ou à cela. Va sans dire que si tu préférais dans l'envoi une autre étude aux Déchargeurs de sable tu pourras la prendre et effacer ma dédicace*[11] *si un autre en veut. Mais je crois que celle là t'ira une fois que tu l'auras regardée un peu plus longtemps.*

Si Laval, Moret et l'autre[12] *veulent bien me faire des échanges, parfait mais surtout je serais satis-*

would be especially satisfied if they wanted to do their portraits for me.

You know, Bernard, it always seems to me that if I want to do studies of brothels, I'd need more money than I have; I'm not young or womanizer enough[13] for them to pose for me for free. And I can't work without a model. I'm not saying that I don't flatly turn my back on reality to turn a study into a painting—by arranging the color, by enlarging, by simplifying—but I have such a fear of separating myself from what's possible and what's right as far as form is concerned.

Later, after another ten years of studies, I'm not saying so, but in very truth I have so much curiosity for what's possible and what really exists that I have so little desire or courage to search for the ideal, in so far as it could result from *my* abstract studies.

Others may have more clarity of mind than I for abstract studies—and you might certainly be among them, as well as Gauguin and perhaps myself when I'm old.

But in the meantime I'm still living off the real world. I exaggerate, I sometimes make changes to the subject, but still I don't invent the whole of the painting; on the contrary, I find it ready-made—but to be untangled—in the real world.

But you'll probably find these studies ugly, I don't know. In any case, neither you nor anyone else should do an exchange grudgingly.

My brother writes that Anquetin's back in Paris;[14] I'm curious to know what he's made. When you see him you'll give him my kind regards.

The house will seem more lived in now that I'll see the portraits in it.

How happy I would be to see you there yourself this winter; it's true that the trip costs rather a lot. Nevertheless, may one not risk those expenses by taking one's revenge by working? Work's so difficult in the north in winter. Here too, perhaps; I've hardly had the experience yet and it remains to be seen.

But it's damned useful to see the south, where life is lived more in the open air, in order to understand the Japanese better.

And that touch of the haughty and the noble that certain places have down here will suit your book very well. In The Red Sunset, the sun should be imagined higher, outside the painting, let's say just at the level of the FRAME.[15] Because it so happens that an hour, an hour and a half before it sets, the things on the earth still keep their colors like that. Later the blue and the violet color them darker, as soon as the sun sends out rays that are more horizontal. Thanks once again for what you sent me, it really warmed my heart.

And a good handshake in thought, and write to me the day of your departure so that I know when you'll be in Paris; address in Paris still avenue de Beaulieu 5, isn't it?[16]

Ever yours,
Vincent

fait de mon côté s'ils voulaient me faire leurs portraits.

Tu sais Bernard, il me semble toujours que si je veux faire des etudes de bordels, il me faudrait plus d'argent que je n'en aie, je suis pas jeune et chair à femme[13] *assez pour qu'elles posent pour moi à l'oeil. Et je ne peux pas travailler sans modèle. Je ne dis pas que je ne tourne pas carrément le dos à la nature pour transformer une étude en tableau—en arrangeant la couleur, en agrandissant, en simplifiant—mais j'ai tant peur de m'écarter du possible et du juste en tant que quant à la forme.*

Plus tard après encore dix ans d'études je ne dis pas, mais vrai de vrai j'ai tant de curiosité du possible et du réellement existant que j'ai si peu le désir et le courage de chercher l'ideal en tant que pouvant résulter de mes *études abstraites.*

D'autres peuvent avoir pour les études abstraites plus de lucidité que moi—et certes tu pourrais être du nombre ainsi que Gauguin et peut etre moi-même quand je serai vieux.

Mais en attendant je mange toujours de la nature. J'exagère, je change parfois au motif mais enfin je n'invente pas le tout du tableau, je le trouve au contraire tout fait—mais à démêler—dans la nature.

Mais probablement tu trouvera laides ces etudes, je ne sais.—Dans tous les cas, que ni toi ni personne ne fasse d'échange à contre coeur.

Mon frère écrit qu'Anquetin est de retour à Paris,[14] *je suis curieux de savoir ce qu'il a fait. Lorsque tu le verras tu lui diras bien des choses de ma part.*

La maison va me sembler plus habitée maintenant que j'y verrai les portraits.

Que je serais content de t'y voir toi-même cet hiver, il est vrai que le voyage coute un peu cher. Pourtant ne peut on pas risquer ces frais-là en se vengeant en travaillant? L'hiver, dans le nord, le travail est si difficile.—Peutetre ici aussi, je n'en ai encore guère l'experience et ce sera à voir.

mais c'est bougrement utile de voir le midi, où la vie se passe davantage en plein air, pour mieux comprendre les japonais.

Puis le je ne sais quoi d'altier et de noble qu'ont de certains sites d'ici ferait bien ton affaire. Dans le Coucher de soleil rouge, le Soleil doit être supposé plus haut, hors du tableau, mettons juste à la hauteur du CADRE.[15] *Car il y a qu'une heure, une heure et demie avant son coucher, les choses à terre gardent leurs couleurs ainsi encore. Plus tard le bleu et le violet les colorent davantage en noir dès que le soleil envoie des rayons plus horizontaux. Merci encore une fois de ton envoi qui m'a bien rechauffé le coeur.*

Et bonne poignée de main en pensee et écris moi le jour de ton depart pour que je sache quand tu sera à Paris, adresse à Paris toujours avenue de Beaulieu 5 n'est ce pas?[16]

t. à t.
Vincent

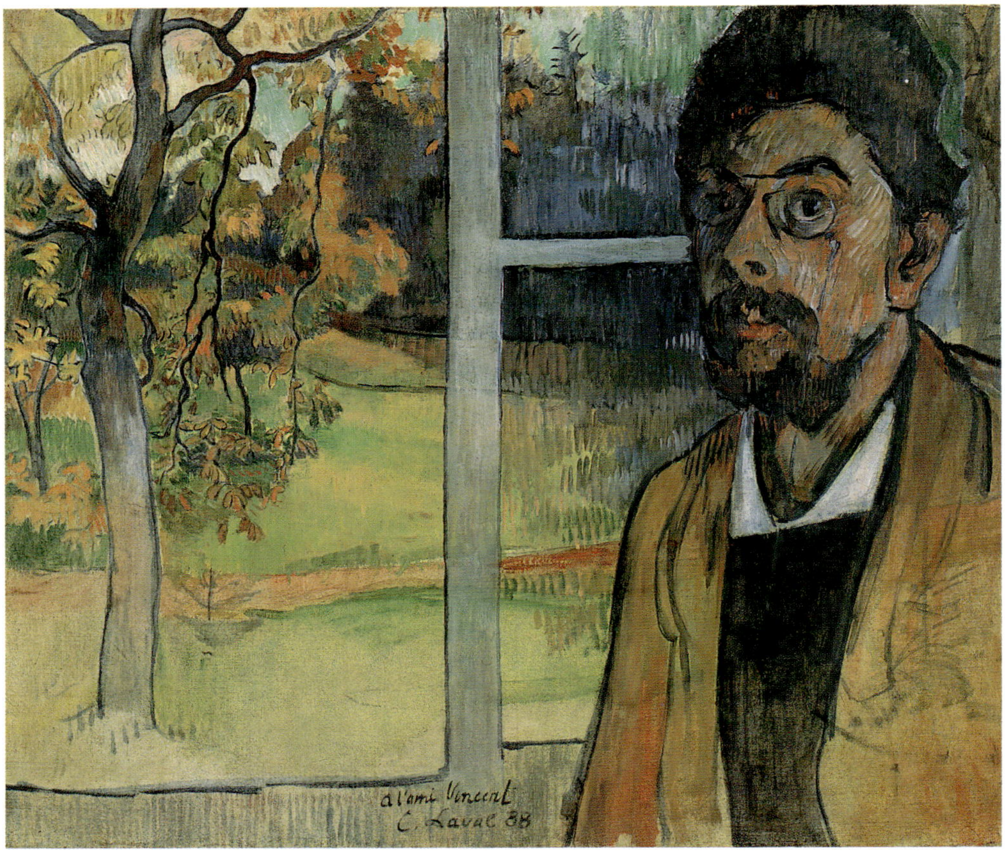
à l'ami Vincent
C. Laval 88

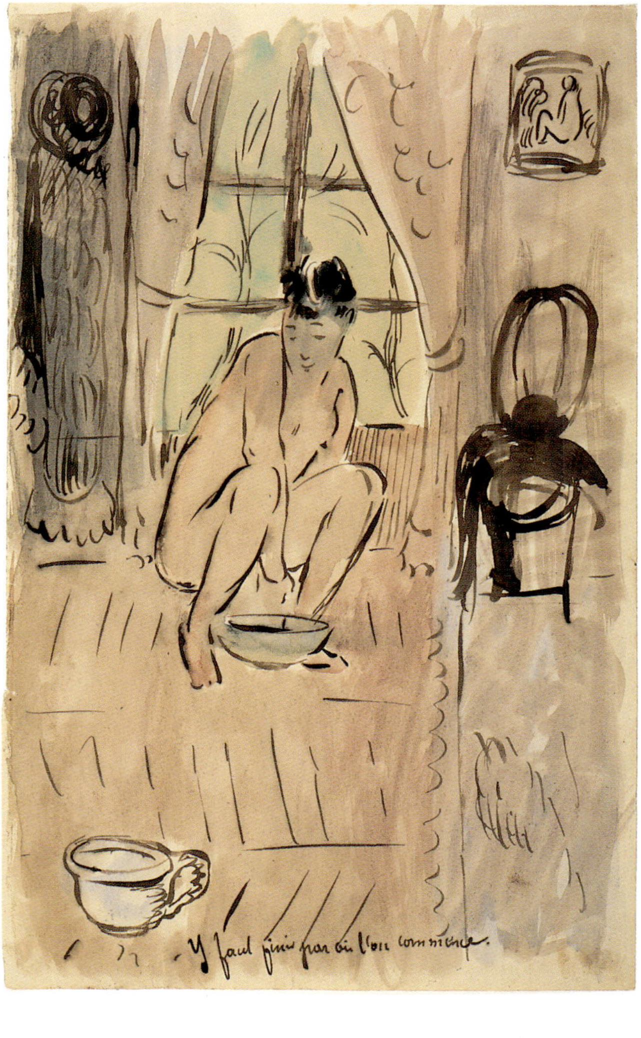
Y faut finir par où l'on commence.

Annotations to Letter 19

Arles, ca. Friday, 5 October, 1888

Textual Note
a. trop < tros

1. Van Gogh received Gauguin's *Self-Portrait with Portrait of Bernard, "Les misérables"* (W309/W239; Fig. 72) and Bernard's *Self-Portrait with Portrait of Gauguin* (Fig. 73); see Letter 16, n. 1.

Van Gogh sent seven studies to Pont-Aven (see letter *CL* 553). Two of them—*Self-Portrait* (F 476 / JH 1581; Fig. 74) and *Quay with Men Unloading Sand Barges* (F 449 / JH 1558; Fig. 71), respectively, were intended for Gauguin and Bernard in return for their self-portraits; see Letter 16, n. 1. See also nn. 8 and 11 below.

The other five works were intended for the new exchange with Bernard, Laval, Moret, and Chamaillard. Two can be identified for certain: *Thistles* (F 447 / JH 1550; Fig. 79) and *The Old Mill* (F 550 / JH 1577; Fig. 88), which went to Moret and Chamaillard, respectively. See Bernard 1994, vol. 1, p. 307, and n. 10 below. Two of the other three studies probably went to Bernard and one to Laval, who sent his *Self-Portrait* (Fig. 89) in exchange. There was certainly a "red sunset." Going by van Gogh's descriptions in Letter 18 of the studies he was thinking of sending, the remaining two could have been chosen from the following three: "a study of a little garden of multicolored flowers," "a still life of old peasants' shoes," or "a small landscape of nothing at all, in which there's nothing but a bit of an expanse."

The "study of a little garden" was *Garden with Flowers* (F 578 / JH 1538; Fig. 78) which van Gogh probably did send to Pont-Aven, given the provenance, which isn't the family collection. See Roskill 1971, p. 159 (n. 89). Feilchenfeldt thought that it was the painting of a garden that Jo van Gogh-Bonger sold to Cassirer in March 1908, but that was another work, *Garden* (F 814 / JH 2107). See Feilchenfeldt 1988, p. 105, and *Account Book* 2002, pp. 52, 148.

It is impossible to identify the last work that he sent. The "still life of old peasants' shoes" was *A Pair of Old Shoes* (F 461 / JH 1569; Fig. 80), but since that was owned by Jo van Gogh-Bonger, one can conclude that it was not sent. It is not clear what the "small landscape of nothing at all, in which there's nothing but a bit of an expanse" was (see Letter 18, n. 14). See also Dorn's identification of the works in the batch in Essen and Amsterdam 1990, pp. 110–12.

2. Bernard sent an album, titled *Au bordel* (At the Brothel) on the front, with the dedication *a l'ami Vincent / ces croquis stupides* (to my friend Vincent / these stupid sketches) and signature *EBernard / 1888*. The album measures 15⅞ x 10¼ in. (40.5 x 26 cm) and contains eleven color sketches of brothel scenes. Written on most of them is something said by a prostitute or a title.

89. Charles Laval, *Self-Portrait*, 1888. Amsterdam, Van Gogh Museum (Vincent van Gogh Foundation).
90. Émile Bernard, *A Prostitute Washing Herself*, from the series *At the Brothel*, 1888. Amsterdam, Van Gogh Museum (Vincent van Gogh Foundation).

3. The two drawings van Gogh discussed here are *A Prostitute Washing Herself*, which has the inscription *Y faut finir par où l'on commence* (You have to finish where you begin; Fig. 90), and *Two Prostitutes at a Table*, inscribed *Y en a pas deux comme moi pour travailler un homme* (I'm second to none when it comes to taking it out of a man; Fig. 91).

4. Bernard wrote the following poem on the inside back cover of the album.

Disgust is the healthiest, and to the red ray of dusk
I prefer a gas-lamp in a sordid bar,
With girls on green couches, bare-breasted,
Kissing stupid strangers' lips.
Ugliness is the infernal thing that can stir the soul,
And we have truly ceased loving women
With a languid gaze, like a nude by Fragonard.
Let us prefer flaunted flesh to great art
(Which, as we know, consists of great *machines*
In which queens, virgins, murderesses move,
Joan of Arc or *Catherine* de' Medici,)
I don't dispute their indefinable charms,
That's everyone's right—. But the more we plunge into the chasm,
The more the concept pervades our brain;
For beneath the oceans' eternal depths,
In the blackest, bitterest of abysses,
The pearl sleeps among the monsters and the weeds;
The violet, beneath the rotted heap of bouquets,
Exudes a sweet scent that intoxicates intensely—.
It's the hideous, then, that's the sole element—
The crucible from which a world of an abyss escapes
Whose form is ugliness, whose essence the Sublime.

–.–

That is why I like recreating myself in ghastliness,
And when my weary mind refuses to create,
I go to those forbidden haunts where drunkenness is flaunted
To find for my brain the divine caress
Given to our gaping heart by the misunderstood
Bleak, vast revelation of Nothingness.

(L'horreur c'est le plus sain, et je préfère au rouge
Rayon d'un crépuscule un bec de gaz de bouge
Avec, sur des bancs verts des filles les seins nus
Baisant les lèvres de stupides inconnus.
Le laid c'est l'infernal qui sait remuer l'âme,
Et nous avons vraiment fini d'aimer la femme
A l'oeil languide ainsi qu'un nu de Fragonard.

Qu'on préfère la chair à l'étal, au grand art
(Qui consiste l'on sait en de grandes machines
Où se meuvent des reines, vierges, assasines
Jeanne Darc ou Cathérine *de Medicis,)*
Je n'en discute pas les charmes indécis,
C'est le droit de chacun—. Mais plus au gouffre on plonge
Plus dans notre cerveau le conceps s'allonge;
Car sous les profondeurs eternelles des mers
Dans les abîmes les plus noirs, les plus amers,
La perle dort parmi les monstres et les herbes;
La violette sous le tas pourri des gerbes
Répand un doux parfum qui grise fortement—.
Donc c'est que le hideux c'est l'unique élément—
Le creuset d'où s'échappe un monde d'un abîme
Dont la forme est le laid et le fond le Sublime.

–.–

C'est pourquoi dans l'affreux j'aime a me recréer
Et quand mon esprit las se refuse a créer
Je vais aux lieux bannis où s'étale l'ivresse
Pour mon cerveau chercher la divine caresse
Que donne l'incompris à notre coeur béant
Révélation morne et grande du Néant.)

Note: We have restored any missing accents.

5. Van Gogh had written to Bernard about his painting *The Night Café* (F 463 / JH 1575; Fig. 75) in a letter that is now lost and in Letter 16.

6. This study is not known. On the basis of the dimensions, it could be *Brothel Scene* (F 478 / JH 1599; Fig. 92), which is on a no. 6 canvas (13 x 16⅛ in.; 33 x 41 cm). Van Gogh said, however, that he had set the study in the night café, where he had painted F 463, and the interior in F 478 does not resemble it. On top of that, the scene does not match van Gogh's description. It is more likely, then, that F 478 is the rough sketch that van Gogh painted in November 1888 and mentioned in letter *CL* 561. See also Dorn 1990, p. 249 (n. 52), and Chicago and Amsterdam 2001–2, pp. 195, 387 (n. 114).

7. Vincent told Theo about his second, abortive attempt to paint a Christ without a model on 21 September: "For the second time I have scraped off a study of a Christ with the angel in the Garden of Olives. Because here I can see real olive trees. But I cannot, or rather I do not wish, to paint it without models. But I have it in my mind with color—the starry night, the figure of Christ blue, the strongest blues, and the angel broken lemon yellow" (*J'ai pour la deuxieme fois gratté une etude d'un Christ avec l'ange dans le jardin des oliviers.— Parceque ici je vois les oliviers vrais. Mais je ne peux ou plutot je ne veux pas non plus le peindre sans modèles. Mais j'ai cela en tête avec de la couleur—la nuit etoilée, la figure du Christ bleue, les bleus les plus puissants, et l'ange jaune citron rompu; CL* 540). He wrote about his first attempt at the beginning of July 1888: "a *Garden*

of Olives—with a white and orange Christ, a yellow angel—a piece of red earth, green and blue hills. [. . .] I scraped it off because I tell myself it's wrong to do figures on this scale without a model" (*un* jardin des oliviers—*avec une figure de Christ bleue et orangé, un ange jaune—un terrain rouge, collines vertes et bleues. [. . .] Je l'ai grattée parce que je me dis qu'il ne faut pas faire des figures de cette portée sans modèle; CL* 505). As it happens, at the beginning of September he had painted "a poet" with a starry night after a model: *Portrait of Eugène Boch* (F 462 / JH 1574; Paris, Musée d'Orsay).

8. Van Gogh wanted Bernard to have *Quay with Men Unloading Sand Barges* (F 449 / JH 1558; Fig. 71). The latter's attachment to it is clear from the fact that at first he did not want to sell it, nor the *Self-Portrait with Straw Hat* (F 526 / JH 1309; The Detroit Institute of Arts), because "I'm attached to it as much as a souvenir of friendship as I am as a painting" (*j'y tiens autant comme souvenir d'amitié que comme peinture*). Unpublished letter from Bernard to his father, 28 January 1900, Getty Center, Los Angeles; with thanks to Fred Leeman. In an act of homage to van Gogh, Bernard portrayed himself in front of that painting in his *Self-Portrait* of 1892 (private collection).

9. The study in red and green would have been the "red sunset" mentioned later in this letter (see n. 15). Van Gogh described it in Letter 18 as "a landscape angry with a nasty mistral" (*un paysage en colère de mistral méchant*).

10. *The Old Mill*, which once belonged to Chamaillard (see n. 1). See *Correspondance Gauguin* 1984, p. 503. It is not known whether van Gogh received anything in return. Theo's estate contained an oil sketch by Chamaillard, *View of a Harbor*, but that is dedicated *à l'ami Gauguin.*

11. The painting *Quay with Men Unloading Sand Barges* (F 449 / JH 1558, Fig. 71) is signed and dedicated *Vincent / à Émile Bernard* (most of the inscription has been removed).

12. Ernest Ponthier de Chamaillard.

13. Van Gogh first wrote *amoureux assez* (amorous enough).

14. Anquetin had spent the summer in Etrépagny (Normandy).

15. This painting, a study in red and green (*étude en rouge et vert;* see n. 9) is not known, but it might be the work described in letter *CL* 535 as "a landscape with factory, and an enormous sun in a red sky, above red roofs, in which nature seems to be in a rage, on a day of nasty mistral" (*un paysage avec usine et un soleil enorme dans un ciel rouge au-dessus des toits rouges où la nature semble être en colère un jour de mistral méchant*), but the descriptions do not completely match. It is possible that in the meantime he had worked on it again and had painted out the sun.

16. 5, avenue de Beaulieu was the Bernards' address in Asnières.

---

91. Émile Bernard, *Two Prostitutes at a Table,* from the series *At the Brothel,* 1888. Amsterdam, Van Gogh Museum (Vincent van Gogh Foundation).

92. Vincent van Gogh, *Brothel Scene,* 1888 (F 478 / JH 1599). Merion, PA, The Barnes Foundation.

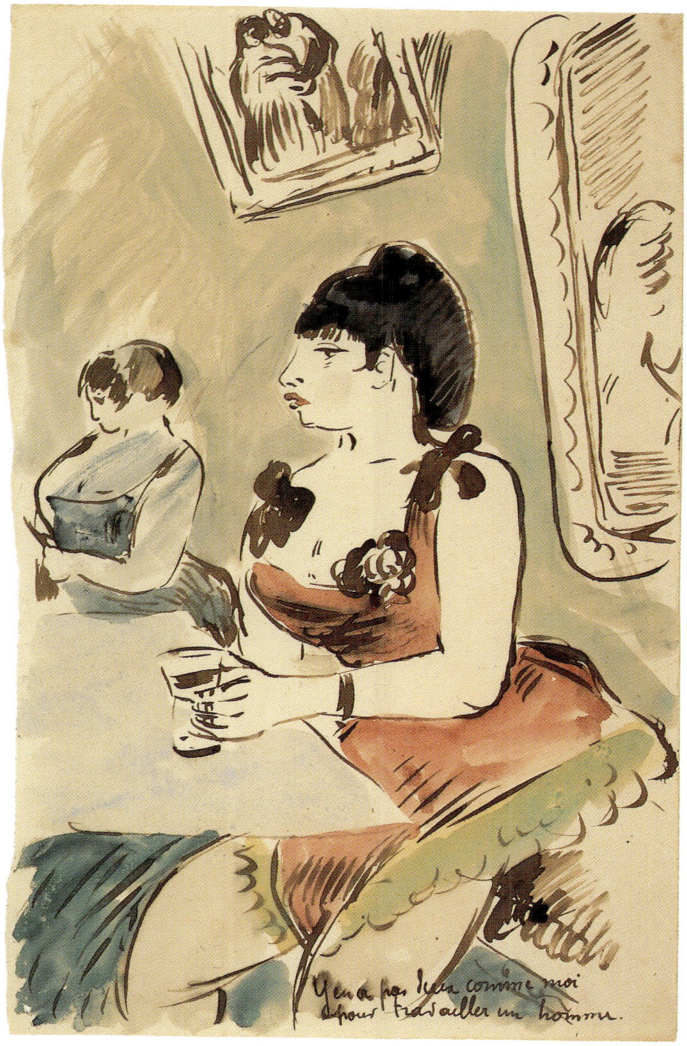
Y en a pas bien comme moi
pour travailler un homme.

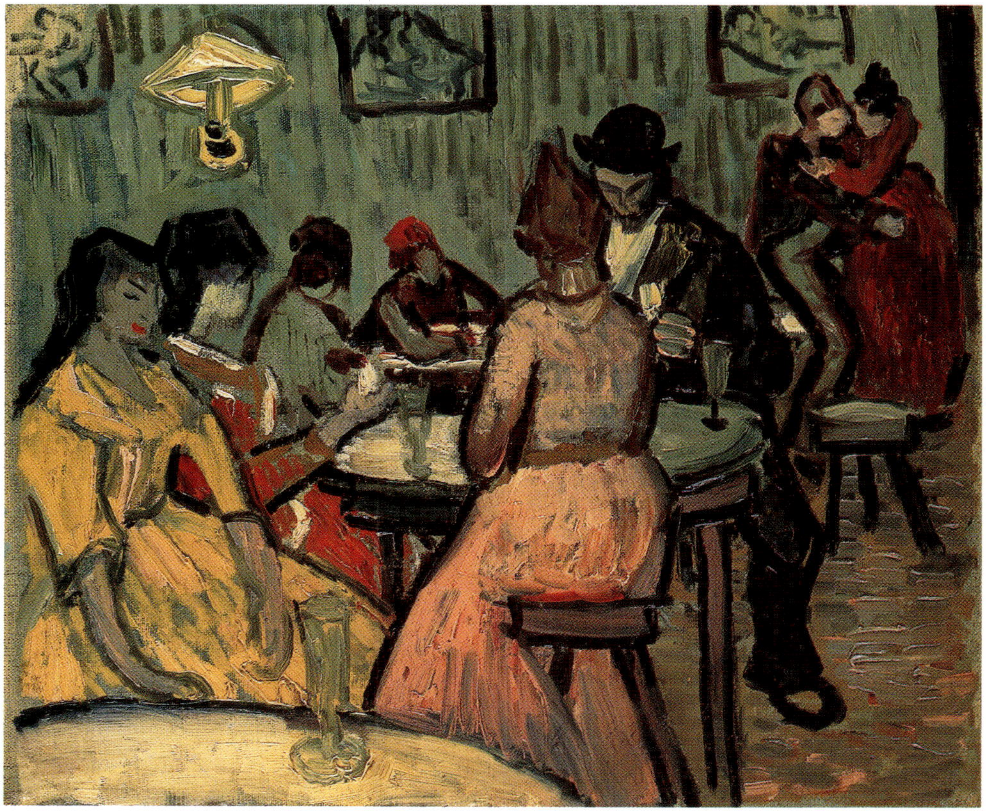

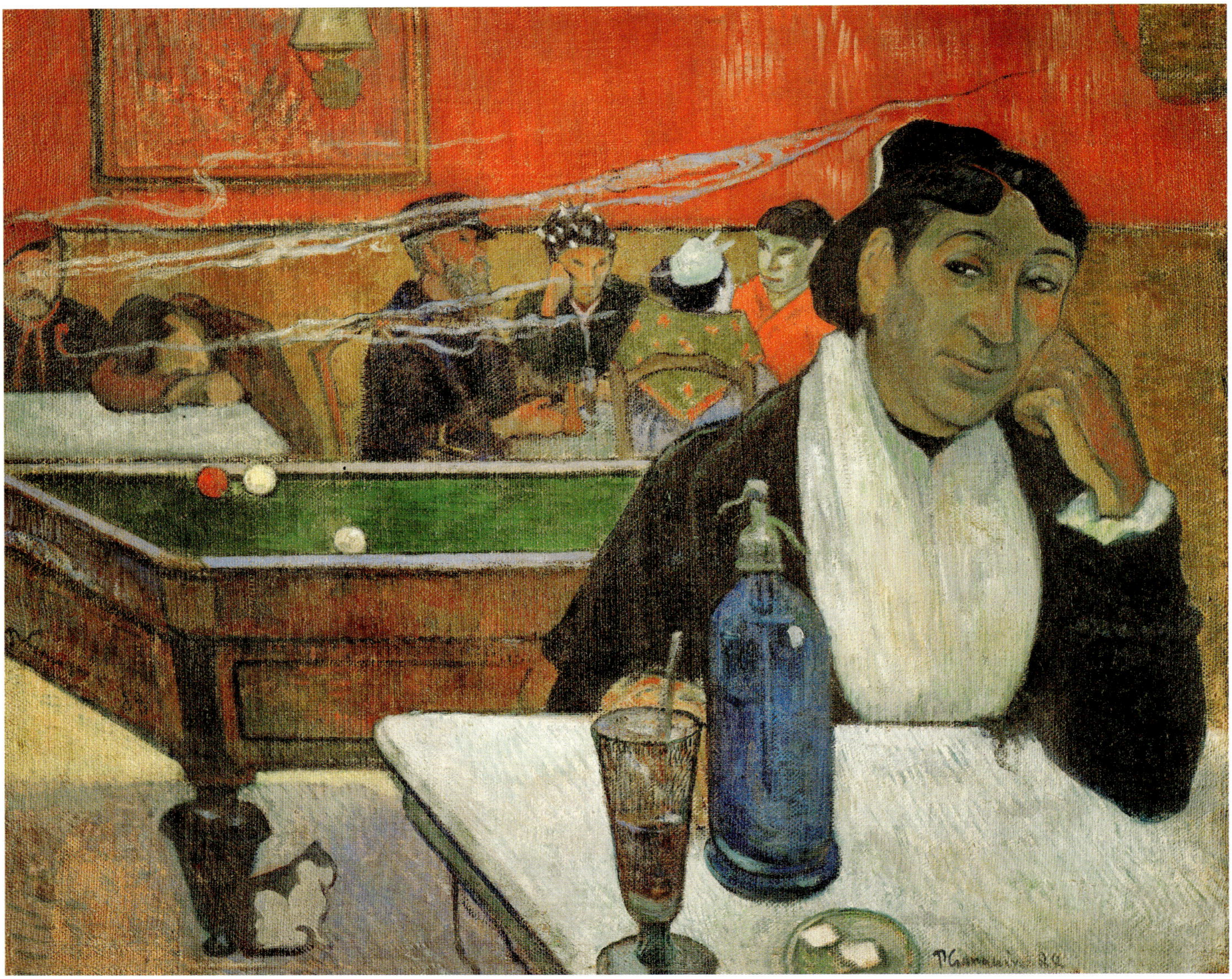

Letter 20

~

Written by Vincent van Gogh and Paul Gauguin; Arles, Thursday, 1, or Friday, 2 November, 1888

Source
Reproduction

Location
Unknown

Date
This letter must precede letter *CL* 559 to Theo of ca. 3 November. In that one, van Gogh announced that he had begun work on a red vineyard, and because he gave quite a detailed description of what he was doing in the present letter without mentioning that painting, it can be assumed that he had not yet started it. On the other hand, this letter could not have been written before 1 November, which was the day Milliet left for Africa (see the present letter and letter *CL* 558b). It is for these reasons that we have dated it Thursday, 1, or Friday, 2 November, 1888.

Additional details
Bernard gave this letter to Aurier when he was preparing his article "Les isolés: Vincent van Gogh" for the *Mercure de France*. Aurier incorporated a passage from this letter in his article (see n. 2).

The constellation had shifted. Gauguin finally left Brittany and moved into the Yellow House on 23 October. Bernard remained behind in Pont-Aven and was to return to Paris in mid-November.

Van Gogh spent the weeks before Gauguin's arrival working on the decoration of his room, which had become a point of honor. In addition to the two canvases of sunflowers hanging there, he wanted four of "the poet's garden." He complained several times about tired eyes and felt that he was about to fall ill. Gauguin got the same impression and wrote to Theo a few days after arriving in Arles: "Your brother is indeed somewhat troubled, and I hope gradually to calm him."[1]

The first week that the two men spent together (up until then they had spent at most a few hours in each other's company) gave van Gogh confidence, and he was clearly elated. In addition, Gauguin had brought along Bernard's *Breton Women in the Meadow* (Fig. 103). Van Gogh ran out of superlatives when speaking of it, describing it to Theo as "a magnificent canvas" (*CL* 557), "superb" (*CL* 562), and "simply masterful" (*CL* 558a).

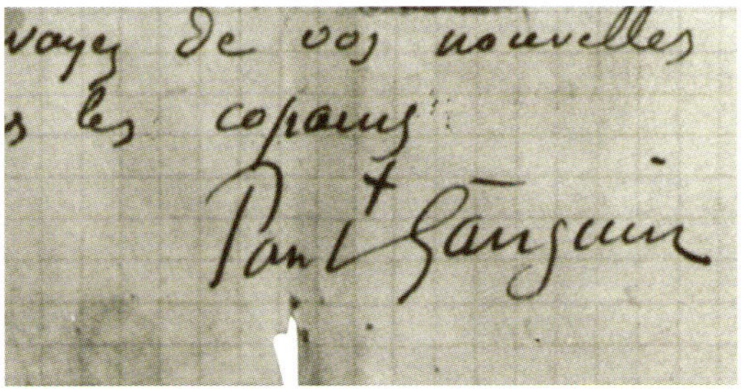

The future was now looking rosier, for Theo had succeeded in selling work by Gauguin. On top of that, Gauguin's arrival had breathed new life into the ideas about a renaissance of art and an association of artists. Gauguin's stories about the tropics convinced van Gogh that it was there that the future lay for "a great renaissance of painting."[2] If he had been younger, he too would have gone there, but now he would remain in the Yellow House, midway between Africa and the tropics and the people of the north (*CL* 558b).

93. Paul Gauguin, *Night Café,* 1888 (W318 / W305). Moscow, Pushkin State Museum of Fine Arts.

Translation of Letter 20 / Written by Vincent van Gogh and Paul Gauguin; Arles, Thursday, 1, or Friday, 2 November, 1888

My dear old Bernard,
We have done a great deal of work these past few days, and in the meantime I've read Zola's Le rêve,[1] so I've hardly had time to write.

Gauguin interests me greatly as a man—greatly. For a long time it has seemed to me that in our filthy job as painters we have the greatest need of people with the hands and stomach of a laborer. More natural tastes—more amorous and benevolent temperaments—than the decadent and exhausted Parisian man-about-town.

Now here, without the slightest doubt, we are in the presence of an unspoiled creature with the instincts of a wild beast. With Gauguin, blood and sex have the edge over ambition. But enough of that, you've seen him close at hand longer than I have, just wanted to tell you first impressions in a few words.

Next, I don't think it will astonish you greatly if I tell you that our discussions are tending to deal with the terrific subject of an association of certain painters. Ought or may this association have a commercial character, yes or no? We haven't reached any result yet, and haven't so much as set foot on a new continent yet.

Now I, who have a presentiment of a new world, who certainly believe in the possibility of a great renaissance of art. Who believe that this new art will have the tropics for its homeland.[2]

It seems to me that we ourselves are serving only as intermediaries. And that it will only be a

---

Transcription of Letter 20 / Written by Vincent van Gogh and Paul Gauguin; Arles, Thursday, 1, or Friday, 2 November, 1888

Mon cher copain Bernard[a]
Ces jours ci nous avons beaucoup travaillé et entre temps j'ai lu le rêve de Zola,[1] *ce qui fait que je n'ai guère eu le temps d'écrire.*

Gauguin m'intéresse beaucoup comme homme—beaucoup.—Il m'a depuis longtemps semblé que dans notre sale métier de peintre nous avons le plus grand besoin de gens ayant des mains et des estomacs d'ouvrier.—Des gouts plus naturels—des tempéraments[b] *plus amoureux et plus charitables—que le boulevardier parisien décadent et crevé.—*

Or ici sans le moindre doute nous nous trouvons en présence d'un être vierge à instincts de fauve. Chez Gauguin le sang et le sexe prevalent sur l'ambition. Mais suffit, tu l'as vu de près plus longtemps que moi, seulement voulais en quelques mots dire premieres impressions.

Ensuite je ne pense pas que cela t'epatera beaucoup si je te dis que nos discussions tendent à traiter le sujet terrible d'une association de certains peintres. Cette association, doit ou peut elle avoir oui ou non un caractère commercial? Nous ne sommes encore arrivé à aucun resultat et n'avons point encore mis le pied sur un continent nouveau.

Or moi qui ai un pressentiment d'un nouveau monde, qui crois certes à la possibilité d'une immense renaissance de l'art. Qui crois que cet art nouveau aura les tropiques pour patrie.[2]

Il me semble que nous mêmes ne servons que d'intermédiaires. Et que ce ne sera qu'une génération suivante qui réussira à vivre en paix. Enfin, tout cela, nos devoirs et nos possibilités d'action ne

subsequent generation that will succeed in living in peace. Anyway, all that, our duties and our possibilities for action could become clearer to us only through actual experience.

I was a little surprised not yet to have received the studies that you promised in exchange for mine.[3]

Now something that will interest you—we have made some excursions in the brothels, and it's likely that we'll eventually go there often to work. At the moment Gauguin has a canvas in progress of the same night café that I also painted, but with figures seen in the brothels.[4] It promises to become a beautiful thing.

I've made two studies of falling leaves in an avenue of poplars, and a third study of the whole of this avenue, entirely yellow.[5]

I declare I don't understand why I don't do figure studies,[6] while theoretically it's sometimes so difficult for me to imagine the painting of the future as anything other than a new series of powerful portraitists, simple and comprehensible to the whole of the general public. Anyway, perhaps I'll soon get down to doing brothels.

I'll leave a page for Gauguin, who will probably also write to you, and I shake your hand firmly in thought.

Ever yours,
Vincent

---

sauraient nous devenir plus clairs que par l'expérience même.

J'ai été un peu surpris de ne pas encore avoir reçu tes études promises en échange des miennes.[3]

Maintenant ce qui t'interessera—nous avons fait quelques excursions dans les bordels et il est probable que nous finirons par aller souvent travailler là.—Gauguin a dans ce moment e[n][c] *train une toile du même café de nuit que j'ai peint aussi mais avec des figures vues dans les bordels.*[4] *Cela promet de devenir une belle chôse.*

Moi j'ai fait deux études d'une chûte des feuilles dans une allée de peupliers et une troisieme étude de l'ensemble de cette allee, entièrement jaune.[5]

Je déclare ne pas comprendre pourquoi je ne fais pas d'études de figure[6] *alors que théoriquement il m'est parfois si difficile de concevoir la peinture de l'avenir comme autre chose qu'une nouvelle serie de puissants portraitistes simples et comprehensibles à tout le grand public. Enfin peutetre je vais sous peu me mettre à faire les bordels.*

Je laisse une page pour Gauguin qui probablement va t'ecrire aussi et te serre bien la main en pensee.

t. à t.
Vincent

Milliet the 2nd lieut. Zouaves has left for Africa, and would be very glad if you were to write to him one of these days.

[CONTINUED BY PAUL GAUGUIN]

You will indeed do well to write him what your intentions are, so that he could take steps beforehand to prepare the way for you.

Mr. Milliet, *second lieutenant of Zouaves*, Guelma, Africa.

Don't listen to Vincent; as you know, he's prone to admire and ditto to be indulgent. His idea about the future of a new generation in the tropics seems absolutely right to me as a painter, and I still intend going back there when I find the funds.[7] A little bit of luck, who knows?

Vincent has done two studies of falling leaves in an avenue, which are in my room and which you would like very much. On very coarse, but very good sacking.[8]

Send news of yourself and of all the pals.

Yours,
Paul Gauguin

Milliet le sous off. Zouaves est parti pour l'Afrique et aimerait bien que tu lui ecrives un de ces jours.—

[CONTINUED BY PAUL GAUGUIN]

Vous ferez bien en effet de lui écrire quelles sont vos intentions afin qu'il prenne les devants pour vous préparer la voie.—

Mr Milliet, sous lieutenant de Zouaves, *Guelma, Afrique.—*

N'écoutez pas Vincent, il a comme vous savez l'admiration facile et l'indulgence dito.—Son idée sur l'avenir d'une génération nouvelle aux tropiques comme peintre me paraît absolument juste et je continue à avoir l'intention d'y retourner quand je trouverai les moyens.[7] Qui sait, un peu de chance?—

Vincent a fait deux études de feuilles tombantes dans une allée qui sont dans ma chambre et que vous aimeriez bien. sur toile à sac très grosse mais très bonne.[8]

Envoyez de vos nouvelles et de tous les copains.

t—
Paul Gauguin

---

94. VINCENT VAN GOGH, *The Alyscamps, Avenue at Arles,* 1888 (F 486 / JH 1620). Otterlo, Kröller-Müller Museum.

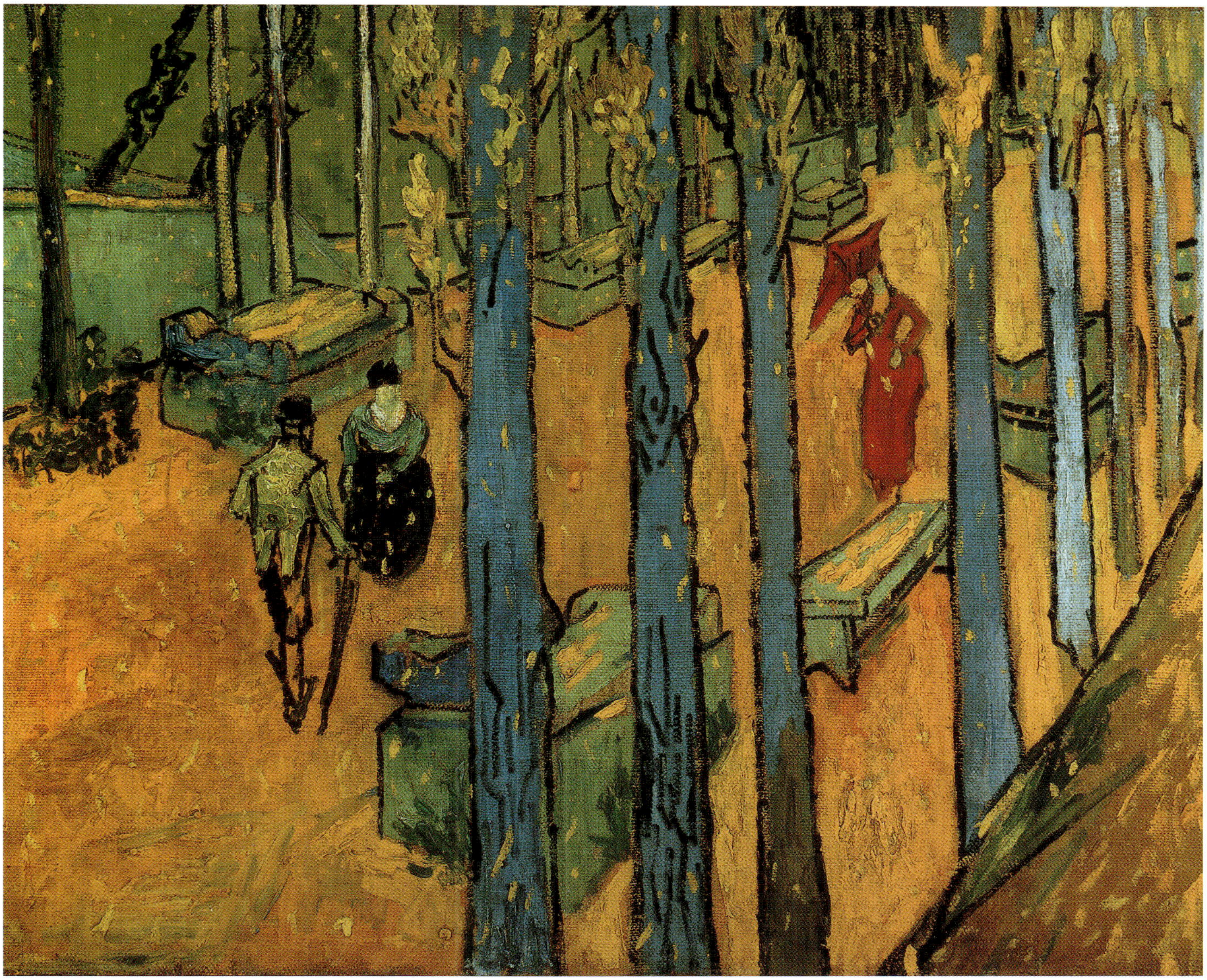

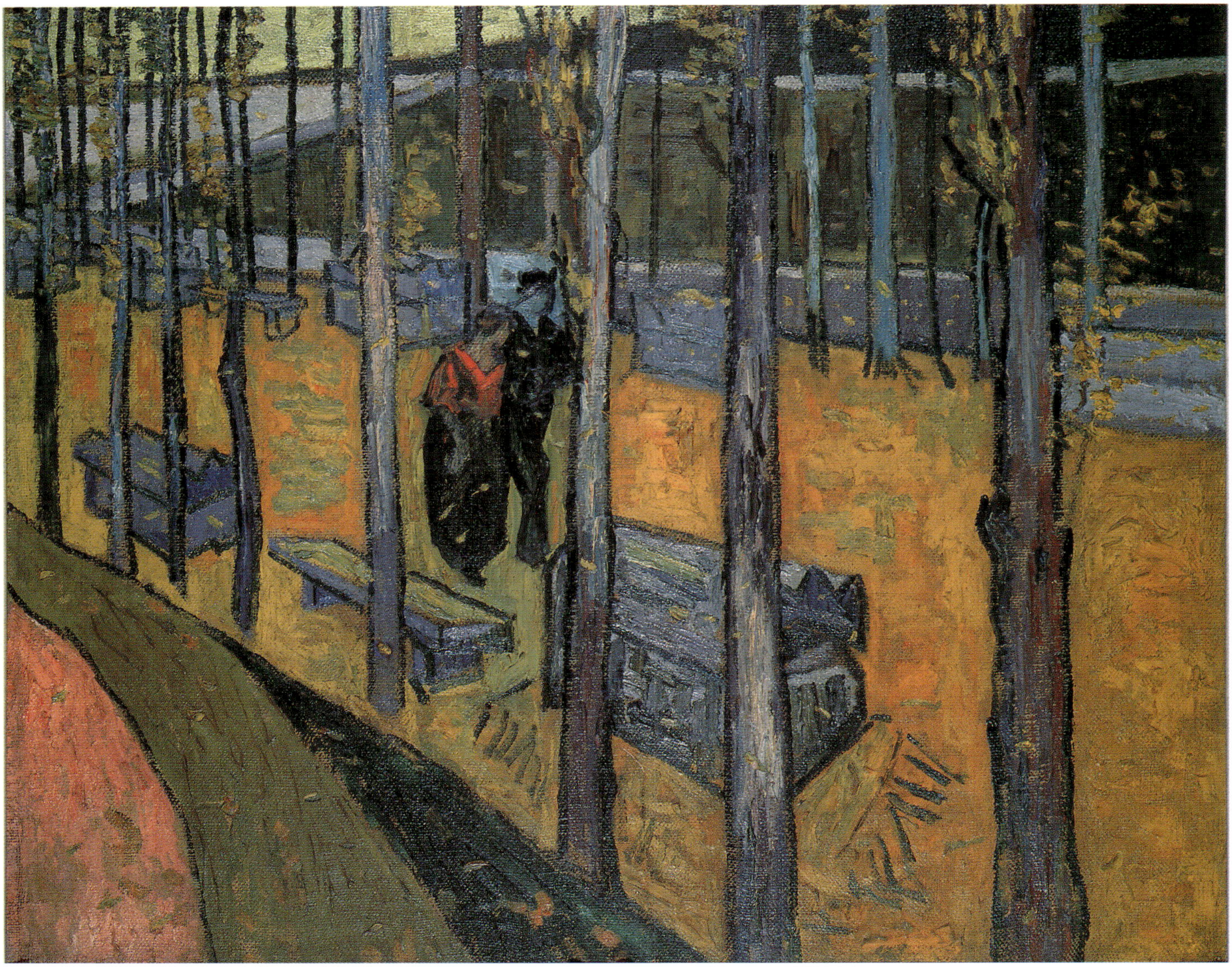

Annotations to Letter 20

Written by Vincent van Gogh and Paul Gauguin;
Arles, Thursday, 1, or Friday, 2 November, 1888

Textual Notes
a. *Bernard* < *(Possibly added by another hand.)*
b. des tempéraments < Des tempéraments
c. e*[*n*]* < *(Text lost due to paper damage.)*

1. *Le rêve* (1888), Émile Zola's most recent novel in the Rougon-Macquart series, was published on 11 October 1888. It is the story of the orphan Angélique Marie, who spends her time making embroideries of the lives of saints and dreaming about Prince Charming, who then materializes in the shape of Félicien. At the height of her happiness, however, after the wedding mass, she dies in the arms of her bridegroom. Alienation from reality and coping with disillusion are recurrent themes in Zola's work.

2. Aurier reworked this passage in his "Les isolés: Vincent van Gogh" in the *Mercure de France* of January 1890 to provide the following characterization of van Gogh: "a dreamer, an exalted believer, a devourer of beautiful utopias, who lives on ideas and illusions. For a long time he has taken delight in imagining a renovation of art made possible through a displacement of civilization: an art of tropical regions" (*un rêveur, un croyant exalté, un dévoreur de belles utopies, vivant d'idées et de songes. Longtemps, il s'est complu à imaginer une rénovation d'art, possible par un déplacement de civilisation: un art des régions tropicales*). See Rewald 1978, p. 342 and n. 74.

3. Van Gogh used the plural *miennes,* so Bernard had evidently told him that he had taken two works from the batch that van Gogh had sent. They must have been two of the following three: "red sunset," *Garden with Flowers* (F 578 / JH 1538; Fig. 78), and an unidentified work (see Letter 19, n. 1).

4. Paul Gauguin, *Night Café* (W318/W305; Fig. 93). Van Gogh's painting of Café de la Gare is *The Night Café* (F 463 / JH 1575; Fig. 75).

95. Vincent van Gogh, *The Alyscamps, Avenue at Arles,* 1888 (F 487 / JH 1621). Private collection.

5. The two studies of falling leaves are *The Alyscamps, Avenue at Arles* (F 486 / JH 1620; Fig. 94) and *The Alyscamps, Avenue at Arles* (F 487 / JH 1621; Fig. 95). The "entirely yellow" study was probably *The Alyscamps, Avenue at Arles* (F 568 / JH 1622; Fig. 96). It could also be *The Alyscamps, Avenue at Arles* (F 569 / JH 1623; private collection), although there the yellow is not as dominant.

6. The most recent figural works that van Gogh had made, leaving aside the *Self-Portrait* that he exchanged with Gauguin (F 476 / JH 1581; Fig. 74), dated from September: the portraits of Eugène Boch and Lieutenant Milliet (F 462 / JH 1574; Paris, Musée d'Orsay, and F 473 / JH 1588; Otterlo, Kröller-Müller Museum, respectively).

7. Gauguin had lived on Martinique with Laval from May to November 1887, and in Arles he was making plans to return to the tropics. He finally left for Tahiti on 1 April 1891. See Washington and elsewhere 1988–89, pp. 45, 50, 205.

8. Soon after arriving in Arles, Gauguin bought 20 meters of "very strong canvas" (*toile très forte*), as Vincent informed Theo in letter *CL* 559. It was coarse jute. Van Gogh and Gauguin divided it equally between themselves and worked on it almost exclusively until it was used up in December. For the paintings made on this jute, see Chicago and Amsterdam 2001–2, pp. 354–69.

96. VINCENT VAN GOGH, *The Alyscamps, Avenue at Arles,* 1888 (F 568 / JH 1622). Private collection.

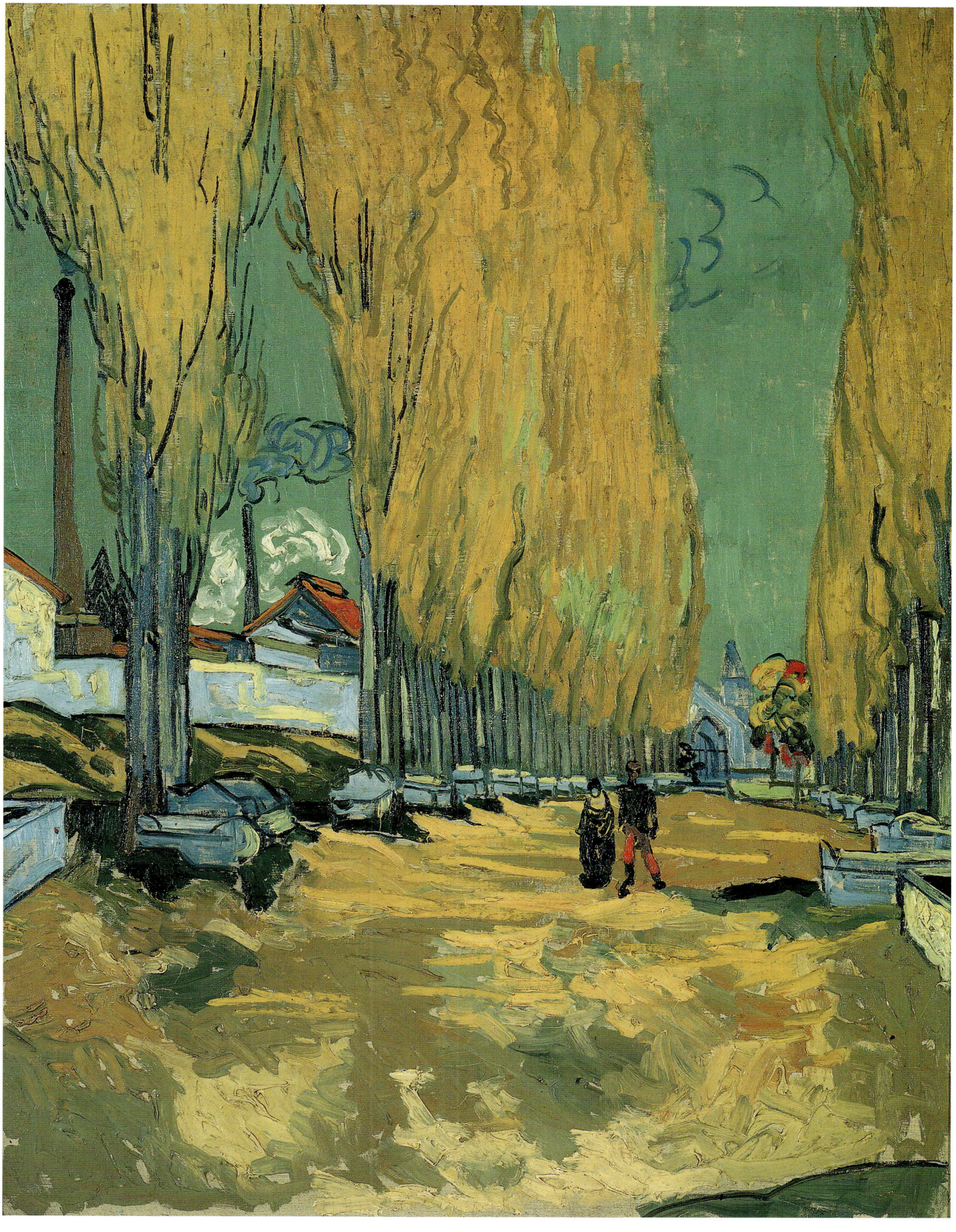

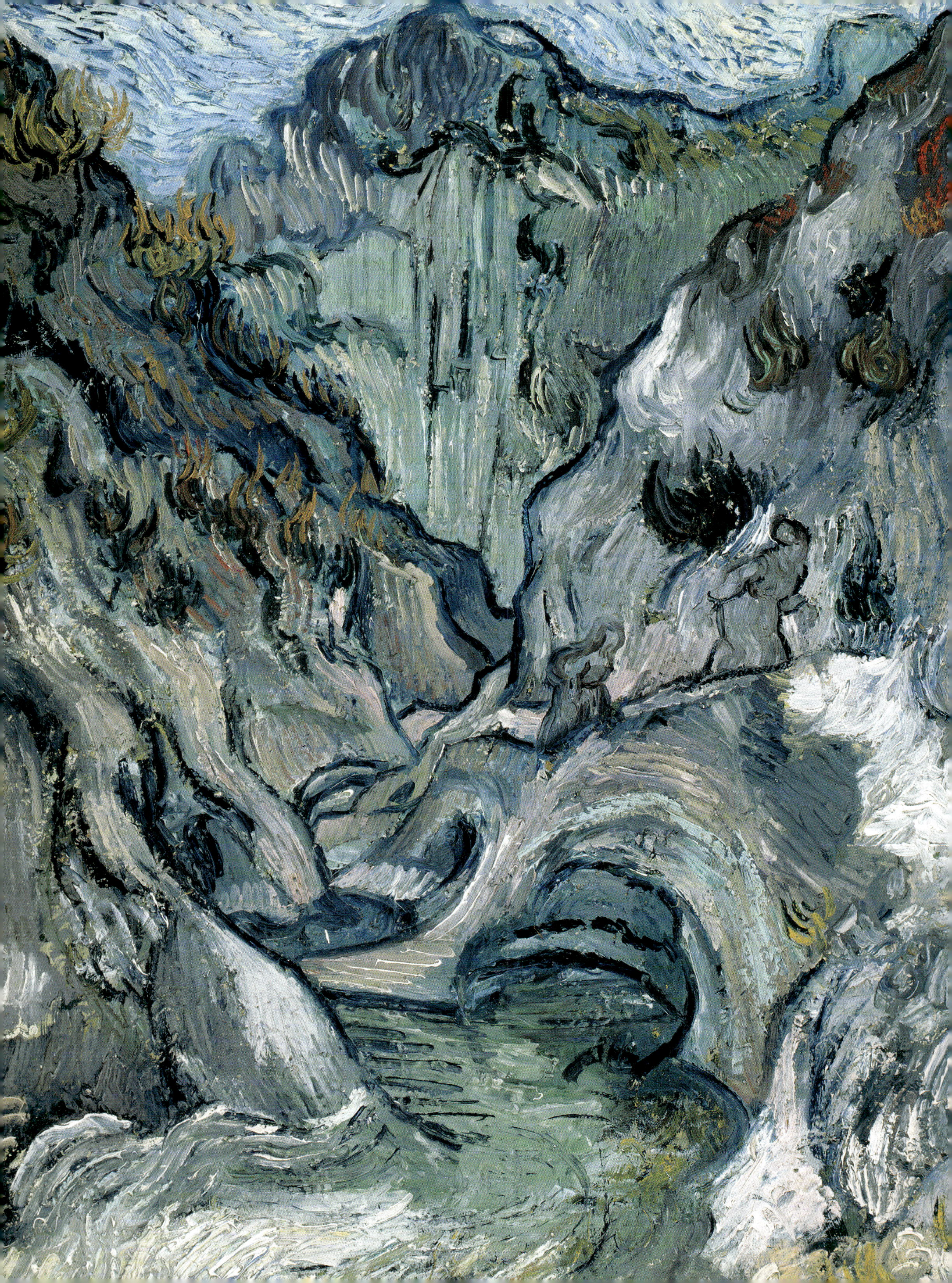

Letter 21

Saint-Rémy, ca. Tuesday, 8 October, 1889

Source
Original manuscript

Location
New York, Thaw Collection, The Morgan Library & Museum

Date
This letter was enclosed with *CL* 610 to Theo, which dates from ca. Tuesday, 8 October, 1889. We have therefore given it the same date.

Additional details
Like the letters to Joseph Isaäcson and Paul Gauguin, this was enclosed with letter *CL* 610 to Theo, who was asked to pass them on at his convenience.

Almost a year had passed since the last letter to Bernard. Van Gogh was now being cared for in the Saint-Paul-de-Mausole asylum in Saint-Rémy-de-Provence, which he had entered voluntarily because of his illness. He was suffering from epilepsy and mental breakdowns.

Van Gogh's first crisis came on 23 December 1888, when he cut off part of his left ear. Gauguin immediately left for Paris, where he told Bernard what had happened. The latter in turn wrote to Albert Aurier on 1 January 1889, giving him a detailed account of the events and expressing his great concern: "My dear friend Vincent is mad. Since I learned that, I'm almost mad myself. [. . .] I have lost my best friend and one of the most wonderful and powerful minds I have known."[1] In the following months van Gogh spent much of the time in the hospital in Arles because of his recurrent attacks.

He occasionally received news of Bernard through Gauguin. In January 1889, for example, the latter wrote to say that Bernard would probably not have to do his military service after all, because his chest was too narrow, and that his father was putting all sorts of obstacles in the way of his painting (letter GAC 35). In February Vincent received news from Bernard himself (*CL* 578), but he asked Theo to tell him that he could not reply. "Tell him to ask Gauguin for advice, but shake his hand firmly from me."[2]

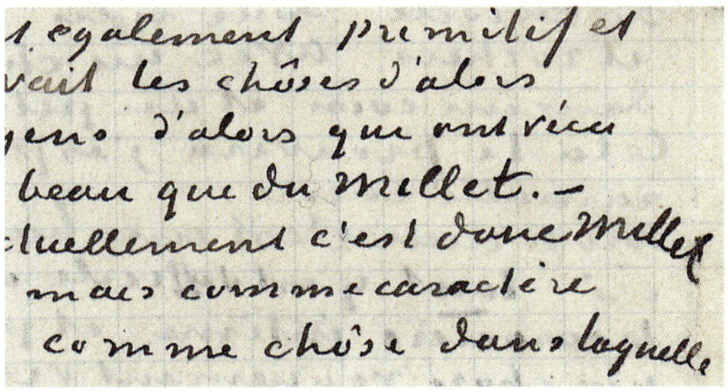
1. egalement primitif et
vait les choses d'alors
gens d'alors qui ont vécu
beau que du millet. –
tuellement c'est donc Millet
mais comme caractère
comme chose dans laquelle

Detail of Fig. 99.

In May he asked Theo to give both Gauguin and Bernard a version of *La Berceuse* as a token of friendship (*CL* 592).

On the occasion of the world's fair, the Groupe Impressionniste et Synthétiste under Gauguin's leadership held an exhibition in Café Volpini from June to October 1889. Bernard and Émile Schuffenecker were closely involved in the preparations and took over the organization when Gauguin left for Brittany at the end of May. Vincent decided not to take part after hearing Theo's criticism of the way it was being mounted. He did, though, defend his friends. "For me it is beyond doubt that Gauguin and Bernard have great and real merit. It remains, however, perfectly understandable that for beings like them, really alive and young, who *must* live and seek to carve out their path, it is impossible to turn all their canvases to face a wall until it pleases people to admit them somewhere, in the official show."[3]

Translation of Letter 21 / Saint-Rémy, ca. Tuesday, 8 October, 1889

My dear friend Bernard,

The other day my brother wrote to me that you[1] were going to come to see my canvases; so I know that you're back, and I'm very pleased that you thought of going to see what I've done.[2]

For my part, I'm extremely curious to know what you have brought back from Pont-Aven.[3]

I hardly have a head for writing, but I feel a great emptiness in no longer being at all up to date with what Gauguin, you and others are doing. But I really must have patience. I have another dozen studies here,[4] which will probably be more to your taste than the ones from this summer that my brother will have shown you.

Among these studies there is an entrance to a quarry, pale lilac rocks in reddish earth, as in certain Japanese drawings.[5] In terms of design and the division of color into large planes, it's quite closely related to what you're doing in Pont-Aven.

I had more control over myself in these latest studies, because my state of health had firmed up. So there's also a no. 30 canvas with broken lilac plowed fields and a background of mountains that go all the way up the canvas; so nothing but rough ground and rocks, with a thistle and dry grass in a corner, and a little violet and yellow man.[6] That will prove, I hope, that I haven't yet gone soft.

Dear God, this is a pretty awful little part of the world, *everything's* hard to do here, to disentangle its intimate character, and so that it's not something vaguely true, but the true soil of Provence. So to achieve that, you have to toil hard. And so it naturally becomes a little abstract.

Transcription of Letter 21 / Saint-Rémy, ca. Tuesday, 8 October, 1889

Mon cher ami Bernard,

l'autre jour mon frère m'a écrit que vous[1] viendriez voir mes toiles, je sais donc que vous êtes de retour et cela me fait bien plaisir que vous ayez pensé à aller voir ce que j'ai fait.[2]

De mon côté je suis extrêmement curieux de savoir ce que vous avez rapporté de Pont Aven.[3]

Je n'ai guère la tête à la correspondence mais je sens un grand vide de ne plus être au courant du tout de ce que Gauguin, vous et d'autres font. Mais faut bien que je prenne patience. J'ai encore une douzaine d'etudes ici[4] qui seront probablement plus de ton gout que celles de cet été que mon frère vous aura montrées.

Il y a parmi ces etudes une entrée de carrière, des rochers lilas pâle dans des terrains rougeâtres comme dans de certains dessins Japonais.[5] Comme dessin et division de la couleur par grands plans cela a pas mal de rapport avec ce que vous faites à Pont Aven.

J'ai été plus maître de moi dans ces dernières études parceque mon état de santé s'était raffermi. Ainsi il y a aussi une toile de 30 avec des terrains labourés lilas rompu et fond de montagnes qui montent tout en haut de la toile, donc rien que des terrains rudes et rochers avec un chardon et herbes sèches dans un coin et un petit homme violet et jaune.[6] Cela te prouvera j'espère que je ne suis pas ramolli encore.

Mon dieu c'est un bien mauvais petit pays ici, tout *y est difficile à faire, pour demêler le caractère intime et pour que cela ne soit pas une chose vaguement vraie, mais du vrai sol de Provence. Alors pour arriver à cela c'est qu'il faut labourer dur. Et alors ça devient naturellement un peu abstrait. Car*

Because it will be a question of giving strength and brilliance to the sun and the blue sky, and to the scorched and often so melancholy fields their delicate scent of thyme. The olive trees down here, my good fellow, they'd suit your book; I haven't been fortunate this year in making a success of them, but I'll go back to it, that's my intention. It's silver against orangish or purplish earth, under the great blue sky. Well now, I've seen some by certain painters, and by myself, which didn't render the thing at all. Those silver grays are like Corot first of all, and that, above all, hasn't been done yet—while several artists have been successful with apple-trees, for example, and willows.

So there are relatively few paintings of vineyards, which are nevertheless of such changing beauty. So there's still plenty for me to fiddle around with here.

Look here, what I very much regret not having seen at the Exhibition is a series of houses of all the nations;[7] I think it was Garnier or Viollet-le-Duc who organized it. Well, could you, who will have seen it, give me an idea, and especially a sketch with the color of the primitive Egyptian house? It must be very simple, a square block, I believe, on a terrace—but I should like to know the coloring too. I was reading in an article that it was blue, red and yellow.[8]

Did you pay attention to it? Please inform me without fail! And it must not be confused with the Persian or the Moroccan; there must be some that are more or less it, but not it.

Anyway, for me the most wonderful thing that I know in terms of architecture is the cottage with a mossy thatched roof, with its blackened hearth. So I'm very fussy. I saw a sketch of ancient Mexican houses in an illustrated magazine; that, too, seemed primitive and really beautiful. Ah, if only one knew the things of those days, and if one could paint the people of those days who lived in them—it would be as beautiful as Millet. Anyway, what we do know that's solid these days, then,

---

il s'agira de donner au soleil et au ciel bleu sa force et son eclat, aux terrains brulés et si melancoliques souvent, leur fin arome de thym. Les oliviers d'ici, mon bon, ca ferait votre affaire, j'ai pas eu de chance cette annee pour les reussir mais j'y reviendrai à ce que je me propose. C'est de l'argent sur terrain orangeatre ou violacé sous le grand ciel bleu. J'en ai ma foi vu, de certains peintres et de moi-même, qui ne rendaient pas du tout la chôse.—C'est comme du Corot d'abord ces gris argent, et surtout cela n'a pas encore été fait—tandis que plusieurs artistes ont reussi les pommiers par exemple et les saules.

Ainsi il y a relativement peu de tableaux representant les vignes qui pourtant sont d'une beauté si changeante. Il y a donc encore assez à tripoter ici pour moi.

Dites donc, ce que je regrette beaucoup de ne pas avoir vu à l'exposition c'est une serie d'habitations de tous les peuples,[7] je crois que c'est Garnier ou Violet le Duc qui ont organisé cela. Eh bien pourriez vous, qui l'aurez vu, me donner une idée et surtout un croquis avec la couleur de la maison Egyptienne primitive?—Ça doit être fort simple, un bloc carré je crois sur une terrasse—mais je voudrais savoir la coloration aussi.—Dans un article je lisais que c'etait bleu, rouge et jaune.[8]

Avez vous fait attention à cela? Prière de me renseigner sans faute! Et faut pas confondre avec le Persan ou le marocain, il doit y en avoir qui sont à peu près cela mais pas cela.—

Enfin pour moi en fait d'architecture ce que je connais de plus admirable c'est la chaumière au toit de chaume moussu avec son foyer noirci. Je suis donc très difficile.—J'ai vu un croquis dans une illustration des habitations anciennes mexicaines, cela paraît egalement primitif et bien beau. Ah si on savait les chôses d'alors et si on pouvait peindre les gens d'alors qui ont vécu là-dedans—ce serait aussi beau que du Millet.—Enfin ce qu'on sait de solide actuellement c'est donc Millet, je ne dis pas pour la couleur—mais comme caractère, comme chôse significative, comme chôse dans laquelle on a foi solide.—

is Millet; I'm not talking about color—but as character, as something significant, as something in which one has solid faith.

Now, about your service; will you go? I hope you'll go to see my canvases again when I send the studies of autumn, in November. And if possible let me know what you've brought back from Brittany, because I'd really like to know what you yourself believe to be your best things. So I'll write again soon.

I'm working on a large canvas of a ravine; it's a subject just like the study with a yellow tree that I still have from you,[9] two bases of extremely solid rocks, between which a trickle of water flows, a third mountain that closes off the ravine.[10] These motifs certainly have a beautiful melancholy, and it's enjoyable to work in really wild sites where you have to bury your easel in the stones so that the wind doesn't send everything flying to the ground.

Handshake.

Yours,
Vincent

---

maintenant pour ton service est ce que vous partirez? J'espère que vous irez voir mes toiles de nouveau lorsque j'enverrai en Novembre les études d'automne. Et si possible faites moi savoir ce que vous avez rapporté de Bretagne car je tiens à savoir ce que vous croyez vos meilleures chôses vous-même. Alors bientôt j'ecris de nouveau.

Je travaille à une grande toile d'un ravin, c'est un motif tout à fait comme l'etude avec un arbre jaune que j'ai encore de vous,[9] *deux bases de rochers excessivement solides entre lesquels coule un filet d'eau, une troisieme montagne qui ferme le ravin.*[10] *Ces motifs ont certes une belle melancolie, puis cela est amusant de travailler dans des sites bien sauvages où il faut enterrer le chevalet dans les pierres pour que le vent ne vous fiche pas tout par terre.*

Poignée de main.

b. à. t.
Vincent

---

97. Vincent van Gogh, *Entrance to a Quarry,* 1889 (F 635 / JH 1767). Private collection.

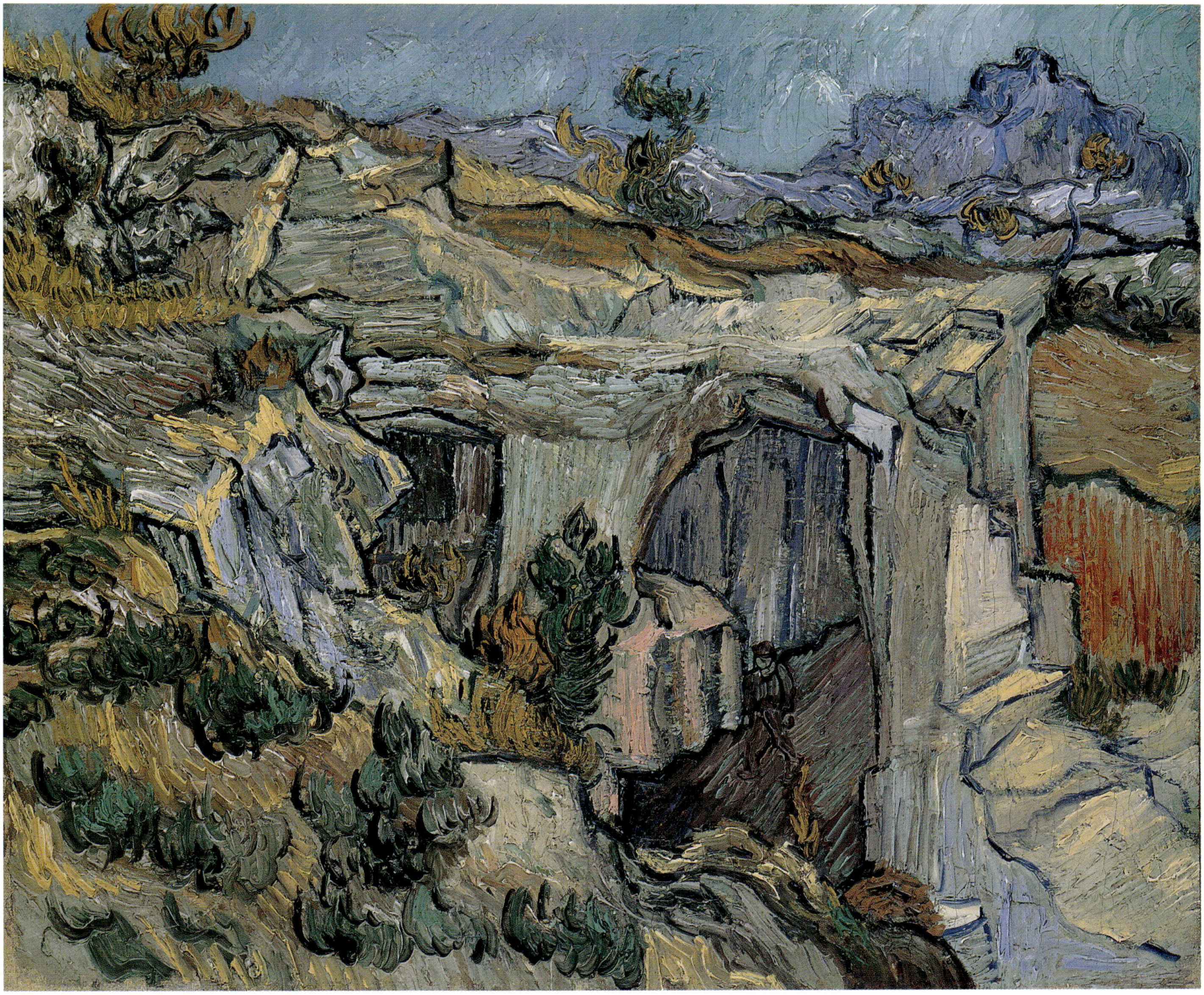

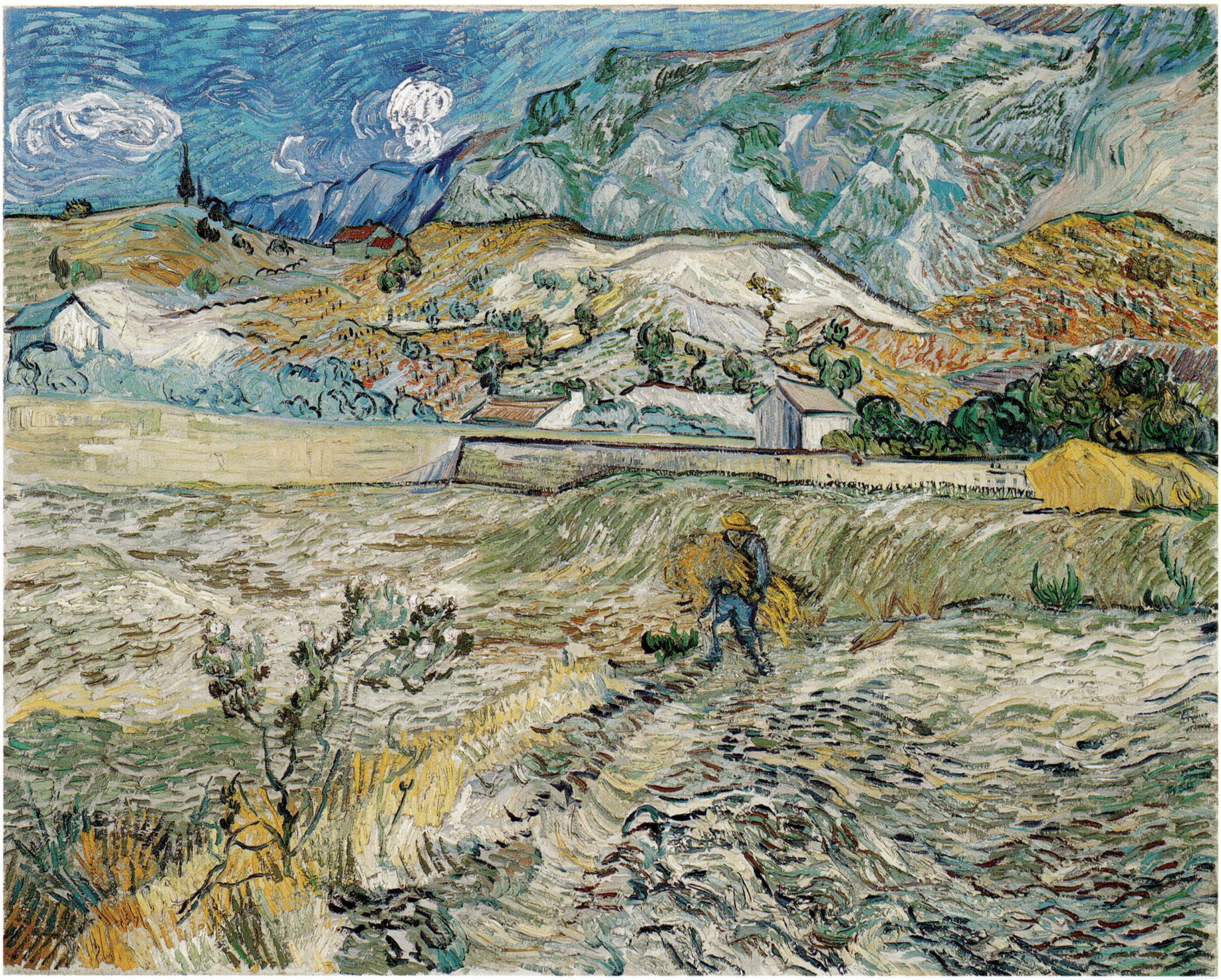

Annotations to Letter 21

Saint-Rémy, ca. Tuesday, 8 October, 1889

1. It is noteworthy that van Gogh now occasionally addressed his "pal" Bernard with the formal *vous.* In all his previous letters he used the familiar *tu.* See also additional details of Letter 22.

2. Theo had announced on 4 October that Bernard was coming to look at Vincent's paintings (letter *CL* T18). That same month, incidentally, Bernard wrote to Theo saying that he was very short of money and asked if he could perhaps work at Boussod, Valadon & Cie., "to retouch photo-engraving or some other procedure taking place" (*pour retoucher de la photogravure ou autre procédé en cours;* Amsterdam, Van Gogh Museum, inv. no. b827).

   Since van Gogh spoke of "the ones from this summer" in the present letter, he must have been referring to the paintings that he sent Theo from Saint-Rémy at the end of September. That consignment contained eight works he had painted in the summer: *Self-Portrait* (F 627 / JH 1772; Paris, Musée d'Orsay), *Olive Trees in a Mountain Landscape* (F 712 / JH 1740; New York, Museum of Modern Art), *Mountains with Dark Hut* (F 622 / JH 1766; New York, Guggenheim Museum), *Mountain Landscape Seen Across the Walls* (F 611 / JH 1723; Copenhagen, Ny Carlsberg Glyptotek), "olive trees," which was probably *Olive Grove* (F 715 / JH 1759; Kansas, Nelson-Atkins Museum of Fine Art), *Orchard and House with Red Roof* (F 511 / JH 1386; Amsterdam, Van Gogh Museum), *Entrance to a Quarry* (F 744 / JH 1802; Amsterdam, Van Gogh Museum) and a "study of flowers," possibly *The Iris* (F 601 / JH 1699; Ottawa, National Gallery of Canada).

3. Bernard had spent some time in Saint-Briac during the summer of 1889. He did not go to Pont-Aven, where Gauguin was staying. Bernard's father thought that Gauguin had a bad influence on his son and forbade any contact between them. Gauguin alluded to this in a letter to Bernard of August 1889: "I thought you were in Paris and you're at Saint-Briac on your father's orders, inasmuch as you're forbidden to come to Pont-Aven" (*je vous croyais à Paris et vous êtes à St-Briac par ordre de votre père en tant qu'il vous est défendu de venir à Pont-Aven*). See *Gauguin lettres* 1946, p. 162.

4. In addition to the three studies that van Gogh described in this letter (see nn. 5–6, 10), the recent studies included *Mulberry Tree* (F 637 / JH 1796; Pasadena, The Norton Simon Museum), *Two Poplars with a Background of Mountains* (F 638 / JH 1797; Cleveland Museum of Art), *Trees in the Garden of the Asylum* (F 642 / JH 1798; private collection), *Trees in Front of the Entrance to the Asylum* (F 643 / JH 1799; Los Angeles, Armand Hammer Museum) and *Woman with a Baby, Sitting at the Fireside* (F 644 / JH 1805; private collection). *Trees in the Garden of the Asylum* (F 640 / JH 1800; private collection) and *Trees in the Garden of the Asylum* (F 730 / JH 1841; private collection) were probably also included.

98. Vincent van Gogh, *Enclosed Field with Farmer Carrying a Bundle of Straw,* 1889 (F 641 / JH 1795). Indianapolis Museum of Art.

5. *Entrance to a Quarry* (F 635 / JH 1767; Fig. 97).

6. *Enclosed Field with Farmer Carrying a Bundle of Straw* (F 641 / JH 1795; Fig. 98).

7. The world's fair was held in Paris from 5 May to 5 November 1889. Charles Garnier (not Eugène-Emmanuel Viollet-le-Duc) built a street of thirty-nine dwellings that ran from Champ de Mars to Trocadéro. Each house or hut represented a culture and a stage in residential history from prehistoric to modern times. The homes were built almost at full size with authentic materials. This section of the fair (*Dessins et modèles d'architecture*) was titled *Histoire de l'habitation.* See Paris 1889, p. 104, and Paul Greenhalgh, *Ephemeral Vistas: The Expositions Universelles, Great Exhibitions and World's Fairs, 1851–1939,* Manchester 1988, p. 20.

8. The illustrated magazines devoted a lot of space to the *Histoire de l'habitation,* so it is impossible to identify the article from which van Gogh got his information about the Egyptian house. The sketch of Mexican houses that he mentioned a little further on was not in *L'Illustration,* in any event.

9. Bernard's *Yellow Tree* (Rennes, Musée des Beaux-Arts) matches this description and is accordingly often dated to 1888. However, it is dated ca. 1892 on stylistic grounds in Mannheim and Amsterdam 1990, p. 136. If that is correct, it is not clear which painting this could have been.

10. *A Path Through the Ravine* (F 662 / JH 1804; Fig. 99), which measures 28⅞ x 36¼ in. (73 x 92 cm). Gauguin and Bernard saw the painting at the Indépendants show in Paris in March 1890. Gauguin was so impressed that he wanted to make an exchange with van Gogh for it (letter GAC 40).

---

99. Vincent van Gogh, *A Path Through the Ravine,* 1889 (F 662 / JH 1804). Boston, Museum of Fine Arts.

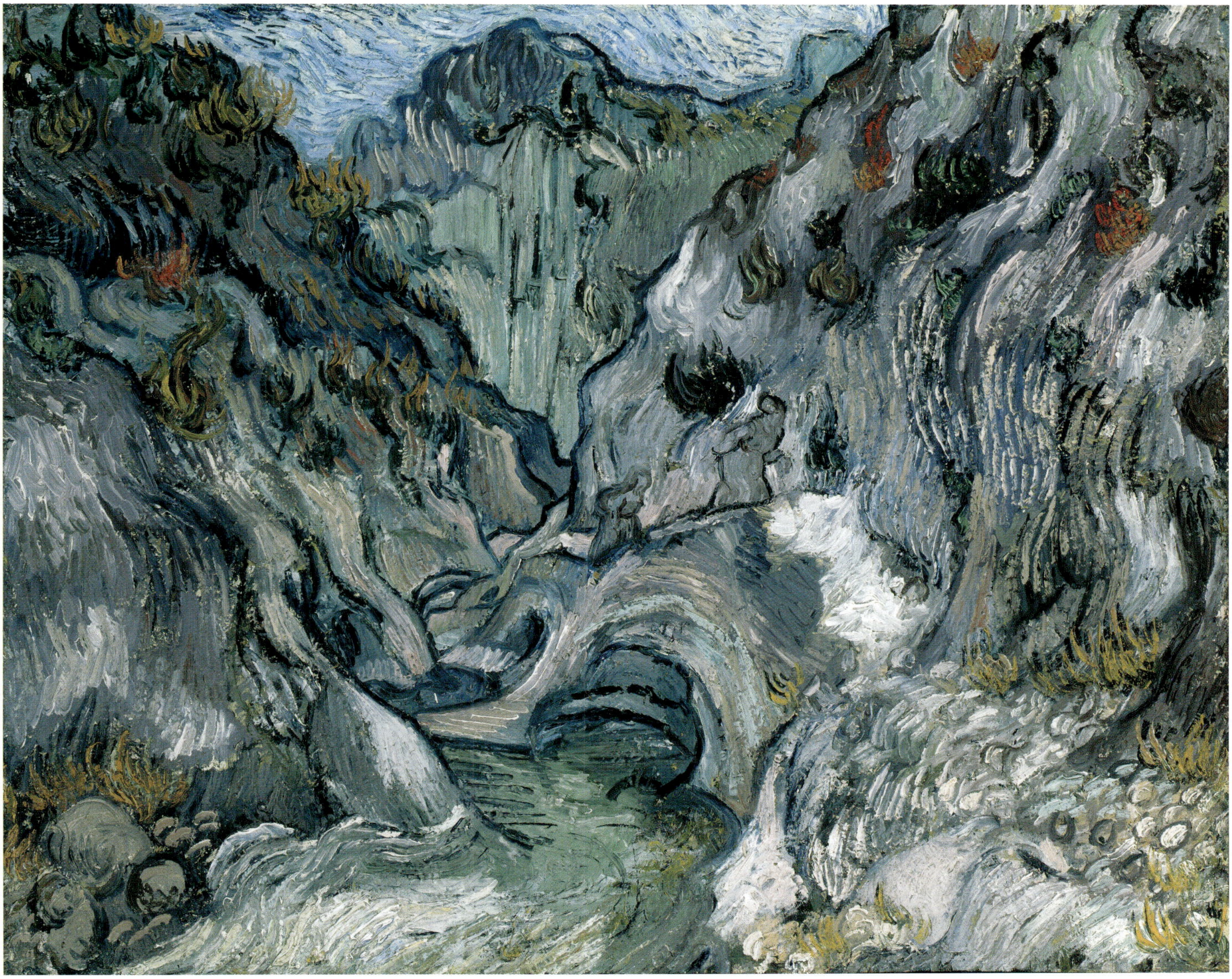

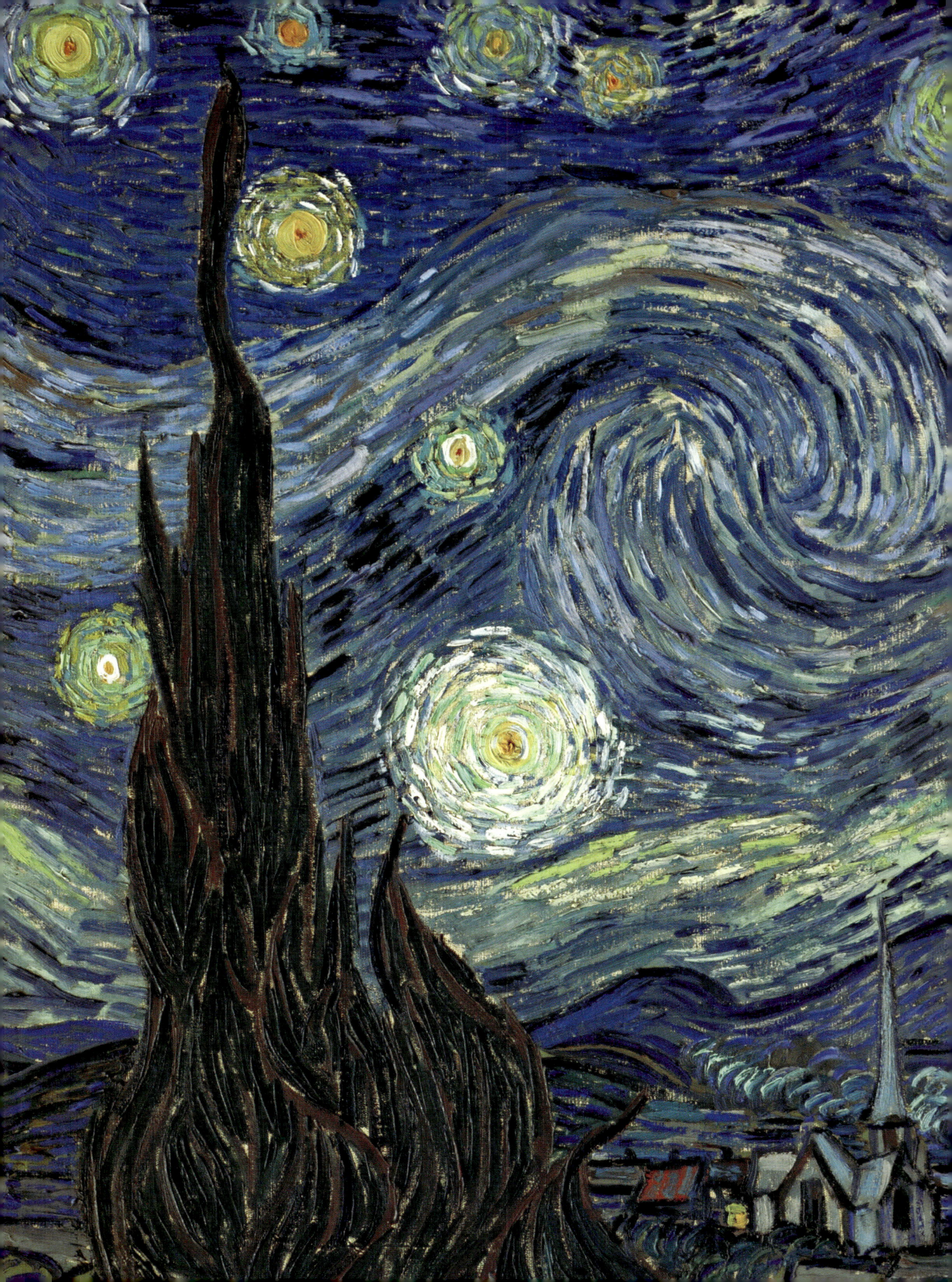

Letter 22

Saint-Rémy, ca. Tuesday, 26 November, 1889

Source
Original manuscript

Location
New York, Thaw Collection, The Morgan Library & Museum

Date
Van Gogh reported that he had finished five no. 30 canvases of olive groves. He wrote the same in letter *CL* 615 to Theo, which dates from 26 November 1889, so we have assumed that the present letter was written around the same time, in other words, ca. Tuesday, 26 November, 1889.

Sketches
1. *Reclining Girl,* after Émile Bernard, *Madeleine in the Bois d'Amour* (F - / JH -), letter sketch
2. *Three Trees,* after Émile Bernard, *Red Poplars* (F - / JH -), letter sketch

Additional details
Bernard wrote the following note to accompany this letter in the Vollard edition: "This letter, the last I received from Vincent, was written after a long silence explained by his state of health. One will notice the oddity in it of the mixture of *tu* and *vous* in the sentences." (*Cette lettre, la dernière que je reçus de Vincent, me fut écrite après un long silence motivé par son état de santé. On y remarquera l'étrangeté de ces* tu *et de ces* vous *mêlés aux phrases*). See *Lettres à Bernard* 1911, p. 143.

This strongly worded letter brought an end to the correspondence between van Gogh and Bernard. Van Gogh's cutting remarks about Bernard's *Christ in the Garden of Olives* (Fig. 106), among others, must have contributed to the estrangement. Nor did he approve of Gauguin's painting of the same subject (West Palm Beach, Norton Gallery and School of Fine Art; W326), of which he had received a sketch. As it happens, van Gogh had himself made unsuccessful attempts to depict the same subject in Arles (Letter 19).

In the letter to which this is the reply, Bernard must have written frankly about the awkward position he was in at home. "Bernard also wrote to me, complaining about a heap of things while resigning himself like the good boy he is, but not happy at all; with all his talent, all his work, all his sobriety, it appears that home is often a hell for him."[1]

Even before receiving photographs of Bernard's recent paintings, Vincent doubted that he would like them, having heard what Theo had to say: "I don't know, but I fear that his biblical compositions will make me wish for something else." Van Gogh himself opted to paint not Christ in the Garden of

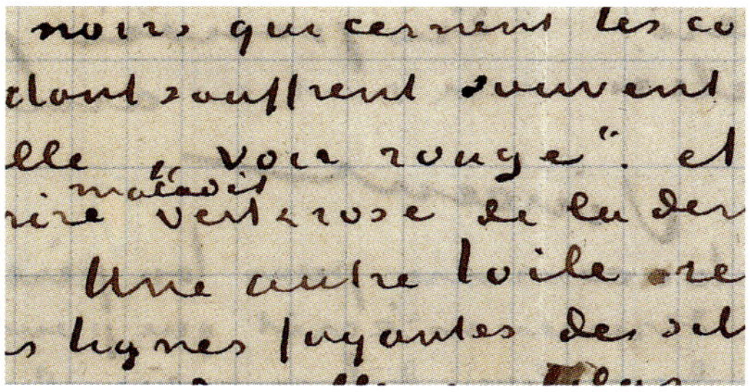
noirs qui cernent les co
dont souffrent souvent
lle "voix rouge". et
rire vert rose de la der
Une autre toile re
s lignes fuyantes des sol

Olives but olive picking as it was done in Saint-Rémy, "and then, nevertheless, giving the correct proportions of the human figure in it, that would perhaps make people think of it."[2]

The old discussion about painting from life or from the imagination and about the relationship between realism and religious scenes, was thus still going on. Van Gogh had experimented with abstraction a year previously, but now he firmly rejected it. To put it in his own words, he had "matured in the storm (*CL* 544)."

Detail of Fig. 110.

Translation of Letter 22 / Saint-Rémy, ca. Tuesday, 26 November, 1889

My dear friend Bernard,

Thank you for your letter, and thank you especially for your photos, which give me an idea of your work.[1]

Incidentally, my brother wrote to me about it the other day, saying that he very much liked the harmoniousness of the color, a certain nobility in several figures.[2]

Look, in the adoration of the shepherds, the landscape charms me too much for me to dare to criticize, and nevertheless, it's too great an impossibility to imagine a birth like that, on the very road, the mother who starts praying instead of giving suck, the fat ecclesiastical bigwigs, kneeling as if in an epileptic fit, God knows how or why they're there,[3] but I myself don't find it healthy.

Because I adore the true, the possible, were I ever capable of spiritual fervor; so I bow before that study, so powerful that it makes you tremble, by *père* Millet—peasants carrying to the farmhouse a calf born in the fields.[4] Now, my friend—people have felt that from France to America. After that, would you go back to renewing medieval tapestries for us? Truly, is this a sincere conviction? No, you can do better than that, and you know that one has to look for the possible, the logical, the true, even if to some extent you had to forget Parisian things à la Baudelaire. How I prefer Daumier to that gentleman!

An annunciation of what———I see figures of angels, elegant, my word, a terrace with two cypresses, which I like very much; there's an enormous amount of air, of clarity in it. . . . [5] but in the end, once this first impression is past, I wonder if it's a mystification, and these secondary characters

---

Transcription of Letter 22 / Saint-Rémy, ca. Tuesday, 26 November, 1889

Mon cher ami Bernard,

merci de ta lettre et surtout merci de vos photos qui me donnent une idée de vos travaux.[1]

Mon frère d'ailleurs m'a l'autre jour écrit là-dessus, disant qu'il aimait beaucoup l'harmonieux de la couleur, une certaine noblesse dans plusieurs figures.—[2]

Tenez, dans l'adoration des bergers le paysage me charme trop pour oser critiquer et néamoins, c'est trop fort comme impossibilité de supposer un enfantement comme ça sur la route même, la mère qui se met à prier au lieu de donner à têter, les grosses grenouilles éclesiastiques agenouillés comme dans une crise d'épileptiques sont là dieu sait comment et pourquoi,[3] *mais je ne trouve pas ça sain moi.*

Parceque moi j'adore le vrai, le possible, si toutefois je sois capable d'un élan spirituel; et alors m'incline devant cette étude, forte à faire trembler, du père Millet—les paysans qui portent à la ferme un veau né dans les champs.—[4] *Or—mon ami—cela depuis en France jusqu'en Amérique les gens l'ont*[a] *senti. Apres cela viendrez vous nous renouveler les tapisseries moyen âge? Vraiment est ce une conviction sincère? NON, vous savez mieux faire que ça et vous le savez qu'il faut chercher le possible, le logique, le vrai, dussiez vous un peu oublier les chôses parisiennes à la Baudelaire. Comme je préfère Daumier à ce monsieur-là!*

Une annonciation de quoi———je vois des figures d'anges ma foi élégantes, une terrasse avec deux cyprès que j'aime beaucoup, il y a là énormement d'air, de clarté. . . . [5] *mais enfin, cette première impression passée je me demande si c'est une mystification et ces figurantes ne me disent plus rien.—*

Mais suffit pour que tu comprennes que je soupirerais de savoir de toi des choses comme le tableau

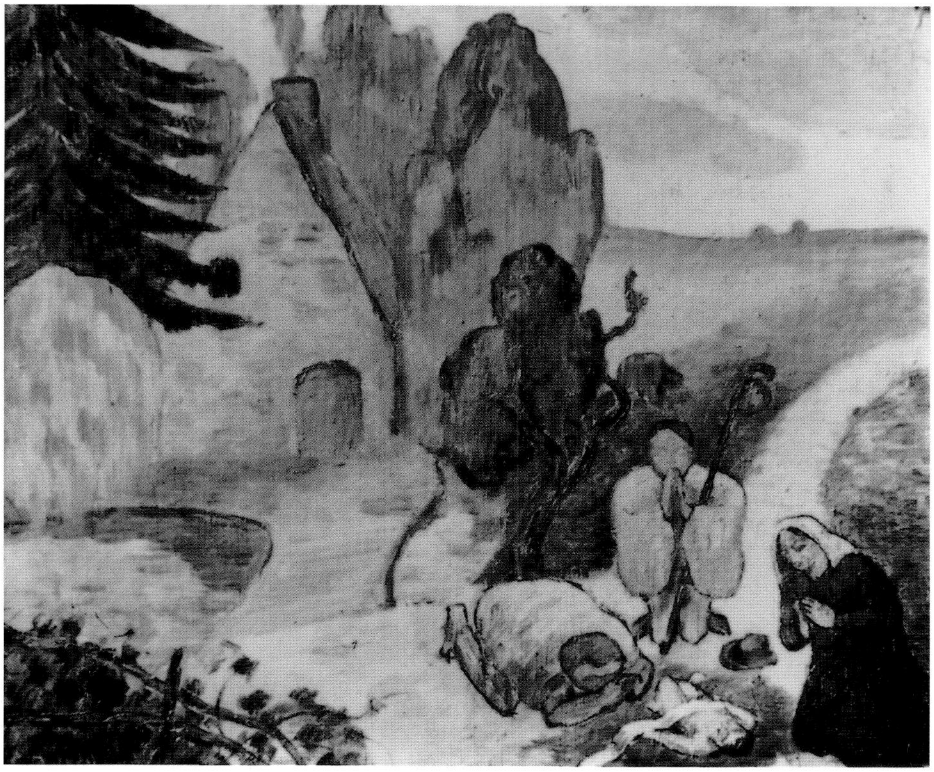

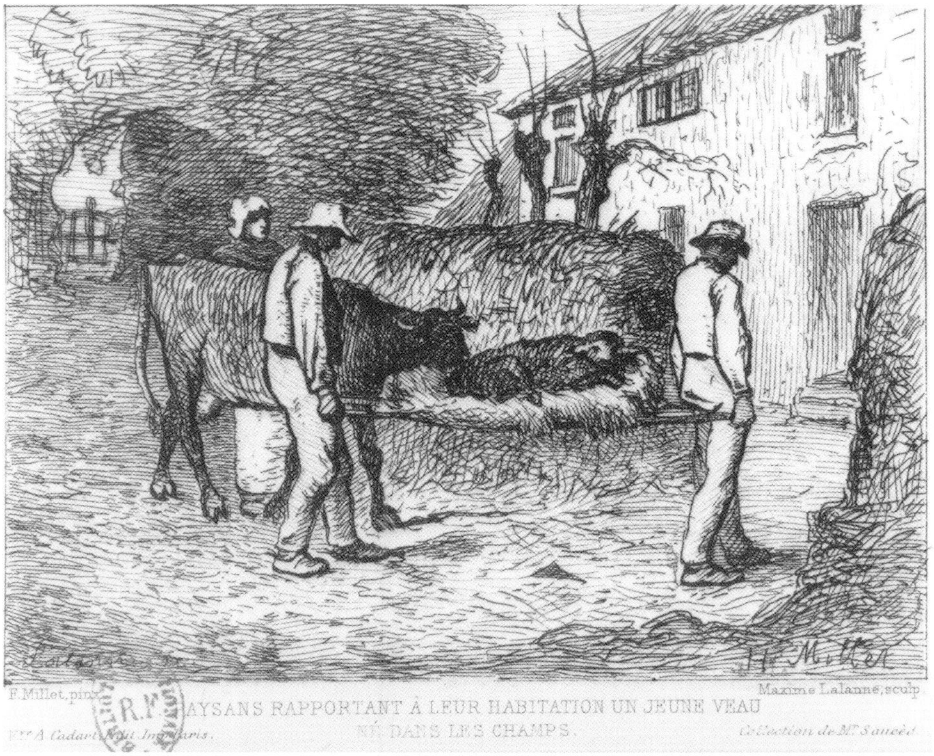

100. Émile Bernard, *The Adoration of the Shepherds,* 1889. Private collection.

101. Jean-François Millet, *Birth of the Calf.* Engraved by M. Lalanne. Published in Alexandre Piedagnel, *J.-F. Millet: Souvenirs de Barbizon.* Paris, 1876.

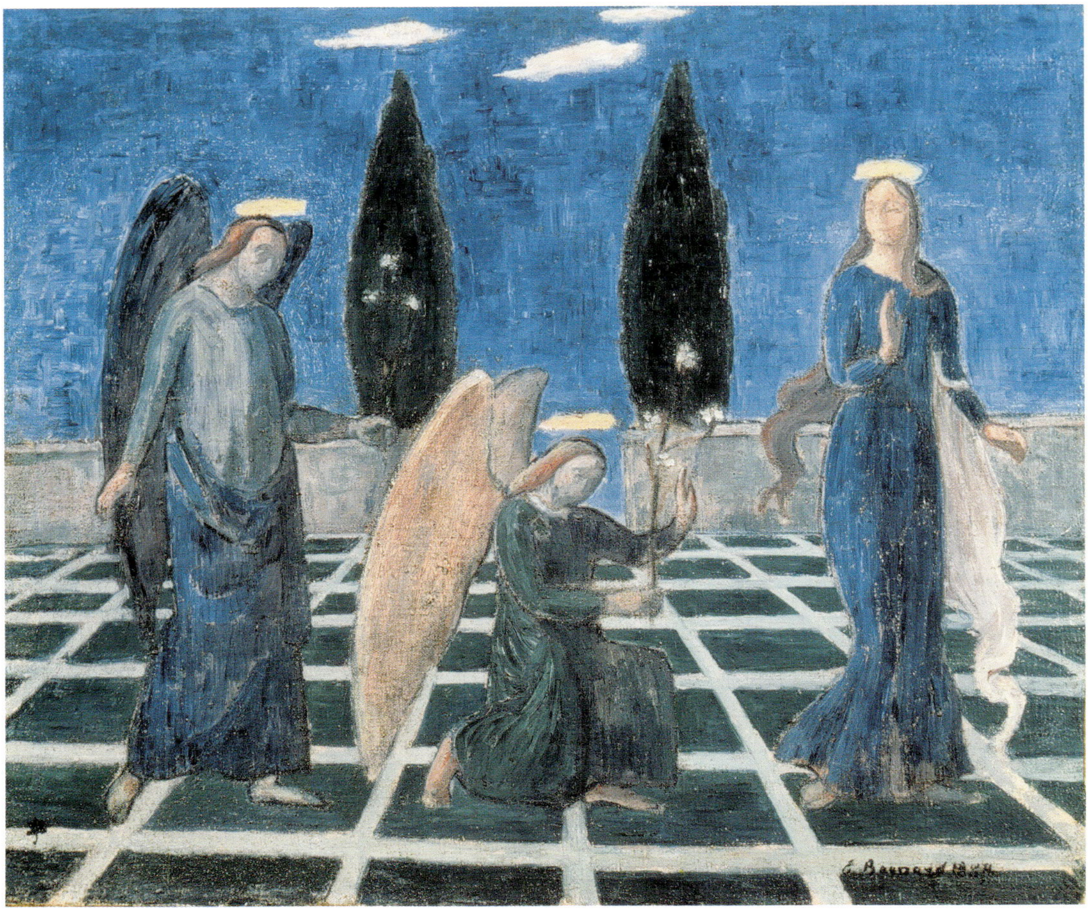

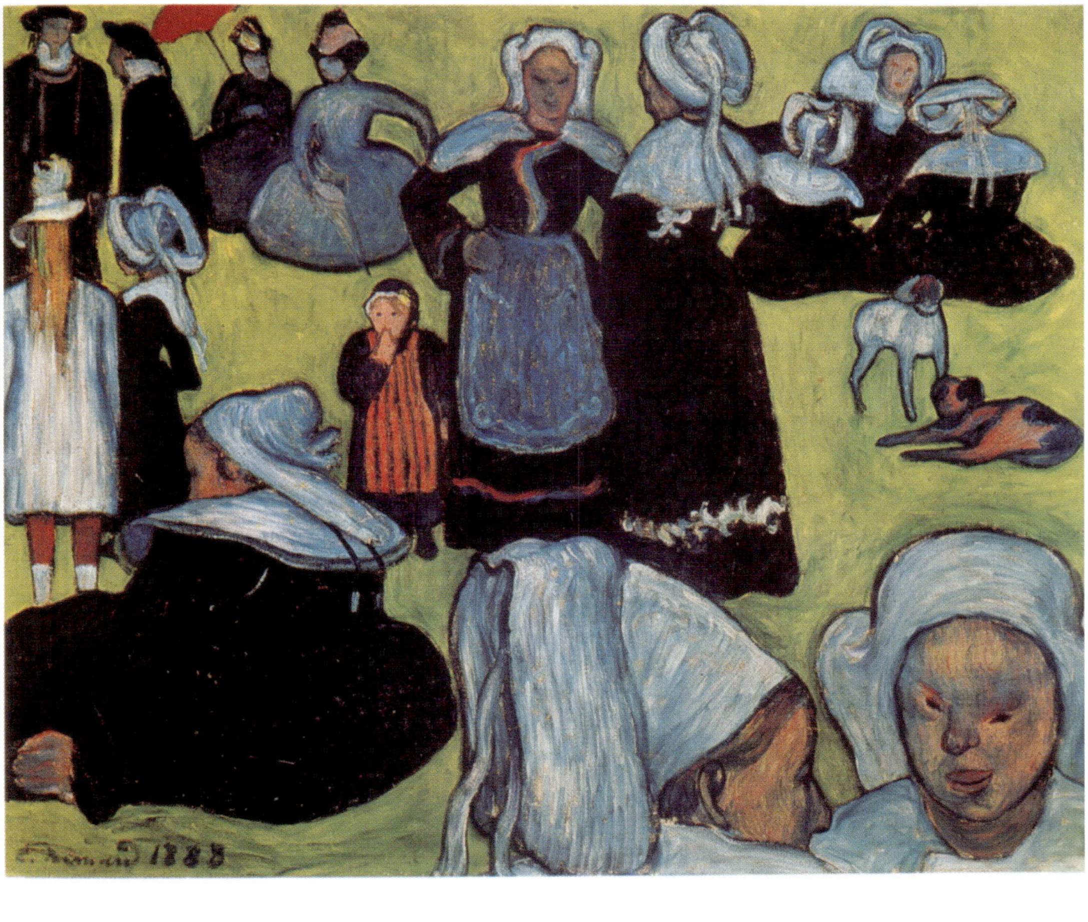

no longer tell me anything.

But this is enough for you to understand that I was longing to get to know things from you like the painting of yours that Gauguin has, those Breton women walking in a meadow,[6] the arrangement of which is so beautiful, the color so naively distinguished. Ah, you're exchanging that for something—must one say the word—something artificial—something affected.

Last year, from what Gauguin was telling me, you were doing a painting more or less like this, I imagine.[7] *[sketch]* Against a foreground of grass, a figure of a young girl in a blue or white dress, lying full length. Behind that: edge of a beech wood, the ground covered in fallen red leaves, the verdigrised trunks crossing it vertically—I imagine the hair a colorful note in the tone required as complementary to the white dress: black if the clothing was white, orange if the clothing was blue. But anyway, I said to myself, what a simple subject, and how he knows how to create elegance with nothing.[8]

Gauguin spoke to me of another subject, nothing but three trees, thus the effect of orange foliage against blue sky, but still really clearly delineated, well divided, categorically, into planes of contrasting and pure colors—that's the spirit![9] *[sketch]* And when I compare that with that nightmare of a Christ in the Garden of Olives,[10] well, it makes me feel sad, and I herewith ask you again, crying out loud and giving you a good rocket with all the power of my lungs, to please become a little more yourself again.

The Christ Carrying His Cross is atrocious.[11] Are the splashes of color in it harmonious? But I will not let you off the hook for a COMMONPLACE—commonplace, you hear—in the composition.

When Gauguin was in Arles, I once or twice allowed myself to be led into abstraction, as you

---

qu'a de toi Gauguin, cette promenade de Bretonnes dans une prairie[6] *d'une si belle ordonnance, d'une couleur si naivement distinguée. Eh, tu échanges cela contre du—faut il dire le mot—du factice—de l'affection.—*

l'année passée vous faisiez un tableau d'après ce que me disait Gauguin à peu près je suppose ainsi.[7] [sketch] *Sur un avant plan d'herbe une figure de jeune fille en robe bleue ou blanche etendue tout de son long. Un second plan—lisière de bois de hêtre, le sol couvert de feuilles rouges tombées, les troncs vert de grisés le barrant verticalement—la chevelure je la suppose une note colorée du ton necessité comme complementaire de la robe blanche, noire si le vetement etait blanc, orangée si le vetement etait bleu.— Mais enfin, je me disais, quel motif simple et comme il sait faire de l'elegance avec rien.—*[8]

Gauguin me parla d'un autre motif, rien que trois arbres, ainsi effet de feuillage orangé contre ciel bleu mais encore bien nettement delinéé, bien divisé cathegoriquement en plans de couleurs opposées et franches—à la bonne heure.—[9] [sketch] *Et lorsque je compare cela à ce cauchemar d'un christ au jardin des oliviers,*[10] *ma foi je m'en sens*[b] *triste et te redemande par la présente à hauts cris et t'engeulant ferme de toute la force de mes poumons de vouloir bien un peu redevenir toi.—*

Le christ portant sa croix est atroce.[11] *Sont elles harmonieuses, les tâches de couleur là-dedans? je ne te fais pas grace cependant d'un* PONCIF*—tiens poncif—dans la composition.*

Lorsque Gauguin était à Arles, comme tu le sais une ou deux fois je me suis laissé aller à une abstraction, dans la berceuse, une liseuse de romans noire dans une bibliotheque jaune,[12] *et alors l'abstraction me paraissait une voie charmante. Mais c'est terrain enchanté*[13] *ça—mon bon—et vite on*

---

102. ÉMILE BERNARD, *The Annunciation*, 1889. Private collection.

103. ÉMILE BERNARD, *Breton Women in the Meadow*, 1888. Private collection.

know, in a woman rocking a cradle, a dark woman reading novels in a yellow library,[12] and at that time abstraction seemed an attractive route to me. But that's enchanted ground,[13]—my good fellow—and one soon finds oneself up against a wall. I'm not saying that one may not take the risk after a whole manly life of searching, of fighting hand-to-hand with reality, but as far as I'm concerned I do not want to rack my brains over that sort of thing. And the whole year, have fiddled around from life, hardly thinking of impressionism or of this or that.

However, once again I'm allowing myself to do stars too big, etc., new setback, and I've enough of that.[14]

So at present am working in the olive trees, seeking the different effects of a gray sky against yellow earth, with dark green note of the foliage; another time the earth and foliage all purplish against yellow sky, then red ocher earth and pink and green sky.[15] See, that interests me more than the so-called abstractions.

And if I haven't written for a long time, it's because, having to struggle against my illness and to calm my head, I hardly felt like having discussions, and found danger in these abstractions. And by working very calmly, beautiful subjects will come of their own accord; it's truly first and foremost a question of immersing oneself in reality again, with no plan made in advance, with no Parisian bias. Besides, am very dissatisfied with this year, but perhaps it will prove a solid foundation for the coming one. I have let myself become thoroughly imbued with the air of the small mountains and the orchards. With that, I'll see. My ambition is truly limited to a few clods of earth, some sprouting wheat. An olive grove. A cypress; the latter not easy to do, for example. You who love the primitives, who study them, I ask you why you appear not to know Giotto. Gauguin and I

---

se trouve devant un mur.—Je ne dis pas, après toute une vie mâle de recherches, de lutte avec la nature corps à corps, on peut s'y risquer mais quant à moi je ne veux pas me creuser la tête avec ces chôses-là. Et toute l'année ai tripoté d'après nature ne songeant guère à l'impressionisme ni à ceci ni à cela.

Cependant encore une fois je me laisse aller à faire des étoiles trop grande &c., nouvel echec et j'en ai assez.[14]

Donc actuellement travaille dans les oliviers cherchant les effets variés d'un ciel gris contre terrain jaune avec note vert noir[c] *du feuillage, une autre fois le terrain et feuillage tout violacé contre ciel jaune, puis terrain ocre rouge et ciel rose & vert.—*[15] *Va, ca m'intéresse davantage que les abstractions ainsi nommés.*[d]

Et si je n'ai pas écrit depuis longtemps, c'est qu'ayant à lutter contre ma maladie et à calmer ma tête je ne me sentais guère envie de discuter et trouvais du danger à ces abstractions. Et en travaillant tout tranquillement les beaux sujets viendront tout seuls, il s'agit vraiment surtout de bien se retremper dans la realité sans plan conçu d'avance, sans parti pris parisien. Suis d'ailleurs fort mecontent de cette année mais peutêtre prouvera-t-elle un fondement solide pour la prochaine. Je me suis bien laissé pénétrer par l'air des petites montagnes et des vergers.—Avec ça je verrai. Mon ambition se borne bien à quelques mottes de terre, du blé qui germe. Un verger d'oliviers. Un cyprès, le dernier par exemple pas commode à faire. Toi qui aimes les primitifs, qui les étudie, je te le demande, pourquoi tu sembles ne pas connaitre Giotto.—Gauguin et moi avons encore vu un tout petit panneau de lui à Montpellier, la mort d'une bonne sainte femme quelquonque.[16] *là les expressions de douleur & d'extase sont*

---

104. Émile Bernard, *Madeleine in the Bois d'Amour,* 1888. Paris, Musée d'Orsay.
105. Émile Bernard, *Red Poplars,* 1887. Present whereabouts unknown.

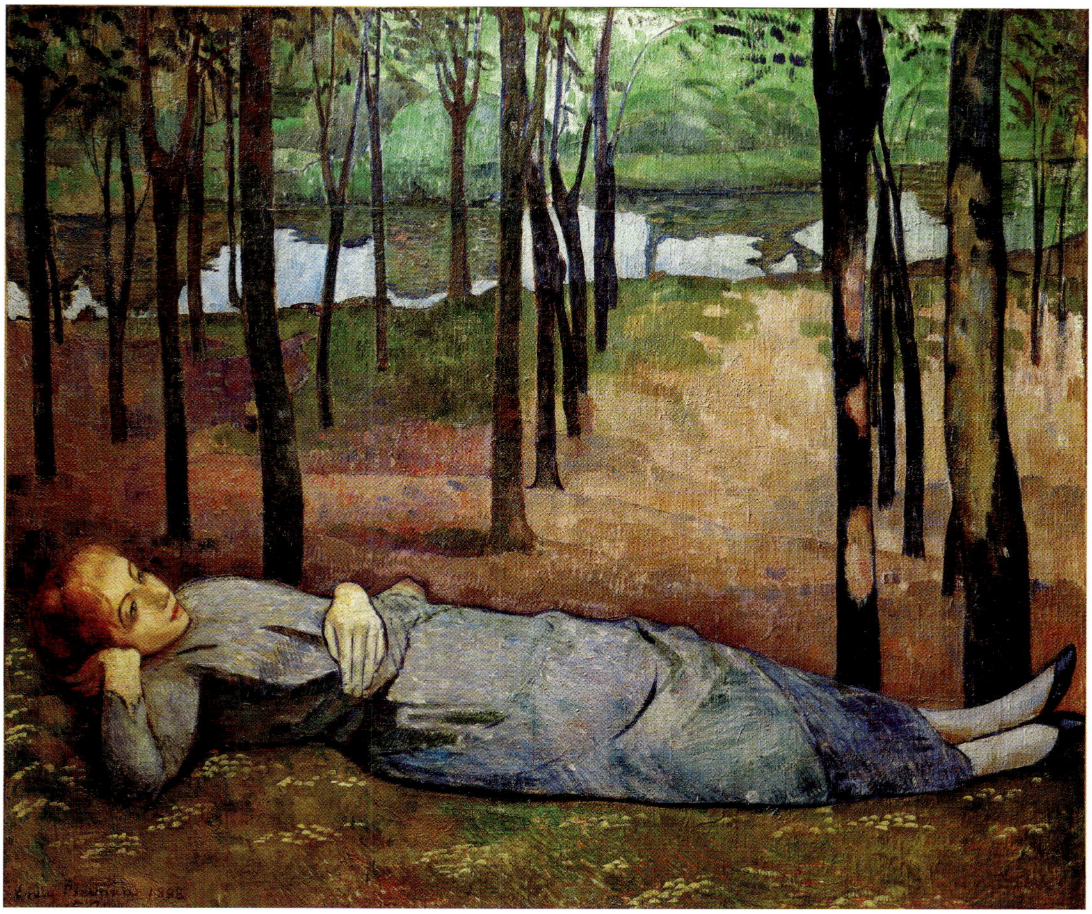

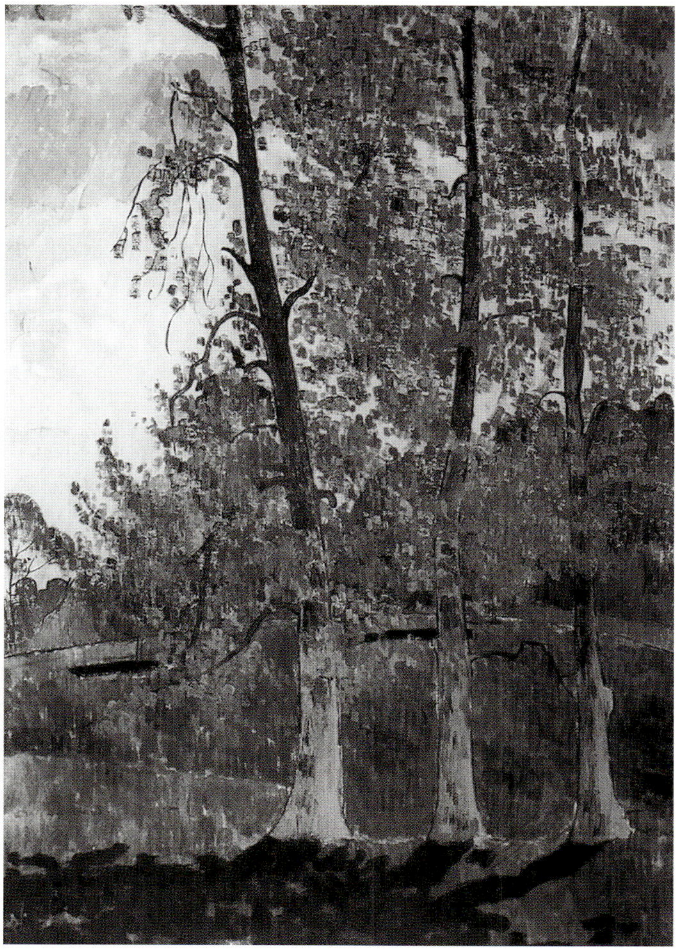

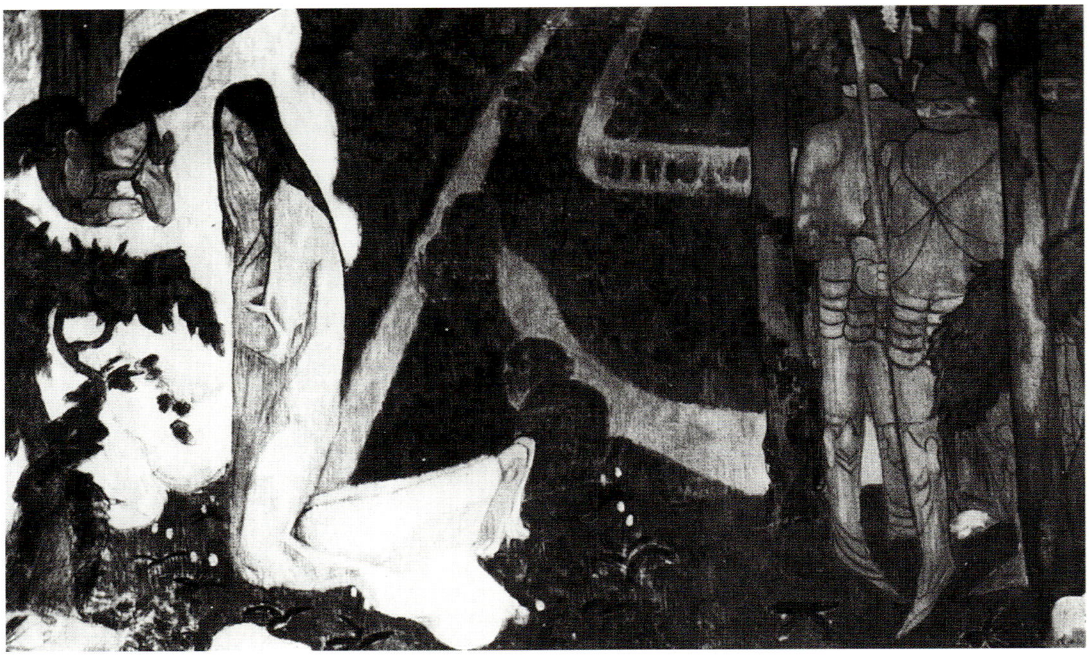

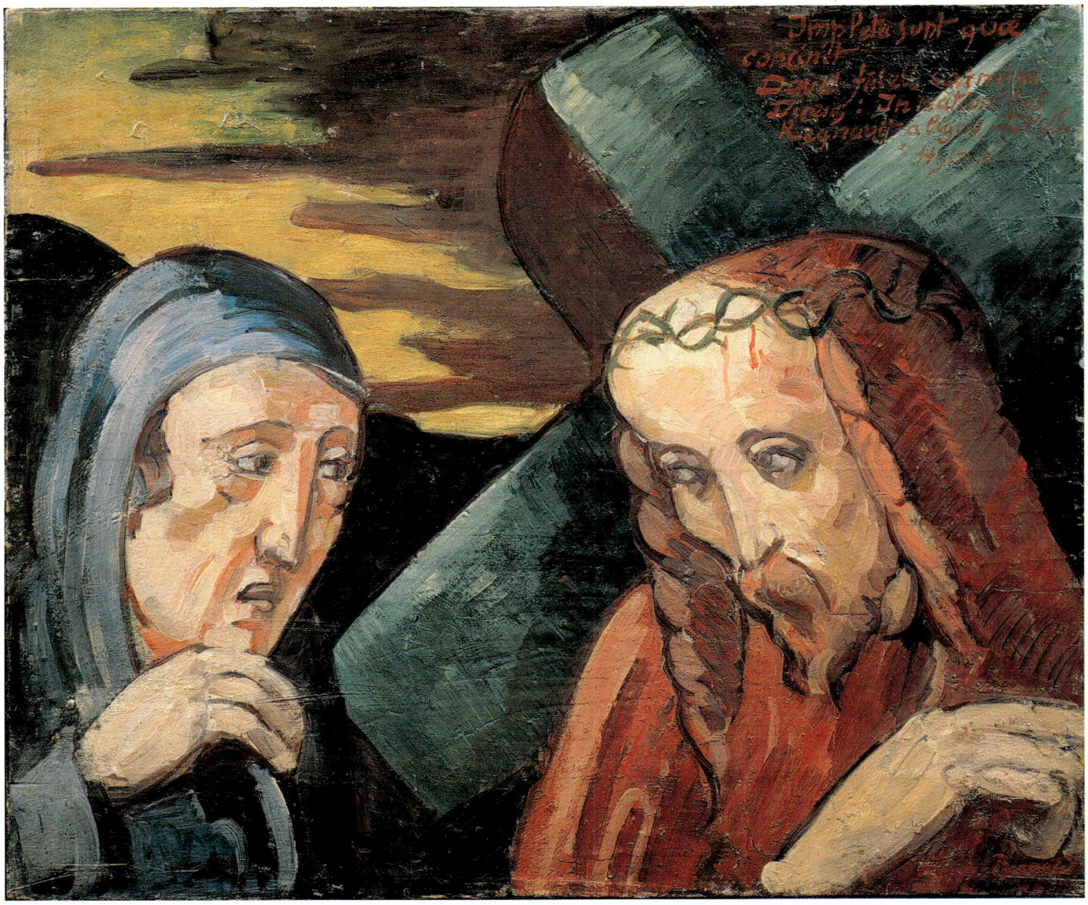

106. Émile Bernard, *Christ in the Garden of Olives,* 1889. Present whereabouts unknown.

107. Émile Bernard, *Christ Meeting His Mother,* 1889. Private collection.

saw a tiny panel of his in Montpellier, the death of some sainted woman or other.[16] The expressions in it of pain and ecstasy are human to the point that, nineteenth century though it may be, you feel you're in it—and believe you were there, present, so much do you share the emotion. If I saw your actual canvases, I believe the color could nevertheless excite me. But then you speak of portraits that you have done, and have captured precisely; that's something that will be good, and where you will have been yourself.

Here's a description of a canvas that I have in front of me at the moment. A view of the garden of the asylum where I am, on the right a gray terrace, a section of house, some rosebushes that have lost their flowers; on the left, the earth of the garden—red ocher—earth burnt by the sun, covered in fallen pine twigs. This edge of the garden is planted with large pines with red ocher trunks and branches, with green foliage saddened by a mixture of black. These tall trees stand out against an evening sky streaked with violet against a yellow background. High up, the yellow turns to pink, turns to green. A wall—red ocher again—blocks the view, and there is nothing above it but a violet and yellow ocher hill. Now, the first tree is an enormous trunk, but struck by lightning and sawn off. A side branch thrusts up very high, however, and falls down again in an avalanche of dark green twigs.

This dark giant—like a proud man brought low—contrasts, when seen as the character of a living being, with the pale smile of the last rose on the bush, which is fading in front of him. Under the trees, empty stone benches, dark box. The sky is reflected yellow in a puddle after the rain. A ray of sun—the last glimmer—exalts the dark ocher to orange—small dark figures prowl here and there between the trunks.[17] You'll understand that this combination of red ocher, of green saddened

---

humains à tel point que tout dixneuvieme siecle qu'on soit, on s'y sent—et croit avoir été là, présent, tant on partage l'émotion. Si je voyais tes toiles mêmes, je crois que neamoins la couleur pourrait me passionner.—mais alors tu parles de portraits que tu as fait et serré de près, voilà ce qui sera bien et où tu auras été toi.—

Voici description d'une toile que j'ai devant moi dans ce moment. Une vue du parc de la maison de santé où je suis, à droite une terrasse grise, un pan de maison, quelques buissons de roses déflories, à gauche le terrain du parc—ocre rouge—terrain brulé par le soleil couvert de brindilles de pin tombées. Cette lisière de parc est plantée de grands pins aux troncs & branches ocre rouge, au feuillage vert attristé par un mélange de noir. Ces hauts arbres se détachent sur un ciel du soir strié de violet sur fond jaune. le jaune tourne dans le haut au rose, tourne au vert. Une muraille—ocre rouge encore—barre la vue et n'est dépassé que par une colline violette et ocre jaune.—Or le premier arbre est un tronc énorme mais frappé par la foudre et scié. Une branche laterale cependant s'élance très haute et retombe en avalanche de brindilles vert sombre.

Ce géant sombre—comme un orgueilleux défait—contraste en tant que consideré comme caractère d'être vivant, avec le sourire pâle d'une dernière rose sur le buisson qui se fâne en face de lui. Sous les arbres des bancs de pierre vide, du buis sombre. le ciel se reflète jaune après la pluie dans une flaque. Un rayon de soleil—le dernier reflet—exalte jusqu'à l'orangé l'ocre sombre—des figurines noires rodent cà et là entre les troncs.[17] *Tu comprendras que cette combinaison d'ocre rouge, de vert attristé de gris, des traits noirs qui cernent les contours, cela produit un peu la sensation d'angoisse, dont souffrent souvent certains de mes compagnons d'infortune, qu'on appelle "voir rouge."*[18] *et d'ailleurs le motif du grand arbre frappé par l'éclair, le sourire maladif vert & rose de la derniere fleur d'automne, vient*

with gray, of black lines that define the outlines, this gives rise a little to the feeling of anxiety from which some of my companions in misfortune often suffer, and which is called "seeing red."[18] And what's more, the motif of the great tree struck by lightning, the sickly green and pink smile of the last flower of autumn, confirms this idea. Another canvas depicts a sun rising over a field of new wheat. Receding lines of the furrows run high up on the canvas, toward a wall and a range of lilac hills. The field is violet and green yellow. The white sun is surrounded by a large yellow aureole.[19] In it, in contrast to the other canvas, I have tried to express calm, a great peace.

I am speaking to you of these two canvases, and especially the first, to remind you that in order to give an impression of anxiety, you can try to do it without heading straight for the historical garden of Gethsemane; in order to offer a consoling and gentle subject it is not necessary to depict the figures from the Sermon on the Mount[20]—ah—it is—no doubt—wise, right, to be moved by the Bible, but modern reality has such a hold over us that even when trying abstractly to reconstruct ancient times in our thoughts—just at that very moment the petty events of our lives tear us away from these meditations and our own adventures throw us forcibly into personal sensations: joy, boredom, suffering, anger or smiling. The Bible—the Bible—Millet was brought up on it from his childhood, used to read only that book and yet never, or almost never, did biblical paintings.[21] Corot did a Garden of Olives with Christ and the star of Bethlehem: sublime.[22] In his work you feel Homer, Aeschylus, Sophocles too, sometimes, as well as the gospels, but how sober and always giving due weight to modern, possible sensations common to us all. But, you'll say, Delacroix—yes, Delacroix—but then you'd have to *study* in a very different way, yes, *study* history before putting things in their place like that.

---

confirmer cette idée.—Une autre toile représente un soleil levant sur un champ de jeune blé.—Des lignes fuyantes de sillons montent haut dans la toile vers une muraille et une rangée de collines lilas. Le champ est violet et jaune vert. Le soleil blanc est entouré d'une grande auréole jaune.[19] *Là-dedans j'ai par contraste à l'autre toile cherché à exprimér du calme, une grande paix.*

Je te parle de ces deux toiles, surtout alors de la première, pour te rappeler que pour donner une impression d'angoisse, on peut chercher à le faire sans viser droit au jardin de Ghetsemané historique, pour donner un[e] *motif consolant et doux il n'est pas nécessaire de representer les personnages du sermon sur la montagne*[20]*—ah—il est—sans doute—sage, juste, d'être ému par la bible mais la réalité moderne a tellement prise sur nous que même en cherchant abstraitement à reconstruire les jours anciens dans notre pensée—juste alors même les petits evenements de notre vie nous arrachent à ces meditations, et nos aventures à nous nous rejettent de force dans les sensations personelles, joie, ennui, souffrance, colère ou sourire.—La bible—la bible—Millet dès son enfance etait eduqué là-dedans, ne faisait que lire ce livre-là et pourtant jamais ou presque jamais ne fit des tableaux bibliques.—*[21] *Corot a fait un Jardin des oliviers avec le Christ et l'étoile du berger, sublime.*[22] *dans son oeuvre on sent Homere, Aeschyle, Sophocle aussi parfois, comme l'évangile, mais combien discret et préponderant toujours les sensations modernes, possibles, communs à nous tous.—Mais, diras-tu, Delacroix—oui Delacroix—mais alors tu aurais encore tout autrement à* étudier, *oui* étudier *l'histoire avant de mettre les chôses à leur place comme ça.*

Donc, c'est un échec mon brave, tes tableaux bibliques mais. . . . il y en a peu qui se trompent comme ça et c'est une erreur mais le retour de cela sera j'ose croire épatant, et c'est en se trompant

So, they're a setback, my dear fellow, your biblical paintings, but. . . . there are few who make mistakes like that, and it's an error, but your return from it will be, I dare to say, astonishing, and it's by making mistakes that one sometimes finds the way. Look, avenge yourself by painting your garden as it is, or anything you like. In any case, it's good to look for what's distinguished, what's noble in figures, and your studies represent an effort that's been made, and so something other than wasted time.

To know how to divide a canvas into large, tangled planes like that, to find contrasting lines and forms—that's technique—trickery, if you like, but anyway, it means you're learning your craft more thoroughly, and that's good. No matter how hateful and cumbersome painting may be in the times in which we live, the person who has chosen this craft, if he nevertheless practices it with zeal, is a man of duty, both sound and loyal. Society sometimes makes existence very hard for us, and from that too comes our impotence and the imperfection of our works. I believe that Gauguin himself suffers greatly from it, too, and cannot develop as he yet has it in him to do.

I myself suffer in that I'm utterly without models. On the other hand, there are beautiful sites here. Have just done five no. 30 canvases of the olive trees. And if I still stay here it's because my health is recovering greatly. What I'm making is harsh, dry, but it's because I'm trying to reinvigorate myself by means of rather arduous work, and would fear that abstractions would make me soft. Have you seen a study of mine with a little reaper? A field of yellow wheat and a yellow sun.[23] It isn't there yet—but in it I have again attacked this devil of a question of yellow. I'm talking about the one that's impastoed and done on the spot, not about the repetition with hatching, in which the effect is weaker. I wanted to do it in pure sulphur. I'd have plenty more things to tell you—but

---

qu'on trouve parfois le chemin. Va, revenge t'en en peignant ton jardin tel qu'il est ou ce que tu voudras. En tout cas c'est bon de chercher du distingué, de la noblesse dans les figures et tes etudes representent un effort fait et donc autre chôse que du temps perdu.

Savoir diviser une toile ainsi en grands plans enchevêtrés, trouver des lignes, des formes faisant contraste—c'est de la technique—des trucs si tu veux de la cuisine mais enfin, c'est que tu aprofondis ton metier et cela c'est bien. Quelque haïssable que soit la peinture et encombrante au temps où nous sommes, celui qui a choisi ce métier, s'il l'exerce quand même avec zele, est homme du devoir et solide et fidèle. La société nous rend parfois l'existence bien penible et de là aussi vient notre impuissance et l'imparfait de nos travaux. Je crois que Gauguin lui-même en souffre beaucoup aussi, et ne peut pas se developper comme pourtant c'est en dedans de lui de pouvoir le faire.

Moi je souffre de ce que je manque de modèles absolument. Par contre il y a des beaux sites ici. Viens de faire 5 toiles de 30 des oliviers. Et si je reste ici encore, c'est que ma santé se refait beaucoup. Ce que je fais est dur, sec, mais c'est que je cherche à me retremper par du travail un peu rude et craindrais que les abstractions ramollissent. As tu vu une étude de moi avec un petit faucheur? Un champ de blé jaune et un soleil jaune.—[23] *Ca n'y est pas—et pourtant là-dedans j'ai encore attaqué cette diable de question du jaune.—Je parle de celle qui est empatée et fait sur place, non de la repetition à hachures où l'effet est plus faible. Je voulais faire cela en plein souffre. J'aurais encore bien des chôses à te dire—mais si j'ecris aujourd'hui que ma tête s'est un peu raffermie, auparavant je craignais de me l'échauffer*

although I write today that my mind is somewhat stronger, previously I was afraid of overheating it before I was cured. In thought a very warm handshake, to Anquetin too, to other friends if you see them, and believe me,

Ever yours,
Vincent

No need to tell you that I regret, for you as well as for your father, that he did not approve of your spending the season with Gauguin. The latter wrote to me that for reasons of health your service has been postponed for a year.[24] Thank you anyway for the description of the Egyptian house.[25] I would still have liked to know if it was larger or smaller than a cottage back home—the size relative to the human figure, in short. I was looking for information about the coloring in particular.

---

avant d'être gueri. En pensée poignée de main bien cordiale, aussi à Anquetin, aux autres amis si tu en vois et crois moi,

t. à t.
Vincent

pas besoin de te dire que je regrette pour toi comme pour ton père que celui ci n'aie pas trouvé bon que tu passe la saison avec Gauguin. Ce dernier m'écrit que pour cause de santé ton service est remis à un an.[24] *Merci quand même de la description de la maison Egyptienne.*[25] *J'aurais encore voulu savoir si elle était plus grande ou plus petite qu'une chaumière de chez nous—enfin la proportion relativement à la figure humaine. C'était surtout pour la coloration que je demandais le renseignement.*

---

108. Vincent van Gogh, *La Berceuse,* 1888–89 (F 508 / JH 1671). Boston, Museum of Fine Arts.
109. Vincent van Gogh, *Woman Reading a Novel,* 1888 (F 497 / JH 1632). Private collection.

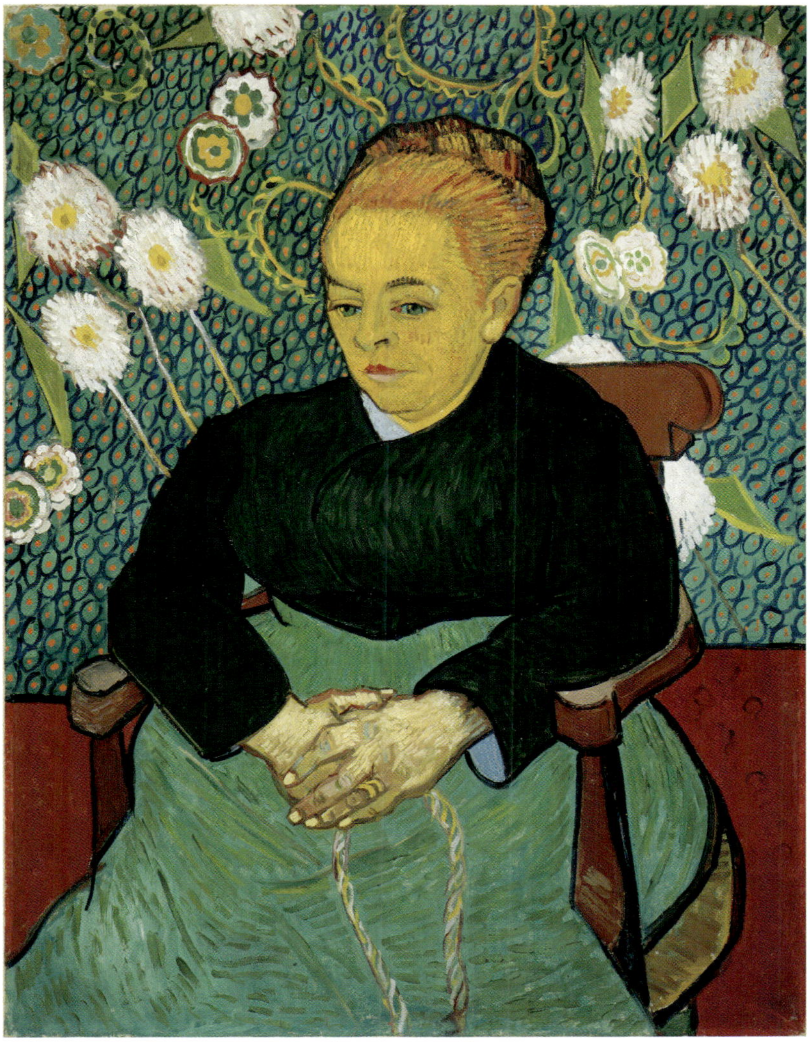

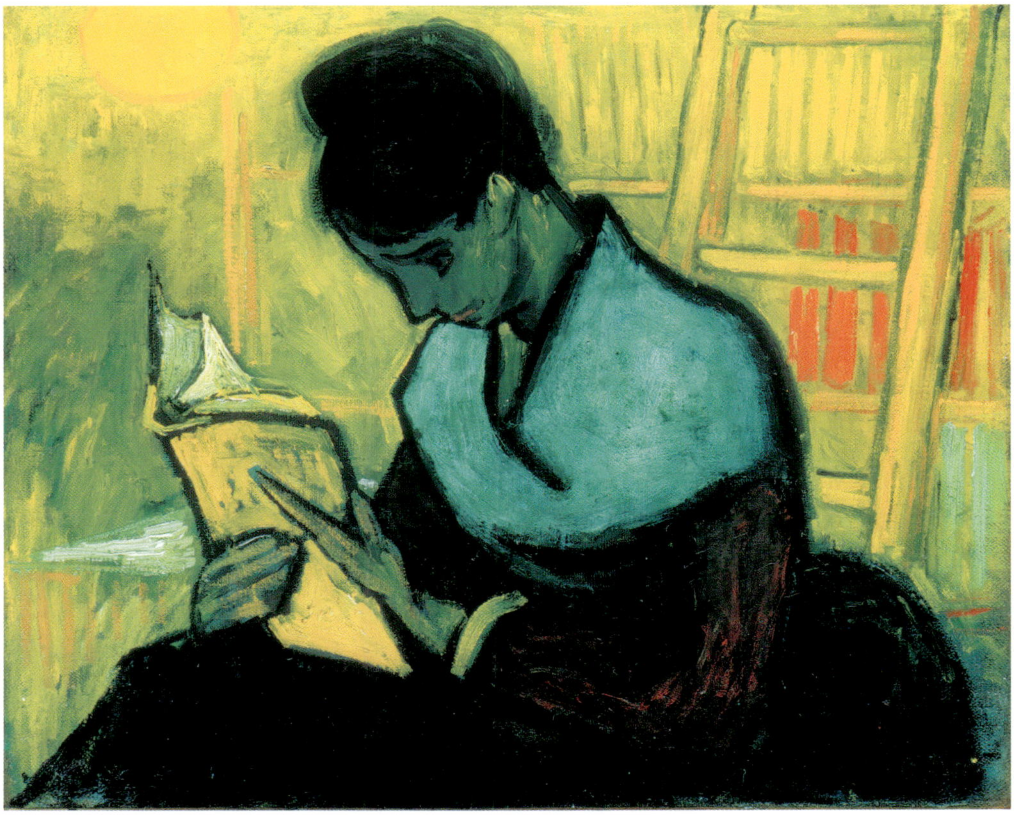

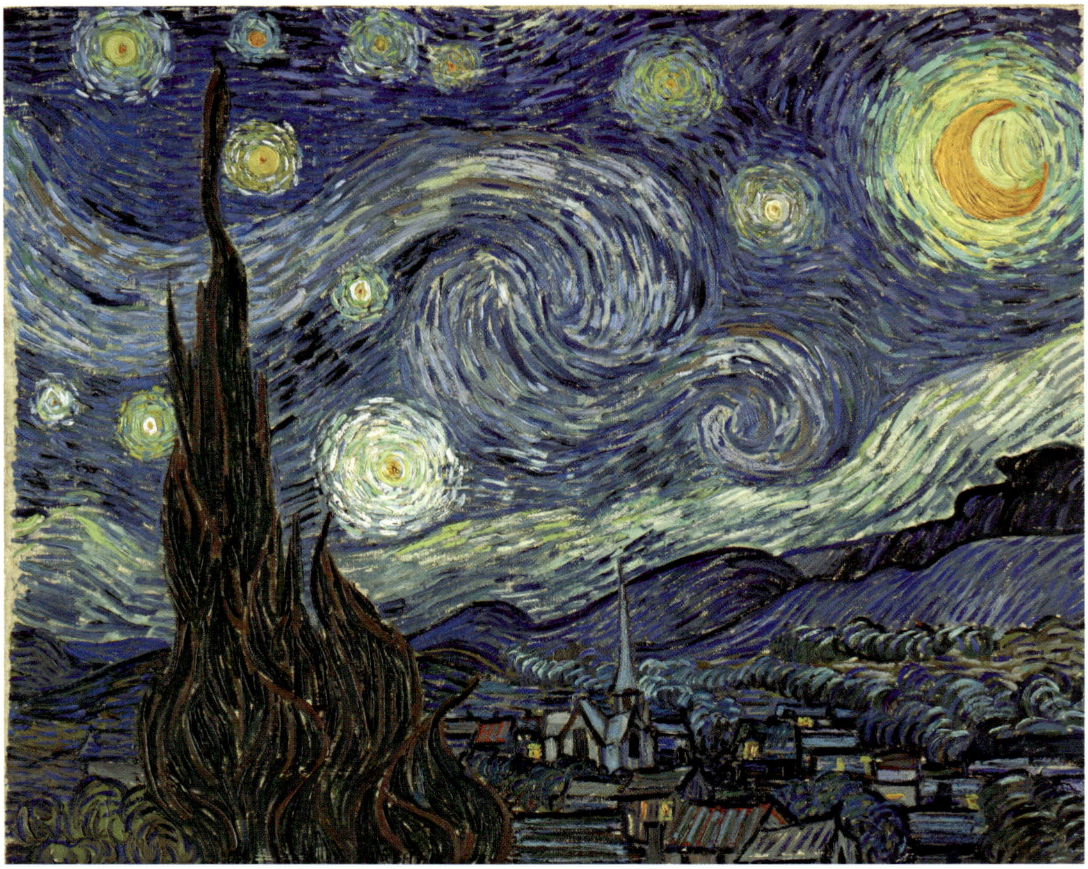

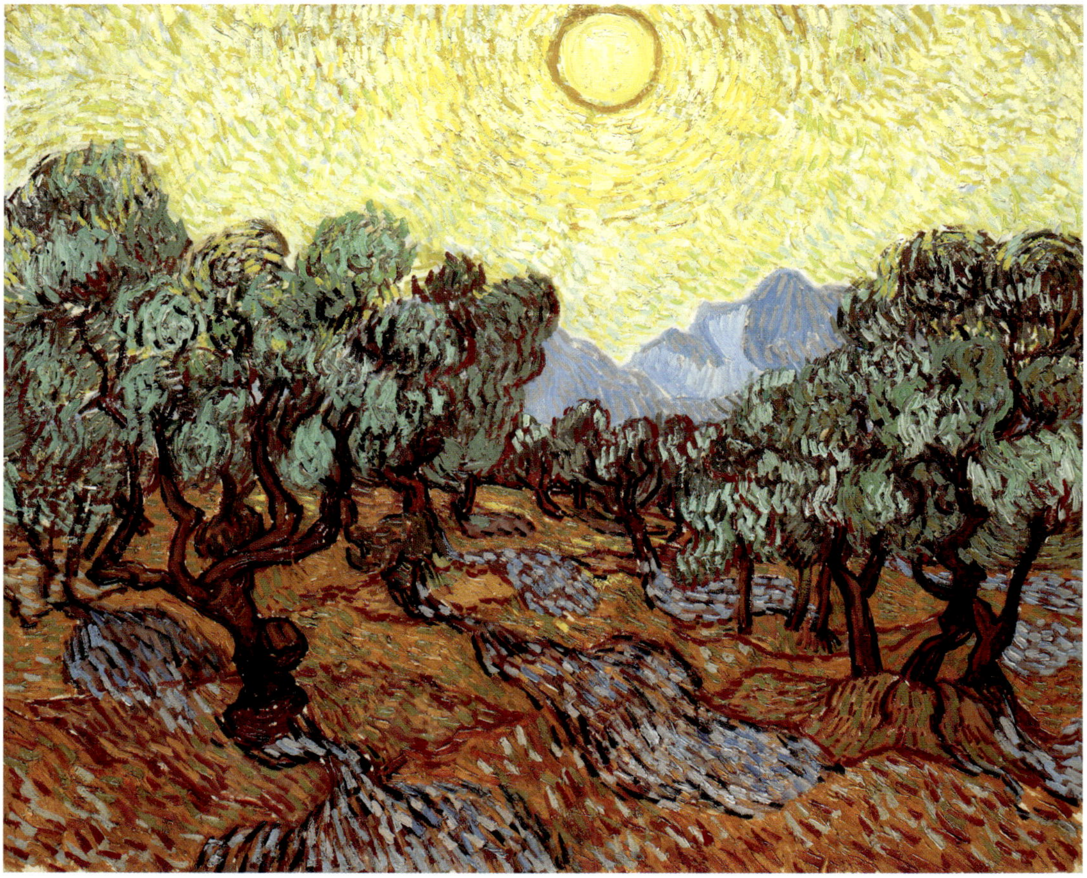

Annotations to Letter 22

Saint-Rémy, ca. Tuesday, 26 November, 1889

TEXTUAL NOTES
a. l'ont < l'on
b. sens < sans
c. This should be read as *vert foncé* (dark green).
d. This should be read as *ce qu'on appelle des abstractions* (the so-called abstractions).
e. un < une

1. Vincent told his sister Willemien that Bernard had sent six photographs of recent paintings (letter *CL* W16). Four of them are discussed in the present letter. He probably also received a photograph of Bernard's *Deposition from the Cross*, 1889–90 (private collection; see Luthi 1982, p. 44, no. 267).

2. Theo wrote the following to Vincent on 16 November about Bernard's paintings *The Annunciation* and *Christ in the Garden of Olives*: "I have been to Bernard's this week, and he showed me what he has done lately. I consider he has made a lot of progress. His drawing is less determined but it's there all the same. There is more flexibility in his touch. With him there is a more direct influence from the primitives, thus he has done a kneeling figure surrounded by angels. The ground is in large squares, and the figures are posed as if on a chessboard, but there is one angel figure that really has nobility. He has also done a Christ in the Garden of Olives. A redheaded, violet Christ with a yellow angel. It is very difficult to understand, and the search for style often lends something ridiculous to his figures, but he will perhaps get something good out of it." (*J'ai été cette semaine chez Bernard qui m'a montré ce qu'il a fait dans le dernier temps. Je trouve qu'il a fait beaucoup de progrès. Son dessin est moins déterminé mais n'existe pas moins. Il y a plus de souplesse dans sa touche. Chez lui il y a une influence plus directe des primitifs, ainsi il a fait une figure agenouillé entouré d'anges. Le terrain est à grands carraux et les figures sont posées comme sur un échiquier mais il y a une figure d'ange qui a vraiment de la noblesse. Lui aussi a fait un Christ au jardin des oliviers. Un Christ violet à cheveux rouges avec un ange jaune. C'est bien difficile à comprendre et la recherche du style donne souvent quelque chose de ridicule à ses figures mais il en sortira peut être quelque chose de bien;* letter *CL* T20). For the paintings, see nn. 5 and 10.

3. Van Gogh must have received a photograph of *The Adoration of the Shepherds* (Fig. 100), which Bernard had just painted (see Luthi 1982, pp. 36–37, no. 217). An unpublished inventory by Bernard from 1895 shows that it was executed in 1889. With thanks to Fred Leeman.

4. He is thinking of Millet's *Birth of the Calf*, ca. 1864 (private collection), which had already been acquired by an American collector. Van Gogh may have seen a replica, but the scene was best known through the engraving made after it by Maxime Lalanne for the catalogue of the Alfred Saucède sale in

110. VINCENT VAN GOGH, *The Starry Night*, 1889 (F 612 / JH 1731). New York, The Museum of Modern Art.
111. VINCENT VAN GOGH, *Olive Grove with Mountains and Sun Disk*, 1889 (F 710 / JH 1856). The Minneapolis Institute of Arts.

1879 (Lugt 1938–87, no. 38966). It was also reproduced in Alexandre Piedagnel, *J.-F. Millet: Souvenirs de Barbizon*, Paris, 1876, facing p. 61, with the title *Peasants Carrying Home a Young Calf Born in the Fields* (Paysans rapportant à leur habitation un jeune veau né dans les champs; Fig. 101).

5. Émile Bernard, *The Annunciation* (Fig. 102). See Luthi 1982, no. 216; Mannheim and Amsterdam 1990, pp. 209–13, no. 62.

6. This is Bernard's *Breton Women in the Meadow* (Fig. 103). Bernard himself explained the role of this work in the 1911 edition of his letters: "This is the canvas of which I once spoke in the *Mercure de France: 'Breton women in the meadow,'* in my article *Histoire de l'École dite de Pont-Aven,* and which brought about such a change in technique and assumptions in Gauguin. In 1888 he had exchanged it with me for a painting of his of the same size, and had taken it to Arles, where Vincent saw it and made a copy of it" (*Il s'agit ici de la toile dont j'ai parlé autrefois au* Mercure de France: "Les Bretonnes dans la Prairie," *dans mon article:* Histoire de l'École dite de Pont-Aven, *et qui détermina chez Gauguin un tel changement de technique et de parti-pris. Il me l'avait échangée en 1888 contre un tableau de lui de même dimension et l'avait portée à Arles où Vincent la vit et en fit une copie*). See *Lettres à Bernard* 1911, p. 144. Van Gogh had made his watercolor copy in December 1888, while Gauguin was in Arles: *Breton Women* (F 1422 / JH 1654; Fig. 7).

7. The letter sketch was based on Gauguin's description in the autumn of 1888, possibly amplified with a sketch, of Bernard's painting *Madeleine in the Bois d'Amour* (Fig. 104).

8. At this point in his edition of the letters, Bernard once again took the opportunity of clarifying his position vis-à-vis Gauguin in a footnote: "The exactitude of the description shows how much Gauguin had appreciated the painting" (*L'exactitude de la description, prouve à quel point Gauguin avait goûté le tableau.*) See *Lettres à Bernard* 1911, p. 144.

9. The letter sketch was based on Gauguin's description in the autumn of 1888, possibly amplified with a sketch, of Bernard's painting *Red Poplars* (Fig. 105).

10. Émile Bernard, *Christ in the Garden of Olives* (Fig. 106). Bernard also sent a photograph of this painting to Gauguin, who, unlike Vincent, applauded it: "the Christ seems to me not only better, but even more beautiful. Overall, the canvas breathes a purposefulness, an imaginative style that I find quite amazing. The disproportionate length of the figure at prayer is very bold and adds to its movement. You were right to exaggerate it, at least one doesn't think of the model, or of that bloody reality. The soldiers well arranged. In the photograph you can see a head of Judas that vaguely resembles me. Rest assured, I don't see anything wrong in it" (*le Christ me paraît non seulement meilleur, mais encore fort beau. La toile respire d'un bout à l'autre une volonté, un style imaginatif que je trouve tout à fait épatant. La longueur démesurée de la figure en prière est très hardie et ajoute à son mouvement. Vous avez bien fait de l'exagérer, au moins on ne pense pas au modèle et à cette sacrée nature. Bien disposés les guerriers. On aperçoit une tête de Judas qui me ressemble vaguement dans la photographie. Soyez tranquille je n'y vois pas de mal.*). See *Gauguin lettres* 1946, p. 178.

---

112. Florentine school / school of Giotto, *The Death and Assumption of the Virgin.* Montpellier, Musée Fabre.
113. Vincent van Gogh, *A Corner of the Asylum and the Garden with a Heavy, Sawn-Off Tree,* 1889 (F 659 / JH 1850). Amsterdam, Van Gogh Museum (Vincent van Gogh Foundation).

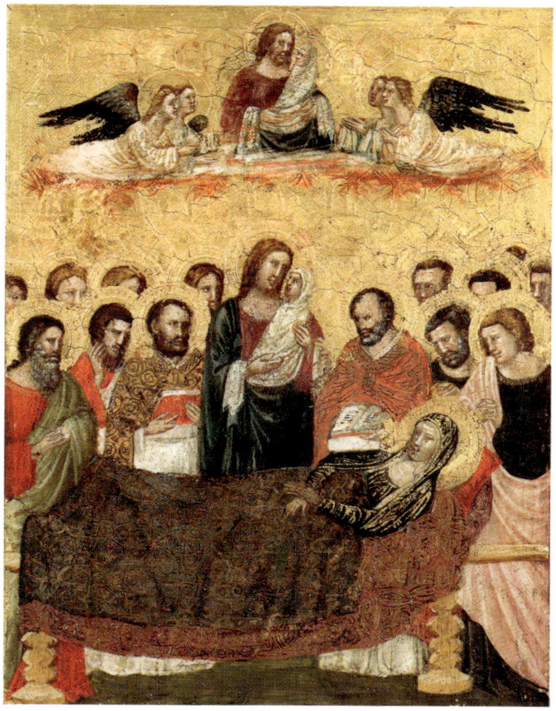

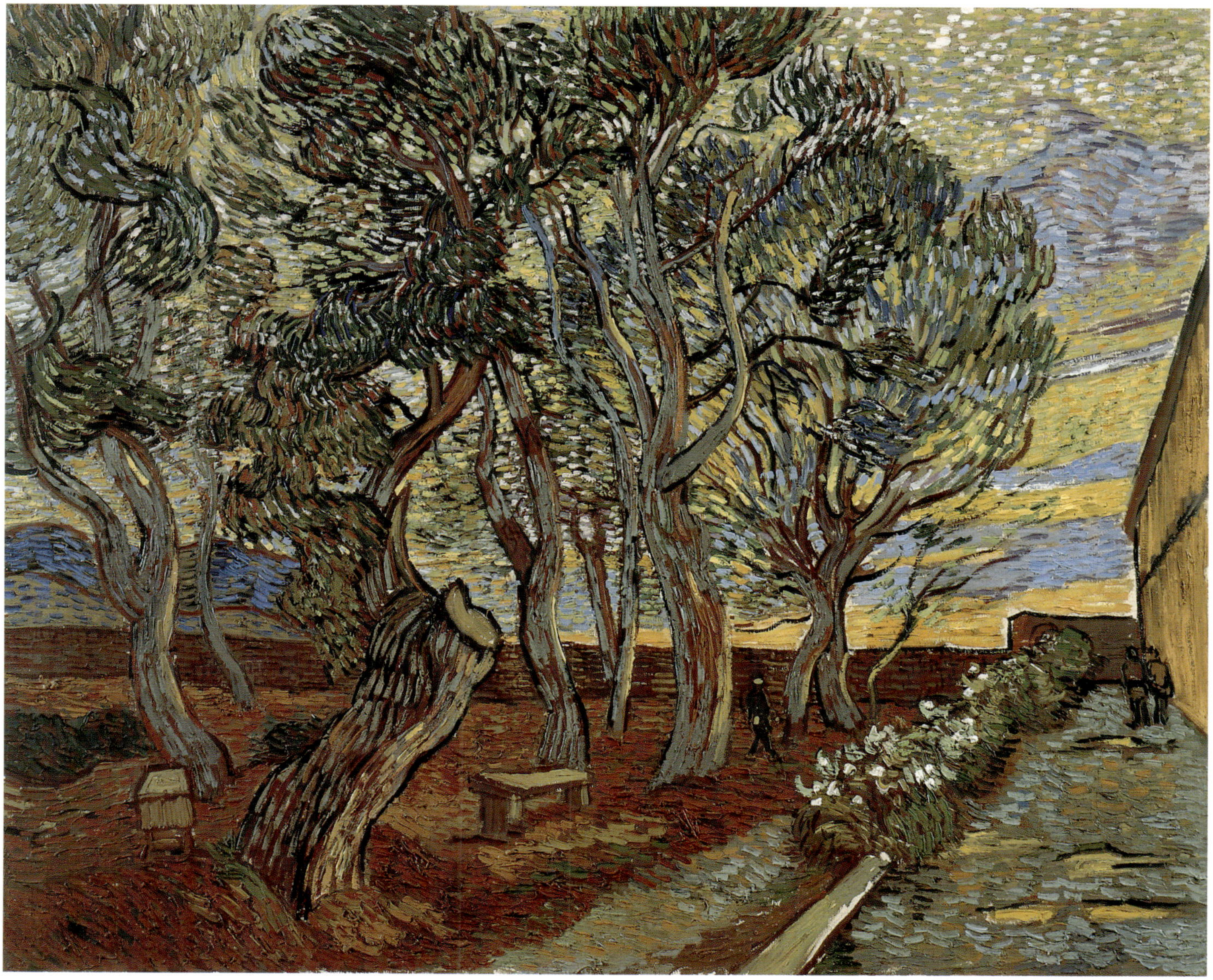

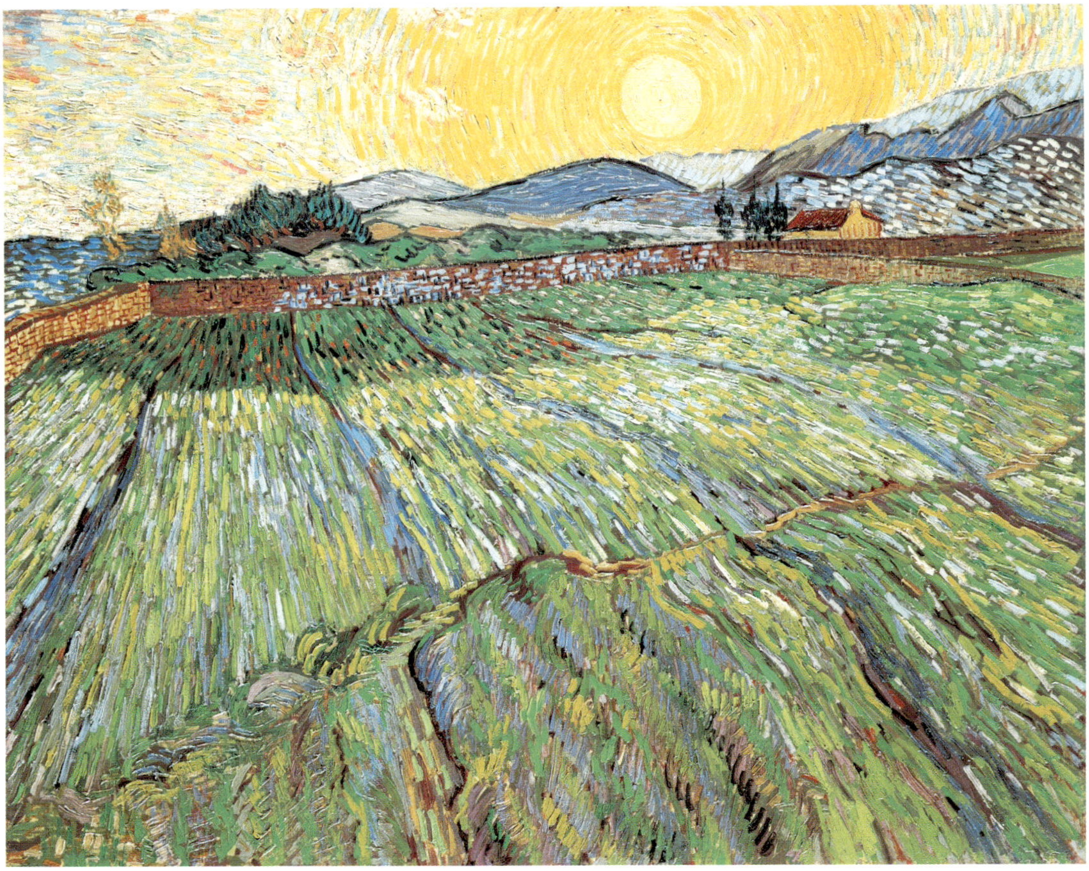

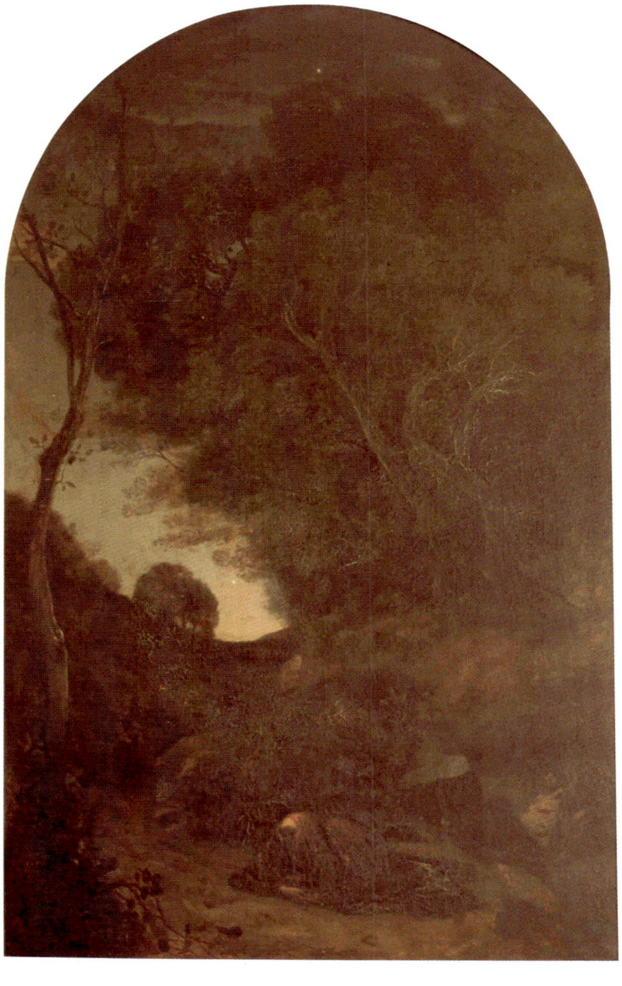

11. Probably Émile Bernard, *Christ Meeting His Mother* (Fig. 107). It does not date from 1891, as stated by Luthi, but from 1889. With thanks to Fred Leeman.

12. While Gauguin was in Arles, van Gogh had started on the first version of *La Berceuse* (F 508 / JH 1671), which he finished in January 1889 (Fig. 108). See Kristin Hoermann Lister, "Tracing a Transformation: Madame Roulin into *La berceuse,*" *Van Gogh Museum Journal 2001,* Amsterdam and Zwolle 2001, pp. 62–83. The other work is *Woman Reading a Novel* (F 497 / JH 1632; Fig. 109).

13. "Enchanted ground" is a term frequently encountered in John Bunyan, *The Pilgrim's Progress from this World, to that Which Is to Come* (1678), which van Gogh had read when he was younger. It is a metaphor for the sham, the mendacious, the wrong path.

14. Van Gogh appears to have been referring to *The Starry Night* (F 612 / JH 1731), which he had painted in June that year (Fig. 110). He was not so critical of it in earlier letters, however, and actually defended it against Theo, who had remarked, "I clearly sense what preoccupies you in the new canvases like the village in the moonlight or the mountains, but I feel that the search for style takes away the real feeling of things" (*Je sens bien ce qui te préoccupe dans les nouvelles toiles comme le village au clair de lune ou les montagnes mais je trouve que le recherche du style enlève au sentiment vrai des choses; CL* T19).

15. A little later in the letter van Gogh said that he had made five no. 30 canvases of olive groves. They were *Olive Grove* (F 707 / JH 1857; Amsterdam, Van Gogh Museum), *Olive Grove* (F 708 / JH 1855; New York, The Metropolitan Museum of Art), *Olive Grove with Mountains and Sun Disk* (F 710 / JH 1856; Fig. 111), *Olive Grove with a Man and a Woman Picking Olives* (F 587 / JH 1853; Otterlo, Kröller-Müller Museum) and *Olive Grove* (F 586 / JH 1854; Gothenburg, Konstmuseum).

16. In December 1888, van Gogh and Gauguin had gone on a trip to Montpellier, some 40 miles (65 km) west of Arles, to visit the Musée Fabre. Among the works there were some by van Gogh's beloved Delacroix. The "tiny panel" is *The Death and Assumption of the Virgin* (Fig. 112). It was attributed to Giotto at the time but has been reassigned to Florentine school or School of Giotto. See Montpellier 1904, p. 207, no. 743.

17. The canvas that van Gogh described in such detail here is *A Corner of the Asylum and the Garden with a Heavy, Sawn-Off Tree,* of which there are two variants: F 660 / JH 1849 (Essen, Museum Folkwang) and F 659 / JH 1850. Van Gogh was very likely describing the latter (Fig. 113). See Hendriks and van Tilborgh 2001, esp. pp. 154–56.

18. This expression has always been read incorrectly as *noir-rouge,* and is often cited as such. The expression *voir rouge* can be read without any difficulty at all in the manuscript, and means "to be in a state of violent psychological or emotional agitation" (*TLF*).

19. *Enclosed Field with Young Wheat and Rising Sun* (F 737 / JH 1862; Fig. 114).

---

114. Vincent van Gogh, *Enclosed Field with Young Wheat and Rising Sun,* 1889 (F 737 / JH 1862). Private collection.
115. Camille Corot, *Christ in the Garden of Olives,* 1849. Musée de Langres.

20. Van Gogh was merely taking this as an example. Bernard is not known to have made a painting of the Sermon on the Mount (Matt. 5–7, Luke 6:16).

21. According to Millet's biographer Sensier, it was the Bible that Millet "considered the painters' book, the book in which the most moving paintings are found in imposing forms" (*considérait comme le livre des peintres, le livre où se trouvent sous les formes grandioses les tableaux les plus émouvants*). See Sensier 1881, p. 66. Sensier's biography, in turn, became a bible for van Gogh.

22. Camille Corot, *Christ in the Garden of Olives* (Fig. 115).Van Gogh had seen this work in Paris back in 1875, when it was in a major Corot exhibition held in the École Nationale des Beaux-Arts after the painter's death. Van Gogh had written about it to Theo, saying: "I'm glad he painted that" (*ik ben blij dat hij dat geschilderd heeft;* letter *CL* 27).

23. *Enclosed Wheat Field with Reaper* (F 617 / JH 1753; Fig. 116) was with Theo in Paris, as was the repetition, *Enclosed Wheat Field with Reaper at Sunrise* (F 618 / JH 1773), which van Gogh mentioned a little further on (Fig. 117).

24. Gauguin had written about Bernard's father and the postponement of their friend's military service in letter GAC 37 of ca. 8 November.

25. Van Gogh had asked for this information in Letter 21.

---

116. Vincent van Gogh, *Enclosed Wheat Field with Reaper,* 1889 (F 617 / JH 1753). Otterlo, Kröller-Müller Museum.
117. Vincent van Gogh, *Enclosed Wheat Field with Reaper at Sunrise,* 1889 (F 618 / JH 1773). Amsterdam, Van Gogh Museum (Vincent van Gogh Foundation).

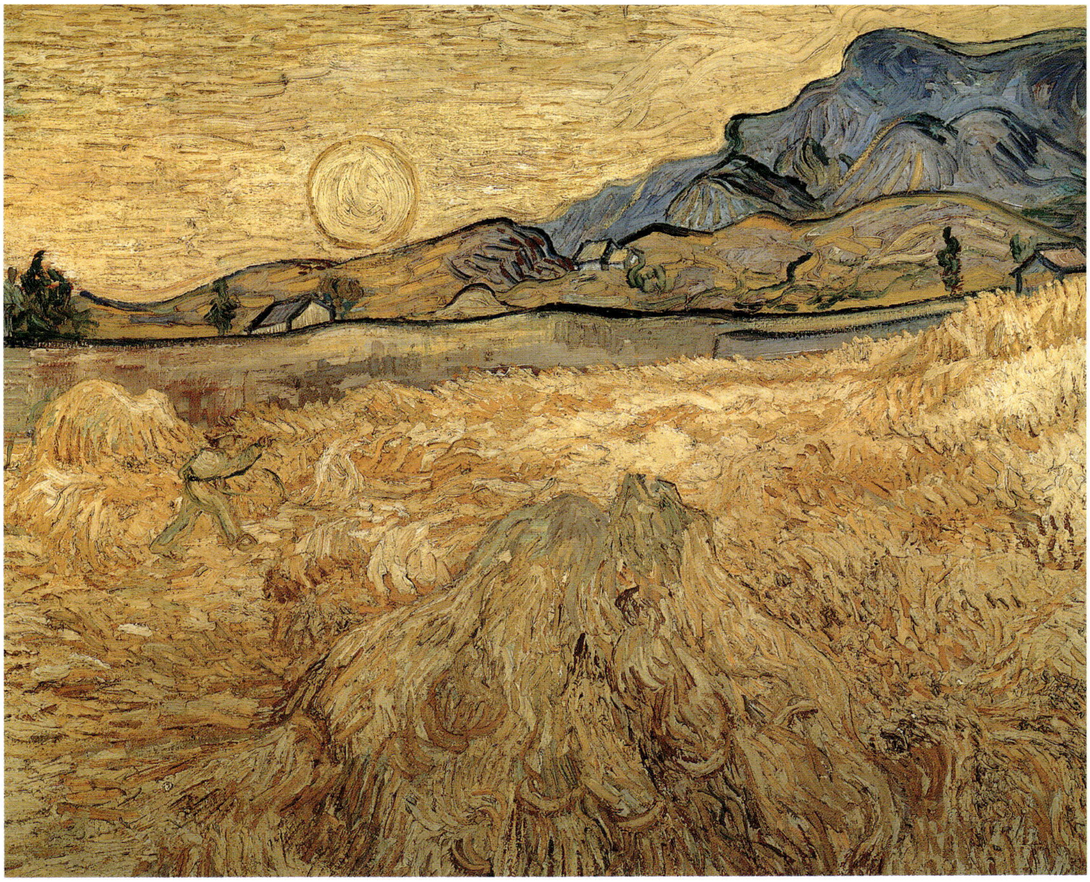

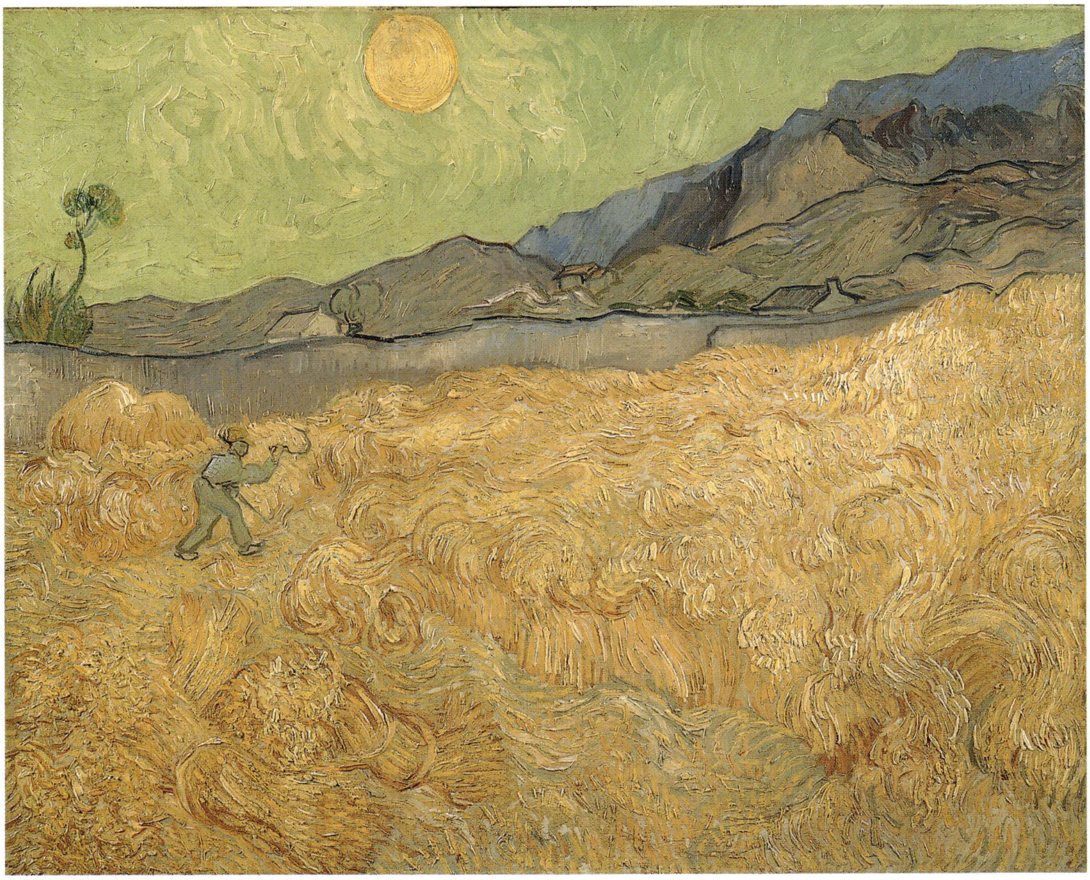

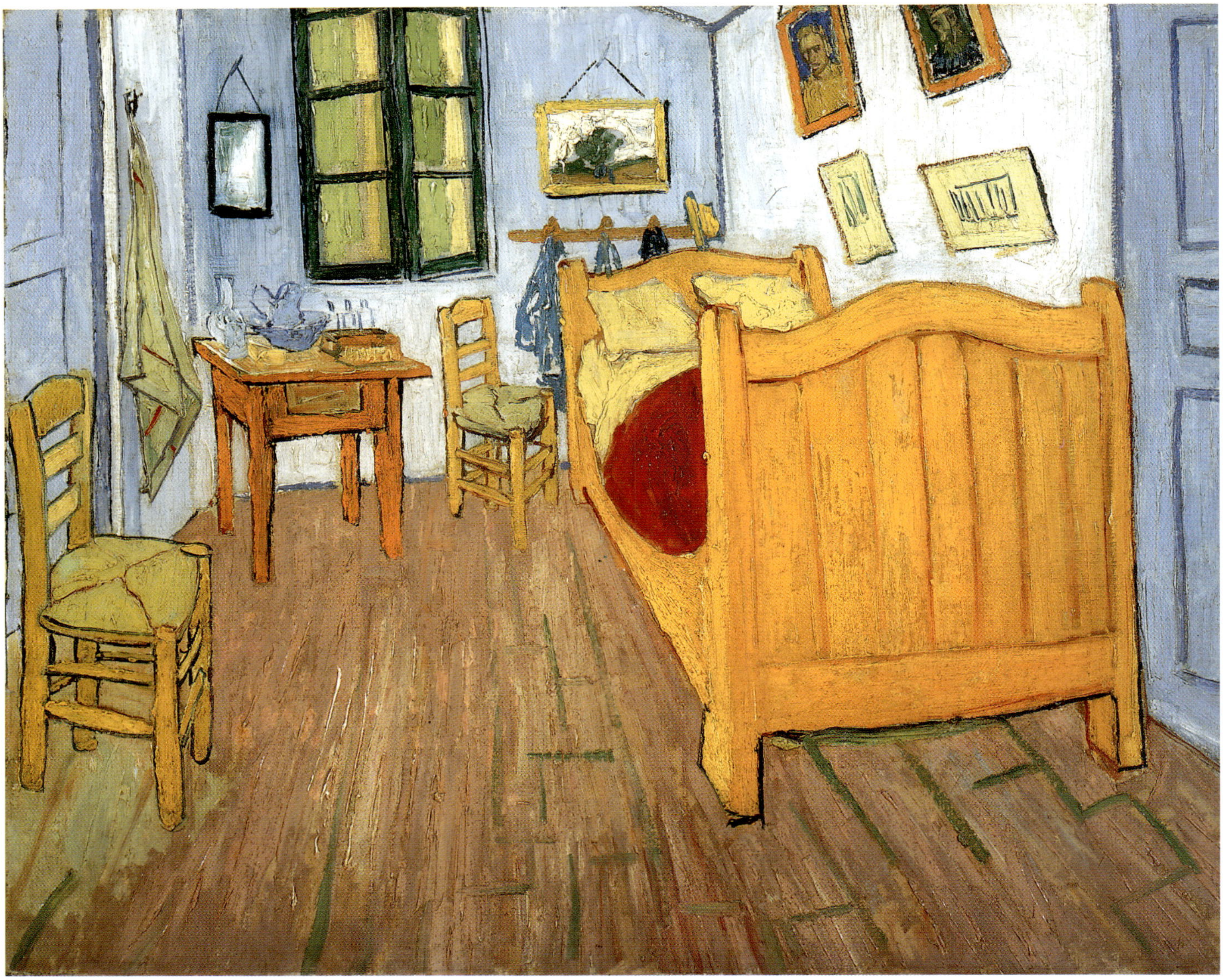

Epilogue

Van Gogh related to Theo that he had written to both Bernard and Gauguin about his reaction to their religious paintings: "that I thought thinking and not dreaming was our duty, that I was therefore astonished when looking at their work by the fact that they had let themselves go to that extent."[1] So he had also criticized Gauguin's painting, but although it was another two months before Gauguin wrote to him again, they still kept in touch. Van Gogh also expected to hear from Bernard, as he wrote to his sister Willemien on 20 January 1890. "Have you met Émile Bernard now—I would very much like him to come and see some of my canvases one of these days. I ought to write to him, but just now I'm expecting a letter from him at any moment."[2] As far as is known, however, he never got one, nor did he himself write again.

Although there was no contact between them during the eight remaining months of van Gogh's life, it seems that neither regarded the break in the correspondence as the end of their friendship. In late April 1890, Vincent asked Theo how Bernard was and proposed another exchange with him. Bernard, for his part, continued to be interested in van Gogh's work. He and Aurier called on Theo in March 1890 to look at Vincent's recent canvases (*CL* T29); at around the same time Gauguin said that Bernard, like Aurier and himself, was full of praise for Vincent's paintings in the Indépendants exhibition (letter GAC 40).

On 27 July 1890, van Gogh shot himself in the chest in the fields outside Auvers-sur-Oise, dying two days later. He was buried on 30 July. Bernard was present on that sad occasion, which was also an homage to van Gogh, for his paintings were placed around the coffin and many artists attended the service. It was not over for Bernard, though. He kept the flame of friendship burning and proved to be an indefatigable champion of his friend's artistic bequest to the world—not just the superb drawings and impressive paintings but also the unique epistolary legacy.

Appendix 1

Letter from Vincent van Gogh to Paul Gauguin / Arles, Wednesday, 17 October, 1888

This letter was included in *Lettres à Bernard* as number 22, and subsequent editions have consequently retained this misleading B number. Bernard explained his reason for including it: "I did not believe I should omit this interesting letter, decorated with a drawing" (*Je n'ai pas cru devoir omettre cette intéressante missive orné d'un dessin; Lettres à Bernard* 1911, p. 151). Merlhès has suggested that the letter came into Bernard's possession because it arrived after Gauguin had left Pont-Aven (Merlhès 1989, p. 124). Another possibility is that Gauguin gave it to Bernard. The document is now in the Thaw Collection, The Morgan Library & Museum.

Date
The letter was written after van Gogh had heard from Gauguin that he was coming to Arles on 20 October. We have assumed that van Gogh replied immediately, otherwise there would not have been time for the letter to reach Gauguin before he set out. Since it is unlikely that Vincent had received Gauguin's letter on 16 October (if he had, he would have told Theo about it when he wrote to him that evening, *CL* 554), we have dated this letter Wednesday, 17 October, 1888.

Sketch
Vincent's Bedroom (F - / JH 1610), letter sketch

118. Vincent van Gogh, *The Bedroom*, 1888 (F 482 / JH 1608). Amsterdam, Van Gogh Museum (Vincent van Gogh Foundation).

Appendix 1: Translation of Letter from Vincent van Gogh to Paul Gauguin / Arles, Wednesday, 17 October, 1888

My dear Gauguin,

Thanks for your letter, and thanks most of all for your promise to come as early as the twentieth.[1] Agreed, this reason that you give[2] won't help to make a pleasure trip of the train journey, and it's only right that you should put off your journey until you can do it without it being a bloody nuisance. But that apart, I almost envy you this trip, which will show you, in passing, miles and miles of countryside of different kinds with autumn splendors.

I still have in my memory the feelings that the journey from Paris to Arles gave me this past winter.[3] How I watched out to see "if it was like Japan yet"! Childish, isn't it?

Look here, I wrote to you the other day that my vision was strangely tired. Well, I rested for two and a half days, and then I got back to work. But not yet daring to go outside, I did, for my decoration once again, a no. 30 canvas of my bedroom[4] with the whitewood furniture that you know. Ah, well, it amused me enormously doing this bare interior.

With a simplicity à la *Seurat. [sketch]* In flat tints, but coarsely brushed in full impasto, the walls pale lilac, the floor in a broken and faded red, the chairs and the bed chrome yellow, the pillows and the sheet very pale lemon green, the bedspread blood red, the dressing table orange, the washbasin blue, the window green. I had wished to express *utter repose* with all these very different tones, you see, among which the only white is the little note given by the mirror with a black frame (to cram in the fourth pair of complementaries as well).

Anyway, you'll see it with the others, and we'll talk about it. Because I often don't know what I'm doing, working almost like a sleepwalker.

It's beginning to get cold, especially on the days when the mistral blows.

I've had gas put in the studio, so that we'll have good light in winter.

Perhaps you'll be disillusioned with Arles if you come at a time when the mistral's blowing, but wait. . . . It's in the long term that the poetry down here soaks in.

You won't find the house as comfortable yet as we'll gradually try to make it. There are so many expenses, and it can't be done in one go. Anyway, I believe that once here, like me, you'll be seized with a fury to paint the autumn effects, in between spells of the mistral. And that you will understand that I've insisted that you come now that there are some very beautiful days. Au revoir, then.

Ever yours,
Vincent

Appendix 1: Transcription of Letter from Vincent van Gogh to Paul Gauguin / Arles, Wednesday, 17 October, 1888

Mon cher Gauguin

merci de votre lettre et merci surtout de votre promesse de venir déjà le vingt.[1] *Certes cette raison que vous dites*[2] *doit ne pas contribuer à faire un voyage d'agrément du trajet en chemin de fer et ce n'est que comme de juste que vous retardiez votre voyage jusqu'à que vous puissiez le faire sans emmerdement. Mais à part cela je vous l'envie presque, ce voyage qui va vous montrer en passant des lieues et des lieues de pays de diverse nature avec les splendeurs d'automne.*

J'ai toujours encore présent dans ma mémoire l'emotion que m'a causé le trajet cet hiver de Paris à Arles.[3] *Comme j'ai guetté "si cela etait déjà du Japon!" Enfantillage quoi.*

Dites donc je vous ecrivais l'autre jour, que j'avais la vue etrangement fatiguée. Bon je me suis reposé deux jours & demi et puis je me suis remis au travail. Mais n'osant pas encore aller en plein air, j'ai fait toujours pour ma decoration une toile de 30 de ma chambre à coucher[4] *avec les meubles en bois blanc que vous savez. Eh bien cela m'a enormement amusé de faire cet interieur sans rien.*

D'une simplicité à la Seurat. [sketch] *A teintes plates mais grossierement brossées en pleine pâte, les murs lilas pâle, le sol d'un rouge rompu & fané, les chaises & le lit jaune de chrome, les oreillers et le drap citron vert très pâle, la couverture rouge sang, la table à toilette orangée, la cuvette bleue, la fenetre verte. J'avais voulu exprimer un* repos absolu *par tous ces tons très divers vous voyez, et où il n'y a de blanc que la petite note que donne le miroir à cadre noir (pour fourrer encore la quatrième paire de complementaires dedans).*

Enfin vous verrez cela avec les autres et nous en causerons. Car je ne sais souvent pas ce que je fais, travaillant presqu'en sonnambule.

Il commence à faire froid surtout les jours de mistral.

J'ai fait mettre le gaz dans l'atelier pour que nous ayons une bonne lumière en hiver.

Peutêtre serez vous desenchanté d'Arles si vous y venez par un temps de mistral mais attendez. . . . C'est à la longue que la poésie d'ici pénètre.

Vous ne trouverez pas encore la maison aussi comfortable que peu à peu nous chercherons à la rendre. Il y a tant de dépenses et cela ne peut pas se faire d'une seule haleine. Enfin je crois qu'une fois ici vous allez comme moi etre pris d'une rage de peindre, dans les intervalles du mistral, les effets d'automne. et que vous comprendrez que j'aie insisté pour que vous veniez maintenant qu'il y a de bien beaux jours. Allons, au revoir.

t. à v.
Vincent

Annotations to Appendix 1

Letter from Vincent van Gogh to Paul Gauguin / Arles, Wednesday, 17 October, 1888

1. Gauguin would arrive in Arles on 23 October 1888. This must be a reference to a new letter from Gauguin and not the one van Gogh said that he had received in letter *CL* 553, otherwise he would undoubtedly have told Theo that Gauguin wanted to come on 20 October. His journey from Pont-Aven to Arles took from Sunday afternoon to Tuesday morning, as Gauguin reported to Schuffenecker on 25 October 1888. See Merlhès 1989, pp. 124–27.

2. Gauguin was still in poor health (see Letter 6, n. 13). He told Schuffenecker on 8 October that he had had another attack of dysentery. See *Correspondance Gauguin* 1984, pp. 247–49.

3. Van Gogh had made the journey from Paris to Arles on Sunday, 19, and Monday, 20 February, 1888.

4. *The Bedroom* (F 482 / JH 1608; Fig. 118). The painting measures 28⅜ x 35½ in. (72 x 90 cm). Vincent also sent Theo a sketch of the bedroom (letter *CL* 554).

Appendix 2

Autograph Manuscript of an Article on Vincent van Gogh by Émile Bernard and the Cover Letter to Albert Aurier

Albert Aurier was a symbolist writer and critic who founded a small, short-lived review, *Le Moderniste Illustré,* of which he was editor-in-chief from April 1889. Bernard hoped that he would run an article on van Gogh in his publication. Bernard's letter was written at Saint-Briac, probably in July or August 1889. It is possible that the article remained unpublished because Aurier received it only shortly before *Le Moderniste Illustré* ceased publication. Several months later Aurier himself wrote an article on van Gogh entitled "Les isolés," which was published in the *Mercure de France,* January 1890, pp. 24–29. These documents are in the Morgan's collection of literary and historical manuscripts; MA 4148. They were first published and annotated in Mannheim and Amsterdam 1990, pp. 381–83.

Appendix 2: Translation of Autograph Manuscript of an Article on Vincent van Gogh by Émile Bernard and the Cover Letter to Albert Aurier

Article

Impressionists[1]
Vincent van Gogh
Two years ago, Vincent van Gogh had organized a sort of exhibition of impressionism in a large working-class restaurant on the avenue de Clichy. The room was huge and provided a surface on which over a thousand canvases could hang: so Vincent asked for assistants; and there came to join him—Louis Anquetin, Koning (since returned to Holland) and Émile Bernard.

The establishment's regular customers were a little alarmed by this sudden exhibition (a little out of place, it's true, in this location, but one takes what one finds, and wasn't it better than nothing?). But incapable as they were to appreciate either good or bad, they tolerated it and continued to eat there (not, however, without being a little taken aback both by the off-putting appearance of the paintings and by the painters) among all that polychromy. A certain number of artists, among whom I mention at random Pissarro, Gauguin, Guillaumin, Seurat, etc., dropped in, as well as some dealers, then fairly well disposed toward the revolutionaries, who made some purchases; among others I mention Monsieur Georges Thomas (of the boulevard Malesherbes), on the right track at that time but who has since sacrificed to the golden calf in support of certain facile paradoxes. . . .

Appendix 2: Transcription of Autograph Manuscript of an Article on Vincent van Gogh by Émile Bernard and the Cover Letter to Albert Aurier

Article

Impressionnistes[1]
Vincent van Ghogh
Il y a deux ans passés, dans un grand restaurant Populaire de l'avenue de Clichy. Vincent Van Ghogh avait entrepris une manière d'Exposition d'impressionnisme. La salle etait immense et offrait une surface où pouvaient pendre plus de mille toiles: Vincent demanda alors des aides; et à lui vinrent se joindre—Louis Anquetin, Koning (depuis retourné en Hollande) et Émile Bernard.

Les habitués du lieu furent tant soit peu effrayés de cette soudaine exhibition (peu dans son milieu il est vrai, en cet endroit, mais on prend ce qu'on trouve et cela ne valait-il pas mieux que rien?) Mais inaptes qu'ils etaient tant au mal qu'au bien ils la tolérèrent et continuerent à prendre leur repas (non sans être toutefois un peu interloqués et par la mine rebarbatives des peintures et des peintres) parmi ces polychromies. Un certain nombre d'artistes en lesquels citons au hasard, Pissaro, Gauguin, Guillaumin, Seurat etc. y passa et quelques marchands assez bien disposés alors à l'egard des revolutionnaires y firent quelques achats citons entre autres Monsieur Georges Thomas (du Boulevard Malesherbes) en bonne voie à cette epoque, mais qui depuis a sacrifié au veau d'or à l'appui de certains paradoxes faciles. . . .

Là Vincent s'etalait dans toute l'ampleur de son tempérament vigoureux. On devinait deja le style,

There Vincent displayed himself in all the breadth of his vigorous temperament. You could already foresee the style, the willpower, the boldness of his latest productions: in his portrait of *Père* Tanguy (the colorman of the rue Clauzel), so delightfully jovial, in his Clichy factories that smelled so strongly of coal and gas, and in his sunlit Asnières landscapes.

Intensity of life was the striking aspect of these canvases, and if a certain hastiness undermined the brain's activity, one nevertheless felt the powerful mark of logic and knowledge in them.

About a hundred of Vincent's canvases hung on the walls, and the overall impression of the room derived directly from him, and it was a gay, vivid, harmonious impression.

Later on, he appeared more legitimately in the Independents' Exhibition (in 1888).

All I remember of his canvases is a large Montmartre landscape, like this: sheds surrounded by large, very yellow sunflowers rise in tiers on the hill, from the top of which the Moulin de la Galette summons into its arms the so depraved young apprentices of the capital. A leaden sky presses down on the landscape flooded by a torrid sun.

And another exhibit: a large display of very yellow books among which a rose (symbol) opens in a glass.

But these few paintings could not give any firm idea of the artist, because, chosen hastily from a heap by his brother and sent by him the day before the exhibition opened, they did not yet embody the qualities of his most recent works.

Vincent van Gogh is thirty-five years old and leads a very simple life.

He has a primitive's fanatical admiration for works of art. His faith is limitless, he's a true believer.

---

la volonté, la hardiesse de ses dernières productions: dans son portrait du Pere Tanguy (le marchand de couleurs de la rue Clauzel) d'une jovialité si delectante, dans ses usines de clichy qui sentaient tant le charbon et le gaz, et dans ses paysages ensoleillés d'asnières.

L'intensité de la vie etait le coté frappant de ces toiles et si quelquefois une certaine hativité de travail trahissait l'activité du cerveau on y sentait neanmoins la trace puissante de la logique et du savoir.

Une centaine de toiles de Vincent pendait aux murs et l'impression generale de la salle derivait de lui directement, et c'etait une impression gaie vibrante, harmonieuse.

Depuis, plus legitimement il a figuré à l'Exposition des indépendants (en 1888).

Je ne me souviens d'entre ses toiles que d'un grand paysage montmartrois tel: des cabanes ceintes de grands soleils fleuris, très jaunes s'etagent sur la butte du haut de laquelle le moulin de la galette appelle dans ses bras les si dépravées jeunes apprenties de la capitale. Un ciel de plomb pèse sur le paysage qu'inonde un soleil torride.

Puis d'un autre envoi: grand etalage de livres très jaunes parmi lesquels une rose (symbole) dans un verre s'epanouit.

Mais ces quelques peintures ne pouvaient donner de l'artiste aucune idée certaine, car choisies hativement dans un tas par son frère et envoyées par lui la veille de l'ouverture de l'Exhibition, elles ne renfermaient encore pas les qualités de ses plus recentes choses.

Vincent van Ghogh a trente cinq ans et même[a] *une vie très simple.*

Il a l'admiration fanatique d'un primitif pour les oeuvres d'art. Sa foi est illimité, c'est un vrai croyant

Je lui ai vu faire des lieues à pied sous un soleil devorant, pour peindre un motif à son goût, aucun

I've seen him do leagues on foot under a broiling sun to paint a subject that pleased him, no trouble bothers him. Rain, wind, dew, snow, he braves everything. He gets down to work at any hour of the day or night to paint either a starry sky or a midday sun.

He hiked all over Holland (his native country), went into the mines, lived in those insalubrious hovels among the peasants. You find traces of his journey in some old sketches, and in his paintings too; he often depicts the shoes he wore on his explorations.

His good taste reached everywhere and everything. I have seen him cover the walls of the café he patronizes, on the pretext that they were an unpleasant color, with Japanese prints, and personally paint his house and furniture.

I met him during his time at Cormon's studio, where he stayed two months and left behind the reputation of a raging revolutionary.

He would make three studies each session, getting bogged down in impastos, constantly starting all over again on new canvases, painting the model from all sides, while the pathetic students who laughed at him behind his back took eight days to make an idiotic copy of a foot.

The Vingtiste committee of which Mr. Maus is the principal member has just, I think, invited Vincent to take part in its next exhibition.

That's a decision that pleases all painters who know and love the works of this indefatigable artist.

Note: Canvases by Vincent etc. can be seen at the premises of Mr. Tanguy, 14 rue Clauzel, or by application to Monsieur van Gogh, Maison Goupil (Boussod et Valadon) Boulevard Montmartre.

---

derangement ne lui coûte. pluie, vent, rosée neige il brave tout. à n'importe quelle heure du jour ou de la nuit il se met au travail, soit pour peindre un ciel etoilé ou un soleil de midi.

Il a parcouru à pied la Hollande (sa patrie) est descendu dans les mines, a veçu des[b] *ces huttes malsaines parmi les paysans. Dans d'anciens cartons on trouve des traces de son voyage et aussi dans ses peintures souvent il represente les chaussures qui lui ont servi à ses explorations.*

Son bon goût s'est etendu partout et sur tout. Je lui ai vu tendre lui même de crepons Japonais les murs du café qu'il frequente sous pretexte que le ton en etait déplaisant, et peindre personellement sa maison et ses meubles.

Je l'ai connu lors de son passage à l'atelier Cormon où il est resté deux mois et a laissé le renom d'un revolutionnaire endiablé.

Il faisait par seance trois etudes, s'embourbant dans des pâtes, recommencant incessamment sur de nouvelles toiles, peignant le modèle sur toutes ses faces, alors que les piteux éleves qui lui riaient dans le dos mettaient leurs huit jours à copier imbecilement un pied.

Le comité vingtiste dont Mr Maus est le principal vient, je pense, d'inviter Vincent à participer à sa prochaine exposition.

C'est là une decision qui fait plaisir à tous les peintres qui connaissent et aiment les travaux de l'infatigable artiste.

En note. On peut voir des toiles de Vincent etc. . . . chez Mr Tanguy, 14 Rue clauzel, ou en s'adressant à Monsieur Van Ghogh, maison Goupil (Boussod et Valadon) Boulevard Montmartre.

Letter

My dear Aurier—

Herewith a little article on my friend Vincent. If you think it necessary to place it in *Le Moderniste*, do so. As much as possible, I am eager that my good friend should be talked about a little, in the sense that he is truly an artist who ought to be spoken of in our times, not that his work is something absolutely complete, but nevertheless because of the surprising insights that he sometimes has.

I thought that it would be good, always supposing you were inclined to do so, if you were to supplement the article yourself with a critique of the canvases that he has at Tanguy's, creating the hope that his brother will not hesitate someday to let them be seen, either in an exhibition organized by himself—which would be easy—or with Goupil.

He seems to persist in this idea of not wishing to believe in his brother Vincent's talent at all—I don't know if you agree with me on this point. In any case, do as you wish. But it might be very interesting to consider in that way a certain number of young or old impressionists through a series of articles written by themselves, one about another. . . .

I hope you are in good health. Write to me and send me—the Pleiade and the Modernistes that have appeared. (Do you have our plates?) so that I could relieve myself of some boredom in this silent corner of Brittany.

I offer you my hand, kind regards to Madame

E. Bernard

—Excuse this slightly primitive correspondence, but I am short of everything at the moment.

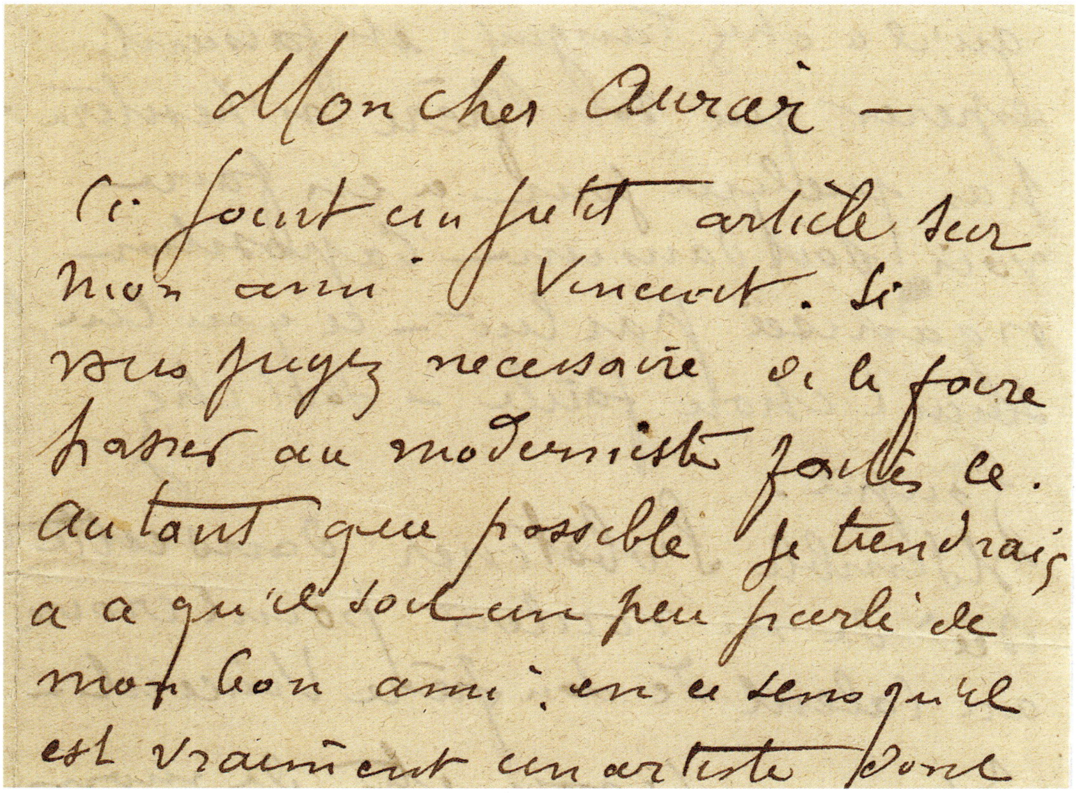
Mon cher Aurier —
Ci joint un petit article sur
mon ami Vincent. Si
vous jugez necessaire de le faire
passer au moderniste faites le.
autant que possible je tiendrais
a a qu'il soit un peu parlé de
mon bon ami; en ce sens qu'il
est vraiment un artiste dont

Detail of Appendix 2.

Letter

Mon cher Aurier—
Ci joint un petit article sur mon ami Vincent. Si vous jugez necessaire de le faire passer au moderniste faites le. Autant que possible je tiendrais à ce qu'il soit un peu parlé de mon bon ami, en ce sens qu'il est vraiment un artiste dont il doit etre fait mention à notre epoque. non pas que son oeuvre soit quelquechose d'absolument complet, mais à cause neanmoins des apercus surprenants qu'il a parfois.

J'ai pensé qu'il serait bon si toutefois vous etes d'avis de faire cette chose, que vous completiez vous même l'article par une critique des toiles qu'il a chez Tanguy et faisant esperer que son frère n'hesitera pas quelque jour à en faire voir soit dans une Exposition organisée par lui—ce que lui serait chose facile—soit chez Goupil.

Il semble s'obstiner dans cette idée de ne vouloir point croire au talent de son frère Vincent— J'ignore si vous etes de mon avis sur ce point. faites en tous les cas comme vous voudrez. mais il serait peut être très interessant de passer en revue comme cela certain nombre d'impressionnistes jeunes ou vieux en suite d'articles ecrits par eux mêmes, l'un sur l'autre. . . .

J'espere que vous etes en bonne santé. ecrivez moi et m'envoyez—la Pleiade et les Modernistes parus. (avez vous nos clichés?) que je puisse un peu me dessennuyer en ce taciturne coin Breton.

Bien à vous la main mes amities a Madame

E Bernard

—Excusez cette correspondance tant soit peu primitive mais je suis en ce moment tres à court de tout.

Annotation to Appendix 2

Autograph Manuscript of an Article on Vincent van Gogh by Émile Bernard and the Cover Letter to Albert Aurier

Textual Notes
a. Bernard probably meant *mène.*
b. For *des* read *dans.*

1. The initial title was "Les peintres impressionistes." Various corrections and improvements were made to the manuscript, most of them while the article was being written, so we assume they are Bernard's.

List of Works Exchanged by van Gogh and Bernard

N.B. All the works listed below as being in the Van Gogh Museum are from the van Gogh family collection.

The van Gogh brothers owned the following paintings by Bernard:

1. *Portrait of Bernard's Grandmother* (Amsterdam, Van Gogh Museum; Fig. 63) Exchanged for *Self-Portrait with Straw Hat* (F 526 / JH 1309); see letter *CL* 553.

2. *Vase with Flowers and a Cup* (Amsterdam, Van Gogh Museum)

3. *Figure Sitting in the Grass* (Amsterdam, Van Gogh Museum)

4. *Ragpicker Fishing* (Amsterdam, Van Gogh Museum) Possibly identical to no. 7.

5. *Self-Portrait with Portrait of Gauguin* (Amsterdam, Van Gogh Museum; Fig. 73) Exchanged for *Quay with Men Unloading Sand Barges* (F 449 / JH 1558; Essen, Museum Folkwang; Fig. 71); see Letter 19.

6. *Les saltimbanques (La parade*; Montevideo, Museo Nacional de Bellas Artes) Was in Theo van Gogh's possession in 1888; see letter *CL* 502.
Bernard included this work in his *"inventaire inédit,"* adding that it had once belonged to Vincent. See Luthi 1982, p. 14, no. 65.

7. A "marine"
Mentioned in letter *CL* 562.
Possibly identical to *Ragpicker Fishing* (Amsterdam, Van Gogh Museum).

8. An unknown "study with a yellow tree"
Mentioned in Letter 21. See note 9 to the letter.

The van Gogh brothers owned the following drawings by Bernard:

1. *Figures in a Street* (Amsterdam, Van Gogh Museum)

2. *Portrait of Bernard's Grandmother* (Amsterdam, Van Gogh Museum)

3. *Girl in a Paris Street* (Amsterdam, Van Gogh Museum) See Letter 5; Fig. 25.

4. *Brothel Scene* (Amsterdam, Van Gogh Museum) See Letter 8; Fig. 38.

5. *Lane in Brittany with Figures* (Amsterdam, Van Gogh Museum) See Letter 12.

6. *Breton Woman in an Orchard* (Amsterdam, Van Gogh Museum) See Letter 12.

7. *Breton Woman with an Umbrella* (Amsterdam, Van Gogh Museum; Fig. 48) See Letter 12.

8. *Women Bathing* (Amsterdam, Van Gogh Museum) See Letter 12.

9. *Female Nude Reclining on a Bed* (Amsterdam, Van Gogh Museum; Fig. 49) See Letter 12.

10. *Female Nude Seated on a Bed* (Amsterdam, Van Gogh Museum) See Letter 12.

11. *A Woman Washing Herself* (Amsterdam, Van Gogh Museum) See Letter 12.

12. *Breton Woman in a Chapel* (Amsterdam, Van Gogh Museum) See Letter 12.

13. *Breton Woman* (Amsterdam, Van Gogh Museum) See Letter 12.

14. *Lubricity* (Amsterdam, Van Gogh Museum; Fig. 47) See Letter 12.

15. *Meadow with Figures and Animals* (Amsterdam, Van Gogh Museum) See Letter 17.

16. *Idyll at Asnières* (Amsterdam, Van Gogh Museum) See Letter 17.

17. *Figures by the Riverside* (Amsterdam, Van Gogh Museum; Fig. 76) See Letter 17.

18. *Brothel Scene and Two Sketches of Prostitutes* (Amsterdam, Van Gogh Museum; Fig. 77) See Letter 17.

19. Album with 11 sketches, *Au bordel* (Amsterdam, Van Gogh Museum; Figs. 90–91) See Letter 19.

Bernard owned the following paintings by van Gogh:

1. *Quay with Men Unloading Sand Barges* (F 449 / JH 1558; Essen, Museum Folkwang; Fig. 71)
Exchanged for *Self-Portrait with Portrait of Gauguin;* see Letter 19, note 8.

2. *Self-Portrait with Straw Hat* (F 526 / JH 1309; The Detroit Institute of Arts) Exchanged for *Portrait of Bernard's Grandmother* (Fig. 63); see letter *CL* 553. Letter from Bernard to his father, 28 January 1900, Getty Center, Los Angeles: *"le portrait de Van Ghog en chapeau de paille."* With thanks to Fred Leeman. See also Letter 19, note 8.

3. *Nude Woman, Reclining* (F 330 / JH 1214; Merion, PA, The Barnes Foundation) Archives Vollard, MS 421, Registre des entrées et sorties de juin 1904 à décembre 1907, no. 3399: *"Femme nue étendue (ovale), T. [Toile] 50 x 74,"* purchased from Émile Bernard.
See also Feilchenfeldt 2005, pp. 117–18.

4. *Nude Woman, Reclining* (F 329 / JH 1215; private collection, on loan to Otterlo, Kröller-Müller Museum) Archives Vollard, MS 421, Registre des entrées et sorties de juin 1904 à décembre 1907, no. 4367: *"Femme nue couché, T. [Toile] 24 x 41,"* purchased from Émile Bernard.
See also Feilchenfeldt 2005, p. 118, and *The Paintings of Vincent van Gogh in the Collection of the Kröller-Müller Museum.* J. ten Berge et al., eds., Otterlo 2003, pp. 165–67.

5. *Blue and White Grapes, Apples, Pears, and Lemons* (F 382 / JH 1337; The Art Institute of Chicago)
Letter from Bernard to his mother, Cairo, ca. June 1894, BCMN (Bibliothèque Centrale des Musées Nationaux): *"les raisins et les pommes."*
With thanks to Fred Leeman.

6. *Self-Portrait* (F 319 / JH 1333; Basel, Kunstmuseum)
Archives Vollard, MS 421, Registre des entrées et sorties de juin 1904 à décembre 1907, no. 3452: *"Portrait de l'artiste par lui-même, T. [Toile] 44 x 35,"* purchased from Bernard's mother.
See also Feilchenfeldt 2005, p. 115.

7. *Self-Portrait* (F 366 / JH 1345; Zürich, Foundation E.G. Bührle)
Archives Vollard, MS 421, Registre des entrées et sorties de juin 1904 à décembre 1907, no. 3515: *"Portrait de l'artiste, T. [Toile] 48 x 35,"* purchased from Bernard's mother.
See also Feilchenfeldt 2005, p. 115.

8. *L'Arlésienne (Madame Ginoux)* (F 540 / JH 1892; Rome, Galleria Nationale d'Arte Moderna)
Archives Vollard, MS 421, Registre de caisse, consignant les entrées et sorties 1894–1900, 7 January 1899: *"arlesienne par Van Gogh,"* purchased from Bernard's mother.
See also Feilchenfeldt 2005, p. 119.

9. *Olive Picking* (F 654 / JH 1868; private collection)
Letter from Bernard to his mother, Cairo, ca. June 1894, BCMN: *"cueillette d'olives."* With thanks to Fred Leeman.
Archives Vollard, MS 421, Registre de caisse, consignant les entrées et sorties 1894–1900, 7 January 1899: *"cueillette d'olives,"* purchased from Bernard's mother.

10. *The Drinkers* (F 667 / JH 1884; The Art Institute of Chicago)
Archives Vollard, MS 421, Registre de caisse, consignant les entrées et sorties 1894–1900, 7 January 1899: *"d'après Daumier Buveurs,"* purchased from Bernard's mother.

11. *Still Life with Oranges, Lemons, and Blue Gloves* (F 502 / JH 1664; Upperville, VA, Collection Mr. and Mrs. Paul Mellon)
Gift from Jo van Gogh-Bonger to Bernard in 1890 (Documentation Centre, Van Gogh Museum, FR b3055).
Archives Vollard, MS 421, Registre de caisse, consignant les entrées et sorties 1894–1900, 7 January 1899: *"citrons et gants,"* purchased from Bernard's mother.

12. *Augustine Roulin (La Berceuse)* (F 508 / JH 167; Boston, Museum of Fine Arts; Fig. 108)
Letter from Bernard to his mother, Cairo, ca. June 1894, BCMN: *"la berceuse."*
With thanks to Fred Leeman.

BERNARD MAY ALSO HAVE OWNED THE FOLLOWING PAINTINGS BY VAN GOGH:

1. *Woman with a Scarlet Bow in Her Hair* (F 207 / JH 979; private collection)
See Faille 1970.

2. *Woman, Strolling in a Garden* (F 368 / JH 1262; private collection)
See Faille 1970.

3. *The Seine with a Rowboat* (F 298 / JH 1257; private collection)
See Faille 1970.
This may be the *"frühes schönes Flussbild mit Booten"* (early, beautiful river scene with boats) in the possession of Bernard's mother, as mentioned in Meier-Graefe 1904, vol. 1, p. 120 (note 1).

4. *A Factory at Asnières* (F 318 / JH 1288; Merion, PA, Barnes Foundation)
Possibly the work referred to in a letter from Bernard to his mother, Cairo, ca. June 1894, BCMN: *"les usines."* With thanks to Fred Leeman.

BERNARD OWNED THE FOLLOWING DRAWINGS BY VAN GOGH:

1. *Zouave, Half-Length* (F 1482 / JH 1487; New York, The Metropolitan Museum of Art; Fig. 37)
See Letter 10.

2. *Newly Mown Lawn with Weeping Tree* (F 1450 / JH 1509; private collection)
See Letter 10.

3. *Fishing Boats at Sea* (F 1430 / JH 1505; Berlin, Nationalgalerie)
See Letter 10.

4. *Street in Saintes-Maries* (F 1435 / JH 1506; New York, The Metropolitan Museum of Art; Fig. 41)
See Letter 10.

5. *Sower with Setting Sun* (F 1442 / JH 1508; private collection)
See Letter 10.

6. *Canal with Women Washing* (F 1444 / JH 1507; Otterlo, Kröller-Müller Museum)
See Letter 10.

7. *Harvest in Provence* (F 1485 / JH 1540; Berlin, Nationalgalerie)
See Letter 10.

8. *Wheat Field* (F 1481 / JH 1515; New York, The Metropolitan Museum of Art; Fig. 42)
See Letter 10.

9. *Wheat Field with Sheaves* (F 1488 / JH 1517; Berlin, Nationalgalerie)
See Letter 10.

10. *View of a River, Quay, and Bridge* (F 1507 / JH 1469; private collection)
See Letter 10.

11. *Rocks with a Tree* (F 1554 / JH 1518; private collection)
See Letter 10.

12. *Haystacks Near a Farm* (F 1426 / JH 1514; Budapest, Szépmüvészeti Museum)
See Letter 10.

13. *Wheat Field with Sheaves and Arles in the Background* (F 1491 / JH 1516; Washington National Gallery of Art)
See Letter 10.

14. *Drawbridge with a Lady with a Parasol* (F 1471 / JH 1420; Los Angeles County Museum of Art; Fig. 43)
See Letter 10.

15. *Wheat Field with Setting Sun* (F 1514 / JH 1546; Winterthur, Kunstmuseum)
See Letter 10.

16. *Mousmé, Sitting in a Cane Chair, Half-Length* (F 1504 / JH 1520; Moscow, Pushkin State Museum of Fine Arts)
See Letter 10.

BERNARD MAY ALSO HAVE OWNED THE FOLLOWING DRAWING BY VAN GOGH:

1. *Orphan Man with Umbrella, Seen from the Back* (F 978a / JH 240; present whereabouts unknown)
See Faille 1970.

Descriptions of the Manuscripts[1]

Condition

Not unexpectedly, van Gogh's letters to Bernard have suffered from the normal wear and tear of personal correspondence—scattered smudges and fingerprints from reading and re-reading, small tears and ruptures from folding and unfolding, and the occasional stain and crumple. Traces of additional handling for purposes of inventory, editing, and photography also remain: numbers, years, names, small crosses, (marginal) marking lines, underscores, brackets, or instructions, such as the framing around the sketches on p. 1v:3 of Letter 6, which corresponds exactly with the illustration in *Lettres à Bernard* 1911, p. XLVIII. Around this frame the text was covered with pencil zigzags. In the lower margin the instruction appeared: *"la partie encadrée seulement"* ([print] only what's within the frame). Most of these additions by others are in (blue) pencil, and some have been erased; a few are in black ink. Finally, because of the presence of preliminary sketches for popular painted works, several of the letters have been damaged by the tacks and adhesives used for their display. Exposure to light through prolonged exhibition has exacerbated the gradual darkening of van Gogh's inexpensive stationery, with the result that the papers now vary from cream to dark tan.

With the exception of Letters 11 and 15, the letters were bound together in an album structure with sturdy paper "flanges" adhered to the fold line or left edge of each (see Introduction, p. 23). Because the heavy paper flanges from the previous binding obscured some text and interfered with the full opening of the folded letters, they were removed. Previous repairs to edge tears and other minor damages were not altered.

Materials and Technique

The letters were written with pen and, in most cases, a ferro/gallous complex ink that was originally black but has faded over time to a brown/black or light tan. Inks with a predominantly carbon-based formulation have remained truly black.

The stationery appears to have been obtained locally and includes examples of formal writing papers as well as student-grade graph or composition papers.[2]

(Note: The first measurement indicates the orientation of the writing on each sheet.)

Letter 1
One vertically folded sheet. 10½ x 8⅛ in. (26.6 x 20.5 cm); cream, machine-made laid paper; chain line interval ¾ in. (1.9 cm).
Pen and blue ink.

Letter 2
One sheet. 5¼ x 8 in. (13.2 x 20.3 cm); cream, machine-made laid paper; chain line interval 1 in. (2.4 cm).
Watermark: L-J D L.[3]
Pen and brown/black ink.
One sketch on p. 1r:1: *Drawbridge with Walking Couple*
5¼ x 3¼ in. (13.2 x 8.3 cm).

Letter 3
Originally one vertically folded sheet. Presently two sheets. Both 5¼ x 8⅛ in. (13.3 x 20.7 cm); cream, machine-made laid paper; chain line interval ⅞ in. (2.3 cm).
Pen and brown/black ink.
(p. [1r:1] in graphite pencil, lower right, *Darmes Alibaud*)
One sketch on p. [1v:3]: *Orchard Surrounded by Cypresses*
8⅛ x 5¼ in. (20.7 x 13.3 cm).

Letter 4
Originally one vertically folded sheet. Presently two sheets. Both 5¼ x 8⅛ in. (13.3 x 20.7 cm); cream, machine-made laid paper; chain line interval ⅞ in. (2.3 cm).
Pen and brown/black ink.
One sketch on p. [1r:2]: *Orchard and House with Orange Roof*
3 x 3⅝ in. (7.5 x 9.2 cm; framed by van Gogh).

Letter 5
One vertically folded sheet. 10⅜ x 8 in. (26.3 x 20.3 cm); cream, machine-made laid paper; chain line interval 1 in. (2.4 cm). Watermark: L-J D L & C°.
Pen and brown/black ink.

Letter 6
Three sheets. Sheet 1: Originally one vertically folded sheet. Presently two sheets. Both 14⅛ x 9⅛ in. (35.8 x 23.2 cm); cream, machine-made laid paper; chain line interval 1 in. (2.5 cm).
Watermark: ORIGINAL PALET MILL below a unfurled ribbon surmounted by a crown.[4]
Pen and black ink.

Two sketches on p. 1v:3:1. *Cabane in Saintes-Maries* 2⅜ x 1 in. (6.0 x 2.5 cm; framed by Van Gogh); 2. *Woman with a Parasol* 3⅜ x 2⅞ in. (8.5 x 7.3 cm; framed by van Gogh). Handwriting in graphite pencil (unknown hand) around the sketch.

Six sketches on two separate sheets: Sheet 2: 7 x 5⅝ in. (17.9 x 14.2 cm); cream, machine-made laid paper; chain line interval 1 in. (2.5 cm). Watermark: Unfurled ribbon surmounted by a crown.
Pen and black ink, with sketch no. 3 (recto) and nos. 4–6 (verso): 3. *Street in Saintes-Maries* 7 x 5⅝ in. (17.9 x 14.2 cm); 4. *Fishing Boats at Sea* 5¼ x 3¾ in. (13.2 x 9.5 cm); 5. *Landscape with Edge of a Road* 1¾ x 2½ in. (4.3 x 6.5 cm); 6. *Farm Along a Road* 1¾ x 1 in. (4.3 x 2.5 cm); including inscription below: 1¾ x 1⅝ in. (4.3 x 4.0 cm).

Sheet 3: 7 x 3½ in. (17.9 x 9.0 cm); cream, machine-made laid paper; chain line interval 1 in. (2.5 cm). Watermark: ORIGINAL PALET MILL.
Pen and black ink, with sketch no. 7 (recto) and no. 8 (verso):
7. *Fishing Boats on the Beach* 7 x 3½ in. (17.8 x 9.0 cm);
8. *Still Life with Coffeepot* 7 x 3½ in. (17.8 x 9.0 cm).

Letter 7
Two sheets. Both 8⅛ x 10½ in. (20.5 x 26.8 cm); cream, machine-made laid paper; chain line interval 1 in. (2.4 cm). Watermarks in both: LAROCHE-JOUBERT/ANGOULÊME surmounted by a crown above a branched flourish.
Pen and black ink.

One sketch on p. 1r:1: *Sower with Setting Sun* 5¾ x 4½ in.; (14.5 x 11.4 cm; framed by van Gogh).

Two sketches on p. 1v:2: 1. *Wheat Field with Setting Sun* 6⅜ x 4¼ in. (16.2 x 10.8 cm; framed by van Gogh); 2. *Leg of an Easel with a Ground Spike* 2⅛ x 1¼ in. (5.5 x 3.2 cm).

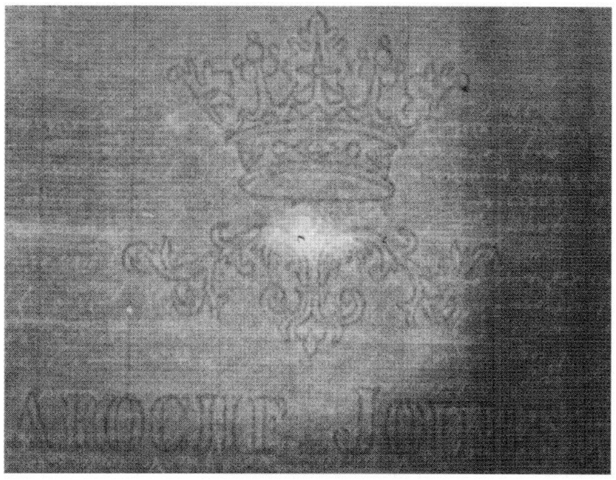

Letter 8
Two sheets. Both 8⅛ x 10½ in. (20.6 x 26.8 cm); cream, machine-made laid paper; chain line interval 1 in. (2.4 cm). Watermarks in both: LAROCHE-JOUBERT/ANGOULÊME surmounted by a crown above a branched flourish.
Pen and black ink.

Letter 9
Two sheets. Sheet 1: 8⅛ x 10½ in. (20.6 x 26.8 cm); cream, machine-made laid paper; chain line interval 1 in. (2.4 cm). Watermark: LAROCHE-JOUBERT/ANGOULÊME surmounted by a crown above a branched flourish.
Pen and black ink.
Sheet 2: 8 x 5¼ in. (20.3 x 13.2 cm); cream, machine-made laid paper; chain line interval 1 in. (2.4 cm). Watermark: L-J D.
Pen and black ink.

Letter 10
One vertically folded sheet. 10⅝ x 8¼ in. (26.9 x 21.0 cm); white wove, blue squared (5/16 x 5/16 in.; 8 x 8 mm) paper.
Pen and brown/black ink.

Letter 11
One vertically folded sheet. 8⅝ x 6⅞ in. (21.8 x 17.3 cm); cream, machine-made laid paper; chain line interval 1⅛ in. (2.7/2.8 cm). Watermark: TRADE MARK / HULPMILL, separated by a lion.
Pen and black ink. On p. 1r:4, lower left, in another hand, the inv. no. *i 8727.*

Letter 12
Originally one vertically folded sheet. Presently two sheets. Both 5¼ x 8 in. (13.2 x 20.2 cm); cream, machine-made laid paper; chain line interval 1 in. (2.4 cm). Watermark: L-J D L & C°.
Pen and black ink.

Letter 13
One vertically folded sheet. 16½ x 10⅝ in. (41.8 x 26.9 cm); white wove, blue squared (3/16 x 5/16 in.; 4 x 8 mm) paper.
Pen and black ink.

Letter 14
Two sheets. Sheet 1: vertically folded 16½ x 10⅝ in. (41.9 x 26.9 cm); white wove, blue squared 3/16 x 5/16 in.; 4 x 8 mm) paper.
Pen and black ink.
On p. 1r:1, upper right, in an unknown hand, a sailboat.
Sheet 2: 5¼ x 8 in. (13.2 x 20.2 cm); cream, machine-made laid paper; chain line interval 1 in. (2.4 cm).
Pen and black ink.

Letter 15
One vertically folded sheet. 10½ x 8¼ in. (26.6 x 21.0 cm); white wove, blue squared (5/16 x 5/16 in.; 8 x 8 mm) paper.
Pen and black ink.
In another hand on p. 1r:1, upper margin, with a purple copy pencil, *publiée sous le numéro XIX.* Followed by, in pencil: *dans l'ouvrage de Bernard—Lettres de V. Van Gogh / a Émile Bernard.*

Letter 16
One vertically folded sheet. 10½ x 8¼ in. (26.6 x 21.0 cm); white wove, blue squared (5/16 x 5/16 in.; 8 x 8 mm) paper.
Pen and black ink.

Letter 17
One vertically folded sheet. 10½ x 8⅛ in. (26.8 x 20.7 cm); white wove, blue squared (3/16 x 5/16 in.; 4 x 8 mm) paper.
Pen and brown/black ink.

Letter 18
One vertically folded sheet. 10½ x 8⅛ in. (26.8 x 20.7 cm); white wove, blue squared (3/16 x 5/16 in.; 4 x 8 mm) paper.
Pen and brown/black ink.

Letter 19
One vertically folded sheet. 10½ x 8⅛ in. (26.8 x 20.7 cm); white wove, blue squared (3/16 x 5/16 in.; 4 x 8 mm) paper.
Pen and brown/black ink.

Letter 20 (present whereabouts unknown; information derived from a black-and-white photograph)
One sheet. White wove, (probably) blue squared paper.
Pen and (probably) brown/black ink.

Letter 21
One sheet. 5⅛ x 8 in. (13.1 x 20.3 cm); white wove, blue squared (3/16 x 3/16 in.; 4 x 4 mm) paper. Watermark: [partial D] L & C°.
Pen and brown/black ink.

Letter 22
One vertically folded sheet. 16¼ x 10½ in. (41.4 x 26.6 cm); white wove, blue squared (3/16 x 5/16 in.; 4 x 8 mm) paper.
Watermark: L-J D L & C°.
Pen and brown/black ink.

Two sketches on p. 1v:2: 1. *Reclining Girl* 3⅜ x 1⅜ in. (8.5 x 3.5 cm; partially framed by van Gogh); 2. *Three Trees* 1⅜ x 1⅞ in. (3.4 x 4.8 cm; partially framed by van Gogh)

Appendix 1
One vertically folded sheet. 10⅜ x 8¼ in. (26.3 x 21.0 cm); white wove, blue squared (3/16 x 3/16 in.; 4 x 4 mm) paper.
Pen and brown/black ink.
One sketch on p. 1v:2: *The Bedroom* 5⅝ x 3½ in. (14.2 x 9.0 cm).

Appendix 2
Three sheets. Sheet 1: One vertically folded sheet. 20.4 x 15.3 cm (irregularly folded and torn); cream newsprint.
Sheets 2 and 3: Two vertically folded sheets. Both 31.0 x 19.8 cm (irregularly folded and torn); cream newsprint.
Pen and brown / black ink.

Notes

Introduction

1. *Lettres à Bernard* 1911, p. 41: *"là on le trouverait tout, palpitant."*
2. Auden 1961, p. [5].
3. Bukowski 1994, p. 30.
4. Bernard 1994, vol. 1, p. 251, and *Lettres à Bernard* 1911, p. 12.
5. See Hendriks and van Tilborgh 2008 for this episode in van Gogh's life and for the meeting with Bernard.
6. See Sjraar van Heugten, "Working in Black-and-White and Color: Van Gogh's Regard for Tonality and Technique," in Amsterdam 2003, pp. 123–32.
7. See Mannheim and Amsterdam 1990, p. 95.
8. Bernard 1994, vol. 1, pp. 26–27: *"pour la première fois à l'atelier Cormon. Puis chez Tanguy, cette ardente petite chapelle dont le vieux prêtre a le bon sourire de l'honnêteté incomprise. Quand il émergea de l'arrière-boutique, ce front haut et large, j'eus presque peur tant il flamba; mais vite nous fûmes amis et s'ouvrirent les cartons de Hollande et les portefeuilles d'études. [. . .] Sur la table, parmi des crépons japonais, des boules de laine dont les fils entrelacés jouaient des symphonies imprévues."*
9. *Lettres à Bernard* 1911, p. 12.
10. Those works are now in the collection of the Van Gogh Museum.
11. See Bernard 1994, vol. 1, p. 274. On van Gogh and the "petit boulevard," see also St. Louis and Frankfurt 2001.
12. See Toronto and Amsterdam 1981.
13. See van Rappard-Boon et al. 1991. Bernard later wrote that Segatori gave van Gogh free meals in return for paintings, mainly flower still lifes, and the walls of the restaurant were covered with his studies; see Bernard 1994, vol. 1, p. 167.
14. On Bing and his activities as a dealer, see Richmond and elsewhere 1986–87 and Amsterdam and elsewhere 2004–6.
15. In December 1887, for example, he exhibited work by Pissarro, Gauguin, and Guillaumin, and in January 1888 pastels by Degas and works by Gauguin. See Amsterdam and Paris 1999–2000, p. 187.
16. On Montmartre in this period, see Richard Thomson, "The cultural geography of the Petit Boulevard," in St. Louis and Frankfurt 2001.
17. *"As tu vu les études que Bernard a rapportées de Bretagne. Gauguin m'en a racconté bien des chôses. Lui en a une qui est simplement magistrale. Je crois qu'en lui en achetant une, à Bernard, on lui rendrait service et qu'il le mérite réellement."*
18. For a list of the works that van Gogh and Bernard exchanged, see p. 366.
19. Van Gogh's other correspondence shows that he received at least twelve letters from Bernard.
20. *"Je garde tous les lettres de Bernard, ils sont quelquefois vraiment interessants, tu les liras un jour ou un autre, cela fait déjà tout un paquet."* He wrote the following to Theo in March 1888 on the subject of keeping letters: *"il sera peutêtre intéressant de garder la correspondance des artistes"* (*CL* 471).
21. *Lettres à Bernard* 1911, p. 14: *"Je lui répondais non moins longuement, remplissant aussi mes lettres des croquis de mes toiles en train. Nous avions formé ce projet de dessiner comme on écrit et avec la même facilité que le feraient un Hokousaï ou un Outamaro."*
22. See *Gauguin lettres* 1983, p. 33.
23. See Letter 5 and note 1 thereto.
24. *"J'étudie le petit Bernard que je connais moins que vous; je crois que vous lui ferez du bien et il en a besoin. Il a naturellement souffert et il débute dans la vie rempli de fiel, entrainé à voir le mauvais côté de l'homme. J'espère qu'avec son intelligence et son amour de l'art il s'apercevra un jour que la bonté est une force contre les autres et une consolation pour nos malheurs propres. Il vous aime et vous estime, vous pouvez donc avoir une bonne influence sur lui.—Nous avons besoin d'être très unis de coeur et d'intelligence si nous voulons que l'avenir nous mette à notre vraie place."*
25. Harscoët-Maire 1997, pp. 162–63: *"En arrivant j'ai trouvé une lettre de Vincent très intéressante que j'ai lue et relue pour me distraire car avec le vent qu'il fait, la pluie et le froid, le pays quoique très sauvage est encore bien triste. Vincent me félicite de ma décision pour l'Algérie et me dit que lui-même ira peut-être aussi pour m'y voir. Il me donne le conseil de me fortifier avant d'aller au service, ce que je crois aussi très nécessaire quoique je sois d'une constitution moins gaillarde que j'en ai l'air. C'est en somme un très bon ami, très sincère et toute son exubérance méridionale se traduit (en homme du nord) par une profonde sincérité. Seulement, (il y a toujours un seulement), il s'emporte trop vite pour des choses insignificantes. Il m'a parlé beaucoup des vers que je lui ai envoyés et me dit 'ce n'est pas si bien que ta peinture, mais il faut sûrement continuer les sonnets. Il y a beaucoup de copains qui croient qu'écrire est mauvais. Eh bien! Moi je dis qu'il est aussi intéressant de peindre avec la parole qu'avec le pinceau. Continue donc'."*
26. Harscoët-Maire 1997, p. 174: *"C'est un garçon d'un tempérament artistique très large, mais trop indépendant, d'un côté scientifique approfondi, malgré cela je ne désespère pas de le voir revenir avec de fort bonnes choses. Il a la compréhension facile et en somme a le côté artiste très développé (cela est si rare!)."*
27. See p. 360ff. After a few fragments from the article had been published and quoted here and there, it first appeared in its entirety in Mannheim and Amsterdam 1990, together with the letter to Aurier and with references to previous publications of fragments.
28. Albert Aurier, "Les isolés: Vincent van Gogh," *Mercure de France* 1 (January 1890), pp. 24–29. It also appeared in a shortened form in *L'Art Moderne* of January 1890.
29. Letter *CL* 626a.
30. For Bernard's letter to Aurier, see Pickvance 1992, pp. 32–38 (with facsimile, English translation, and commentary). Aurier followed Bernard's suggestion and wrote "a few lines" for the *Mercure de France*, but the journal had already typeset Julien Leclerq's article "Vincent van Gogh," ready for publication in the December issue. See Stein 1986, pp. 234–35.
31. Bernard 1994, vol. 1, pp. 26–29, especially p. 26: *"d'une insigne laideur et d'une vie inquiétante."*
32. Bernard 1994, vol. 1, pp. 26–27: *"une manière decisive, [. . .] une technique personnelle très picturale"*; *"une symbolisme naissant"*; *"son égale turbulence vitale lui crée une unité qui, à la longue, le démontre très équilibré, très logique, très conscient. En des toiles dernières, d'aucuns virent la folie. Mais qu'est-elle lorsqu'elle se fait deviner sous la forme présente, sinon le génie."*
33. Bernard 1994, vol. 1, p. 34: *"Roux de poil (barbiche de bouc, moustache rude, toque capillaire rase), le regard d'aigle et la bouche incisive comme pour ainsi parler; la taille moyenne, trapu sans toutefois d'excès commun, le geste vif, la marche saccadée, tel van Gogh avec, toujours, sa pipe, une toile ou une gravure, ou un carton. Véhément dans le discours, interminablement explicatif et développeur d'idées, peu prêt à la controverse, encor lui tout cela; et des rêves, ah! des rêves! expositions géantes, phalanstères philanthropiques d'artistes, fondations de colonnes dans le Midi, et ailleurs, envahissement progressif des milieux publics pour la fameuse rééducation des masses qui ont pourtant connu l'art dans le Passé."*
34. Bernard 1994, vol. 1, p. 318: *"intriguait tout le monde par son air féroce et absorbé."*
35. *Lettres à Bernard* 1911, pp. 19–20: *"L'opposition crée souvent de ces contrastes inattendus et les résoud dans une tragédie intime, dérobée aux yeux de tous. [. . .] exaltation solaire [. . .] la mélancholie."*
36. *Lettres à Bernard* 1911, p. 10: *"frénésie de l'expression."*
37. *Lettres à Bernard* 1911, pp. 19–21: *"je ne la décrit point sans compatir à son horreur et comprendre combien l'incomplet de son art, marqué d'un incontestable génie, demande d'indulgences et de pardons. [. . .] La technique le préoccupe moins, il peint mieux parce qu'il ne fait plus de gammes, mais suit le développement de ses intimes visions. Son mysticisme va vers une pitié qui lui fait aimer ses frères douloureux, les inférieurs et les pauvres, les derniers de l'humanité, les malades, les perdus; dans la nature même, il s'attendrit sur le vieil arbre entouré de lierre, sur la vasque du parc, d'où l'eau est absente et que les feuilles emplissent de leur manteau fané."*

38. The extent of van Gogh's correspondence is well known. The surviving letters by him number around eight hundred, but that is probably only half or one-third of what he actually wrote. Bernard's letters are not so famous, but it seems from what has been preserved in public and private collections that he, too, was an active correspondent.
39. *Lettres à Bernard* 1911, pp. 12–13: *"le lien qui nous réunit; elles nous firent nous aimer, nous connaître, durant cette absence. Il se plaisait à m'écrire longuement. J'étais, je crois, après Gauguin, son seul ami; j'ai vu les lettres qu'il adressait à ce dernier, elles étaient plus brèves, parce que plus respectueuses. Gauguin était son aîné et à ses yeux occupait une situation supérieure à la sienne: il avait connu les impressionistes et lutté avec eux. Il ne s'abandonnait donc entièrement qu'à moi; j'étais plus jeune de quinze années, et quoiqu'il me parlât des travaux de mes dix-huit ans avec considération, il pouvait prendre vis-à-vis de ma jeunesse une parole conseillère et protectrice; c'est pourquoi, malgré ma parfaite indépendance de toute influence, on trouvera dans ces lettres le ton permis à un homme d'âge mûr vis-à-vis d'un jeune homme."*
40. He did, of course, meet artists staying in or near Arles, such as Christian Mourier-Petersen, Eugène Boch, and Dodge MacKnight, but those encounters were brief and far less intimate.
41. Bernard 1994, vol. 1, p. 41: *"Autant de théologie que de sociabilité. Autant de critique que de peinture. Enfin comparez ces lettres les unes aux autres, et voyez comme elles forment bien les analogues anneaux d'une même chaîne et cette harmonie qui naît de l'analogie. Les plus grand génies y sont sans cesse cités. Noms de dieux, de saints, d'apôtres, de savants, de peintres, Jésus, Rembrandt, Giotto, Delacroix, etc. Chacun de ces noms évoque un monde d'idées qui se répondent, se complètent, et, formant unisson, vous conduisent vers le sublime."*
42. Letter from Émile Bernard to his parents, 16 May 1888. See Harscoët-Maire 1997, p. 168: *"En définitive qui a souffert, aimé, s'est battu, a vécu, a vécu grandement. Lutter c'est vivre. L'éternel bon accord est certainement admirable mais il est inerte; il n'engendre rien. Il faut le flux et le reflux en tout c'est la loi, le rythme, la mesure."*
43. *Lettres à Bernard* 1911, p. 13.
44. He said as much to Theo in February 1889; see letter *CL* 578, from which it appears that Bernard had written to him again.
45. See, for example, letters *CL* 578 and *CL* 579.
46. These words from Zola's *Mes haines* are quoted three times in the correspondence; see also Letter 11.
47. Letter 22. Van Gogh thought that some of the figures looked as if they were having epileptic seizures.
48. See Mannheim and Amsterdam 1990, pp. 98–99.
49. See Pickvance 1992, p. 33.
50. See Van Gogh Museum, inv. no. b947 V/1962.
51. See Mannheim and Amsterdam 1990, pp. 100, 292–93 (for the address, see Van Gogh Museum, inv. no. b833 V/1962).
52. See *Account Book* 2002, pp. 24–25. In 1891 Bernard also had photographs taken of twelve works by van Gogh that he offered for sale in order to raise money for an exhibition. On this, see Larsson 1993, pp. 127–28.
53. *Lettres à Bernard* 1911, p. 7: *"Je l'avais conquis à Vincent dès ma première rencontre avec lui, à Saint-Briac [in the summer of 1888]. [. . .] Je lui avais montré [. . .] les lettres de van Gogh que je venais de recevoir, dont les dessins le séduisirent et dont le texte le captiva."*
54. See Jansen et al. 2002, pp. 26–29.
55. *Lettres à Bernard* 1911, pp. 40–41: *"tenter de faire apprécier Vincent en révélant son esprit, sa lutte, sa vie. Ses lettres étaient ce qu'il y avait de plus puissant. Après les avoir lues, on ne douterait ni de sa sincérité, ni de son caractère, ni de son originalité; là on le trouverait tout."*
56. *Mercure de France* 4 (April 1883), p. 329: *"C'était le plus noble caractère d'homme qu'on puisse rencontrer, franc, ouvert, vif au possible, avec une certaine pointe de malice drôle; excellent ami, inexorable juge, dépourvu de tout égoïsme et de toute ambition, comme le prouvent ses lettres si simples, où il est aussi bien lui-même que dans ses innombrables toiles."* Bernard's introductions to this series and to the one with letters to Theo (see below) were reprinted in *Lettres à Bernard* 1911.
57. Amsterdam, Rijksprentenkabinet, inv. no. F 735: *"J'ai recopié une partie des lettres c'est un travail très long et tres minutieux. Je suis souvent forcé de completer des phrases inachevées et de suivre les idées a travers des labyrinthes inextricables. d'autres fois cela est clair comme de l'eau de roche. Que pensez vous par exemple de cette idée: Luther c'est la grande lumière du moyen-age. Luther au moyen age et une telle assertion cela pourrait nuire a Vincent [. . .] faut il mettre ces choses? Dites moi franchement votre avis."*
58. *Mercure de France* 4 (May 1893), p. 20. He took a different tack in the Vollard edition, reproducing the passage correctly but adding that he did not share van Gogh's views; see Letter 8, note 23.
59. *Lettres à Bernard* 1911, p. 41: *"Plutôt que d'en publier d'abord la totalité, il fallait, pour ainsi dire, n'en tirer que l'essence, afin que par un contact prudent de l'esprit public avec l'esprit de van Gogh le but désiré soit atteint. Je pris donc, dans la publication des fragments faits au* Mercure de France, *le parti de ne rien reproduire qui put blesser par la brutalité du langage, la crudité de l'expression, de ne rien publier de relatif à moi-même, de ne donner que les initiales des amis mêlés à nos existences d'alors."*
60. Bernard asked her for reproductions and permission to have a look at other letters, which she sent him in 1893. He did not return them until 28 June 1896, from Cairo, adding: "God grant that one day they will be edited fittingly and in their entirety" (*Dieu permette qu'elles soient editées un jour dignement et en leur entier;* Amsterdam, Van Gogh Museum, inv. nos. b830-831 V/1962). Alfred Vallette, the publisher of the *Mercure de France*, asked Jo's brother Andries Bonger to translate the fragments from the Dutch letters into French.
61. *"pour soldes de tout compte de l'édition des lettres à lui de Vincent van Gogh."* This and the following information about the preparation and sales of *Lettres à Émile Bernard* has been taken from the Vollard archives preserved in the Documentation Department of the Musée d'Orsay in Paris.
62. *Lettres à Bernard* 1911, pp. 41–42.
63. *Letters to Bernard* 1938, p. 7. Degas would have known what had been said about him in Letter 14, for the passage had appeared in the *Mercure de France* of May 1893 (p. 12).
64. Cooper called himself Douglas Lord in that edition, a photographic reprint of which was recently published; see *Letters to Bernard* 2003.
65. Another part of van Gogh's correspondence has appeared in an annotated edition: the letters he received from Paul Gauguin. The editor was once again Douglas Cooper; see *Gauguin lettres* 1983.
66. Douglas Cooper's papers (Los Angeles, Getty Research Institute) provide a glimpse behind the scenes regarding the preparation of his edition. Aside from the difficulties with the two publishers, it is telling that Bernard asked for and received 6,000 francs, despite the fact that he no longer had title to nor copyright of the letters. He also wanted his preface from the Vollard edition to be included "for sentimental reasons" (*par droit de sentiment*), but Cooper was not prepared to indulge him. He wrote about Bernard: "He is a very greedy and difficult person who is only interested in capitalizing all he can with regard to his now famous friends." Cooper also referred to him as "a professional trouble maker" (letter to The Museum of Modern Art, 27 December 1937). The actual owner of the copyright at that time, van Gogh's nephew V. W. van Gogh, gave his permission for the publication free of charge, merely asking for a few complimentary copies. The copy that Cooper presented to him is now in the library of the Van Gogh Museum.
67. See Rewald 1978, p. 358, note 74.
68. With thanks to Victor Merlhès for this information. The letter was not published until the first complete edition of van Gogh's correspondence, *Verzamelde brieven van Vincent van Gogh*, ed., J. van Gogh-Bonger and V. W. van Gogh, 4 vols., Amsterdam and Antwerp 1952–54.
69. Contrary to what the title promises, the book (which is presented as "tome 1") does not contain any letters by Huysmans or Barrès.
70. This is based on the following sentence: "Among the letters kept religiously ever since my youth, I have therefore selected those from people now dead which may show us something of themselves and recall their struggles and their suffering" (*Parmi les lettres pieusement conservées depuis ma jeunesse, j'ai donc choisi celles des défunts qui peuvent nous montrer quelque chose d'eux-mêmes et rappeler leurs luttes et leurs souffrances; Lettres à Bernard* 1926, p. [8]).

71. *"Gegessen bei Baby Goldschmidt-Rothschild am Pariser Platz. Acht bis zehn Personen, kleines Diner, äußerster Luxus, vier unschätzbare Meisterwerke von Manet, Cézanne, van Gogh, Monet an den Wänden. Dreißig Briefe von van Gogh in einem überreichen, häßlichen Einband wurden nach Tisch zu Zigaretten und Kaffee herumgereicht. Armer van Gogh! Man empfindet schließlich pogromhaft: diese Leute müßte man totschlagen. Nicht Neid, sondern Ekel über die Verfälschung und Verflachung geistiger und künstlerischer zu bloß materiellen Werten, zu Gegenständen des 'Luxus'."* Kessler 1961, p. 604.
72. *Letters to Bernard* 1938, p. v. Cooper unequivocally refers to the baroness as the "owner" in a letter of 17 December 1937 to Alfred H. Barr (Los Angeles, Getty Research Institute).
73. When the letters arrived at their present location, the sheets still bore clear traces of their attachment in the album in the shape of glue remnants and white strips that had been pasted onto them. Some sheets, which had been folded over as a sort of cover, had been torn along the folds, separating the two halves of the pages. Restoration has now removed many of those traces. See Description of the Manuscripts, pp. 368.
74. With thanks to Walter Feilchenfeldt.
75. See *Connaissance des Arts* no. 614 (May 2004), pp. 58–63.

NOTES TO THE READER
1. See van der Veen 2002 for an analysis of van Gogh's French.
2. On this edition, see the Introduction, p. 22. Cooper's method of annotation broadly coincides with our own. His focus, however, was a little narrower, concentrating more on van Gogh alone. We have taken a broader view.

LETTER 3
1. Letter *CL* 471: *"la petite tête de Bretonne."*

LETTER 4
1. Letter *CL* 477: *"J'ai eu une lettre de Bernard avec des Sonnets qu'il a fabriqués parmi lesquels il y en a qui sont réussis, il arrivera à faire un bon sonnet, ce que je lui envie presque."*

LETTER 5
1. See Harscoët-Maire 1997, p. 166: *"je n'ai guère le temps de faire les bêtises de mon âge."*
2. See Harscoët-Maire 1997, p. 166: *"Je ferai une espèce de série de portraits de tous les gens du pays; à ce tableau la famille Lemasson et bien d'autres inconnus de vous, y figureront."*
3. See Harscoët-Maire 1997, p. 168: *"une entre autres très grande qui représente Saint-Briac en fleurs. C'est une pluie, une neige d'arbres fruitiers, pommiers, abricotiers, poiriers, cerisiers en fleurs, ça et là apparaissent des murs de vergers, des prairies, des arbres sauvages et des groupes d'habitations."*

LETTER 6
1. Letter *CL* 499: *"La Méditerranée—a une couleur comme les maquereaux c'est à dire changeante—on ne sait pas toujours si c'est vert ou violet—on ne sait pas toujours si c'est bleu—car la seconde aprés le reflet changeant a pris une teinte rose ou grise."*
2. Letter *CL* 500: *"Si Gauguin venait ici lui & moi pourraient peutêtre accompagner Bernard en Afrique lorsque celui là y ira faire son service."*
3. See Harscoët-Maire 1997, pp. 172–73: *"C'est bien embêtant tout de même une grande toile faite dans les conditions de la mienne, les modèles sont irréguliers, posent mal, ne sont pas vêtus comme il le faudrait et quoiqu'ils témoignent de leur bonne volunté, ne manquent pas de mauvaise."*

LETTER 7
1. Letter *CL* 501: *"J'ai eu une lettre de Bernard qui dit qu'il se sent bien isolé mais qui travaille tout de même—et a encore fait une nouvelle poésie sur lui-même dans laquelle il se blague d'une façon assez touchante. Et il demande: 'à quoi bon travailler'? Seulement il demande cela lui* en travaillant, *il se dit que le travail ne sert absolument à rien* en travaillant—*ce qui n'est pas du tout la même chôse que de le dire en ne travaillant pas. Je voudrais bien voir ce qu'il fait. Je suis curieux de savoir ce que fera Gauguin et si Bernard n'ira pas le rejoindre à Pont Aven; je leur ai donné les adresses de part et d'autre déjà auparavant parceque ils pourraient avoir besoin l'un de l'autre."*

LETTER 8
1. Letter *CL* 502: *"pour l'accrocher à côté des saltimbanques que tu as de lui,"* and *"Bernard en est à la meme question."*
2. Harscoët-Maire 1997, pp. 170–71, 174–75.

LETTER 9
1. Letter *CL* 503: *"Les employés de la poste ont donc eu en me renvoyant la lettre ouverte le plaisir de pouvoir s'édifier en contemplant le bordel de Bernard."*
2. Letter *CL* 503: *"complètement remanié."*

LETTER 10
1. Letter *CL* 509: *"un intérieur nu, 4 murs blancs et des pavés rouges par terre."*
2. Harscoët-Maire 1997, p. 176: *"Je fais une décoration de 4 mètres de long sur 2 m de haut. J'ai choisi un sujet religieux,* L'adoration des bergers, *il y a environ 20 figures double nature à l'heure où je vous écris, je suis en plein travail, car je n'en démords pas depuis deux jours. La couleur est de la couleur à bâtiment. Je fais cela avec trois bleu, blanc, rouge et je parviens à des choses amusantes comme tons. Jamais je ne me suis senti si courageux que depuis que j'ai entrepris cela. C'est pour moi un excellent exercice, et jamais non plus je n'ai fait meilleur, je crois."*

LETTER 11
1. Letter *CL* 513: *"malade et découragé."*
2. Harscoët-Maire 1997, p. 180: *"que vous allez venir, Mère et toi, avec moi à Pont-Aven."*

LETTER 12
1. Letter *CL* 514: *"J'ai reçu de Bernard 10 croquis comme son bordel, il y en a 3 qui sont à la Redon, enthousiasme qu'il a pour cela que moi je ne partage pas trop. Mais il y a une femme qui se laves bien rembrandtesque ou à la Goya et un paysage avec figures tres étrange. Il me défend expressément de te les envoyer, seulement tu les recevra par même poste."*
2. Letter GAC 30: *"que Russel avait une grande admiration pour moi et qu'il devait aller à Belle Isle.—Je ne comprends pas très bien qu'un homme riche n'achète pas ce qu'il admire.—Enfin espérons."*
3. Letter *CL* 513: *"doigts de peintre se dégourdissent,"* and *"je bois un verre de trop pour m'étourdir."*

LETTER 13
1. Letter GAC 30: *"L'art est une abstraction, malheureusement on devient de plus en plus incompris,"* and "sans exécution, *comme les crépons japonais."*
2. Letter *CL* 514: *"Si un peintre se ruine le caractère en travaillant dur à la peinture qui le rend stérile pour bien des choses, pour la vie de famille &c. &c. Si conséquemment il peint non seulement avec de la couleur mais avec de l'abnégation et du renoncement à soi et le coeur brisé. Ton travail à toi non seulement ne t'est pas payé non plus mais te coute exactement comme à un peintre cet effacement de la personalité, moitié volontaire moitie fortuit."*

LETTER 14
1. Letter *CL* 521: *"Ce que dit Gruby se priver de femmes et bien se nourrir, c'est vrai cela fait du bien et si on dépense en travaillant de la tête tout de même sa cervelle et sa moelle, c'est très logique de ne pas se dépenser en faisant l'amour plus que nécessaire."* David Gruby was the brothers' doctor in Paris.

LETTER 15
1. Letter *CL* 518: *"En attendant je suis dans ma peau et ma peau dans l'engrenage des Beaux Arts comme le grain entre les meules."*
2. Letter *CL* 523: *"Je viens de recevoir une lettre de Bernard qui depuis quelques jours a rejoint Gauguin, Laval et encore un autre à Pont aven. Dans cette lettre qui d'ailleurs est très bonne il n'est cependant pas dit une syllabe de ce que Gauguin aurait l'intention de me rejoindre et pas davantage une autre syllabe de ce qu'on me demandait là-bas. Toutefois la lettre était tres amicale. De Gauguin lui-même pas un mot depuis à peu près un mois."*
3. Letter *CL* 526: *"Ils s'amusent bien à peindre, à discuter, à se battre avec les vertueux anglais, il dit beaucoup de bien du travail de Bernard et Bernard dit beaucoup de bien du travail de Gauguin."*

Letter 16

1. Letter *CL* 527: *"parlent maintenant de faire "de la peinture d'enfant'."*

2. Letter *CL* 539: *"Aujourd'hui tout en travaillant j'ai beaucoup pensé à Bernard.—Sa lettre est empreinte de vénération pour le talent de Gauguin—il dit qu'il le trouve un si grand artiste qu'il en a presque peur et qu'il trouve mauvais tout ce que lui, Bernard, fait en comparaison de Gauguin. Et tu sais que cet hiver Bernard cherchait encore querelle à Gauguin. Enfin quoi qu'il en soit et quoi qu'il arrive, il est tres consolant que ces artistes-là sont nos amis et j'ose le croire le resteront n'importe comment tournent les affaires. [. . .] Il a dit qu'il me ferait l'échange de son portrait pour une étude de moi. Mais il a dit qu'il* n'ose pas *faire Gauguin comme je le lui avais demandé parcequ'il se sent trop timide devant Gauguin. Bernard est au fond un tel temperament!! il est quelquefois fou et méchant mais certes ce n'est pas moi qui aie le droit de lui reprocher cela parceque je connais trop moi-meme la même névrose et je sais que lui ne me reprocherait pas non plus."*

Letter 17

1. Letter *CL* 541: *"Les études actuelles sont réellement d'une seule* coulée de pâte. *La touche n'est pas divisée beaucoup et les tons sont souvents rompus. et enfin involontairement je suis obligé d'y empâter à la Monticelli.—Parfois je crois réellement continuer cet homme-là, seulement je n'ai pas encore fait de la figure amoureuse comme lui."*

2. See letter *CL* 543. Part of this letter (including the passage referred to here) will be transferred to another one in the scholarly edition of the complete correspondence.

3. Letter GAC 32: *"Je ne suis pas en état de le faire, attendu que ce n'est pas une copie d'un visage que vous désirez mais un portrait tel que je le comprends. J'observe le petit Bernard et je ne le possède pas encore. Je le ferai peut être de mémoire mais en tous cas ce sera une abstraction. [. . .] Quant au logement; en dehors de la vôtre, Laval et Bernard pourraient avoir une petite chambre meublée à proximité.—J'aime bien la disposition de votre maison rêvée et l'eau m'en vient à la bouche de la voir."*

4. Letter *CL* 543: *"Que je pense à toi et à Gauguin et à Bernard, à tout moment et partout. Tellement c'est beau et tellement je voudrais y voir tout le monde."*

Letter 18

1. Letter GAC 33: *"Le masque de bandit mal vêtu et puissant comme Jean Valjean qui a sa noblesse et sa douceur intérieure."* Jean Valjean is the hero of Victor Hugo's novel *Les misérables* (1862).

2. Letter *CL* 544: *"Il dit aussi que Laval viendra également et que ces deux autres ont le désir de venir. Je ne demanderais pas mieux mais lorsqu'il s'agira de la vie en commun de plusieurs peintres je stipule avant tout qu'il faudrait un abbé pour y mettre l'ordre et que naturellement cela serait Gauguin. Raison pourquoi je désirerais que Gauguin fût ici encore avant eux [. . .]. La lettre de Bernard est encore une fois remplie de la conviction que Gauguin est un bien grand maître et un homme supérieur absolument quant au caractère et l'intelligence."*

Letter 19

1. Letter *CL* 545: *"Le Gauguin est remarquable d'abord mais moi j'aime fort celui de Bernard, c'est rien qu'une idée de peintre, quelques tons sommaires, quelques traits noiratres mais c'est chic comme du vrai vrai Manet. Le Gauguin est plus étudié, poussé loin. [. . .] Voilà qu'en fin j'ai l'occasion de comparer ma peinture à celle des copains."*

2. Letter *CL* 545: *"J'ai ecrit à Gauguin en reponse à sa lettre que s'il m'etait permis à moi aussi d'agrandir ma personalité dans un portrait j'avais, en tant que cherchant à rendre dans mon portrait non seulement moi mais en general un impressioniste, j'avais conçu ce portrait comme celui d'un bonze, simple adorateur du Bouddha éternel. Et lorsque je mets à côté la conception de Gauguin et la mienne, le mien est aussi grave mais moins désesperé."*

Letter 20

1. See *Correspondance Gauguin* 1984, p. 266: *"Votre frère est en effet un peu agité et j'espère le calmer petit à petit."*

2. Letter *CL* 558b: *"une grande renaissance de la peinture."*

Letter 21

1. Quoted from the auction catalogue *Manuscrits du XVe siècle. Livres anciens et modernes. Autographes.* Paris, Nouveau Drouot, 29 March 1985, lot 48: *"Mon cher ami Vincent est fou. Depuis que j'ai appris cela, je le suis presque moi-même. [. . .] Je viens de perdre mon meilleur ami et un des cerveaux les plus admirables et puissants que j'aie connu."* See also Chicago and Amsterdam 2001–2, p. 260.

2. Letter *CL* 579: *"Dis lui de demander conseil à Gauguin mais serre lui bien la main pour moi."*

3. Letter *CL* 595: *"Il est indubitable pour moi que Gauguin et Bernard ont du grand et reel mérite. Qu'à des êtres comme eux bien vivants et jeunes et qui* doivent *vivre et chercher à se frayer leur sentier, il soit impossible de retourner toutes leurs toiles contre un mur jusqu'à qu'il plaise aux gens de les admettre dans quelque chôse, dans le vinaigre officiel, demeure pourtant fort compréhensible."*

Letter 22

1. Letter *CL* 614: *"Bernard aussi m'a écrit, se plaignant d'un tas de chôses tout en se résignant en bon garçon qu'il est mais pas heureux du tout; avec tout son talent, tout son travail, toute sa sobriété, il parait que la maison est souvent un enfer pour lui."*

2. Letter *CL* 614: *"je ne sais mais je crains que ses compositions bibliques me feront désirer autre chôse,"* and *"et alors quand meme, donnant la proportion juste de la figure humaine là-dedans, ça y ferait peutêtre songer."*

Epilogue

1. Letter *CL* 615: *"que je croyais que la pensée et non le rêve était notre devoir, que donc j'étais étonné devant leur travail de ce qu'ils se laissent aller à cela."*

2. Letter *CL* W19: *"as tu rencontré Emile Bernard maintenant—je voudrais bien qu'il vienne un peu voir mes toiles de ces jours ci, je dois lui écrire mais justement j'attends un peu tous les jours une lettre de lui."*

Descriptions of the Manuscripts

1. This was done in collaboration with Margaret Holben Ellis, Director of the Thaw Conservation Center, The Morgan Library & Museum.

2. Information on Laroche-Joubert papers graciously provided by Claire Bustarret, Institut des Textes et Manuscrits Modernes, CNRS, Paris, and Denis Peaucelle, Musée Atelier du Papier "Le Nil," Angoulême, France.

3. The watermark belongs to the Laroche-Joubert paper company located in Angoulême, France, a venerable papermaking region since the fifteenth century.

4. The watermark belongs to the Laroche-Joubert paper mill, which is adjacent to place du Palet in Angoulême.

Concordance of Published Letters from van Gogh to Bernard

Present Edition	Cooper and English Editions	Graber	Vollard
1	B 1	1	I
2	B 2	2	II
3	B 3	3	III
4	B 4	4	IV
5	B 5	5	V
6	B 6	6	VI
7	B 7	7	VII
8	B 8	12	XI
9	B 9	13	XII
10	B 10	17	XVIII
11	B 11	14	XIII
12	B 12	10	X
13	B 13	8	VIII
14	B 14	9	IX
15	B 15	16	XIX
16	B 16	11	XVI
17	B 17	15	XIV
18	B 18	18	XV
19	B 19	19	XVII
20	B 19a	-	-
21	B 20	20	XX
22	B 21	21	XXI
Appendix 1	B 22 (to Gauguin)	-	XXII

Works Cited in Abbreviated Form

LITERATURE

Account Book 2002
Chris Stolwijk and Han Veenenbos, *The Account Book of Theo van Gogh and Jo van Gogh-Bonger,* Leiden, 2002.

Auden 1961
W. H. Auden, ed., *Van Gogh: A Self-Portrait: Letters Revealing His Life as a Painter,* New York and Greenwich, 1961.

Baedeker 1889
K. Baedeker, *Paris et ses environs: Manuel du voyageur,* 9th ed., Leipzig and Paris, 1889.

Bernard 1898
Émile Bernard, *Le voyage de l'être. Poèmes d'évolution,* Cairo, 1898.

Bernard 1994
Émile Bernard, *Propos sur l'art,* 2 vols., Paris, 1994.

Bovero 1961
Anna Bovero, *Tutta la pittura del Crivelli,* Milan, 1961.

Bredius 1969
Abraham Bredius, *Rembrandt: The Complete Edition of the Paintings,* revised by H. Gerson, London, 1969.

Bukowski 1994
Charles Bukowski, *Screams from the Balcony: Selected Letters 1960–1970,* Santa Rosa, 1994.

Coquiot 1923
Gustave Coquiot, *Vincent van Gogh,* Paris, 1923.

Correspondance Gauguin 1984
Victor Merlhès, *Correspondance de Paul Gauguin: Documents, témoignages,* Paris, 1984.

Daudet 1986–94
Alphonse Daudet, *Oeuvres,* Roger Ripoll, ed., 3 vols., Paris, 1986–94.

De brieven 1990
De brieven van Vincent van Gogh, Han van Crimpen and Monique Berends-Albert, eds., 4 vols., The Hague, 1990.

de Dijn 2002
Rosine de Dijn, *Liefde, leed en passie: De vrouwen van Rubens,* Leuven, 2002.

d'Orléans 1923–27
Charles d'Orléans. Poésies. Pièrre Champion, ed., 2 vols., Paris, 1923–27.

Dorn 1990
Roland Dorn, *Décoration, Vincent van Goghs Werkreihe für das Gelbe Haus in Arles,* Hildesheim, Zürich, and New York, 1990 (Studien zur Kunstgeschichte, Band 45).

Dorn 1998
Roland Dorn, "Refiler à Saintes-Maries? Pickvance and Hulsker Revisited," *Van Gogh Museum Journal 1997–98,* Amsterdam, 1998, pp. 14–25.

Dorn 1999
Roland Dorn, "Van Gogh's *Sunflowers* Series: The Fifth Toile de 30," *Van Gogh Museum Journal 1999,* Amsterdam, 1999, pp. 42–61.

Faille 1970
J.-B de la Faille, *The Works of Vincent van Gogh: His Paintings and Drawings,* Amsterdam, 1970.

Feilchenfeldt 1988
Walter Feilchenfeldt, *Vincent van Gogh & Paul Cassirer, Berlin: The Reception of van Gogh in Germany from 1901 to 1914,* catalogue of the drawings compiled by Han Veenenbos, Zwolle, 1988 (Cahier Vincent 2).

Feilchenfeldt 2005
Walter Feilchenfeldt, *"By Appointment Only," Schriften zu Kunst und Kunsthandel: Cézanne und Van Gogh,* Wädenswil, 2005.

Fromentin 1902
Eugène Fromentin, *Les maîtres d'autrefois. Belgique–Hollande,* Paris, 1902.

Fromentin 1981
Eugène Fromentin, *The Masters of Past Time: Dutch and Flemish Painting from van Eyck to Rembrandt.* Horst Gerson, ed., Oxford, 1981. (Translation of Fromentin 1902.)

Gauguin lettres 1946
Maurice Malingue, *Paul Gauguin, lettres à sa femme et à ses amis,* Paris, 1946.

Gauguin lettres 1954
Pierre Cailler, ed., *Lettres de Paul Gauguin à Émile Bernard 1881–1891,* Geneva, 1954.

Gauguin lettres 1983
Douglas Cooper, *Paul Gauguin: 45 lettres à Vincent, Theo et Jo van Gogh,* The Hague, 1983.

Greer 2000
Joan Greer, *The Artist as Christ: The Image of the Artist in The Netherlands, 1885–1902, with a Focus on the Christological Imagery of Vincent van Gogh and Johan Thorn Prikker,* dissertation, University of Amsterdam, 2000.

Harscoët-Maire 1997
Laure Harscoët-Maire, "Lettres d'Émile Bernard (1886): de Cancale à Saint-Briac"; "Lettres d'Émile Bernard (1887): de Cancale à Saint-Briac"; "Lettres d'Émile Bernard (1888): à Saint-Briac," in *Le Pays de Dinan* no. 17 (1997), pp. 113–38, 139–59, 160–83.

Hendriks and van Tilborgh 2001
Ella Hendriks and Louis van Tilborgh, "Van Gogh's 'Garden of the Asylum': Genuine or Fake?" *The Burlington Magazine* 143 (March 2001), pp. 145–56.

Hendriks and van Tilborgh 2008
Ella Hendriks and Louis van Tilborgh, eds., *Vincent van Gogh Paintings 2. Antwerp and Paris,* Amsterdam, 2008.

van Heugten 1996
Sjraar van Heugten, ed., *Vincent van Gogh Drawings 1: The Early Years, 1880–1883, Van Gogh Museum,* Amsterdam and Wormer, 1996.

Hoogewerff 1947
G. J. Hoogewerff, *De geschiedenis van de St. Lucasgilden in Nederland,* Amsterdam, 1947.

Hulsker 1996
Jan Hulsker, *The New Complete van Gogh: Paintings, Drawings, Sketches.* Revised and enlarged edition of the catalogue raisonné of the works of Vincent van Gogh, Amsterdam and Philadelphia, 1996.

Hulsker 1999
Jan Hulsker, "Facts instead of suppositions. Roland Dorn revisited," *Van Gogh Museum Journal 1999,* Amsterdam, 1999, pp. 25–28.

Jansen et al. 2002
Leo Jansen, Hans Luijten, and Fieke Pabst, "Paper Endures: Documentary Research into the Life and Work of Vincent van Gogh," *Van Gogh Museum Journal 2002,* Amsterdam and Zwolle, 2002, pp. 26–39.

Johnson 1981–89
Lee Johnson, *The Paintings of Eugène Delacroix: A Critical Catalogue,* 6 vols., Oxford, 1981–89.

Kendall 1999
Richard Kendall, " 'I Kept on Thinking about Degas . . . ': Vincent van Gogh and 'the Little Lawyer,' " *Van Gogh Museum Journal 1999,* Amsterdam, 1999, pp. 30–41.

Kessler 1961
Harry Graf Kessler, *Tagebücher 1918–1937,* Wolfgang Pfeiffer-Belli, ed., Frankfurt, 1961.

Kōdera 1990
Tsukasa Kōdera, *Vincent van Gogh: Christianity Versus Nature,* Amsterdam and Philadelphia, 1990.

Kris and Kurz 1979
Ernst Kris and Otto Kurz, *Die Legende vom Künstler: Ein geschichtlicher Versuch,* Frankfurt, 1979.

Larsson 1993
Håkan Larsson, *Flames from the South: The Introduction of Vincent van Gogh in Sweden Before 1900,* dissertation, Lund University, 1993.

Letters to Bernard 1938
Vincent van Gogh, Letters to Émile Bernard, edited, translated, and with a foreword by Douglas Lord (Douglas Cooper), London, 1938.

Letters to Bernard 2003
Van Gogh on Art and Artists: Letters to Émile Bernard, Mineola, N.Y., 2003 (photographic reprint of *Letters to Bernard* 1938).

Lettres à Bernard 1911
Lettres de Vincent van Gogh à Émile Bernard, Émile Bernard, ed., Paris, 1911.

Lettres à Bernard 1926
Lettres de Vincent van Gogh, Paul Gauguin, Paul Cézanne, J.-K. Huysmans, Léon Bloy, Elémir Bourges, Milos Marten, Odilon Redon, Maurice Barrès à Émile Bernard, Tonnerre, 1926.

L'indicateur marseillais 1888
L'indicateur marseillais: Guide de l'administration et du commerce: Annuaire du département des Bouches-du-Rhône, G. Allard et Bertrand, eds., Marseille, 1888.

Lugt 1938–87
Frits Lugt, *Répertoire des catalogues de ventes publiques intéressant l'art ou la curiosité,* 4 vols., The Hague, 1938–87.

Luthi 1982
Jean Jacques Luthi, *Émile Bernard: Catalogue raisonné de l'oeuvre peint,* Paris, 1982.

Meier-Graefe 1904
Julius Meier-Graefe, *Entwicklungsgeschichte der modernen Kunst: vergleichende Betrachtung der Bildenden Künste, als Beitrag zu einer neuen Aesthetik,* 3 vols., Stuttgart, 1904.

Merlhès 1989
Victor Merlhès, *Paul Gauguin et Vincent van Gogh 1887–1888: Lettres retrouvées, sources ignorées,* Tahiti, 1989.

Mercure de France
Mercure de France, Serie moderne, Paris, 1890–97.

Météo-France
Annales du bureau central météorologique de France, publiées par E. Mascart, année 1888–90, and *Bulletin annuel de la commission météorologique du Département des Bouches-du-Rhône,* année 1888–90 (Marseille 1889), Paris, Bibliothèque Météo-France.

Milner 1988
John Milner, *The Studios of Paris: The Capital of Art in the Late Nineteenth Century,* New Haven and London, 1988.

Montpellier 1904
Catalogue des peintures et sculptures exposées dans les galeries du Musée Fabre de la ville de Montpellier, Montpellier, 1904.

Paris 1886
Tableaux modernes de premier ordre: Collection John Saulnier de Bordeaux, Vente après décès, auction catalogue, Paris (Hôtel Drouot), 1886.

Pickvance 1992
Ronald Pickvance, *"A Great Artist is Dead": Letters of Condolence on Vincent van Gogh's Death,* Sjraar van Heugten and Fieke Pabst, eds., Zwolle, 1992 (Cahier Vincent 4).

Provvido 1972
Sandra di Provvido, *La pittura di Vittore Crivelli,* L'Aquila, 1972.

van Rappard-Boon et al. 1991
Charlotte van Rappard-Boon et al., *Catalogue of the Van Gogh Museum's Collection of Japanese Prints,* Amsterdam and Zwolle, 1991.

Rewald 1978
John Rewald, *Post-Impressionism: From van Gogh to Gauguin,* 3rd, revised ed., London, 1978.

Rewald 1986
John Rewald, *Cézanne: A Biography,* London, 1986.

Roskill 1970
Mark Roskill, *Van Gogh, Gauguin, and French Painting of the 1880s: A Catalogue Raisonné of Key Works,* Ann Arbor, 1970.

Roskill 1971
Mark Roskill, "Van Gogh's Exchanges of Work with Émile Bernard in 1888," *Oud Holland* 86 (1971), nos. 2–3, pp. 142–79.

Sensier 1881
Alfred Sensier, *La vie et l'oeuvre de J.-F. Millet,* manuscrit publié par Paul Mantz, Paris, 1881.

Silverman 2000
Debora Silverman, *Van Gogh and Gauguin: The Search for Sacred Art,* New York, 2000.

Silvestre 1864
Théophile Silvestre, ed., *Eugène Delacroix: Documents nouveaux,* Paris, 1864.

Slive 1970–74
Seymour Slive, *Frans Hals,* 3 vols., London, 1970–74.

Stein 1986
Susan Stein, ed., *Vincent van Gogh: A Retrospective,* New York, 1986.

Sund 1992
Judy Sund, *True to Temperament: Vincent van Gogh and French Naturalist Literature,* Cambridge, 1992.

Thomson 2005
Richard Thomson, "Maisons closes," in National Gallery of Art, Washington, and The Art Institute of Chicago, *Toulouse-Lautrec and Montmartre,* catalogue by Richard Thomson et al., 2005.

Thoré 1858–60
E. J. T. Thoré (under pseudonym W. Bürger), *Musées de la Hollande: Amsterdam et La Haye,* Paris, 1858, and *Musées de la Hollande: Musée Van der Hoop, à Amsterdam et Musée de Rotterdam,* Paris, 1860.

TLF
*Trésor de la langue française. Dictionnaire de la langue du XIX*e *et du XX*e *siècle (1789–1960),* publié sous la direction de Paul Imbs, 16 vols., Paris, 1971–94.

Vasari 1822
Opere di Giorgio Vasari: Pittore e architetto, 5 vols., Firenze, 1822.

van der Veen 2002
Wouter van der Veen, " 'En tant que quant à moi': Vincent van Gogh and the French Language'," *Van Gogh Museum Journal 2002,* Amsterdam, 2002, pp. 63–77.

Vellekoop and Zwikker 2007
Marije Vellekoop and Roelie Zwikker, eds., *Vincent van Gogh Drawings 4. Arles, Saint-Rémy, and Auvers 1888–1890,* Amsterdam, 2007.

Werness 1972
Hope Benedict Werness, *Essays on Van Gogh's Symbolism,* dissertation, University of California, Santa Barbara, 1972.

Wildenstein 1963
Georges Wildenstein, *Gauguin I: Catalogue,* Paris, 1963.

Wildenstein 1996
Daniel Wildenstein, *Monet or the Triumph of Impressionism: Catalogue Raisonné, Werkverzeichnis,* 4 vols., Köln, 1996.

Wildenstein 2001
Daniel Wildenstein, *Gauguin, Premier itinéraire d'un sauvage: Catalogue de l'oeuvre peint (1873–88),* Paris, 2001.

Wingfield Scott 1936
Mary Wingfield Scott, *Art and Artists in Balzac's Comédie Humaine,* dissertation, University of Chicago, 1936.

Zola 1966–70
Émile Zola, *Oeuvres complètes*, ed. établie sous la direction de Henri Mitterand, 15 vols., Paris, 1966–70.

Exhibitions

Amsterdam 1990
Rijksmuseum Vincent van Gogh, Amsterdam, *Vincent van Gogh: Schilderijen*, catalogue by Evert van Uitert et al., Sjraar van Heugten and Louis van Tilborgh, eds., 1990.

Amsterdam 1994
Van Gogh Museum, Amsterdam, *Pierre Puvis de Chavannes*, catalogue by Geneviève Lacambre et al., 1994.

Amsterdam and Paris 1999–2000
Van Gogh Museum, Amsterdam, and Musée d'Orsay, Paris, *Theo van Gogh 1857–1891: Art Dealer, Collector, and Brother of Vincent*, catalogue by Chris Stolwijk and Richard Thomson, with a contribution by Sjraar van Heugten, 1999–2000.

Amsterdam 2003
Van Gogh Museum, Amsterdam, *Vincent's Choice, The Musée Imaginaire of Van Gogh*, catalogue by Chris Stolwijk et al., 2003.

Amsterdam and elsewhere 2004–6
Van Gogh Museum, Amsterdam, Museum Villa Stuck, Munich, CaixaForum, Barcelona, and Musée des Arts Décoratifs, Paris, *The Origins of Art Nouveau: The Bing Empire*, catalogue edited by Gabriel P. Weisberg et al., 2004–6.

Amsterdam and New York 2005
Van Gogh Museum, Amsterdam, The Metropolitan Museum of Art, New York, *Vincent van Gogh: The Drawings*, catalogue by Colta Ives, Susan Alyson Stein, Sjraar van Heugten, and Marije Vellekoop, 2005.

Arles 1999–2000
Museon Arlaten, Arles, *Arlésienne: Le mythe?* catalogue by E. Rouquette-Mathé et al., 1999–2000.

Bremen 2002–3
Kunsthalle, Bremen, *Van Gogh, Fields: The "Field with Poppies" and the Artists' Dispute*, catalogue by Wulf Herzogenrath and Dorothee Hansen, 2002–3.

Chicago and Amsterdam 2001–2
The Art Institute of Chicago and Van Gogh Museum, Amsterdam, *Van Gogh and Gauguin: The Studio of the South*, catalogue by Douglas W. Druick and Peter Kort Zegers in collaboration with Britt Salvesen, 2001–2.

Essen and Amsterdam 1990
Museum Folkwang, Essen, and Van Gogh Museum, Amsterdam, *Vincent van Gogh en de moderne kunst*, catalogue by Roland Dorn et al., 1990.

Mannheim and Amsterdam 1990
Städtische Kunsthalle, Mannheim, and Van Gogh Museum, Amsterdam, *Émile Bernard 1868–1941: A Pioneer of Modern Art (Ein Wegbereiter der Moderne)*, MaryAnne Stevens et al., 1990.

New Brunswick 1988
Jane Voorhees Zimmerli Art Museum, New Brunswick, *Émile Bernard (1868–1941): The Theme of Bordellos and Prostitutes in Turn-of-the-Century French Art*, catalogue by Bogomila Welsh-Ovcharov, 1988.

New York 1984
The Metropolitan Museum of Art, New York, *Van Gogh in Arles*, catalogue by Ronald Pickvance, 1984.

New York 1986–87
The Metropolitan Museum of Art, New York, *Van Gogh in Saint-Rémy and Auvers*, catalogue by Ronald Pickvance, 1986–87.

Paris 1875
École nationale supérieure des beaux-arts, Paris, *Exposition de l'oeuvre de Corot*, with a "Notice Biographique" by Philippe Burty, 1875.

Paris 1889
Catalogue général officiel. Exposition universelle internationale de 1889 à Paris, 1889.

Paris 1988
Musée d'Orsay, Paris, *Van Gogh à Paris*, catalogue by Françoise Cachin and Bogomila Welsh-Ovcharov, 1988.

Paris 1998–99
Musée d'Orsay, Paris, *Millet/Van Gogh*, catalogue by Louis van Tilborgh and Marie-Pierre Salé, 1998–99.

Paris and Quimper 2003
Musée du Luxembourg, Paris, and Musée des Beaux-Arts, Quimper, *L'aventure de Pont-Aven et Gauguin*, catalogue by André Cariou et al., 2003.

Richmond and elsewhere 1986–87
The Virginia Museum of Fine Arts, Richmond, The Joslyn Art Museum, Omaha, John and Mable Ringling Museum of Art, Sarasota, and The Cooper-Hewitt Museum, New York, *Art Nouveau Bing: Paris Style 1900*, catalogue by P. A. Loar and G. Weisberg, 1986–87.

St. Louis and Frankfurt 2001
St. Louis Art Museum and Städelsches Kunstinstitut und Städelsches Galerie, Frankfurt, *Vincent van Gogh and the Painters of the Petit Boulevard*, catalogue by Cornelia Homburg et al., 2001.

The Hague 1994–95
Royal Cabinet of Paintings Mauritshuis, The Hague, *Paulus Potter: Paintings, Drawings and Etchings*, catalogue by Amy Walsh et al., 1994–95.

The Hague and Schwerin 2004–5
Royal Cabinet of Paintings Mauritshuis, The Hague, and Staatliches Museum, Schwerin, *Carel Fabritius 1622–1654*, catalogue by Frederik J. Duparc, with contributions by Gero Seelig and Ariane van Suchtelen, 2004–5.

Toronto and Amsterdam 1981
Art Gallery of Ontario, Toronto, and Rijksmuseum Vincent van Gogh, Amsterdam, *Vincent van Gogh and the Birth of Cloisonism*, catalogue by Bogomila Welsh-Ovcharov, 1981.

Washington and elsewhere 1988–89
National Gallery of Art, Washington, The Art Institute of Chicago, and Grand Palais, Paris, *The Art of Paul Gauguin*, catalogue by R. R. Brettell, 1988–89.

Washington and elsewhere 1989–90
National Gallery of Art, Washington, Royal Academy of Arts, London, and Frans Hals Museum, Haarlem, *Frans Hals*, catalogue by Seymour Slive et al., 1989–90.

Index

The index comprises the names of individuals and works of art mentioned in the Introduction, English translations, annotations, and the List of Works Exchanged by van Gogh and Bernard. The only book titles included are those mentioned by Vincent van Gogh.

Works of art by Vincent van Gogh, Émile Bernard, and Paul Gauguin are listed under their names. Because their names occur throughout the text, they are not listed separately. The same applies to Vincent's brother Theo van Gogh (1857–1891) and Bernard's parents, Ernest Bernard (1841/1842–1911) and Héloïse Bernard-Bodin (1838/1839–1909).

Page references in italics refer to illustrations.

A

Aeschylus (525–456 B.C.), 344

Anquetin, Louis (1861–1932), 10, 131, 145, 173, 179, 185, 212, 260, 306, 312, 361

The Mower at Noon (Fig. 31), *181*, 185

Old Peasant (Fig. 46), 218, *219*

Portrait of Émile Bernard (Fig. 6), *17*

Auden, Wystan Hugh (1907–1973), 7

Aurier, Albert (1865–1892), 13–14, 18–19, 23, 147, 315, 321, 325, 357, 360–61, 364, 370nn27–28, 370n30

B

Balzac, Honoré de (1799–1850), 16, 239, 255, 263

Baudelaire, Charles (1821–1867), 16, 183, 187, 226, 231, 238, 242, 336

Bernard, Émile (1868–1941)

Acrobats, 189, 366

The Adoration of the Shepherds (Fig. 100), 18, *337*, 349

The Annunciation (Fig. 102), *338*, 349–50

Au bordel (At the Brothel; Figs. 90, 91), *308*, 309–11, *313*, 366

Breton Woman, 231, 366

Breton Woman in a Chapel, 231, 366

Breton Woman in an Orchard, 231, 366

Breton Woman with an Umbrella (Fig. 48), *228*, 231, 366

Breton Women in the Meadow (Fig. 103), 11, 273, 315, *338*, 350

Brothel Scene (Fig. 38), 186, 189, *198*, 200, 203–4, 209, 366; detail, *188*

Brothel Scene and Two Sketches of Prostitutes, 287, 366

Catalogue for the van Gogh Exhibition at Galerie Le Barc de Boutteville, Paris (Fig. 8), *20*

Christ in the Garden of Olives (Fig. 106), 18, 335, *342*, 349–50

Christ Meeting His Mother (Fig. 107), *342*, 353

Deposition from the Cross, 349

Female Nude Reclining on a Bed (Fig. 49), *229*, 231, 366

Female Nude Seated on a Bed, 231, 366

Figures by the Riverside (Fig. 76), *283*, 287, 366

Figures in a Street, 366

Figure Sitting in the Grass, 366

Front cover of *Lettres de Vincent van Gogh à Émile Bernard* (Fig. 9), *20*

Girl in a Paris Street (Fig. 25), 165, *165*, 366

Idyll at Asnières, 287, 366

Lane in Brittany with Figures, 231, 366

Lubricity (Fig. 47), *224*, 231, 247, 366

Madeleine in the Bois d'Amour (Fig. 104), 335, *341*, 350

Meadow with Figures and Animals, 287, 366

Portrait of Bernard's Grandmother (Fig. 63), *253*, 259, 366

Portrait of Bernard's Grandmother (Fig. 64), *253*, 259

A Prostitute Washing Herself (Fig. 90), *308*, 310

Ragpicker Fishing, 366

Red Poplars (Fig. 105), 335, *341*, 350

Self-Portrait, 312

Self-Portrait with Portrait of Gauguin (Fig. 73), *277*, 279, 309, 366

Still Life: Earthenware Pot and Apples (Fig. 62), *250*, 259

Still Life: The Blue Coffeepot (Fig. 61), *250*, 259

Two Prostitutes at a Table (Fig. 91), 310, *313*

Two Sketches of Prostitutes (Fig. 77), *286*, 287, 366; detail, *280*

Vase with Flowers and a Cup, 366

A Woman Washing Herself, 231, 366

Women Bathing, 231, 366

Yellow Tree, 332

Bernard, Madeleine (1871–1895), 211, 220, 269, 273

Bing, Siegfried (1838–1905), 10, 370n14

Blanc, Charles (1813–1882), 173, 186, 227, 232

Boch, Eugène (1855–1941), 249, 281, 371n40

Boggs, Frank Myers (1855–1926), 10

Bol, Ferdinand (1616–1680), 241

Bonger, Andries (1861–1936), 19, 371n60

Borch, Gerard ter (1617–1681), 239, 241

The Swearing of the Oath of Ratification of the Treaty of Münster (Fig. 57), *243*, 245

Botticelli, Sandro (1444/1445–1510), 192

Boulanger, Georges (1837–1891), 173

Bracquemond, Félix (1833–1914), 173

Bruant, Aristide (1851–1925), 10

Bukowski, Charles (1920–1994), 7

Bürger, W. *See* Thoré, Étienne Joseph Théophile

C

Cassirer, Paul (1871–1926), 21, 23, 309

Cézanne, Paul (1839–1906), 16, 205, 209, 220–21, 256

Chamaillard, Ernest Ponthier de (1862–1930), 289, 297, 303, 309, 312

View of a Harbor, 312

Charles d'Orléans (1394–1465), 216

Chevreul, Michel Eugène (1786–1889), 173

Cimabue, Cenni (Benciviene) di Pepo (1240–1302), 171, 174, 252

Codde, Pieter (1599–1678): *The Company of Captain Reynier Reael and Lieutenant Cornelis Michielsz Blaeuw ("The Meagre Company"*; with Frans Hals), 246

Constant, Benjamin (1845–1902), 194, 200

Cooper, Douglas (1911–1984), 22–23, 371nn64–66, 372n72

Coppée, François (1842–1908), 151

Cormon, Fernand (1845–1924), 8, 10, 363

Corot, Camille (1796–1875), 327, 344

Christ in the Garden of Olives (Fig. 115), *352*, 354

Courbet, Gustave (1819–1877), 227, 254, 260

Cranach, Lucas, the Older (1472–1553), 148, 192, 196, 202

Crivelli, Carlo (1430/1435–1495), 212, 216

Crivelli, Vittore (1440–1501/1502), 216

D

Dante Alighieri (1265–1321), 241, 247

Daubigny, Charles-François (1817–1878), 130

Daudet, Alphonse (1840–1897), 133, 168, 183

Aventures prodigieuses de Tartarin de Tarascon, 152, 173

Le nabab, 187

Tartarin sur les Alpes, 152

Daumier, Honoré (1808–1879), 240, 252, 256, 336

Degas, Edgar (1834–1917), 22, 139, 226–27, 254, 260, 370n15, 371n63

Delacroix, Eugène (1798–1863), 8, 14, 16, 127, 133, 173, 190, 194, 196, 200, 204, 228, 239–40, 245, 255, 263, 276, 344, 353

Christ Asleep During the Tempest (Fig. 33), *191*, 199–200, 235

Dickens, Charles (1812–1870), 16

Doré, Gustave (1832–1883), 187

Dujardin, Édouard (1861–1949), 185–86

Durand-Ruel, Paul (1831–1922), 19

Dürer, Albrecht (1471–1528), 148, 196, 202

E

Étude d'herbe (Fig. 87), *300*, 301

Eyck, Jan van (ca. 1390–1441), 148, 192, 252

F

Fabritius, Barent (1624–1673), 247

Fabritius, Carel (1622–1654), 241, 247

Fantin-Latour, Henri (1836–1904), 128
Fourment, Hélène (1614–1673), 260
Fromentin, Eugène (1820–1876), 171, 174, 227, 232, 235, 276

G
Garnier, Charles (1825–1898), 327, 332
Gauguin, Paul (1848–1903)
Among the Mangoes (W250/W224; Fig. 18), 11, *157*, 163
Christ in the Garden of Olives (W326), 335
Night Café (W318/W305; Fig. 93), *314*, 321
On the Shore of the Lake, Martinique (W252/W222; Fig. 17), 11, *157*, 163
Self-Portrait with Portrait of Bernard, "Les misérables" (W309/W239; Fig. 72), *272*, 279, 289, 309
Vision of the Sermon (W308/W245), 273
Young Wrestlers (W298/W273), 237
Gaujean, Eugène (1850–1900), 232
Geffroy, Gustave (1855–1926), 19
Gérôme, Jean-Léon (1824–1904), 171, 174, 276
Gigoux, Jean (1806–1894), 263
Giotto, school of / Florentine school: *The Death and Assumption of the Virgin* (Fig. 112), *351*, 353
Giotto di Bondone (1267/1275–1337), 16, 171, 174, 252, 260, 266, 270, 340
Gloanec-Morvan, Marie Jeanne (1839–after 1890), 152
Gogh, Vincent van (1853–1890)
The Alyscamps, Avenue at Arles (F 486 / JH 1620; Fig. 94), *319*, 322
The Alyscamps, Avenue at Arles (F 487 / JH 1621; Fig. 95), *320*, 322
The Alyscamps, Avenue at Arles (F 568 / JH 1622; Fig. 96), 322, *323*
The Alyscamps, Avenue at Arles (F 569 / JH 1623), 322
L'Arlésienne (Madame Ginoux; F 540 / JH 1892), 367
Basket with Lemons (F 384 / JH 1425; Fig. 21), *161*, 164
The Bedroom (F 482 / JH 1608; Fig. 118), *356*, 360
La Berceuse (F 508 / JH 1671; Fig. 108), *347*, 353, 367
Blue and White Grapes, Apples, Pears, and Lemons (F 382 / JH 1337), 366
Breton Women, After Bernard (F 1422 / JH 1654; Fig. 7), *17*
Brothel Scene (F 478 / JH 1599; Fig. 92), 311, *313*
Cabane in Saintes-Maries (F - / JH -), 166
Café Terrace at Night (F 467 / JH 1580), 297
Canal with Women Washing (F 1444 / JH 1507), 215, 367
Corner of a Garden with Flowers and Butterflies (F 460 / JH 1676), 270
A Corner of the Asylum and the Garden with a Heavy, Sawn-Off Tree (F 659 / JH 1850; Fig. 113), *351*, 353
A Corner of the Asylum and the Garden with a Heavy, Sawn-Off Tree (F 670 / JH 1849), 353
Cypresses (F 620 / JH 1748), 14
Drawbridge with a Lady with a Parasol (F 1471 / JH 1420; Fig. 43), *214*, 215, 367
Drawbridge with Carriage (F 397 / JH 1368; Fig. 11), *136*, 137; detail, *132*
Drawbridge with Carriage (F 571 / JH 1392), 137
Drawing with Walking Couple (F - / JH 1370), 133, 137
The Drinkers (F 667 / JH 1884), 367
Enclosed Field with Farmer Carrying a Bundle of Straw (F 641 / JH 1795; Fig. 98), *330*, 332
Enclosed Field with Young Wheat and Rising Sun (F 737 / JH 1862; Fig. 114), *352*, 353
Enclosed Wheat Field with Reaper (F 617 / JH 1753; Fig. 116), 354, *355*
Enclosed Wheat Field with Reaper at Sunrise (F 618 / JH 1773; Fig. 117), 354, *355*
Entrance to a Quarry (F 635 / JH 1767; Fig. 97), *329*, 332
Entrance to a Quarry (F 744 / JH 1802), 331
A Factory at Asnières (F 318 / JH 1288), 367
Farm Along a Road (F - / JH 1464), 166, 174
Farmhouse with Wheat Field Along a Road (F 408 / JH 1417; Fig. 23), *162*, 165, 174; detail, *154*
Field with Flowers (F 409 / JH 1416; Fig. 22), *161*, 164
Fishing Boats at Sea (F - / JH 1464), 166, 174
Fishing Boats at Sea (F 417 / JH 1453; Fig. 29), 174, *175*
Fishing Boats at Sea (F 1430 / JH 1505), 215, 367
Fishing Boats on the Beach (F - / JH 1461), 166, 174
Fishing Boats on the Beach (F 413 / JH 1460; Fig. 28), *172*, 174
Garden (F 814 / JH 2107), 309
The Gardens of Montmartre (F 316 / JH 1246), 139
Garden with Flowers (F 578 / JH 1538; Fig. 78), *288*, 298, 309, 321
The Green Vineyard (F 475 / JH 1595; Fig. 84), *296*, 297, 301
Harvest Landscape (F 412 / JH 1440), 177
Harvest Landscape (F 1485 / JH 1540), 215, 366
Haystacks Near a Farm (F 425 / JH 1442), 177, 209
Haystacks Near a Farm (F 1426 / JH 1514), 215, 367
The Iris (F 601 / JH 1699), 331
Joseph Roulin, Head (F 433 / JH 1524; Fig. 68), *262*, 263
Joseph Roulin, Sitting in a Cane Chair (F 432 / JH 1522; Fig. 67), *261*, 263; detail, *248*
Joseph Roulin, Sitting in a Cane Chair (F 1723 / JH 1523), 216
La Crau, Seen from Montmajour (F 1420 / JH 1501; Fig. 44), 216, *217*
Landscape Near Montmajour with Train (F 1424 / JH 1502; Fig. 45), 216, *218*
Landscape with the Edge of a Road (F - / JH 1464), 166, 174
Landscape with the Edge of a Road (F 567 / JH 1419; Fig. 24), *163*, 165, 174, 298
A Lane in the Public Garden (F 470 / JH 1582), 297
A Lane in the Public Garden (F 471 / JH 1613), 297
Leg of an Easel with a Ground Spike (F - / JH -), 177
Lieutenant Milliet (F 473 / JH 1588), 279, 322
Little Blossoming Pear Tree (F 405 / JH 1394; Fig. 16), 152, *153*
Meadow with Poppies (F 576 / JH 1423), 298
Mountain Landscape Seen Across the Walls (F 611 / JH 1723), 331
Mountains with Dark Hut (F 622 / JH 1766), 331
La Mousmé (F 431 / JH 1519), 225
Mousmé, Sitting in a Cane Chair (F 431 / JH 1519; Fig. 55), *234*, 235
Mousmé, Sitting in a Cane Chair (F 1504 / JH 1520), 215–16, 220, 225, 367
Mulberry Tree (F 637 / JH 1796), 331
Newly Mown Lawn with Weeping Tree (F 428 / JH 1499; Fig. 82), *292*, 301
Newly Mown Lawn with Weeping Tree (F 1450 / JH 1509), 215, 301, 367
The Night Café (F 463 / JH 1575; Fig. 75), *278*, 279, 297–98, 311, 321
Nude Woman, Reclining (F 329 / JH 1215), 366
Nude Woman, Reclining (F 330 / JH 1214), 366
The Old Mill (F 550 / JH 1577; Fig. 88), *302*, 309, 312
The Old Peasant Patience Escalier, Head (F 443 / JH 1548; Fig. 69), *264*, 265, 269
The Old Peasant Patience Escalier with Walking Stick (F 444 / JH 1563), 269
The Old Peasant Patience Escalier, Head (F 1460 / JH 1549), 269
The Old Peasant Patience Escalier with Walking Stick (F 1461 / JH 1564), 269
Olive Grove (F 586 / JH 1854), 353
Olive Grove (F 707 / JH 1857), 353
Olive Grove (F 708 / JH 1855), 353
Olive Grove (F 715 / JH 1759), 331
Olive Grove with a Man and a Woman Picking Olives (F 587 / JH 1853), 353
Olive Grove with Mountains and Sun Disk (F 710 / JH 1856; Fig. 111), *348*, 353
Olive Picking (F 654 / JH 1868), 367
Olive Trees in a Mountain Landscape (F 712 / JH 1740), 331
Orchard and House with Orange Roof (F - / JH 1401), 147
Orchard and House with Orange Roof (F 406 / JH 1399; Fig. 15), *146*, 152
Orchard and House with Red Roof (F 511 / JH 1386), 331
Orchard Surrounded by Cypresses (F - / JH 1390), 139, 145
Orchard Surrounded by Cypresses (F 513 / JH 1389; Fig. 12), *141*, 145, 152; detail, *144*
Orchard Surrounded by Cypresses (F 554 /

JH 1388; Fig. 14), *142*, 145
Orchard with Blossoming Apricot Trees (F 555 / JH 1380), 152
Orchard with Blossoming Plum Trees (F 556 / JH 1383), 152
Orchard with Blossoming Plum Trees (The White Orchard; F 403 / JH 1378), 152
Orchard with Blossoming Plum Trees and Factory (F 553 / JH 1387), 152
Orchard with Cypresses (F 551 / JH 1396; Fig. 13), *141*, 145, 152
Orphan Man with Umbrella, Seen from the Back (F 978a / JH 240), 367
A Pair of Old Shoes (F 461 / JH 1569; Fig. 80), *291*, 298, 309
A Path Through the Ravine (F 662 / JH 1804; Fig. 99), 332, *333*; detail, *324*
Piles of French Novels and a Glass with a Rose (F 359 / JH 1332), 139
Pink Peach Trees (F 404 / JH 1391), 152
Plowed Field (F 574 / JH 1586; Fig. 85), 297, *299*, 301
Portrait of Eugène Boch (F 462 / JH 1574), 312, 322
The Potato Eaters (F 82 / JH 764; Fig. 70), 14, 265, *268*, 269
Public Garden with Round Clipped Shrub and Weeping Tree (F 468 / JH 1578; Fig. 81), *292*, 297, 301
Quay with Men Unloading Sand Barges (F 449 / JH 1558; Fig. 71), 270, *271*, 279, 298, 309, 312, 366
Reclining Girl, after Émile Bernard, *Madeleine in the Bois d'Amour* (F - / JH -), 335
Rocks with a Tree (F 1554 / JH 1518), 215, 367
The Seine with a Rowboat (F 298 / JH 1257), 367
Self-Portrait (F 319 / JH 1333), 366
Self-Portrait (F 366 / JH 1345), 367
Self-Portrait (F 476 / JH 1581; Fig. 74), 187, *277*, 279, 298, 303, 309, 322
Self-Portrait (F 627 / JH 1772), 331
Self-Portrait with Straw Hat (F 526 / JH 1309), 312, 366
Sower with Setting Sun (F - / JH 1472), 177
Sower with Setting Sun (F 422 / JH 1470; Fig. 30), *176*, 177, 185, 204, 209
Sower with Setting Sun (F 1442 / JH 1508), 215, 367
The Starry Night (F 474 / JH 1592; Fig. 83), *296*, 297, 301
The Starry Night (F 612 / JH 1731; Fig. 110), *348*, 353; detail, *334*
Still Life with Coffeepot (F - / JH 1428), 166, 174
Still Life with Coffeepot (F 410 / JH 1426; Fig. 20), *158*, 164, 174
Still Life with Oranges, Lemons, and Blue Gloves (F 502 / JH 1664), 367
Street in Saintes-Maries (F - / JH 1463), 166, 174
Street in Saintes-Maries (F 420 / JH 1462; Fig. 27), *169*, 173–74
Street in Saintes-Maries (F 1435 / JH 1506; Fig. 41), *210*, 215, 367
Thistles (F 447 / JH 1550; Fig. 79), 270, *291*, 298, 309
Thistles (F 447a / JH 1551), 270
Thistles Along the Road (F 1466 / JH 1552), 270
Three Cottages in Saintes-Maries (F 419 / JH 1465; Fig. 26), *169*, 173
Three Trees, after Émile Bernard, *Red Poplars* (F - / JH -), 335
Trees in Front of the Entrance to the Asylum (F 643 / JH 1799), 331
Trees in the Garden of the Asylum (F 640 / JH 1800), 331
Trees in the Garden of the Asylum (F 642 / JH 1798), 331
Trees in the Garden of the Asylum (F 730 / JH 1841), 331
Two Cut Sunflowers (F 375 / JH 1329), 11
Two Cut Sunflowers (F 376 / JH 1331), 11
Two Poplars with a Background of Mountains (F 638 / JH 1797), 331
Vegetable Gardens in Montmartre (F 350 / JH 1245), 139
View of a River, Quay and Bridge (F 1507 / JH 1469), 215, 367
Vincent's Bedroom (F - / JH 1610), 357
Walking Couple (fragment) (F 544 / JH 1369; Fig. 10), *136*, 137
Wheat Field (F 411 / JH 1476), 209
Wheat Field (F 1481 / JH 1515; Fig. 42), *214*, 215, 367
Wheat Field with Setting Sun (F - / JH 1474), 177
Wheat Field with Setting Sun (F 465 / JH 1473; Fig. 32), *184*, 186, 209
Wheat Field with Setting Sun (F 1514 / JH 1546), 215, 367
Wheat Field with Sheaves (F 558 / JH 1481), 209
Wheat Field with Sheaves (F 561 / JH 1480), 209
Wheat Field with Sheaves (F 1488 / JH 1517), 215, 367
Wheat Field with Sheaves and Arles in the Background (F 545 / JH 1477), 185, 209
Wheat Field with Sheaves and Arles in the Background (F 1491 / JH 1516), 215, 367
Woman, Strolling in a Garden (F 368 / JH 1262), 367
Woman Reading a Novel (F 497 / JH 1632; Fig. 109), *347*, 353
Woman with a Baby, Sitting at the Fireside (F 644 / JH 1805), 331
Woman with a Parasol (F - / JH -), 166
Woman with a Scarlet Bow in Her Hair (F 207 / JH 979), 367
The Yellow House (F 464 / JH 1589; Fig. 86), 297, *299*, 301
Zouave, Half-Length (F 423 / JH 1486; Fig. 36), 189, *195*, 200
Zouave, Half-Length (F 1482 / JH 1487; Fig. 37), *198*, 200, 215, 367
Zouave, Sitting, Full-Length (F 424 / JH 1488; Fig. 35), 189, *195*, 200
Zouave, Sitting, Full-Length (F 1443 / JH 1485; Fig. 34), *191*, 200
Gogh, Vincent Willem van (1890–1978), 371n66
Gogh, Willemien van (1862–1941), 18, 130, 237, 349, 357
Gogh-Bonger, Jo van (1862–1925), 19, 21, 298, 309, 369, 371n60
Goldschmidt-Rothschild, Marianne (née Von Friedländer-Fuld; 1892/1894–1973), 23, 25
Goncourt, Edmond de (1822–1896), 254, 259
Goncourt, Jules de (1830–1870), 254, 259
Gonse, Louis (1846–1921), 301
Goya y Lucientes, Francisco de (1746–1828), 225, 238, 245
Portrait of Ferdinand Guillamardet, 245
Gruby, David (1810–1898), 249
Guillaumin, Armand (1841–1927), 10, 127, 130, 139, 167, 361, 370n15

H

Hals, Frans (1581/1585–1666), 240–41, 245–46
The Company of Captain Reynier Reael and Lieutenant Cornelis Michielsz Blaeuw ("The Meagre Company"; with Pieter Codde), 246
Family Group in a Landscape, 246
Family Portrait, 246
Family Portrait in a Landscape, 246
Gipsy Girl (Fig. 59), *244*, 246
Malle Babbe and a Smoker (attribution), 246
Marriage Portrait of Isaac Massa and Beatrix van der Laen (Fig. 60), *246*, 247
The Merry Drinker, 246
Portrait of a Man Wearing a Cuirass, 245
The Regentesses of the Old Men's Alms House, 246
The Regents of St. Elizabeth's Hospital, 246
The Regents of the Old Men's Alms House (Fig. 58), *243*, 246
Willem van Heythuysen, 247
Young Woman with a Glass and Flagon, 247
Hippocrates (ca. 460–370 B.C.), 287
Hokusai, Katsushika (1760–1849), 11
Holbein the Younger, Hans (1497–1543), 196, 202, 252
Homer (ca. 800–ca. 750 B.C.), 344
Hooch, Pieter de (1629–ca. 1683), 241
Hugo, Victor (1802–1885), 215
Huysmans, Joris Karl (1848–1907), 179, 371n69
En ménage, 186

I

Ingres, Jean-Auguste Dominique (1780–1867), 235
Isaäcson, Joseph (1859–1942), 325
Israëls, Jozef (1824–1911), 178, 185

J

Jastrau, Viggo (1857–1946), 216

K

Kessler, Harry (1868–1937), 23
Koning, Arnold (1860–1945), 10, 131, 361

L
Lalanne, Maxime (1827–1886), 349
Laval, Charles (1862–1894), 174, 265, 281, 289, 293, 303, 305–6, 309, 322
Self-Portrait (Fig. 89), *308,* 309
Leclerq, Julien (1865–1901), 370n30
Lemasson, Madame, 147, 211
Lemasson, Marie, 155, 211
Leonardo da Vinci (1452–1519), 228
Loti, Pierre (pseudonym of Julien Viaud; 1850–1923), 183
Madame Chrysanthème, 187, 211, 235
Louis XIV (1638–1715), 196, 203
Luther, Martin (1483–1546), 19, 196, 202–3

M
MacKnight, Dodge (1860–1950), 216, 249, 371n40
Maes, Nicolaas (1632/1634–1693), 241
Manet, Édouard (1832–1883), 303
Mantz, Paul (1821–1895[?]), 200
Massenet, Jules (1842–1912), 187
Maupassant, Guy de (1850–1893), 183, 187
Maus, Octave (1856–1919), 363
Mauthner, Margarethe, 21
Mauve, Anton (1838–1888), 14, 178, 185
Mauve-Carbentus, Jet (1856–1894), 185
Michelangelo Buonarotti (1475–1564), 241
Michelet, Jules (1798–1874), 202
Millet, Jean-François (1814–1875), 16, 178, 185, 190, 204, 227, 240, 270, 327–28, 336, 344, 354
Birth of the Calf (Fig. 101), *337,* 349–50
Milliet, Paul Eugène (1863–1943), 180, 186–87, 203, 218, 279, 315, 318
Mohammed (570–632), 228
Monet, Claude (1840–1926), 139, 183, 187, 196, 202
Monticelli, Adolphe (1824–1886), 133, 139, 145, 221, 276, 281
Moret, Henri (1856–1913), 289, 293, 298, 303, 305–6, 309
Mourier-Petersen, Christian Vilhelm (1858–1945), 133, 216, 371n40
Musset, Alfred de (1810–1857), 242

O
Ostade, Adriaan van (1610–1685), 239, 241
Portrait of a Family (Fig. 56), *236,* 245

P
Pissarro, Camille (1830–1903), 10, 139, 361, 370n15
Potter, Paulus (1625–1654), 197, 221, 223, 241
The Piebald Horse (Fig. 40), *201,* 203
Puvis de Chavannes, Pierre (1824–1898), 196, 252–54
The Beheading of St. John the Baptist (Fig. 39), *201,* 202
Portrait of a Man (Eugène Benon) (Fig. 65), *258,* 260
Portrait of a Woman (Portrait of Madame M. C. [Maria Cantacuzène]; Fig. 66), *258,* 260

R
Raphael (1483–1520), 241
Rappard, Anthon van (1858–1892), 15, 23, 232
Redon, Odilon (1840–1916), 225
Rembrandt van Rijn (1606–1669), 14, 16, 190, 197, 202, 221, 225–28, 231, 235, 238–42, 247, 251, 259, 266
The Agony in the Garden, 199
Bathsheba Bathing, 247
Christ at the Column (Fig. 50), *230,* 232
The Evangelist Matthew Inspired by an Angel (Fig. 54), *234,* 235
Self-Portrait as Zeuxis, 235
Self-Portrait at the Easel (Fig. 53), *233,* 235
The Slaughtered Ox (Fig. 51), *230,* 232
The Supper at Emmaus, 199, 247
Susanna Bathing (now regarded as copy after Rembrandt), 247
Renan, Ernest (1823–1892), 203
Richepin, Jean Auguste Jules (1849–1926), 199
Rochefort, Henri (1831–1913), 173
Roulin, Joseph (1841–1903), 237, 249, 263, 269
Roulin, Marcelle (1888–1980), 263, 269
Roulin-Pellicot, Augustine (1851–1930), 263
Rubens, Peter Paul (1577–1640), 254–55, 260
Ruisdael, Jacob van (1628/1629–1682), 221, 241
Russell, John Peter (1858–1931), 10, 147, 167, 177, 216, 225, 249
Portrait of Vincent van Gogh (Fig. 1), *8*

S
Saulnier, John (?–1886), 200
Schuffenecker, Émile (1851–1934), 203, 269, 325, 360
Segatori, Agostina (1841–1910), 10, 370n13
Seneca (ca. 4 B.C.–A.D. 65), 287
Sensier, Alfred (1815–1877), 185, 270, 354
Seurat, Georges (1859–1891), 10, 130, 358, 361
Signac, Paul (1863–1935), 10–11, 127–28, 130, 133
Silvestre, Armand (1837–1901), 187
Silvestre, Théophile (1823–1876), 200, 260, 263
Eugène Delacroix. Documents nouveaux, 130, 240, 245
Sisley, Alfred (1839–1899), 139
Socrates (469–399 B.C.), 228, 266, 269
Sophocles (496–406 B.C.), 344
Springer, Anne-Marie, 25

T
Taine, Hippolyte (1828–1893), 260
Tanguy, Julien (1825–1894), 8, 10, 256, 362–64
Tersteeg, Hermanus Gijsbertus (1845–1927), 139
Thaw, Eugene, 25
Thomas, Georges (?–after 1908), 212, 218, 361
Thoré, Étienne Joseph Théophile (writing under pseudonym of W. Bürger; 1807–1869), 227, 232, 247, 259
Tolstoy, Leo (1828–1910), 127
A la recherche du bonheur, 130
Toulouse-Lautrec, Henri de (1864–1901), 10, 131, 133, 139, 218

U
Utamaro, Kitagawa (ca. 1753–1806), 11

V
Vallette, Alfred (1858–1935), 371n60
Vasari, Giorgio (1511–1574), 260
Velázquez, Diego (1599–1660), 192, 227, 238–39, 245
Gathering of Thirteen Characters, 245
Portrait of a Priest of Toledo, 245
Portrait of Philip IV of Spain, 245
Portrait of the Infanta Maria Margarita, 245
Portrait of the Infanta Maria Theresa, 245
Vermeer, Johannes (1632–1675), 227, 232, 241, 251, 259
Woman in Blue Reading a Letter (Fig. 52), 232, *233*
Viollet-le-Duc, Eugène-Emmanuel (1814–1879), 327, 332
Vollard, Ambroise (1865–1939), 14, 21–22, 269

W
Wagner, Richard (1813–1883), 173
Williame-Mahé, Eliane, 23

Z
Zola, Émile (1840–1902), 16, 18, 223, 239, 241, 316, 371n46
Le rêve, 321

Credits

Every effort has been made to trace copyright owners and photographers. The publishers apologize for any unintentional omissions and would be pleased in such cases to add an acknowledgment in future editions.

Letters

Letter 11, Collection Frits Lugt Institut Néerlandais, Paris; Appendix 2, The Pierpont Morgan Library, New York; Letter 20, present whereabouts unknown; Letter 15, private collection; Letters 1–10, 12–14, 16–19, 21–22 © Thaw Collection, The Pierpont Morgan Library, New York.

Collections

Fig. 88, Albright Knox Art Gallery, Buffalo, New York, bequest of A. Conger Goodyear, 1966; Fig. 81, Mr. and Mrs. Lewis Larned Coburn Memorial Collection, The Art Institute of Chicago, photography © The Art Institute of Chicago; Fig. 39, The Barber Institute of Fine Arts, The University of Birmingham; Fig. 92, photograph © reproduced with the permission of The Barnes Foundation™, all rights reserved, BF104; Fig. 101, Bibliothèque nationale, Paris, France; Fig. 45 © copyright the Trustees of The British Museum; Fig. 74, courtesy of The Fogg Art Museum, Harvard University Art Museums, bequest from the Collection of Maurice Wertheim, Class of 1906, 1951.65, © 2004 President and Fellows of Harvard College; Fig. 68, photograph © 1997 The Detroit Institute of Arts; Fig. 58, Frans Hals Museum, Haarlem; Fig. 98, Indianapolis Museum of Art, Gift of Mrs. James W. Fesler in memory of Daniel W. and Elizabeth C. Marmon (44.74); Figs. 11–12, 21, 30, 94, 116, Collection Kröller-Müller Museum, Otterlo, The Netherlands; Fig. 61, Kunsthalle Bremen; Figs. 26, 78 © 2006 Kunsthaus Zürich, all rights reserved; Fig. 32, Kunstmuseum Winterthur, presented by Dr. Emil Hahnloser, 1922; Figs. 40, 54, 59, 93, 104, Erich Lessing/Art Resource, NY; Fig. 43, Los Angeles County Museum of Art, George Gard De Sylva Collection, photography © 2004 Museum Associates/LACMA; Fig. 41, The Metropolitan Museum of Art, bequest of Abby Aldrich Rockefeller, 1948 (48.190.1), photograph ©1998 The Metropolitan Museum of Art; Fig. 37, The Metropolitan Museum of Art, gift of Emanie Philips, 1962 (62.151), photograph ©1982 The Metropolitan Museum of Art; Fig. 42, The Metropolitan Museum of Art, gift of Mrs. Max J. H. Rossbach, 1964 (64.125.3), photograph ©1983 The Metropolitan Museum of Art; Fig. 33, The Metropolitan Museum of Art, H. O. Havemeyer Collection, bequest of Mrs. H. O. Havemeyer, 1929 (29.100.131), photograph ©1984 The Metropolitan Museum of Art; Fig. 80, The Metropolitan Museum of Art, purchase, The Annenberg Foundation Gift, 1992 (1992.374), photograph ©1993 The Metropolitan Museum of Art; Fig. 111, The Minneapolis Institute of Arts, The William Hood Dunwoody Fund; Fig. 66, Musée de Beaux-Arts, Lyon; Fig. 112, Musée Fabre, Montpellier Agglomération; Fig. 115, Musée de Langres; Fig. 71, Museum Folkwang Essen, Succession Picasso, Paris; Figs, 64, 67, 108, photograph © 2007 Museum of Fine Arts, Boston; Fig. 110, The Museum of Modern Art, New York, acquired through the Lillie P. Bliss Bequest (472.1941), digital image © The Museum of Modern Art/Licensed by SCALA/Art Resource, NY; Fig. 57 © National Gallery, London, Picture Library; Fig. 55, image © Board of Trustees, National Gallery of Art, Washington, Chester Dale Collection; Fig. 69, Norton Simon Art Foundation, Pasadena, CA; Figs. 118, 119, The Pierpont Morgan Library, New York, MA 4148; Fig. 24, Pommersches Landesmuseum, Greifswald; Figs. 105, 106, present whereabouts unknown; Fig. 103, Prêteurs anonyms; Figs. 10, 13–15, 20, 27, 65, 82, 95–97, 102, 109, 114, private collection; Figs. 51, 53, 56, 62, 83, Réunion des Musées Nationaux/Art Resource, NY; Figs. 52, 60, Rijksmuseum, Amsterdam; Figs. 7, 29, Scala/Art Resource, NY; Figs. 1–2, 5, 8, 16–18, 22–23, 25, 28, 34, 36, 38, 44, 47–49, 63, 70, 72–73, 76–77, 85, 86, 89–91, 113, 117–18, and back cover, Van Gogh Museum (Vincent Van Gogh Foundation); Figs. 3–4, 6, 19, 46, 50, Van Gogh Museum; Figs. 9, 87, Van Gogh Museum Library; Fig. 31, Bogomila Welsh; Fig. 100, photograph courtesy of Wildenstein Institute, Paris; Fig. 75, Yale University Art Gallery, bequest of Stephen Carlton Clark, B.A. 1903.

Photography

Fig. 66 © Alain Basset; Fig. 51, Gerard Blot; Fig. 112, Frédéric Jaulmes; Fig. 56, C. Jean/J. Schormans; Fig. 74, Katya Kallsen; Figs. 53, 62, 83, Hervé Lewandowski; Figs. 20, 96, Mr. Peter Schibli; Fig. 31, Bogomila Welsh; front cover, Letters 1–10, 12–14, 16–19, 21–22, Appendix 2, Joseph Zehavi.

Authors' Acknowledgments

The editors would like to thank those individuals who have made vital contributions to this book. Heading the list are Fred Leeman, who kindly shared his knowledge of Émile Bernard with us, Wouter van der Veen, who was always ready to answer questions about van Gogh's French, and Imogen Forster and Michael Hoyle for their very skillful translations.

We are most grateful to Egbert Haverkamp-Begemann, who championed this project from its inception; the staff of The Morgan Library & Museum, in particular Charles E. Pierce, Jr., Jennifer Tonkovich, Margaret Holben Ellis, Karen Banks, and Patricia Emerson; and our colleagues at the Van Gogh Museum, above all Suzanne Bogman, Chris Stolwijk, Louis van Tilborgh, and Axel Rüger as well as our former director, John Leighton.

We are indebted to Anne-Marie Springer and to the Fondation Custodia in Paris, especially Hans Buijs, for their enthusiastic cooperation on this publication. Finally, we would like to thank Walter Feilchenfeldt, Martin Royalton-Kisch, Susan Alyson Stein, and Belinda Thomson, who assisted us in various stages of the project, as well as Andrea van Leerdam, who was extremely helpful with the picture editing and research.

Exhibition at The Morgan Library & Museum
28 September 2007–6 January 2008

This publication was made possible by a generous grant from the International Music and Art Foundation.

Support for *Vincent van Gogh ~ Painted with Words: The Letters to Émile Bernard* was provided by the Robert Lehman Foundation and by the National Endowment for the Arts.

NATIONAL ENDOWMENT FOR THE ARTS
A great nation deserves great art.

Published by Rizzoli International Publications, Inc.
300 Park Avenue South
New York, NY 10010
www.rizzoliusa.com

in association with The Morgan Library & Museum
225 Madison Avenue
New York, NY 10016-3405
www.the morgan.org

and Van Gogh Museum
Paulus Potterstraat 7
1071 CX Amsterdam
www.vangoghmuseum.com

2007 2008 2009 2010 2011 / 10 9 8 7 6 5 4 3 2 1

Project staff

THE MORGAN LIBRARY & MUSEUM
Karen Banks, Publications Manager
Patricia Emerson, Senior Editor
Elizabeth Moore, Editorial Assistant
Marilyn Palmeri, Manager, Photography and Rights
Jennifer Tonkovich, Curator, Drawings and Prints
Isabelle Dervaux, Translation Consultant

VAN GOGH MUSEUM
Suzanne Bogman, Head of Publications
Michael Hoyle, Translation of Introduction/Translation Editor
Imogen Forster, Translation of van Gogh's Letters
Wouter van der Veen, Translation Consultant

RIZZOLI INTERNATIONAL PUBLICATIONS, INC.
Ellen Cohen, Editor
Designed by Pirtle Design

ISBN–13: 978-0-8478-2993-4
ISBN: 0-8478-2993-6
Library of Congress Catalogue Number: 2007927304

Frontispiece: Vincent van Gogh, *Orchard and House with Orange Roof* (Fig. 15; detail)

Printed in China